HOW TO
BUILD YOUR OWN HOME

Acknowledgments

Ink sketches used throughout the text were by Carol Reschke. All photos were by the author except where otherwise noted or implied in the captions.

Special thanks is due each of the organizations listed in Appendix B. We are particularly indebted to the building product manufacturers and trade associations included in this listing. The inference here is that these organizations will be responsive to inquiries from prospective owner-builders. And these organizations have developed useful instructional booklets designed for guiding owner-builders, as indicated in the Appendix.

HOW TO
BUILD YOUR OWN HOME

Robert C. Reschke

Structures Publishing Company 1976
Farmington, Michigan

Manufactured in the United States of America

Edited by Shirley M. Horowitz

Book design by Richard Kinney

Current Printing (last digit)
10 9 8 7 6 5 4 3 2 1

International Standard Book Number: 0-912336-18-8 (cloth)
0-912336-19-6 (paper)

Library of Congress Catalog Card Number: 75-40522

Structures Publishing Co.
Box 423, Farmington, Mich. 48024

Library of Congress Cataloging in Publication Data

Reschke, Robert C
  How to build your own home.

  (Successful books)
  Bibliography: p.
  Includes Index.
  1. House construction—Amateurs' manuals. I. Title.
TH4815.R48   690.8   75-40522
ISBN 0-912336-18-8
ISBN 0-912336-19-6 pbk.

I know you believe
you understand
what you think I said,
but I'm not sure you realize
that what you heard
is not what I meant to say.
                              Anon

At one time long ago, a single carpenter-craftsman would build a home almost entirely by himself, with the aid of just a laborer or two. The emphasis then was on the ability of such a craftsman to use his hands to perform a very considerable variety of jobs.

Today, with a sometimes bewildering array of all kinds of building tradesmen, "skilled" or "unskilled" are mostly trade union terms which may or may not reflect wide variations in working capability. Still, most of the public believes that the key part of constructing a new home is the ability to use one's hands to do the work.

That is a misconception. The single most important personal quality that a professional home-builder has today is his ability to communicate. It is this ability to put things into words and writing so that it is properly understood, and so that other's communications are properly received, that results in a successful and well-expedited job. For the professional home-builder and also for the first-time owner-builder, the word is . . . communicate to move the job ahead.

The Author

Contents

Preface

Some people purchase a new home that is already completed, or nearly so, when they first see it.

But many, many others reach the moving-in stage only after going through a frustrating and hectic period during which the home is under construction. There are four common ways in which an owner becomes involved in the building of his new home:

(1) he hires an architect to draw up plans and supervise the building work done by separate contractors;

(2) he signs with a builder-contractor for a standard-plan home or for duplication of a previously built model;

(3) he acts as his own general contractor, obtaining plans, taking subcontractor bids and supervising the subcontractors;

(4) he acts as owner-builder with some subcontractors helping, but doing much of the construction work himself.

This book is especially directed toward the latter two types of new home owners; however, though aimed primarily to such owner-builders, it will also provide a wealth of information and guidance for other new home owners-to-be. Information and guidance which will prove valuable in communicating with the people who do the supervising and building work on a new home.

To be as helpful as possible, the author has attempted in nearly every chapter to bring better understanding of current home-building practices. And, in addition, he's tried to touch those bases which will be of the most aid to the owner in making the almost endless series of decisions that someone must make in the course of planning and constructing a home. An effort has been made to provide:

- A continuity of sequence . . . in construction progress from the initial home concept to completion and occupancy;

- Explanation of changes . . . pinpointing the newer and better ways of doing things in contrast to the older, once-acceptable methods, thus keeping up with building trends;

- Practical data on building materials-products . . . and the owner-builder decisions in his choice of materials-products . . . including factors such as availability or need to special-order;

- Indication of home-buyer preferences . . . in areas where such data is available, including practices of professional home-builders;

- Building code requirements . . . that must be met particularly with respect particularly to structural and mechanical work in order to meet provisions of a national code or HUD-FHA minimum property standards (MPS's);

- A focus on simpler techniques . . . emphasizing methods that speed the construction and help eliminate tedious jobs—plus explanations of procedural steps so the owner-builder understands why something is done as well as how;

- Minimum excess or repetitive detail . . . an assumption that once basics are told, the owner-builder can apply common sense in carrying out instructions, and does not need to have each and every body move spelled out in boring repetitious detail;

- An alertness to timing . . . with indications of prerequisite work needed or the delay of further work advancement due to considerations of other work performance;

- A guide to cost-saving options . . . with indications as to different cost or quality levels and cost-levels that might be appropriate to each type of home.

The comprehensive treatment of each building trade's work and the wide range of building products that can be utilized in new home construction makes the book useful to others considering a new home . . . it can be a guide in helping a family to decide *not* to build their own as well as a key tool for those who do follow the owner-build procedure.

Throughout the text, where applicable, product or information sources are given. In addition, the appendix contains a carefully selected list of organizations and building product manufacturers having special publications or instruction data available to owner-builders on request.

Introduction

Close your eyes . . . dream a little . . . about a new home.

If you're like a very large and growing number of Americans age 20 to 55, the vision materializes quickly. You've thought about it so often and for so long that your ideal house has by now become clear and distinct.

It might be a small, but not too small, home with ample yard space and much shrubbery. Plants indoors and out. Ground-hugging appearance, though it may be a split-level or two-story. A home of many conveniences, minimal irritations, and easy upkeep. A home that's headquarters for varied family activities, but with room enough for privacy and the accommodation of individual desires, needs, and tastes.

Welcome to the new-home dream scene! You're among the friends and neighbors who in decades past were called the ivy-covered-cottage crowd.

Motivation: $$$$$$

New-home dreams are shattered in inflationary times by the reality of rapid rises in building costs. In the five years since 1970 construction costs have risen more than 56 percent. The U.S. Department of Commerce's composite construction-cost index with a base year of 1967 = 100 had a First Quarter 1970 level of 117.5 and a First Quarter 1975 level of 184.4, or almost double the costs in 1967.

During this same period, the median selling price of new homes rose from $23,900 in early 1970 to $36,500 in early 1975, an increase of nearly 53 percent. Each thousand-dollar increase in a new home's cost makes it impossible for the very substantial number of people whose incomes rise much less rapidly to afford adequate new housing.

The motivation for acting as your own general contractor for building your own new home is primarily the dollars you save. Doing some or nearly all of the administration work plus 10 percent to as much as 85 percent of the actual construction work brings savings that may range from a low of $3,000 to 5,000, to as much as $12,000 to 15,000 on a 1500 to 1800 square foot single-family home.

Or, in higher priced homes with selling prices in the $50,000 to 65,000 range for 2200 to 2600 square feet of living space, an owner-builder actively participating as bid taker and job supervisor, but having all work done by subcontractors, stands to eliminate architectural fees and/or general contractor profits that may run between 5 percent and 20 percent of the home's total price. The actual amount is difficult to pinpoint for any specific case. Building professionals do obtain lower figures from subcontractors than individual owners do; but there are also some professionals whose overall contract prices may include considerably more than the traditional 7 to 10 percent fee or profit.

When you consider that inflation is going to add another 6 to 10 percent with new labor rates and material price increases during the year-or-less period during which your home is under construction, it is easy to see why growing numbers of prospective home buyers are becoming owner-builders.

Brainwork, Not Brawn

There's a dark side owner-builders must consider. Dream homes can turn into nightmares unless *you* keep watchful control. There are many turning points in the course of construction where obstacles and delays can occur and prove costly. You solve most of them *before* they occur by being prepared in advance to deal with them. And in these dealings—your communications with officialdom and businessmen—the least effective tools are anger and threats.

An owner-builder should ascertain his exact legal rights and obligations at the outset. They will probably vary from one locality to another. So hire as your first subcontractor a local-area lawyer who will investigate and report to you the rights you will have in building and working on your own property.

When you build your own, you may think of doing every last bit of labor by yourself. That won't be likely. One obvious example of why you won't want to is the digging of a water-supply well several hundred feet into the ground.

The ratio of manual labor that you do . . . either alone or the two of you, man and wife, man and man, or woman and woman . . . whether it be most, some, or little of the work, is not that important. What *is* important is applying one's brain and common sense to the task so it gets done on a reasonable schedule, and employing assistance in the areas most needed due to your own lack of knowledge and/or lack of time. Forget lack of manual skills. With suitable guidance, they can be acquired in a surprisingly short period of time.

One key ingredient is confidence. You gain this by a combination of knowledge and practice. You learn by inquiring and you learn by doing. Take with a grain of salt any admonitions you might hear about the four-year apprentice periods that would-be carpenters, plumbers, and other skilled tradesmen are forced to live through. Those requirements were designed to protect union journeymen and to accommodate grade-school dropouts. In today's context, the much broader capability factor is forcefully demonstrated in thousands of home center and lumber-hardware retail establishments across the country in which structural and mechanical building components and parts are being sold from shopping-center display counters and racks. The manufacturers of these building products incorporate easy installation aids. They package materials with installation accessories and detailed instruction sheets. And these building products are not collecting dust on the shelves—people like yourself are buying them and learning by doing.

Your Attitude

You'll find fewer roadblocks, less frustration, and more cooperation in your contacts if you get used to the idea of yourself as the "builder" or "contractor."

The unvarnished fact is that if you decide to go ahead and do some or most of the work yourself, you *are* a builder. For this job, no one else is asking a subcontractor to look at the plans and give a price. No one else is asking the building inspector when you can get your permit. And no one else is burning the midnight oil listing estimated costs and scheduling work on this job. *You* are.

There are practical reasons for adopting the role of builder or contractor and downplaying the fact that you're also the owner. There's the matter of discounts. Many building supply retailers dispense special prices and extra service to builders and contractors. The service may include deliveries at key times . . . free deliveries. And discounts of 5 to 10 percent have been common in the past although growing numbers of large cash-and-carry chain merchandisers have diminished the amount of builder discounting being done.

One thing about discounts: if you are a new customer you have to claim or ask for them. "By the way, I get a builder's discount on these materials, don't I?" And the particular order involved or inquiry should indicate to the supplier that you expect to get all the items for this part of the work in a single order. After establishing a supplier-builder relationship on one or two orders, discounts on subsequent orders usually come routinely.

Adopt A Move-Forward Course

As an overall recommendation, it is suggested that you outline a home-building procedure that involves a division of labor. Certainly among the family members age ten or more, but also with the key subcontractors in the mechanical field—electrician, plumber, and heating contractor. You can get expert counseling on the work you will do yourself if you hire these subcontractors to handle the more critical parts. And you will avoid snags in getting the necessary official local permits and approvals if you can point to these professional subcontractors in your employ.

You can divide the labor, too, in other ways. As implied earlier, it is more satisfactory to work in pairs than alone. You exchange knowledge and know-how, and beat the weariness and discouragement that inevitably occur. The work is not easy, but can be satisfying.

Use your head to avoid the tedious. Take digging, for example. By hand, it's a slow body-and-mind-tiring process. Remember that once your septic system or house excavation is done and backfilled, there is nothing to see. So save the time and the backpains by subcontracting the digging to those who specialize in that work and who have the equipment to do in a day or less what could easily take you a month or more.

The crux of this text, then, lies in two words . . . compromise and expedite. The words work together. For example, the counsel given here is that you use standard stock house plans selected from a multitude of home plan books. These are readily available from lumber suppliers or on newsstands. By so doing, you'll compromise in that you may not get the exact home of your dreams. But you'll be saving a significant amount of time and cost by *not* holding out for the literally "individual custom home." There are some additional and perhaps more important compensations. The home you build will be uniquely yours because almost everywhere you look when it is done you will see the evidence of your labors, and the special touches added.

Savings Realized

How much will you really save doing some or a major part of your own building and administrative work? A rough guide may be drawn from the following list. By building your own as much as possible and doing some subcontracting, you can cut the labor percentage to about 10 percent.

land, title, survey	10 percent
plans, mortgage fees, services	2 percent
taxes, permits, insurance, etc.	3 percent
building materials	35 percent
construction labor	45 percent
builder and subcontractor profit	10 percent

1 Money Comes Before Land

Few people are able to finance all the things that go into the building of a new home without resorting to borrowed money unless, of course, they are selling or have sold a previous home in which they held a high amount of equity. The usual form of loan on a completed new home is a first mortgage loan secured by the property—meaning that if you default on the loan, the property may be transferred to the lender or to the mortgage holder through a process of foreclosure.

When a home is being built, money is provided for the work in the form of a construction loan which later changes into a permanent mortgage loan. In many cases a lending institution will arrange a single mortgage loan package whereby loan proceeds are paid out as the building work proceeds, but the permanent mortgage is not issued until the home has been satisfactorily completed. Home mortgages carry benefits of varying values to owners but one immediate and ongoing benefit is that of tax deductibility for mortgage interest paid.

Types of Mortgages

Mortgages on single-family homes are nearly always of the amortized type. This means the setting up of a series of monthly payments covering reduction of principal and payment of interest. In the early years of the mortgage, a greater proportion of your monthly payment goes for interest. Later on in the mortgage term, less goes for interest and more to reduce the principal. So, the more you pay as you go along, the larger the degree of ownership or equity that you have.

Talk about the possibility of a loan with mortgage lenders even before you acquire your building site. Let's take a moment to explore the logic of this.

First, you will probably wish to shop for a mortgage, or you may be forced to. The availability of loan funds for mortgages varies considerably from time to time. Your own ability to qualify for a loan may be seen as favorable by some lenders, or not favorable by others depending upon the general mortgage-money situation at the time or the current policies of the lender.

Second, as an owner-builder, you will have to practice up on your salesmanship. Not all lenders are eager to fund a home construction job to someone inexperienced in building.

Inquire In Person

In shopping early for mortgage loan possibilities, you may be inclined to use the telephone. This will not get you very far, at least not until the loan officer of the lending institution has seen you and had a chance to size you up. Don't try too hard to sell yourself. Don't try to show how knowledgeable you are. Sincerity, conscientiousness, and a sense of determination are the best qualities to display. And let the lending officer know you're still shopping around for a money source.

One of the most satisfactory ways of leading up to a mortgage loan is to open a savings account in a lending institution that makes mortgage loans. Talk to the lending officer at the time the account is opened to let him know you're aiming this account at home ownership and to expect you back before too long to discuss it with him.

Home Mortgage Information in booklet form will help owner-builders prepare for their mortgage loan discussions with lenders. Shown above are some popular guides: (l to r) U.S. Dept. of HUD's guide on mortgage insurance, quick mortgage facts from Mortgage Guaranty Insurance Corp., booklets on home ownership loans by the Farmers Home Administration and a guide to a conventional savings/loan mortgage.

Before arranging your first mortgage discussion, try to get a line on which lending institutions in your area are most active in home mortgages. Ask a few real estate brokers or home builders. Some lending institutions are much more active in offering home loans than others and you are likely to save time and shoeleather by going to those first. Find out when you talk to a lender how many homes they finance annually, what types of mortgage loans they make, and what geographic boundaries, if any, they observe in making loans.

There are a great many details that must be touched upon in arranging a loan secured by real estate. Right from the beginning you should have a fairly clear understanding of these various items. When you eventually sign the mortgage and related papers, there will be an accounting that includes an assortment of fees and charges. (See Chapter 47, "Opening Your Mortgage Loan".)

How Home Loans Are Arranged

A mortgage lender is willing to make a loan that amounts to a certain percentage of the overall value of home and land. Conservative lending institutions may loan only up to perhaps 50 or 60 percent of the appraised value or an estimate of such value made before the home is completed. The length of term for such low-ratio mortgage loans is usually relatively short, 12 to 15 years.

At the opposite end are high-ratio loans where the loan amount and term might go to 90 or 95 percent of appraised value for 30 or 40 years.

Understand that low-ratio loans are safer risks for the lender. But they mean that you have to put more money in

Monthly Payments per Thousand Dollars Loan Amount

Interest rate (Percent)	Payment period				
	10 yrs.	15 yrs.	20 yrs.	25 yrs.	30 yrs.
6	$11.11	8.44	7.17	6.45	6.00
6-½	11.36	8.72	7.46	6.76	6.33
7	11.62	8.99	7.76	7.07	6.66
7-½	11.88	9.28	8.06	7.39	7.00
8	12.14	9.56	8.37	7.72	7.34
8-½	12.40	9.85	8.68	8.06	7.69
9	12.67	10.15	9.00	8.40	8.05
9-½	12.94	10.45	9.33	8.74	8.41
10	13.22	10.75	9.66	9.09	8.78

Monthly Payments per Thousand Dollars of mortgage loan are indicated in this chart which is a rough guide for owner-borrower trying to decide how much loan he can afford in terms of payment per month.

SOURCE: Home and Garden Bulletin # 182, U.S. Department of Agriculture, "Selecting and Furnishing a Home"

cash into the deal. This means usually a larger downpayment in cases where a home is purchased. It may not pose as much of a problem to an owner-builder doing a considerable amount of his own work which will, once the loan is formally signed, take the place of a downpayment.

In this connection, it might be noted that there are other types of loans sometimes available. Some lending institutions will make land loans with the understanding that a portion of the proceeds goes to acquiring the land, another portion for improving it. Often the latter is intended for such items as sewer and water supply or access road work but may also include construction work on the home.

Prepare a Presentation

The most convincing argument in your favor in gaining approval of a lender for a morgage-and-construction loan is, as always, a relatively high rating in your net worth, income, and past credit performance records. The second persuader, and especially necessary in a build-your-own project, is evidence that you have done your planning in detail: you know exactly what work you will do yourself; you know which subcontractors will assist you; you can put down a rough schedule of work, and your house plans are completed.

Obviously, all of the many details involved in planning the home will not be finalized by the time you first talk to a mortgage lender. But gather together as many of the specifics as you can in advance. Or partial specifics. There should be many items on which you are still in doubt and you can tell the lender you will be getting further advice on them.

Bring along some data on yourself. Perhaps a job resumé and/or something that indicates your present level of income. Information about your family, and about present companies with whom you've established credit, will help. The lender you eventually work with will, of course, ask for all and more of these evaluation specifics later. But it is not a bad idea to give him a quick rundown on your resources during your initial discussion.

Be prepared also to give him any preferences you may have arrived at insofar as your home site is concerned. Assuming you have not already purchased a home site, a lender may have some suggestions that could be helpful in land selection. And it could also be that he has preferences of his own concerning the location of properties on which he is willing to make mortgage loans.

How Much Loan, How Much Home?

How you rate as a credit risk will probably determine or at least figure into how much of a home your lender believes you can afford and how much of a loan he is willing to provide on such a home. But, assuming you have average-or-above credit rating and income for the kind of home you have in mind, then other factors may enter into consideration.

The lender may be willing to lend a greater proportion of a home's appraisal figure if the loan is to be insured or guaranteed by a private or government agency. Savings-loan institutions make extensive use of private mortgage insuring firms, and the Veterans Administration and U.S. Department of Housing & Urban Development (HUD) offer VA-guarantees and FHA-insurance on mortgage loans to qualified owners.

Studies of families having mortgages indicate that the amount of income-after-taxes going into monthly payments and home operating-maintenance costs range from:

- 15 to 22 percent for moderate income families, with the lower amounts for older age groups;
- 25 to 39 percent for low-incomers with the lower amounts for the younger age groups.

The lending institutions you contact in your area will provide guidelines to the amount of home they believe suited for different levels of income. In your own calculations for estimating possible monthly payments, you should consider housing costs with additions for taxes, insurance, repairs, utilities, and other home services as well as the principal/interest payments for the mortgage. When considering types of mortgage loans, you may initially be attracted to the longer terms and higher loan-to-value ratios of government insured loans. These are the loans some lenders prefer because the government insures them (the lenders) against losses in case the mortgage is defaulted. For the home occupant they usually mean lower monthly payments and a longer time over which to spread the payments.

But there are disadvantages in FHA/VA insured loans, too. They are quite apt to involve processing delays. You will be expected to follow HUD's Minimum Property Standards which are a bit more stringent in requirements than many local building codes. And in a very large number of

metropolitan areas as well as nearly all rural areas, not many lending institutions are involved with FHA/VA loans.

If your new home is to be located in the country or in a smaller town or city *not* part of a Standard Metropolitan Statistical Area and under 20,000 population, you may qualify under the direct lending program of the Farmers Home Administration (FmHA).

These FmHA loans are direct, meaning the government provides the money, not merely the insurance for the mortgage. The program is handled through FmHA agents in most counties and the financing of single-family homes is under Section 502 of the authorizing act. Emphasis in the program is on smaller homes for low-to-moderate income families which, in most cases, means homes on the order of 800 to 1200 square feet of living area. The major advantage for the borrower is the 40 year term of these loans, which means low monthly payments. A relatively low interest rate applies without the complication of discount points used as an adjustable market factor in FHA/VA loans.

Recommended Procedure. If your home is to be located in an outlying rural area or small town and your income is about $8,000 to $9,000 annually or less, by all means inquire about the Farmers Home direct loan program by sending for literature and then making contact with the agent in the county in which you plan to be located.

If your income is higher than $9,000, you are more likely to be able to work out a complete home-building and long-term financing arrangement with a savings and loan association (in some areas called building and loan or simply savings association). Such institutions are geared to residential mortgages and most are oriented to working closely with individuals in connection with home loans.

Savings and loan companies may also be able to offer you high-ratio loans of 90 or 95 percent of appraised value at lower fees and much less red tape than is involved in FHA-insured loans. These loans are privately insured, but often only for the early part of the loan period.

2 Choosing a Home Site

The scenic home site high on a hilltop with a view extending miles in every direction may require added expenditures of $250 or higher for lightning rod protection. That little plot of ground with gardening area in the valley may be under water at times during the April flash-flood period. The sidehill site with an attractive stone irregularity may be underlaid with solid rock that will add hundreds of dollars to excavating, grading, and driveway work.

So, plan to investigate the land surrounding your prospective home site. Plan to compromise and try to avoid the expense and delays that problem building sites can cause.

Similar in nature but not so visually apparent as the above mentioned potential trouble makers are a long list of location and site factors that an owner-builder should give some thought and careful consideration to when selecting a spot for his home. Here are the major items:

☐ water-table and drainage patterns in the area;
☐ whether or not location is in a flood-plain district;
☐ location factors with respect to future assessments;
☐ limitations due to zoning or building requirements;
☐ water supply;
☐ soil factors relating to absorption or stabilization;
☐ true values and limiting controls in a subdivision;
☐ location characteristics with regard to marketability;
☐ status of present ownership or title to the property.

A Closer Look

First on your checklist should be the laws regarding those zoning and building regulations by the governing jurisdiction which limit what you are legally able to do with the property. A similar set of rules may also apply to the property as a result of a subdivider or developer having recorded such guidelines as part of the deed or other instrument of ownership transferral.

Neighborhood

Size up and perhaps obtain local counsel regarding the proximity of present and future homes. Look also to the quality of new construction and cost level of recently built homes. Favor locations where existing homes in the area tend to be newer. And where they tend to be larger or a little more luxurious than your initial plans call for. It is better to be the least expensive house in a better area than the most expensive house in a less advantageous area.

Facilities

Check those public services which your family will need. Foremost facility is, of course, the school situation with a look at both present and future needs. Other facilities of varying importance to different families but worthy of checking include churches, food-necessity shopping centers, less frequent big-ticket shopping proximity, recreational features, organized sports, and irritants. Are there conditions about the location not readily apparent? Frequent noise or unpleasant odor conditions? Rail grade crossings without signals? Ordinances that govern pets or keeping of animals? And so on.

Appraisals

Your mortgage loan may require home site appraisal. An appraisal is an impartial opinion of the value of real estate prepared by an expert who knows the relevant factors and local characteristics. While the appraiser's work generally concerns land and buildings, it is possible to obtain an appraisal on a parcel of vacant land for a reasonably low fee.

The point is, an appraiser can help you reach a decision

for or against buying a particular home site. And he can probably be of some service in guiding you to desirable home sites in the geographic area you have selected. If you have been talking to a lending institution in a given area, the mortgage loan officer can offer a name or two of appraisers you may wish to contact.

Buying A Subdivision Lot

In addition to the newly subdivided tracts in which developers are actively promoting lot sales, there are in nearly all parts of the country an assortment of lesser known and somewhat older subdivisions still having vacant lots. By the time a subdivision has homes on about 75 percent of its lots, the developer is usually no longer actively involved except for possibly a lot or two. The remaining lots are likely to be in the hands of individual owners whose plans for building are still in the future if they are planning at all. Occasionally such owners are valuable contacts if you are interested in living in the area, because you may chance upon a bargain.

The principal merit in purchasing an improved subdivision lot lies in the word "improved." This usually means that the prime necessities such as sewer and water supply plus electricity and perhaps natural gas are readily available. Or that the lots themselves can accommodate individual water supply wells or septic disposal systems. Improved subdivision lots may also have added value due to paved streets or other community facilities or services that are not available with many individual land parcels or acreage.

Some lot owners, however, play the waiting game. Like the owners of homes for sale, they have asking prices above what they are actually willing to take—most of the time. So, bargain with them if the area interests you. First, try to get a verbal indication that the owner might come down on the price. Later, if you wish to test and are ready to buy, do so by making a bona fide offer. Bona fide in most areas means accompanying the offer with an earnest money de-

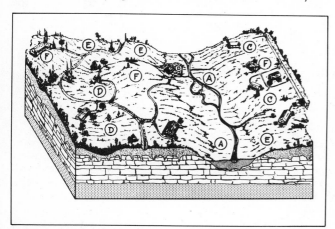

Common Topographic Positions are shown in this sketch, adapted from the SCS booklet: (A) flood plain; (B) alluvial fan of deposits near mouth of a contributing creek which may be subject to flash floods; (C) an upland waterway collecting water from surrounding higher land will need diversion measures; (D) depressed areas where water accumulates may be soft and continuously spongy; (E) steep hillsides may be shallow to rock or subject to slippage and erosion; (F) well-drained soil on ridges or gentle hillsides have fewest water problems and are usually best home sites.

posit, a nominal sum which may be forfeited, however, if you fail to complete the deal after acceptance.

In buying property, scepticism may serve you well. Your stand on buying any site is simply that your wish is to have all the facts in hand before making your decision. And you're going to go wherever it may be necessary in order to resolve any doubts.

A home-site buyer needs to be especially wary in the purchase of property on which he desires to build a fairly remote country home, vacation/leisure, or retirement home. The rural-resort areas of the country are swamped with home sites for sale and a sizable proportion of them are no better than swamps for home building purposes. Misrepresentations by sellers of this type of home site real estate occur with much more frequency than is the case with sellers of vacant land in suburban and small town areas.

Sewers and Soils

The single most important aspect of your home site purchase as far as accommodating a home is the ability to dispose appropriately of household liquid and solid wastes. While there are a few space-age substitute or alternative methods for handling wastes, this text will recommend you avoid them and bypass home sites where no municipal or community sanitary sewers are available for connection or where limitations indicated by soil percolation tests hint that the ground is unsuited to septic disposal field installations.

The fact that a sewer main runs in front of the vacant property you are interested in does not mean that you will be able to connect to it when you wish. Some communities have inadequate sewage treatment facilities and have declared moratoriums on further connections to existing sewers. Other communities apply the phrase "inadequate facilities" to any of a number of community services as an excuse to slow down the rate of building for one reason or another, and the reasoning is, no doubt, occasionally valid. Sewer connection permits sometimes become a home-building control, the rationed-out permits acting as reins on the rate of new home construction.

In still other communities and areas, the expansion of sewage treatment or disposal facilities is being delayed by court actions and other activities initiated by environmentalist groups or by federal and state environmental protection agencies.

Do not assume that in buying a large lot of acreage away from sewer lines you will encounter no problems with an individual sewage disposal system, a septic tank, and a distribution field. Your first roadblock to such a system may be unsuitable soil and/or a relatively high level of ground water table. If you clear those conditions, the supervisory agency such as the state board of health or possibly the department of conservation may have rules and regulations you must observe. And then, of course, the local building-zoning authorities may have their own special requirements for septic systems.

There is still another septic disposal field matter worth inquiry while you are making the foregoing checks, and that is your neighbor's disposal field. It could, depending on your lot size and condition, be located in such a way so as to interfere with either your water-supply well installation or your septic field in case your state health department or local building code has minimum distance requirements that must be observed.

There are other aspects of home site soil conditions to look into, of course. Soil hazards need not be 100 percent avoided since some can be corrected or compensated for so that chances of damage or trouble are minimized. Sump pumps, for example, can be depended upon as one protective measure. And erosion can be reduced in several ways to manageable levels, but it does cost money to do so.

In a great many locations, you can obtain detailed and reliable guidance on soil matters through county offices of the U.S. Department of Agriculture's Soil Conservation

Factors Involved in Selecting A Homesite range from subsoils to school convenience. Among the sources of information are the various organizations issuing educational booklets such as these: U.S. Soil Conservation Service, U.S. Dept. of HUD, American Land Title Association and the Society of Real Estate Appraisers. Where to send for such booklets is indicated in the source reference, Appendix B.

Natural Hazards to Homesites are shown in this series of photos taken from the Soil Conservation Service's booklet "Know the Soil You Build On". Shown upper left is a home site where the soil's high water table presents a problem for the home's septic disposal field. At right, a group of small homes have been built on a flood plain subject to periodic flooding. Below, there may be high erosion hazard present even on shallow slopes and with some slopes, soil slippage may be difficult and costly to prevent.

Service. Many counties have been completely surveyed and county maps published showing locations of different kinds of soils and describing just what land uses they may be appropriate for, and what their limitations may be.

Among the common hazards in certain soils and locations, beyond lack of absorptivity and flooding, are seasonally high water table levels. During the wet season, such conditions can lead to basement flooding, inoperative septic disposal fields and damages to plants and shrubs that cannot tolerate much water.

Certain kinds of clay soils are prone to uneven settlement or soil shifting which can result in foundation movement and development of cracks or openings. Shrinking-swelling movement as water content varies may cause a home's foundation walls or floors to move as much as an inch or two and create interior wall damage.

Certain soil types are poor at bearing sustained loads without special foundation measures. Avoid them. Another factor is erosion by rain and storm-water runoff. Erosion in your home site may eat away continually at your topsoil and lawn. Erosion in a nearby area may bring sediment deposits and can cause other damage to your property unless the site drainage pattern is revised. Similarly, erosion-protection measures for drainage downstream of your site may cause water backup or flooding damages to your site.

Also of prime importance is feasibility of a water-supply deep well if your lot is not served by a municipal or community water system. While some soil specialists may provide well information, the best up-to-date counselor is likely to be the well-digging contractor who does regular work in that area.

Except for some special and limitied situations where a safe water supply may be obtained with shallow wells and direct driven pipe taps or well points, the recommended procedure is a deep drilled well with an outer casing and a submersible pump.

When obtaining a bid price from a well-digging contractor, the quotation is often given at a figure of so much per foot of depth. The contractor may make an educated guess but he cannot be sure to what depth he will have to go to give sufficient volume of flow. Nor can he guarantee drinking water quality.

The installation should include drilling, installation of casing, well pipe and pump and the well-head to house connection in a below-frost trench. With sandy or silty soils, well-strainers are needed. Also advisable: deal with a well digger who will warranty the materials and workmanship and who will also be able to offer after-completion services to solve any problems that may arise.

There may be occasions where the land or home site location desirable to you is within a flood plain district. First inquire about the National Flood Insurance program based upon the Flood Disaster Act of 1973. Since many private insurance companies will not offer protection against flood damage, this Act authorizes federally subsidized flood insurance for all types of buildings and their contents at rates lower and with coverage more generous

than in the original program of 1968. The Act cuts back the extent of haphazard construction on land known to be flood prone. All identified flood-prone communities must enter the program by mid-1975, adopting appropriate land-use measures to regulate and protect construction in such high-risk areas.

Property Transfer And Rights

Ownership of a piece of land or a developed home site passes from its previous owner in the form of a deed. But this transferring instrument is no assurance to you of the quality or condition of the title thus conveyed.

Title Insurance. Widely used today, title insurance provides protection to real estate buyers from the hazards involved in clouded titles and defects in ownership records. A title or abstract company conducts a title search through previous ownership records to see that the property is free of encumbrances and then issues a title insurance policy for a single one-time premium or fee.

With title insurance you should understand that there are differing interests. A title policy may be one whose principal purpose is to protect a lender's interest in the property. Be certain in arranging a title search that the resulting title insurance policy is one that will protect the buyer's (your) interests. A property seller's title search and insurance, even if recent, may not be adequate for you as the buyer and new owner.

Advisable: the use of an attorney in closing the purchase of a home-site or parcel of land. By all means, choose a lawyer who practices regularly in real estate transactions and is familiar with local and state laws, policies, and procedures.

Check Your General Soil Map if you can. Many but not all counties in which soil-water conservation districts have been established have been surveyed by the Soil Conservation Service and a general soil map published. A map with vari-colored areas representing different types of soils, plus a description of these soils, gives indications of each soil's limitations and its suitability for selected uses.

Your lawyer may offer to conduct the title search. What he is offering is the search of public records for possible title defects. He can then give you the facts as he finds them. In contrast, a title insurance policy offers you protection against nonrecorded defects and defects that may develop subsequent to the purchase. Some of these non-public-record defects that may apply are:

□ false representation and/or forged signatures;
□ instruments signed under expired/revoked powers of attorney;
□ delivery of a conveyance after the death of a grantor;
□ dower rights of a previous spouse;
□ undisclosed heirs;
□ deeds by a corporation without proper or legal authority;
□ misrepresentation of marital status;
□ errors of recording officials or in legal interpretations;
□ fraud in obtaining of signatures.

Additional Limitations. Be alert for possible claims other than those of previous owners before signing a purchase contract for a home site. One notable exception on many pieces of property is the right to extract various minerals. Mineral rights are commonly separated from property rights where the land is suspected of having some resource value for minerals such as oil or uranium.

Another exception in some areas is that pertaining to water. Whatever water can be welled from below or removed from the surface of your home site, land may belong partially or wholly to someone else.

A third common form of exceptional external rights is the control for certain purposes expressed in easement rights. Easements occur where utility companies run poles and wires or underground pipes/cables across the property. Easements may also be utilized by their owners to cross your property legally by roads or access ways including recreational paths or routes.

Finally, there are strictures concerning your home's proposed size or appearance, and perhaps other factors, because of deed restrictions. Usually, this will involve approval of your home's working drawings by an architectural control committee or agent.

3 Choosing Your Home Plans

There have been many homes erected by home builders based on little more than a couple of sheets of paper, one sheet containing floor-plan dimensions, the other sheet, four house elevations. Even where such minimal "plans" might still be acceptable to some local building officials, it is in the best interests of the home occupant to have the home built from a proper set of working drawings and specifications.

Your plans and specifications have value in the arrangement of mortgage loans as well as in obtaining building permits and other necessary approvals. So the working drawings should consist of approximately the following: plot plan, foundation plan, first and second floor plan, exterior elevations, typical wall section, key structural details, fireplace and chimney details, and interior elevations of kitchen and bath walls. In some localities, accepted practice may be to also include a heat-duct drawing and a plumbing diagram.

For the owner-builder, the fastest, simplest, and least expensive way to obtain working drawings and specifications or materials lists is through design companies called stock plan services. These firms prepare catalogs or plan books containing simple floor-plan drawings and architectural renderings (sketches) of homes. A dozen up to more than a hundred different designs can be found in plan-books, which are nominally priced and sold in many newsstands, home centers and lumber-supply dealer stores. You look through plan books until you find the home design that appeals to you. Then, if you decide to follow that design in the building of your new home, you look for instructions in the back of the plan book, send in an order with a check for either a single set of plans or for multiple sets as may be needed. Some companies base their initial price on a package of four sets. An individual set or minimum package may range in cost from $35 to $150 depending on house size and complexity. Additional sets of plans are available at low cost, about $10 to $15 per set.

The Value of Plan Services

Using stock plans and buying sets from the stock plan services has a number of advantages. First, these design specialists stay pretty up-to-date in connection with building code changes. Most stock plan companies conform all their plans to recognized national codes such as the One-and-Two-Family Dwelling Code sponsored by the three major organizations of building code officials and the HUD-FHA Minimum Property Standards.

The trouble with trying to design your own home from scratch is that there are certain fundamentals that should be adhered to, certain dimensions that should for various reasons be standard. Stairways and halls should be a minimum of 3 feet in width. But little is gained if they are wider. Ceilings of 8 feet are considered standard although 7 feet 6 inches is considered satisfactory for certain areas. But this height is a minimum and the designer must allow for finished materials installation so dimensions from rough floor to finish ceiling are often established at 8 feet plus 1-½ or 2 inches.

Such details in planning and a multitude of others are already taken care of in stock plan house designs. There's another element included in stock plans, too—economy. Dimensioning of rooms and spaces for suitable structural members are made with a minimum amount of waste using standard-length lumber. Dimensions used also tend to be economical in their use of sheet materials. This would be a virtually impossible task for a first-time owner-builder unless he had a professional home designer standing alongside and telling him what to do every step of the way.

Hiring an architect or home designer to plan a custom home will involve substantially more cost and time in developing plans and specifications than use of a stock plan service. Actually, only relatively few architects are involved in daily home design work and of those who are, most develop plans and specifications primarily for luxury homes. For small to medium sized homes, the plan service firms probably offer *better* designs (because of their specialization) than could be worked out by architects. This is not meant to convey the idea that stock plans are available only for smaller homes. Not a bit. Plans and designs come in all sizes and styles.

Some lumber dealers and other retail outlets offering plan books for sale sometimes have their own draftsman or designer who can make alterations or modifications in stock plans. You may run across a stock plan in a plan book that you like very much except you would like just a few changes made.

Nevertheless, such modifications should be looked at very closely before making them and in most cases, not made. The reason is the domino effect. Make a little change here, and you affect other related items that then require changes on other drawing sheets or materials lists. Even what seems to be a minor change can have a snowball effect.

Instead, try hunting a bit more in plan books. Get more plan books produced by other companies. The few dollars they will cost is far less than probable cost of the revised drawing work.

Stock plans are prepared by experienced home design experts who have accumulated a broad range of planning ideas over a considerable length of time. Some are licensed and practicing architects. Others are architecturally trained or have come from the field of industrial design. But most have acquired considerable skill in planning homes and in avoiding troublesome construction details.

Incidentally, when you stop by such retail building materials suppliers such as home centers and lumber dealers seeking out plan books, it's a good time to inquire about that supplier's other services, availability of components,

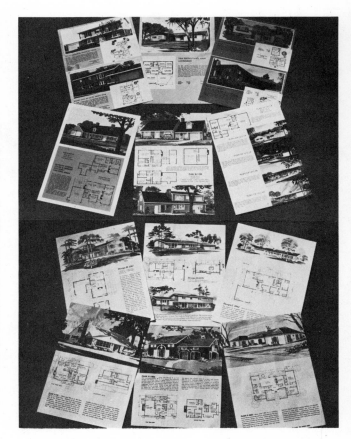

Typical Pages in Plan Books are shown to indicate common practice of design firms. The plan books are comparable to catalogs from which you choose products. They offer 50 to 100 or more different home designs. You can pore over and study these various home designs to find a home whose floor plan and design appeal to you. Each page contains an architectural sketch of the home's exterior plus a floor plan and also a brief description of the home's main features. Some plan books specialize in presenting certain types of home designs; others give a broad assortment of designs for all styles or types of homes.

and the counseling that they might be able to furnish you during the course of construction. Shop for guidance as well as plan books.

Looking At House Plans

In a recent comprehensive survey of current consumer and home builder attitudes towards new homes, a number of revealing feelings surfaced. Conducted by the National Family Opinion Research Company and the research affiliate of *Professional Builder* magazine, the survey indicated a very, very strong preference persisting for single-family detached homes. But high premiums on good home locations and convenient community services were also evidenced. With respect to types of single-family homes, the degree of preferences expressed were: one-story ranch

Selected Home Plan Books are available at nominal cost from design companies that also offer complete blueprint and specifications services. Shown here are planbooks issued by Master Plan Service, Garlinghouse Home Plans Division, Home Planners Inc., and Home Building Plan Service. Addresses are provided in Appendix B.

home, over 50 percent; 22 percent for two-story; 18 percent for split- or bi-level homes; and 8 percent for one-and-a-half story.

Other specific home features indicated as desirable in the survey, and borne out by other similar research studies in recent years, include strong preference for full basements, an extra bedroom beyond immediate needs, laundry facilities on the first floor, and a two-car garage. Also quite popular among new home buyers are separate dining rooms, fireplaces, air conditioning, wall-to-wall carpeting, and fuel-saving measures through extra insulation.

In plan books, each design is accompanied by a home size given in square feet. This figure is usually calculated from the plans and is sometimes referred to as "living area." What is meant is the interior living space involved in rooms, halls, closets and stairs, but not unfinished space in basements, garages, or carport areas and additional area outside the home but roofed in, such as entry porches, terraces, or outdoor decks.

A home's living area in square feet may be used as a rule-of-thumb figure for residential costs for your local area. These rule-of-thumb figures are often not very accurate. But they will give you at least a rough or ballpark amount as a guide.

Although the level of square foot costs may vary one job to another within a given area and vary even more one area to another reflecting different levels of construction wage rates, the current typical square foot costs reported by home building professionals is running in the range of $18 to $20 per square foot in lower cost areas such as small towns and far-out metro fringes. In small-to-medium cities, single-family wood-frame construction is more apt to be in the $20 to $22 range and perhaps $25 or more in large metro and well-established suburban areas. These are approximate cost levels in the mid-seventies and tend to reflect costs in north-central, northeast, and far west states. Square foot costs in other areas are apt to be slightly less.

When looking at house plans, try to judge whether a home is easier or harder to build than most others you've looked at. To judge, look at the number of corners in walls and partitions. Where there are wall projections, odd angles, curves . . . in short many zigs and zags . . . such a home design is going to be relatively difficult to frame and finish.

And skip hurriedly past those more complex designs having zooming roof angles or changing roof slopes and the off-beat shapes that architects and builders are prone to develop for their custom-home clients. Being different and being spectacular in home design usually means doubling the costs.

Choose for your first owner-built home a plan that comes closest to meeting your immediate needs. There are some sound reasons, too, for planning a basic one-story home that offers easy expansion space at a later date, such as in an unfinished attic or basement, or lower level of a bi-level.

Check house sizes carefully. Use a square foot cost rule-of-thumb as a guide to affordable house size. Deduct on the order of $2 to $5 per square foot from your area's

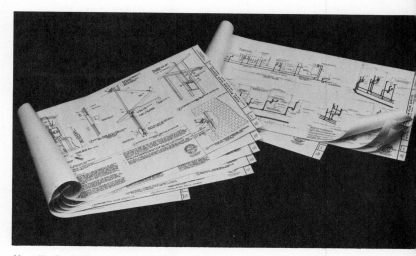

How-To-Do-It Plumbing and Wiring Diagrams prepared by professionals are available at low cost to supplement the drawings-specifications services of Home Building Plan Service. The diagrams are color-coded and give many supplementary informative details about owner-builder procedures in plumbing and electrical work.

thumb figure as the rough amount that you'll save. It's easy to be carried away with your dreams as you look at plan books. Use a thumb cost figure to keep your thoughts in rein. It's silly to be dreaming and planning a 2900 square foot home when your credit rating, income, and mortgage lender says that at most you should be considering a $24,000 cost level.

Try to narrow your choices to about six house plan designs. Then, you and your family should start trying to find fault with them. Discard designs that appear to have excessive hallway space. Favor plans that have convenient entrances, particularly entrances from garage to house. Avoid plans that indicate a number of small closets in what appear to be odd locations. Rather, choose a plan that tends to group closet storage areas along one wall or two walls so that the closets serve as noise reducers between rooms. Walk-in closets for the master bedroom are a plus.

Pick a plan that has what the home-and-garden magazines refer to as "good circulation." This phrase indicates ease in moving from one place to another in the home. And it means that access to each room from a central or entrance hallway is direct and relatively short. Look for good room relationships rather than foot traffic paths . . . dining areas convenient to kitchen serving areas, powder rooms convenient to living or family rooms, baths convenient to bedrooms, and so on.

Materials List or Specifications

Working drawings indicate part of the information needed to build. Materials lists and/or specifications indicate more specific details relating to the grade and quality of the materials. The practice has been, increasingly, to supplement and annotate some good working drawings and perhaps to some degree to duplicate the detail provided in the specifications and materials list. The drawings do this by notations that explain or elucidate how the product or material is to be installed and what practices in that connection should be observed. A typical example taken from a floor plan drawing with the following notation in the garage floor area: "4 inch thick concrete floor slab (1:2:4 mix, 3,000 pound compressive strength) over compacted earth; slope up 4 inches from front to rear."

So, plans and specifications or materials lists work together; as you go over them there will be side aspects to which you will want to give consideration. Three of the more important considerations in recent years include sav-

ings in fuel to heat, cool and light the home; reduction of noise transmission from outside the home and between certain rooms; and safety and security or protection within the home against intrusion, fire, and accident.

Energy Savings

The amount of fuel used is in inverse proportion to the thermal insulation value incorporated into a home. The better insulated, weatherstripped and thermal-glass-equipped, the better a house offers an effective barrier to the outside and thus needs less energy to keep it warm or cool.

Three major areas require extra attention in providing insulation:

(1) walls, floors, ceilings—where insulations such as mineral wool or fiberglass are used, the degree of insulating performance increases with thickness. Use "full" thicknesses (meaning up to stud or joist depths) in walls and ceilings. Check a heat transfer resistance chart as a guide to thickness usage (further details in Chapter 26);
(2) window and door glass—the use of double-paned insulating glass or a built-in window storm sash is recommended. A separate storm sash that is removable is also acceptable.
(3) edge-sealing of windows and doors—used to be handled by weatherstripping but today's windows and thermal-type entrance doors come with built-in stripping (see details in Chapter 18)

You will no doubt hear or read about the great strides being made in these energy-conscious times by companies or individuals with practical solar heating-cooling systems for homes. But beware! Investigate exactly what is meant by "practical" if you're interested in these solar energy approaches.

Recommendation: At present writing, the counsel is "no" on solar energy devices for general heating-cooling unless you live in particular geographic areas. Although there has been some excellent research and development work in this field, it's a field crowded with scientists, not home design experts, so that many residential solar energy systems to date must be labelled "unproven" either in performance or estimates of cost, some of which can run unusually high.

Safety and Security

Home safety, particularly with respect to possible fire hazards, has been scrutinized to an extensive degree in just the past two years. During this period, many building codes and construction standards have added mandatory provisions for the interior use of smoke detection devices. There presently appears to be a possibility that certain widely followed model building codes may soon be requiring the installation of sprinkler systems in one-and-two family construction.

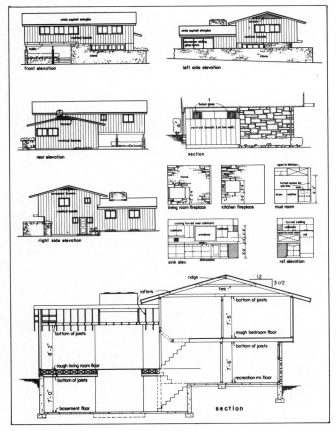

Working Drawings for a Home, also called "Blueprints." Today these drawings are printed up black on white paper with a more up-to-date process than blueprinting. Typically, such working drawings will contain scale drawings of each floor level, elevations (as shown above) of each of the four sides of a home's exterior, elevations of the walls of kitchen and bathroom and a full cross-section through the home to show portions of the structural framing. Working drawings may also include diagrams relating to plumbing and heating installations, house foundations and perhaps other details such as stairways or fireplaces.

One safety precaution, simple though it may sound, should be observed in all one- and two-story homes. Provide at least one window in each sleeping room with sufficient size in its ventilating opening to allow exit by an adult or child in case of emergency.

Wood-frame construction is in itself not especially subject to fire hazards despite the prejudiced viewpoints of people and officials having some relationship with masonry or fire-resistant materials and methods. But in any frame home, there are certain areas that are more subject to accidents and perhaps to the origin of fires just as there are parts of a home that are more subject to damage by windstorms. The greatest protection is for the owner-builder and occupant to be aware of such locations. Added safety measures can easily be applied during construction at relatively slight increases in cost. Several such areas will be described in chapters to come with suggestions made on how to increase safety. Here's a brief listing of some of the more important safety-consideration factors.

(1) energy-consuming appliances—specifically the furnace, water heater and other heavy-duty electrical loads such as clothes dryers, ironers, air conditioners;
(2) rooms where portable electrical appliances are frequently used or where such appliances are involved with the presence of water—kitchen, bath, laundry areas;
(3) stairways where falls may be serious;
(4) large glass areas where breakage may readily occur and the use of safety glass is often indicated, particularly with sliding patio doors;
(5) places where floors are apt to be slippery at times;
(6) basement or utility areas where instantly flammable items might be stored in close conjunction with easily burning rags, clothes and paper;
(7) proper electrical grounding of wiring circuits particularly certain hazardous circuits inside and out;
(8) rooms in which decorating materials include carpeted

floors and wind draperies whose fabrics have low flammability or flame-spread characteristics;
(9) entrance locking devices that offer better resistance to intruders and other occupant-protective devices.

Noise Reduction

Just as thermal insulation will reduce transfer of heat or cold through walls, roofs, and floors, so there are acoustical materials which can help reduce the transmission of noise throughout structures and also lower other noise conditions within a home.

If a home is well insulated thermally, it will be a quieter home. But sometimes it is desirable to isolate certain rooms to reduce transmission between them. Or to muffle noises within a room, such as the rattling of pans in a kitchen.

Isolation by cushioned mounting of noisy equipment can help. And in some cases, further steps can be taken to produce quieter operation; for example, the wrapping of heating or cooling ducts to reduce fan or blower sounds. Some of a typical home's more serious noise offenders are:

(1) lower decibels but fairly continuous noise—furnace blowers, air circulators, fans, air conditioners, refrigerators, and clothes dryers;
(2) mid-range noisiness but under 60 decibels—dishwashers, clothes washers, vacuum cleaners, food mixers, sink disposal grinders, sewing machines, electric shavers;
(3) most noisy and above 80 decibels—yard-care tools, shop tools, children's or adult's electronic entertainment equipment.

So, in checking home plans and material lists or specifications, be alert for materials and products that provide assistance with their fuel savings, safety-security, and noise-reduction properties. Check manufacturer's literature for their performance and be willing to spend a small additional sum money for materials or products designed to aid in these areas and to improve living comfort and health.

CONSTRUCTION PLANS

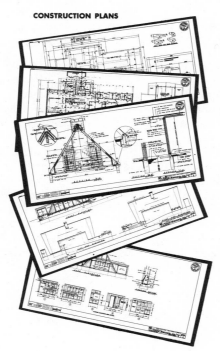

MATERIALS LIST

Among the materials listed:
• Masonry, Veneer & Fireplace • Framing Lumber • Roofing & Sheet Metal • Windows & Door Frames • Exterior Trim & Insulation • Tile Work, Finish Floors • Interior Trim, Kitchen Cabinets • Rough & Finish Hardware

SPECIFICATION OUTLINE

• General Instructions, Suggestions and Information • Excavating and Grading • Masonry and Concrete Work • Sheet Metal Work • Carpentry, Millwork, Roofing, and Miscellaneous Items • Lath and Plaster or Drywall Wallboard • Schedule for Room Finishes • Painting and Finishing • Tile Work • Electrical Work • Plumbing • Heating and Air

Blueprints, Specifications and Materials Lists are the principal planning aids that plan book design companies offer to owner-builders. Blueprints and specifications come in sets so that copies can be submitted to local building department, lender, and subcontractors estimating portions of the work. Blueprint and specs cost around $40-50 per set depending on company and type of house design involved.

4 Planning Your Construction Work

Your home plans, consisting of working drawings, specifications, and materials list as discussed in the previous chapter, are your basic communication tool in talking with and getting prices or estimates from suppliers and subcontractors. They are also a primary persuasion factor in obtaining approvals from zoning boards or building departments and any other agency that may be involved in a particular locality. The plans and specifications indicate primarily what you propose to construct and the quality of that construction.

Consequently, you will require a number of sets of drawings and specifications. A typical distribution list for these sets might be: one for the building-zoning department; one for the lender; one for each subcontractor with whom you will work; one for your components supplier; one for your principal materials supplier; a file copy; and a working copy for yourself. You had better order an added set or two if you're going to get a few competitive subcontract bids (ten to fifteen copies should start you off with no difficulty). Some of the sets you put out to subcontractors and suppliers can, of course, be returned to you.

To the sets of drawings that you obtain from a stock plan service, you will have to add one drawing, a plot plan drawing, to each set going to agencies or subcontractors interested in the work related to the building site. This plot plan drawing can be prepared by the engineer handling your survey.

As you become involved with certain aspects of the construction you may wish to add a few supplemental drawings, usually referred to as shop drawings or diagrams and used in connection with mechanical work, plus a plumbing diagram showing line runs of drainage-waste-vent and water piping, a heating duct layout drawing showing main supply, branches, registers and plenums, and an electrical circuit diagram to aid in properly connecting wiring runs to outlet boxes. Other simpler sketch drawings you may also make up yourself will assist in using materials effectively, such as a plywood sheet layout sketch for floor and roof decks. You will also need accurately dimensioned shop drawings for certain items where it may be desirable to measure from actual job conditions rather than from working drawings. One example might be the drawing prepared for shop fabrication of kitchen counter assemblies.

Using Partial Subcontracts

Reaching possible subcontractors to assist you with certain types of installations is not particularly difficult. You will find that many individually owned subcontracting businesses are quite willing to assist you on a partial basis where they perform key or critical parts of the work and guide you in doing the balance. Here are three ways to contact suitable subcontractors:

☐ use supplier recommendation—every time you talk with lumber and material suppliers, ask about subcontractors and initiate a subcontractor prospect list;
☐ look in neighborhood or community newspaper ads and yellow pages for names of smaller and moonlighting tradesmen;
☐ visit home-builder sites to see subcontractor trucks with names-numbers—stop, observe, talk with subcontractors, who can often recommend someone even if they are not interested in doing the work.

When talking to a potential subcontractor, explain that you essentially need guidance in installation as well as having someone do the more critical portions of the work. Later, once you have reached a decision on the subcontractor you want, ask about his ideas on suitable division of work. Prepare a letter of agreement about such division to go with a signed contract that includes a fixed price. Do not proceed with any work simply on the basis of a verbal agreement or verbal price figure. Get in writing the scope of the work and just what the subcontractor will supply and do.

A further suggestion as you deal with a subcontractor or supplier. If he does not so indicate, inquire about his usual method of receiving payments. You'll receive better attention and more cooperation if you agree to pay him on a certain basis or at certain times and then follow through with prompt payments. Tell him how a payment schedule has been set up with your lender.

Most lenders providing construction or what is often called "interim" funds, prefer to set up a system of payouts to be made during the construction period. These are often called "draws" against the construction account and the payments are authorized by the borrower for work performed or materials delivered. Rather than make individual payouts, a schedule usually calls for a group of payments to be made:

□ when foundations or basement walls have been completed;
□ when the house is roofed in and closed against the weather;
□ when an inspector has approved plumbing-heating-electrical rough;
□ when interior finish and trim work has been completed;
□ following final clean-up and inspection.

Contracting

For the owner-builder who expects to do as much of his own work as possible or practical, the following line-up of partial subcontract jobs should be considered:

Foundation Walls. Pouring of concrete footings and laying up concrete masonry blocks for your foundation wall is considered well within the capabilities of an owner-builder, but if for any reason you plan to have your foundation walls of poured concrete, it is recommended you have a concrete subcontractor do the footings and the walls. This way you will avoid the rather touchy job of erecting wall forms and the subcontractor will probably use smooth reusable forms that result in a uniform and smooth concrete surface, especially worth attention for homes with basements.

Masonry. Laying of concrete block foundation walls and brick veneer as exterior siding are both relatively straightforward jobs that an owner-builder can accomplish without problems. The same applies to a block chimney for use as a heating vent. But fireplace chimneys are more difficult. The easiest, fastest way to build a fireplace is to use a prefabricated fire-box with or without a heat-circulation feature and to follow with a prefabricated metal chimney. If an all-brick or all-stone fireplace and chimney is contemplated, also consider letting a subcontract on it.

Electrical Wiring. Your twofold aim here is to hire an electrician to install the heavy-duty part including the meter base, main disconnects, feeder and distribution panel. Then, have him agree to guide you in the branch-circuit wiring and fixture-receptacle installation. He can also aid in purchasing supplies and handling needed inspections.

Plumbing. Working from the same principle here, hire a plumber to install the soil pipe and main stack if using cast iron pipe with poured lead joints. If waste lines are to be of copper or plastic you will still benefit by having a plumber install the sewer connecting part and fabricate the main stack so that you will have his guidance in the balance of the drain-waste-vent connections and on the water supply piping. Again, the plumber may be helpful in purchasing of supplies and arranging inspections. You may also need his guidance on sump pump installation and individual water supply systems. And he will be the information source you fall back on in case of problems with the fixture installation. Keep in mind that many plumbing subcontractors are also dealers for plumbing ware and will be interested in furnishing fixtures to you along with the information.

Heating, Air-conditioning. A division of labor for this work might involve a subcontractor handling shop fabrication of your plenum and main duct run; count on him also for final fuel and electrical connections to the equipment and start-up adjustments. Arrange for his guidance on branch ducts, registers-grilles and return air ducts. You can also handle duct insulation work if needed. Also, with this tradeoff, remember that the subcontractor is often a dealer for certain brands of equipment and will therefore have an interest in providing you with that make of equipment.

There are two areas of early construction work stages for which you will be wise to arrange full, not partial, subcontracts. For *excavating and backfill*, machine digging cannot be matched by manual work and good digging equipment is not readily available on a rental basis. Opt for a complete digging-backfill subcontract. For *outside sewer-water work*, if your lot requires a septic tank and disposal field, subcontract it. If you can connect to a sanitary sewer in the street, hire a sewer subcontractor to install the connection and to run the line to the house. In some areas, plumbers also do this portion of the work and include it in the subcontract. Water supply line connection to the street main can be handled simultaneously in the same trench.

Dealing With Material Suppliers

It takes time to go the shoeleather route and to shop thoroughly among building material suppliers. Keep in mind that you are trying to find a principal supplier who can be helpful throughout the course of construction. And it is also desirable to deal with a principal supplier carrying a broad range of products as well as extensive stocks in types, sizes, patterns, colors, and so on. A one-stop source of supply, or nearly so, is especially convenient with respect to structural components, sheet and exterior materials.

How far to shop? The range of doing business in building materials and supplies has broadened. Most supply firms now service at least one county and many extend their deliveries out to serve a marketing area within a 35-to-40 mile radius. When it comes to major building components such as roof or floor trusses and wall panels, suppliers may be fewer in number in any given area but will generally service building jobs within 100-to-150 miles of their fabricating plant.

There is another category of component suppliers who specialize in furnishing complete home packages with a broad assortment of optional items. Such panelized package suppliers offer a wide selection of house designs in different sizes and styles. The assembly-erection procedure is usually quite rapid, with only a period of two or three days from delivery until the home is closed against the weather and ready for interior work. The delivery is made following preparation of the foundation and the balance of materials for finishing the home is either stored inside or shipped in a second truckload.

For the owner-builder who wishes to speed up his completion time, the packaged-panelized home is an excellent way to go. Not all such package producers will deal directly with owner-builders because they may have obligations to distribute only through builder-dealers in each local area. However, some such firms not only sell direct to owner-builders but have field representatives who aid the owner in his planning and construction.

Keep in mind that more help, better service, and considerably more awareness of local building requirements and conditions are apt to come from supplier firms whose backgrounds have been in the lumber and home-building

businesses. To a great degree, such lumber and building supply retailers continue to supply a substantial number of home builders and contractors. It is this type establishment that will be equipped to handle a complete bill of materials and from whom you may have the opportunity of obtaining a builder's discount. Other building supply retailers focus their merchandising efforts more on the consumer, do relatively little business with builders and contractors, and when you buy from them it is cash or bank card, and no discounts. Still, such retailers do have good buys in certain materials from time to time.

Then, there are specialized suppliers for plumbing, heating and sheet-metal, electrical, floor coverings, and painting and wallpaper. These specialized companies can be of aid in making contact with subcontractors and also for reliable instructional information.

One important facet you should remember about these material sources who regularly do business with builders and subcontractors. They can guide you to certain jobs that their customers have in progress so that you can visit such jobs and observe first-hand work being done. This will help acquaint you with procedures. Seeing an expert tradesman do his job is extremely helpful. You can quickly grasp the essential details, and you can ask questions about things that puzzle you.

A vital necessity for everyone involved in planning and building a home is a pocket notebook carried at all times to briefly jot down facts, names and phone numbers, brand

A Componentized House is shown in break-away sketch indicating various subassemblies or components available. This particular combination of components and materials can be obtained from many of the 262 retail home supply centers operated by Wickes Lumber. This type of new home service can save an owner-builder much time and running around while getting his home under roof.

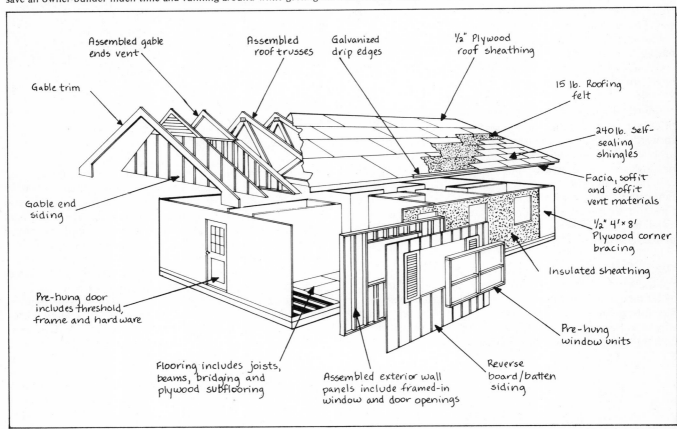

names of products, addresses of jobs in progress, color-pattern-source of a material you like, and so on.

Something that will help your day-in and day-out planning and purchasing is a job progress schedule set up in conjunction with a calendar. This can be done with ruled accounting sheets that have multiple vertical columns and horizontal rulings in groups. In the left-hand index area, list the general work headings in the approximate order that the work will be done, you might use the chapter headings in this book. Leave blank lines for the detailed specific jobs that you, a subcontractor, or supplier will do. The vertical columns progress week by week. As you go along, use a colored ink pen to mark jobs you plan to do during the two-week period ahead. Use a second color for partial jobs completed. Make notes about calling suppliers or subcontractors. Fill in the entire block area when that specific job is entirely done. You get the idea. Apply your own particular system as long as it reminds you and alerts the people who must furnish you with goods and services.

On this progress chart, it's also a good idea to have some extra room for noting down small jobs, last minute details and changes. Try to avoid changes from the plans, and changes of your mind. They're costly in time, trouble and dollars. Use your progress chart to form the basis for thinking about the tasks about to be done. You'll do the job better and faster for having thought it out in advance.

With subcontractors and with all major suppliers, continued help and cooperation will depend upon your performance in paying them. If you have set up a schedule of payouts with your lender, be sure to advise and discuss this payment schedule with your subs and suppliers. Indicate that their billings to you must be accurate but that you will act as promptly as possible in getting their billings paid in accordance with the lender's payout schedule.

In connection with payments, be a bit cautious, too. Especially in connection with a final payment. It is fairly common practice in many areas to hold back partial funds from a final payment until the work has been found acceptable by you as the owner-builder or by inspecting authorities who must give their official stamp of approval.

Your Working Tools

For the most part, you'll be using carpenter tools. Rather than try to anticipate fully in advance just what you need in working tools, buy as you go along. As you consider each task and buy materials, ask for advice on proper tools.

To begin your probable first work with concrete footing forms, poured footings, and concrete block foundations, here are the essential tools:

(1) professional quality carpenter's claw hammer;
(2) medium weight long-handle sledge hammer;
(3) large ball of regular-duty woven mason's line;
(4) powdered chalk-line in retractable container;

(5) professional quality crosscut type handsaw;
(6) steel square;
(7) large size pry bar;
(8) contractor's high-side wheelbarrow;
(9) mason's mortar-mixing hoe;
(10) professional quality mason's pointed trowel;
(11) mason's joint tool;
(12) professional quality 4 foot level;
(13) 100 foot steel tape;
(14) 6 foot steel pocket tape or folding rule;
(15) short-handled square-end steel shovel;
(16) short-handled pointed-end steel shovel.

About tool quality. All kinds of places sell tools and a high proportion have low prices and poor quality. They're not fit for continued usage. The chances are that long after your home is finished you will still be using most of the tools required to build it. So, buy good quality. Ask suppliers and subcontractors for their recommendations on the brands and types of tools you should have and where you can get them. Most tradesmen now combine the use of hand or manual tools with power tools or equipment. Be alert for such tools and where they can be rented if you don't wish to purchase them. Among the portable electric tools with which you will want to equip yourself are (at a minimum) 7-¼ inch circular saw, ¼ or 3/8 inch electric drill, jig saw. If you expect to go into your own cabinet work, there will be other pieces of equipment worth considering. To help you decide yes or no on power tool purchases, check yellow pages for tool-rental agencies in your area and obtain by phone information about tool availability and rental rates.

In working with unfamiliar tools take the time at the beginning to do some trial work. Attempt to get the feel of the tool as something that works with your hand cooperatively and simultaneously. Each hand tool operation has a little knack and a little rhythm that assists accurate usage. When a particular tool seems awkward despite advance practice, start your work in a less noticeable area. You'll find your workmanship improving quite rapidly despite a slow start.

Recommendations

You will note, going through this text, that it is suggested you opt for the systems approach and utilize building components and fabricated subassemblies for the structural portions of the home. If you want to gain further speed and less site work, then shop among the panelized packaged-home manufacturers serving your area. But bear in mind that one of your objectives is to save money by doing your own construction labor. The more labor that goes into a bought building component or factory package, the less you will have to do at the site but by the same token, the less money you will be apt to save.

5 Lot Surveys, Elevations, Drainage

Plot Plans

When you buy a home site, one of the documents that's a part of the transaction is an engineer's drawing often referred to as a "plat." Its primary purpose is to indicate the exact ownership boundaries with appropriate reference marks and lot line or boundary distances.

The information contained on such a boundaries plat, which is often a duplicate of the official recorded plat in the county office, needs to be transferred to and supplemented by additional information on a plot plan drawing. This drawing then becomes a part of your working drawings set for your home.

To accomplish this plot plan drawing, you'll require the services of an engineer-surveyor qualified for local civil engineering practice. The engineer-surveyor or one of his staff should visit the lot with you to consider three major aspects of positioning the home on the property:

(1) placement to comply with zoning regulations;
(2) placement for sufficient ground-absorption septic disposal field if no street sewer line is available;
(3) choice of a suitable ground-floor elevation to permit lot grading that will assure proper surface drainage.

In connection with zoning regulations, or building requirements in areas not controlled by zoning ordinances, your submitted plans in seeking to qualify for a building permit will be studied carefully to see that minimum front and side yard dimensions have been observed. These are distances from the nearest portion of the house measured perpendicularly to the lot line. The dimension to the front lot line is called the "set-back."

With respect to side yard minimums, these are established primarily for fire safety and maintenance considerations. For example, the HUD Standards apply different minimums for a primary wall, a secondary wall and a windowless wall. The primary wall contains windows of living-dining-family room or main entrance while secondary walls have windows for kitchen or bedrooms. The minimum distances applicable then are:

□ primary—6 feet plus 2 feet for each story in height plus 1 foot for each 10 feet of wall length;
□ secondary—2 feet plus (as noted above) 1 foot plus 1 foot, with a minimum of 5 feet;
□ windowless—0 feet plus (as noted above) 1 foot plus 1 foot, with a minimum of 5 feet, or 3 feet for a garage.

In addition to the engineer's responsibility for seeing to it that your home's placement will meet regulations, he should be willing to advise you on certain other matters. Here are just some of the points which might be considered or be applicable in connection with siting a new home:

(1) elevation of the street sewer in relation to the elevation of your home and your house sewer flow;

Lot Clearing Work, preparatory to new home construction, is best done by a combination of hand labor and machine. On any home site, weeds and brush need to be cleared as well as tree felling and stump-removal within the area where the home will stand. For sites with many small trees and thick bushes a bulldozer will be well worth your rental and operator costs. Shown also is a level-transit in position to assist in the stake-out of the excavating area as soon as clearing work is completed.

(2) existence of a natural drainage channel through your property and how it might be modified if desirable;

(3) need for a basement or crawl space sump pump in areas of high water tables;

(4) need for a sump or other outlet for foundation drain tile around home's outer perimeter;

(5) how to deal with steep slopes or other erosion areas;

(6) driveway location factors with respect to curvature, turning radii, turn-around area, grade or slope variations;

(7) water-supply well considerations, proximity to septic field and maintenance accessibility;

(8) recognition and allowance for easements that may be recorded on the property.

Plot Plan Details

Once you've discussed the various site conditions and problems they may pose, the engineer-surveyor will probably have recommendations for you to follow with respect to home positioning, sewer connections or sewage disposal systems, water supply, house elevation, grading and other elements related to the site. Ask him to incorporate provision for as many of these as possible into the home's plot plan.

One purpose here is to indicate on the plot plan the essentials needed in construction work so that they may be communicated to others. Attention to these details will also indicate to the lending institution that your planning work is taking proper cognizance of conditions with which the lending officer may already be familiar due to financing of other properties in the area or to his local knowledge.

The showing on plot plans of topographic lines, those irregular curves of equal points of elevations, is included routinely for hilly or irregular home sites but they are not included when the site is nearly flat. The topographic lines should be given for any home site where suitable drainage provisions should be made either by the grading of dirt around the home or by revision and supplementation of the present drainage pattern. Such rough grading work and revision of drainage channels should be done at the time the home's foundation is being backfilled.

The plot plan prepared by the engineer-surveyor should include notations about specific reference marks that he has placed in proper position at the site; for example, lot corner stakes as shown on the drawing with distances indicated between stakes, or the bench mark for elevation reference, usually placed at some point within reasonable distance from the house position, so that excavation can proceed without disturbing the mark.

The plot plan will also indicate the accessibility of various services or utilities such as electrical poles or underground service, existing sewer-water mains and storm drainage system, telephone lines, fire hydrants. The finished drawing original should be blueprinted or white-printed in sufficient copies so that one drawing goes with each complete set of plans. A few extra copies will take care of needs of excavating or sewer subcontractors who do not need to see complete sets of drawings.

The cost of lot survey, staking, preparation of the plot plan drawing, and consultation will vary considerably according to the site characteristics and other factors. In choosing an engineer-surveyor, it is a good idea to ask about engineers who have been doing work in the nearby vicinity. Such engineers often have familiarity with the local conditions, know the plats involved, and may already have certain check points from work done on adjacent or nearby properties.

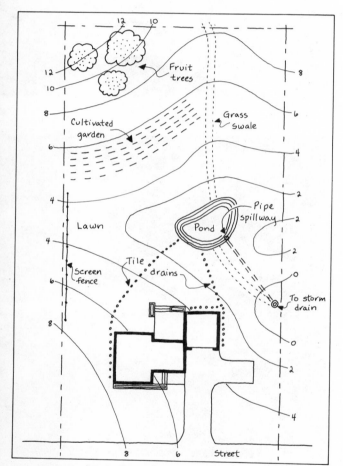

Home Site Grading-Drainage Plan shown here has been adapted from an example given in a Soil Conservation Service booklet. It indicates some of the factors in choosing the exact location of your home on the lot, and other facilities that should be provided to assist in handling water drainage. A screen fence helps provide visual privacy for the rear outdoor living area but is not made of wire screening. More appropriate are fences made of thin cedar poles, wide boards or other hard-to-see-through materials. In this home site plan, the topographic lines give ground elevations and a small pond has been planned for the low-lying area of the site with overflow connections to a storm drain outlet. A grass swale in the rear area helps channel storm water flowing down from higher ground areas.

Lot Clearing Work

Before doing any lot clearing work, it may be advisable to check into your rights with respect to clearing and construction work if the lot has not been purchased outright and fully paid for. Home sites are often purchased on land contracts and time-payment plans. Have your lawyer look at the fine print and advise you as to just what rights are yours in going ahead with the work before you actually start.

If your home site is relatively open and free of trees, bushes and other natural growths, little work is required of you in advance of excavation. One step you can take is to arrange street or road entrance access so that cars and trucks can get off the road and into your home site within a drive of 35 to 50 feet. This may mean such preliminary provisions as placing a metal culvert pipe in the street's drainage ditch and covering it with crushed stone. And extending the crushed stone base along the course of the future driveway for a distance sufficient for cars or trucks to reach solid ground. It may also mean, in the case of a paved street with curb, breaking out the curb concrete to make driving in easier.

Cut down brush, small bushes and weeds along the home's perimeter outline sufficiently so the excavator can set a few flagged stakes to indicate to machine-digger operators the outer points of excavation. If there is topsoil that you wish to save, clear away an area to one side so a topsoil pile can be made.

If there are trees to be removed, they should come down and be removed or cut up before the excavator comes. The excavating subcontractor will know of a tree removal expert. You can, of course, rent or buy a chain saw and do considerable tree removal and cutting up for firewood yourself. But there's a line to be drawn here. About 18 to 20 inches of tree diameter is where you begin separating the men from the boys. Beyond this tree size it may be desirable to have some upper branches removed before felling a tree. This is work for the tree expert, not you.

Small trees with shallow or limited roots can be cut off at grade. Larger trees need the main stump removed. Stump removal can be done by the excavator's bulldozer if there's been sufficient height left in the trunk base for the dozer to get some leverage with.

In connection with clearing work on wooded home sites, be sure to mark trees you want saved. The usual practice is to tie a red rag around the trunk about head height. A better practice is to obtain some 1X6 or 1X8 third-rate or old inch boards about 8 feet long. Stand them up around the trunk and bind them in place with some heavy wire. Mark "SAVE" in large letters. Red letters. It sometimes takes quite a bit of effort to catch the attention and regard of machine and truck operators.

With a legal check completed, the bench mark in, brush and trees cleared and entrance from the street or access road made possible, you're all set to go ahead and break ground.

Excavating for Basement with a power shovel. Owner-builders should save themselves this back-breaking labor by choosing an excavating subcontractor with proper equipment for handling residential excavations. In foreground, hauling trailer for the shovel, which can complete the job in less than a day. Below, excavating work completed, the entrance drive area has also been dug out and filled with a base course of crushed rock to permit easy access to site by ready-mix trucks.

6 Building Permits and Approvals

At the very outset, before any construction work proceeds, a building permit issued by the local government agency having jurisdiction for your home site location is necessary. Within an incorporated town, village or city, the local municipality has jurisdiction. And it usually has a building inspector or department that issues the permits and administers the local building and/or zoning requirements.

Larger municipalities of 10,000 or more people are likely to have a department headed by an engineer. And many counties in which an increasing amount of residential building is done are also apt to have a building department directed by an engineer to cover homes and other buildings that are outside local town or city limits.

Building permits are issued on the basis of an application accompanied by a complete set of working drawings and the plot plan mentioned in the previous chapter. A set of specifications should accompany the plans so that determination can be made as to whether or not construction materials and quality will meet the code requirements.

A substantial and constantly growing number of building department officials and inspectors now observe in their local codes an adaptation of or specific reference to uniform model building codes sponsored by each of the three following organizations: Building Officials and Code Administrators International (BOCA), International Conference of Building Officials (ICBO) and the Southern Building Code Congress (SBCC). Within recent years, these three code official organizations have agreed to follow the same building code on detached homes and that code is called the "One-and-Two-Family Dwelling Code." This text will make occasional references to a few of that code's rules.

Codes, and a wide variety of construction standards to which the codes frequently refer, are designed to protect new home buyers and owners from the hazards of faulty construction materials and methods. And especially so with respect to any materials or methods that relate to an occupant's health or safety. Observance of the required standards in construction assures the owner that the home is not a hazard nor does it contain construction or products which might endanger the occupant's safety.

Another set of requirements sometimes used as a quality construction reference similar to a building code is the Minimum Property Standards issued and maintained by the U.S. Department of HUD. HUD-MPS's are the construction and location criteria set up for the approval of mortgage loans for FHA/VA loan insurance or guarantee. This set of requirements for one- and two-family homes (1973 edition) and its related Manual of Acceptable Practices (also 1973) have been used as guidelines in this text.

Even though a local municipality or jurisdiction may have adopted a major model building code such as those mentioned, it may still have in effect certain local ordinances or requirements which it continues to enforce and which generally take precedence over model code provisions relating to that topic. It is therefore apparent that in building your home you must deal with the local building authority and what his interpretation of the local or model code might be.

The areas or installations of the home that are perhaps more subject to extensive regulations are usually these:

☐ structural strength and load-carrying capabilities;
☐ electrical system for lighting and household appliances;
☐ heating equipment and distribution method;
☐ waste-drainage-vent piping and water supply system;
☐ sewage connections and individual sewage disposal system;
☐ provision for the storage and removal of garbage/trash.

There may also be additional requirements controlling what are considered to be hazardous conditions in some areas. This type of requirement might include issues related to ground subsidence or earthquake, flooding, erosion, high ground water levels, springs, unstable soils, and hazards posed by nearby industrial plants.

Obtaining Your Permits

In many less-populated locations, the building permit is the only local document needed to proceed legally with construction. In some rural areas, the permit is routinely issued by the town clerk and that's it . . . no further contacts, no inspections, just go ahead and build.

Red Tape

That simplicity is being lost as a growing number of county-state-federal agencies are making site development and home building the focus of environmental protection measures. Just what agencies may be involved and what new rules employed for residential development and building vary considerably. The antigrowth and antidevelopment proponents have made significant progress in a number of areas. If your local building official is a fulltime professional, he will undoubtedly be aware of your local situation in relation to such policies. He will know what additional approvals you should seek with respect to your particular property and intentions.

Recommendations. From the beginning, make personal contact with the head of the building department if you're in a small area and with the chief building inspector if you're in an area of substantial population. One reason is that it's a likely place to learn some of the things you need to know. Also, if you display a willingness to learn, to be conscientious and to do things the way they're supposed to be done, your chances of getting the approved inspections you need are better. Arguments hardly ever work, even for the professionals who deal daily with code and inspection requirements. For an amateur like you, arguing is futile.

Professional home builders and contractors can cite innumerable instances of bureaucratic delays, obstinacy and bull-headedness on the part of their building department; they may have occurred, but probably not without some blame or provocation on the part of the builder or contractor. A large number of building officials are well informed and professional in their contacts and actions.

If you have a complaint to make when dealing with a building department or building inspector, know what you're talking about. And make your complaint count—do it at a high level. The person who answers the phone is probably *not* the person who can tell you the "why" of whatever it is you're inquiring about. Reach the right person. Hold in your frustrations and anger at the red tape. Make your point diffidently, ask for appropriate action and try to avoid confrontations as much as possible. Be sure to find out exactly what it is expected of you and is considered correct so that you can proceed again after you have had a chance to cool off.

Fees will be required in connection with approvals for your plans and for the various services that building departments provide. They can be considerably high in some cases. Building permit fees are usually based upon a scaled rate of so much per thousand dollars of estimated construction cost. The minor fees and charges are usually on a flat rate basis for such items as sewer connection, water-main tap, meter charge, driveway permit and perhaps others. You can also expect when the time comes for electric service or

gas connection that these utility companies will also have a charge for their initial service installation work. Inquire about such charges and fees so that you will be prepared for them.

Don't assume when you make application for a building permit that you can just wait a few days and go down to pick it up. It may occasionally happen, but building departments in most areas are more often than not noted for delays and especially so if you're in a town where a lot of home building is being done.

There may be times when the rule of screaming

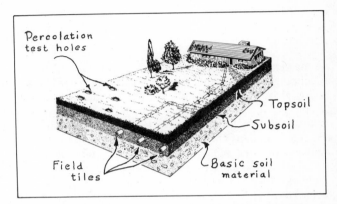

Septic Tank and Disposal Field for single-family home requires an adequate open treeless area for field tiles and suitable absoption characteristics for the soil. Suitability is measured by advance percolation test holes. Obtain details of this test method from your state Board of Health or in U.S. Dept. of Agriculture Information Bulletin No. 349 titled "Soils and Septic Tanks". Tight soil layers such as clay, hard rock or moistness from high water table in upper 4 ft. of soil depth usually make the location unsuitable for sewage disposal fields.

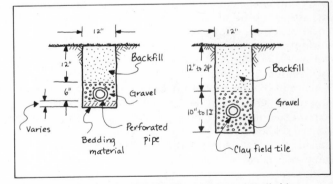

Sewage Disposal and Water Drainage trenches are installed in a similar manner although field tiles are intended to disperse effluent into the soil while drain tiles are intended to collect excess water and carry it away. At left, in soils characterized by good dispersion and fast percolation test rates, a shallow trench with piping material installed on a quite shallow bed of sand or mixed sand-gravel will do a good job. In denser soils where percolation is slower, the deeper trench shown on the right with a deeper gravel layer is likely to be more suitable.

applies . . . service to him that honks loudest. In the building department, however, persistence and frequency of inquiry are most expeditious. Dragging of official feet on permits is one method that has been employed in some areas to lower the pace of development. In other areas, moratoriums and complete stoppage of permit issuance have occurred pending the outcome of certain political actions or public improvements to existing service. No matter how loud you honk you will not be able to overcome such obstacles. It is better instead to check into such conditions before committing yourself to a lot, and to look elsewhere if necessary.

Series Of Inspections

After completing discussions with your building department and learning of the procedures with which you must comply, you can incorporate notations about official inspections into your plans. You might wish to make a separate inspection schedule that pinpoints the items that the inspectors will be looking at. Practices vary on inspections from one municipality or jurisdiction to another. Whatever the procedure may be, you should make it clear that you wish to obtain notice in writing of some kind to indicate that the inspection has been made and found satisfactory. Three of the typical times during construction that inspections are made are:

☐ when foundation work has been completed but before backfill;

☐ when plumbing and electrical rough-in work has been done;

☐ final inspection after all is finished and equipment has been installed.

In many larger towns or suburbs having well-staffed building departments, you may encounter a more frequent schedule of visits—and more details to be covered by the inspector. He'll want certain things left in inspectable condition or work done just to a certain stage.

Perhaps another set of times will come from your lending or mortgage-insuring agency. In each case, be certain to find out approximately how much advance notice these inspection people wish to be given before they come out so that progress on your job will not be held up unnecessarily. Use caution in observing these inspection rules. It's well within the realm of possibility that if not observed, the penalty can be time-consuming as well as costly.

A further cautionary note. Many municipal agencies are quite sensitive about owner-builders moving in and occupying a home before what they consider to be the proper time, namely, after final inspection and issuance of a certificate of occupancy. Exceptions to rules can sometimes be accomplished diplomatically, but be aware that the time of occupancy may be a milestone signalling an increase on the property tax rolls, a change in conditions for insurance coverage, and perhaps additional changes of importance.

Flexibility In Requirements

Hold little hope of being able to make any immediate change or modification in building requirements or standards. The people in charge just do not function this way with regard to any one individual job. They may possibly give you some indication they will "be looking the other way" on some item that you're concerned about. But you will not be able to obtain any official say-so in writing that such and such requirement will be waived in your case, or that you will not be held responsible until a later date.

One thing you can do to try to shift slightly the code-meeting responsibility you have concerns the purchase of materials and products, particularly subassemblies or building components. Indicate to your supplier at time of purchase that you expect that these items will be prepared and delivered so that they meet the code requirements applicable to your building site. And that you'd like to receive from them some sort of statement of this fact.

In connection with the mechanical trades, a further method of sharing responsibility has already been suggested in the form of partial subcontracts with plumbing, heating and electrical subcontractors. Your agreement with them should include provision that you expect them to assist you in ensuring the entire installation will be in compliance with the code and building department regulations.

Somewhere, no matter how careful you've been, the building inspector is likely to find something that you or one of your subcontractor helpers has not done according to the rules. If you and the inspector have had reasonably pleasant relations or contacts, the error or oversight is apt to be a very slight or unimportant infraction to which he wants to call your attention. It is politic for you to offer to correct this right away if possible, and make good on your word if you promise him something. Once you have done it, call him to let him know.

Keep in mind that in the long run of the job, a building inspector who wants to be tough will be able to find all kinds of things that are "wrong." He probably won't have to justify them to anyone but himself. So the way to move your job forward in such a case is . . . acquiesce. Swallow your pride. Forget you may be right. Tell yourself, "This time, to keep things moving, we'll do it *his* way without complaint." You will in the end anyway.

7 Excavating and Foundation Footings

With your various approvals out of the way, you have the go-ahead to break ground. The only thing that can hold you back is the weather. You need dry weather for excavating work and nonfreezing weather for concrete and masonry work.

Prior to this time in the course of your planning, you will have made your choice between poured concrete foundation walls and concrete block. Poured concrete tends to be favored in metro and suburban areas because there are concrete contractors who specialize in footing and foundation work. Masonry block foundations in such areas tend to be fewer in number and relatively higher in cost because of union rates and/or unwillingness of some mason contractors to lay concrete blocks. In outlying or rural areas, the reverse is true; more concrete block foundations and fewer poured concrete are the rule.

The choice between them makes little difference as far as the utilization of basement areas is concerned. Both types of walls can be painted or insulated and covered with wallboard. Neither is affected more by dampness or moisture penetration. Concrete has a slight advantage in load-carrying capacity but for wood-frame structures of two stories or less in height, there is essentially no difference between the two types of foundation walls.

One suggestion, however. If you've elected to have a poured concrete foundation, do not try separating the labor—you handling the footings, the subcontractor the walls. Concrete subcontractors are not inclined to consider such a separation. They would much prefer setting foundation wall forms on footings they've prepared. If asked to submit a bid on divided work, they're apt to indicate they wish to do the entire job and that you won't save much by doing the footings yourself.

Preparation for Excavation

The first step of preparatory work is insuring yourself, your family and outsiders against accidents on the site that cause injuries. A family accident policy will protect you and yours. But for outside delivery and working men you need to provide yourself with liability insurance. A little later, as the home takes form, you will need a comprehensive home-owner's policy for protection against home damage by fire, windstorm and other contingencies. So, have a talk with your insurance counselor.

This is a good time, too, to consider on-the-job safety and what steps you should initiate from the beginning to help prevent accidents and injuries. Most building tradesmen follow simple little practices almost automatically, such as turning lumber with protruding nails nail-side down and replacing sharp-edged tools in toolboxes. You're not in this habit and need to consider details more attentively.

A clean job is the safest kind. Keep debris collected. Avoid letting tools and waste lie in the foot traffic pattern around the job. Keep children under ten away from the building site if possible. Use a little extra care when placing planks for walkways, when using ladders and providing scaffolds.

Tools

To accurately position your home's foundation you will need a level-transit. This surveyor's instrument is rather expensive for the limited use you will require of it, so inquiry should be made about borrowing or renting the instrument. Sometimes called simply "the instrument" by construction men, the level-transit serves a variety of functions in measuring angles, distances and other mathematical field needs. Your prime purpose for it, however, is simple alignment and height reference marks.

The instrument screws to a tripod and the mounting includes adjustment devices for leveling the sighting piece so that it remains level when revolved to sight in any direction. The instrument is essentially a telescope with vertical and horizontal cross-hairs in the lens and an adjusting dial to permit focussing for various distances.

Also important are batter boards. These 1X6's or 2X4's are nailed to ground stakes slightly above the ground in a

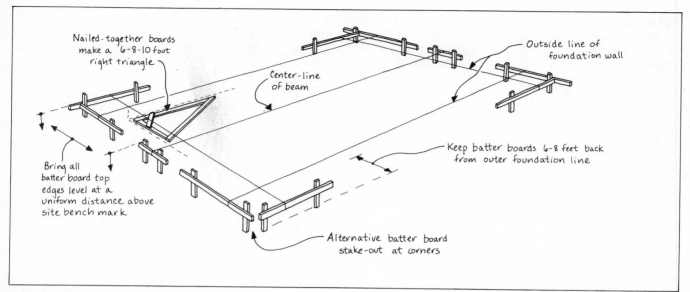

Nailed-together boards make a 6-8-10 foot right triangle

Center-line of beam

Outside line of foundation wall

Keep batter boards 6-8 feet back from outer foundation line

Bring all batter board top edges level at a uniform distance above site bench mark

Alternative batter board stake-out at corners

Batter Boards, nailed to carefully placed stakes at building corners and midpoints, act as fastenings when stretching mason's line cords between board pairs and give proper alignment and height for your home's excavation, footings and foundation walls.

The boards themselves need not be in perfect alignment but their top edges must be exactly level. This means nailing up the boards by means of a level-transit so that each board's top edge is a uniform height above the home site's reference bench mark.

Batter boards should be set at least 6-to-8 feet back from the outer foundation wall face. After boards have been placed and brought to levelness, line cords should be stretched and adjusted for a position that will be directly above the outer face of the foundation wall.

At this position, drive a nail partially into each board's top edge where the line cord crosses. Drive a second nail to the outside of the first nail by the footing projection distance. The second nails will then provide alignment for the footing forms. Line cords can be removed for excavating work and later easily replaced in proper position alongside the nails when setting footing forms and starting the foundation wall.

horizontal position (see illustration). They're placed at building corners and perhaps some intermediate points. When mason's line is stretch between marks on the batter boards, the line marks the proper position of the outside face of the foundation wall. When a set of batter boards have been placed so their top edges are all horizontal and at the same elevation, then the stretched lines also become reference points for determining the proper and accurate height of footings and foundation walls.

The general principles followed in setting batter boards is to set up the level-transit in positions where it can be helpful in sighting and measuring:

(1) for lot lines between survey stakes and measurement from the lines to building corner where the home is to be sited, and verification of this measurement from the opposite lot line;

(2) for transferring proper height information from the bench mark to the building batter boards.

The Excavator's Work

Shallow excavations of only 18 inches depth or less can probably be dug by hand. The easy way would be with a bulldozer. By hand, you need a pointed shovel for sandy-gravelly soils, a clay spade for clay soils and a square-edged shovel for leveling. Anything deeper, you'll save much time, trouble and hard labor by hiring an excavating subcontractor, one who has suitable specialized digging equipment. A dozer for shallow work and grading or backfill, a power shovel or backhoe for deeper foundations and for trenching.

The bulk of what the excavator needs to know will be on either the plot plan or foundation drawings. The former will give him dimensions and rough location, the latter will give him depths, foundation shape, basement or crawl space areas, unexcavated areas such as under garages or porches and the entrance stoop locations. These details guide him in digging the main hole and adjacent spaces.

Practice varies on guiding the excavator. Where the soil is easily dug and there is not a great amount of earth to be removed, batter boards can be set for building corners prior to digging. But probably the most common practice is to delay setting the boards until the hole has been dug. In such a case, the owner-builder should set flagged stakes at the points outside the building corners to which the excavation should extend. A usual provision is to excavate to at least 2 feet outside the outer face of the foundation wall. If the soil is sand or not self-binding, to have 2 feet outside space at the desired depth will involve going a foot or two wider at grade level. Indicate to the excavator what your flagged stakes represent and he can adjust his digging accordingly.

Whereas homes have long been built resting on wood or concrete piers, on hillside stilts and on concrete slabs-on-grade, these methods of structural support for a home are to be avoided by the first-time owner-builder. Done properly, these foundation methods can provide sound support but they bring extra considerations and special problems that are difficult for the amateur to contend with. Settle this time for a less-sloping home site and the simpler perimeter wall foundation.

Depth

The depth of excavating work is guided by typical frost penetration depth for the locality. The bottom of the footings should be at a level to which frost never penetrates. Inquiry in your local area will quickly indicate what depth is considered suitable. The U.S. Weather Bureau data shows that extreme frost penetration may range from only 5 inches at mid-state points in South Carolina, Alabama, Louisiana, Mississippi, and Texas, to 90 inches or more in upper Minnesota and Maine.

Obviously, in northern areas of the country where wall footings must go down 5 feet or more below grade to suit frost conditions in winter, it is quite economical to include provision for a basement. In states like West Virginia, Missouri, Ohio, Indiana, Oklahoma, and Colorado, where portions of the state have penetrations in the 40 to 50 inch depth, crawl-space foundations are an economy worth considering.

Recommendation: for the relatively slight extra cost, include in your plans at least a partial basement regardless of your location. This is low-cost space and it will prove useful for a variety of purposes.

One arrangement you should work out with the excavator is where to put the dug-up dirt. Have him try to keep it in just two or three piles rather than stringing it out. You'll need room between piles for access by ready-mix trucks. The trucks usually need at least two different locations adjacent to the hole so that their chutes can reach all footing points.

Sewer and Water Installations

Depending upon the area in which your new home is located, your excavator may or may not be in the practice of digging trenches for sewer lines and septic systems and laying the pipe in these trenches. If so, you will want to hire a sewer subcontractor who can handle such digging and pipe-laying whether it be for a street sewer connection or the installation of a septic tank and field. In either case, such subcontractors utilize specialized trenching machines and perhaps other equipment that are beyond the scope of or availability to the owner-builder.

If your home is to have a septic disposal system, it can wait until the home is nearly completed. This presumes that you have already ascertained that your soil is suited to such a system, that your lot dimensions will permit proper placement of it, and that you have a permit from the local sanitation authority.

If your home is to be connected to a street sewer, this connection should be made at the present excavating or foundation stage of construction. The sewer line is generally run from house to street with a slope of ¼ inch per foot to give proper flow. It usually runs under a wall footing to the main stack location. The sewer subcontractor brings it underground to this point and with a sanitary Y-joint and additional pipe length, if needed, brings it to just above basement floor or crawl space grade level.

If a septic system will be used, the same sanitary sewer pipe installation must be made from septic tank location to the stack location wtihin the foundation. If septic tank and field are to be done later, make a suitable sleeve-access hole through the footing or crawl space foundation wall to permit entry of the sewer line.

For single-family homes septic tank dimensions usually require a hole about 7 to 8 feet in diameter and 6 to 8 feet deep. Tanks vary somewhat by area. Both round and rectangular tanks are used, generally of about a 500-gallon capacity. Inlet and outlet are near the top of the tank. The outlet line runs to a "disposal field" that consists of several rather shallow trenches containing drain tile laid on a gravel base (see illus. Chap. 6). The 4 inch clay drain tile are placed at a depth of about 2 to 3 feet below grade. More gravel is

Sewer Subcontractor trenching and laying house sewer lateral to street main connection. Shown ready for use are "no-hub" sewer pipes which simply tap together without filling of hub with mortar cement. At right, workman shovels out dirt from hole-drilling machine which spirals its way under the street pavement to the sewer main on the other side. For an owner-builder whose home sites has sewer mains available for connection, time and trouble are saved by employing a specialized sewer subcontractor.

added above the tile and the trench backfilled. Overall trench length and the area needed for the field depends upon the soil absorption characteristics as determined by percolation testing. If there is any question about absorption ability on a particular home site, the percolation tests should be run before you are committed to the purchase. Tight clay soils have the poorest absorption capacity while sandy-gravel soils have the best.

In hiring a septic installation subcontractor, have your agreement specify that the installation shall meet health and building department regulations on tile depth and trench spacing. Indicate also that you will need a copy of the percolation test report. Include in this subcontract the trenching, tile-laying, backfilling and the trench and sewer installation from tank to house.

With regard for the proper installation of the house sewer line, you should have made your selection of a subcontractor for the rough plumbing. Talk with him about your main stack location and just where he wants the sewer subcontractor or septic system man to bring the sewer line. You may need him at this stage to install part of the sewer line. In some areas, there is strict observance of union trades jurisdiction lines and for sewer and plumbing work, the dividing line is the house foundation wall . . . outside the foundation wall, it's the work of the sewer or septic man, while inside is the plumber's territory.

During this discussion with your plumbing subcontractor, one further item should be brought up: sewer line depth. A septic disposal system may be too high for a house sewer line running below the basement floor. Often the simplest solution is to avoid any sanitary drain in the basement (no toilets, wash basins or laundry equipment). Then, the house sewer run can be suspended under the

floor joists and run through an opening cut in the foundation wall. The same can be done with a crawl space foundation.

The alternative is a sewer lift pump installation to raise the sewer line's floor from below basement floor to the level of the tank input. The equipment for a lift is not inexpensive and not immediately available in all areas.

Before allowing your sewer or septic subcontractor to backfill his trenches, be certain that you know whether the local building department or inspector must take a look at the sewer tap or sewer line installation. This may be an inspection point, and the inspector's office should be properly notified.

At the same time you're talking with your plumbing subcontractor about the house sewer, find out how he suggests the water supply entrance be made, whether it comes from a street main or an individual water supply pump. If from a street main, the water pipe can often be placed on a ledge in the same trench with the sewer line. The ledge or shelf is on one side of the sewer trench and only deep enough to avoid danger of freezing. If the water supply main is at the street but no sanitary sewer is there, your plumbing subcontractor will be able, usually, to handle the trenching work as well as the water tap-in and pipe run to the house.

In connection with the water supply installation, you may or may not have a choice about meter location. In some areas you may have a curb meter below ground, near

Do Measuring Accurately by using appropriate, good-quality rule or tape. Here, different types of Lufkin-made measures: (top) a general purpose folding wood rule especially useful in marking lumber for cutting; (middle) a 100 foot long steel tape suited to layout measuring where longer lengths are involved; (bottom) a 25-inch steel rule, spring retractable, convenient for measuring openings and short distances in all kinds of positions.

The Key Tool in residential carpentry work is the hammer. Your hammering rhythm and accuracy will be helped by the right type and weight of hammer. These Stanley-made hammers are: (left) all-purpose claw type with curved nail-pullers; (right) three fiberglass-handled hammers from top to bottom—claw, hammer with straight claws, and a ball-pien hammer for use with metals.

the street main tap-in point. Such location speeds meter reading and requires no entry to the home. In some municipalities, curb meters are required. Otherwise, traditional practice is to place the water meter at the point of entry of the water supply line just inside the house—in the basement if a basement home, in a nonfreezing location if a nonbasement home.

If you're having an individual water supply well installed by a well-digging subcontractor, the well-digger will handle the supply line from the well location to the house at the time the well is drilled. He will also advise on electrical circuitry needed for a remote-from-house or submersible pump. Initial contact with well-diggers should be made early; some areas have limited well-digging service and you may find you can get the well dug only as the digger makes his rounds, rather than exactly when you want it done.

With any of the foregoing plumbing and sewer installations, make sure you protect the inside-the-hole parts against damage during footing and foundation work. Protect pipe stubs with stakes, wrap pipe ends with plastic film.

Setting Footing Forms

Footings are the simplest of all concrete structures to form and pour. They rest on the ground and are simply formed by upright wood planks back-supported by wood stakes. Not at all complicated. For a typical rectangular house about 24×50 feet, the footing forms can be set in less than a day by two persons and the concrete pour from a ready-mix truck is a matter of not much over 2-½ hours, if that.

The first step in setting forms is ordering out the lumber you'll need. With the planks used just once for the footing pour, you might consider where they can be used permanently afterward, since they'll still be in quite good shape after removal from the sides of the footings. Most footings are 8 inches deep so that 2X8's can be used. Or 2X10's with a bit of undisturbed earth left between planks to keep the footing depth of 8 inches (no sense in using more concrete than you have to). If the 2X8's are given a light coating of thin oil before setting and the concrete is cleaned off them following removal, the planks can easily serve as floor joists or other rough framing work. If their lumber grade is not suited for framing purposes, they can still serve for construction walkways and scaffolding. For oil, use a few cans of SAE new crankcase oil thinned somewhat with kerosene or paint thinner. Use a paint brush to coat planks on both sides and both edges.

Your lines and height for footing forms come from lines stretched over the batter boards erected at the corners of your building (see illustration). Usual practice is for the batter board marks to be made for the outside surface of the foundation wall. From this line, you will have to measure the distance of the footing projection to the out-

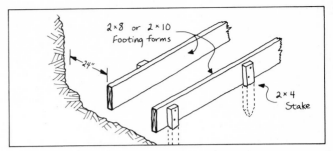

Footing Forms are set parallel with top edges level and at uniform depth measured down from line cord stretched between batter board pairs. Actual depth will depend upon height of foundation wall and the elevation of the first floor level above the reference bench mark.

Where footings of different levels meet, such as a basement area adjoining a crawl space or unexcavated area, the common practice is to end the footing at each level with ends as nearly vertical one over the other as the soil condition will permit. At end points, short planks should be nailed to the parallel side forms.

If form planks are set so their bottom edges are a half inch or more above grade, avoid loss of concrete by placing earth fill on outer sides of forms to keep the concrete from flowing out.

side in order to obtain the line of the outer edge of the footing.

After getting your first outer plank form along one wall length, come back to your starting corner and place the inner side form measuring the right distance for the overall footing width . . . the foundation wall thickness plus two projections. When driving stakes for the form planks, use 2X4 pieces that have been pointed with a handaxe. Two-sided points are sufficient, not four-sided.

Stakes need penetrate the earth only about 6 inches to get a firm hold for nailing although greater depth might be needed if the soil is quite sandy. Get good alignment of the planks when driving the stakes. Then get the proper height measurement to the batter board line. Lift or lower the planks to get a uniform measurement to the line all along the wall length. When inner planks have been staked, use hand level from outer plank form to obtain correct height for plank's top edge. Nail stakes to planks using double-headed scaffold nails driving through stakes into planks. Hold a sledge behind planks when hammering so that nails drive easier and planks positionings are undisturbed.

Proceed around the house perimeter wall length by wall length keeping footing forms at edges only so that concrete around a corner will be continuous. Footing will also be needed for foundation walls around nonexcavated portions of the home, for attached gargages and for entrance porches or stoops. These additional footing forms are handled in the same way as for regular walls. Keep their thicknesses and widths the same, but they need not go down as deep as basement wall footings. Just far enough so the footing bottom is below frost depth.

When starting to set the first footing forms, double

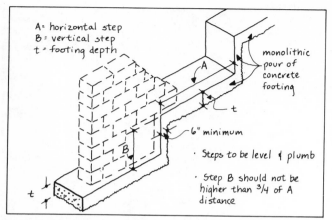

A = horizontal step
B = vertical step
t = footing depth

monolithic pour of concrete footing

A

t

6" minimum

- Steps to be level & plumb
- Step B should not be higher than 3/4 of A distance

B

t

Stepped Footings are required to be continuous under some building codes; in such cases, the earth base must be dug to grade on the different levels with vertical sections spaded smoothly. Form board or plywood is nailed to long stakes to form the vertical wall face for the footing and this form must be well-braced to withstand the concrete pressure during pouring.

When pouring stepped footings, begin at lowest level and pour continuously. Don't let ready-mix chute deliver concrete directly into vertical portions. Pour the concrete onto the flat portion and then shovel it down into the vertical portion.

check your engineer-surveyor plot plan drawing for the height-of-building reference. The reference bench mark may have this elevation noted as zero or a plus or minus number, depending on local practice or referring to other bench marks involved. The plot drawing, with house location indicated, should also have a notation with respect to the foundation wall top or the first floor level—how much above or below the bench mark it is in feet and inches. With this height of foundation top or floor known, you will then have to deduct the height of foundation wall and perhaps floor depth to arrive at the height that is proper for your footing form plank top edges. This height should be level all around the perimeter and you should check the levelness out using the transit-level. Test each building corner footing form edge with the bench mark.

Emphasis is made here on footing depth and levelness. Accuracy in height is needed in order for the home to have proper grading and drainage. Footing levelness is important for proper construction of foundation walls. Accuracy on footings is needed for the top surfaces. If the sides of the footing are a little misaligned or if there are openings below the form planks where concrete can run out, no matter. Just shovel a bit of dirt against the outside of the form. But the ground within the forming area should remain undisturbed earth.

If the adjustments needed to get the plank forms to the proper height are relatively small, you don't have to pull and redrive the nails. If the form must go down slightly, put one foot on the plank edge while you tap the stake with a

sledge. If the form must be raised just a little, use a pry bar to lift the form near a stake, then sledge down the earth around the stake.

Normally, you will use planks that are 12, 14 or 16 feet long with stakes placed at about 3 to 4 foot intervals. Join planks by butting and placing a splice block on the side away from the footing. Outer planks don't have to be cut exactly at the corner; one plank may extend beyond if there is excavation space. Where there are changes in the level of footings such as one part of a home with a basement and another part unexcavated, blocking of footing form ends is done simply by a short plank length nailed to the ends of the parallel form planks (see illustration). No forming or concrete pouring is done for the vertical portion.

Pouring the Footings

While you may be a little worried about the pour if this is your first one, remember footings are really the easiest of any concrete work and there's really not much that can go wrong. You'll need helpers for this work because the ready-mix people don't like delays. The driver just moves the truck to position and connects the chute on the truck end. You need helpers to shove and to help move the chute lengths and to add lengths to reach farther spots.

Down in the hole, there should be two shovelers who work near the chute end. You start your pour just beyond a building corner away from the truck. Fill the forms to the top surface, your shovelers leveling it off as they proceed to shovel concrete ahead. Keep pouring and moving the front flow forward towards the truck. The driver will help control the flow so it doesn't come too fast or too slow or overflow the forms. As you come to porch or entrance footings, pour them also. Keep progressing with the main-footing pour passing the truck and going beyond until you've reached the extent the chutes will reach. Then, it's time to move the truck to a new location.

As a rule, you want to work rapidly. The steel chute gets hot in warm weather and concrete that rests in it a little while begins to harden. Use a board or shovel to clean out the chute while pouring work is stopped for short periods.

Footing concrete tends to be a little on the wet side so that it will flow rather easily. This means it may take a little while to set up before you finish the top surface. It will be about ready for finishing when the water sheen or glaze has disappeared. Use a float to finish it. This is a cement finisher's tool that consists of a flat wood rectangle with a handle. The flat side is applied to the concrete surface in an arm-sweeping motion with just a slight liftup of the float's leading edge. It smooths out minor irregularities in the concrete surface. It also raises water to the surface, so too much floating is not advised.

If the concrete has been poured with insufficient leveling off to the form top edges, it should be "struck off" before floating. This is done with a short length of 2X4 held on

Pouring Your Footings is a relatively fast job but you need two or three helpers. Procedure is highlighted in this series of photos: (1) completing the footing forms with stake-driving of pier forms in crawl space area; (2) using ready-mix truck's long chute connections to reach lower part of foundation area; (3) floating the top of the footing to level off and smooth the concrete; and (4) concreting completed including pier pads in both basement and crawl space areas. Note change of levels in noncontinuous footing.

edge across the top edges of the two footing forms. Zig-zag the 2X4 back and forth across the forms to move along the excess concrete and leave a surface roughly even with the form top edges and ready for floating once set up.

8 Foundation Walls and Backfill

Mentioned briefly in the preceding chapter was the choice between poured concrete and concrete masonry block foundation walls. This decision may rest on several of the factors mentioned. Sometimes, the time element alone is a deciding factor.

In small cities and suburban locations in metropolitan areas, there are concrete subcontractors specializing in home foundation work. If your home fits their schedule and the subcontractor doesn't have too many jobs going, the sequence of foundation work may run like this: come to excavated home site and set footing forms in a day or less; follow with footing pour, perhaps same day; then a day to day-and-half setting wall forms; pour walls following day, and on the next, strip the forms and apply dampproofing. Weather and schedule permitting, a poured concrete foundation may by installed and completed in a 5 day period but is more likely to extend over 7 or 8 working days due simply to scheduling of other work.

Time in doing your own footings and block foundation walls is apt to follow this schedule (weather permitting): set footing forms in a day or less with you and one helper; pouring footings in a half day with three helpers; lay concrete blocks with one helper for a period of about 12 working days for a basement foundation on a home of about 1200 square feet or about nine days for a crawl space foundation on about the same size house. On this basis, there is not too much time difference. But your own working time may be limited. And good weather doesn't always come in stretches of two to three weeks at a time.

If you're a little bit worried about your block laying capability, you might investigate two alternative methods.

One alternative would be a partial subcontract with a mason contractor or journeyman. Every block or brick

Wood Foundation Procedures when built at the site. Top photo shows panels being nailed together after gravel fill has been evenly spread. Treated wood supplied by the Koppers Company. In bottom photo, panels have been tilted up into position and outside surfaces covered with black polyethylene plastic film and a dampproofing material.

laying job involves a "helper" or laborer who does mortar mixing, carrying of mortar and block to where they are convenient to the mason. The helper also stretches mason's lines and other light-duty chores around the job. If you inquire at a concrete block supply firm, you can probably obtain from them the names of three or four subcontractors or moonlighting masons who might be willing to work with you, you serving as their helper.

The second alternative would be to use a wood foundation wall. That's right, wood. Within recent years, wood-preservative people have developed a method of treating structural wood members so they are resistant to the chemicals in soils. Treated lumber and plywood is being sold increasingly to building component fabricators who are assembling foundation wall panels in their shops.

Wood foundation panels, if available, would provide a builder-owner with a foundation that is simpler to build and faster to erect than either a masonry block or poured concrete foundation. The wood panels rest on a relatively thick gravel bed (see illustration) and there is no need for poured concrete footings. The panel methods will still permit installing of a concrete basement floor. The system, properly executed, meets the Department of Housing and Urban Development Minimum Property Standards (HUD-MPS's) and probably will soon have the approval of major model building codes.

One factor to check before deciding. Being relatively new, wood foundation panels are not readily available. For your particular job you may find the nearest supplier to be quite a distance away. Inquire about delivery service, shipping cost, price and other factors. Also about any nearby ongoing jobs you can observe.

Preliminary Needs

If you've never laid a concrete block or brick, you can stand spending half a day observing a block-laying job. Check your yellow pages for concrete block suppliers and stop by one or two of them. You'll do better in person obtaining the names locations of two or three jobs than you will trying to obtain the information by phone. At the same time, you have a chance to size up a block supplier as a potential supplier for your job.

Mortar

In observing a residential block mason at work, note the economy of movements and the way the helper coordinates in keeping materials at hand. Watch the mason's manipulation of the trowel, the way he butters block ends with mortar and where he grasps the blocks to handle them effectively. Watch, too, the trimming of mortar after the block has been tapped to final position, the use of this trimmed mortar to butter another block or to add to the mortar bed. Witness block procedure, the building up of courses at corners and the laying of intermediate blocks between corners with the aid of a mason's line.

Talk a bit with both the mason on the job and the block

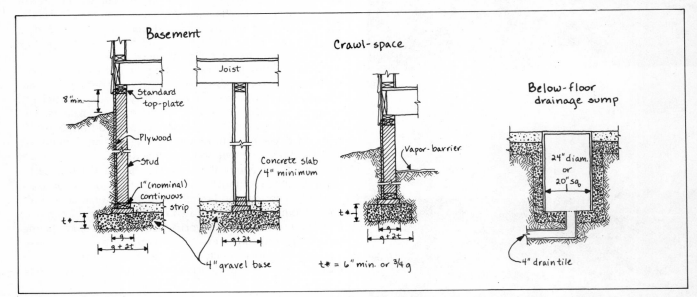

All-Wood Foundations are now approved by some major building codes and by government loan-insuring agencies. Wood foundations have been developed because of their high resistance due to pressure treatments. In the sketches, the wood parts having diagonal lines are pretreated.

Wood foundation panels can be built at the site using pressure-treated lumber. However, time and trouble will be saved by finding a manufactured housing fabricator or components producer who will supply foundation wall sections in panelized form. Information on wood foundations obtainable from American Plywood Association, American Wood Preservers Institute, and the Koppers Company.

supplier about mortar cement mixing. There are two ways to go: follow the traditional mason's method of mixing mortar cement with damp loose sand in a mortar box or mortar mixer, adding water and allowing to rest then rehoeing or retempering for use; or, purchase ready-mixed dry ingredients in bag-form, requiring just the addition of water for immediate use.

The former method is used by tradesmen and the materials cost less than with the latter dry ready-mixes. But, if you're working with minimum help and at a rather slow pace, the ready-mix method might be suitable despite a somewhat higher cost. Whatever the method, be certain you provide on-job covering protection for the materials.

Don't underestimate the part that a helper plays in masonry work. Alone, mixing mortar takes more time and you've got to be careful not to mix up too much in mortar box or mixer for use before the mortar begins its hardening process. Use of a helper lets you concentrate on putting blocks into place. And the work goes much faster. More speed is yet possible with *two* block layers, each working at

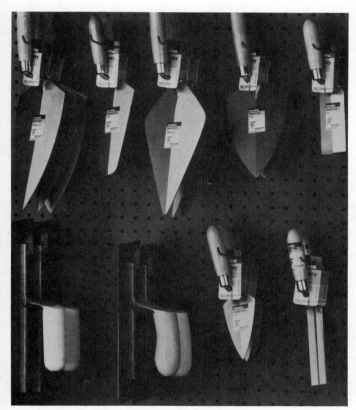

Assorted Mason's Trowels included in the line made by the Coastal Abrasive & Tool Co. Choose proper trowels for the specific jobs you have to do. Shown here in the top row are: brick Philadelphia-pattern trowel, a 7-inch gauging trowel, a 10-inch general purpose pointed trowel, a 7-inch tiling trowel and a 2X5 margin trowel. In the lower row; 12-inch and 10-inch cement finisher's trowels, 5-inch pointing trowel and a joint-tooling trowel.

opposite wall ends. And a good helper will be able to keep both supplied with mortar and blocks. Incidentally, when the blocks are purchased specify that you want the pallet loads of block distributed around the foundation hole. Most suppliers will have truck-unloading cranes that will permit placement of the pallets and thereby save your and your helper a lot of carrying work and back pain.

A small mortar mixing box for your one-time block-laying job is easily made. Stop by a sheet metal shop and get a piece of galvanized sheet about 3X6 feet. Take a pair of 2X8's about 4 feet long, cut the ends at 60° angles, an opposite pair. Place the long edges down and separate the 2X8's by about 3 feet. Center the sheet metal piece over the wood members and mark ends for a 60° bend and foldover at the top. Make the crease and the fold at ends of the sheet metal piece then replace on the 2X8's and nail to them using roofing nails.

The mixing box saves money, but if you will have a couple helpers and another block layer, you would probably be better off paying for the rental of a mortar mixer. A mixer very much simplifies the mortar preparation. The mixer keeps the mortar better, slowing down the drying out process as a batch is being used up.

For general masonry use, mortar is mixed 1 part masonry cement to about 2-¼ to 3 parts of masonry sand in damp loose condition. Thorough mixing is desirable and this requires sufficient time.

If mixed manually in a mortar box:

(1) the sand-cement should be hoed through the box twice, once in each direction lengthwise before adding water;
(2) then add water progressively as a third hoeing through the box is done;
(3) continue to hoe and mix for five to eight minutes to make sure all dry pockets are eliminated;
(4) avoid too much water and a soupy mix.

If mixing with a rental mixer:

(1) be sure you're getting a mixer suited to mortar rather than to concrete;
(2) check the gas supply in the tank;
(3) clean out mixer with water initially and after each batch, but empty water before dumping in dry ingredients;
(4) again add water, cautiously so that the mix does not become soupy;
(5) once right consistency is reached, mix for about three to five additional minutes;
(6) after delivering mortar to mortar stands, shut off mixer;
(7) restart and mix for a minute or two before reapplying the mason.

On hot sunny days, cover mortar box or mixer with plastic film. Wet down mortar board and keep mortar supply film-covered to help maintain workability. Mix mortar in batches suited to your crew size and rate of laying. Mortar left standing for over about 2-½ hours should not be used and retempering should be limited to just once after the initial preparation.

Block Masonry

Working tools needed for block masonry work are relatively inexpensive and a few will be useful in later jobs other than masonry. Here's a minimal list:

- ☐ mortar mixing box and hoe or rental mixer;
- ☐ deep-tray wheelbarrow for bringing materials from dump site to mixing location and thence to mortar boards;
- ☐ 30-inch square, ½ inch plywood piece mounted on a pair of short 2X4's on edge will serve as a mortar pallet or board;
- ☐ professional quality pointed mason's hand trowel;
- ☐ mason's line cord (you have from footing work) and a pair of line cord tension clips;
- ☐ joint-smoothing tool;
- ☐ brick mason's straight-claw hammer for chipping and cutting of blocks;
- ☐ couple pair noncloth working gloves because concrete blocks are extremely abrasive to fingers;
- ☐ 4-foot mason's level.

Window and Door Supplies

Before starting work, you will have checked your block supply to make sure of the correct proportion of corner and stretcher blocks as well as other supplemental block types which needed for any particular job (see illustration). Your block supplier will guide you on quantities needed and application of special block units for window jambs, lintels and other needs.

Your block supplier or building materials dealer will usually be able to supply basement windows. These are generally steel windows with frames designed to be set in masonry walls. If you plan a sliding patio or entrance door for a walk-out basement, you'll have to select the brand and size which provide correct wall opening dimensions. Regular basement windows are set as the blocks are laid; the entrance door units are generally installed later into correctly sized openings.

With a conventional door entrance, provision is made for use of a wood-frame unit. This is installed in the course of block-laying. Frames are anchored to walls by small galvanized anchor clips nailed to the frame's back and penetrating into mortar joints.

Recommended Procedure. Consider window-door installation in block foundation walls as separate situations from those of the home's above-ground doors and windows. Ask for advice about windows and doors suited to masonry construction and order them in sufficient time even though sliding or entrance units may not be installed until later. By so doing, you'll be certain to make proper wall provision by having the manufacturer's instructions at hand.

When frames are to be installed, set the units in approximate position when correct masonry course has been reached. Check the measurements for the opening. Block the frame up so its base is at the correct height and then

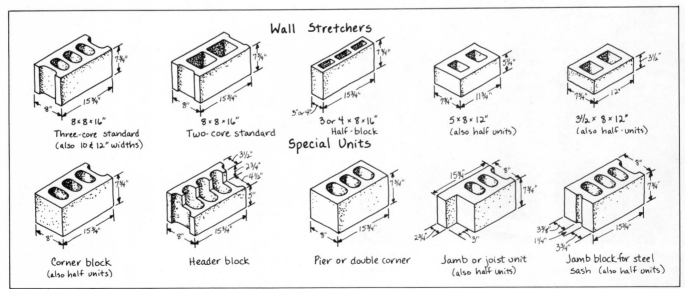

Commonly Used Types of Concrete Blocks and their dimensions are fairly uniform throughout the country. However, the number and shape of the core holes vary somewhat in different areas. Some block plants also produce an additional variety of shapes or sizes, particularly in fractional units. Visit block plant in your area to discover local practices and pinpoint block needs for your foundation.

brace with a 2X4 running from frame top to the ground an nailed to a stake. Fill in below frame with concrete block units trimmed to proper height, and remove blocking.

At time of window selection with block supplier, he will also enter on your order an appropriate number of end-slotted jamb blocks that allow easy slide-in insertion of basement windows. At same time, depending on window size and height as well as outside ground condition, he

Complete Basement Foundation of 12 masonry block courses with front entry cheek walls finished off two courses below plate level: (1) A close-up of (2) a reinforced concrete lintel formed-and-poured in place to span the rear basement opening for a sliding patio door. Another close-up (3) of the insertion of a steel basement sash unit in jamb block slots with the top of the head member flush with the top of the final block course.

should include appropriately sized galvanized window wells attached to the outside of the foundation to keep backfill away from windows and allow daylight in.

Lintels, the horizontal load-carrying supports spanning across basement window and door openings, must also be considered. These may be provided by lintel blocks into which reinforcing bars are placed and concrete poured, or they may be entirely of concrete either poured at the job or precast. Discuss your needs with the supplier and he'll suggest what he feels the most suitable method.

For crawl-space block foundations, there will normally be no window or door openings. But there will be ventilation openings. Most codes or standards will require a free-vent area (reduced from vent size by the area of intermediate bars or supports) of 1/1500 of the ground area of the crawl space. When the surface of the crawl space is to be covered with a vapor barrier such as polyethylene film (to prevent upward penetration of ground moisture), cross-ventilation of the crawl space is required.

If you're in a middle-to-northern climate and trying to conserve heating fuel, choose the type of block ventilator that can be closed from outside during cold weather. And insulate the foundation walls and joist-space perimeter as indicated in Chapter 26. Block vent units of metal are usually available to fit block coursing for both full, 8 inch block heights or half-block heights of 4 inch.

Lay-Up Procedures

The secret to obtaining good-quality and goodlooking concrete block walls is two-faceted: first is the use of properly mixed mortar, and use of the proper amounts in all the right places; second, proper block alignment horizontally and vertically in order to assure uniform width of mortar joints.

Proper mixing has been mentioned. Alignment ease is the reason for corner buildup for line-stretching guidance. Corner blocks are laid up first at the corners with alternate courses going in two directions (see illustrations). Lay up the blocks for a corner to about four or five courses high to start. Care must be used to get the blocks accurately lined up for wall length but also to get them plumb vertically and level horizontally. It's particularly important to get the first or base course in proper position so that slight errors in corner buildup don't progressively increase. It becomes apparent why extra effort was suggested in trying to get your wall footings level around the building.

With two wall corner buildups carefully laid up, you're ready to try to somewhat speed up laying the intermediate blocks. The following procedural tips will help you do a faster and better job:

□ Use plywood mortar pallets or boards that rest on a pair of upturned blocks rather than on the ground; the slight added height makes the mortar easier to reach.
□ With a straight wall section, place continuous rows of

mortar so that the outer edges are about block width apart; the rows should be about an inch thick and about 2 inches wide. Lay out the rows sufficiently to receive about six or seven block units. Then, proceed block by block to butter inside and outside end faces setting the block down in the mortar rows with the buttered faces adjacent to the end of the previously laid bottom-course block.

□ After the sixth or seventh block, come back to the starting point and proceed similarly with the next course. And the one after that until you're four or five courses high.

□ Now, go to the end of that section and begin again with your mortar rows for the bottom course and follow through with another section. Adjust the blocks laid per section to the overall wall length so that, for example, a

Block-Laying Steps recommended by the Portland Cement Association in its booklet on the subject from which this series of photos was taken. The highlights are: (1) with blocks ready nearby, trowel mortar into two rows on the top of the footing; (2) using two hands to lift, put mortar-buttered block into position. Each block is placed into a mortar bed, and needs one end spread or buttered with mortar so that this end may be placed against the block unit previously placed.

Use the mason's level (3) to make sure blocks are level, tap down (4) blocks at points where block remains slightly above the stretched mason's line cord. Blocks at building corners are laid up first to provide line stretching clips a fastening base. With one edge of the trowel (5), excess mortar is bladed off. The level is in almost constant use to check face straightness (6) as well as level and plumb.

When mortar begins hardening, the joint tool is used to give each mortar joint a slight indenting pressure and a smooth surface (7). When proper course height is reached, masonry anchor bolts (8) or metal clips are set and block core holes fill with mortar. And in (9) a final step, outer surface of the wall is given a cement coat (parging).

40 or 45 feet wall length is divided into about four lay-up sections.

□ After getting your initial wall section up to four or five courses high, go on to your next building corner for corner buildup followed by intermediate laying in of sections.

□ The standard thickness for most masonry wall mortar joints is 3/8 inch. You gradually become accustomed to approximating this by eye, but to start, have a convenient 3/8 inch thick block of plywood as a guide.

□ Your alignment guide in laying up intermediate blocks is a mason's line stretched from buildup corner to buildup corner. Small clips that hold the line in tension also hold the clip in accurate position at the corner so that the line follows the top edge of the buildup block for which the matching course is being laid. The intermediate blocks

are lowered into the mortar and tapped level to just reach the line with their upper edge.

□ Keep a 4 foot level always handy for quick and frequent checks of block levelness and face plumbness.

□ Initially, you'll be bothered by getting too little or too much mortar in the rows and in your buttering of the block ends. Take your time and adjust mortar amounts. Remove excess with trowel cut across face and return excess to mortar board, add to mortar rows, or use to end-butter.

□ In using trowel to cut off mortar at joints leaving the joints flush, don't worry about immediate joint tooling. Tooling is best done after the mortar has started to set. Many times you can do a full wall length five courses high before going back to do tooling.

□ Take an occasional moment to step back and admire your work. Not just for satisfaction but also to detect possible misalignments or face adjustments that might be made.

Supplemental Considerations

Wall Stiffeners or Supporters

The thickness of most concrete masonry walls used for foundations is 8 inches. However, where basement walls are built in tight soils subject to lateral pressure and carrying heavier loads, building codes may require increased thicknesses to 10 or 12 inches at various depths below grade. One method of strengthening basement walls where such earth pressures are present is to build in integral pilasters.

Pilasters are column-like projections on the inner side of the basement running from floor or first course up to foundation top. They should have a minimum width of one block length, 16 inches. And they should be laid as the wall

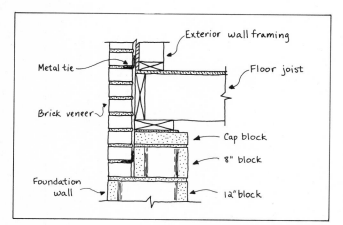

Foundation Wall Detail for masonry veneer construction, showing 12-inch thick concrete blocks for foundation wall to provide full support for veneer brick.

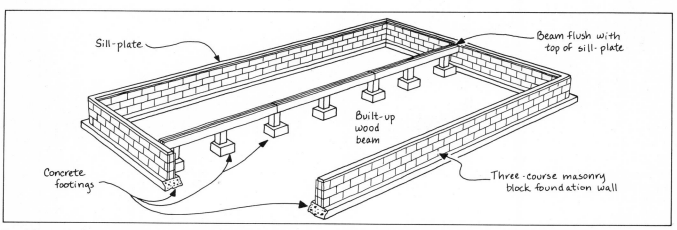

Crawl Space Block Foundation with central beam, piers and footing pads all ready to receive floor joists. In this sketch, sill plates have been placed and anchor bolts or clips (not shown) have been started or tacked but not tightened. Purpose here is to leave plates slightly

loose so that after floor joists have been nailed up, the deck framing may be brought up to level by wedges between the sill plates and foundation top. After such leveling, the anchor bolts or clips are firmly tightened or nailed.

goes up, meshing the pilaster block into the wall. Pilaster practices vary somewhat with local building departments. The more or less standard practice is that no pilasters are needed with 12 inch thick walls. With 10 inch thick blocks, and walls over 36 feet long, the distance between pilasters or between pilaster and end-wall should not exceed 18 feet. With 8 inch thick blocks and walls over 30 feet, pilaster spacing or pilaster-end-wall distance should not be over 15 feet.

Some codes may permit wall stiffeners to be used, in which the stiffener is a reinforcing bar placed in block cores from footing to wall top and with the cores filled with mortar. Spacing of stiffeners may be 15 feet with 10 inch blocks and 12 feet with 8 inch blocks. Some codes in areas where earth pressures are apt to be mild provide for tempo-

rary stiffening during construction by means of wood plank or timber bracing on the interior to aid in resisting back-filling pressure or possible water pressure. Your local code official will advise on wall stiffening measures he considers appropriate.

Dampproofing

Following block lay-up, allow a few days for the foundation wall mortar to set or cure. In most areas the practice is to provide a dampproofing coat on the outer foundation

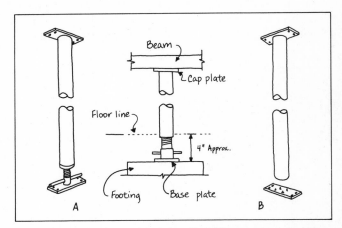

Steel Basement Posts may be of the adjustable type shown in (A) or nonadjustable as indicated in (B). These steel columns may be used with either steel or wood beams. Where steel is used, the fabricating supplier will precut and predrill the beam to exact dimensions shown on plans and the columns will bolt to the beam. Where wood is used, lag screws are used to fasten the column plates to the beam.

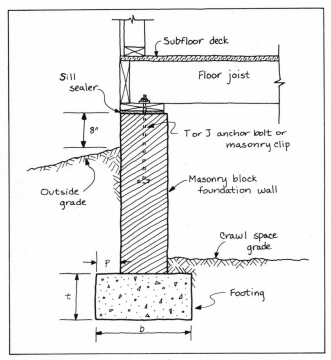

House Foundation Support and the parts or materials involved are shown in this sketch. Floor construction must be anchored to foundation wall by use of bolts or appropriate metal clips.

The height and thickness of a block foundation wall generally follow code requirements prevailing in any given area. Check with your block supplier.

With respect to concrete footings, their thickness (t), base width (b) and projection from the face of the foundation wall (p), will be determined by the height of the building and whether or not a basement is involved. In FHA's Manual of Acceptable Practices, footing thickness may be 6 inches minimum for one-and-two story homes, but 8 inches on a two-story with basement if built of masonry or masonry veneer. Footing projection of 3 inches is suited to no-basement frame construction while 4-inch projection is needed for basement or masonry homes. Again, check your local building official for footing-dimension requirements.

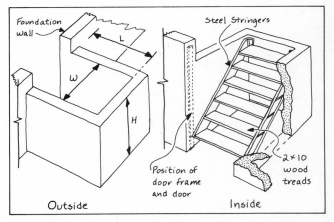

Outside Basement Stairs can be provided for by a properly sized opening in the foundation wall and the addition of enclosure walls dimensioned to suitable stair width and to metal basement door units. The length, width and height of the foundation walls are determined according to the particular model of basement door unit selected. See Chapter 48 for further details.

wall face. It's called waterproofing in some areas but both terms refer to the same type of asphaltic compound. The application may be brush or spray. Your block supplier will know what compounds are suitable.

Dampproofing may be a single coating unless some severe water or moisture problem is present. In such cases, it may be desirable to provide a parging coat, a 1/4-to-3/8 inch thick application of troweled-on portland cement and sand mix. The Portland Cement Association recommends such parging to be applied uniformly over the outer surface when the basement is to receive interior wall finish and use as a habitable room such as a family room or bedroom (see

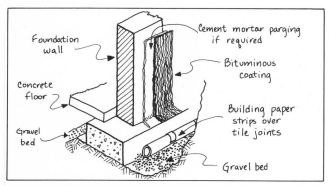

Foundation wall

Cement mortar parging if required

Bituminous coating

Concrete floor

Building paper strips over tile joints

Gravel bed

Gravel bed

Finished Foundation Wall and Footing in cross-section to indicate supplementary factors: the position of the concrete floor to be poured later, the location of foundation drain tile and the provision of dampproofing on the outer side of the wall. A coating of cement on masonry block foundations is desirable (sometimes mandatory by code) when the interior side of the wall is living space such as a basement room or lower level of a bi-level home.

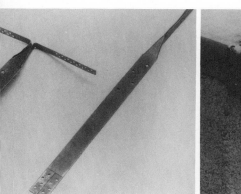

Metal Anchor Clips fold over the top and nail to sill plates, making sill anchoring easier than using bolts which require predrilling of plate members. To meet with FHA requirements, clips or bolts must be spaced a maximum of 8 feet and at each wall end, a clip or bolt must be no more than 1 foot and no less than 3 inches from the outer wall face on each side of the corner. Clips or bolts must be embedded downward 15 inches in masonry or 6 inches in poured concrete. With hollow-core masonry units, the sill plates must be of a width sufficient to cover the core holes.

illustration). Both parging and the subsequent dampproof coating should extend down over the footing projection and face.

Practices vary widely on dampproofing compounds. It may be cold-applied compound. Or it may be a cut-back type asphalt or bituminous mix that needs heating. A hot mix may be awkward without proper heating equipment. If such a hot-applied coating is required, call in a dampproofing or roofing subcontractor to do it. It's a quick job and does not cost much.

Backfilling

Backfilling is done quickly by bulldozer or bucket-equipped tractor. If the foundation includes a basement and no internal bracing or wall strengthening is required, backfilling by machine requires some care to avoid putting too much pressure on the new block walls. You had better count on doing one of the following before backfilling: provide internal plank or timber bracing at about 15 foot intervals; or, install the central longitudinal support beam and first floor joists and deck. As a general rule, backfill height from footing to grade should not exceed 7 feet.

Before backfilling but after dampproofing, foundation drain tiles are a common provision except in the dryest and highest ground locations. Drain tiles, 4 inch diameter clay field tiles, are laid on a gravel base along the exterior sides of the footings. Ordinarily they run along the two long sides of the foundation, join together at one endwall nearest the low elevation side of the lot and run in a drainage trench to a ditch or storm drain (see illustration).

As indicated in the drawing, small pieces of felt building paper are placed over the top halves of the tile butt joints to keep sediment from penetrating. Gravel is placed over the tile. If no appropriate outlet is readily available, the drain tile can lead to a dry well or seepage pit in some dry part of the lot or to a sump from which a submersible pump can lift the draining water for surface disposal.

Don't let the backfilling dozer come too close to the foundation wall. It can exert a lot of pressure. The leveling off of backfill should be done at a point about 2-to-4 inches above what you want final grade to be. There will be that amount of settling or compaction. At time of backfilling, have the excavating subcontractor also move excess excavated dirt to a smooth sloping-out grade around the house so no piles remain (except possibly a topsoil pile) to block drainage or to interfere with the remaining work.

The interior side of concrete block walls can easily be painted later on with a wide choice of easily applied masonry paints. If basement space will see use as a recreation room, laundry or workshop, it may be desirable to provide additional thermal values to the walls. This can be done in those areas by a mineral type fill insulation placed in the block voids as the block units are laid up. A more effective method of insulating would be the use of furring strips on the interior side for application of wallboard or paneling

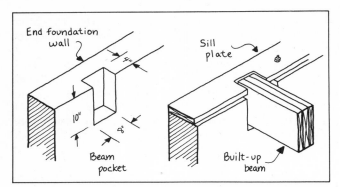

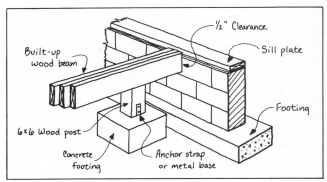

Beam End Recess in masonry wall to provide supporting base for the central longitudinal beam or girder is usual practice for basement foundations. The recess should provide at least 4 inches support base and the width-depth of the recess should be determined by the size of the beam or girder. The 10-inch depth shown in the sketch is suitable for a built-up beam of 2X12's. This depth will allow the beam top to be approximately flush with the top of the sill plate.

In some localities, the code or building official may not permit pocket-bearing points when hollow-core masonry units are used. In some cases an additional pier or column adjacent to the wall may be required, or an integral pilaster may have to be laid up using regular wall block.

A possible alternative is to use solid masonry blocks for at least two courses below the bearing point.

Beam-End Piers, an alternative to wall pocket bearing for central support beam or girder. Shown here is a typical pier and footing adjacent to the foundation wall on a crawl space home. The wood post is easier to anchor but such piers may also be built of block units or of poured concrete. If blocks are used, solid masonry units should be used although in some areas it is common practice to use square chimney blocks for building piers.

Footings for piers are made of same thickness as wall footings and they are usually about 2 feet square for one-story homes and 30-to-36 inches square for split-level and two-story homes. Refer to your set of working drawings to check pad size and location.

Backfill the Foundation carefully to avoid too much lateral pressure on the freshly built wall. If masonry blocks have been used for a basement foundation, the walls should be well-braced inside the basement area using 2X10's or 2X12's against the face of the wall at about 6 feet high with diagonal 2X6's running down to well-implanted ground stakes. In any case, ask the tractor operator to approach wall at right angles, keeping tractor weight off the backfill area that's within a few feet of the wall face.

and the filling of spaces between strips with a urethane or styrene foam type insulation board.

Beams

One final part of your foundation installation and support for first floor joist framing is a central longitudinal beam. This can be a solid timber, or a built-up timber usually of three or four layers of 2X12's properly nailed together or a steel beam. Use of steel I-beams has increased because of easier handling; wood beams even in sections are heavy, and awkward to handle. Steel beams are now generally available from foundation material suppliers, those establishments principally serving the contractor trades and sometimes known as "hard materials" dealers. The fabricated steel beams come in sections with bolt-together fastening and with steel support columns as indicated on the drawings.

Support beam ends, whether wood or steel, should have ample bearing space on foundation end-walls. This can be done with properly sized beam pockets in the wall (see illustration) or by means of integral pilasters laid as the foundation walls go up.

9 First or Ground Floor

Before getting into the floor framing work for the main or ground floor, you may be wondering about your basement floor, if your home is being built with one. Should it be poured now before floor framing work is done?

It is really your option, and may perhaps depend more on the basement ground condition at this time. If the ground is dry, it's quite appropriate to go ahead and pour the basement floor now. However, frequently the ground is mushy and each rain accumulates water in the basement area. In such cases, it's desirable to hold off pouring until the home is under roof and the basement area pumped out and given a chance to dry. If you do desire to go ahead now with the floor, check the suggestions in Chapter 46. Ordinarily, pouring of the basement floor can await completion of outside rough grading so that all flat slab work, the walks, entrance stoop, driveway, and basement or garage floors can be poured all during a short one-to-three day period.

Working around a basement area that's a mushy mess can be a headache. Although pouring can wait, if you have the chance before floor framing work to level off the basement grade and have the gravel floor base material delivered and spread, do so. Same applies to leveling work in crawl spaces or unexcavated areas. This leveling-grading work can be done much more easily at this time than later after the floor deck and rest of the structure has been completed.

Floor Decks

Approach the floor deck construction with complete confidence. There's no part of residential framing work so simple to build as the ground floor deck. Note the use here of the word "deck" instead of subfloor, which has been commonly used in the past. There's a reason. Building products keep being refined and improved. There are now several alternatives to the former traditional double-floor construction consisting of subfloor inch boards later covered with hardwood flooring. The choice of double-

Guidelines to New Lumber Sizes

| What You Order | What Size You Get | | What You Used to Get |
	Dry or Seasoned*	Green or Unseasoned**	Seasoned or Unseasoned
1×4	3/4× 3-1/2	25/32× 3-9/16	25/32× 3-5/8
1×6	3/4× 5-1/2	25/32× 5-3/8	25/32× 5-1/2
1×8	3/4× 7-1/4	25/32× 7-1/2	25/32× 7-1/2
1×10	3/4× 9-1/4	25/32× 9-1/2	25/32× 9-1/2
1×12	3/4× 11-1/4	25/32× 11-1/2	25/32× 11-1/2
2×4	1-1/2× 3-1/2	1-9/16× 3-9/16	1-5/8× 3-5/8
2×6	1-1/2× 5-1/2	1-9/16× 5-5/8	1-5/8× 5-1/2
2×8	1-1/2× 7-1/4	1-9/16× 7-1/2	1-5/8× 7-1/2
2×10	1-1/2× 9-1/4	1-9/16× 9-1/2	1-5/8× 9-1/2
2×12	1-1/2× 11-1/4	1-9/16× 11-1/2	1-5/8× 11-1/2
4×4	3-1/2× 3-1/2	3-9/16× 3-9/16	3-5/8× 3-5/8
4×6	3-1/2× 5-1/2	3-9/16× 5-5/8	3-5/8× 5-1/2
4×8	3-1/2× 7-1/4	3-9/16× 7-1/2	3-5/8× 7-1/2
4×10	3-1/2× 9-1/4	3-9/16× 9-1/2	3-5/8× 9-1/2
4×12	3-1/2× 11-1/4	3-9/16× 11-1/2	3-5/8× 11-1/2

* 19% moisture content or less
** over 19% moisture content
SOURCE: Folder prepared for Republic Lumber Market, Chicago

New Actual Sizes of Lumber are shown for both green and dry lumber. The column at left lists the nominal sizes of all common framing lumber. Before a recent change in lumber standards, all lumber whether seasoned or unseasoned was milled to the same actual size. For a 2×4, it was 1-5/8 inches by 3-5/8 inches. Under the new system, there are different milling sizes and these actual dimensions are listed in columns two and three.

floor or single-floor construction is up to you. In the following paragraphs you'll find some specifics to help you make up your mind.

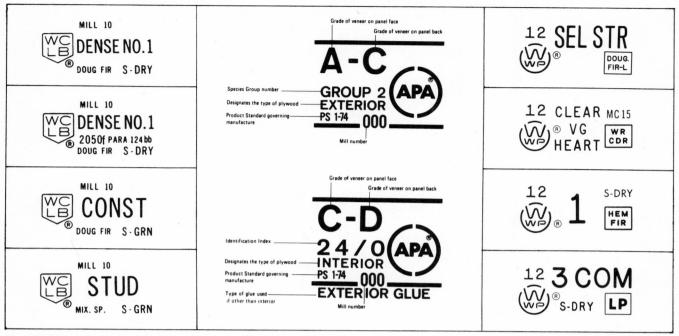

Samples of Lumber-Plywood Grade Marks used by mills to indicate quality of wood and its suitability for varied construction purposes. Shown at left, some common grade marks used by the West Coast Lumber Bureau. In the center, two of many plywood grades used under the rules of the American Plywood Association, with explanation of the designations. At right, sample grade marks used by members of the Western Wood Products Association.

One of the advantages in using fabricated components is that the fabricating plants carefully design components to use proper lumber-plywood grades and the components produced are of uniform high quality. In contrast, it has been the practice in the past for shipments to lumber dealers to be not only of certain commonly used grades but also of mixed grades. When purchasing, economize by ordering the lowest grade or lowest-priced species capable of doing the particular job. But choice is more often than not limited by what a lumber supplier has in stock.

It's now required that all framing lumber be stamped with its appropriate grade mark to indicate the species, condition of moisture, and identity number of the producing mill. In a few marks, more than one species may have the same mark. One common example is with "HemFir" grades whose marks may be applicable to both fir and hemlock; shipments of such lumber often contain mixed species.

Regarding moisture conditions, producing mills may surface lumber in green or unseasoned condition but the size has to be sufficiently larger so that when it dries out naturally it will be of the same size as lumber grade-marked dry. Dry lumber is stronger than green but in some marketing areas the unseasoned type still predominates for construction uses. Green lumber is also more apt to develop warping or twisting and should generally be avoided by the owner-builder if possible.

Single-Floor Decks versus Subfloor plus Hardwood

A single-floor deck makes good sense today in view of the newer materials available and the opportunity to save both time and money. A single-floor system is designed to combine the subfloor function with the underlayment sheet material into a single operation suitable for direct application of resilient types of floor coverings or wall-to-wall carpeting. Such a single-floor deck usually has some provision for a little greater stiffness than the usual subfloor, less chance of joint unevenness, and a smoother surface comparable to that provided by underlayment sheets.

If you opt for extensive use of hardwood flooring as a finish material, then the traditional subfloor is quite suitable. But for smaller owner-built homes where time, expense and degree of skill each play a part, it's suggested that hardwood floors be limited in favor of three now generally accepted floor coverings, all of which can be applied directly over properly installed single-floor construction: resilient tile or sheet goods; wall-to-wall carpeting; and ceramic tile laid in adhesive. (See illustrations of various floor surfaces in Chapters 37 and 38.)

An important factor in the above suggestion is the ease of installation. The single-floor construction with floor coverings applied directly provide good-quality methods and materials with worthwhile savings as opposed to double-floor construction.

It is recognized that hardwood finish flooring, with many of the new plank, strip, parquet and block styles, rates highly in the preferences of many people planning

Fastener Schedule for Structural Members

Description of Building Materials	Number & Type[1] of Fasteners[2,3,5]	Spacing of Fasteners
Joist to sill or girder, toe nail	2-16d	—
1″ × 6″ subfloor or less to each joist, face nail	2-8d	—
	2-staples, 1-¾″	—
Wider than 1″ × 6″ subfloor to each joist, face nail	3-8d	—
	4-staples, 1¾″	—
2″ subfloor to joist or girder, blind and face nail	2-16d	—
Sole plate to joist or blocking, face nail	16d	16″ o.c.
Top or sole plate to stud, end nail	2-16d	—
Stud to sole plate, toe nail	4-8d or 3-16d	—
Doubled studs, face nail	16d	24″ o.c.
Doubled top plates, face nail	16d	16″ o.c.
Top plates, taps and intersections, face nail	2-16d	—
Continued header, two pieces	16d	16″ o.c. along each edge
Ceiling joists to plate, toe nail	2-16d	—
Continuous header to stud, toe nail	4-8d	—
Ceiling joist, tas over partitions, face nail	3-16d	—
Ceiling joist to parallel rafters, face nail	3-16d	—
Rafter to plate, toe nail	2-16d	—
1″ brace to each stud and plate, face nail	2-8d	—
	2-staples, 1-¾″	—
1″ × 6″ sheathing to each bearing, face nail	2-8d	—
	2-staples, 1-¾″	—
1″ × 8″ sheathing to each bearing, face nail	2-8d	—
	3-staples, 1¾″	—
Wider than 1″ × 8″ sheathing to each bearing, face nail	3-8d	—
	4-staples, 1¾″	—
Built-up corner studs	16d	30″ o.c.
Built-up girder and beams	20d	32″ o.c. at top & bottom & staggered 2-20d at ends & at ea. splice
2-inch planks	2-16d	at each bearing
Roof rafters to ridge, valley or hip rafters, toe nail	4-16d	—
face nail	3-16d	—
Collar ties to rafters, face nail	3-8d	—

Nailing Sizes for Various Materials to be nailed to framing members are shown in this chart reproduced from the "One-and-Two Family Dwelling Code." Also given are appropriate sizes of staples for certain fastening applications for which they are considered suitable.

Description of Building Materials	Description[1] of Fasteners[2,3,5]	Spacing of Fasteners	
		edges	intermediate supports[4]
Plywood subfloor, roof and wall sheathing to frame:			
1/2 inch - 5/16 inch	6d staple 16 ga.	6"	12"
5/8 inch - 3/4 inch	8d smooth or 6d deformed	6"	12"
7/8 inch - 1 inch	8d	6"	12"
1-1/8 inches - 1-1/4 inches	10d smooth or 8d deformed	6"	12"
Other wall sheathing[7]			
1/2" Fiberboard Sheathing	1-1/2" galvanized roofing nail 6d common nail staple 16 ga. 11/8" long	3"	6"
25/32" Fiberboard Sheathing	1-3/4" galvanized roofing nail 8d common nail staple 16 ga. 1-1/2" long	3"	6"
1/2" Gypsum Sheathing	1-1/2" galvanized roofing nail 6d common nail staple 16 ga. 1-1/2" long	4"	8"
Particleboard wall sheathing (Exterior-Type 2-B-1)			
3/8" - 1/2"	6d common nail	6"	12"
5/8" - 3/4"	8d common nail staple 16 ga. 1-1/2" long	6"	12"
Combination subfloor-underlayment to framing			
3/4 inch and less	6d deformed	6"	10"
7/8 inch - 1 inch	8d deformed	6"	10"
1-1/8 inches - 1-1/4 inches	10d smooth or 8d deformed	6"	6"

1. All nails are smooth-common, box or deformed shanks except where otherwise stated.
2. Nail is a general description and may be T-head, modified round head or round head.
3. Staples are 16 gauge wire and have a minimum 7/16 inch O.D. crown width.
4. Nails shall be spaced at not more than 6 inches o.c. at all supports where spans are 48 inches or greater. Nails shall be spaced at not more than 10 inches o.c. at intermediate supports for floors.
5. The number of fasteners required for connections not included in this Table shall be based on values set forth in Section S-26.402.
6. Four foot X 8-foot or 4-foot X 9-foot panels shall be applied vertically.
7. Structural sheathing shall comply to applicable standards listed in Chapter 26 and be approved by the Building Official.

new homes. Maintenance of such floors is minimal and their appearance enhances many rooms. The foregoing single-floor construction method does *not* preclude the eventual use of hardwood finish flooring. You may elect to go the single-floor route now and then decide after a period of occupancy to install the hardwood flooring of your choice.

Recommended Method. The single-floor plywood deck method, with glue-nailed application as developed by the American Plywood Association, is best. This glue-nailed system uses underlayment type of plywood having tongue-groove edges and provides a firm underfooting. It will take slightly longer to install than a regular plywood subfloor and cost slightly more for materials. But not significantly so, and not for the dual function it performs. It results in a more rigid, squeakless floor construction with sufficient "give" for comfort. A saving in time and materials also results, because with the glue-nailed application no bridging between floor joists is needed.

Sill-Plate And Sealer

The initial preparatory step in building your main floor deck is installing the foundation sill-plate around the building perimeter. In the case of an 8 inch thick concrete block foundation wall, use of a 2X8 sill-plate covers the block voids and eliminates the need for filling these top-course voids with mortar or concrete. With poured concrete foundation walls, the normal sill-plate is of 2X6's.

You can order out the sill-plate members at the same time that your basement posts and beam are ordered. The two jobs more or less go hand in hand. Also order out sufficient sill-sealer material for the perimeter of the house. This is ½ inch thick insulating material in 4-inch-wide rolls. Placed atop the foundation wall before the sill-plates are secured, the sealer gives a tight fit over minor irregularities in the foundation top and prevents infiltration of air or moisture. Setting the sill-plate and tightening it down with anchor bolt nuts or anchor clips will compress the sealer for a tight joint.

If you've installed T- or J-bolts into the block foundation for anchoring, you'll have to predrill the 2X8 sill-plates at the correct bolt positions before putting them into place. Mark the bolt locations accurately on the sill-plate member by putting the 2X8 in position along the side of the anchor bolts. Then, measure distance in of the bolt from the out foundation wall face less the sheathing thickness (see illustration). This short distance is apt to vary from bolt to bolt, so adjust accordingly.

A simpler anchoring procedure for the sill-plates is possible if plate-anchoring metal clips are used. The clips or bolts need to be set in the block voids as the last course of blocks is completed. HUD-MPS requirements indicate such anchors need to penetrate downward from the block top at least 15 inches. When setting sill-plates on foundation walls where the anchor clips have been used, the twin arms of the

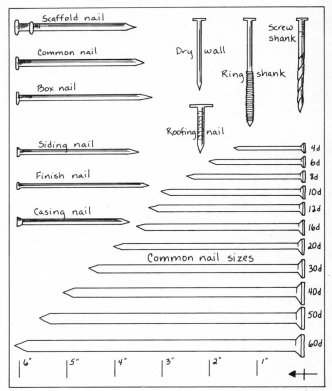

Nails for Residential Applications (called "box") are shown in sketch form in the upper portion; sizes of common nails are indicated below. Nail or fastener cost for a single home being built is relatively low so owner-builders should attempt to obtain the best quality most appropriate nails.

Nail size is indicated by "penny," the abbreviation for which is "d." For example, a nail 3 inches long is a 10-penny nail which is written "10d." This applies regardless of head or shank configuration. The shank diameter of nails generally increases with length. Most used are the common and box nails used usually for framing work. Box nails with thinner shanks are less apt to split lumber. In many areas, lumber suppliers furnish common or box nails that are "coated" with a thin film that tends to increase nail holding power.

Double-headed or scaffold nails are useful for temporary fastening of braces, concrete forms, and other applications where the work being nailed up must later be dismantled. Nails for drywall and roofing uses generally have broader heads and shanks suited to the specific purpose for which they're intended. Nails with deformed shanks have extra holding power and are difficult to loosen once in place. Siding, casing, and finish nails are alike in that they have smaller heads which are not noticeable when left exposed. The small heads are also suitable for "setting" or driving below the surface of the material and then filling the holes remaining with wood filler.

Nails that are used for exterior materials should not corrode. Residential-application nails are zinc-coated (galvanized) or aluminum nails.

clip are bent down flat to the foundation top, the sill-plate is placed, and the metal clip arms are bent back around the plate member and nailed to it. There's no premarking or drilling of the plate needed.

Now, give consideration to your central longitudinal support beam. With wood central beams, it's common practice to install and support the beam so that its top surface is flush or even with the top surface of the sill-plates. With steel central support beams, the practice is to install them so their top surface is even with the foundation wall top. This is to allow placement on top of the beam's flange, a 2X6 or 2X8, to facilitate the toe-nailing of floor joists.

Usually, wide-flange I-beams are furnished by your block or hard materials supplier for this purpose. The size beam and flange width will vary according to design load which the supplier can determine from your working drawings or specifications. The wood plate member should be a bit wider than the steel I-beam flange. Fastening to the beam is done by metal clips, adhesive or often just a simple row of nails along the flange edge driven from below into the wood plate with the head portion bent around the flange. The principal stress here is in a downward direction and once the joists have been lapped or spliced and toe-nailed to the plate, there is little chance of any side-slip.

At this point you may want to check the levelness of the sill-plate installation before the anchor nuts or clip arms are fastened down. There are two schools of thought on this procedure. One school says do your level check with the level-transit now before the joists are set so that you can wedge up the sill-plates more easily. The other school says hold off with your bolts, clip-nailing and leveling until all the joists have been installed and you're ready to apply the deck material; this lets you level the floor as well as the sill-plates. But after the joists have been nailed into place, it's considerably harder to wedge up the plate and joists to bring them level, and there's a possibility of damage to the foundation wall if pry-bars are used. So, take your choice as to the time of leveling. Both choices have advantages and disadvantages.

In either case, set up your level-transit instrument again

Floor Trusses, used extensively in recent years on apartment buildings, are seeing increased use in single-family homes where they can eliminate the need for central support beams and basement posts. These fabricated trusses have been shop-assembled using Gang-Nail connector plates. Inquire from your components supplier about possible cost or time savings with floor trusses.

in a position where various points on the sill-plates or floor-joist tops can be sighted. Start with one corner of the building and proceed around to find the high corner if any. Inspect it. If the sill-plate is flat atop the foundation and won't go down, then this corner becomes the reference point and the other corners are shingle-wedged up to level. Now check intermediate points about every 10 or 12 feet along the house perimeter. Wedge as needed. Now the same along the central support beam. Here's where use of adjustable basement posts comes in handy. If plain posts are used, wedge with metal, asbestos-board or stones at the *bottom* of the support posts. A tolerance of plus or minus 1/8 inch is considered acceptable. Projecting ends of shingle wedges should be broken or sawn off flush.

At this point, you may wish to verify your house elevation reference point (top of foundation wall or first floor level) with the surveyor's bench mark. The reference point, if your footing and masonry course work have been adequate and your height calculations correct, should be within about 1/2 inch plus or minus of the height shown on the plot plan drawing.

Shimming up of sill-plate of only 1/8 to 1/4 inch usually won't disturb the sill-sealer. More than that it may. Inspect around the perimeter after shimming for any openings. If there are stretches where the sill-sealer is not down close to the foundation top, the opening should be caulked.

Joists

Selection

The size of floor joists you use will depend upon the span of distance from your central beam to the outer walls. This span, with respect to normal residential floor loadings, is given consideration by the home's designer and is reflected in the joist size and spacing and grade of lumber he indicates in the drawings and specs. In ordering your floor joists, make a notation of the species and grade that are specified and if any other grade-species is to be supplied, make certain your supplier gives you assurance that it is a suitable material for substitution for that which is specified. There's sometimes a slight tendency on the part of lumber suppliers to belittle this insistence on proper grade-species. You may elicit such comments as: "Oh sure, this grade we're supplying you with is just as good. You don't have to worry." Don't trust such offhand comments. Make them give you a statement in writing to the effect that they're substituting such-and-such lumber for what has been specified and that it has the required strength values.

In connection with load-carrying capacities, you'll hear the terms "live load" and "dead load." The latter refers to the weight of the materials themselves. The "live load" is the people load. HUD-MPS's and the One-and-Two-Family Dwelling Code have identical requirements in this connection: 40 pounds per square foot live load is the live load

Sill Plate Sealer of soft fiberglass material comes in 4 inches wide rolls to prevent air infiltration between sill plate and foundation tops.

provision to be made for floors other than sleeping and attic areas, where a 30 pound live load provision is the minimum. Dead load in either case, for wood-frame residential floors, is generally figured at 10 pounds per square foot.

If the recommended APA glue-nailed single-floor system is used, the descriptive booklet on this system which is listed in this text's references contains complete joist size information for you and your supplier. The glued procedure has a composite action which adds a measure of stiffness. The span tables given in the booklet can also be used in conjunction with double-floor construction.

Normally, your supplier knows the lumber you're ordering out is intended for joists but it is worth a check to verify that you will receive lumber having one square-cut end. The normal practice is that joists in standard lengths suited to the span distance are supplied somewhat longer in the knowledge that they will be overlapped where they join side-by-side over the central support beam. At the overlapping end, the ends need not usually be cut. Thus, quite often buying joists that have one square-cut end means you have no cutting to do. They can be put into place just as they come.

Installation Necessities

For floor joist assembly work, the following tools will prove useful: claw hammer, handsaw, electric circular saw, sawhorse, nails and sledge-hammer. You may wonder about the sledge. You'll learn there are times with almost any kind of job when something has to be moved an eighth, a quarter, or a half inch. And when you strike it with an ordinary hammer, it stays right there staring at you from the exact same position; you need a sledge to budge it.

Permit a bit further discourse on tools at this point. You'll be using your claw hammer for a long time. Buy top quality. Buy a hammer only after hoisting a number of them. You'll find different ones have a different "feel." Buy one whose head seems slightly heavy at first, then comes to feel comfortable in your hand. Buy two different kinds. You'll need an extra for the helper to use.

A handsaw whose teeth are cut and set eight teeth per inch is called an 8-point saw. This is a good general-purpose saw for normal cutting of lumber and wood across the grain. For most cuts of 2 inch nominal (1-1/2 inch actual) dimension lumber, your basic tool should be a portable electric circular saw. Saw manufacturers commonly offer circular saws in 7-1/4 inch size having a vertical cutting depth of about 3-½ inches and a 45° angular cutting depth of about 2-3/4 inches. This is adequate for most cuts in dimension lumber. But in selecting a saw, consider an 8 inch model for slightly deeper cutting and additional power. These models are nearly as light, handle as easily as the 7 inch models, and may perform better.

Electric saws, electric drills and sanders have become general merchandise in recent years and are seen on the shelves of all kinds of retail stores. Don't go for bargain prices. Buy brands that are well known to carpenters and home builders . . . Skil, Black & Decker, Milwaukee. Buy a saw that's just under the top-of-the-line model—the top model often has one or two special features that tend to be of use or value for only special kinds of work. Good performance and durability can be expected without frills in the next-to-highest priced model. A combination blade is usually provided with the saw. You might wish to inquire about a carbide-tipped blade; its value lies in longer wear, in remaining sharp longer.

A basic "tool" for carpentry work throughout the construction work will be a sturdy and easily moved working table. This is best provided in the form of a pair of sawhorses plus two or three planks about 7 feet long, 2X10's or 2X12's, and reasonably straight and smooth. Just let the planks lie loose across the sawhorses. Later, when wallboard is being marked and cut, you may wish to add a smooth piece of 4X8 foot plywood atop the planks to allow easier shifting of the wallboard sheets.

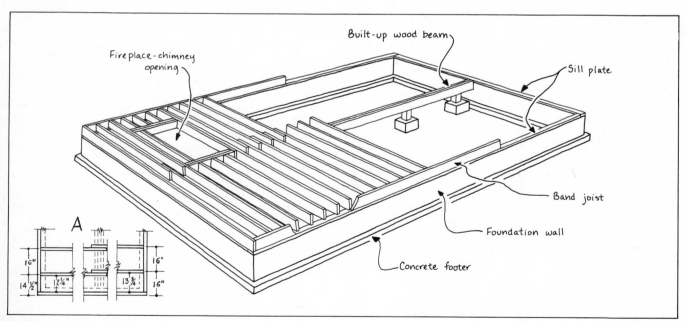

First Floor Framing work progressing from one end of the home towards the other end. Shows how headers and trimmer joists are doubled around larger floor openings such as those for stairs and fireplace chimneys. Complete nail-up should be done as work proceeds. After completion of all cross-joists and band joists, the levelness of the installation should be checked with a level-transit. If any area is out-of-level by more than 1/8 inch, the low areas should be raised to high areas using wood shingle wedges driven between the sill plates and the foundation wall top or between the central beam and the supporting piers. This wedging should be done before securing anchor bolts or clips, and nut-tightening or clip nailing should be done immediately following the leveling procedure.

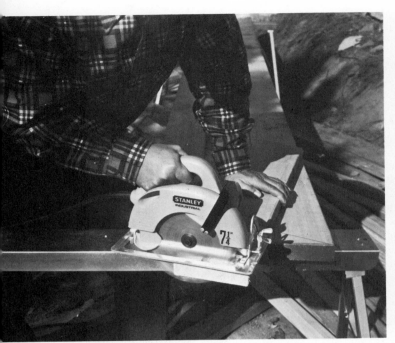

Electric Handsaw is a "must" for saving cutting time at the building site. Use sawhorses to provide a support for lumber to be cut. Shown is a Stanley 7¼-inch saw that weighs only 12 lbs and is double-insulated. It has base adjustments for mitering and angle-cutting such as shown in right photo. Notched stops provide easy adjustment to 45 and 90 degrees.

Nails. For floor joists, you'll need two sizes. Use large 16d (16 penny) steel common nails for butted joints where you nail through the side of one member into the end of another, and 10d common nails for toe-nailing of joists into sill-plates and beam-plate (see illustration and chart). Order 8d common or 6d deformed shank nails for fastening the plywood subfloor or underlayment plywood in the glue-nail procedure.

Installation Steps

Joist installation begins at one end of the building and moves toward the other end. Choose the end away from any floor opening as your starting point. Note the slight adjustment in dimension that must be made for the lapping of joists (see illustration). The spacing interval of joists is 16 inches, and at this starting end your measurement goes from the center of the first interior joist to the outer edge of the box or band joist. The lapped joist on the other side of the central support beam will have a lesser dimension by 1-1/2 inches.

You begin by marking joist positions at this starting end. It is a simpler practice to mark where the *edge* of a joist is to be positioned than where the center of it is to come. Then, when you set the joist, you adjust it to the mark.

The best practice is to proceed with all marking on both sill-plates and central beam plate before starting with the joists. Work with the working drawing of the home's first floor plan at hand so that you can include marking of floor

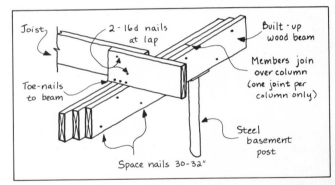

Floor Joists Crossing Beam with nailing together of lapped joists indicated as well as toe-nailing to beam which occurs on both sides of the joists. Also indicated: nail spacing for built-up beam which can be assembled at site prior to placement or, in some cases, can be furnished in assembled form by a components supplier.

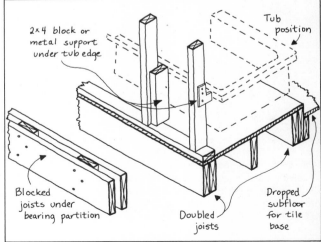

Doubled Floor Joists may be needed at certain locations. Two such places are where joists occur under and parallel to a bearing partition and where support is needed in bathrooms under cast iron bathtubs. Shown in this detail, too, is the method of lowering the subfloor in a bathroom in order to provide depth for a cement ~~~~~~ ~~ ~~~~~~~~ ~~~~ ~~~ ~ ~~~~ ~~~~~

openings such as for stairs or chimney. With the marking completed, you can now proceed with the placement and nailing, as you go along, of the joist units. First, determine what joist cutting may be necessary. Each joist should be long enough to rest fully on the beam width. But the projection of each joist beyond the beam should be kept to

about a foot. If cutting is needed, do it for all joists at once. Then, proceed to put them in place as follows:

(1) Take two joists each having two square-cut ends and place in position at a building corner, one along one sill-plate, the other at 90th along the other sill-plate. Nail together with four nails. Shift the butted box-

Floor Deck Nailing goes faster with one or two helpers. Shown in this group of photos are various nailing details: (1) nailing joists to the marks on the sill plate; (2) a close-up of nailing procedure fastening band joist so that its top edge meets the top edges of previously placed cross joists; (3) using a pneumatic cartridge nailer for fastening the plywood deck sheathing saves time; nailer and the necessary compressor to run it may be obtainable on rental basis; (4) deck sheathing work being completed with one man setting the unset nail heads and the second man using an electric handsaw to trim off projecting portion of the deck plywood.

joists so each side sets flush with the outer edge of the sill-plate and toe-nail in this position along the length of each box-joist;

(2) Proceed to place additional box-joists on end of building and around corner on opposite side. Where box-joists butt, toe-nail each into the sill-plate and then toe-nail top edges, one nail in each direction. Nail wood tie or splice board over butted joint of box-joists along end-wall;

(3) Begin setting interior joist at edge marks, proceeding in pairs. When first member is in place, nail through box joist from outside and into butt end of first joist. Then, place paired joist on other side and nail through box joist. Complete the pair by nailing together the overlap and toe-nailing the two joists into the sill-plates and beam plate.

(4) Proceed down the house length by joist pairs until you come close to a floor opening. Floor opening for basement stairs or to accommodate a chimney must have doubling of the framing members. To do this, set the two joists at the 16 inch spacing marks that are closest to the opening marks. Set second joist members flush to first ones and on the opening side if there is room. Check measurements and if there is still adequate room, prepare to nail joists to each other at each side and then toe-nail to plates. If one double-joist is close or just past the opening mark, shift it slightly so that the face towards the opening is on the mark. If both sides are within 3/4 inch of the opening mark, shift them to the mark.

(5) What you did above was double-frame the sides of the opening; now, you must double-frame the ends. This is done in steps. First measure-mark where the ends of the opening occur. Mark on top edges of the doubled joists. Next, cut to this inner distance between faces of the doubled joist, four trimmer-joist members, two for each end.

(6) Nail one trimmer-joist at each end of the opening coinciding with the opening marks and matching them to the inner faces of the trimmers. Now, measure the exact opening width placing marks on the trimmer-joist top edges and cut a final trimmer member or two as needed to fit between the trimmer-joists running parallel to the doubled-joist sides.

(7) Nail side-trimmer up by nailing through trimmer-joists into the trim member's ends. Now complete the opening frame by nailing up the second trimmer-joist at each end.

With other floor openings, the procedure is similar. When you approach the building end, cut and nail the final box-joist. Check the whole joist installation by walking around perimeter and looking for any discrepancy in the parallelness of the members. At each building end, stoop down and sight along top edges of joists to see if any protrude upward or downward from the others or if any curves are evident indicating joist warp.

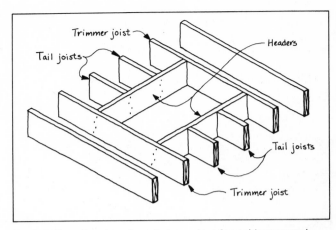

Framed Floor Opening of small size such as for a chimney can be single-framed; sketch indicates names of various framing members around opening. For larger openings, see double-framing method in next drawing.

Most rough-framing carpenters, as a matter of general habit, take a sighting along each framing member to check for excessive warp or curve. A slight curve is of little concern. When placing floor joists, such minor curves should placed so the convex side is up so that it will tend to straighten as the deck material is applied. Don't use warped or twisted joists.

When the foundation has been backfilled, you may find joist-setting can be done from outside the foundation standing on grade. Your helper will be at the center-lap position with narrow stances on the beam or beam-plate. However, most framing carpenters like to work from the joist platform itself and use a few planks or plywood sheets atop the joists for standing and kneeling as they handle and nail the joists.

Glued Plywood Floor System recommended for residential use by the American Plywood Association is shown in this series of photos. (1) A caulking gun is used to apply a glue bead to joists and band joists. Then (2), the tongue-and-grooved plywood sheets, 4X8 feet in size, are positioned. Next in (3), a bead of glue is run down the grooved edge and after the next plywood sheet is placed, it is driven home (4) tongue into groove using a sledge hammer and a protective 2X4 block. A handy plywood sheet spacing gauge can easily be site-built using a 2X4 with handles (5) and two flat pieces of metal 1/16-inch thick nailed to the sides of the 2X4. This gauge will give proper spacing between sides and ends of plywood sheets. After spacing of sheets, nailing should be done placing nails 6 to 8 inches apart along sheet edges over joists and 10 to 12 inches apart over intermediate joists (6).

Full details on glued plywood system including proper grades of plywood are covered in a 16-page booklet (No. U405-874) issued by the American Plywood Association. The glue-nail technique results in a stiffer floor construction, eliminates the need for double floor layers yet provides a squeakless base for resilient and soft floor coverings. It is a system recommended for the owner-builder who will take extra trouble to obtain a better floor installation.

Certain building codes may require a doubling of joists in places other than around openings. Two common places for such doubling requirements are under bearing partitions running parallel with the joists and under cast-iron bathtubs in bathrooms (see illustration). The parallel bearing partition doesn't occur very often in home plans. When such doubling is necessary, keep in mind that the doubled joists don't have to be tightly together. They can be separated by 2X4 blocks so that there's a central opening through which wiring or piping can be run from below into the partition above.

Plywood Application

Plywood subfloor sheathing in 4X8 sheets is quickly laid in place and nailed. The 8 foot dimension runs perpendicular to the joists. Sheet ends are butted over joists. At building ends, allow plywood to extend over edge of box-joist, adjusting it for the joist location where the plywood sheet butts to the next one.

The plywood suitable for deck sheathing is "C-D Interior" grade; having an identification index marking of 32/16, when the subfloor installation is made. These figures refer to the grade as being suitable for roof sheathing with rafter spacing of up to 32 inches and for floor sheathing with joist spacing up to 16 inches. If plywood materials installed are likely to have considerable exposure to the weather, it may be advisable to order plywood with exterior-type glue used in its laminations. The C-D grade noted means one surface is better than the other. Place the plywood so the better, C, side is up. When butting the plywood end to end or side by side, allow a 1/8 inch open space along long edges and 1/16 inch where butt ends meet over joists.

If you have elected to use the APA glue-nailed method of underlayment plywood, the accompanying series of photos illustrates the principal procedural steps in application, and appropriate specific guidelines are given in the caption.

The final step in any deck application after all nailing is completed is the trimming work. This is easily done at box-joint and opening edges by use of an electric saw. Keep the saw over the framing member with the excess plywood to the right. Cut flush with the outer edge of the box-joist or opening framing member. You may also wish to add a safety step. Nail in a temporary framing member or two in floor openings and tack a spare piece of plywood over the opening. Keep the cover in place until work related to the opening is started.

10 First-Floor Wall Framing

Frame residential walls have long been differentiated into two kinds . . . load-bearing and non-load-bearing. Since in practice the two kinds of walls are built in exactly the same way, this division is of importance primarily from a design standpoint.

The widespread use of roof trusses in frame homes has focussed designer calculations for wall-bearing strength on exterior walls since trusses are designed to bear complete loads across the space they span from exterior wall to exterior wall. In practice, when interior partitions are placed at intermediate points between floor and ceiling, the loading on the trusses tends to spread to the partitions as well as the exterior walls. The designer's calculations for wall and truss strength do not, however, take this spreading factor into account.

The point is that with a trussed roof on a small home, the exterior wall framing can be done first, the trusses placed, the roof finished, and the home closed in against the weather before the interior partitions are put into place. This procedure has been followed by many home builders on small homes of simple rectangular design.

Despite fast assembly, the above procedure doesn't always work out as well in many new homes because it is frequently easier for one reason or another to put the interior partitions in place as the exterior walls are erected. Partition panels, without wall covering on either side, are simple to fabricate or assemble and their use tends to minimize the amount of temporary bracing work that needs be done when exterior walls only are put up.

Whatever the wall-framing alternatives may be, they should partly reflect the supplier's usual practices. Owner-builders, when shopping for lumber, should visit suppliers who offer preassembled building components and discuss with them their wall-framing procedures. What they tell you can be taken into consideration when choosing the supplier.

The components may be in simple rough form . . . just roof trusses and studs-sheathing exterior wall panels. Or the supplier may be a producer of panelized house packages, with complete subassemblies and parts for a series of standardized home designs. Or he may be a lumber dealer equipped to fabricate trusses, wall panels, partition panels, window-door assemblies and various subassemblies such as roof rake ladders and garage-door headers. Lumber dealers involved with components are usually well-equipped to work with owner-builders using home plans selected from one of the stock home plan services.

Whenever the owner-builder arranges with his supplier to furnish partition lumber or preassembled units at the same time as the exterior wall panels, the two types of wall units are most easily erected if done together, with exterior wall erection slightly preceding that of interior partitions.

For simplicity in this text, partitions are dealt with separately in connection with other framing details in Chapter 21.

Exterior walls must carry the structural load of ceilings and roof plus a lateral load of wind pressure. The component or home fabricator takes these factors into account and will furnish exterior wall panels that meet code requirements on load-carrying.

In some areas, a fabricator may offer to furnish panels with stud spacings at 24 inches center to center (or "on center" as the abbreviation "o.c." on plans or drawings indicates). The fabricator will say this wider-than-the-normal 16 inch spacing provides a saving in lumber and still meets loading or stress requirements. There is a slight savings in lumber. But the recommendation here is that the owner-builder favor 16 inch spacing for exterior and partition wall panels. The reason is that most exterior sidings and interior sheet materials will be a little easier to apply with 16 inch spacings, and the lumber saving is not that significant with respect to a single home. It's a somewhat different picture, however, with roof member spacings, particularly if they're roof trusses. The 24 inch spacing of trusses is now a widely accepted method and one in which the lumber savings is probably worthwhile. But be guided here, too, by local practice. It's better to go the 16 inch spacing route using extra lumber if that's what your local building department expects.

Framing Work Details illustrated in this series: (1) the wall panel supplier in this custom home used two 2X12 headers for all openings in both partitions and exterior walls to save cutting of cripples and extra nailing effort; (2) when trusses are being raised, exterior walls must be well-braced and nailed so that they are plumb and in proper position for truss nailing; (3) showing typical panel opening for a fireplace chimney, the 2X4 to be cut out when chimney work begins; (4) long header across garage door opening is actually a preasembled flat truss furnished by the component supplier. Headers can also be assembled at the site for this purpose using nail-together connector plates.

Variances In Wall Framing

Before getting into some of the details of wall panel assembly work, you should understand the overall framing procedures as they may vary for ranch, bi-level or two-story, split-level and expansion-attic. Below are brief considerations with respect to each of these types of homes.

Home Types

Ranch. Two types of framing are common, the trussed type with preassembled roof trusses bearing on exterior walls and the ceiling-joist-and-rafter type in which the individual lumber pieces are cut and assembled. The truss method is faster but the joist-and-rafter method more suited to steeper-pitched roofs and more complex floor plans.

Bi-level. Sometimes called a "split-foyer" home, this type of home has two living levels. Usually, the lower living level is of basement or semi-basement construction using a concrete slab-on-ground floor. Wood framing extends from about mid-point on the lower-level walls upward. The second floor and wall-roof framing is nearly identical with that of the ranch home. One specialized form of the bi-level is often called a "walkout-basement" home and is built on a hillside. Normal foundations and one-story wall framing on the high side are combined with low foundations and two-story framing on the low side. The end-walls are often of partial-height framing above stepped foundations.

Two-story. Plans may be similar in room arrangement to a bi-level but this type has complete two-story wall framing all around. It may be built on basement foundations (for a third level), on crawl-space foundations with wood first-floor construction or on concrete slab-on-grade foundations. The principal difference in framing for a two-story from that of a bi-level is the need for a first-floor bearing partition to support the second-floor joists. This bearing partition occurs directly over the central first-floor joist support beam. Roof framing over the second floor may be either with trusses or ceiling joists and rafters; in the latter case, a second-floor bearing partition is used.

Split-level. Foundation work and framing are almost as though a bi-level home were being built next to and touching a one-story ranch, except that at the touching point, one foundation wall and one framed wall are used instead of two. Split-level framing requires certain minor adjustments be made and the stair work is just a bit more complex, but most split-level homes can be framed without difficulty either in shop-fabricated panel form or at the site.

Expansion Attic. Main floor and wall framing are the same as for ranch home construction with just one exception, the need for a central first-floor bearing partition as mentioned above for two-story construction. Rafter framing of the roof is necessary instead of trusses. Roof slopes of 8 or 10-inch-12 (10 inch height for every foot of horizontal run) results in the second floor being only partially usable for living space. Near the exterior walls where roof rafters rest, half-height knee walls are framed. Usable floor area can be enlarged somewhat through the use of dormers. A common practice is to build only window dormers in front (no added floor area) but a nearly full length dormer at the rear side of the home which does add substantial floor space. This type also requires a first-floor bearing partition. Panel components can be used for first-floor framing and second-floor partitions but preassembly work is not practical for the roof framing. Rafter and dormer-framing on an expansion-attic home take more time and lumber than for typical one- and two-story homes but are not particularly difficult to frame.

The so-called Cape Code style traditional home is a form of expansion-attic home. A word of explanation about use of the term "expansion-attic"—it indicates, as one sees immediately upon looking at floor plans, a home that has complete living quarters including at least one bedroom on the first or ground floor. The same is generally true for bi-level homes.

This has some significance for the owner-builder. It means that with a bi-level or expansion-attic home he can easily postpone a portion of the construction and finishing work until a later date when he is occupying the home. It's highly unlikely that a mortgage lender or building department won't accept as "finished" and ready for occupancy a home of this type where main floor facilities are completely done but the attic or lower level remains unfinished.

Supply Variances

With a large number of component fabricators, the supplying of exterior wall panels is done on a "studs-and-sheathing" basis. The panels are shop-framed on jig tables with bottom plates and single top plates nailed to stud ends. Proper sized openings are included for accommodating windows and doors. Panel size will usually range from 4 to 8 feet if the panels are to be erected manually and longer if the supplier has a small chassis-mounted hydraulic hoist on his delivery truck to assist in erection.

Some fabricators will install windows and prehung door units in the panels during the fabrication process. If offered, this procedure is desirable for the owner-builder. It helps get the job closed in faster, so it is safe against the weather or vandalism. Panel fabricators can usually adjust their work easily enough to different types of homes so that you receive semi-fabricated or subassembly components for use with the regular panels with the different types of homes described above.

There are some variations in fabricator practices and delivery methods. This applies in some cases to floor construction as well as walls and roofs. Some fabricators pre-

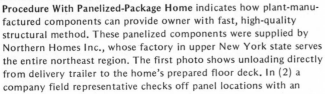

Procedure With Panelized-Package Home indicates how plant-manufactured components can provide owner with fast, high-quality structural method. These panelized components were supplied by Northern Homes Inc., whose factory in upper New York state serves the entire northeast region. The first photo shows unloading directly from delivery trailer to the home's prepared floor deck. In (2) a company field representative checks off panel locations with an owner-builder. Next (3) panel erection starts with exterior walls placed at a building corner. Then as indicated in (4) the partition panels are set as the exterior wall panel work proceeds. This minimizes the need for temporary wall bracing. In nailing together panels constantly check accuracy of panel position on the floor layout, and plumbness of the panel once the right floor position has been established.

66

Varied Practices of Component Suppliers are shown in this group of pictures. In (1), wall sections may be full length because the supplier delivers them with a truck having a convenient unloading crane; (2) some component producers preinstall windows in their plant-produced panels and some producers may also fabricate foundation wall panels of pressure-treated wood as well as the home's regular wall panel sections; (3) in many West Coast areas, siding is applied directly to studs without sheathing and building codes in some areas permit stud spacing of 24 inches o.c. for single-story frame-bearing walls.

pare floor framing and decking in panelized form. Others do not. In recent years, a growing number of fabricators have begun fabricating low-height flat trusses designed for floor use and spanning from foundation wall to foundation wall. If the supplier or fabricator that you reach offers such floor components or trusses, you should investigate them thoroughly since they can make the floor deck work even simpler than the site procedure described in the previous chapter.

With wall panel fabricators, the common practice has become one of furnishing stud-and-plate panels (no wall finish) at the same time as exterior wall panels. This is another desirable choice for the owner-builder because of time saved, particularly where the supplier assists in erection with a truck hoist or hydraulic crane.

Wall Erection Procedure

Before your load of wall panels arrives, you should prepare in two ways: clean and mark the deck, and have at hand (or know it's coming with the load) a floor plan sheet that indicates the panel numbering or identification system the fabricator uses so that you place pieces in the correct position. Quite often, the identification system marked on the panels will also indicate the correct sequence of placement. If not, you should have discussed with the fabricator the sequence he believes is best.

While certain panel handling and placement details may vary in different localities or with different types of panel fabricators, the overall procedure is just about the same no matter where you are or with whom you are dealing. Here are the highlights of most panel erection methods:

(1) Starting at a building corner, position the two panel sections intended for each side of the corner. Place the panel sill-plate on the floor near the edge of the deck and tilt up; have a helper hold it upright while the second panel is being tilted up. Slide panels so they meet properly at the corner and the sheathing face is flush with the edge of the deck and box-joists on each side. While helpers continue to hold firm, nail through into box-joists near the corner; then nail one nail partially through corner stud into stud of other wall section.

(2) With step-ladder, check evenness of the top-plates of the two sections, then if two sections are properly meeting at the top-plate, toe-nail the sections together, step down the ladder and drive two or three more nails through corner stud into other corner stud. Now go outside with ladder and drive four or five nails through outer corner studs. Follow with nailing of sill-plate.

(3) At studs next to the end stud away from the building corner on each side, nail a diagonal board brace from near the top of the wall stud to the floor deck using a wood block nailed to a joist and the brace nailed to the block. Use double-headed nails for easy later re-

moval. Check plumb of wall section before nailing brace to block.

(4) Place next exterior wall panel on the shorter side of the house. Tilt up. Slide or drive to proper floor position. Nail sill-plate near panel juncture. Nail studs at panel juncture near top of wall after checking top-plate alignment. Nail studs at intermediate points. Complete with sill-plate nailing and, if judged necessary, another brace.

(5) Continue on same wall with another panel section or two, reaching the next building corner and proceeding to make the next corner assembly in the same way as the first.

(6) At this point, if panel fabricator has supplied partition panels for erection, locate proper partition panel (or perhaps two panels if there are three rooms along house end-wall). Place this panel in proper position where the doubled studs have been incorporated in the exterior wall panel. Adjust so panel edges conform to floor marks. Slide tight to exterior wall keeping bottom edge at marks. Nail through partition sill-plate near exterior wall so that nail is angled into box-joist. Check plumb of partition panel near exterior wall and nail end stud into studs of exterior wall. Check top-plate juncture and toepnail. Complete stud nailing at juncture. Complete sill-plate nailing into floor joists keeping plate to marks.

(7) When attempting to bring one panel section close and in correct floor position to meet adjacent panels, your most useful tool is a sledge-hammer. But use care. A panel will move easier with a few light taps of a sledge than with a long series of hard hand-hammer blows. Tap with the sledge at bottom and top plate points.

(8) Continue along home perimeter placing first an exterior wall section or two, then an interior partition panel. As partition panels are placed, diagonal board braces can be removed. If just exterior walls are being placed, keep diagonal braces in place and not more than about 15 or 16 feet apart.

(9) Where especial care is needed in handling panels is in connection with the sheathing. Depending upon the fabricator's practice, the sheathing may extend below the sill-plate and it will also extend above the top-plate if the latter is just a single member. Watch these projecting edges when handling, when tilting, when nailing and sledging.

(10) Be sure to check plumbness with your 4 foot level as you proceed. It's much easier to verify plumbness as each brace or each partition panel is placed than to have to come back later, remove nails, and plumb.

(11) Complete nailing of each panel as you go. A panel left partly nailed is very likely to be forgotten and left in temporary-nailed condition.

(12) Place partition panels adjacent to exterior walls. When final stretch of exterior wall is being erected, move balance of partition panels inside the house and complete the exterior panel erection.

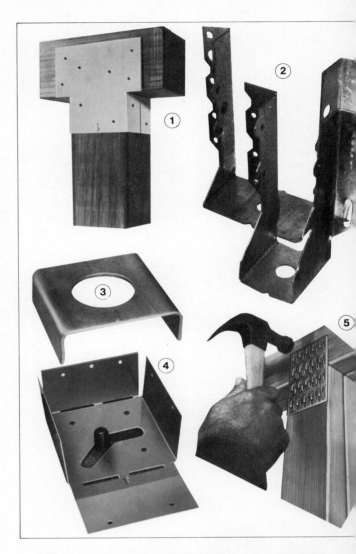

Metal Clips for Framing Connections can allow faster construction and assure good-quality connections. Such metal devices are available for tops-bottoms of wood posts or columns, for support of single or doubled joists and for other specialized purposes. Clips shown here are part of the complete line of framing-anchoring devices made by the Panel Clip Company. Item 1 is used to attach a 4X4 post to a beam. Item 2 shows joint hangers, available single or double. Items 3 and 4 are used to attach posts to concrete for porches, carports, etc. Item 5 is a top plate tie which can be used to fasten walls and partitions together without the conventional pocket and lap of the 2X4 top plate.

(13) The exterior wall placement should be completed at a building corner since it is easier than fitting the final panel into a straight wall portion. At the final corner, place one panel in position and put a couple nails through the sill-plate but not fully driven. Brace the panel so that it has a slight outward tilt. Then, bring the second corner panel into position, partly nailing the sill-plate. Now, working from outside the building, bring the panel tops together. Check top-plate alignment and toe-nail. Complete sill-plate nailing and complete corner-stud nailing as well as that to adjacent panel sections.

The foregoing panel assembly procedure will usually be done with a fair amount of speed and your supplier's truck, once freed of its load, can return. You and your crew of three-to-five men have now completed the bulk of the work and you can get along for the balance with just a helper.

Now quickly check exterior wall alignment, and plumb. Next, install the second 2X4 top-plate on exterior walls if that member was not included as part of the panel assembly. In applying the top-plate, remember that it's supposed to provide a bonding or tie function. It should overlap other panels at building corners and it should allow the top-plates on partitions to overlap the exterior wall (see illustration).

If the partitions were supplied by the fabricator, completion work is largely a matter of being correct in identifying which panel goes where. After you're sure of identity and fit to floor marks, nail bottom plates first, followed by check of top-plate conformance and nailing. Then, nail studs. Use your 4 foot level freely to verify plumbness, which needs double-checking at all door openings.

If your framing work involves placement of exterior panels only, with partitions to be framed later, your first-floor wall work is finished with the placement of exterior walls. Roof trusses come next. But if your home is designed for, or you've decided instead, on the use of joist-rafter roof framing, then you must complete the first-floor wall work with installation of the load-bearing partition, usually a single partition near the central part of the home and running lengthwise or parallel to your home's longest dimension.

The bearing partition may consist of part stud wall and part ceiling beam. The latter is commonly used for relatively wide openings in the partition such as might occur between living room and dining room, between kitchen and family room, or where a hallway occurs. In any case, the partition framing involving studs should be erected first. The end stud at a partition wall opening is a support stud on which rests the beam that spans the opening. The end stud will be cut shorter by the amount of the beam depth so that when the beam is put into place, resting on the two shorter studs at each side of the opening, the beam top will coincide with the top of the bearing partition's top-plate. As previously indicated, this second or top top-plate should overlap with the top-plates of intersecting partitions and exterior walls.

First Floor Panel Assembly work begins with an accurate layout of partition locations on the floor deck. As indicated by the dashed lines in this sketch, floor deck should be marked with lines representing both sides of the partition framing with all doors or other openings accurately positioned. Such marking not only facilitates placement of panels but also helps with location of temporary braces so conflict is avoided between braces and panels yet to be erected.

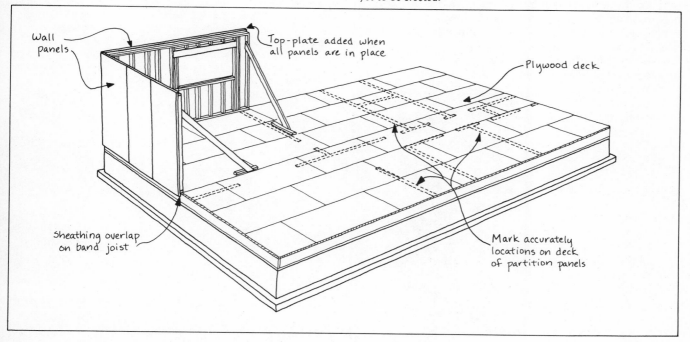

Wall panels

Top-plate added when all panels are in place

Plywood deck

Sheathing overlap on band joist

Mark accurately locations on deck of partition panels

As a final step in panel assembly work, follow through with a level check. Use a long straight 2X6 with your 4 foot level. Place the 2X6 across building corners and check the level. Do the same with partitions. Put the 2X6 along the midpoint of exterior walls and check levelness. With any discrepancy in wall levelness or plumb, correct with shingle wedges before further work proceeds.

Wall Assembly On The Job

Without preassembled wall panels, the framing work takes more time and care. The extra care needed is principally in preparing wall openings for doors and windows so that they are in the proper position and of the proper size. Most of the extra time comes in checking of plans, measuring and cutting of framing members. The nailing together of framing members is best done in a flat on-the-floor-deck position. Studs are laid out on edge to their marked positions on the bottom and top plates.

The frame at the site procedure requires that you preselect your window and door units so that you can obtain the exact rough opening dimensions needed to accommodate these units.

If you've been unable to find a reasonably convenient supplier of panel components or for some other reason choose to do your own wall framing at the job site, you may wish to seek the guidance of a carpenter contractor. In and near many metropolitan areas there are residential framing specialists—carpenters who concentrate most of their effort on structural framing jobs. In rural areas, carpenters doing all kinds of work may also be willing to work with you at hourly rates and guide you over the more sensitive areas. It's not so much that the job is difficult, as it is that you must avoid mistakes which would create later fitting problems or require you to dismantle and rebuild. Once you've been guided to a correct initial practice, there's usually sufficient repetition for you to handle the remainder without assistance.

For on-the-job framing, your principal needs are a good pair of sturdy sawhorses and planks. Your circular saw is really a prime necessity and to use it you will have to arrange for a power source. By far the simplest power source to arrange is a neighbor's existing home, from which you simply run a long extension cord . . . with the neighbor's permission, of course. A second alternative is to rent a small portable gasoline generator. These are usually available from rental or tool companies. A third possibility is for the electric utility company to run conductors to a temporary pole with a suitable receptacle for plug-in of electric power tool cords. The provision of temporary construction electricity varies somewhat from one utility company to another. In practically every case, however, there will be a certain fee for making the installation as well as a charge for the use of the electricity.

In cutting your own framing members, a two-step procedure is involved: measure and mark lumber; cut accurately to the mark. When repetitive cuts of the same length are to be made it will save time to use a marking pattern. And it usually saves time to do one thing repetitively for a while then shift to another step and do that repetitively. When using one board or piece of lumber as a pattern to cut other members of the same length, cut your pattern shy by about 1/32 inch. This allows for the marking pencil width. In cutting, be consistent either cutting directly over the mark or, more desirable, always cutting just outside the mark.

Some areas allow compromise. As a compromise between on-site cutting and framing and the preassembled shop-fabricated panels, a few lumber suppliers may be able

Wall Building At the Site is easier when done horizontally on the floor deck and then tilted up into position. On-site panel assembly proceeds best if a cutting platform is used and one person does all precutting while two others lay out the panel members and nail them together. Sheathing should also be applied while the panel assembly is on the floor deck. Average size home of one story construction will take 3-to-5 days to frame out all exterior walls and partitions.

to furnish you with precut lumber, door or window units in framed panel mounts, precut and assembled opening headers, corner posts and built-up beams. Inquire, inquire. These are time savers.

Sheathing Considerations

Practices with respect to sheathing vary somewhat from one locality to another. In many places all sheathing,

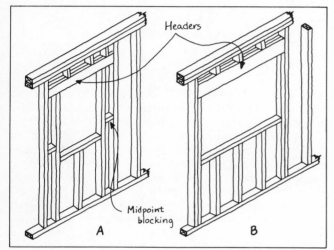

Doubling Frames Around Openings is a normal requirement with woodframe homes. This is done with doubled studs at jambs and doubled headers. Sill members need not be doubled. The depth of the doubled headers will depend upon the opening width. Such headers can extend up to plate level. Jamb doubling may be done with midpoint blocking as in (A) or with nailed together studs as in (B).

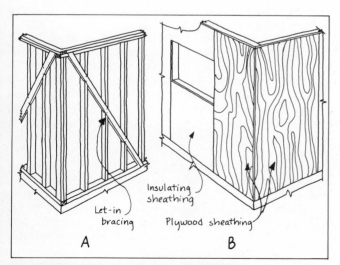

Bracing of Home Corners is required by most building codes and can be accomplished in several ways. Most common practice is shown in sketch (B) where single 4X8 sheets of plywood sheathing are used on each side of the corner. The let-in bracing shown in sketch (A) may be done on either the exterior or interior side of the walls. As can be seen from the sketch, notching in of the 2X4 studs and plates to accommodate the diagonal 1X4 braces is a job that takes considerable cutting-fitting time whereas the use of plywood sheet bracing needs no cutting of the framing at all, just a nail-up of the sheets.

whether it be for floor decks, walls or roofs, is plywood. In many other places, the standard or commonly used form of sheathing is a fibrous light-density 3/4 inch board material in 4X8 sheets or 2X8 T&G (tongue-and-groove) type either being called "insulating sheathing." It is usually furnished with an asphaltic impregnation or coating that's moisture resistant. A third type of sheathing readily available but not used as extensively as the other two is a denser fiberboard material, usually in 1/2 inch thickness and available in large 8 foot wide sheets up to perhaps 14 feet in length. A newer type of insulating sheathing is a 1 inch thick board of styrene foam, having high thermal resistance value.

If sheathing for insulation is to be used most building codes, as well as the HUD-MPS's, require bracing at building corners. In some areas, this is commonly done by diagonal "let-in" braces. From the top of the wall at the house corner, they run down on each side at a 45° angle (except where windows or doors interfere) to the bottom of the sill-plate. They are "let-in" to the studs they cross by cutting a notch so the brace's face matches the face of the studs. They may be inside or outside stud faces. The braces are usually of 1X4 material. Cutting the notches diagonally and inserting the braces tends to be time-consuming, so many home builders and fabricators now use insulating sheathing over most of a wall area but single sheets of 4X8 plywood sheathing at the building corners, because the plywood provides the bracing strength sufficient to eliminate the let-in braces (see illustration).

The insulation sheathings do provide a measure of thermal protection. The 3/4 or 25/32 inch thick insulating boards have a thermal resistance value of R = 2.06 which is roughly two to three times the values of other sheathings in the thicknesses which are generally used for residential frame buildings.

Some suppliers offer a choice of three types of insulation sheathings:

(1) Regular—usually having the most insulating value;
(2) Intermediate—added strength provided;
(3) Nail-Base—designed for the direct application of wood shingles or shakes.

Like most sheet materials, these come in 4X8 size but may also be available in 4X9 sheets so that continuous coverage from top surface of top-plate to the bottom of the foundation sill-plate is provided. One of the factors here is the HUD-MPS's; some codes have a provision requiring some special metal-strap wall anchoring devices at top-plates and sill-plates where the sheathing material is not continuous from top to bottom.

With the large sheet size, the 25/32 inch thick material or the nail-base type can be used without let-in corner bracing if properly nailed to studs using 8d common, 1-3/4 inch long roofing nails or staples.

11 Second-Floor Planning

Wall framing work on the second floor of a two-story home will be essentially a duplication of the framing assembly on the first floor. This is particularly true when the framing is done using shop-fabricated wall and partition panels as described in the previous chapter. The principal difference will be that on the second floor, the panels will not include any having an entrance door opening unless the home happens to have an outdoor deck at this level.

The initial step in two-story work is the installation of the floor deck. In this case, the joists serve not only to support the floor load above but also the ceiling installation on the under side. This necessitates a few relatively minor changes for the installation work done on the first floor joists. One frequent change is with respect to beams needed for support of joists across open rooms below. Such a condition might occur over larger rooms below, such as

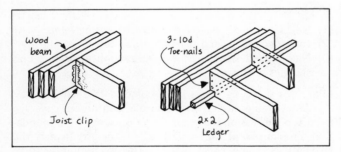

Joist and Beam Connections where the joist tops or bottoms should be flush even with the top of bottom of a supporting beam occur frequently in second-floor framing or ceiling-floor construction, especially with L- or T-shaped floorplans. Also in conjunction with various floor openings or for spanning wide wall openings. Shown above are the two common methods for providing suitable support for joists that butt to beams. At left, the convenient metal clip or joist hanger method in which the hanger has nail holes for nailing on both sides to both the joist and the beam. At right, the ledger method in which a 2X2 or 2X3 is first nailed to the beam side near the bottom and then each joist is notched to rest over the ledger strip.

living or family rooms. It's generally desirable to keep a first-floor ceiling flat except where room spaces adjoin such as a living room and dining room. In order to keep a flat ceiling where a beam must cross a room, joists can be end-butted to the beam and rest on a ledger strip. An easier butt connection is made with metal joist hangers (see illustration). The same type of hangers may be used in double-framing of floor openings such as that for a stairway.

On two-story construction, your first-floor framing will have included a central bearing partition whether the balance of the interior partitions was installed or not. On second floor work, the bearing partition is the point of overlap or floor-ceiling joists just as the basement or crawl-space central support beam was for the first floor.

Cutting, assembly and nailing of floor-ceiling joists is done in the same manner as for the first floor deck. Floor openings and other details are handled in the same way. There is one additional step that is not usually included in the first floor framing. That is the matter of providing backing or blocking between floor-ceiling joists and above interior wall partitions.

Wherever such interior partitions run parallel to the floor-ceiling joists, a continuous nailer member should be nailed to the top of the partition top-plate and cross 2X4 backing blocks nailed between joists over the nailer board (see illustration). Similarly, where interior partitions run perpendicular to floor-ceiling joists, 2X8 members should be cut to fit between joists and be nailed to top-plates. A similar backing-blocking is done on one-story homes between ceiling joists or trusses. The purpose of this backing and blocking is to provide a rear solid surface for the nailing of ceiling drywall or other board material in the room wall-ceiling corners.

About warped floor-ceiling joists. In Chapter 9, it was indicated that a slight joist curvature was acceptable and that it might be used placed with the convex edge up. With floor-ceiling joists, the same applies, but to a lesser extent—extent of curve that is. Be more selective and discard any floor-ceiling joists that curve more than about 1/4 or 5/16 inch overall. Reason: the underside of the joists will receive ceiling finish materials and any substantial curvature of a floor joist could result in noticeable ceiling unevenness.

Framing for Roof Slopes

There are certain specialized kinds of homes having two floors with habitable rooms. The most common is the traditionally styled Cape Cod cottage. In many areas, it is referred to as a one-and-a-half story home and in other areas, with a more contemporary style, it may be known as an expansion-attic home. A very practical home for a first-time owner-builder, it enjoys widespread popularity.

Less known and much less widely built are homes having gambrel and mansard roofs. (Check your nearest dictionary to find out the difference between them.) Both roof types have roofs with two different slopes, a steep slope portion in the lower areas and a shallow slope portion in the upper areas. A gambrel roof is somewhat akin to the gable roof of a Cape Cod home in that it has end-walls, while the mansard roof is similar to a hipped roof, being four-sided on a rectangular building.

In the past few years, there has been something of a revival among professional home-builders in the use of gambrel and mansard like roofs. More accurately, gambrel-like or mansard-like roofs. Many builders use an adaptation in which the second floor walls are framed over the first-floor walls and sheathed as in ordinary two-story homes. Then, the steep-sloping portion of the roof is framed by add-on rafters and soffit blocking. The shallow upper roof portions are framed by resting rafters or trusses atop the wall plates. In any case, true gambrel/mansard roof framing as well as the add-on type is considered inadvisable for the first-time owner-builder, and will not be covered in this discussion.

However, one-and-a-half story or expansion-attic construction is a popular style and within the owner-builder's scope whether framing components can be supplied or not. A brief outline of on-site framing work with these homes is included later in this chapter.

Completing The Floor Deck

The first and second floor joist-and-decking assemblies that you have by now completed, following the procedures in this text, are known as "platform framing." The floor construction rests on wall and beam supports like a platform. This is the most widely-used framing technique for one-to-three story residential buildings, for both single- and multi-family homes.

There is one characteristic that sometimes goes with platform framing if floor or floor-ceiling joists with relatively high moisture content are used. This lumber is subject to shrinking when the home gradually dries out due to interior heating. Minor cracks can develop from the shrinkage; they may occur at certain points in the wall-

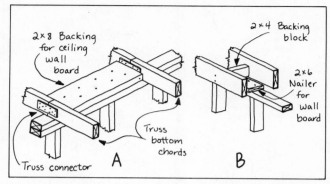

Nail Backing for wallboard application is generally needed at ceiling level for all types of woodframe homes and this most often occurs where trusses are spaced at 2 feet o.c. and cross partitions as indicated in (A). Some builders provide this type of backing blocks where trusses or joists are spaced 16 inches o.c. but it is not usually considered necessary for the shorter spacing. Another common situation that calls for backing blocks is that shown in (B) where a partition runs parallel to joists or trusses.

board near wall-ceiling corners. A fairly common point of occurrence for shrinkage cracks is in the wallboard on walls that form stairwell sides. The shrinkage cracks are *not* evidence of serious structural problems. The joists will stabilize. The cracks can be filled and repainted, or covered with moldings. Avoid joist shrinkage by purchasing good-quality lumber with a desirably low moisture content, and keeping it covered when stored at the building site. The possibility of such shrinkage occurring is another factor in the builder's desire to get the home under roof as fast as is practical.

Be aware of the possibility of using a slightly smaller joist size for floor-ceiling use in one-and-a-half story or expansion-attic construction. This may be possible due to reduced live loading allowance to 30 pounds per square foot instead of 40 as required for first-floor joists. Check with your supplier on this.

With respect to the second floor sheathing or subfloor, your choice of material should reflect consideration for the rooms on the floor. If they will be principally bedrooms, with carpeting or resilient floor coverings to be applied, you will save time and cost by using the APA glue-nailed underlayment plywood as recommended for the first floor deck. If the second-floor space won't be finished off for some time and you're not yet sure of what room space or type of floors the area will have, you'll save slightly by use of ordinary plywood sheathing, nonmatched with tongue-groove edges, and simply nailed in place. In either case, a small extra expense after roof framing work is completed will prove very worthwhile with plywood surfaces that are to remain uncovered for some time. Get a couple gallons of penetrating sealer and apply with a wide brush. It will take an hour and a half or less and be well worth its cost and time by minimizing collection of dust and dirt and simplifying sweeping of the floor surface.

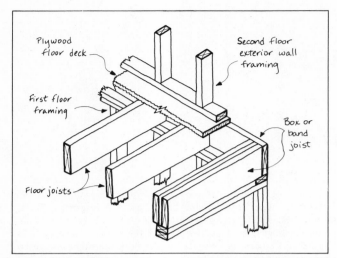

Plywood floor deck

Second floor exterior wall framing

First floor framing

Box or band joist

Floor joists

Second Floor Joists are positioned and assembled in a manner that is essentially a duplicate of the joist construction on the first floor. The top plate of the first floor's exterior walls and central bearing partition simply take the place of foundation sill plates and bearing beam. Second floor joist work proceeds much the same way except that work may require use of ladders and more safety awareness due to height.

At this point in construction, there is another small extra job that's worth the effort. You will want to provide decent temporary climbing facilities in the stair opening. The first inclination here is to wonder if you can get the staircase installed—not advised, because your building work is not finished nor closed in against the weather. A stair alternative is easily built in little more than an hour.

Cut a pair of stair stringers from two long 2X12 planks. Use your steel square to mark tread and riser notches once they have been cut to length so they rest on the first floor deck near where the bottom of the stairs will occur, and against the floor-ceiling joist framing at the stairway's top opening. The slope of the stringers should be steeper than normal for a stairway. Using the steel square as a marking tool, and having divided up the overall height to have equal riser segments of between 7 and 8 inches with tread space of 5-to-7 inches, cut the riser-tread notches with your electric saw. Nail the stringers in the stair opening each about 6 inches away from the side-walls. Nail stringer tops to the floor-ceiling joists at the top and to the first-floor deck at the bottom. First nail a 2X4 or 2X6 flat block to the floor deck in front of the stringer edges so that no sliding can occur. Then nail down the stringer bottoms.

Cut treads from 2X6's. If your stairs are to be 3 feet wide in finished form, cut these temporary treads to about 2 feet 6 inches, just enough to extend a little over the stringer edges. Nail them to the stringers. Now you have a solid set of stairs for hauling up of tools and materials. And they won't interfere with the placing of wallboard sheets when that time comes.

Expansion-Attic Walls and Roof

The focus in the balance of this framing description will narrow down to the on-site framing of a straight-gabled roof for a one-and-a-half story or expansion-attic home. Most of the framing here involves roof rafters but there are vertical end-walls to be built also.

With this type home, the second floor joist framing is done just a bit differently. The box- or band-joists around the perimeter are eliminated. At the building ends, the first joists are placed at or just inside the *inner* face of the doubled top-plates of the first floor wall.

The installing of the deck material can follow the same procedure as on the first floor using the suggested glue-nailed underlayment plywood or the subfloor sheathing plywood with just a nailed application. A steel square will come in useful in rafter marking and calculations although the pattern method for rafters is faster and less subject to error.

If you wish to follow this pattern rafter procedure, here is how you transfer pertinent information from the working drawings to obtain the correct angles and cuts for the rafter pattern:

(1) Obtain from working drawings the accurate roof slope usually given in printed form near the typical house cross-section. Using a large separate sheet of paper and drawing to scale of 3/4 or 1-½ inch equals 1 foot, draw two parallel lines representing the rafter edges; scale down distance between lines for actual rafter width, probably 2X6 or 2X8 sized lumber (actual of 5-½ or 7-½ inches). Make length of the lines a foot or so longer than the distance from ridge top to eave as shown on house elevation.

(2) Near one end of the parallel lines (say the right end) draw a vertical line representing the angle at which the rafter fits to the vertical ridge board. You obtain this angle by drawing two lines at right angles to each other. A horizontal line 12 inches long and, at the right end, rising vertically, a second line 10 inches long. These are for a 10-in-12 roof slope. Join the free ends with a diagonal line which will be at something less than a 45° angle with the horizontal. This diagonal line then represents the bottom edge of the rafter. If you continue the vertical line upward, you'll have the angle for proper cutting of the rafter end to make the ridge cut.

(3) But before using this angle for rafter marking, you should complete your scale drawing for the balance of cutting information . . . for the horizontal eave soffit cut and for the bird's mouth cut. You want to extend the vertical ridge cut line downward so that it forms one leg of a right triangle. The other leg is horizontal. The distances of these two leg lines are: for the vertical leg, the distance from the top of the ridge board and rafter down vertically to the level of the first floor wall top-plate; and, the horizontal distance from the building center to the *inner* edge of the wall top-plate. If

these distances and angles are correctly drawn, the two right angle legs will join with the *lower* rafter edge line to form a triangle.

(4) On your scale drawing at the left where the above horizontal line meets with the lower edge slope line, let the intersection point represent the upper inside corner of the top-plate. Extend the horizontal line left for 3-½ inches to scale (surface of top-plate) then draw the other three lines to complete the cross-section of the top-plate.

(5) From the top-plate's outer edge on the drawing, measure to scale the amount of eave overhang as indicated on the drawing, say a foot. Then at 12 inches to the left of the top-plate's outer edge, draw a parallel vertical line. If necessary extend the two rafter lines to intersect this vertical.

(6) Now check the cross-section or elevation drawings to obtain the height of the eave soffit. On your drawing use the top of the top-plate as a reference and measure down an appropriate distance that will give the proper soffit height. Draw a horizontal line at this point representing the soffit level and intersecting the rafter edge lines. This will be the mark for the eave end horizontal cut.

Your rafter scale drawing for preparation of a pattern rafter is now complete. It has the top vertical ridge cut, the eave vertical and flat cuts and it has the two bird's mouth cuts—the top surface line of the top-plate cross-section, and the left or outer edge of the top-plate which line needs to be extended downward slightly to intersect with the rafter's bottom edge line. Now, lay out your pattern rafter using this scale drawing and transfer its dimensions and angles to the pattern rafter-to-be.

One further detail. A board serving as a pattern always results in slightly oversize marking of a member. To accommodate this pencil-point thickness, make your pattern rafter cuts so your marked lines on each cut just barely disappear. Then, after making the marks on the regular rafter members following the pattern lines, you can cut in the usual manner of having the saw blade go just barely *outside* the marked line.

Go through a saw check before cutting your pattern rafter and the following ones. Verify that the electric saw's foot is adjusted to zero angle tilt so that your saw blade cuts vertically at 90° through lumber. Next, check the depth-of-cut adjustment so that it is set for maximum. This allows pulling back in the bird's mouth cuts and leaving nearly vertical cut edges.

Use the pattern rafter to make marks and cut another rafter. With your helper's aid, take the pair and set them temporarily in position so the ridge cuts butt. Have your helper on a ladder at the ridge with a 2X4 block taking the place of the ridge board. Everything look OK? Take your ruler out or a measuring stick and measure the distance rafter top to floor. Does it mesh with that indicated on the drawings? All right, then you're ready to proceed.

Your rafter sawing will go faster if you set up to cut them all at once. With an accurate pattern for marking, your helper can do this while you saw. Using the sawhorse and plank table, see if you can't establish a routine for making the same cuts in order on each rafter. Try beginning with the fish-mouth horizontal, then the vertical. Slide the rafter slightly to then make the eave vertical cut going downward. Switch position to make the eave horizontal. Then shift the rafter and yourself to the other end to complete the rafter with the ridge cut. In connection with the marking, mark the pattern rafter with the word "TOP" on one side so that the marking is always done with the same size up. Have your marker check each rafter for curve or warp. Any member that's more than a 1/2 inch out of line or has a slight twist should be put aside for other use, or discarded.

Before starting to set rafters, check your ridge boards. In some areas of the country, it's common practice to use inch boards for this purpose, 1X8's or 1X10's. In other areas, nominal 2 inch dimension lumber is used. The latter offers a better nailing base. And where there are dormers to be built, the 2 inch lumber makes for a stiffer ridge which won't be bent out of alignment when rafters are erected on only one side. When starting and when completing the rafter setting, permit the ridge board to extend outward beyond the end or rake rafters, and cut them flush after the end-walls have been completed.

On a 2X8, the diagonal ridge cut for a 10-in-12 roof slope will have a cut surface about 8-1/4 inch long. For a slope of 12-in-12, the cut surface will be about 10-½ inch long. HUD-MPS's require ridge boards to extend down sufficiently to cover the full cut surface. So 2X10 ridge boards are suited to the 10-in-12 slope and 2X12's to the 12-in-12.

When starting to set rafters and ridge boards you can use at least two, preferably four, helpers. Two of you each hold a rafter in paired position. A third holds up the inward end of the ridge board on a ladder while the ridge board holding device (see illustrations) is at the end-wall of the home holding up the ridge boards' outer projecting end. This is easier if you begin with the rafter pair that is in from the end-wall by two or three joist spaces. While the rafter pair are being held thus, yet another person should position next to the joist and on top of the top-plate with the bird's mouth cut tight against the top-plate edge. Then nail to the joist. One nail for the time being. Same for other rafter.

Next with another ladder, nail and toe-nail through the top rafter ends into the ridge board. Test plumb along side of rafter and adjust slightly before placing second rafter pair down near other end of ridge board. Nail with single nails into joists and single nail at ridge board not fully driven. Go back to the initial rafter pair and with a vertical 2X4 test for plumbness of rafter side with bottom of 2X4 edge atop floor joist edge (judge by sheathing nails). Run a diagonal brace now from the ridge board (nailing into its side) down towards the center of the floor to a floor block. Now, proceed with rafter pairs.

When adding another length of ridge board, it should butt to the first and the joint should be spliced with plywood pieces on each side. In hoisting this next ridge board member, follow the same procedure with the free end as you did with the initial ridge board. After the first few rafters are in place to hold the ridge board up, mark at 16 inch intervals. An alternative to this, because the ridge board marks may be hard to see as you are readying to nail the rafters, cut a short 2X4 to 14-½ inch length and use as a measuring block between the last rafter and the one being placed.

At the ends of the building, you will need two end rafters, one whose outer face is flush vertically with the outer face of the first floor top-plate, and another that may be about 6 to 10 inches farther out to serve as a rake rafter. Check your drawings to see just what this rake projection is. The flush end rafters are set like the others. Place the lower end so its outer face is flush with the top-plate's outer face. Nail to the top-plate since there will not be a ceiling joist there for attachment. At the ridge board, first get the measured distance from the last regular rafter down at the top-plate. Then mark that distance off at the ridge to fix the position of the end rafter there.

In placing the rake rafter, the usual practice is to wait until after the roof sheathing has been nailed up and made longer than the rake projection. Then the rake rafter is nailed to the ridge board and the eave end joined with the fascia board nailing through it into the rake rafter. Some carpenters knowing in advance the difficulty in holding up the rake rafters for nailing, see to it that the wall top-plate at the corner extends out sufficiently to allow resting the lower end of the rake rafter on it for nail-up. The top-plate extension is then trimmed off.

End-Wall and Knee-Wall Framing

The second floor attic end-walls involve cutting of various lengths of studs to fit under and be nailed to the end rafters (see illustration). The owner-builder is advised to begin with the studs near the center, which usually involve framed openings for a window and, in all probability, a ventilator above the window. Use care to get the openings framed to proper window and vent dimensions.

The notching cuts in the studs are to allow the stud outer edges to be flush with the outer face of the rafter as well as with the outer edge of the wall top-plate and first-floor studs. They're easiest done by cutting each stud a little long, then putting it into correct marked position for measuring. Marks are made along both upper and lower edges of the end rafter. These studs should be toe-nailed to the wall top-plate then nailed through the end rafter into the notched part of the stud.

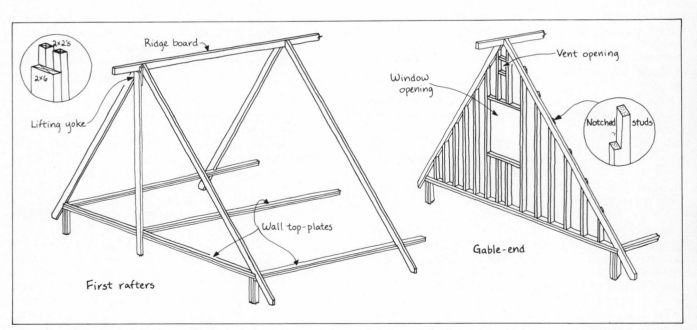

Rafter Framing work proceeds in much the same way for any pitch or slope of roof. In the sketches here, intended to show the start and finish of roof framing, the ceiling-floor joists (ordinarily installed prior to rafter setting) have been omitted. Inset upper left shows a site-made lifting yoke which can be helpful in holding up the end of the ridge board when the initial rafters are placed. The yoke extends downward along face of the first floor wall and is nailed to it; ridge board is positioned so that its end projects beyond house end and this end is cut off only after completion of rafter and gable-end work. Sketch at right indicates typical gable-end framing for a story-and-half home. Gable studs extend down to wall plates and end ceiling-floor joist rests against stud faces. Inset shows notching detail for tops of gable studs.

After completing both end-walls, install collar ties, sometimes called collar beams. They usually occur at every fourth rafter pair (4 feet o.c.), meeting HUD-MPS's on this point. These collar ties, when later supplemented by similar ties at intermediate rafter pairs, can serve as ceiling joists for the room ceiling wallboard. Thus, use care in placing them so that they are horizontally level and their bottom edges are at the correct ceiling height. HUD-MPS's permit a 7 foot 6 inch ceiling height for this space. The required height, HUD says, must apply to half the room space when there are sloping ceilings, and no part of the sloping ceiling should be below 5 feet.

The latter height, then should be your guide to the height of the knee-wall. Knee-walls need have only single top-plates. Cut the studs. Place them with the top and bottom plates on the floor. Nail through plates into studs. Build in two sections for easier fitting. Tilt up to position. Nail through the bottom plates into joists and drive nails from under side of top-plate, through it and into rafters.

If the foregoing work on a straight dormerless gable roof sounds just a bit complicated, in practice it will seem somewhat harder still. You might well consider the possibility of obtaining the part-time or full-time help for a few days of a good framing carpenter experienced in making the proper calculations, marking and cuts. This course is definitely recommended for an expansion-attic roof which has either single window dormers or a nearly house-length shed-roof dormer in the rear.

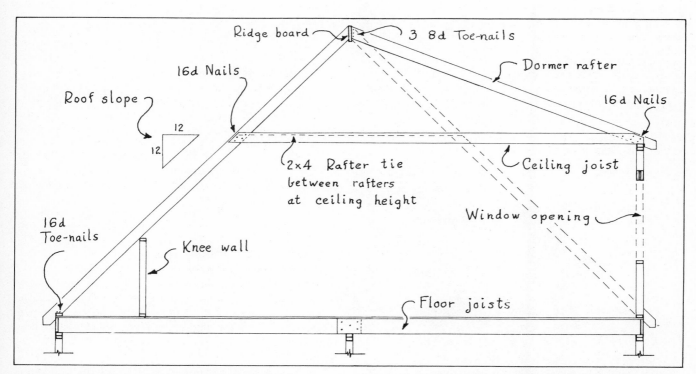

Story-and-Half Framing shown in cross-section indicates how shed-type dormer can extend usable floor space and full height ceiling area. Such dormers are usually used only on the home's rear or backyard side. Where this second-floor space is left unfinished for the time being, the rafter tie and ceiling joist members need not be placed with each rafter pair; instead shorter collar beams may be used and placed horizontally every 48 inches or every fourth rafter pair. Normal rafter to sole-plate nailing involves three 16d toe-nails, two on one side, one on the other. Metal anchor clips may also be used. If area is subject to excessive wind pressures, an 18-gauge inch-wide metal anchor strap over the top of rafters and carried down the outside edge of the stud may be desirable for added uplift resistance.

12 Roof Trusses and Gable Framing

Roof Trusses

The house plans you've chosen may or may not indicate roof trusses (sometimes called trussed rafters) as the method of roof framing. The use of trusses has become very widespread in recent years but the method does have some

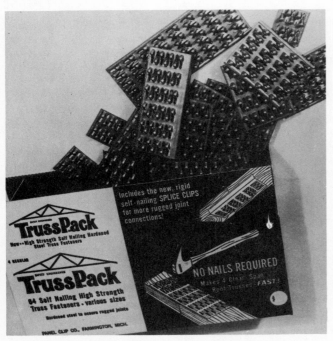

Truss Assembly Work by owner-builders can be accomplished more easily using TrussPack kits of self-nailing connector plates. In areas where shop-fabricated trusses may not be available to owners or where an owner-builder desires to save the cost of shop labor, he can set up his own truss jig and use these connectors to form a rigid truss. The packaged kit contains connector plates for making four residential type trusses. Truss designs and other details are obtainable from the Panel Clip Company.

limitations. Trusses are generally used for gabled and hipped roofs whose slopes fall in the range between 3-in-12 and 6-in-12 pitches (3 inch or 6 inch rise for every foot of horizontal run or distance).

With flat roofs, the ceiling joists serve the dual function as rafters. Their loading strength must be calculated to support both ceiling and roof loads. In application, flat-roof joist-rafters are set and assembled almost in the same exact manner as floor joists. Plywood sheathing is used as a roof deck materials and the flat surface receives a gravel surfacing applied with hot asphalt or pitch.

Steeper sloped roofs such as those in one-and-a-half story construction are not trussed because their objective is to provide livable attic space. In homes using trusses, the attic space is practical only for limited storage use accessible either through a closet scuttle opening or a hallway-located pull-down attic stairway.

Keeping in mind work that an owner-builder can accomplish without outside assistance, the roof truss method of framing is advisable and preferred over joist and rafter framing. Think twice if you've chosen a home style with complicated roof framing, because you will probably need the help of a framing carpenter to do a correct measuring and cutting job.

Discuss roof framing requirements and desired simplicity with your building supply retailer as you're looking at house plans. He'll advise you, prior to ordering of working drawings, whether the home you've selected is one that lends itself to truss construction. In the past few years, increasing use of computerized design methods by truss fabricators has broadened the applications of trusses. Within the range of roof slopes mentioned above and for the dimensions of most single-family homes, you'll be hard-pressed to choose a house plan for which a capable fabricator cannot work out truss application.*

*For information on truss packages, write to Panel-Clip Company, Box 423, Farmington, Mich. 48024.

Preliminary Truss Procedures

Savers of time and money, roof trusses today are generally fabricated with all members in one flat plane and with no overlaps. Bottom chords are in straight alignment and ceiling materials are applied directly to them. Where sloping ceilings are desired in living-dining-kitchen areas, trusses of the scissors type can be used in which the lower chords form a shallow inverted vee.

An owner-builder in a location where no truss fabricator is readily available can cut and assemble his own trusses. Or if he has a suitable small fabricating area, he may choose to approach his roof framing in this way. Whether or not it is advisable depends upon the particular house design. Trusses for a simple rectangular gabled roof are fairly easy to fabricate. On homes whose roof may be more complex, such as a hipped roof for an H-floorplan home, making your own trusses may be a formidable job. If you can't find a suitable truss fabricator for such homes, the joist-and-rafter method is probably preferable.

Once the trusses are fabricated, installing them becomes simple and fast process. Here's the step-by-step:

(1) Mark wall top-plates on long sides of home for proper truss positions. Depending on home design or length of span, trusses are usually spaced 24 or 16 inches o.c. The usual practice is to set trusses so that, at 4 foot intervals, the truss falls nearly or directly over wall studs. Do a little pencil figuring to find the number of truss spaces, and for gable end trusses make allowances at building ends where truss space may diminish.

(2) Make marks for truss edges rather than centers and if metal anchor clips are being used, nail at edge marks nailing base of clip into wall-plate with proper consideration for which side of clip the truss is placed.

(3) If trusses are delivered by a hoist-equipped truck, have the driver-operator place them in groups of four or five trusses resting on wall-plates along the building, ridge peaks upward. Brace one truss in each group from the ground and let the others lean slightly against it.

(4) If no truck hoist is available and the trusses have just been dumped near the house, one-at-a-time placement is best, carrying them into the home to lift up if partitions have not yet been installed; lifting the trusses up from outside if partitions are in place.

(5) Start setting trusses near one end. You'll need a minimum of two helpers. Station two persons at the outside walls with ladders and hammer, and have them place trusses one at a time to the mark and toe-nail them into the wall top-plate, or nail the metal anchor clip into the truss. A third person will be "on top," and it helps if he has good balance. At the placement of the first two or three trusses, he places a relatively short inch board across the truss top-chords at about midspan on each side of the ridge. The board is simply tacked temporarily to the trusses to help hold them erect and without regard for spacing.

(6) After about seven or eight trusses have been put into position and nailed at the top-plates, you stop to apply proper bracing. With the aid of the helpers, this is done by first placing a long 2X6 or 2X8 on each side of the ridge so that they are lying flat on the top edges of the lower chords of the trusses—two walking platforms. Then, using a ladder you get up on one walking plank near the starting end and a helper hands up a long 14 or 16 foot 1X6 or 2X4. You place this across the top-chords down about 3 to 4 feet from the ridge. Let the board or 2X4 project over the end of the house and, using a scaffold nail, nail it to the first truss placed. Now move so that with a properly cut spacing measure block you can adjust the second truss to the first and nail the board-brace to it with a scaffold nail. And so on down to the last truss placed, if your brace reaches that far. Next, begin again with another board-brace on the opposite side of the ridge and repeat the nail-space-nail process on that side.

(7) Continue setting truss after truss, nailing to wall top-plates and on top nailing to board-braces after proper spacing measure. When end of brace-boards is reached, set a couple more trusses, then get additional brace-board lengths overlapping previous ones by one or two truss spaces and proceed. The person on top slides the walking planks along and helps position the tops of the trusses, and also handles the nailing of brace-boards to the truss chords.

(8) When all trusses have been set and brace-boards nailed to them, take additional 2X4's for row bracing of the lower chords. Two rows are placed atop lower truss chords at approximately the midpoints between the center of the building and the exterior walls. These are permanent braces and should be nailed tightly using 16d common. Leave upper chord bracing in place until necessary to remove as roof sheathing work reaches that point.

Adapting End Trusses

On small homes where economy is a main consideration, gable-ends are kept simple and the easiest way to handle them in conjunction with a trussed roof is to use a truss as a gable end by providing it with vertical members to which siding can be nailed.

Assuming the trusses are flat-plane trusses as mentioned previously, simply lay a standard truss down on a level ground area and cut 2X3's or 2X4's to run at 16 inch intervals from slightly below the bottom chord to the sloping top edge of the top chord. These are laid flat-wise on the truss members and nailed perpendicular to the bottom chord. Begin at the truss center with the first two vertical members spaced properly to provide the sides of a ventilator opening. After these verticals have been nailed, cut cross pieces for top and bottom of the opening and place to avoid diagonal truss members. If the trusses are of the king-post type with a vertical member at the center, this member should be cut to fit the edges of the top and bottom cross pieces.

With respect to the lower projections of the verticals, the idea is simply this. The trusses probably have top-chords that continue the downward slope beyond the wall top-plates to form an eave overhang. The lower ends of these truss tails may have flat-cut bottoms for placement of soffit blocking. You want your gable-end verticals to come down below the bottom chord this far so that the bottoms of the verticals will line up with the flat-cut bottoms of the truss tails. When the gable-end truss is then set in place, these vertical projections are nailed to the wall top-plates.

In addition, when setting the gable-end trusses, toe-nail the bottom chord to the wall top-plate between the vertical members. Then go up on top to test the gable-end plumbness and to nail the projecting brace-boards to it.

Other Gable-End Types

Where the home's design shows a distinct rake overhang or projection that ranges between 6 inches and up to perhaps as much as 30 inches beyond the face of the end-wall sheathing, then a different type of gable-end treat-

Truss Placement Details are illustrated in this group of photos. In the large picture (1), save handling time and trouble by arranging to unload the trusses directly from the delivery truck onto the house for immediate nail up. (2) A row of trusses is shown with 1X8 braces tack-nailed to their top chords to hold them firmly in position. Trusses are (3) toe-nailed to wall top plates by one man moving along each wall plate and a third man moving down the center to hold trusses and nail the braces. Metal clips to anchor trusses to wall plates provide a better nailed connection. In photo (4), the fabricated gable-end component has been placed above the flat truss garage-door header which was also shop-fabricated by the components producer for this job.

ment is necessary. With such rake projections, the common practice is for soffit material to follow the rake slope.

Two methods are possible both using assemblies that are called "ladders." They consist of two parallel long members spaced the amount of the projection. Plus cross-members between the long ones spaced 16 in. o.c. All members are usually of the same size as the truss top-chords, 2X4's or 2X6's. When joist-and-rafter framing is used the rake ladders are sized the same as the rafters. A ladder assembly is applied at each roof slope or two per gable-end.

One type of rake ladder is for short projections and the assembly is placed along the outer face of the gable-end truss top-chord, top edges flush, and nailed to it. A second type is to prepare a rake ladder that is cantilevered over a sloping-plate gable-end stud wall (see illustration).

This second type of framing is suitable for homes having longer rake projections. The inner side of the rake ladder is nailed to the first inboard truss. Gable-end stud walls (in one or two sections) and rake ladder assemblies can be furnished in preassembled component form by many suppliers of trusses and other building components.

It is a fairly simple procedure to site-build rake ladders when necessary. For long members, cut same as rafters except that the bird's mouth cut to fit wall top-plates can be omitted on the outer pair. Begin cross-piece spacings about a foot downslope from the ridge and continue at 16 inch intervals taking care to avoid conflict of a cross-piece at the top outer edge of the top-plate where the bird's mouth cut is. Nail through the long members into the cross pieces. Set in place with one person holding the bottom at the eave while you nail the top long members into the

projecting ridge board and the inner long member to the truss top-chord or rafter. Now, following placement of gable-ends and rake ladders, the projecting ridge boards at each end can be cut off flush with the outer face of the rake ladder or gable-end verticals.

In some areas where truss or rafter tails along eaves are left without soffit treatment, rake projections using ladders are unsuitable. In such cases, the usual practice is to keep the rake projection relatively short, a foot or so perhaps, and to nail the rake rafters to the ridge board. This is done after the roof has been sheathed and the sheathing left projecting sufficiently beyond the end truss or rafter. While the rake rafter is temporarily supported at its bottom end, the sheathing is nailed to its top edge with closely spaced nails. Later the fascia board is extend to the rake rafter, nailed to it and it helps provide the support needed. This leaves sheathing exposed on the under side as it is between rafter tails. On such jobs, the row of sheathing sheets along eaves and rakes should be of exterior grade plywood with a suitable finish on the under side.

Joist/Rafter Considerations

Cutting Rafters

If for one reason or another you have elected to frame your roof using ceiling joists and rafters, your first step

Rake Ladder Components are first hoisted, then positioned over the gable-end and nailed to the adjacent truss chord and to the gable-end.

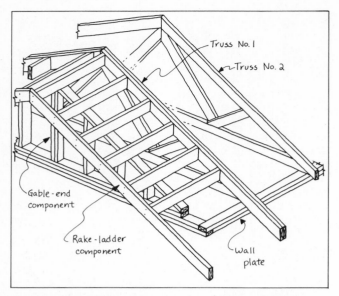

Endwall Roof Projections or rake overhangs can be furnished by most components suppliers. These are sometimes called rake ladders and they are furnished in pairs for each side of the ridge on a single endwall. As indicated in the sketch, the ladder components rest on (or cantilever over) a gable-end component. Their inboard end nails to the upper chord of the first truss. The ladder members are toe-nailed to the sloping top plate of the gable-end component.

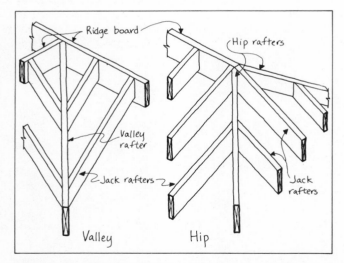

Valley and Hip Framing for hipped roofs is the most difficult part of rafter framing work done at the site. These hip and valley jacks require precision measuring and cutting on complex angles. Fortunately for owner-builders who desire hipped roofs, most roof truss fabricators are now capable of prefabricating truss components that assemble at the site to form hipped roofs and eliminate the need for precision on-site cutting.

should be an inquiry to your principal supplier or a local truss shop whether or not they can furnish precut rafter members. Ceiling joist placement is no more of a problem than with the first-floor joists. But rafter cutting is precise work and takes time, even when done with an electric saw at the building site. Some lumber suppliers or truss shops may be willing to take your plans and precut rafters for you. This is helpful for a straight gable roof but almost mandatory for a more complex roof frame, such as on an H or T plan house or for a hipped roof. Here, listed in order of increasing difficulty or complexity of roof framing, is a comparison of different types of homes.

(1) straight gable roof;
(2) gable roof on L, T or H plan;
(3) rear shed dormer on one-and-a-half story;
(4) dormered-window one-and-a-half story;
(5) hipped roof, rectangular plan;
(6) hipped roof on L, T or H plan;
(7) any roof on home having acute or obtuse angles (non 90°)

Recommendation. If this is your first owner-built home, your experience with portable electric saws is limited and you don't have a comfortable feeling with geometric math, so avoid roof framing complexities. Or obtain the help of a framing carpenter.

Setting Procedure

If you desire to proceed with you own rafter cutting at the building site, refer to the use of pattern rafters in the preceding chapter. On a straight gabled roof, once the rafters are cut, the setting procedure is quite easy and resembles that described for a one-and-a-half story or expansion-attic home. Gable-ends are also dealt with in a low-pitched roof frame much as they are with a one-and-a-half story except that the windows are not normally included in gable-ends of lower pitched roofs.

Incidentally, it probably should be mentioned here that gabled roofs are much the same as hipped roofs as far as their under-supports are concerned. This means that you can, in all probability, revise a home design whose floor plan you like but whose roof style you don't. But this does require changes in working drawings, as well as in materials lists.

One further detail about joist-rafter roof framing is worth attention when installing ceiling joists. This is where the procedure differs slightly from that of floor joists. Ceiling joists should be positioned so that when rafters are set, they lap the joists and the two are nailed together over the wall plates. Now, consider that rafter pairs are supposed to align with each other and meet opposite each other at the ridge, while ceiling joists lap each other over the bearing partition. If the joists lap the rafters on the same side, the joists will run at a very slight angle off the perpendicular to the exterior walls. This may be sufficient to interfere with the proper butting of ceiling sheet materials.

In order to obtain good joist alignment and perfect perpendicularity with exterior walls, the addition of short 1-½ inch thick blocks (of joist depth) between the joists at the point of lapping will correct the deviation. One joist then is lapped on one side of the rafter pair while the opposite side's joist is lapped on the other side of the rafter pair, resulting in a straight alignment.

Final Roof-Frame Details

If you used square-cut joist members, bringing them out (as directed) to the outer edge of the wall plates, and later proceeded to set rafters alongside and to nail the lapped joist-rafter connection together, you will have a small triangle of joist at the upper outer corner which projects above the upper edge of the rafter. This triangle will have to be trimmed off at each joist-rafter connection to allow proper seating of the sheathing. You can saw it with a handsaw or an electric saw. Many carpenters simply use a sharp handaxe to chip it off, chipping downslope.

Your roof frame will probably have openings that need to be trimmed with cross pieces, somewhat similar to the framed openings described in the previous chapter for window and ventilator in gable-end walls. Two added types of openings must be provided for.

The first is an opening for a chimney, whether it be a small square one for a prefabricated metal chimney, a slightly larger opening for a masonry chimney, or a still-larger rectangle for a combined heating-plant and fireplace chimney. Or for a fireplace alone. For a prefabricated chimney, the small opening can usually fit well within existing framing members. It's just a question of adding cross members of the same depth as the joists or lower-chords at the ceiling level, and members of rafter or upper-chord depth at the roof-slope level. These small openings do not need to be double-framed as described in the earlier description of floor framing. A similar framed opening between existing framing members can be provided in a hallway or closet where it is desirable to provide an attic scuttle for access into the attic space.

However, where larger chimneys that do not fit between trusses or rafters and joists are involved, a modification is necessary. Before you proceed to change the framing, however, check your drawings again to ponder whether the masonry chimney might be shifted slightly, reduced somewhat in size at the ceiling level, or possibly corbelled to fit the framing condition. A "corbel" is a process that involves shifting the vertical faces of masonry by stepped coursing. Keep in mind that most building codes require the framed openings around chimneys to have a 2 inch clearance between the outer surface of the chimney and the framing members. Some prefabricated chimneys having internal flues and outer jackets are approved for zero clearance.

If chimney adjustment seems impractical, then proceed to modify your trusses or joist-rafter construction at the chimney location. Doubled cross framing members are needed for larger openings. If you have a wide chimney that cuts across two or even three framing spaces, you may need to double the trusses or joist-rafter framing at the sides of the opening as well as for cross-members. Check this with your supplier when planning the truss installation of ordering the joists and rafters.

Also double-framing may be required if you plan to use a larger ceiling opening for attic access such as can be accomplished with a fold-down attic stairway. With such an installation, obtain rough opening dimensions from the stairway supplier and follow the manufacturer's instructions with regard to preparing the opening.

13 Chimneys, Fireplaces, Veneers

Every home needs a flue gas vent. This is the outlet for various types of heating appliances, including warm-air furnaces, hot-water boilers and coal-fired stokers. Don't laugh at the latter. In a few areas at present, automatic-operating coal-fired heating plants are being installed in homes. They've been developed partly as a result of continued concern for natural gas shortages and mounting fuel oil prices.

These same energy considerations have tended to darken the future of electricity for home heating and cooling. Electric heating, which requires no flue-gas escape route and thus no chimney, has grown in residential use for more than two decades. Today's building codes require all other fuel-burning appliances to be connected to an approved vent to outside air for disposal and dispersion of the products of combustion.

There are available specialized metal vent pipes in smaller sizes that are code-approved and suited for use with small-capacity individual units such as wall furnaces, room heaters, water heaters and certain kinds of oil-fired appliances. However, in most single-family homes, central heating systems predominate and the venting of equipment for these systems must be done through larger-sized flues incorporated in a masonry chimney or provided with an outer shell casing as in a prefabricated metal chimney.

In most residential installations today, domestic water heating units are located in close proximity to the home's heating plant so that a heater's vent pipe can be connected to that of the heating plant and share a single flue.

For the first-time owner-builder, use of prefabricated metal chimneys and prefabricated fireplace units is suggested as a real time saver and a much easier installation job than with a masonry chimney and fireplace. Any of three situations are common today with the use of prefabricated chimneys and fireplaces:

(1) Home with no fireplace—prefabricated metal chimney chosen to fit ceiling-roof style and serving both heating plant and domestic water heater in basement or first-floor utility room or closet;

(2) Home with fireplace and basement—two prefabricated metal chimneys, one for a fireplace and one for heating/water-heating can be combined in a single chimney housing framed of wood and plywood;

(3) Home with fireplace built over crawl space—while a few floor plans may back up a heating closet to a fireplace, most plans will separate them; use of separate, prefabricated chimneys is indicated.

Building Codes and Safety

Danger is everpresent with fuel-burning appliances. Codes have detailed guidelines for proper installation of such appliances and the chimneys which vent the combustion gases. Local building codes may vary considerably from the major One-and-Two-Family Dwelling Code or the set of HUD Minimum Property Standards which, while not a code, sometimes functions as though it were.

One typical code requirement may affect the location of the chimney and thus the location of the heating appliances connected to it. That is a requirement that the chimney be extended through the roof a minimum of 3 feet above the highest point of pass-through and at least 2 feet above any portion of the building within 10 feet horizontally. To indicate one apparent result of this latter requirement, it's advisable on a split-level home to keep any chimney related to the ground-level portion of the home beyond the 10 foot distance from the nearest wall of the split-level or second floor part of the home. Otherwise an unusually high chimney will be needed to meet code requirements. Most professionally done home plans such as those found in widely distributed plan books will take such factors into account in their plans.

Care is advised in building fireplaces, too, for similar fire safety and code reasons. Probably, as shown by results of investigations of fires originating with fireplaces, the real hazard is not so much the fireplace construction as it is misuse . . . overloading, burning of trash and carelessness with fire screens for containing sparks. For details on proper fireplace operation, obtain a fireplace fact sheet from the U.S. Consumer Product Safety Commission.

Chimney-Fireplace Planning

In considering your chimney or chimneys, bear in mind that prefabricated units have flexibility. Made in sections that fit tightly together, chimney weight is supported by floor or ceiling joists or by sloping rafters in cathedral ceiling rooms (see illustration). In recent years, there has been increasingly widespread use of metal chimneys erected within wood-framed and plywood-covered enclosures. These have an attractive exterior appearance equalling, for many people, the appearance of masonry chimneys.

Framing

Framing work for such a wood chimney is commonly tied in with the wall framing up to roof level, and then becomes four-sided above the roof. Metal chimney assembly within the enclosure is done before the enclosure siding is applied. Wood chimneys require flashing details quite similar to those of other chimneys. The plywood utilized should be exterior grade and most chimneys of this type employ plywood whose exterior finish has a rustic texture. These enclosures, or "chases" as they're sometimes called, can accommodate more than a single chimney.

Recommendation. First check your local building code concerning prefabricated chimneys, prefabricated fireplaces and wood-plywood chimney enclosures. If the code permits these installations, we advise use of these products to save both time and trouble. Weigh the following benefits of prefabricated chimneys-fireplaces against your desires for a masonry fireplace:

- ☐ flexibility in placement of chimney so that it can go up through framing members with minimal adaptation;
- ☐ with a prefabricated fireplace unit, you can still design the interior fireplace face and hearth as you wish;
- ☐ if an odd size or shape is desired in the fire-box and fireplace opening area, you can achieve this with a prefabricated chimney and it will still be easier to erect on the masonry base than will a masonry chimney;
- ☐ a prefabricated fireplace unit with a heat circulation system is desirable as emergency backup in case of heating fuel shortage, these units can be incorporated into a masonry fireplace shell and chimney.

One accessory for a wood-burning fireplace that an owner-builder might wish to include is a gas lighter for starting wood fires; this requires installation of a branch gas line to the fireplace opening. There are available certain fireplace units designed for connection to gas or electric lines. These units give off substantial heat and some incorporate ceramic "logs" that glow, supposedly like a real fire. Just guessing, but probably very few people having the gumption and energy to build their own home would be able to abide the idea of an artificial fire. However, the units are available.

Prefabricated metal fireplace units come in both wall and corner models. In case the terminology is confusing: a wall-type metal unit can be framed to set in the corner of a room and it can also be used for placing the fireplace in a room divider; a "corner-model" fireplace unit is not intended for use in a room corner. The latter unit has a fire-box open not just in front but also on one side, either right or left.

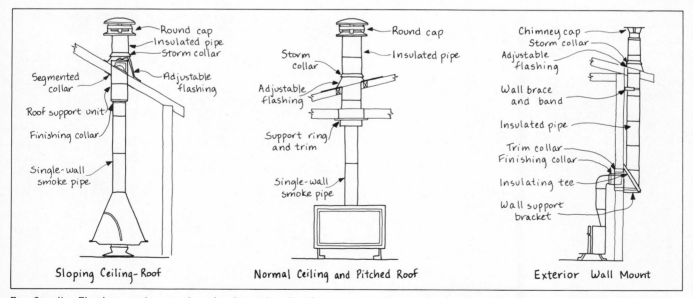

Free-Standing Fireplaces are least costly and easiest to install and should be given serious consideration by owner-builders even with a tight construction budget. A fireplace can be excellent "insurance" against power blackouts and fuel shortages. Shown here are typical free-standing units with different chimney accessories to accommodate the most common types of installation.

In planning a heat-circulating fireplace, consideration should be given for room air intake into the circulation channels and output from the unit back into the room. Output grilles can be on the wall face above the fire-box or may be on the sides of an enclosure (see illustrations). Intake openings are near the floor and their location depends on the type of unit.

Metal fireplace manufacturers provide complete installation instructions with their products. The descriptive literature gives ordering details such as range of sizes available, clearance information, and hearth details. Check to make sure that the unit you choose indicates what clearances are needed with other building or framing materials. Your work will probably be simpler if a unit has been approved by Underwriters Laboratories for zero clearance, meaning that it can touch any other adjacent construction. This type unit uses air spaces and fire-box throat insulation to prevent excessive heat buildup.

Metal Fireplace Installation

Conventional stud walls surround the fire-box and throat assembly. Above this height, the framed enclosure can narrow down to a size to accommodate the prefabricated chimney (see illustrations). Or, the larger enclosure can continue up to ceiling or roof as desired, according to the fireplace location.

The same framework built for the fireplace facing wall may include bookshelves, wood bin, closets, or other flues from floor below—just so these enclosure built-ins occur at the sides or above the fire-box and throat assembly. The manufacturer's instructions will provide details on completing and trimming the opening and framing.

Alternative positions for setting the fire-box may be offered: face flush with the facing wall, or projecting beyond it so that mantel support is provided. Facing materials of brick, tile, marble, glass, stone or other noncombustibles can be used to trim the fireplace opening if the manufacturer's self-trim method is not desired. Such facing trim should extend a minimum of about 6 inches at the top and 5 inches at the sides, and greater distances are satisfactory.

The metal fireplace unit may be raised above floor level if desired to accommodate a raised hearth. In such raised

Metal Heat-Circulating Fireplace unit shown in this series is a Heatilator-made unit that comes complete with chimney sections, roof housing, ceiling sleeve and firebox including damper and fire-screen. (Note: model shown in assembly of items in first photo is not the heat-circulating type.) Photo (2), the installation begins by marking on the floor the proper location of the firebox; in this case, framing has been prepared for a raised hearth. Then, in (3), the heat-circulating firebox is set and photo (4) shows the framing surround work which may be partial height as shown or extend fully to the ceiling. Round metal duct sections and elbows (5) are brought to the register openings in the framing. Finally (6), the finished facing of the fireplace can be done in almost any style desired.

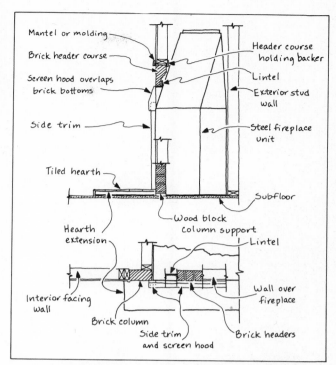

Fireplace Framing Details are shown in this typical cross-section of a steel firebox enclosure (top sketch) and partial plan (bottom sketch). This installation includes face brick trim around fireplace opening plus a ceramic tiled hearth projection. Owner-builders are well-advised to use built-in metal fireplace units such as this rather than laying up a complete masonry fireplace. Its easier, faster, safer and surer to produce good results.

installations, use care that the air intake units of a heat-circulating fireplace are not blocked.

Caution is also advisable in regard to the fireplace hearth. Not the bed of the fire-box, but the floor on which the unit rests and the heat-protective base that may extend forward for a wall fireplace or around it for a free-standing unit.

Inspect the manufacturer's literature for a hearth extension accessory. Or look at recommended alternative methods in the manufacturer's installation drawings. A notching of floor joists may be needed if the unit's hearth extension is to have its surface flush with the room's finished floor. This is not recommended, however, since a raised hearth, even if raised only an inched or two, provides a better juncture with floor coverings, and makes hearth sweeping easier. Raised to a height of 10 to 14 inches the hearth can act like a casual bench; the height brings the burning fire almost to eye-level of people seated in the room, and can be dramatic.

Hearth extensions, it should be noted, add a measure of safety in that they help contain fire sparks, catching embers that sometimes penetrate fire screens and keeping them from alighting on adjacent carpeting. The extension accessory for a fireplace unit is also of metal in pan form, to accommodate covering material of tiles, brick, slate or similar noncombustibles.

About free-standing metal fireplace units. There's a constantly growing variety of shape and design, available from a number of manufacturers. They can set by themselves anywhere in a room although certain types similar to the old Franklin stoves are designed for placement with their backs near to a wall.

Quite popular in free-standing units are the different conical and European styles, offering a wide choice of shapes and materials. One line of ceiling-suspended fireplace hoods provides a "fire-in-the-round" concept and supplements its hoods with steel base bowls, circular fire-screens and fire grates. Some of these prefabricated fireplace units can run into substantial money. Most are offered in special matte black finishes and some in a range of baked-on enamel colors. The chimney pipe sections for use below the ceiling come in a matching finish.

Free-standing metal fireplace units require a hearth installation of noncombustible material. Building code ap-

Free-Standing Metal Fireplaces come in a wide range of different styles including these two designs by Temco. Once used predominantly for vacation homes, the free-standing units are becoming increasingly popular in new prime homes. Shop for them in lumber supply home centers, hard building materials dealers and in urban fireplace boutiques. The models illustrated are wood-burning models with provision for adding gas logs. The units come in choice of satin black, burnt orange, autumn red and aspen gold finishes.

Prefabricated Metal Chimney with its various parts identified. This sketch has been adapted from the descriptive installation instructions issued by the William Wallace Co., makers of Metalbestos chimney units for a wide range of residential applications. Chimney models and installation accessories are available to meet virtually any framing condition encountered in woodframe homes. The insulated and stainless steel chimney pipes are suitable with home heating furnaces or air conditioners and also with fireplace units.

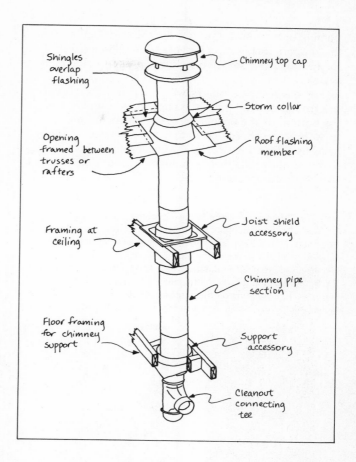

proval for specific models may depend upon the use of supplementary heat shields. Local code requirements should be checked while in the planning stage.

Prefabricated Chimney Details

Approved prefabricated chimneys usually employ an insulated double pipe, one chimney wall inside another with insulating material between. Stainless steel or similar corrosion-resistant metal is used. Chimneys come in short 18- to 36-inch sections and various diameters depending upon which manufacturer's product is selected.

Manufacturers of prefabricated chimneys alone are relatively few in number but they offer a wide range of diameters to meet varying needs. In contrast, prefabricated chimneys are also offered by prefabricated fireplace manufacturers, but the chimney sizes they offer tend to be limited to those suitable for use with their own fireplaces.

Prefabricated metal chimneys need corrosion-resistant materials because of their inaccessibility once installed, and to minimize the possible effects of the condensation that sometimes occurs as flue gases are exhausted. Typical inside pipe diameters range from 6 to 14 inches; the smaller sizes are suited to venting individual appliances while the larger sizes accommodate fireplaces.

The most common practice in home design and preparation of home plans is to have chase space for a heating-plant chimney indicated in the floor plans although it may not be so labelled. It will usually be adjacent to a closet or hallway. If not shown, such a chimney can be run up through a closet but its enclosure must be framed off from the closet space.

To help avoid coming too close to the roof ridge and, in some cases, to avoid conflict with roof framing, a prefabricated chimney can be ordered with accessory elbows that permit a shift in the vertical axis of the chimney (see illustration). Added support should be provided for the vertical portion above the offset.

Main support for the metal chimney is by a framed joist opening. An accessory wall bracket is available from the chimney manufacturer for supporting an external chimney just outside the home's exterior wall. When ordering chimney parts, include information about your roof slope so that a properly sloped roof-flashing component is included.

It might be noted here that typical single-wall flue or smoke pipes from furnace or water heater to the chimney

should not come closer than 18 inches to combustible materials such as wood framing or wall-ceiling board. Prefabricated chimneys of approved double-wall type may require small clearances by local codes. As indicated earlier this is a critical point, to be verified locally by the owner-builder before proceeding to order the chimney or to build the masonry. The latter in most cases does require 2 inch spacing away from all framing and combustibles. If such clearance is needed for prefabricated chimneys, the manufacturer has an accessory spacer or shield assembly for that purpose.

Chimney Installation

Assembly of a prefabricated metal chimney at the building site once the chase and framing work have been completed is a relatively fast job, but requires attention to detail to obtain proper section-by-section seating and seal. The procedure will vary somewhat one manufacturer's product to another.

As a rule, the chimney support device is keyed to joist or rafter conditions. For horizontal joists such as start of the chimney in the first-floor joists for a basement connection, the metal supporting unit is simply nailed to the prepared framing open from below and the chimney sections rest on the support. Below, the joists, a tee-section extends down for heating plant smoke pipe and the other opening serves as a cleanout.

For basementless homes where the heating plant is on the ground or main floor, the same support unit is nailed to the bottom of the opening prepared in the ceiling joists or truss bottom chords. Where a prefabricated chimney is being used for a fireplace in a living or family room having a sloping ceiling-roof line, a support bracket that adjusts to varying roof slopes is available.

Once the starter section of chimney is in place on the support plate, chimney erection proceeds section by section. The section joints usually incorporate an external locking band or an integral device so that the chimney section is merely twisted to lock it to the section below.

Where the chimney passes through upper floor joists or ceiling joists, an accessory protective shield should be placed around the chimney section and its accompanying metal support plate nailed to the framed opening.

At the roof level, the chimney section is followed by a roof flashing member slipped over the section and flashing

Masonry Chimney Construction using brick for interior facing and firebox plus concrete block for the exterior chimney are shown in this photo group. First photo indicates prepared openings in wall and roof. In (2) a start is made on the outside with thin block units laid atop the prepared foundation wall. Inside, work begins with the fire brick hearth and brick wall facing. Next photo (3) shows the layup work proceeding on the exterior with the block enclosure of 4 inches thick units, 8X16 inches in face size. Interior photo (4) shows firebox work completed, with damper built in and rear voids filled with block and rubble. Notice the sloping corbel of brick to narrow the firebox top to dimensions needed for placement of flue-liner. Outside (5), the chimney is narrowed by block units laid at an angle and in (6) the chimney is shown in nearly completed condition. The tubular steel scaffolding shown is convenient for chimney work and in most areas can be rented from contractors' supply firms.

baffle. Additional sections are placed to required height and followed by the chimney's round top. If the height above roof is more than about 4 feet, check the chimney instructions for use of a chimney brace to the roof.

Above the roof lines, the chimney may be left exposed. Or, for improved appearance, a square roof housing can be supplied by the chimney manufacturer. These housings come preassembled or in kit form. They are of metal or asbestos-cement panel construction and sometimes have a simulated brick finish on the exterior. The roof housings seem to look best, however, when painted. A builder-owner can also opt for a wood-frame and plywood-sided enclosure. A roof cap for a custom-built enclosure can be made by any sheet metal shop. But the chimney cap used should be the same type as that furnished with the chimney.

Masonry Chimneys and Veneers

Masonry fireplaces and their chimneys come in standard, traditional and contemporary styles and range widely in design and size. Custom-designed brick and stone fireplaces frequently require the special knowledge that comes from first-hand experience. If your home will have a large custom masonry fireplace, two fireplaces in one masonry assembly, or an otherwise complicated design, you will need the guidance of an experienced mason, and a partial or full subcontract with him is advised.

The full range of detailed planning considerations for fireplaces and chimneys of masonry construction along with information relating to trims, mantels, various designs and construction options are contained in the *Book of Successful Fireplaces* authored by R.J. and Marie-Jeanne Lytle (see appendix).

Despite the foregoing warnings about fireplace and chimney complexity and counsel to obtain aid from a mason subcontractor, there are two masonry installations found in some homes which are within a typical owner-builder's skills. These are (1) a square or rectangular single-flue chimney for heating/water-heating connection which can run upward through a chase or closet without modification of the floor, ceiling or roof framing; (2) a single fireplace of modest dimensions with the above characteristic or one which is located on the outside of an exterior wall whose chimney rises through an eave or rake overhang.

Both these fireplace or chimney styles involve straight masonry work in which either bricks or concrete blocks can be used. And the fireplaces can be easily corbelled below ceiling level to allow a smaller chimney to penetrate the roof with a minimum of modification of framing work.

As implied in the preceding paragraph, straight course brick and block work is easy; it can also be fun! Consequently, an owner-builder who desires to have a brick veneer exterior on his home might well consider this work within his capabilities.

Planning Considerations

Following are several points to keep in mind when deciding about veneer work. One way to speed and simplify veneering jobs is to cut the siding area roughly in half. Very frequently the exterior veneering purpose and decorative

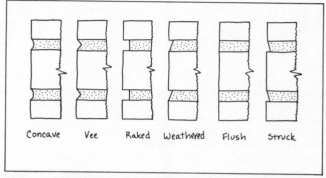

Brickwork Joints can be varied to give different appearance to the masonry wall. The first three types at left are the most commonly used and the concave style is recommended to owner-builders doing their first masonry lay-up job.

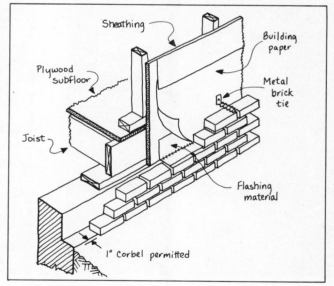

Brick Veneer Exterior Walls for woodframe homes keep approximately 3/4 to 1 inch of space between the inner faces of the bricks and the building-paper covering of the sheathing. In laying up the bricks do not fill this void with mortar, although it will not be harmful if a few mortar drippings fall into the crevice. In the course where the flashing penetrates, weep holes should be provided every 4 feet by omitting a portion of mortar from vertical joints. The flashing material should extend up the wall at least 6 inches behind the building paper; the flashing material can be light-gauge copper or galvanized or 30 pound roofing felt.

appearance can be served by a wainscot instead of full-wall height veneering. A wainscot of brick presents an usually good appearance when windows in the home are mostly of the same height so that the brick work can be brought up to sill height and then trimmed in continuity with the window sills. Such wainscot brick-laying is easily done from the ground without scaffolds.

Then, consider hipped-roof versus gabled-roof homes. With hipped-roof homes, the brick work rises to eave soffit height which is continuous around the home. It's very simple to provide brick trim at the top by a single trim strip

(see illustration). On the other hand, where the brick work must run up the end-walls to reach the gable rake, the high brick-laying and meeting the roof slope angle involves more difficulty. A better alternative is to project the gable-end framing out sufficiently so that when it is sided with sheet material, the latter will extend downward just covering and concealing the top edge of the masonry veneer which has been brought to eave level all around.

With two-story construction, yet another way of minimizing the high level brick work is to provide a brick veneer only for the ground floor and use wood, plywood or

Brick Veneer Lay-Up, like the concrete block foundation work, starts at building corners with carefully leveled and plumbed units that provide a base for stretching mason's line to give a straight edge for intermediate coursing to follow. In the large photo (1), veneer work has begun and brick ties have been nailed to the studs ahead. Loose brick are conveniently piled nearby and mortar mixed and ready for use from any of several mortar boards placed on folding-leg supports to be at convenient work height. Then (2), two brick

layers work well together on a residential wall with a third person providing a continuous supply of mortar and bricks. In the lower photos, beginning at the left, a continuous offset of veneer brick provides the outer face of a fireplace chimney integral with the wall veneer. Center photo shows staggered brick ends where day's work finishes off and next day begins. Last photo indicates completed wall; tubular scaffolding in place was used for higher courses; rental mortar mixer is in foreground.

hardboard siding materials on the second floor. In such cases, it is advisable to follow a simple framing modification for handling the juncture of the brick and other siding material. Cantilever the second floor out and bring the veneer brick up to this second floor projection. The amount of cantilever can be just sufficient to cover the brick-mortar width of 4 inches or it may be greater with soffit material applied to the underside of the second floor joists, just as normally done for a roof's eave soffit.

Some builders put up a brick veneer facing on the front elevation of a home. Don't do it. It makes the home look worse that it would without any brick veneer. Be economical by using a wainscot all the way around . . . not by placing all your brick on one side of the house with the other sides looking like poor relatives.

There are some communities in which subdivisions are approved with quite small lots and the homes are relatively close. Many such communities won't permit use of any siding materials other than brick. There are also some communities in which appraisers view a brick veneer home as having more value than a home having conventional sidings.

But short of such local situations favoring brick, you will in all probability gain just as much satisfaction in the long run from the wide choice of other exterior sidings, most being just as attractive and maintenance-free as brick veneer.

Like the concrete block basement or foundation walls, veneer work is started at the corners by carefully setting up and plumbing several brick courses on each side of the building corners. Stretcher brick are laid to a mason's line as were the concrete blocks. If there is a fireplace whose shell enclosure and chimney project beyond the exterior wall, the veneer brick can course and interlock with that of the fireplace back, sides, and chimney.

Corrugated galvanized metal strips with prepunctured nailing holes are used to tie the masonry veneer to the frame wall. The 22-gauge 7/8 inch wide strips are embedded at least 2 inches into the mortar joint and their wall ends nailed through sheathing into studs with 8d nails . . . a row of ties every six courses of brick.

In veneer work, there's only one wythe (thickness) of brick and therefore no need for any bonding with other wythes. Lay-up in any pattern other than the standard staggered-joint method is not advised because slight errors in brick placement or joint thickness tend to show up more where a specialized brick pattern is being followed.

Cutting off mortar joints with the trowel's edge leaves a rough cut or flush joint. Other types of joints are made by tooling the mortar with a joint tool of one type or another (see illustration). In selecting the joint style some are more difficult to make uniform than others. Recommended for the owner-builder is either the rounded concave joint or the vee.

One final note on brick veneers. During the past two decades, a variety of different manufacturers have introduced brick-like siding materials in both panel and individual brick form. Most of these simulated bricklike products are relatively thin and employ some type of nailing application in which the nail-heads are hidden as "mortar" joints are filled or as additional panels are placed. A few of these brick products are actually fired ceramics just about identical in composition to normal sized bricks. Others are of molded plastic.

It is possible that a few such products might be suitable for exterior veneer work. Check the manufacturer's literature for limitations. Properly executed, some of these simulated brick products (or real ones) can give an excellent appearance inside or out. They're worth investigating because of lower cost and easier application.

14 Roof Deck and Fascia-Soffit-Rake

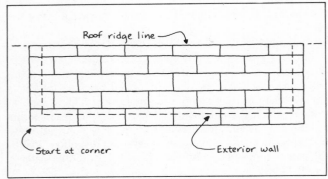

Half-Roof Plan of Sheathing Sheets as they are applied to roof trusses or rafters with joints staggered and occurring over truss top chords or raft centers.

First check your roof trusses or rafters. They should still be braced as they were when set. And your walkway planks on lower chords or ceiling joists should still be in place.

Now verify your truss or rafter spacing. You need to determine whether over the bulk of the roof area, the spacings are accurate enough to have the 4X8 sheets of plywood sheathing, when laid with long edges perpendicular to the framing members, butt-join each other over the framing members.

An easy way to make a quick check is cut yourself a 2X4 or 1X6 exactly 8 feet in length and make a mark at midpoint if your member spacing is 24 inches or 16 inches o.c. Test both sides of the ridge, once near the ridge and again near the eaves. Go down the house laying out the measuring board. Put one end at a member center and see where both the midpoint mark and the other end fall. If at or close to member centers, it's OK and you can move the board across to test the next set of members.

If a truss or rafter is slightly out of position for making a plywood joint, loosen the bracing board or rafter ridge nailing and adjust the member if possible. If the discrep-

ancy is serious and the truss or rafter can't be adjusted that much, take a 2X3 or 2X4 the length of the chord or rafter and nail it to the member flush with top edge. Then, the plywood butt-joint can fall on the 2X3 or 2X4.

Your advance preparation might include the drawing of a sheathing layout sketch. It can be for half the roof if the roof is symmetrical (see illustration). It will help in determining the starting point in one corner with a proper sized sheet. It's not really a necessity for simple rectangular or L-shaped roofs but the drawing can be useful in minimizing plywood cutting and waste on a more complex roof. The idea, of course, is to use full-size 4X8 sheets as much as possible and cut off as little as possible.

Choice of Decking

At the time you arrange deliveries with your lumber-plywood supplier, check on the grade of plywood you are to receive for roof sheathing. You want to be certain that the grade is suited to the spacings of your trusses or rafters. Plywood sheathing is grade-marked to give the quality of its surfaces but sheathing grades are also provided with an identification index number such as 24/0 or 32/16. The first part of the index number tells the maximum spacing in inches that support members can be for that grade and thickness when used for roof sheathing. The second part of the number tells the maximum spacing of supports when the sheathing is used for subfloors.

For roof sheathing, a suitable grade is "C-C INT," an interior type of plywood intended for nonexposed usage with C-grade veneers on both surfaces. With an identification index of 24/0, it is suitable for roof member spacings of up to 24 inches o.c. but is not suitable for subfloor use.

If your home's eave and rake overhangs are to remain open or exposed with uncovered rafter tails, you'll be advised to use plywood of the exterior type (with waterproof glue in its laminations) and in the ½ inch thickness to keep roofing nails from penetrating to the exposed under surface. This type plywood is needed only for the sheets along the eaves and rake. Discuss this point with your supplier if exposed soffits and rakes are used.

Use of the correct grade and thickness of plywood means economy. Better grades and thicker plywood cost more. But the specific grades indicated should be viewed as minimums and there should be no hesitation about using better grades or thicknesses if they are readily available and the specified ones are not. Remember that local suppliers follow local or regional preferences and requirements in respect to different applications. And the difference in cost between 3/8 and 1/2 inch sheathings, for example, is not going to make a world of difference on a single home.

Deck Application Procedures

For applying the 4X8 roof sheathing sheets you will want one helper to assist in moving the sheets into approximate position while you do the preliminary nailing; another helper to finish out the nailing will speed completion.

If your house is a split-level, a two-story or bi-level with attached garage or otherwise has roof surfaces at different heights, plan to sheath the lowest height first so it will be a stepping stone for handling the materials up to upper roof levels.

The easiest way to lift plywood sheets (aside from a hydraulic hoist or lift truck) is to slide them up a pair of sloping 2X4's or 2X6's leaned from the ground against the rafter or truss tails to which the 2X4's or 2X6's are temporarily nailed. Plank walkways on the lower truss chords or joists allow handling and nailing of the first row or two of sheathing sheets but then the deck itself becomes the better working platform. With relatively steep slopes, have a few short 2X4's to nail above sheathing to framing members; these serve as working toeholds. Now, you're ready to begin initial placement and preliminary nailing in the following manner.

(1) Start near a lower corner so the initial sheet's long edge just meets the top ends of the truss or rafter tails. Using 6d coated common nails or deformed shank nails, tack the sheet into framing members in three or four spots, but do not fully drive nails. Bring in a second sheet placed at the end of the first also along the truss-rafter tail edges. Again, three or four partly driven nails. Now a third sheet centered above the first two and adjusted so its edges fall near framing member centers. And three or four nails. The butted sheets shouldn't fit tight; leave about 1/16 inch nail thickness between sheet ends and about 1/8 inch between sheet long sheet ends and 1/8 inch between sheet long edges.

(2) Check the sheets placed for alignment, slight openings between ends and edges and how the ends appear to fall at framing member centers. Make any slight adjustment and then drive nails home. Move along eave to add third and fourth eave edge sheets followed by additional second row sheets. Again use four to six

nails a sheet at sheet edges and ends. Continue to check closely on lower row joints centering over framing members. Same for second row.

(3) At building ends, the plywood sheets should project sufficiently for the particular rake treatment and trim. Rake edges will be trimmed off later after the complete slope has been sheathed and rake rafter and trim has been installed. Continue with full 4X8 feet and half 4X4 feet sheets staggering joints and maintaining your watch on butt-end and long-edge spacings.

(4) Follow the same procedure on the other slope or slopes leaving the narrower sheets that occur along the ridge until last. Cutting these sheets right on the roof with your portable electric saw is fine with low roof slopes but on steeper roofs, measure the width needed and do the cutting on the ground.

Methods For Handling Roof Sheathing are shown. Top photo indicates the easier way, unloading directly from the truck to the roof with workers applying the first few sheets and partially nailing them in order to obtain a temporary resting place for the balance of the sheets. Below, on another house, the leaning plank at the left permits easy shove-up of plywood sheathing sheets. Note that the 1X4 fascia trim board is applied as soon as the sheathing is in place, in order to finish off rake edge.

(5) Use care in cutting the sheets along the ridge. The joint should be a lapped joint with the first sheet cut to meet the slope of the opposite side's framing member top edges. The ridge sheet for the opposite side is then cut to lap the edge of the first sheet and trimmed off to meet that sheet's top surface. Trimming for a close match can usually be done with a sharp hand plane.

(6) At the rake edges after the rake ladder or rake rafter has been installed, you can allow for the rake trim board by simply temporarily nailing in an inch board under the projecting plywood and sawing along its edge with the electric saw. Then, the trim board can be applied later with other exterior trim materials.

(7) One of your roof sheathing helpers should be with your handling sheets and helping you position and nail temporarily. The other should follow in the nailing with the proper frequency of nails both along the sheet edges and at intermediate points. Incidentally, most roof framing carpenters find it less tiresome and more productive to nail from a stooped but standing position on their feet rather than on their knees.

If you have an unusually large roof area to sheath and have difficulty getting helpers, you might check your nearest tool rental agency to see if they can rent you a pneumatic tacker-nailer with a small portable air compressor. These automatic fastening tools, with proper-sized nails or staples, can make short work of the nailing.

Where there are roof deck openings such as for chimneys, roof vents or fireplaces, cut the sheathing around the opening as the sheet is placed. Once an opening has been covered, it is an extra bother to find the right place to cut for a flush edge.

Application of Fascia-Soffit Materials illustrated in these four photos: (1) plywood soffit sheets being spot- or tack-nailed with the 2X4 blocking installed previously in order to provide a trim nailing base when brick veneer comes up to the blocking; (2) nail up of 1X6 fascia board with lapped joints used temporarily until board bottom edges can be lined up for the entire house length; (3) now nailing work is completed on the soffit sheets; (4) final step is sawing the fascia boards where they lap over a rafter or truss tail member; saw both boards at the same time in order to give a neat, well-fitted butt joint after removal of the waste piece underneath.

Fascia and Soffits

All along the ends of the truss or rafter tails on the vertical cuts of those members, an exterior trim board called the fascia is applied. At building ends, similar-sized trim boards follow the roof slope and are nailed to the rake rafter.

Fascia and rake boards are chosen for size according to the rafter or truss-chord size and the length of the vertical cut. The object is to have a fascia-rake trim width such that the board extends downward below the rake rafter bottom edge or the bottom edge of the truss-rafter tails' vertical cut by at least a half inch. This downward projection allows insertion of the soffit material.

With the present high cost of clear trim lumber, many home builders use tight-knotted dimension boards for exterior trim—species such as spruce, larch or fir in lieu of the traditional white pine. Seek your supplier's advice on this since he can undoubtedly recommend a local practice. You should again obtain only straight, unwarped pieces because the roof edge boards are easily seen and curves become visually apparent. For this reason apply the fascia trim by tacking before nailing, and visually sighting the board's lower edge before nailing into place.

In this connection, you can obtain tight end-to-end fascia board joints by applying uncut boards with overlapped ends. A 3-to-4 inch overlap. Nail temporarily with overlap directly over a truss-rafter tail. Align lower edges by sighting. Mark with a try-square the cut at the overlap centering the mark on the tail. Use a portable saw running upward to make the cut through both boards and pull out the small waste piece. The same overlapping method can be used at the rake peak vertical cut where your level can be used to obtain an exact vertical mark.

Some home builders try to cut a corner by using the end or rake rafter as trim. This practice makes it difficult to obtain a finished appearance at the cornice or eave-rake corner and is not recommended even though part of this corner may later by concealed by the roof gutter.

The joint of the trim boards at the eave-rake corner varies. These meet directly when truss-rafter tails are left exposed and the neatest joint is a mitered one. With eaves having soffit material, the common practice is to provide a cornice return enclosure. This is most simply handled by first support-blocking, then nailing up of a vertical board or piece of plywood the width of the rake soffit. This is brought down plumb at the eave corner so that its outer surface (facing downslope) is aligned with the wall sheathing. Horizontal blocking from this vertical board to the rake rafter tail then provides a nailing base for extension of the soffit material beyond the end-wall to meet the line of the inner edge of rake trim. Then a wide cornice trim board covers the end opening of the above-soffit space meeting the eave fascia. Rake trim and rake soffit material is then brought down to meet this wide cornice board and the vertical board. It sounds complex, but is not. Observe this

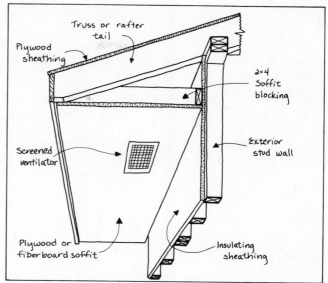

Boxed Eave Overhang and Soffit is probably the most common method for finishing off roof overhangs except in many Western states where rafter tails are left exposed. In some areas its common practice to use special fascia boards pregrooved on one side to receive the edge of the soffit material. At house ends, boxed overhang is usually finished with a cornice return. After application of siding material, the soffit-wall corner is trimmed with a cove mold. Readily available, but not recommended for the first-time owner-builder, are metal soffit-and-vent systems. Joints in the soffit material should occur where lookout blocking will provide a nailing base for both sheet ends. Normal practice is to leave soffit nail heads exposed but with entire soffit receiving a paint finish.

cornice treatment on another home under construction and you'll grasp the procedure easily.

Final trimming of the eaves and rakes is done by applying soffit "material." This word is in quotes because there exists a variety of different materials for this purpose. What may be a common soffit material in one area is practically unheard of in another area. Plywood is commonly used in many areas; fibrous building boards are used in other areas. In suburban metropolitan fringes, aluminum soffit systems incorporating eave ventilators and trim are used. The old-time porch ceiling boards (narrow-grooved T&G 1X6's) are sometimes seen in rural areas. Asbestos-cement boards have been used and there have been some homes built with gypsum drywall board used for soffits.

Almost any of the above can be used successfully. The main object is to get a good permanent base for paint. The first-time owner-builder is apt to find plywood of the exterior type with one good-grade smooth surface easiest to work with. Another excellent material due to similar ease in use is an exterior grade of fiber building board.

Before soffit material can be applied, you'll need horizontal blocking from the truss-rafter tails to the wall sheathing. Short 2X4's are commonly used with their sides nailed to lap the truss-rafter tail sides. At the wall sheath-

Vinyl Plastic Soffit System consists of V-grooved panels in either perforated (for ventilation) or nonperforated types. These panels, produced by Bird & Son, are adaptable for sloping soffits as well as horizontal installations.

Some manufacturers of soffit and siding materials of rigid vinyl offer a full assortment of accessories such as base flashings, starter strips, inside-outside corner units, window-door caps and so on. With a small and simple one-story home, the cost of these materials may be minimal and justified by their easier application. For larger and more complex homes having more corners, different eave heights and greater areas involved, the extra costs of these materials may be considerably more than conventional wood-based sheet materials with wood trim.

ing, first install a 2X4 horizontal strip whose bottom edge is at soffit height. Nail it through the sheathing into studs. This strip then provides a nailing base for the inboard ends of the 2X4 blocking pieces which are toe-nailed to the strip.

A similar 2X4 or 1X4 strip is applied over the gable-end sheathing so that the bottom edge of the strip is even with the bottom edge of the rake rafter. This serves as an inboard nailing base for the rake soffit material.

A somewhat different blocking method is needed for brick veneered exterior walls and it is easier to install before the veneering is done. Instead of the horizontal strip nailed over wall sheathing, short 2X4 blocks about a foot long, depending on roof slope, are nailed in vertical position on edge. Their bottom ends come about 2 inches shy of soffit level and the blocks are nailed to wall top-plates and studs through the sheathing. The 2X4's width should be just over brick width. Then, the horizontal strip is nailed to these blocks and becomes the inner trim board for the soffit. Its bottom edge should be even with the fascia board's bottom edge (see illustrations). When the brick veneer is laid up, it's carried up so that the top course just barely fits behind the inner strip.

The best method is to install soffit ventilators as the soffit material application progresses. The vent units need openings cut in the soffit material and this can be done more accurately and easily on the ground.

Some home builders provide a continuous opening, perhaps 2 or 2-½ inches wide, near the fascia board for soffit ventilation. This strip opening needs to be screened. The idea is sound but often does not work out satisfactorily because of the difficulty in getting the screening to lie evenly and uniformly. A better way to provide a continuous vent opening along the fascia board or slightly inboard from it is by means of a louvered aluminum strip that nails to the soffit blocking before the soffit material is applied. This strip, like most soffit ventilating units, is screened behind the louvers.

15 Roof Flashings and Accessories

A home's roof acts as a giant siphoner of and track for rain water and the water resulting from melting snow. The water does not stand around unless, possibly, on a flat roof. The water, unseen but flowing, will be channeled by the roofing plus certain accessories until the stream reaches ground level where it may enter drainage tiles or simply be dispersed on the surface, away from the building.

During the course of this substantial amount of water travel, some may have the chance to penetrate the roofing surface and leak into the house. Especially vulnerable are such points around various roof penetrations . . . chimneys, soil or vent stacks, and roof ventilators. There are also key points in the roofing material at roof edges, slope changes and valleys. The various types of roof flashing are installed to protect and guard against such leakage.

These considerations are routine when preparing installation of any kind of roofing material. However, the subject is emphasized here for the owner-builder for another reason—the job schedule. Roof flashing must be done before the roofing shingles can be applied. And the roofing shingles are an important milestone in the construction progress because they usually bring the job's progress to the point of being "closed in against the weather" or in the terminology of many builders: under roof. The reasons for reaching this stage as quickly as possible are:

☐ to protect the already completed construction work from extensive damage due to rain, snow and exposure;
☐ to provide cover and enclosure so that further construction work can proceed despite bad or colder weather;
☐ to be able to lock the home and provide a safe-against-theft place for materials delivered and tools left on the job;
☐ to eliminate the job as a play area for the neighborhood's young people.

In order that roof flashing work can proceed without delay or complication, two related tasks should be completed first. They are the installation of stack and vent plumbing lines and their extension through the roof with pipe flashings in place, the installation of heating and fireplace flues whether they be in the form of prefabricated metal or masonry chimneys.

Both of the above roof penetrations can be installed after the roofing shingles are applied. It's a matter of folding back shingle tabs, cutting pipe holes, trimming shingles and then folding them back down and securing with roofing cement. The trouble is that asphalt shingles fold easily enough but they often crack in so doing. A much better job results from fitting the shingles to the roof penetrations when the flashings are already in place.

Chimney and Side Flashings

With prefabricated chimneys, the roof flashing is a component accessory that comes with the chimney and is put into place as the chimney is installed (see illustration in Chapter 14).

With masonry chimneys, flashing is done usually with sheet copper. For general purpose flashings, the 2/100 inch thickness is appropriate. Inquire in advance at local sheet metal shops how they ordinarily handle chimney flashing materials. If possible order relatively small sized sheets to avoid on-job cutting.

For this flashing work, two types of flashing sheets are used—base or flange flashing and lap or counter flashing.

The base flashing sheets must be sized to give proper breadth of coverage on the roof sheathing and proper height on the chimney face (see illustration). You form a right-angle bend in these sheets to fit the chimney-sheathing corner. Using appropriate bronze roofing-type nails which the sheet metal shop can probably supply, the base flashing sheets should be lapped over as you proceed to position them going upslope. Simply tack each sheet once to hold and don't drive nails home. The object is to position temporarily so that counter flashing sheets can be placed. Later, when roofing strips are brought to the chimney, the base flashing sheets will be adjusted to the shingle coursing and at that time permanently nailed to the sheathing.

Counter flashing sheets have a 3/4 to 1 inch margin at the top edges which is bent at right angles to project into horizontal masonry joints. Starting at the bottom portion of the chimney side, position each sheet to leave at least 6 inches from the top of the base flashing to the counter flashing top margin. Mark and cut the bottom portion of the counter flashing to parallel the roof slope, at about 3 inches above it.

To install the counter flashing sheets, rake out the masonry joint mortar using a raking tool or small pointed

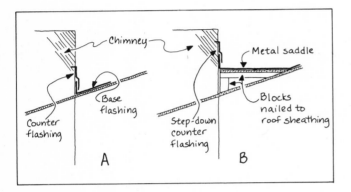

Chimney Flash and Counter-Flash Details for a typical brick chimney meeting a sloping roof. Flashing begins with folding up of roofing felt along face of chimney followed by folded thin-gauge sheets of copper or galvanized steel which are placed first at lower side of chimney and succeeding sheets lapped over preceding ones. These are nailed with roofing nails only at the top roofside edges. Then, roofing shingles are brought up to butt to the chimney face flashing. After completion of shingling, the metal counter-flashing sheets have their top edges folded for insertion into brick joints in step fashion. Joints are raked out to about 1 inch depth and after position of lapped counter-flashing, are filled with caulking.

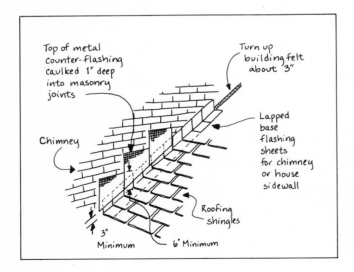

trowel. Rake to about an inch depth but only for a horizontal distance the same as that of the counter flashing sheet. Place the sheet's bent margin into the raked-out joint, press the margin downward, and fill the joint again with caulking compound.

The flash-counterflash method can also be used on the lower side of the chimney (no staggering of the flashing sheets). The same method can be used on the chimney's high side if the latter is no more than 30 inches wide, according to HUD-MPS's. Wider chimneys will require a roof saddle. This is supplementary blocking up above the roof sheathing with additional small pieces of sheathing cut to fit the saddle (see illustration). The blocking is built something like a miniature gable from the main roof slope with a ridge running to the central point of the chimney face. From this point, step flashing down each side of the slope is handled in the same manner as the step flashing on the main-slope chimney sides.

At points where a roof surface meets a house side-wall, as with a split-level home or two-story with attached garage, flashing sheets should be installed at the juncture. The base flash method can be done here in much the same way that the chimney sides were flashed except that base flashing sheets can also be nailed to side-wall sheathing. No counter flashing is needed since the house siding will come down over the base sheets.

While the door and window heads are not part of the roof, installation of roof flashing work is a good time for the owner-builder to make a check of his window-door head situation if these units are already installed. Narrow strips of base flashing material should be applied along the top edges of doors and windows. If these units have drip caps, the flashing need extend just sufficiently to cover the top of the drip cap. Flashing at these points helps prevent infiltration of wind-driven moisture. If the doors and windows have not yet been installed in the openings, tack the strips up. Strips should be about 6 inches wide.

For window-door head flashing and also for house side flashing where masonry mortar is not involved, the flashing material can be galvanized metal in a 26 or 28 gauge thickness.

Other Roof Flashings

With respect to flashing of soil and vent pipes that penetrate the roof, check with your plumbing subcontractor. He should supply these pipe flashings at time the pipes are installed. The type of flashing used for this purpose is a preformed flashing, usually of lead, which fits over the projecting pipe end. It has an integral flange that lies flat on the roof sheathing. The upper part of the flashing folds down into the interior of the pipe or the flashing may be designed for a tight tension fit into the slip-over portion that surrounds the pipe.

If you're handling the rough plumbing work yourself, be certain that your pipe supplier furnishes the preformed stack and vent flashings at the time he furnishes the rough-in pipe.

Hips and ridges are dividing points in roof water flow and are not subject to serious leakage except possibly on unusually low-sloped roofs. Common roofing practice is simply to provide a self-covering of the top-course shingle edges (see illustration in Chapter 16).

Valleys, being water collectors, do need added protection of flashings. Galvanized metal sheets can be used for open valleys or aluminum sheets in the .019 or .020 inch thickness. Used in conjunction with wood shingle or shake roofs, the valley flashings should be 24 inches wide for low roof slopes (less than 4-in-12 slope), 18 inches wide for medium slopes (up to 7-in-12) and 12 inches wide for steeper slopes.

For open valley wood shingling, the shingles are kept back from the point of the valley so there are 4 inches or more near the slope bottom between the shingle edges along each side of the valley. The metal flashing is left exposed in this open area. A closed valley may also be used and metal flashing sheets can be interlaced across the valley with the shingle courses. Each valley shingle must have its lower edge trimmed to meet the shingle edges on the opposite side of the valley.

With asphalt shingle roofs the practice differs considerably. Increasingly common is the strip-shingle interwoven method. The flashing material consists of a 36 inch wide roll of 55 pound mineral-surface roofing; a strip is laid down the valley, mineral surface down. Then, as the strip asphalt shingles are laid, they are permitted to carry across the valley in alternating directions weaving the strips together (see illustration in next chapter).

Asphalt shingle valleys may also be open or closed types and the practice is to use 36 inch wide roll roofing with closed valley shingles, and apply two thicknesses of 85 pound mineral-surfaced roofing for open valleys—first an 18 inch wide strip laid mineral surface down, followed by a 36 inch wide top strip with mineral surface up.

Roofs having 5-in-12 or steeper slopes don't usually have roof edge problems due to moisture backup or ice damming. The flow of moisture and water off the roof is fast enough to avoid such problems. The only flashing, if it can be called that, is conventionally provided by the use of shingle starter strips. However, in many areas metal roof edge flashing strips are provided because they neatly trim the edges of the roof sheathing and also furnish a sharp drip edge that keeps moisture drips dropping within the gutter instead of backing up under the sheathing.

For 4-in-12 or lower roof slopes, these metal edging strips should be installed. The preformed strips are available at any sheet metal shop either in galvanized or aluminum. They come in 10 feet lengths and local practices vary as to whether they should have lapped or butted joints. If you butt them to have a bit neater appearance, place another small piece of metal over the joint before applying the shingle starter strip.

Keep the metal edging about a quarter or half inch away

Assorted Residential Ventilators for attic and crawl space airing include in the group at the left (top to bottom): brick-size vent, soffit grille, round siding or soffit vents and square-edged block size vent. At right on top, a typical gable-louver vent and a roof-cap vent for hipped roof homes available with or without an electric exhaust fan. All of these as well as other types are produced by Leigh Products Company.

from the face of the fascia board. Good practice here calls for a 1X2 wood strip back here at the edge projection if interior type plywood is being used for roof sheathing or in areas subject to wind-driven rains.

Mentioned earlier were eave soffit vents. Proper circulation of air through the attic prevents moisture condensation in the attic and possible damage to structure and insulation. But venting the eaves alone is not sufficient. Warm air circulates upward and vent openings somewhere near the top of the attic space should have sufficient free-opening area to match that of the eave soffit vents.

Upper roof vents can be any of several types or a combination of types needed to have the desired area for vent openings. The general rule in meeting most code requirements is for a free ventilating area (open area only, not counting louver or support space) that is 1/300 of the horizontal ceiling area below the attic or structural space. Through circulation must also be provided for porch spaces and false gable spaces. Half of the free ventilating area must be near the top of the ventilated space at least 3 feet above the level of the soffit or cornice vents that provide the other half.

In a gabled house, the most common types of vent units are aluminum or wood louvered gable-end vents and aluminum soffit vents. In a hipped roof, the soffit vents match up with a series of roof dome vents mounted near the ridge and on the rear side of the home. Another very effective type of high level ventilator is a continuous aluminum ridge vent which saddles to the roof peak and may be used instead of the gable-end or roof dome vent units. Yet another possibility for homes not equipped with air conditioning but in warm climate areas are electric roof-vent units whose circular bladed fans can assist the air circulation through the attic space and help maintain a cooler home interior.

Discuss soffit-roof ventilators with your supplier by inquiring about local practices and reports back from other customers on successes or failures. Aluminum vents of various types are quite easy to nail to the framing of prepared openings. Yet, an owner-builder should look twice at aluminum combined soffit-and-ventilator materials. Aluminum materials of this type are usually formed from thin-gauged sheets and they need careful handling to avoid accidental bends and damage.

All ventilator units installed on the roof or in gable-ends should be designed to shed rain and snow, not permitting the penetration of either to the interior. In addition, the free-opening area must be screened to protect against entrance by bugs, bats, rodents, squirrels and similar invaders.

Roof ventilation is also of importance to homes exposed to continuous sunshine and equipped with air conditioning. The vented circulation helps prevent extreme heat buildup within the attic space and thereby tends to reduce the air-conditioning load.

When installing roof or gable-end ventilators, the process is simply one of nailing the flanges down to the framing members earlier provided to prepare the opening. Roof vent units are furnished in a self-flashing design so that no flashings need be added. In many cases, roof vent units need no special framing preparation and will simply fit into openings cut in the roof sheathing between framing members. Check this detail in the vent manufacturer's literature and provide blocking if needed.

Gable-end ventilators usually have house siding butted to them. Allow a slight gap here for caulking as explained in Chapter 19.

Roof Drainage System

Considered at this point because of its obvious relation to roof water collection and disposal, eave gutters and downspouts should not be installed on the home until after the exterior work is entirely completed—all roofing, siding, exterior painting.

Through most of the country sheet metal guttering and downspouts are the commonly used material. Wood gutters are used to limited extent in some western states. Galvanized sheets are used to preform the gutters and downspouts but in recent years there's been a rapid growth in the use of aluminum. And, to a lesser extent, of vinyl plastic roof drainage systems.

Metal gutters should be installed with a slight pitch along the lengths leading to downspouts. The half-round shape of metal gutter is now obsolete, giving way to the box or "O-G" shape of gutter with a high straight back and flat bed. Gutter hanging is usually done by means of metal straps nailed to roof sheathing under first-course roof

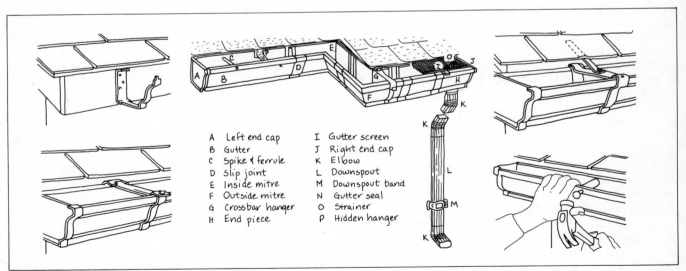

A	Left end cap
B	Gutter
C	Spike & ferrule
D	Slip joint
E	Inside mitre
F	Outside mitre
G	Crossbar hanger
H	End piece
I	Gutter screen
J	Right end cap
K	Elbow
L	Downspout
M	Downspout band
N	Gutter seal
O	Strainer
P	Hidden hanger

Packaged Roof Drainage System, with various components and parts identified in the center portion of this sketch, is offered by several aluminum fabricating companies including the Billy Penn Company and Crown Aluminum Company, from whose brochures these items were sketched. Alternative methods of mounting gutters on roof fascia are shown in the side sketches. At left top, a hanger support that fastens directly to the fascia and has a lock-bar (below) which holds the gutter firmly. At top right, a gutter hanger with extension strap that nails to roof sheathing under the shingles. Bottom right, long spike and ferrule method of fastening to the fascia.

shingles. In many areas this traditional method has been replaced by the use of narrow gutter-width tubes through which long spikes are driven through fascia boards and into truss-rafter tail ends. With the newer aluminum and plastic gutter systems, specialized types of hangers may be used (see illustration).

Don't mix types of metal gutters. Use all accessories and fasteners of the same type of metal. The exception is apt to be with the long spikes, which will probably be available only in galvanized.

Downspouts are usually installed at building corners and the rectangular cross-section shape is usually used. The number of downspouts to properly serve the roof is calculated at the rate of 1 square inch of downspout cross-sectional area for each 100 square feet of roof surface. Use smaller, more numerous cross-sectional areas if you're in a locality with a high intensity of rainfall.

In purchasing roof drainage materials, shop different suppliers to find out just what they will supply. In some cases, a supplier will take your house plans or a roof layout sketch and do all or most of the fabricating work in his shop. In other cases, the system he's selling may be complete with a full range of accessory devices that assist in making on-the-job connections. Sears and Wards have long supplied roof drainage products and in some areas now offer an installation service as well. Shop. You may save both working time and money.

In some areas of the country, roof gutters and downspouts are entirely omitted from many homes. In such areas, it's common practice to furnish some sort of roof edge diversion at house entrance points to avoid eave dripping on stoops and porches. HUD-MPS's call for guttering when the following conditions apply: roof overhangs are less than 12 inches for a one-story home and 24 inches for a two-story; or, the home is located in an area characterized by excessive soil erosion or expansion factors. Aside from these factors, gutterless roof eaves with appropriate overhangs are practical alternatives for homes sited in natural surroundings without specific landscaping, such as vacation or leisure homes.

16 Asphalt Shingle Roofing

The supplier who furnished your framing components, sheathing, and other lumber needs may not be just the right one from whom to buy your roofing shingles. Not if you like to be selective with respect to color, texture, and some of the new shingle looks. At the least inquire about the shingles he stocks and what lines can be ordered. Often, a components producer may handle only one roofing manufacturer's product and perhaps not all weights or all colors in a given weight. The standard quality level for most residential work has been in the range of 210-to-240 pounds per hundred square feet, or per "square" as that area is referred to in roofing circles. In recent years, there's been a steady growth in the use of double-layer strip shingles that give a more textured roof appearance. When surfaced with jumbo mineral granules, these shingles may run to 350 pounds per square.

Another growing trend in the last decade has been more widespread use of fire-resistant shingles. Some building codes require shingles to meet Class A, B or C Standards of Underwriters Laboratories. More fire resistance is provided by the Class A shingles, which are geared to urban needs. Heavier weight shingles and those meeting fire-resistance classifications will be higher-priced as might be expected.

Key Considerations

Because of their good resistance to wind, many homebuilders choose a self-sealing strip asphalt shingle. This is a shingle in which short strips of factory-applied adhesive are positioned in a row to meet the underside of the shingle tabs of the strip above. The shingle weight, with the softening adhesive under the sun, makes a firm connection to keep the shingle tabs from blowing up during periods of high winds. For most normal-sloped roofs of 4-in-12 slope or steeper, strip shingles with self-sealing tabs are recommended. With lower pitches, ordinary nonsealing shingle tabs can be cemented down.

The amount of shingle measuring from the bottom of its butt edge upslope to the next overlapping butt edge is called "shingle exposure." What this distance should be is specified by the manufacturer. Follow manufacturer instructions on exposure so that seal-tab strips occur at the proper points.

Asphalt shingles are available in a wide range of weights, colors and patterns. Shingle lines vary from one manufacturer to another. However, the great bulk of shingles sold are of the strip type, approximately 12 inches wide by 36 inches long with three foot-wide shingle tabs which are separated by real slots or embossed slot simulations. The strip shingles are usually designed for 5 inch exposure and a 2 inch headlap meaning that at any given point in the roof surfacing, there are at least two shingle thicknesses.

Choice in design and appearance of strip shingles has broadened in recent years. Color variations and color blends have expanded. Double-layering and extra felt weights have brought thicker shingle butts. Irregular cutting of the butts has given some shingle designs a random appearance which lends texture to the roofing surface.

Preparation for Roofing

Materials

At the time of purchasing roof shingles, you will have determined your need for building felt underlayment. This is a black asphalt-impregnated 15 pound felt paper. Build-

---

Asphalt Shingle Roofs predominate on single-family homes throughout the country. They're not only the least expensive but also the easiest to apply. Shown here are two completed homes. At the top is a roof using "Timberline" multi-layer made by GAF Corporation, with a rustic appearance and built-in fire resistant properties. Below, bold-textured heavyweight "Architect 70" shingles produced by Bird & Son providing wind resistance and a Class C fire safety rating. Both types employ seal adhesive strips which help seal down the shingle tabs using the heat of the sun once they've been installed.

ing codes and HUD-MPS's indicate no underlayment is needed for double-coverage shingles on 7-in-12 or steeper slopes or for triple coverage shingles on 4-in-12 slopes or steeper. Roofing felt comes in rolls and when applied should have 6 inch end-laps and a head-lap along long edges of 2-to-3 inches. Many felt papers have white stripes for indicating laps and these are also a help in coursing the shingles.

Shingles come in bundles and it's common practice in many areas for the delivery to be unloaded directly to the roof deck. If this is done, be sure the bundles are distributed around in the upper portions of the roof deck with no concentration of load in any given area. Check the bundles or package covers for any special manufacturer instructions. When shingles are stacked in a ground pile, see that they're on a flat wood base clear of ground contact, and it's a good idea to keep them covered.

Most asphalt roofing shingles are nailed into place with corrosion-resistant nails having heads of 3/8 inch or larger, and 11 or 12 gauge shanks. A few building codes may specify that shingle nails having deformed, barbed or threaded shanks be used. Inquire of your roofing supplier about suitable nails for your job.

Special Note. If your home is being built with the western-style exposed rafter tails and underside of roof sheathing, you will have to exercise some care to prevent nail penetration. The best way safeguard is to use a slightly thicker plywood roof sheathing.

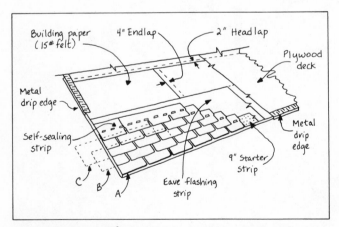

Starting An Asphalt Shingle Roof, begin with application of strips of 15 pound roofing felt. Nail in place galvanized metal roof edging. Next comes the starting strip, a piece of nonmineral-surface roll roofing which runs along the eave edge. First full course of 3-tab shingle strip is then laid at the corner position (A). Roofing nails are applied four per shingle, one just above each tab slot (where it will be covered by the shingle above) and one at each end of the strip (also up sufficiently for concealment by the next shingle). Lay another shingle or two in the bottom course, then begin the second course. Position (B) indicates where shingle of a full strip would come to, but this overhanging portion is cut off before the shingle is placed. Same applies for the third course and position (C).

If your home has a low-slope roof that's less than 4-in-12 but not under 2-in-12, you can still obtain a good asphalt shingle job by using a double-layer coverage of felt underlay and then cementing down the shingles. You start with a 19 inch wide felt strip along the eaves and follow with the 36 inch wide felt strips each lapped 19 inch over the previous layer in order to have 17 inch exposure and assurance at all points that there will be two felt layers.

When applying the roofing felt in areas where there is the annual possibility of roof moisture freezing along the eaves, a good practice to follow and one that is required by some building codes is:

(1) Apply the underlayment felt in a continuous uniform coating of plastic asphaltic cement using a trowel to spread at the rate of about 2 gallons per square.
(2) This cementing goes on top of the starter layer before the full-width felt is applied and from this point on is used between felt layers and carried on up the roof slope to a point that's at least 2 feet inside the interior face of the exterior wall (projected upward).

Installation Guidelines

Your tool and equipment needs for applying asphalt shingles are quite simple: ladders or a simple mobile platform for getting the first few lower courses applied (the remaining work is done from the roof); hammer; roofing nails in your carpenter's pocketed apron; and a chalk-line to snap straight lines.

If your building felt underlayment application is done carefully at the beginning of each felt strip, the felt's white guidelines should be all that's needed to keep the coursing on pure horizontal lines. But a chalkline can come in handy for vertical alignment checks, something that must be particularly watched when shingling hips and valleys.

Some brands of shingles have a notch-type arrangement at the side edges to assist with proper alignment. This is particularly desirable in shingles having irregular butt lines.

Be sure that you have at least a gallon of asphalt roofing cement and a trowel for applying it even though no cementing down of underlayment felt is going to be done. You'll need the cement for seal-down of shingle tabs along roof rake edges and at valleys, hips and ridges. You will also discover that very often the shingle tabs don't lie as flat as you'd like them to. Although many of these are apt to settle down with a little time and sunshine, the cement can come in handy in the meantime.

Usual practice is to start with a starter course along the eave edge. The butt edges of the two overlapped thicknesses project outward at both eave and rake by about 3/8 inch. The top starter course should have its tabs staggered rather than directly over the bottom starter strip. Some roofers remove tabs from the starter bottom strips so that seal-down points are close to the eaves.

Nailing requirements as spelled out in building codes or

Fastener Details for Roof Coverings

FASTENER SPECIFICATIONS

ROOF COVERING MATERIAL	Fastener[2],[3] Style	Min. O.D. Crown	O.D. Leg[1] Lengths		Spacing Specifications[4]
Base Sheet (Roofing Felt)	12 ga. Roofing Nail		7/8	7/8	All metal discs placed and stapled or nailed 12 inches on center
	16 ga. Staple	7/16	3/4		
Composition Shingles	12 ga. 3/8" HD Roofing Nail		1-1/4	1-1/4	(4) Nails or staples per each 36" section of shingle
	16 ga. Staple	3/4	1		
	16 ga. Staple	7/16	1-1/4		(6) Staples per each 36" section of shingle
Composition Ridge, Hip, Caps	12 ga. 3/8" HD Roofing Nail		1-1/4	1-1/4	A minimum of (4) nails or staples are required for ridge capping
	16 ga. Staple	3/4	1		
	16 ga. Staple	7/16	1-1/4		
Wood Shingles	.076 Shingle Nail		1-1/4	1-1/4	16" and 18" Shingle—(2) fasteners per shingle
	.080 T Nail	—	1-1/4		
	16 ga. Staple	7/16	1-1/4		
	.080 Shingle Nail		1-1/2	1-1/2	24" Shingle—(2) fasteners per shingle
	.080 T Nail	—	1-1/2		
	16 ga. Staple	7/16	1-1/2		
Wood Shakes	.0915—Shingle Nail		2	2	(2) Nails or staples per each shake
	.0915 to .099 T Nail		2	2	
	16 ga. Staple	7/16	2		

1. Shingles and shakes attached to roof sheathing having the underside of the sheathing exposed to visual view may be attached in these locations with nails or staples having shorter lengths than specified so as not to penetrate the exposed side of the sheathing.
2. All nails and staples shall be rust-resistant (galvanized-zinc or aluminum).
3. Nails may have T-heads, clipped round heads or standard heads.
4. Roof coverings shall be fastened in an approved manner.

HUD-MPS's specify minimum nailing methods. You may find detailed instructions in the shingle carton or printed on it. Usually there is one nail on each end and one above each slot. In high-wind areas the Minimum Property Standards specify six nails per strip. Nails should be galvanized, large-head roofing nails, at least 3/4 inch long. When using self-sealing strip shingles, be sure your nailing avoids going into the adhesive strips or above the line of them.

After application of the starter course, the subsequent courses require careful alignment in order to maintain uniform shingle exposure and parallel butt lines. Roofer's

Nailing Specifications for various types of roof covering materials are given in this handy chart adapted from a similar one that appears in the One- and Two-Family Dwelling Code. Appropriate types-sizes of nails are given for the coverings listed in the left column and the number or spacing of nails is shown in the right column.

hammers often contain a small device or mark for measuring and checking exposure distance as you go along.

Probably the most common practice used by experienced roofers to progress across with ease across a roof surface when applying shingles is the following. Begin in a lower outer corner of the roof and do not complete the bottom courses, or even run them halfway, before starting at the roof rake or hip with the 3rd, 4th, 5th and 6th course. Maintain shingle strip application running diagonally at roughly a 60° angle with the rake and 30° angle with the eave. Felt underlayment is often simultaneously done with several rolls started at the rake and unrolled just ahead of the shingling. Shingles are laid out in a diagonal line just above the

point where nailing is being done so the shingler can just slide the strips into position without lifting them (see illustrations).

If open valleys are being used, the metal valley flashing may already be in place at roof valleys, or if using mineral-surfaced roll roofing it may be applied as flashing for the valleys just prior to shingling. Where the roll roofing is of a nonmatching color with the shingles, roof appearance and uniformity is helped by use of the interwoven method of

Asphalt Shingling Technique demonstrated: (1) roofing felt has been placed using care to maintain the parallelness of the felt's regular white lines with the eave edge; starter strip and first shingle course shown. Working with a hammer-type tacker (2), building felt is quickly stapled down. After starting shingles in a lower roof corner, work proceeds on the diagonal (3). This is easier for handling shingles and the felt's white lines serve as a constant guide for keeping shingle strips properly positioned. Note that the shingler

works with an adequate supply of loose shingles kept at hand by his helper. At the roof edge (4), a shingle strip is being measured for cutting with the back side up to avoid adhesion of tab seals and it will be cut using a regular utility-type blade-knife. Nailing is done (5) with a shingle hatchet; note shingler holds the nail knuckles down and with his thumb-nail. In the finished roof (6), the multi-ply shingles have a highly attractive thick-butt textured appearance.

applying shingle strips across the valley, a procedure sometimes called "lacing" (see illustration).

When nailing, position the next strip at the edge of the preceding one and place the first nail nearest the shingle just laid and nail in succession across the shingle.

In applying shingles for open valleys, the valley width varies and the following practice is quite common. At the top of the valley, provide a half-tab's width or 6 inches between shingle edges across the valley. Then, increase the open valley width between edges as it descends to the eaves by about 1/8 inch per lineal foot of valley. Measure equally on each side of the valley center. Make marks top and bottom, then snap a chalk line to the marks so you have a shingle edge line down both sides of the valley.

Conventional roofing practice on ridges and hips is to lay shingles up to the point of slope change. Then apply hip-ridge single shingles or cut single tabs from strip shingles (1/3 of a 3-tab shingle strip) and apply along the ridge or hip. Lap these single units and apply in one direction only on ridges as well as hips. Amount of lap is same as the regular shingle exposure and all nails are kept concealed (see illustration). It's helpful if your single units are pre-formed before being applied. Bend them with your hands into a rounded shape but be careful not to break them (slight warming helps). Hip or ridge shingles can also be helped by judicious use of roofing cement.

In fact, the shingle edges wherever they occur at valleys, ridges, hips, roof rakes and dormers are particularly subject to lifting. Cementing the tabs down at these points is routinely done by some roofers. But use care with the asphaltic roofing cements. Spills and drips on the finished shingles may turn into unsightly spots because they're hard to remove fully even with the best of solvents.

Steeper Slopes

On one-and-a-half story homes of expansion-attic or Cape Cod styles, the usual roof slopes of 10-in-12 and 12-in-12 pose no special problem for the owner-builder with respect to the shingles themselves. Open valleys are seldom used, giving way to closed or woven valley shingling. However, you may need more cementing down. Normal application is suitable for roof slopes up to about 21-in-12 slopes. Beyond that, steep slopes such as those encountered

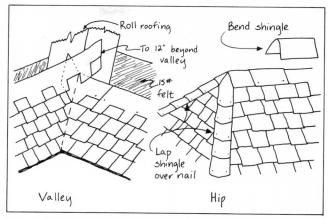

Shingling Hips and Valleys takes some special adaptation. At left in this sketch is method of interleaving asphalt shingle strips across a valley. In some areas, this is called a woven valley. Note than an 3-foot wide strip of roll roofing is placed over the building felt before shingles are positioned to serve as valley flashing. At the right, lapping of single shingles to form a water-shedding cover for the juncture of roof shingles at hips and ridges.

in the lower portions of gambrel and mansard roofs should have extra cementing of the shingle tabs since the effectiveness of the self-sealing strips is less on these steep pitches.

Follow the shingle manufacturer's instructions for steep slope application. This may involve applying an inch-round spot of cement per shingle strip in addition to the self-seal strips.

The one problem that increases with steeper roof slopes is personal safety. Slipping and serious subsequent falls become a hazard that should be specifically dealt with. Use soft-soled shoes. Provide suitable wood foothold members temporarily nailed in place. Use angled small platforms on which to rest loose shingles ready for nailing. A not-bad idea seen on one owner-built Cape Cod was a ladder whose top had blocking attached to fit over the ridge. And not far from the ladder there was also a safety rope over the ridge, fastened to the wall below the other side.

If your home has a steep roof slope, it would be worthwhile for you to observe how roofers move about such a roof before beginning your own shingle application work.

17 Wood Shingles and Shakes

Application may be to solid sheathing such as plywood as provided for asphalt shingles. Or, wood shingles and shakes may be applied to spaced sheathing boards. The spaced-board method calls for the use of square-edge 1X4's or 1X6's. The openings are about 4 inches and should be considered in the light of shingle or shake exposure. The boards should be laid to insure parallel eaves so that shingle coursing can be done with all nail rows penetrating the

sheathing. Also note that warped, twisted boards are unsuited as a shingle base. If you can't find suitable board stock, stick with the simpler and faster-to-apply plywood sheathing since savings by the spaced-board method are not likely to be very significant on a single home.

Selection Factors, Tools

Wood shingles and shakes are produced to meet various grading requirements or standards. Just as lumber and plywood are graded according to strength or quality, so shingles and shakes meet certain standards of suitability for roofing and siding applications.

Most producers of singles conform to the standards

False Mansard Roof with Shakes is really an attractive method of siding the second floor of a two-story home. A sloping framework is first attached to exterior wall sheathing and studs. Plywood sheathing covers the sloping frame and wood shakes are applied as they would be to any sidewall. Actual roofing on this home is of built-up type on a flat deck.

established by the Red Cedar Shingle & Shake Bureau and the packages or bundles from these producers come with labels indicating compliance with the grading rules. The names "Certigrade" for shingles and "Certigroove" for standard shakes identify the graded product while "Certisplit" is used in conjunction with handsplit shakes. The latter are the thick-butted heavy-textured shakes. The foregoing grade names are supplemented by numbers to indicate quality level. These grading practices are adhered to by most western producers in connection with Western Red Cedar lumber. In certain other areas, an owner-builder may encounter cedar shingles cut from other species without grade or identification labelling.

The red cedar grades of shingles are No. 1 Blue Label, Red Label, and No. 3 Black Label. For residential work, your local supplier may carry only a single grade and that's likely to be the No. 1. The standard shakes come only in No. 1 grade. Normal shingles are bundled in 16, 18 and 24 inch lengths with random widths. The length to use depends on the exposure or amount of each shingle not covered by other shingles. And the correct exposure to use depends on roof slope with quality of shingle. Shown are the recommended exposures:

No. 1 GRADE SHINGLES

Slope	16 in.	18 in.	24 in.
4-in-12 or steeper	5 in.	5-½ in.	7-½ in.
3-in-12 to 4-in-12	3-3/4 in.	4-1/4 in.	5-3/4 in.

Wood shingles are normally packed so that four bundles will cover a square of roofing surface. Your shingle supplier will easily calculate your roof surface area from your working drawings and estimate your requirements. He will probably add a fraction more for lower-pitched roofs because of reduced exposures. And he'll add a square for every hundred lineal feet of hips or valleys.

A relatively recent development in cedar shingles and shakes is the availability of a treatment that furnishes sufficient fire-retardant properties so that the shingles or shakes so treated can gain a Class C rating by Underwriters Laboratories. If these same treated shingles or shakes are applied with a special plastic-coated steel foil underlayment (furnished by the shingle-shake manufacturer) over 1/2 inch regular plywood sheathing, the resulting installation can earn a Class B fire-resistance rating.

The very heavy butt and coarsely split shakes that result from hand splitting are beautiful to behold on a home's roof. The 1-1/4-to-1-1/2 inch thick butts represent a lot of lumber and are a costly roof surfacing in comparison to other materials. On typical residential roofs in most areas of the country, handsplit shakes will cost between three and five times as much as asphalt strip shingles.

The handsplit shakes are not especially difficult to apply, their procedure being quite similar to that used with ordinary cedar shingles. For owner-builders desiring to use

Maximum Recommended Weather Exposure For Wood Shingles and Shakes

Shingle or Shake Type	Maximum Roof Exposure	Maximum Wall Exposure **
16" Shingles	5" *	7-½"
18" Shingles	5-½" *	8-½"
24" Shingles	7-½" *	11-½"
18" Resawn Shakes	7-½"	8-½"
24" Tapersplit Shakes	10"	11-½"
18" Straight-Split Shakes	7-½"	8-½"
24" Straight-Split Shakes	10"	11-½"

*Reduce weather exposures on low roof slopes, or if shingle grade other than No. 1 is used.
**Assumes single-coursing application.
SOURCE: Red Cedar Shingle and Handsplit Shake Bureau

How Much Weather Exposure to provide with wood shingles and shakes is given in this chart. The amount of exposure is the measurement from one shingle butt to another in the next course above or below. As can be seen in the chart, longer shingles and shakes can be laid with great amounts of weather exposure.

the handsplits, a copy of the 32-page CertiSplit Manual should be obtained from the Bureau for detailed guidance in application procedures.

Shingling Tools

Nails used for wood shingles vary according to shingle length and the type of application. For new home construction, the common sizes are 1-1/4 inch length 3d nails for 16 and 18 inch shingles and 1-1/2 inch length 4d nails for 24 inch shingles (see chart). Nails should be rust-resistant; commonly available types are zinc-coated (galvanized) and aluminum. Your supplier will indicate the approximate quantity needed.

Regular shinglers use a shingler's hatchet which has both a sharpened cutting edge and a sharpened heel useful in shaving or splitting shingles to desired widths. The hammering end of the hatchet has a rough corrugated finish. Shinglers commonly use two or three strokes to drive a nail, depending somewhat on the rigidity of the roof sheathing. One stroke taps the nail while holding with the fingers. Then a full drive stroke sometimes gets the nail home, but a finishing stroke may be needed. The shingler develops a certain rhythm in a repetitive pattern of placing the shingle, tap nail, drive, tap nail, drive, reach for new shingle, place, and so on.

A straight-edged board, 1X4 or 1X6 about 8 feet long, is needed for temporary nailing into position to obtain even butt alignment (see illustration).

On steeper pitched roofs, shingle-holding platforms are useful to preventing sliding of loose shingles. And plank

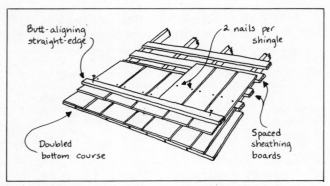

Applying Wood Shingles in the western manner with the use of spaced-out sheathing boards. Note doubled bottom starting course. Shingles are nailed so next course up will cover nail heads by at least 3/4 inch. Nails are placed no nearer shingle edges than 3/4 inch and no matter how wide a shingle is (they come in random widths), only two nails per shingle are used. For alignment of butts, use a temporary straight-edge board tack-nailed parallel to butts of previously laid shingles.

scaffold members hung or suspended from ridge fastenings will provide foothold walkways, moving them from time to time as the shingling proceeds.

Application Procedures

As with asphalt shingles, the start is made with a double layer at the bottom or eave course and beginning in a roof corner. Butts of both shingles should project about a half inch over the sheathing or fascia edge.

Apply shingles side-by-side using random widths. With the following course, there's no special position for the shingle joints except the observing of a minimum 1-1/2 inch distance horizontally from the joints in the course below.

You soon get used to looking slightly ahead and choosing the width shingle that's about right and discarding temporarily a shingle that may cause a spacing problem (too close) for the joint or two ahead.

Use the straight-edged board for tacking to the roof at various points for helping keep butts aligned. Use care in trimming shingles around roof penetrations such as pipes or chimneys, or along hip and valley lines. Straight trim edges are desired. The slight opening where hip or closed-valley shingles meet should be kept to a uniform 1/8 or 3/16 inch. Avoid fitting a trimmed shingle tight to the flashing, to each other or to the faces of house siding.

It appears that the practice with wood shingles and shakes is for using a somewhat narrower open valley than what is commonly provided on asphalt shingle roofs as mentioned in the previous chapter. For wood shingles, the open valley is kept to about 4 inches wide at the base of the valley slope on lower-sloped roofs. On steep slopes, closed valleys are generally used.

Hips and ridges should be formed using shingles of uniform width and preferably laid with the so-called "Boston" hip. This is a simple practice of alternating the cap shingle overlap from one side of the hip or ridge to the other side with succeeding cap courses. Exposure of cap shingles should be the same as that used with field shingles. Reputed but never seen are factory-assembled hip/ridge shingle units. Supposedly they save some time. They should, because this can be a painstakingly slow job.

Adjacent shingles are nailed up with just a slight space between them of about 1/8 to 1/4 inch. Use just two nails per shingle, no more. Keep nails about 3/4 inch from shingle sides and about 1-1/2 inch above the butt line of the course to follow.

Underlayment building felt is generally not used with wood shingles but there may be a requirement included in some building codes for such underlayment to protect eaves where ice formations can be expected.

18 Doors and Windows

The openings in a home for light, air and passage have taken on a number of new angles and twists in recent years. All for the better.

It used to be not very long ago that a window or a door was something an experienced trim carpenter horsed around with for a half day to a day. And that doesn't mean loafing around. It was careful trial-and-error work in which basic procedures in drilling, chiseling, sawing, planing, shingle-wedging, balancing, screw-drivering and maybe some sand-papering were involved. Today, it's mostly a level-plumb, hammer-and-nail job done in 1/10 the time using factory precision-hung door and window units that will give an owner-builder as little difficulty in installing as they do an experienced carpenter.

But more than installation ease, doors and windows have taken on new properties such as the use of insulating glass and thermal exterior door cores that eliminate the twice-annual chore of changing storm windows and screens and the irritating maintenance headaches of keeping them in shape. And in the course of so doing, the windows have become better sealed and easier to operate while the doors have been precision-engineered to eliminate drafts and infiltration, resulting in tighter homes that conserve their use of today's higher priced fuels for heating and cooling.

The practice of preinstalling windows and exterior doors in shop-fabricated exterior wall panels varies from one area to another and from one components fabricator to another. Some do, others don't. As a general rule, the components

Prehung Thermal Entrance Doors are the first choice of most professional home builders. Shown here are a few of the many designs in single-and-double doors produced by the Pease Company, a pioneer firm in developing foam-core steel door construction with magnetic weatherstripping and an adjustable sill. At left, the firm's new factory prefinished doors which come in both bright contemporary colors and more traditional shades. In center and right photos, door units with and without architectural door lights (windows within the door itself).

Prehung Doors Before Installation should keep wrapping in place and be stored flat in an out-of-the-way place. This is a careless way to handle a door, leaving it in an open garage subject to accident or other damage.

fabricator who specializes in fabricating panels for custom home plans or who supplies rough components only, does not preinstall windows or doors.

Even with a components fabricator who will preinstall windows or doors, the choice of type or style and accessories may be limited. Fabricators like to stick pretty much with one window manufacturer's line and just a limited range of units in that company's line. So in talking fabricated wall panels with a supplier, talk windows, too, and find out what choices you have in preinstalled units. And the same applies with prehung entrance doors.

Home Entrance Doors

Every home's front entrance deserves extra attention because this is the part of a home visitors first see and because the entrance design can, if well-handled, add to a home's value and resalability.

Front entrance doors are different in some respects from just plain exterior doors because of attention to details such as the various styles of door caps, the supplementation of entrance foyer daylighting with door sidelight panels, the use of transom sash with some designs and the application of moldings to the door face, plus reeded or fluted pilaster trims at the jambs.

Home security should also be considered in connection with entrance doors. Discussed in more detail in Chapter 43, entrance door security can be provided by proper choice of door hardware. But door style plays a part in the determination, too. With increased use of thermal or insulated doors and the elimination of storm doors at front entrances, it becomes more desirable to have visibility to view visitors before unlocking and opening the entrance doors. At front entrances, this can be accomplished by sidelight panels, by choosing a door style that includes one

or more light inserts in the door, or by use of a small, wide-angle built-in door viewer.

Traditionally, wood doors have been almost universally used in homes, and steel or metal-clad doors used in non-residential buildings because of their greater resistance to fire hazards. However in recent years, largely through the efforts of the Pease Company in its pioneerings of the thermal door concept with its "Ever-Strait" engineered door unit, steel-clad insulating-core entrance doors are in widespread use today. These complete, prehung entrance units in a broad selection of styles and some in completely prefinished form, are now being produced by a number of different manufacturers. The thermal entrance door is now being used front and rear in the bulk of the country's moderate-cost and luxury homes.

The engineered doors are designed first to be free of what was once the principal cause of door replacements in new homes—warps or twists that resulted in improper closure plus air infiltration. The newer thermal door frames provide a thermal break between interior parts of the frame and exterior parts, thereby eliminating winter condensation inside. Other features that apply to some doors . . . adjustable and thermal-break thresholds, magnetic weather-stripping for uniform sealing and fire-resistance in the form of a Class B (1-1/2 hour) fire rating.

Your choice of door style in prehung entrance door units, whether the thermal door or not, is quite wide. Various door panel types fit best with traditionally styled homes while the flush doors blend better with contemporary homes. As a rule, the owner-builder would be well-advised to keep his selection within the style range indicated by the designer in the home's elevation drawings.

Comparing With Interior Doors

Exterior doors serve as weather barriers and noise reducers as well as giving privacy. Interior doors function just in the area of noise-reduction and privacy. And to be effective in each, they should be well-fitted.

Exterior doors in a home are 1-3/4 inch thick and the common sizes are 2 feet 8 inches and 3 feet in width, by 6 feet 8 inches high. Doubled front entrance doors run to 6 feet in width and may be, for some home designs, higher than the standard 6 feet 8 inches. Because of heavier door weights, entrance door hardware is usually of a heavier-duty type than that used for interior doors.

Interior doors 1-3/8 inch thick are standard and come in a range of widths from about 2 feet to 3 feet. Most passageway doors for bedrooms and other principal rooms are 2 feet 4 inches to 2 feet 8 inches. As with exterior doors, the standard height is 6 feet 8 inches. Further considerations with respect to interior doors are given in Chapter 36.

Nonthermal entrance doors usually require the supplementary installation of storm doors on the exterior. The common product used for this purposes today is what's called a "combination" door. Such a door contains interchangeable panels, glass for winter storm door use and screening for summer use. There's no need to install storm doors while the home is still under construction. A few details concerning the use of storm/screen combination units are given in Chapter 43.

Reason For Using Prehungs

The first-time owner-builder is constantly running into apparent "bargains." Often these overstocked items are better evidence of poor purchasing judgment by the merchant rather than good value to the buyer. Or, if the line is being closed out by a manufacturer, replacements will be difficult to find in the future. In connection with many products to be used in his home, the owner-builder will generally do better avoid the bargain offerings. And when it comes to certain new home installations, the owner-builder will do well to say to himself: "Look, this is something that is just going to be done once. It has to be done right! It's going to see a lot of use and I'd better get the very best available!"

When it comes to exterior entrance doors, the "very best" involves selecting doors that offer superior protection and durability features, and provide considerable savings in the time and effort required to produce a first-class installation. These two results are accomplished with the use of prehung insulating entrance doors.

Hanging doors at the site takes time. This is especially true for the novice who has to more or less feel his way. Here is a case where he's trying to speed the work so the building can be locked up and weather-protected. And he's being asked to test his initial door-hanging skills on the most important operating units in the entire home—the entrance and patio doors.

In respect to interior doors, prehungs are also worth serious consideration for the precision that's built into the door by the factory prehanging, plus the time the owner-builder saves. With interior prehungs, the cost differential with blank doors plus unassembled frame units is not all that great while the time-savings with prehungs is evident for the shopping owner-builder, who can see the step-by-step details of installing hinges and locksets.

Steps Installing Prehungs

Prehung entrance doors are furnished in completely wrapped packages although larger double-door units may be delivered to the job in a braced open carton with a see-through plastic wrap. Since many prehung units are pre-finished while others have been smoothed, touched up and otherwise readied for finish painting, the door manufacturer ordinarily includes detailed installation instruction sheets that indicate just where nailing is to be done and how door plumbing is accomplished. So your initial step with a prehung door is to locate the instruction sheet and

read it. Then, approximately the following, though the steps may vary with the individual door manufacturer's suggestions:

(1) Check the plumb and the dimensions of the opening and make certain the prehung unit will fit into the opening. If wall is not quite plumb or opening is otherwise at fault, try to correct before proceeding.

(2) Check the finished floor height with respect to floor finish to be used. Verify door instruction sheet with respect to height of opening and if situation indicates, install blocking, a fill-in plywood strip or board to bring the door sill height to the desired height for door swing to clear finished floor surface or covering. In so checking, be sure to note range of adjustability, if any, that is provided in the door unit's threshold.

(3) Apply two beads of caulking material with a caulking gun completely around the door opening on studs, header and rough sill, one bead near the interior side of the wall and one near the interior. Apply a thickness of bead suggested by the previous measurements of door opening and door unit.

(4) Remove loose trim temporarily tacked in place on the door unit, usually the interior side. Slip unit into position from the exterior by placing the bottom in approximate but not full-in alignment and tilting up the top so interior top edge clears the opening. Then press entire assembly inwards until frame trim is

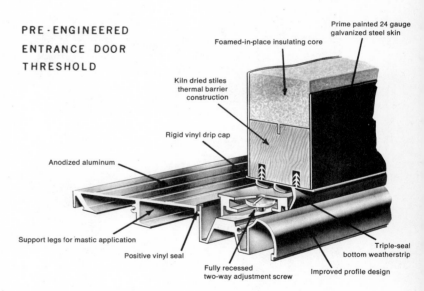

PRE-ENGINEERED ENTRANCE DOOR THRESHOLD

Prime painted 24 gauge galvanized steel skin

Foamed-in-place insulating core

Kiln dried stiles thermal barrier construction

Rigid vinyl drip cap

Anodized aluminum

Support legs for mastic application

Positive vinyl seal

Fully recessed two-way adjustment screw

Improved profile design

Triple-seal bottom weatherstrip

Precision Engineering of Door and Threshold of a thermal prehung door is given in this identification of parts and features included in the metal-clad entrance doors made by Stanley Door Systems. Constructed with polyurethane foam core and kiln dried edges to act as thermal barriers, these units reduce heat loss and eliminate the need for storm doors. Refrigerator-type vinyl seals keep out dirt, drafts and noise; an adjustable bottom weatherstrip is provided in case settling occurs.

against the sheathing (or the frame's outer edge is flush with the sheathing).

(5) Have helper hold door unit while you start casing nails at points indicated by manufacturer's instructions. This will usually be on or near the exterior brick mold, and nail start may need to be on an angle to penetrate into framing stud. Use 16d galvanized casing nails. Check plumb first on hinge side and nail part way top and bottom.

(6) Cut shims 2-to-3 inches wide from wood shingles and place thin edge first between opening and door unit top middle and bottom; objective is to have unit centered in opening with an approximately 1/8-to-3/32 inch clearance between unit's frame and the opening at both jambs and head. With wedges lightly in place, test hinge side plumb in both exterior-interior and side-to-side directions. Lightly tap top nail partly through into framing.

(7) Follow same procedure on the lock side and then test the level of the door head. If needed, apply one or two shims at frame or threshold bottom until head is

Prefinished Wood Windows are factory-assembled in complete easy-installing units, with all hardware mounted and ready for immediate operation. Shown here are the two principal types of wood windows, double-hung in the top photo and, below, casement units formed into a bow combination installation.

level. Retest each jamb and tap lower jamb nails through into framing. Again, retest head level and jamb plumb of the unit.

(8) With door now open, nail through the jamb face into the framing at the points where the shims are on the hinge side; on the lock side first check to see if shims need any tightening or loosening for door to properly meet the weatherstripping. Then proceed with jamb face nailing. Follow by completing the driving of previous partly driven nails. Nail with hammer not quite to jamb face, then use nail set.

(9) Follow with nailing of head frame member in at least two points, being careful to penetrate the header framing, not the center space between header members. Screw door sill to subfloor through predrilled holes in the threshold portion of the door unit.

(10) Check manufacturer's instruction for any adjustments needed at this point for threshold or jamb weatherstripping.

(11) When installing double-door units, follow similar procedure except the nail-up of the secondary nonlockset door should be done first to permit jamb adjustment for assuring a proper fit, with the operating door to the midpoint astragal.* A more thorough check of head level is needed to assure good alignment of the top edges of the two doors.

(12) Pay attention to any manufacturer's recommendation with respect to painting of the door. Avoid painting weatherstrip and avoid using paint that will soften or mark by contact with the weatherstrip material.

Your Choice Of Windows

Windows of poor quality are a longtime headache. You'll cuss when they stick as you're trying to open or close them. You'll nick your fingers on cheap hardware. You'll wonder what's wrong with your eyesight when you peer through poor grades of glass.

There are several good nationally distributed brands of windows, and some good brands distributed only in certain regions. One easily made and reasonably accurate test of window quality lies simply in the product's labelling. Most poor-quality windows do not have a label or even the manufacturer's name on them and without such identification, window quality may be questionable. A window manufacturer that will put his name on the unit usually considers his windows to be of high quality, and most times they are.

Window manufacturers who are members of the National Woodwork Manufacturers Association have for some time used an association-sponsored standard for wood window units. In late 1974, this standard was approved as an American National Standard No. A200.1, and window units whose construction meets the standard requirements are

*narrow, half-round molding

being labelled accordingly. The standard covers such items as the species and grades of wood for various window parts, wood preservative treatments, weatherstripping, hardware, use of insulating glass, other glazing materials, screen and storm insert panels. It also sets minimum strength or loading requirements to be met, amount of air infiltration allowed and other factors affecting overall window quality. The association also has established an industry standard and guarantee for Poderoa Pine wood doors.

Wood windows continue to maintain a high preference level among home buyers and also among home builders. Aluminum, aluminum-clad, plastic-clad metal windows and plastic-clad wood windows are other types being marketed in the residential construction field, but there are many more suppliers of wood windows having immediately available stocks or relatively quick deliveries on special sizes. From the stanpoint of providing a thermal barrier, today's wood windows are probably superior to any type of metal window.

With present-day engineering of wood windows, the typical unit has seen a number of improvements in durability, ease of operation, and paintability. Window maintenance is minimal in comparison with practices of the past. And many wood windows have built-in quality features that go well beyond the mere sash-and-frame constructions of yesteryear. Their joinery is engineered to near perfection. Their moving parts are reinforced or guided in wear areas by nylon or metal inserts. Their hardware is designed to fit both operational and decorative needs. And with controlled minimum air leakage plus availability of insulating glass, today's windows offer an owner-builder the chance to make substantial savings in fuel usage as well as avoiding the bothersome troubles inherent in storm sash.

Tips For Handling Windows

If your windows came preinstalled in exterior wall panels, they are no doubt all preprimed and preglazed and ready for final painting as soon as the balance of the exterior work has been accomplished.

If your window units were selected and purchased separately, they still probably came to the job site with a prime coat, and were preglazed. In all likelihood they also came packaged or wrapped. Here are some suggestions with respect to storing, handling and installing the units:

▢ Store in a dry well-ventilated area to avoid dampness; if wrapped or packaged allow them to remain that way; if not wrapped, cover with a protective tarp or sheet of plastic film.

▢ When handling window units, use clean gloves to avoid staining or finger marks; when carrying, lift the units and avoid dragging them or jarring them since the glazing or seals may be disturbed.

▢ Installation methods vary from one manufacturer to another so look for instruction sheets in the package or stapled to the window unit, and follow them closely.

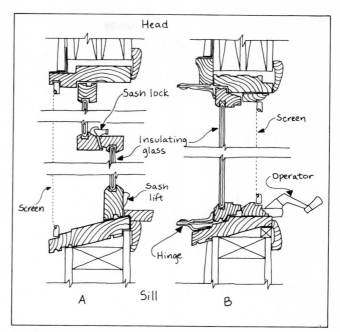

Cross-Section Through Windows with typical double-hung unit in sketch (A) and casement unit in sketch (B). Insulating glass is indicated. Once considered a luxury, the cost of insulating windows with ultra-accurate milling and weatherstripping to minimize infiltration is now thought to be well worthwhile because of reduction in heat transfer and consequent lowering of fuel costs for the home. Storm windows are not usually considered necessary with well-built windows using insulating glass.

▢ Check the squareness of the window frame prior to placing it in the opening and, if need be, apply a temporary diagonal brace across the frame to help maintain squareness while installing.

▢ Use wood shingle shims as spacers and devices to adjust the plumbness of the units; objective is to have the window unit centered in the opening and plumb in two directions, interior-exterior and side-to-side. Plus having the unit level at head and sill.

▢ Check manufacturer's instructions for the exact points at which nails should be placed. This is important to avoid driving nails where they may encounter obstructions, may split the material or may not be driven into the framing members.

▢ Try to avoid all touching or marking of weatherstrip channel or material. If the operating hardware is not already in place, install the locking or operating devices. Leave manufacturer's identification labels on the glass to indicate to all workers that the glazing is in place, and that caution when working nearby is advised.

One special point of attention the owner-builder should clearly understand in regard to window installation is the need for accuracy in the preparation of "rough openings." Every window manufacturer's literature shows the proper dimensions for rough openings that will accommodate his windows. Such rough opening dimensions might be suitable for another brand of window also, but such a situation would probably be an accident or coincidence, not a probability.

So, if you are going to make any changes from the windows shown in your drawings and materials list, you will be sure that in so doing you make a careful check of what rough opening dimensions the windows you're changing to will require.

The rough opening in a wood stud wall is the opening left by the rough framing members *after* doubling of the studs at the jambs and after the header and sill members are in place between the doubled jambs. Headers may range

Wood Window Installation is relatively simple using today's precision-made units. Shown here are the main steps for an Andersen casement type window: (1) the window is set into the frame opening from the outside with exterior casing overlapping the exterior sheathing, using a 3½-inch casing nail partly driven temporarily at one upper corner, with the nail going through the head casing and into the header. In (2), the window is adjusted for

level and a second nail driven in the other top corner. A check for plumbness is made followed by (3) further casing nails spaced about 10 inches apart. All nails are driven at a slight angle inward toward the framing members. Head flashing is applied before siding to extend over head casing and up along face of sheathing. After siding has been applied, complete perimeter of the window is caulked as shown in (4).

from a pair of 2X4's with stud cripples up to plate level to a pair of 2X12's spanning wide openings and used directly below wall-plates without any cripples.

As indicated in Chapter 10, when exterior wall panels are fabricated in a components shop the fabricator must have knowledge of the rough opening dimensions of the specific window units you're planning to use. Problems will seldom occur if the fabricator is also installing the windows and prehung doors, but carelessness in rough opening dimensions quickly shows up when the units are installed at the site. And that's at a time when the framing is relatively difficult and time-consuming to change or adapt.

Sliding Patio Doors

Most new homes built today have at least one sliding glass door, nearly always positioned off the kitchen or family room where the family patio could be expected to be located.

A sliding patio door is something of a cross between an entrance door and an operating window. It has an outer frame much like a prehung entrance door including an integral engineered and weatherstripped door sill. But instead of the simple hinge operation of an entrance door, it employs sliding sash that ride, roll or glide over a narrow track that's also part of the door sill.

Patio sliding doors come in wood and metal types and there are considerable variations in details from one manufacturer to another. The variations here make it very difficult to give even generalized guidelines. Some units come completely ready to set into position and to secure, much like a window unit. Others come in dismantled form with complete step-by-step instructions for assembling panels, frames and hardware down to the tiniest adjustment screw or prepared strip of adhesive. Be certain such detailed instructions come with the door and try if possible to learn installation details in advance.

Once the sliding-door assembly has been accomplished, installation in the rough prepared opening is not unlike that used in placing and fastening entrance doors. But there are certain additional points to check for door position and to avoid binding or obstruction to the operating panel. Most sliding door units have a pair of panels, one fixed, one operating (see illustration). These units can be combined adjacent to each other or the supplier may be able to furnish three- or four-panel units for wide openings.

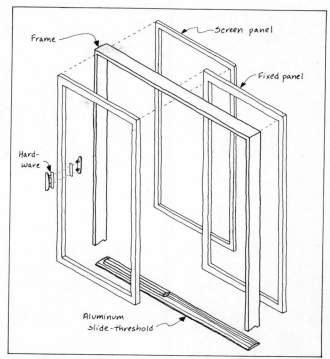

Sliding Glass Doors are in general use in new homes, usually for direct access from living or family rooms to patios or porches. Sliding units are usually of two-panel construction often with just one sliding unit and one fixed panel as shown in this sketch. The door units may come as completely preassembled and prefinished unit or they may be furnished with knocked-down frames for assembly at the job site. Most are furnished with preglazed panels.

The patio door units that come dismantled for job assembly often either enable changing the handing of the operating sash (right or left according to direction of installation) or provide reversibility. These concerns, plus the care needed in assembly work, are chores the first-time owner-builder would do well to avoid by purchase of fully preassembled units.

With respect to sliding patio doors, pay special attention to labels or adhesive taping of the glass at eye levels of adults or children. The Consumer Product Safety Commission has noted a high incidence of household injuries related to architectural glass of this type and is presently developing safety standards for it.

19 Exterior Sidings and Trim

Solid Vinyl Plastic Sidings with insulative properties, impervious to common exterior problems such as peeling, corrosion staining, denting and blistering, are used increasingly for new homes as well as for re-siding old ones. Shown here are vinyl sidings made by Bird & Son: at left, vertical V-groove style for contemporary homes. In center photo, close-up of horizontal clapboard-style siding with color-on-color toning to give woodgrain effect. And at right, bevel siding with windows-doors trimed using decorative vinyl-acrylic shutters that nail into place and are nonoperable.

In finishing the exterior of a wood-frame home, your father probably had a choice between bevel and lap siding, the latter a shortening for the word "shiplap," a form of edge-matching then commonly in use. You, in your new home, may still choose between these two forms of solid wood sidings but also from an expanded assortment of styles as well as a multitude of shapes and sizes of boards.

You will also be able to select exterior siding materials from a constantly broadening line up of sheet materials in plywood and hardboard. Plus some sidings in horizontal or vertical dimensions that are of aluminum, vinyl plastic, fiberboard and simulated brick or stone panels. A literal smorgasboard of sidings.

Discuss this selectivity with your components or lumber supplier. Talk with him about the type of siding indicated on the working drawing elevations and what other types might also be appropriate without really changing the home

design's architectural style. Although you do have a wide choice of sidings, many will be eliminated simply because they're unsuited to the home's architectural treatment. Substitution of other sidings will conflict with the professional designer's intent and sense of appropriate house lines.

With respect to siding costs, those materials in sheet form with textured surfaces or in some cases, prefinishes, are lower priced than the thicker board types or dense specialized sidings with hard, smooth prefinishes. Sheet materials are also easier to apply but because of the recurrence of sheet joints, material is pretty well limited to applications where the exterior design has vertical rather than horizontal lines.

You can discount advertised or promotional literature claims about "maintenance-free" siding materials. There's no such animal . . . if you wish to include appearance as a factor of maintenance. Sidings have seen great improvement

Assorted Plywood Sidings in the U.S. Plywood line testify to the wide range of choice that owner-builders can make for home exterior treatments. Going left to right, the sidings are: (1) prestained in choice of 26 colors, the textured Planktex Kerf sidings give a rustic look; (2) Roughtex lap panels in same range of colors;

(3) Roughtex flat panels with prestained batten strips to match; (4) top photo of regular size Sanspray aggregate-on-plywood with surface scored in grooves 8 inches apart and, bottom, Jumbo aggregate panels with surface giving a rugged chunky appearance; aggregate adhered with epoxy coating.

in providing better bases for paint. Paint properties have greatly improved as have paint durabilities. Factory finishes are great, too. But while many such surfacings have almost interminable durabilities, they all suffer the effects of dust and dirt films and a change in color tone that used to be called "fading" before the days of nonfading chemistry.

Prefinished aluminum has gained in recent years as a residing material and also become acceptable for home construction. A relatively high proportion of aluminum sidings are applied today in both types of work by aluminum siding specialists. Some aluminum building product manufacturers believe that sidings, soffit systems and certain other residential aluminum products should be installed by the skilled specialist, not by a do-it-yourselfer. The view on aluminum from here is that for applications on the exterior of a home, with the possible exception of flashings, aluminum is not as satisfactory a material as many others. It also has a handling disadvantage. It damages easily and damaged portions are hard to smooth out or fix.

The use of solid board lapped sidings has diminished as the use of sheet materials has increased. Today, the most popular types of sidings are those horizontally applied products which have evolved from bevel siding and which may be referred to as strip sidings, and the wide range of plywood, plywood-base and hardboard sidings which may be called sheet or panel sidings. Typical application details for these two principal types will be considered in the following sections.

Wall Preparation

After installation of windows and doors, a check should be made on their head conditions. Many prehung door units and windows include as part of their assembly a drip-cap mold along the door or window head on the exterior side. If this is part of the door-window assembly, fine, nothing further need be added except the flashing.

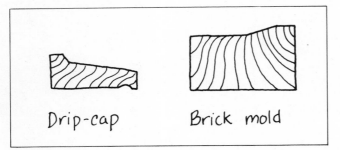

Two Common Exterior Moldings used at heads and jambs of windows and doors for trim. Some windows come with integral drip-cap type heads and do not need this mold. The brick mold, often used as jamb trim with windows in brick veneer walls, is not limited to this application alone. It can be used with any window unit whose jambs do not have sufficient depth for proper butting of the exterior siding.

The same thing applies at the jambs of doors and windows—see that they have integral trim applied and are ready for the butting of the siding material. In the case of many window units, the jambs on the exterior side have a brick mold already applied so that thin sidings or thick veneers can be butted.

Mention was made in Chapter 15 about roof flashings and the fact that when such flashings were being ordered from sheet metal shops sufficient strips for door and window heads should be ordered at the same time. Then when roof flashing work has been done, the head strips are tacked temporarily in place. Now is the time to get those flashing strips properly positioned and permanently nailed into place atop the drip-cap mold.

You do it this way. First cut the strips to project about 1-1/2 inch beyond each end of the drip-cap. The flashing strip should be about 6 inches wide. It may be either copper or galvanized sheet. Use small copper or galvanized nails about an inch in length and having a head diameter of about 1/8 inch. Tack the strip up with equal projections at both ends and with the strip bottom flush with the bottom edge of the drip-cap. Space nails about 2-to-3 inches. Now, fold the metal back towards the siding so that it fits down flat on the sloping upper side of the drip-cap. Near the back edge of the cap, make a crease in the metal so that the balance of the strip lies flat against the sheathing. Holding the strip in folded-creased position close to the drip-cap, nail along the top edge of the flashing strip placing nails 6-to-8 inches apart. Now, come back to each end of the drip-cap; with a sheet-metal shears, cut out corners to allow the excess material to be folded down covering the drip-cap ends and nail these end-folds into place near the bottom edge of the cap. Trim off excess material.

Next comes the question of building paper or building felt, and whether or not such a layer is necessary. It is nearly always used before brick veneer is laid up against the wall. But with strip and sheet siding materials, and if your sheathing is of the insulating type with an asphalt impregnation or outside coating, building felt or paper may be omitted. But this practice varies. Some local building codes require a building felt under all sidings no matter what the type of sheathing used. Check your code or ask your building official about the local practice. If paper is necessary, find out whether the 15 pound or 30 pound felt should be used. This felt paper should *not* be a vapor barrier but instead a "breathing" type paper. It applies easily using a staple-gun. With horizontal strip siding, you can apply the 36 inch wide rolls as you progress with the siding. With sheet sidings, you're better off applying the paper all around the house before starting the siding work.

Final preparation step is consideration for the soffit-sheathing juncture and the soffit-rake or gable-end juncture where the siding is carried up to. Is this a clearly defined line with trim member already in place ready for siding to be cut to it? If not, what trim pieces need be applied first, if any? What trim will follow the siding?

Also taken into consideration at this point are building

corners. Inside corners and outside corners. Are these corners such that the siding material itself will be cut to fit the corners. Or are separate corner molding strips or other corner devices needed. Will they be applied before or after the siding itself is applied? Answers to these questions will depend upon the type of siding selected and whether or not various accessory items are ordered with it.

Applying Horizontal Strip Sidings

At first glance, traditional bevel siding appears to be one of the most popular of all house sidings, but a closer look at the siding situation reveals that there's a lot of *wide* bevel siding being used. Newer kinds of siding materials, cut to wider widths, are seeing increased usage. Hardboard, fiberboard and plywood sidings instead of solid wood. Such materials in 12 inch siding widths are common. And some companies offer siding strips 16 inches wide. The wider the strips, the more area covered per course, the less total labor time. So, the popularity of wider sidings continues to grow.

Still, the narrow siding widths haven't disappeared from the market. They're still in demand for use on Early American styled homes. So, many lumber mills continue to supply siding material in 6 and 8 inch widths and in some cases, material having two narrow 3 or 4 inch courses per siding board. The width you should choose, obviously, is one that best fits your home's design and enhances its appearance.

The widths, thicknesses and maximum stud spacings for these various strip siding materials are given in the accompanying chart, which has been adapted from the HUD Manual of Acceptable Practices, 1973 Edition, to show those dimensions applicable to the HUD-MPS's.

Installation Tips

(1) In readying your siding and nail supply and your sawhorse table for cutting, prepare a measuring strip using a 1X4 or 1X6 long enough to reach from the bottom of the bottom siding course to the soffit level. Measure this distance accurately on the drawings and then verify it on your house. Now proceed around the house and at each window and door, place a mark on one edge where the door-window heads occur and also the window sills. These marks will tell you the levels for certain siding courses for optimum cutting ease around these openings. Remember that course spacings for the siding indicate the minimum lap. You can increase the lap by as much as 50 percent in order to better adjust to head and sill levels. Calculate where the courses fall, mark your measuring pole with a different set of marks in another color to represent the bottom edges of your sidings. Include level adjustments of lap amount to best fit opening heights of most windows and doors. Then, use this measuring device (called a story-pole when

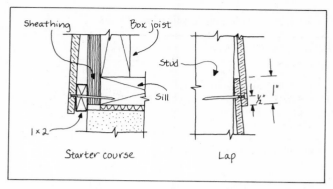

Bevel Siding Details are common to various types of lap sidings—solid boards, plywood, hardboard or particleboard. Nails are shown as commonly practiced in most areas . . . heads driven to just penetrate wood or siding surface and left exposed. Corrosion-resistant nails should be used and in some cases with certain prefinished sidings, color-matched nails are desirable.

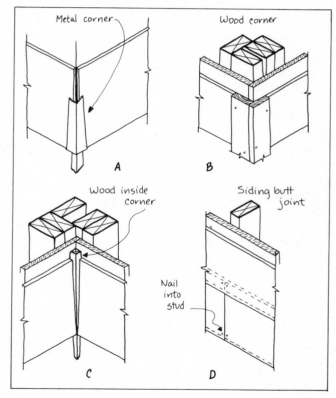

Various Corner Treatments shown here are principally for use with hardboard siding but may also be applicable to other types. The easiest outside corner is in (A), the metal preformed cover plates. Lapped wood strips (B) are simple to apply but joints at each side of corner should be caulked after siding is applied. Same applies to the inside corner strip in (C). Where bevel or lap siding pieces meet to form a butt joint (D), the location should be over the middle of a framing stud and both siding pieces should be nailed into the stud.

Siding Application Details

HORIZONTAL SIDINGS

Maximum Width (Inches)	Over Sheathing		Direct to Framing	
	Minimum Thickness (Inches)*	Max. Stud Spacing (Inches)	Minimum Thickness (Inches)*	Max. Stud Spacing (Inches)
Bevel Siding, Lapped or Rabbeted				
6	7/16		9/16	
8	7/16	24	11/16	16
10	9/16		11/16	
12	11/16		—	—
Drop, Ship Lap, Rustic and Novelty Siding				
8	3/4	24	3/4	16
Vertical application				
12	3/4	**	3/4	**
Plywood, Square Edge Lap Siding				
12	5/16	16	—	—
24	3/8	24	3/8	16
24	1/2	24	1/2	24
Hardboard Lap Siding				
24	1/4	24	—	—

* Butt thickness is shown for bevel siding. Tip thickness should be 3/16″ for beveled wood siding.
** Except when sheathing is nominal 3/4″ board or 1/2″ plywood, vertical siding should be installed over blocking 24″ o.c.

VERTICAL SIDINGS

Minimum Thickness (Inches)	Maximum Stud Spacing (Inches)					
	Over Sheathing			Direct to Framing		
	Plywood Face Grain		Hard-board	Plywood Face Grain		Hard-board
	Vertical	Horiz.		Vertical	Horiz.	
1/4	—	—	24	—	—	16
5/16	16 *	—	—	16	—	—
3/8	16 *	24	—	16	24	—
1/2	24		—	24		—
5/8	16 * **		—	16 **		—

* May be 24″ o.c. when sheathing is not less than 1/2″ plywood or nominal 3/4″ board.
** May be 24″ o.c. for ungrooved siding. Grooved plywood must be 3/8″ at grooves.
SOURCE: *Exterior Wall Finishes* 609.2—HUD Manual of Acceptable Practices

masons use it for brick or block coursing) for marking your sheathing or underlayment paper at key points around the house.

(2) It is important to get the bottom starter course level; the accepted method is to place accurately the starter strip, measuring down from the wall top-plate a uniform distance to the point where the bottom edge of the starter strip should be positioned. After that it's easy to obtain a uniform projection of your bottom siding course below the edge of the starter strip.

(3) Begin the bottom course at a building corner by nailing the bottom row of nails so that they penetrate into the sill-plate. Use rust-resistant nails of a size suited to the siding—6d for thinner materials and 8d for thicker ones, as a general rule.

(4) When driving nails, try to get the knack of driving just enough so the head barely touches the siding surface and follow with one light tap or final stroke to have it depress the siding surface slightly. The objective is to avoid hitting the nail head too much or too hard, a procedure that results in hammerhead dimple marks that become quite noticeable when the siding is painted or given its final finish.

(5) Proceed with the same course until you reach a building corner, then come back the other direction with the next course. Keep checking the level of the bottom course and the exposure of succeeding courses as they meet or come close to the marks you made with the story pole.

(6) Apply nails so they always penetrate into the studs or structural framing. Use care in nailing at ends of siding strips to avoid splitting. A little extra effort can be made here by first blunting the point of the nail with your hammer; put the head on a solid surface and hit the point a straight-on blow. Blunting the point makes the nail break wood fibers rather than spread them and at board ends prevents splitting of the board. If difficulty is still encountered with certain materials in trying to nail close to the edges, predrilled holes may be advisable.

(7) Stagger the vertical strip-end joints along the walls so they fall on studs but in an irregular pattern. Check siding manufacturer's instructions for need to treat or caulk the cut ends.

Recommendation. Use of inside and outside corner moldings or devices, rather than mitering or alternate lapping at building corners. The latter methods look relatively easy when you watch a skilled siding applicator do it but when *you* try to make these cuts it is easy to become confused and end up with a high rate of irregular joints or siding

Siding Thicknesses and Stud Spacings required are indicated in this application chart. Purpose is to provide information for selecting the siding material or suitable thickness for the stud spacing your home will have.

spoilage. The inside-outside moldings and the metal corner units for bevel sidings are much simpler to work with and when the entire job is finish-painted, they look exceptionally neat and workmanlike.

Wood shingles, although they cannot be classified as a strip siding, also have something of a horizontal appearance. Shingles and shakes are used more extensively for both roofs and sidewalls in western states. Siding shingles are applied with wider exposures than roofing shingles and much siding work is done with single coursing. But otherwise the shingle application is done in much the same way as for roofing shingles.

Applying Sheet Sidings

The 4X8 foot sheet size is by far the most common panel size used in sheet siding work. The sheet method allows a minimum of cutting and waste on most jobs, and is therefore very economical of material. It also offers a speed advantage; sheets apply considerably faster and with fewer minor errors than do strip materials.

Before starting your sheet siding application, you should know how the vertical siding joints are going to be concealed. Are the panel edges grooved or treated so that the joints are self-concealing? Or will covering batten strips be needed? And how are building corners to be handled?

Many sheet sidings come in prefinished form but you should still check the nails required in advance. Is a color-matched nail or a nail touch-up compound to be used with the prefinished siding? Also, for some siding patterns nailing in the grooves is desirable and easy; with other patterns face nailing may be necessary.

Installation Tips

☐ Joints and panel edges should fall near the center of framing members. Check instructions for treatment or caulking of joint edges.

☐ Narrow strips of the sheet siding material make good battens and these with prefinished edges come with the siding material, thus assuring a good color match.

☐ Use 6d or 8d galvanized box nails unless siding manufacturer supplies special nails; keep all nails 3/8 inch in from all sheet or panel edges; space nails 6 inches along edges and 12 inches for intermediate nailing into studs.

☐ On shiplap sheet joints, nail both sides through the face; leave 1/16 inch gap or clearance between sheet

---

Figuring Your Quantities of siding materials can be simplified by use of this chart. The important column is the right-hand one giving an area factor. You calculate the wall area, multiply by this factor to give board measure needed and then add 5 percent for waste on simple house-plans, for complex homes with corners, offsets and vari-sized windows.

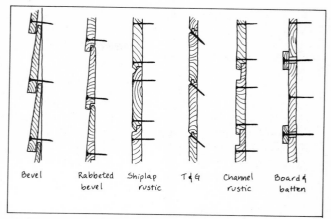

Wood Siding Types commonly used in residential work. The three at the left are generally designed for horizontal application. The tongue-and-groove and channel styles are suited to either horizontal or vertical installation while the board-batten type is limited to vertical use. In applying any of the milled-joint types (the central four), the siding installer should leave a 1/8 inch expansion clearance between each board.

Wood Siding Estimating Aid

	Nominal Size	WIDTH		AREA FACTOR*
		Dress	Face	
SHIPLAP	1 X 6	5-1/2	5-1/8	1.17
	1 X 8	7-1/4	6-7/8	1.16
	1 X 10	9-1/4	8-7/8	1.13
	1 X 12	11-1/4	10-7/8	1.10
TONGUE	1 X 4	3-3/8	3-1/8	1.28
AND	1 X 6	5-3/8	5-1/8	1.17
GROOVE	1 X 8	7-1/8	6-7/8	1.15
	1 X 10	9-1/8	8-7/8	1.13
	1 X 12	11-1/8	10-7/8	1.10
S4S	1 X 4	3-1/2	3-1/2	1.14
	1 X 6	5-1/2	5-1/2	1.09
	1 X 8	7-1/4	7-1/4	1.10
	1 X 10	9-1/4	9-1/4	1.08
	1 X 12	11-1/4	11-1/4	1.07
PANELING	1 X 6	5-7/16	5-7/16	1.19
PATTERNS	1 X 8	7-1/8	6-3/4	1.19
	1 X 10	9-1/8	8-3/4	1.14
	1 X 12	11-1/8	10-3/4	1.12
BEVEL	1 X 4	3-1/2	3-1/2	1.60
SIDING	1 X 6	5-1/2	5-1/2	1.33
(1" 1-a)	1 X 8	7-1/4	7-1/4	1.28
	1 X 10	9-1/4	9-1/4	1.21
	1 X 12	11-1/4	11-1/4	1.17

*Allowance for trim and waste should be added.
SOURCE: Western Wood Products Association

Siding Application on two-story homes requires scaffold equipment that can be rented for short use. The scaffold arrangement shown here is easy to erect and use. It consists of a pair of aluminum ladders for walking platforms between three 4X4 wood posts. The wood posts serve as a climbing base for scaffold jacks and are held in position by roof brackets. The jacks have foot-levers that raise the jack (and the platform) to height needed. Shown here in the process of being applied is rustic prestained plywood.

edges to allow for normal weather expansion and contraction.

☐ On butt edges of sheet joints which are to be covered with batten strips, leave a gap of about 1/8 inch with a similar gap where such edges meet windows and doors.

☐ There are two ways to handle exterior wall heights that run higher than the 8 foot sheet size: butt the sheets with a 1/8 inch gap that's flashed with a Z-shaped sheet metal strip under the upper sheet and over the lower one; or, use waste pieces of siding tacked to the upper portion and apply sheet siding over these random pieces lapping the sheet over the lower sheet by about an inch.

Since about 1950 most wood, plywood, or other types of house sidings have been furnished in paint-primed condition. The exceptions to this practice involve certain species such as redwood or cedar which may be used without any finish and left to weather to a neutral grey color. One of the purposes of having siding preprimed before delivery to the building site is to protect it from dampness and moisture. Even if preprimed, however, store all sidings inside the house under cover.

Another type of exterior siding, needing no finish of any kind, is "simulated brick." Understand that it may be made from plastic or other compounds or it may be and is in some cases a real brick, being a fired ceramic . . . but thin. These simulated bricks either in panel form or in individual thin-brick units are finding acceptance. Some are designed only as interior decorative covering; others are intended for exterior application. Properly applied to the exterior, it's difficult to differentiate between them and a true brick veneer job. If your plans call for brick veneer, you might well investigate several of these simulated brick products that could well serve the purpose with less installation time and cost.

If your siding is not prefinished, you should plan to complete your exterior painting as soon as practicable. Exterior woodwork and trim of all kinds, even though primed for paint, are not fully protected until the final painting has been completed.

Some of the factors involved in paint preparatory work and the choice of exterior paints or stains are discussed in the next chapter. One final item relating to exterior house trim that the owner-builder might also decide on at this time is exterior decorative accessories such as house shutters. If not prefinished, these will need painting along with other house trim.

20 Closing-In Against the Weather

Your home should be made tight and weatherproof before you proceed with interior work. The exterior sealing and finish work can be considered a milestone; professional home builders frequently refer to this stage as being "under roof". What they mean is that the house job is now pretty safe against weather delays and that further work on the home interior can no longer be subject to damage due to exposure.

The initial step for an owner-builder in closing-in his home against the weather is the sealing of all cracks or openings left by the exterior covering materials. Here are various points on the home that may need attention.

- Eaves and rake soffits, particularly the juncture between the soffit material and the house siding where the crack should be caulked or covered with a cove mold;
- Gable-end vent and/or window installations, need caulk-material, especially if sheet siding has been used;
- House walls, if sheet siding is used caulk sheet joints and if strip siding was used, caulk butted joints and on both types check building corners for open cracks to be caulked where corner molds or covers don't provide an air seal;
- All windows and doors, caulking where siding butts including heads and below sills; at heads run caulking bead between siding and head flashing;
- Sill-plates, check crack or opening between siding bottom or siding starter strip and the foundation wall; if not continuously tight, run caulking bead along the crack;
- At points or building lines where exterior siding material changes, run caulking bead to fill crack between two differing materials; if crack is horizontal, the joint should have been flashed with outer edge of flashing carried down over top edge of lower material; caulk joint crack between flashing and upper material.

Caulking compound comes in easy-to-apply tubular form, a cartridge that slips into a caulking gun. Operating a trigger on the gun activates a notched pushing rod whose face-plate enters the back of the cartridge. This pushes out the caulking material through a nozzle in ribbon form. The size of the ribbon or bead depends on how the very tip of the nozzle was cut and on the rate of nozzle movement along the crack.

In using the caulking gun and cartridge, clip off the closed end of the vinyl-plastic nozzle so that about a 1/8-to-3/16 inch opening is provided. If the flow with this size opening seems a bit slow for the amount of crack to be caulked, loosen the push-rod and with your side-cutting pliers, nip off a bit more to make it about a 1/4 inch opening.

Start your caulking in the rear of the house at some point not too noticeable until you acquire a little practice in running a uniform bead. Be careful not to spill the caulking material and use a suitable solvent to clean up spills before they harden or thoroughly stain the material on which they have dropped.

The neatest caulking bead is one which is uniform in size and thus can be wiped easily to provide a smooth-surfaced tight continuous seal. "Wiping" is done by using a solvent-saturated rag and using your number-one finger with the rag covering it to run down the joint.

What Caulking Compound?

There are caulking compounds and sealants galore. Oil-base caulks, flexible sealants, water-based caulks, solvent-based acrylics, and elastomeric sealants . . . an assortment of sealing materials based on neoprene, silicones, poly-sulfides and hypalon. However, most have been developed for specific purposes or because of special properties suited to certain conditions or types of surfaces.

Oil-based caulking material is the traditional kind and used most widely on home exteriors. They're intended for use where the cracks are relatively stable and nonmoving. These caulks are soft and easy to knead or place and have good adherence. Used principally for joints and cracks where there will be very little expansion or contraction, they will generally last for about five years and then begin to dry out and develop hairline cracks in the caulking material. Inexpensive, the oil-base caulks form a surface skin overnight which can then be painted for added protection. And painting does provide added life for the caulking material.

Butyl-based sealants are the most common flexible types, and offer stretchability to cope with temperature shifts. They're most often used in the bedding of glass. Acrylic-latex caulks or sealants are time savers. They can be used where surfaces are damp, may be tooled using water, and paint can be applied over them almost immediately. Similar are polyvinyl-acetate latex-base caulks that dry very hard but which are usually recommended only for interior use.

Solvent-based acrylics take three to four weeks to cure, have a strong odor, a long life expectancy of 20 years, and usually must be heated prior to application. The elastomers have a rubber-like consistency. They also have high resiliency, weathering ability and tenacity. They have a longer life than oil-based caulks and are growing popular for general purpose use. They're available in one-part compounds; simply use the caulk as it comes from the cartridge. They also come in two-part separate containers for mixing when ready to use, but the owner-builder had best avoid this complication. Check the labels on sealants before using because there may be certain limitations. For example, silicone-based sealants may require a primer on some surfaces and should not be used near surfaces that are to be painted since they will affect paint adhesion.

Most sealants and caulking materials function better when they're applied to clean dry surfaces. Any grease should be removed. Also dust. Sealants like space enough to do their job. Acceptable size range for cracks or openings is from 3/16 to 1/4 inch width and depth. Caulking will remain in better contact with primed than bare wood surfaces. When applied to metals, be sure to first wipe off with solvent any film the metal surface may have, or there may be adhesion difficulties. Aluminum is a prime offender in this respect.

You'll probably see puttylike caulking compound available in rope form in supply stores. In roll form, the rope caulks are usually joined together and need pulling apart in single or double strands for application. As a rule, they're not suitable to new home use. Cracks are not uniformly filled. The material is nondrying and does not readily accept paint.

Here are a few other caulking guidelines:

☐ Apply caulks when the outside temperature is 40° or higher;
☐ Don't try to thin the sealing material; use it as it comes from the cartridge and check the label to see if a primer is suggested;
☐ Where joints are deep, use some sort of appropriate filling material;
☐ Clip off the nozzle at an angle and then use the cartridge gun—hold it at a 45° angle to the surface.

Final Exterior Touches and your home is done on the outside. First, you'll want to finish-paint your exterior trim. Some trim items will have come preprimed and all they need is a finish coat. Others need to be primed with an appropriate primer or sealer before final painting. For exterior use, choose paints with good color retention and moisture resistance.

Also important as a final step in weatherproofing the home's exterior is a judicious application of caulking at all corners, edges and material joints subject to wind-rain infiltration. If in doubt, caulk. Modern caulking compounds form a smooth hardened outer film while remaining flexible underneath to conform to material shrinkage or building movement.

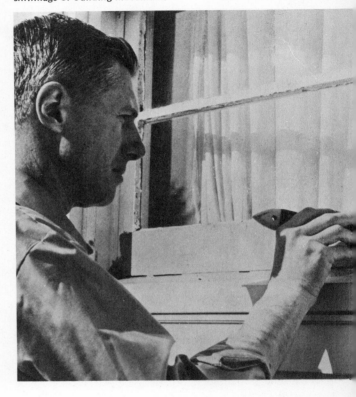

☐ Hold the gun parallel to the crevice and pull it, don't push, along the crevice.

☐ When stopping or pausing, turn the rod handle to release the pressure—otherwise the caulking material will continue to flow out the nozzle; seal the nozzle with tape between periods of usage.

Paint or Stain Selection

Stains

The word "stain" often raises the image of a furniture-like finish that consists of an application of thin fluid, usually dark in color and named for a wood species . . . walnut stain, mahogany stain, oak stain. Applied to bare wood and followed by several coats of varnish, it brings out the grain.

Exterior house stains are not like that at all. House stains are especially suited to textured or rough-surfaced woods although they can also be applied successfully on smooth wood or other surfaces. House stains are usually pigmented stains that have a wide range of colors—colors unrelated to wood species. Further, they are usually heavy-bodied stains that are brush or roller applied.

The pigmented stains are suited to most exterior surfaces, but particularly the textured ones. Such stains are available in the acrylic type for quick drying and easy water cleanup. For redwood and cedar exteriors, the owner-builder should investigate the special stain grades now offered by some companies that enhance the richness and beauty of the natural wood.

The principal difference between paints and stains is that paint finishing often results in the forming of a surface film, while stains tend to penetrate slightly deeper, thereby impregnating the surface rather than covering it.

However, these differences have been minimized in recent years with the development of many new synthetic-based coating materials. The results have shown in thicker flow-on materials that are easier to brush out, have better hiding power, and greater durability. Often, from the consistency in the pail or on the brush, it's difficult to tell a latex or alkyd-based paint from a pigmented heavy-bodied stain. And both have fastness against fading and less need for repetitive maintenance recoatings than do oil-based paints.

Paints

The selection of exterior paints by the owner-builder is best accomplished by visits to several suppliers to see stocks carried, types of paint, enamel or stain for the home's surfaces, and the range of colors available either standard or in custom-mixed formulas.

Of great appeal to the do-it-yourselfer are the latex and acrylic paints. Their primary, well-advertised feature—water

cleanup—could be as important to the owner-builder as the ease of application and good durability these types of paints offer. These water-thinned paints come in flat and semi-gloss or satin finishes. And latex or acrylic enamels are available for gloss finishes on house trim.

Getting the Surfaces Ready

On new construction, there's usually very little that's needed to prepare the exterior surfaces. Bare wood, of course, needs a priming coat. You would probably apply this principally to your roof trim area because nearly all other exterior items are furnished with a prime coat. Before priming, check the surfaces for minor cracks or indentations that need filling or touch-up. The common material for such purposes is putty applied with a putty knife, a straight-bladed tool with a blade width of about 1 to 1-1/2 inches.

Complete painting of the home's exterior, depending on the design and choice of siding materials, may involve several types of paint or stain. It is also apt to require some color coordination. For complete details on various paint and color selection factors as well as painting procedures, the reader is referred to a companion publication, the *Book of Successful Painting* (see bibliography) by Abel Banov and Marie-Jeanne Lytle.

On the other hand, if the owner-builder has elected to use brick veneer or any of a wide range of prefinished sidings, the exterior paint work may consist mostly of trim work, such as roof edges, soffits, windows and doors. Or there may be some brick or block work intended for a paint finish.

Before painting masonry, give it a good wire-brushing to remove particles and dust. If masonry gashes or voids are deep, as in some concrete block units, use a heavy-bodied latex primer or a block filler. Where washability and durability of painted masonry are of principal concern an epoxy coating system may be appropriate; otherwise choose a lower-cost low-luster alkyd enamel or acrylic-latex.

Watch your wood trim corners and edges. Trim boards often have quite sharp edge corners. Use light medium-fine sandpaper to ease off the corner edges and give them a slight roundedness and thus a better surface for paint, stain, or enamel.

Painting Application Tips

☐ Avoid all painting in humid weather; wait for the weather to become clear and dry with temperatures in the 50-to-90 degree range. Don't paint if the temperature goes below 45°;

☐ Exterior paint is usually brush-applied but paint rollers and flat applicators are also suitable and will undoubtedly prove faster, particularly if the surface is coarse or rough;

Exterior Paint and Other Finishes

Surface Types	Oil or Oil-Alkyd Paint	Cement Powder Paint	Exterior Clear Finish	Aluminum Paint	Wood Stain	Roof Coating	Trim Paint	Porch & Deck Paint	Primer or Undercoater	Metal Prime	Latex House Paint	Water Repellent
Wood Surfaces												
Clapboard	X.			X					X		X.	
Natural Wood Siding & Trim			X		X							
Shutters & Other Trim	X.						X.		X		X.	
Wood Frame Windows	X.			X			X.		X		X.	
Wood Porch Floor								X				
Wood Shingle Roof					X							X
Metal Surfaces												
Aluminum Windows	X.			X			X.			X	X.	
Steel Windows	X.			X.			X.			X	X.	
Metal Roof	X.									X	X.	
Metal Siding	X.			X.			X.			X	X.	
Copper Surfaces			X									
Galvanized Surfaces	X.			X.			X.			X	X.	
Iron Surfaces	X.			X.			X.			X	X.	
Miscellaneous												
Asbestos Cement	X.								X		X	
Brick	X.	X		X					X		X	X
Cement & Cinder Block	X.	X		X					X		X	
Concrete/Masonry Porches And Floors								X			X	
Coal Tar Felt Roof						X						
Stucco	X.	X		X						X	X	

· dot at right of X indicates a primer or sealer may be needed before finishing coat is applied

SOURCE: U.S. Department of Commerce

Suitability of Various Paints-Finishes for exterior applications is given in this convenient chart. A dot by the X indicates probable need for a primer, sealer or fill coat.

□ Though roller or applicator may be faster than a brush, a medium-width brush is still needed to skirt the edges, corners and trim; the depth of pile on rollers or applicators affects the amount of paint brought to the surface so choose the roller or applicator accordingly;

□ Paint spraying is the fastest method and pneumatic or electric equipment for such spraying is readily available for purchase or rental. But bear in mind that adjacent areas need protection; you will need eye and skin protection, and spraying may not produce the uniformity or application ease you might expect;

□ Read your paint can carefully; it will tell you preferred application methods and the paint limitations;

□ Alkyd and acrylic paints tend to be faster-drying but this can be something of a handicap if painting in direct sunlight. Plan your work so that you avoid the sun as much as possible;

□ Follow paint manufacturer's recommendations for brush-out or roll-out in spreading the paint. Some paints need the brushing for uniform coverage or suitable penetration while others do not. Some paints brush to uniform smoothness while others appear to flow to it with little brushing;

□ As a general rule, paint from the top down and, in painting across, paint to the raw edge not from it; paint the large surfaces before the trim;

□ Regarding the recommended number of paint coats, remember that your prime coat counts as one coat; most paint manufacturers suggest a three-coat job. Yet many new paints and stains give greater coverage so that one coat over the prime may be sufficient. The final coat can then wait until the home is entirely completed;

☐ Be alert for finger marks around doors and windows; these are grease marks and should be removed before painting or enameling—use a light detergent to avoid damage to the door or window material;

☐ With roof fascia, rake, and soffit trim work, avoid painting too soon after a rain or moist humid weather; wait until the wind or sun has had a chance to dry these surfaces thoroughly;

☐ Don't paint weatherstripping, and remove any drippings that occur on it; with windows and door lights, be sure to paint over the glazing material and extend the paint just slightly onto the glass for later close edging by a razor blade.

Other Outside Clean-Up

When the work on the house proper has been completed, it's time to pause and take stock of the situation.

Normally, with a house under construction, a home builder will have had rough-grading work done when the foundation was backfilled, and with the completion of the exterior finish he will clear and haul away yard debris. But flat-slab concrete in the basement floor, driveway and entrance walks will not be done until the home's interior is completed.

With an owner-builder, there may be other considerations. With the exception possibly of some west coast and southern areas, there may be oncoming cool and colder weather which will involve difficult access or muddy conditions. In such conditions the heat needed for working purposes will spur your desire to get the home heating and perhaps other mechanical systems into operation or partial operation as quickly as possible.

For these and perhaps other more compelling reasons, the owner-builder may at this time choose to install his basement floor slab, entrance walk and stoop. Or he may choose to pour the concrete garage floor slab and install the garage door(s) to complete the closing-in of his home and provide clean, dry material storage and working area. Whatever the choice may be at this time, a check of the procedures involved in this work can be found in Chapter 46.

If the owner-builder is negative on immediate action for the above items, he should at least go ahead with two provisions that will help the work ahead and improve poorer winter working conditions. These two provisions are if not already arranged: have electric utility company provide temporary electricity either to a temporary pole or to your meter location; and, clear your driveway, level it to grade, and bring in suitable crushed stone or gravel base material. In connection with the latter, provide a galvanized steel culvert pipe under the driveway fill material at any point where a drainage channel must pass. This driveway work will accommodate cars and trucks in bad weather without the hazard of stalled engines, and will also help with driveway base compaction and settling before any surfacing or pavement work is done.

With exterior finished and cleanup work done, it's a good time for the owner-builder to sit down with planning pencil in hand and set down on paper his next immediate goals. Among the most important considerations are:

☐ Your requirements, materials, and tools, for interior work and perhaps a change in job procedures now that the house can be closed up and locked.

☐ Steps that should be taken to allow temporary or partial use of the home's mechanical systems—the heating unit, the water supply and the drainage-waste system.

It is with some of these near-future considerations that the next several chapters will be concerned, before proceeding with the other interior construction procedures. And it's not too early to consider your time of occupancy. Local building officials have rules to the effect that no new home shall be occupied until a certificate of occupancy has been issued, a step not usually taken until the home has had its final inspection.

It may be possible for the owner-builder to work around the normal occupancy rules in some way in order to help speed his house completion work. Whatever the individual case, getting your new home under roof and safe against weather and vandalism is a milestone calling for something in the way of a celebration, plus taking stock of the situation in order to fix some new goals for the immediate period ahead.

21 | Partitions and Framing Details

A decision to erect or install interior partitions before doing the roof framing and roof covering work is not only a valid one but a common one. Related to it, of course, is the question of how fast an owner-builder wishes to get the house under roof. And also related to it is the usual practice in a given area or of an individual supplier.

In many cases where the components supplier is furnishing exterior wall panels, he will supply studs-only partition panels at the same time. In other cases, exterior wall panels only are furnished and the house framing and roof-frame work proceeds without partitions . . . if it is a one-story home.

If your home is a one-and-a-half or two-story design, then it requires at the least installation of a load-bearing partition before structural framing work is completed. Later interior partition work consists of fitting the various room or intersecting partitions to this load-bearing partition.

Where partition panels are furnished, be certain your supplier identifies each unit so that you know exactly where it goes. This is ordinarily done with a shop drawing prepared by the components fabricator, a floorplan sketch with the identity numbers of each panel unit marked. The same sort of drawing is needed when the supplier furnishes loose partition studs and plates, but preassembled components for corner posts, headers and beams. You have to have the supplier's component identity to know what goes where.

Preliminary to any partition framing work is cleanup and floor sweeping. You need a clean deck to make accurate marks for partition locations. Work from the working drawings that indicate measurements from the edges of the 2X4's. Mark the sole-plate locations by two parallel lines representing both edges. Be especially careful of your accuracy in marking the partition end and door opening locations.

Floor-Marking Details

If partition panels are being supplied, your principal marking concern is to have floor marks in which true right angles to exterior walls are made since the length or opening accuracy will have been part of the fabrication work. For true right angles, use a 6-8-10 foot board triangle as described in connection with footing layout work. And supplement the triangle with a steel square for the shorter partition lengths.

In most homes, all partition framing will be of 2X4's with the exception of the bathroom plumbing wall containing the waste-vent pipes of two or three plumbing fixtures. Depending on exact bathroom fixture layout, this wall may have 2X6 sole-plates and top-plates with 2X6 studs, or other arrangements that will accommodate the piping thicknesses. In advance of your partition framing work, talk this matter over with your plumbing subcontractor to find out just what wall framing thickness is needed for the type of pipe that will be used. Copper and plastic D-W-V pipe connections don't require as thick a wall as cast iron. When this point is settled with the plumber, you can plan to frame the wall as he might suggest with a single row of studs or with double studs in the area where the pipes occur.

Partition Assembly On Site is a simple job but requires strict attention to the floorplan dimensions for proper partition fitting without later reworking. At top of sketch is position of partition section marked on the floor deck with a door opening at the right. Then, precut studs are laid out on deck along with sole plate and top plate members. First subassembly step is to nail together the doubled 2X4's and header for the door opening (cripple can be added later). Sole plate is positioned near deck markings, plates cut to exact length and marked for stud locations 16 inches o.c. Partition frame is then nailed together using two 16d nails driven through the plates into the studs. When complete, partition is raised into proper floor position and nailed-braced. Note that second top plate will be nailed up to lap partition sections after all have been raised, leveled-plumbed, and nailed.

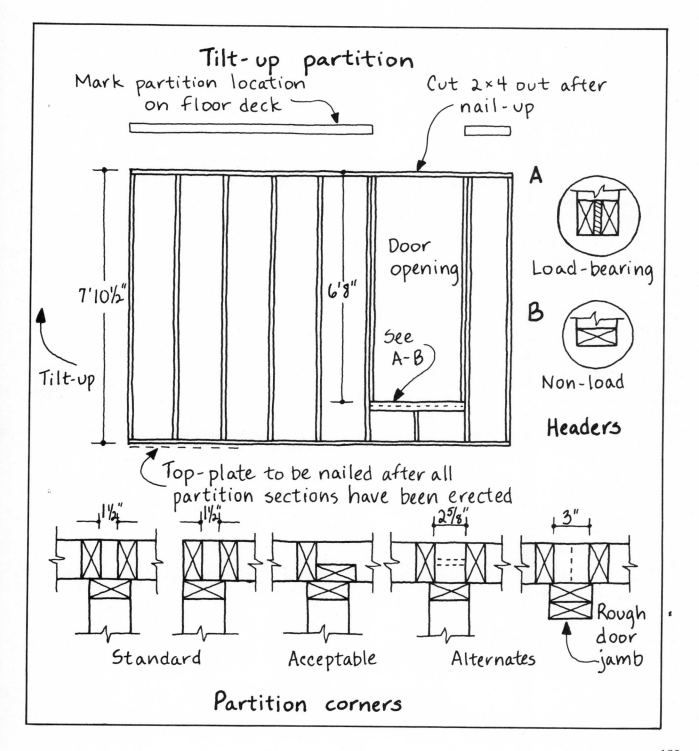

Tilt-up partition

Mark partition location on floor deck

Cut 2×4 out after nail-up

Tilt-up

7'10½"

6'8"

Door opening

See A-B

A

Load-bearing

B

Non-load

Headers

Top-plate to be nailed after all partition sections have been erected

1½" 1½" 2⅝" 3"

Standard   Acceptable   Alternates

Rough door jamb

Partition corners

In marking openings for interior doors, closet doors and other wall openings, use accurate right-angle cross marks. Near center of opening, mark what type of opening or door is there. This helps avoid confusion when there are partition junctures running in several directions with a couple of bedroom doors and a closet door or two all in close proximity.

The purpose here is to avoid little errors as you go along; they can accumulate to the point where it becomes necessary to partially tear out a partition and replace it in order to correct what began as a small error. Make your parallel sole-plate location marks and use a chalk line to give continuous lines. Use a carpenter's crayon or colored pencil for the cross-marks and opening identifications.

Partition Framing and Erection

For purposes of explaining procedures, let's assume here that your home is a single story with a trussed roof for which no partitions or subcomponents have been furnished. The starting point is evident from the plans—one central partition runs the length of the home though not necessarily in an uninterrupted, straight line.

First calculate studs needed and their exact length: floor-ceiling height less 4-½ inches, the thickness of the sole-plate, and two top-plate members. After cutting sufficient studs to proper length, lay them out at 16 inch (approximate) spacings perpendicular to the partition line so that after assembly the wall can be tilted up. Along top and bottom lay out 14- or 16 foot lengths of 2X4's for plates. Beginning at one exterior wall end, mark sole-plate and lower top-plate edges for stud locations including doubled studs at door openings.

The assembly is nailed together on the floor deck with 16d nails driven through plates and into stud ends. Here is the approximate step-by-step procedure:

(1) You will start at one end of the home and build the central partition in two or three sections depending upon openings or offsets in it.

(2) The initial section will run from the home's exterior end-wall, where doubled studs in the framing are located to accommodate the partition, to just beyond the first interior door opening. Measure and cut sole-plate member and lower top-plate so they extend to the center of the 2X4 that doubles the door framing, not the one on the inner side of the opening.

(3) Nail top-plates and sole-plates to the stud ends using two 16d nails driven through the plates into the stud ends.

(4) At the door opening, nail just the inner studs, then cut a pair of 2X4's to door-opening width and nail them together with half-inch plywood blocking between to form the door header; nail this in the door opening at proper opening height driving nails through

the inner jambs and into the ends of the header members.

(5) Nail one doubling jamb stud in place but omit the one at the end of the section; this second doubling stud will be part of the second partition section. Allow sole-plate to remain spanning bottom of the opening; it will be cut out after the partition has been erected and nailed.

(6) With the aid of your helper, tilt the assembly up into position and adjust to floor lines; now take 2X4 that will serve as top top-plate and has been cut one stud space shorter than the lower top-plate and slide it into position atop the partition and under the truss lower chords or ceiling joists. Align the edges of the two plates and, standing on a ladder, nail the upper plate to the lower.

(7) Push partition section tightly to exterior end-wall, test the partition for plumb, check the resting position at floor marks then nail partition end stud into exterior wall studs top and bottom.

(8) At stud space adjacent to door opening near other end of the partition section, adjust sole-plate to floor lines and nail through sole-plate into nearest floor joist judging position by floor sheathing nails.

(9) On ladder near door opening, test plumb of partition and toe-nail top-plate into truss chord or ceiling joist; now proceed to nail sole-plate down the balance of the section, two nails penetrating through floor sheathing and into joists; return on ladder, toe-nailing each truss chord or ceiling joist to the top-plate, at least one nail on each side of the chord or joist.

(10) To complete the partition, cut 2X4 cripple stud for distance from top of door header to bottom of lower top-plate and toe-nail in normal stud position in accordance with 16 inch interval spacing.

The above procedure or a close approximation is followed on remaining sections of the central partition using the same principles of ending a section where doubled studs can be nailed together, allowing for over-lap of upper top-plate (see illustration) and leaving sole-plate to extend across openings for later cut-off.

After the central partition has been nailed into place, follow with the room partitions that are perpendicular to it and finally by the smaller partition sections such as those between closets or at end of halls.

Where a supplier has furnished subcomponents such as partition corner posts, door headers and ceiling beams, procedure will vary somewhat. Include corner posts in your floor nailing on one section but allow for members already part of the corner assembly when making your adjacent section. With respect to ceiling beams that span a wide opening or opening header-beams for wide closet openings, or cased openings between living and dining room or kitchen and family room, these beams should be positioned on the floor, accurately. Where there are a number of cripple studs above such beams, cut these and nail in before tilting the section up. Remember that with the doubled studs at beam or header ends on wide openings, it is common practice to have the inner stud cut *under* the beam to give support while the outer stud is full wall height and is nailed to the beam end. Where a beam is supported by an exterior wall, omit the beam from the partition section and put it into position after the partition section has been erected and temporarily nailed. Finish the nailing after the beam is up.

At interior room corners where partition sections meet, make certain that each corner assembly has three stud members so that adequate nailing base is provided for wallboard on both sides of each inside corner. Each door opening should not be closer than a stud-and-a-half distance (2-1/4 inches) from a room corner.

Be especially careful to align kitchen partitions with respect to right angles and plumbness. Kitchen walls that are out of line and out of plumb will create installation difficulties for cabinets and counter components.

In bedrooms and hallways, there may be certain locations where the partition section occurs only above door height when the full opening spans between two partitions. In such instances, measure distance for door opening height from the floor on each side of the opening, then measure height from door opening to bottom of truss chord or ceiling joist. Then, on the floor assemble a header and cripple component with the usual top-plate members. After nailing it together, have your helper assist with lifting it into position for nailing to adjacent walls and to ceiling framing.

Attention To Plumbing Needs

Mentioned earlier was the need to confer with your plumbing subcontractor about framing of a bathroom wall where fixtures are bunched. In assembling and nailing into place such partitions as well as others where plumbing fixtures are to be located, there are a few framing practices you can follow to minimize the amount of cutting needed to install both waste-vent and water supply lines:

☐ Plumbing diagrams may show exact drainage stack locations, often directly behind or slightly to one side of the water closet; avoid placing of studs within about a foot on each side of the water closet center line;

☐ Where a tub-and-shower recess is being framed, water supply fittings and tub-drain occur at one end; at this end-wall, avoid placing studs within 8 inches of either side of the center line of the tub;

☐ Where a lavatory bowl is to be placed, avoid placing studs within 6 inches of either side of the bowl center line, or within 8 inches of either side of a kitchen sink installation.

The above clearances will permit running of waste con-

nections and water supply lines and air chambers in the spaces between studs and make it easier to attach piping to them.

Other Framing Details

First, about stairs and stairways. In most new homes, the staircases between first and second floors are precision-made in millwork shops. They are made to careful custom-shop drawings and fitted into position after wall finish work has been installed and the interior is about ready for trim work. Attic stairs in an expansion-attic home, though closed off by doors, are similarly built as a millwork item that is shop-fabricated. Same for the open-to-living-area stairs in a split-level home. Basement stairs are generally open stairs and often built using dimension-lumber stringers

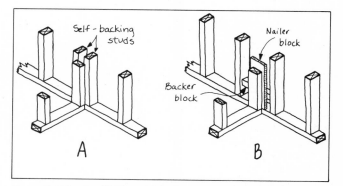

Frame Backing for Wallboard is built into the wall framing in one way or another. In sketch (A), where two walls meet, the triple stud provision gives a nail base for wallboard on both sides of each wall section. In sketch (B), a similar wall juncture meets one wall between stud locations, is provided with backer blocks nailed between studs at high, low and center, with a continuous nailer board nailed to the backer blocks.

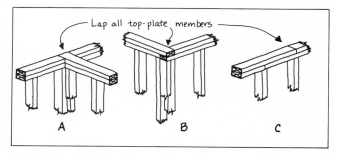

Plate Nailing at Wall Junctures with overlapping members. In sketch (A) a typical partition joining an exterior wall or other partition. Sketch (B) indicates lapping of plates at an exterior wall corner or interior wall corner. In sketch (C), the butting of plate joints is done over studs but not over the same stud for both plate members.

135

with 1-1/4 inch thick tread stock. The latter can easily be built by an owner-builder but this assembly and installation should await completion of the basement floor slab.

However, wall-framing for staircases are installed when other partition work is being completed. The partitions are no different from other partitions. Their sole-plates rest on the floor deck immediately adjacent to floor openings for the stairs. The only complications likely to arise are related to framing of closets under the upper portion of stairs. These usually have low vertical walls rising from floor level, then sloping ceilings that follow the underside of the stair slope. Construction is easy enough if the sidewalls of the closet area are assembled and positioned first.

In addition to under-stair closets, there are a few additional places where added framing or special framing provisions must be made. The most common of these is the soffit framing over kitchen wall cabinets. Sometimes referred to as cabinet furring, it is simply a blocking down over the cabinets to fill the space. Kitchen wall cabinets are wall-hung at heights so their top shelves remain within an average person's reach. This leaves a space between cabinet top and ceiling that is about 10 to 12 inches. Using 2X4 short pieces, vertical members spaced about 16 inches are nailed to the sides of ceilings joists. At their lower ends are horizontal 2X4's that run horizontally attached to wall studs or a ledger board nailed to the studs. Then 1X4's near the ceiling and at bottom corners of the blocking are nailed horizontally to brace the blocking and to serve as base for nailing up of wallboard both on the face of the framing and the underside.

A second type of special framing that may or may not be needed is in connection with the home's heating system. In basementless homes, the ceiling space along hallways may serve as duct space for return air. The framing needed here is simple cutting of 2X4's 7 inches longer than the hall's width between stud edges. The 2X4's are then placed at an appropriate distance below the ceiling, usually 6 or 8 inches, and nailed horizontally across the hall to studs on either side. This shallow but wide duct space is usually installed to permit a floor-to-ceiling height of 7 feet 6 inches.

Similarly, special framing may be needed to provide enclosure in a closet area for a chimney flue. And framing may be needed in connection with fireplace construction (see Chapter 13).

Following completion of above special framing areas, you still have one additional bit of work to finish in connection with partitions. This is the matter of adequate backing. "Backing" in this case refers to the nailing base provided at room corners for nailing up of wallboard. In providing extra studs at partition wall corners, you provided backing for wall sheets. But there are also wall-ceiling corners to be considered. Wall-plates provide suitable nailing for wall sheets, but there is nothing between joists for nailing of ceiling sheets. This is furnished by the installation of dimension lumber to fit between joists, nailed to the top-plates and extending over the top-plate edges sufficiently in order to permit nailing of ceiling sheets (see illustration). So, proceed room by room to check the conditions at the tops of all partitions, those running perpendicular to joists or trusses and those running parallel. Wherever needed, add blocking that will permit nail-up of ceiling sheets on both sides of the partitions.

Backing blocks may be needed at certain other locations. Discover exactly where is best by simply making a thorough inspection of the home's entire framing. Then imagine wall-ceiling sheets being applied and see what nailing bases they will need.

One other type of blocking is likely to occur in one-and-a-half and two-story construction where openings between floor levels occur in stairways and other vertical chases: many building codes require "fire-stops" in these areas. These are simply 2X4's cut between studs and nailed in so that vertical air-flow between studs is interrupted. Check with your local building inspector to find out at exactly what points fire-stops are required.

22 Ducts and Heating Rough-In

Talk of fuel shortages and energy conservation, not to mention constantly rising energy costs, has focussed the building industry attention on home heating systems. The result is a staggering amount of recently issued data and published information on the general topic of saving energy and fuel . . . and making heating plants more efficient.

To sort this flood of recent information out, the owner-builder will have to divide it up. In this text, the subject of energy conservation is discussed in conjunction with the material that can provide the home with the greatest amount of savings, insulation (Chapter 26). With respect to fuel shortages, the owner-builder will have to judge the comparative merits in his local area from the information obtained from utility and fuel supply companies. Here, only a few pertinent general observations on fuel use can be made that might help put the subject into perspective.

Forced warm-air heating with a central furnace and duct distribution system is by far the most common method of heating new homes in all parts of the country. For homes having basements or built over crawl spaces, the usual duct installation involves a relatively large main supply duct called an "extended plenum," which runs lengthwise of the home adjacent to the central support beam; smaller branch ducts lead from this main one to individual room registers. One of several types of provisions assists in bringing return air back to the furnace to complete the air circulation pattern.

Forced warm-air furnaces are available for use with any of three fuels—gas, oil, or electricity. In new homes, gas-fired equipment has predominated. Electric furnaces have been used in limited areas where rates are relatively low. With respect to gas, the larger number of furnaces in new homes use natural gas. But gas-fired equipment can usually be adjusted for the burning of liquified petroleum gases such as propane and many such installations have been made for homes in rural and remote areas that are beyond the range of gas supply lines.

Finding A Subcontractor

Heating, plumbing and electrical work on large construction jobs are often lumped together and called the "mechanical" trades, probably because each involves the application of mechanical engineering principles. But in residential construction they remain separate operations with specialized subcontractors, with each type of installation closely controlled by building codes and building inspection scrutiny.

It's the latter characteristic that makes it advisable for an owner-builder to arrange an agreement with a qualified subcontractor to perform certain minimal installation functions (if not a complete subcontract) and at the same time provide expert guidance for the portion of the heating-plumbing-electrical work that the owner-builder can handle for himself.

These three trades involve a somewhat higher degree of knowledge and skill than most building trades. This is reflected in wage rates a notch above those of most tradesmen. So, whatever work an owner-builder can logically do in these areas, will be a source of savings. The work itself isn't particularly difficult once you learn what needs to be done at what time, and in what manner to gain the building inspector's approval.

In connection with heating-plumbing-electrical work and your efforts to reach a qualified subcontractor to assist and guide you, beware of friends who know somebody or moonlighters recommended by acquaintances. Respond negatively to such offers and hunt up sources as you would with any other building material or service. The difficulty in such good-natured propositions is this: a friend knows a "good air-conditioning man"; you reach him, talk to him, he says "yep, air-conditioning a home is a snap because he's been doing these big commercial and office building jobs for years . . ." He's just the guy you *don't* want. He doesn't know residential work and doesn't know code requirements

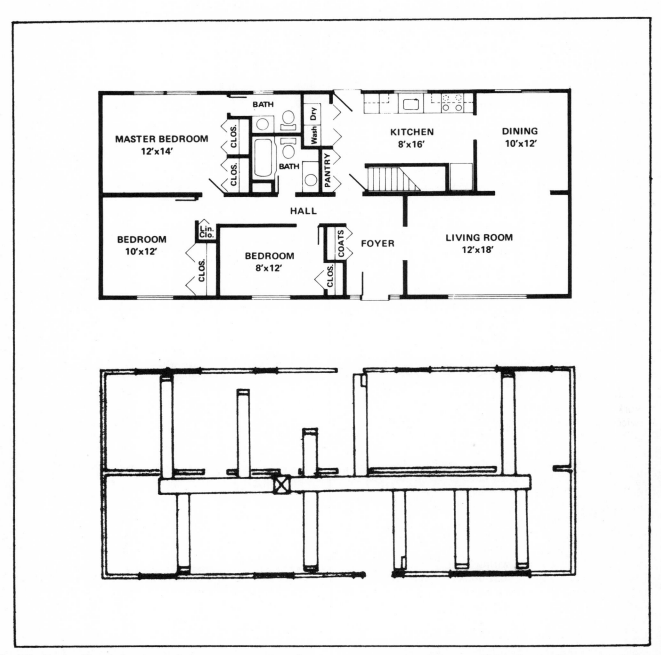

Heat Distribution Plan made using tracing paper over your home's floor plan will help in planning and ordering duct fabrication and accessories. In bottom sketch, main supply duct runs parallel to and near the central floor support beam in the basement. Supply air plenum over furnace is located by the X. Branch lateral ducts run from the main supply duct to floor register locateds indicated by the small rectangles. Note placement in kitchen and bathrooms to avoid cabinets and fixtures. While other duct layouts are possible, this is a straightforward method of bringing heated air into rooms at or near the exterior walls or windows where the warm air counters cool downdrafts. Not shown is return air duct, which can be located on other side of beam for short distance either side of furnace location, and fed by short vertical duct runs from wall grilles in the central lengthwise partition.

for homes and he'll provide very little accurate guidance for you. Similarly, many plumbers are billed as "plumbing and heating contractors" because they install piping and equipment for hydronic heating systems. Such a contractor recommended by a friend will readily admit he can be of no help to you at all on a ducted warm-air system.

In connection with these three trades, you need to scout for a subcontractor who is willing to enter into a written agreement with you for a division of work. The degree of division or proportion of work that each will do depends somewhat on the house design and the complexity of the heating-plumbing-electrical system. For home heating where the living area of the home is about 2,000 square feet or less, the ductwork and single heating plant installation is relatively straightforward. With such an installation, the following approximate division of work might be appropriate:

(1) Your heating subcontractor and you together plan the system layout and draw up a heating distribution diagram showing duct branches and register locations as well as the position of the furnace and return-air provision; in the course of this planning, you learn what parts of the systems are important from a building code standpoint.

(2) With the diagrammatic plan in hand, you talk about the parts of the work you can handle; he agrees to fabricate all duct runs either full-length or in sections; he will supply duct connection devices and sealing tape as well as any hangers or fasteners.

(3) You will handle the installation of the main supply duct and all branch ducts, the transition units to register openings and whatever other in-wall or in-floor work that is needed; he will come to the job once or twice in the course of the work to make sure you're doing it right.

(4) He will suggest the schedule to follow, probably indicating that ductwork within the framing should be done at once, before the plumbing or electrical work, and that the main supply and furnace plenum work that is within the basement or crawl-space area can wait until later when the furance is being set.

(5) When ready to set the furnace, he will come out after the unit has been delivered and help position it, make fuel connections, make wiring connections and otherwise ready the unit for start-up; with his guidance you will then install the furnace plenum, the extended plenum or main supply duct and the smoke pipe connections to the chimney flue.

(6) Later, by your agreement with him, you will install the registers and grilles after completion of wall finish work; you will also run low-voltage wiring from the furnace to the thermostat location.

(7) Finally, with power on, he will come out to check over the entire installation, hook up the thermostat, make initial startup, adjust the controls and the blower, and set the registers for approximate balance.

A part of your agreement may or may not include the furnishing of the furnace and its accessory items. But it should include provision for servicing the unit during the first year following installation.

Planning System Early

Certain early decisions on your home heating must be made. Your partial subcontractor will be of help in making these decisions.

The first is with respect to the type of fuel you desire to use and its availability. Natural gas is the choice of most owner-builders. But first you'll need assurance (in written form if possible) from your local gas utility. Assurance in two ways: that a gas main connection is now or at time of the home's completion will be available to you; and that your home as planned meets with any requirements the utility has in effect with respect to energy-saving construction details.

Another planning factor is your desire for air cooling. Discuss with your heating subcontractor. In a forced warm-air distribution system, the same ductwork can handle distribution of cooled air but it should be sized for the cooling function . . . slightly larger ducts are needed than for heating. Similarly, you should check your heating man on the matter of furnace plenum space for later installation of cooling coils. In some models of furnaces, this space provision is already allowed for and he may suggest purchasing this type of unit if air cooling is to be added relatively soon. Or, he may also suggest that in fabricating your plenum he can provide a covered opening for installing the coil at a later time.

In planning the ductwork, you will want to add to your layout diagram certain pertinent information regarding duct size of each run and the size of register or grille that is to be provided for at each air outlet or intake point. Be sure to include a note and indication for at least one basement register. Duct size and grille size(s) for return-air ducts are important also.

The usual practice when locating the furnace in a basement home is to position it adjacent to a chimney. It may be a heating-only chimney that runs up through a centrally located chase or closet. Or it may be a fireplace chimney which is more often than not located near an end of the home. Ask your heating subcontractor what furnace location he believes will be best in the light of the present chimney plans. And whether it might be perhaps advisable to consider provision for another chimney in a location to better suit the furnace and duct system. In all probability, he will be able to adapt the system to your present plans and drawings without significant changes being necessary.

With respect to the furnace in a crawl-space home, you may have two choices of location. Most house plans for crawl space construction indicate space for furnace and water heater in a first-floor closet. Closet location is desir-

Duct Riser Connection to Register shown from below the floor and indicating the common practice of running duct laterals or branches within the joist space. A metal bracket holds the round duct up. The conversion fitting for the lower part of the register frame is a standard connecting unit.

able because both units can be installed in even the smaller closets, with still sufficient access space for routine servicing. The alternative is to install the furnace in the crawl space itself adjacent to or part of the main supply duct installation. For this purpose, most furnace equipment manufacturers offer horizontal models that can be suspended from floor joists.

Whatever may be determined by your planning talks with the heating subcontractor, you will want to obtain his recommendations with respect to construction adjacent to the furnace location, and the specific requirements in your local building code with respect to this adjacent construction. The code will contain, usually, specific clearances that must be observed. For example, the One-and-Two-Family

Dwelling Code requirements for a gas-fired warm-air furnace are as follows:

- □ a minimum of 6 inches above the top of the casing;
- □ at least 6 inches above and at sides of supply plenum;
- □ a minimum of 18 inches in front of the furnace and 6 inches at the back and sides.

There may also be local code requirements specifying the clearances or installation details with respect to smoke or vent pipes, chimney connections, appliance draft hoods and other aspects of the heating system installation and the flue connection for water heaters. Then, there will also be code provisions covering fuel connections, fuel storage, safety controls, shutoffs and similar operational and safety details.

The principal thing you want to impress upon your subcontractor is that you are counting upon him to see that your installation meets these code requirements and that the installation will pass the inspection of the local building department.

Duct Rough-In Work

As mentioned before, after partition framing, your ductwork comes first in preference over plumbing and electrical. The reason is size. The duct parts and connections within the stud-and-joist spaces take up considerably more room than pipes or wires. So they should be put into position first and then you can find alternative spaces for the plumbing-electrical runs, or run them around the ducts.

Duct runs can be divided into horizontal runs and vertical runs. In a one-story home, the horizontal runs are those coming off the supply plenum or main duct to reach a register. The preferable location for heating supply registers is near room midpoints on the exterior wall. In such cases, the horizontal runs are placed within floor joist spaces. The duct runs are "hung" with simple metal straps that extend under the duct and are nailed to the joists. These ducts are usually rectangular and the standard size in most common use is approximately 4-¼ X 10 inches. Your heating subcontractor may suggest a larger duct size or more than one duct run and register for larger rooms. In some cases, the depth of floor joists will allow the use of round ducts.

Exhaust Ventilator Duct, Fittings must be provided for kitchen fans or hoods and bathroom fans. The aim is to duct the air to the outside. Shown here are four possible routes; which is chosen depends upon the room situation and the fan location. While such fans are sometimes vented using regular rectangular duct sections ordinarily used for heating systems, these sections are often hard to fit into tight quarters and around sharp corners. Shown in the sketches are continuous runs of flexible round metal air duct made by Johns-Manville and other firms. The flexible duct can be worked into areas of limited clearance or access, snaked around structural members and other obstructions. No special fittings or extra joints, and little field cutting work are needed with this flexible ducting.

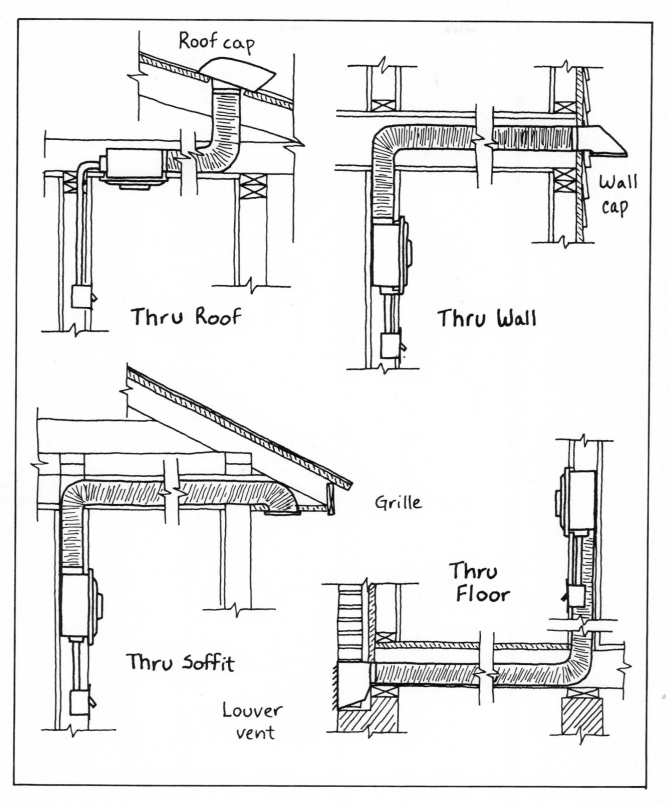

Roof cap

Thru Roof

Wall cap

Thru Wall

Thru Soffit

Louver vent

Grille

Thru Floor

Ductwork Gauges, Insulation, Supports

A. GAGES OR METAL DUCTS AND PLENUMS USED FOR COMFORT HEATING-COOLING FOR A DWELLING UNIT

	Galvanized Steel		
	Nominal Thickness (in inches)	*Equivalent Galvanized Sheet Gage Number*	*Approximate Aluminum B & S Gage*
Round Ducts and Enclosed Rectangular Ducts			
14" or less	0.016	30	26
Over 14"	0.019	28	24
Exposed Rectangular Ducts			
14" or less	0.019	28	24
Over 14"	0.022	26	23

B. INSULATION OF DUCTS[1]

Duct Location		
Roof or Exposed to Outside Air	B and W	
Attics[3]	A	
Underfloor Spaces	A	
Within the Conditioned Space[2]		None Required
Cement Slab or Within Ground		None Required

INSULATION TYPES:

A. One inch of fiber glass or rock-wool insulation with a minimum density of 0.65 pound per cubic foot or two layers of 1/4-inch air cell asbestos or air cell foil.

B. Two inches of fiber glass or rock-wool insulation with a minimum density of 0.75 pound per cubic foot or four layers of 1/4-inch air cell asbestos or 1/4-inch air cell foil, or one-inch fiber glass insulation with a minimum density of one and one-half pounds per cubic foot.

W. Approved weatherproof vapor barrier.

1. Insulation not required for evaporative systems.

2. Insulation may be omitted on that portion of a duct which is located within a vertical wall space if the wall space is directly adjacent to the occupied portion of the building.

3. Vapor barrier should be provided for cooling ducts in attics or areas of high humidity.

C. METAL DUCT SUPPORTS

Duct Type	*Max. Side or Dia.*	*Duct Position*	*Hanger or Strap Size and Spacing*
Circular	10	Vertical	No. 18 gage galvanized steel X 2" @ 12' o.c.
		Horizontal	No. 30 gage galvanized steel X 1" or No. 18 steel wire @ 10' o.c.
Rectangular	24	Vertical	1" X 1/8" teel galvanized strap @ 12' o.c.
		Horizontal	No. 18 gage galvanized steel X 1" @ 10' o.c.

At the register location, a rectangular hole in the floor sheathing must be cut and the duct brought to this opening. This is accomplished by means of a special register elbow that connects to the end of the joist-space duct run. Connections between the elbow and the duct are slip-on connections made secure with sheet-metal screws where the ducts are of galvanized sheet metal.

Vertical duct runs are made in stud walls where the common duct size is about 3-¼ X 10 or 12 inches. And, again, the ducts are held in position by strap fasteners nailed to nearby studs. Except for unusual circumstances, vertical risers are never installed in exterior walls if it is possible to locate a register so that its supply connection can be made through an interior partition. In most homes, vertical risers are limited to use in central partitions of one-and-a-half and two-story homes or split-level designs in which supply runs must be made to upper-level rooms. Vertical runs in central partitions also frequently serve as channels for return air flow down to a return air plenum or duct.

With the vertical risers, there is also provision for right-angle turns at the top. These may be elbow connections or they may be rounded ends plus connection flanges that are fabricated in the heating subcontractor's shop. Or by a sheet-metal shop. These flanged ends either project through beyond stud faces for wallboard to fit around for later register or grille attachment . . . or they serve for connection of a horizontal duct extension through the second-floor joist space.

Bottom ends of vertical risers come down to about the bottom edges of the floor joists and are, for the time being, left open. They will later be connected to either the main supply or main return duct. The same open-end applies to horizontal runs in first-floor joist spaces, the open end being near the central support beam or main supply duct. Your heating subcontractor will have figured this duct run dimension to allow for the transition connection to the main supply or extended plenum.

In short, then, your ductwork installation is a matter somewhat similar to your exterior wall panels. The duct sections and fittings to them have been premeasured and shop fabricated so they can be installed with only a minimum if any, on-the-job cutting.

With the heating supply horizontal runs to registers in place and the vertical risers for supply or return air in place, your ductwork for the home heating system is complete for this stage of construction. The main supply duct, the furnace plenum, the return-air duct, furnace setting and register-grille attachment all come later. But you still have a few little chores to do.

Sizing, Insulation and Support of Ducts can be guided by data contained in these three charts. Chart (A) gives appropriate metal gauges for various duct sizes. Chart (B) provides information on what duct insulation is needed where. Chart (C) gives the suitable types of duct straps or hangers and at what spacing they should be mounted.

The first supplementary chore is to insulate or seal duct runs. This may or may not be applicable to your home. Check with your heating man on these points. Duct insulation is usually provided where there are any duct runs in unheated spaces such as attics. It may be desirable for duct runs in crawl spaces, too. Sealing of duct joint connections with adhesive sealing tape may be a matter of local practice or local code requirements. Running a wrap of wide tape around duct connection joints does provide a good air seal and it tends to quiet the noise of circulating air. Duct insulation also helps to reduce the moving air sound.

The second supplementary chore is to install ventilating ducts. The two common ventilating ducts in nearly every new home serve to exhaust air from the house from kitchen and bathroom ventilating fans. In recent years, the blower-type range hood or oven hood has replaced the kitchen ceiling or wall vent fan. In bathrooms, the vent fan is often part of a ceiling light-and-fan combination. In any case, every fan that is not mounted in an exterior wall opening, needs a duct connection from the fan location to some point on the building's exterior construction for the exhaust grille.

Most range hoods have flanges for easy connection of standard size rectangular ducts. These run up through over-range wall cabinets and at-the-ceiling connection is made with a preinstalled vent duct which may be either round or rectangular. This vent duct runs through ceiling joist or attic space to either the exterior wall or the roof where it connects to a suitable roof cap or wall cap (see illustrations).

Heating Equipment Purchase

There are some nationally known names in warm-air heating and air conditioning . . . Lennox, General Electric, Carrier to name a few. But there are others lesser known or regional in their distribution with quality products that deserve your consideration.

There are two practices with respect to the selling of this equipment. One type of heating subcontractor may be an "exclusive dealer" for an equipment manufacturer. If the heating man you locate is such a dealer, you can buy only one company's product through him. There are other heating subcontractors who have no exclusive arrangement with any manufacturer and are free to purchase for you nearly any kind of equipment you and he choose.

As a generalization, it is probably accurate to say that the exclusive dealerships tend to be the larger heating

Through-Wall Room Air Conditioner is an alternative to central cooling for owner-builders. Hotpoint shown conditioner is one of a line of six cool-only models in capacities ranging from 6,000 to 15,500 Btu/hour. Install these wall models using a metal sleeve that fits into and nails to the framed-in wall opening. A suitable electric outlet is provided nearby. The conditioner is adjusted into its permanent position within the sleeve after exterior and interior wall finishing have been completed.

subcontractors doing a considerable volume of work. There's no harm in approaching such dealers but it's likely this type of dealer will not be interested in a partial subcontract job with you. A smaller heating subcontractor usually has more flexibility. Find a one-man operation and you're likely to receive better guidance not only in installation procedures but also in selection of your heating equipment.

Another source for heating-cooling equipment is the major retailers . . . Sears, Wards, and certain large chain building-supply firms. These are worth checking because many such sources have their own independent installers and you may be able to reach the man suited to your partial-subcontract arrangement through such channels.

23 Plumbing Rough-In Work

Plumbing is the second of the three "mechanical trades" mentioned in the previous chapter. And as earlier indicated, it's advisable for the first-time owner-builder to obtain guidance of a qualified tradesman or subcontractor familiar with local rules and practices.

Most local municipalities require a separate permit to be taken out for plumbing work. Very often, permits are issued only to licensed or otherwise qualified plumbing firms or individuals. Thus, the partial plumbing subcontractor should obtain a permit for you. And, in case there is any question on the part of the local building inspector as to who is doing the work, the plumbing subcontractor should make it clear that the work is being performed under his watchful eye and supervision.

Finding a qualified plumbing tradesman to assist you may require a search. There are three principal sources from which you may obtain the names of men who are able to provide expert assistance to you on either an hourly basis or for a lump sum, resulting from a written agreement concerning just what work he is to perform. The three sources are:

(1) Owners of plumbing firms that specialize in new residential work . . . get names from job foremen on homes under construction in your vicinity;

(2) Local building officials who know many of the plumbing subcontractors in the area, and perhaps know some who have worked with owners under arrangements similar to your conditions . . . building officials often know a few plumbers who are particularly conscientious and do a good job, but in inquiring about such men, avoid mention of the installation role you might play in the work;

(3) Suppliers to plumbing subcontractors usually have knowledge of many of the plumbing firms they supply, and may be able to recommend a few individuals worth calling . . . be sure to go to wholesale plumbing supply houses that regularly do business with plumbers, not to retail places that sell plumbing supplies to consumers.

In making your search, be aware that plumbers and plumbing subcontractors come in all sizes—from an individual one-man operation with answering service, up to a large multi-truck fleet operation with specialist crews who do only certain types of plumbing work. You're more apt to find that the type of individual you want will be either a smaller plumber or a journeyman for a larger firm that specializes in work on new homes for home builders.

When talking with a prospective plumbing subcontractor or tradesman, make sure that you explain your position. That you're building a home of your own and trying to save every penny you can. But you are still doing what is legally required and in the plumbing work you need some expert assistance and guidance.

If the man is interested in working with you on such a partial subcontractor basis, then indicate to him that you expect to draw up an agreement in writing that will spell out just what you want him to do and what work you wish to handle yourself under his guidance. Be sure that you make clear in your agreement the following division of work (or equivalent):

☐ he is responsible for obtaining any permits needed and for calling out inspectors at appropriate times;

☐ he will make installation of house sewer, stack and water line work necessary before foundation work is done, coordinating with the work of the sewer subcontractor as described in Chapter 7;

☐ he will assist in drawing up a plumbing diagram for drainage-waste-vent lines, water supply lines and gas lines;

☐ he will help you in starting the drainage-waste-vent (DWV) and other piping work, guide you in choice of tools and do some work himself in getting you past the rough spots;

☐ he will assist and guide you in the purchase of plumbing supplies and fixtures and later answer questions you have related to fixture installation;

☐ he will keep a watchful eye as the job progresses and you will follow his suggestions . . . basically you are the plumber's helper doing your first complete job under his supervision.

144

There are some baffling terms used in plumbing work. They tend to be confusing until you realize that most of them are names of specific plumbing parts. Pipes and fittings come in an unbelievably large assortment of types, sizes, styles, models, each for a specific type of use. Once you've started to understand the jargon in one type of system, the grasp of the language comes fairly easily. Study of the literature of plumbing supplies manufacturers is of great help in learning the terminology.

For example, let's take a quick run-down on what's involved in a DWV system. You start with soil pipe and soil stack. These terms refer to the large-diameter pipe that serves as the main collector of waste fluids and solids and delivers them outside the house to the sewer or septic disposal field. Toilets or water closets are the only plumbing fixtures that have a full size waste connection made through a fitting known as a "closet bend" to the soil stack. The stack is vertical and it continues upward through the roof; above fixture level, it is called the "soil vent" but the pipe used is the same soil pipe material, either cast iron, copper, or plastic.

This stack and soil vent is sometimes referred to as the "main vent." It must be located near a water closet and normal practice is to attach the waste lines of other nearby fixtures to it, specifically a bathtub and lavatory (see illustration). The waste lines from these fixtures are of smaller pipe, 1-½ and 2 inch diameters in contrast to the 3 and 4 inch soil pipe size. Waste lines run from such fixtures as sinks, laundry trays, dish- and clothes-washers as well as tubs, showers and lavatories. At some point near each individual fixture, and connected to the waste pipe, there must be a vent pipe running upward to a horizontal pipe called the "banch vent." This branch connects the individual vents to the soil vent.

All of this piping is governed by plumbing codes that specify suitable piping materials, the sizes to be used, the allowable distances from fixtures, the slope or pitch of the pipes and other details concerning the installation. In some areas, because of code provisions, you're likely to hear other DWV terms. One is a "wet vent" which occurs where the waste pipe itself is used for venting and this type of venting is frowned upon in most localities. But under some conditions, a vertical wet vent may be permissible. Another venting term is "revent," a term applicable to a secondary vent pipe which is beyond permissable distance from the main vent; it is used for a fixture downstream of the main vent.

The Systems For Plumbing

The piping in a home is often called the plumbing system but actually it is always separated into two systems and sometimes three: the DWV system, the water supply system, and the gas supply system. The first two are the principal components because parts of each must be brought to every water-using fixture or appliance in the home. Each of these systems has different parts and supplies needed to connect it up. The single-pipe gas supply line is, by comparison, a relatively simple installation which usually goes just to the furnace and water heater, the range oven, clothes dryer and possibly a fireplace log lighter or outdoor post-lamp.

It's imperative that you be conscientious in doing your plumbing work correctly and skilfully. The reason is the system's lack of accessibility. Most of the piping is run between framing members where it will become concealed and not readily repairable.

Looking upon each plumbing system individually is advantageous for the owner-builder because there are separate considerations for each. For the DWV system, there may be just a simple run to a septic tank. Or, there may be a municipal or privately owned sewer main to which your house sewer may be connected. In such cases, the tap-in must be done in a certain way and by certain people, often with clearance by a certain agency to whom application must be made.

Similarly, with respect to water supply, connection to an individual well pump may be quite simple while connection to a water main may involve tap-in following a certain established procedure. It's your responsibility in discussions with your plumbing subcontractor to ascertain just what tap-in permits, clearances, fees and procedures need to be observed and handled. With a municipal or privately owned water supply, there is the added factor of metering. Meters are generally furnished by the agency supplying the water but you will bear their cost. The traditional meter installation has been inside the home at a point close to the water supply line entrance. But in many communities, a newer practice calls for meters near the street tap-in point, the installation being in a covered catch-basin to avoid freezing yet allow ready reading of the meter by removal of the basin cover.

It's advisable that you draw up two plumbing diagrams for your home, one for each of the two principal systems. These need not be accurate-to-scale drawings but they should be proportioned roughly to distances of piping runs and complete with respect to the turns and locations of the piping. Your plumbing subcontractor will assist you in making these drawings by inspecting your house working drawings, seeing which wall-floor-ceiling areas it would be advisable to run piping through. The diagrams can be drawn in an isometric style to show three dimensions (as in many illustrations in this text) but just simple lines can be used to represent pipes with short cross-marks to indicate fittings. One of the purposes of such plumbing diagrams is to help prepare accurate lists of different kinds of pipe and fittings. Another purpose relates to your building inspector or official. Although he has a set of working drawings in conjunction with the building permit application, the plumbing diagrams will help him to see the scope of the plumbing work, how it's being laid out and what suggestions he might have with respect to meeting the code requirements. While this may sound a little like asking for trouble, it could be a time saver. It's much simpler for *you* to know the work you're planning will likely meet with his approval rather than to discover later when an inspection is made that "this

Horizontal Waste Pipe Run Support
(Plastic D-W-V Pipe)

Source of Waste	Pipe Sizes		
	1-½ in.	2 in.	3 in.
water closet			4 ft.
bathtub	4 ft.		
lavatory	4 ft.		
stall shower		4 ft.	
laundry tray	4 ft.		
kitchen sink	4 ft.		

SOURCE: Installation Details by Genova Products, Inc.

Pipe Sizes and Support Spacings for plastic pipe. For many years, support spacings have had a rule-of-thumb of 5 feet apart, and this support distance is written in some building codes. It came about because 5 feet was the standard length of cast iron soil pipe. With relatively lightweight plastic pipe, the 5 foot distance between supports would be adequate; this chart indicates 4 feet because the shorter distance is better coordinated with the common 16-inch spacing of wood framing members.

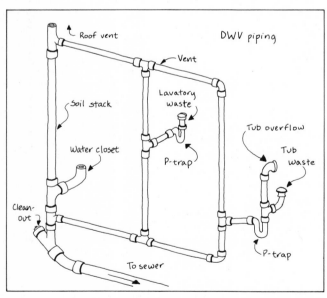

Typical Connections of Fixture Waste-Vent Lines are given. Waste piping runs downward to the main house line, then out to the sewer or septic tank. An upward extension of the same piping connects to each waste pipe near the fixture. These extensions are called vents and they must be extended through the roof or be cross-connected (as shown here) to a stack vent. The piping material for this type installation is called "DWV," an acronym for drainage-waste-vent installations such as this.

isn't the way the code provides so you'll have to tear this out and reinstall it the way it should be".

One thing you'll quickly learn in connection with heating-plumbing-electrical work is that while a certain practice or way of doing things according to a certain building code or set of standards may be all right, it is not "the way we like to have it done." Checking with local officials in advance is the only sensible way to deal effectively with local rules and regulations. There's another objective involved here, too. No matter how well-recommended your plumbing technician or subcontractor may come, he is a relatively unknown quantity to you. He may be an excellent craftsman, a knowledgeable businessman and very good with his crew members or employees. But you're depending on him also for knowledge of the building code and local interpretations of it. He may not know the rules and regulations as well as he should. So the check of plumbing diagrams with your building official protects you against the lack of code knowledge on the part of your subcontractor. It's your money. You want to do the work once, not twice.

One further word on drawing the isometric diagrams. It can be simplified by use of an isometric rule and scale which may be available from drafting supply firms. This is a ruler that runs straight for about two-thirds of its length and then bends upward at a 30° angle. Scale marks run in each direction from the point of the bend. If such a ruler is not available, use a 30-60° triangle. In drawing the piping runs, a vertical line represents a vertical run. Horizontal pipe runs east-west are at 60° with the vertical to the right of it; horizontal pipe runs north-south are at 60° with the vertical to the left. Make notations on the diagrams regarding pipe sizes, run lengths, fittings required.

The Drainage-Waste-Vent System

The system runs from the waste outlet, be it septic field or sewer main, to the plumbing fixture most distant from the outlet. The common practice is to run the house portion of the main soil pipe parallel to exterior walls although it really doesn't matter which direction it runs as long as the flow slope of 1/4 inch per foot is maintained. But running the main parallel to house walls does provide a little simplification in connecting branches at right angles to the main. The main drain or soil line is generally of 4 inch diameter pipe and since the main is usually below the ground or basement concrete floor, the line is usually of cast iron with poured lead joints. Above floor line, stacks are 4 inch if cast iron but may be 3 inch when copper or plastic pipe is used.

In planning the DWV system, your plumbing subcon-

DWV Plastic Pipe Fittings in one-stack bathroom kits are being packaged by the Nibco. Shown is a listing of parts with their sizes and location in the system. A single stack installation is appropriate for small baths with fixtures all located on one bathroom wall.

DWV SUPPLIES FOR 3-FIXTURE BATH

ITEM NO.	NOMINAL SIZE	DESCRIPTION
1	3″ x 4″	Adapter to plastic soil pipe
2	3″	45° Elbow
3	3″ x 3″ x 3″	45° Wye (PxPxP)
4	3″	Fitting & Cleanout w/threaded plug
5	3″ x 3″ x 3″	Sanitary Tee
6	3″	90° Elbow
7	4″ x 3″	3″ Closet Fitting
8	3″ x 3″ x 1½″	Sanitary Tees (Qty. 2)
9	1½″	P Trap w/union (PxSJ)
10	1½″ x 1¼″	Male Trap Adapter
11	1½″	90° Elbow
12	3″	Coupling
13	3″	Neoprene Roof Flashing
14	1½″ x 10′	(ABS or PVC) Pipe
15	3″ x 10′	PVC Pipe (Qty. 2)
16	½ pint	(ABS or PVC) Solvent
17	½ pint	PVC Primer

tractor will indicate most appropriate location of the main drain line in order to minimize piping runs from various fixture locations. Unless bathrooms are back-to-back, soil stacks will be required wherever there is a water closet. Calculations in the planning must include consideration of the house's main drain and necessary slope. The starting point is the depth of the sewer main in the street or the relatively shallow depth of the septic tank inlet. With a 12 foot deep street sewer, problems are not likely. Your home, if not too distant from such a street main, can have a basement floor drain to the below-floor main drain line. If the street sewer is shallower or the distance from it is substantial, the home's main drain may not be able to be placed below floor line in the basement but may have to be run below first-floor joists. Any basement drain outlets then have to be lifted to the main-drain level by pump or a sewage lift installation which can run into extra costs.

One-Piece Tub-Recess Installation is not difficult but must be planned for before completed partition work. As indicated in sketch (A), the tub-recess units are lightweight enough to be handled by two men but they are large enough to perhaps pose a problem going through narrow openings. Once placed in the bathroom framing pocket, the molded units are simply fastened to the framing (B) after proper leveling. Procedures with different types of tub-recess units vary, so be sure to ask in advance for a copy of the manufacturer's installation instructions.

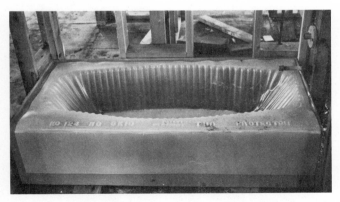

Protect Your Tub, tub damage repairs are expensive. Bathtubs must be positioned, attached to framing, and pipe connections made early. A lot of remaining interior work makes the tub subject to nicks, scrapes, dents and so on. Provide a tub protector such as this, you can obtain them from your plumbing supplier.

Where no street sewer is available for connection, the individual septic disposal system as outlined briefly in Chapter 2 is needed. Whether your home site was appropriate for a septic system should have been determined prior to its purchase. The shallow depth of septic field disposal lines and the house drain input connection is satisfactory for a basementless home or a basement house that is on a site having lower ground for the disposal field and tank. If your depth of tank inlet is not below the basement floor level, your use of plumbing fixtures in the basement may be limited. Consult your plumbing subcontractor how to best handle the problem.

In regard to branch waste-drain lines, the usual practice is to install the piping within the joist spaces. In a basementless or crawl-space home, these branch runs can be just below the joists and hung from them. Branches also slope at 1/4 inch per foot. Waste line risers or vertical runs from the branches are placed in stud spaces of partitions and, when necessary, of exterior walls. The latter usually occurs only in the case of kitchen sinks. Waste lines in exterior walls are to be avoided partly because of consideration for possible freeze-up due to inadequate insulation or close proximity of the pipe to the outdoors. But another factor is the difficulty of venting.

Plumbing Codes

It should be explained that many communities really have four codes: a building or structural code plus separate codes for plumbing, electrical and heating. Plumbing codes are quite strict in their vent requirements. Vents are part of the drainage-waste system. They must be constructed of the same material as that used for the pipe. Standard size for venting of most fixtures is 1-½ inch pipe except for soil stacks. With stacks, the 3 or 4 inch size is used for venting. If 3 inch pipe is used, the code may require an increase to 4 inch at the point where the pipe penetrates the roof.

Another detail of installation that codes have specific provisions for is the matter of clean-outs. These are short pipe extensions at certain critical points in the system. The extension will be fitted with a removable plug. This permits access to the drain line for plumber's snakes or rodders to unblock stoppages. A main system clean-out is usually required. A clean-out is mandatory for certain water using fixtures. But code requirements vary in this respect and the matter should be checked with both your plumbing subcontractor and the building official. With respect to most water-using fixtures, clean-outs can be provided rather easily with a proper choice of fittings. The One-and-Two-Family Dwelling Code requires them at the upper end of the house drain and "at not more than 50 feet on center in horizontal drainage lines, at each change of direction of the house drain which is greater than 45°, at or near the foot of each vertical waste or soil stack and at the junction of the house drain and house sewer."

Any system for handling home wastes involves a health

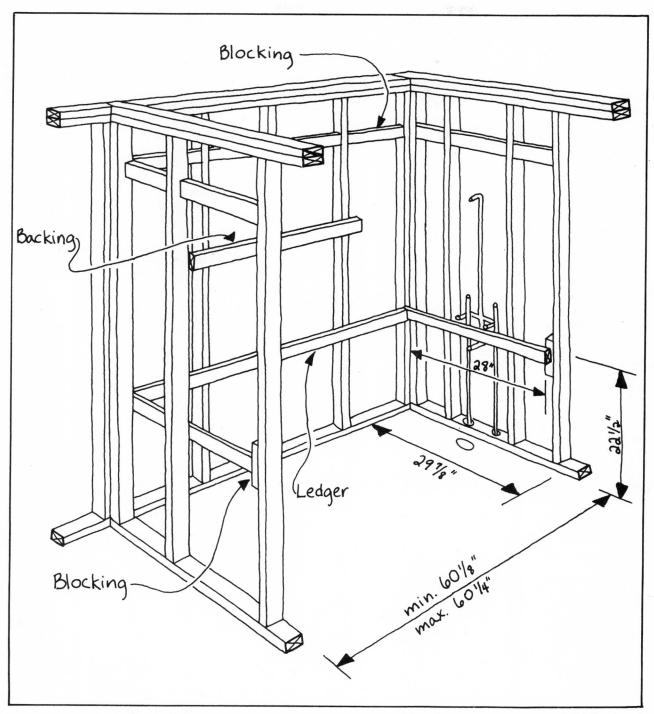

Blocking

Backing

Blocking

Ledger

28"

29⅞"

22½"

min. 60⅛"
max. 60¼"

Framing for A One-Piece Tub-Recess Unit made of molded plastic. A stud-frame pocket of this type must accommodate the newer molded plastic fiberglass-reinforced bathtubs and integral tub-recess surfaces. The pocket must be accurate for dimensions given by the tub manufacturer, plumb, square, and have suitable blocking or ledger support strips. Tub manufacturers will give, in their rough-in instructions, any additional details necessary to wall preparation.

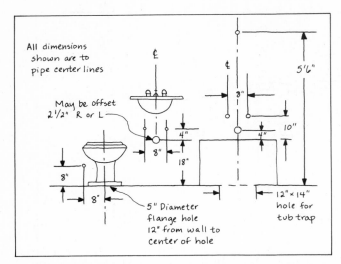

All dimensions shown are to pipe center lines

May be offset 2½" R or L

5'6"

8"

10"

4"

4"

8"

18"

8"

8"

5" Diameter flange hole 12" from wall to center of hole

12"×14" hole for tub trap

Roughing-In Dimensions for Bath Fixtures give the correct locations observed in most areas for closet, lavatory and bathtub. However, keep in mind that a wide range of new fixture designs have come on the market in recent years and its quite possible that a new type of fixture will have different pipe connections and thus the need to bring wall or floor piping to non-standard rough-in distances. Always observe the rough-in pipe locations that the manufacturer of the fixtures you select indicates should apply.

hazard. The aim of plumbing codes is to minimize these hazards and there are a number of them. Aside from the rather obvious hazard of coming into contact with the waste line materials, there are a number that you might not suspect. One example is siphonage. All fixtures are equipped with piping traps that keep a barrier of water filling the pipe within the trap to avoid emission of contaminated air from the waste lines into the house. Under certain conditions, if the waste system is not properly installed, the water in the trap may be siphoned off allowing sewage odors and contaminated air to enter the home.

It's for these health reasons that plumbing codes spell out details and why you should plan to meet each requirement in the way it was intended. Remember, in this case, it's your own family's health that may be threatened by a faulty installation.

Your DWV system may require attention to certain other details in following the code requirements. In some areas where a flooding hazard may be present, your house sewer may be protected by a backwater valve. The code may cover the situation described earlier on below-sewer-level drainage by specifying use of an approved type of vented watertight sump plus a pump to lift it to sewer level.

Venting practices called for by the code may include provisions such as:

□ when vents connect to a horizontal drainage pipe, they should be connected above the center line and ahead of the trap being served;

□ vertical risers must run to a point 6 inches above the fixture's overflow level before being offset horizontally or joining with other vents;
□ vent pipes through the roof should extend at least 6 inches above roof surface and be not closer than 1 foot from any nearby vertical surface;
□ vents should terminate not less than 10 feet from and 3 feet above a window, door or air intake.

Planning Your Water Supply System

A single water supply pipe line runs from the street main or water supply well pump to the house at a depth that is sufficient for protection against ground frost.

First a word of precaution about individual water wells. Start early to make contact with a well digger, sometimes called well-drillers because most installations involve the drilling of a hole, to arrange installation of a casing to prevent hole walls from crumbling, and insertion of a submersible well pump and pipe. The job requires special machinery and well-diggers are scarce in many areas. The well-digger may have a schedule to which he adheres; he may visit certain areas only at certain times of year.

From tap-in at street main or from water supply pump, the underground line entering the building is usually done through foundation wall openings provided by a sleeve in the course of wall construction. Timing of the tap-in on the main varies with local communities. Tap-in may be permitted early to meet the need for construction water for concrete or masonry mixing. However, some plumbing inspectors and building departments require procedures for temporary water and prefer the main tap be delayed until entire piping system has been installed, pressure-tested and approved.

Minimum size water supply line is normally 3/4 inch pipe of galvanized iron, copper or plastic according to what the code may permit. The order given here is approximately in declining order of material costs. Where a long run to the home from a street main is needed, the pipe size may have to be increased to 1 inch. Consult the water supply source on this with and at the same time find out what special provisions or accommodations must be made including details with respect to the water meter.

In making plans for water line trenching with sewer or excavating subcontractor, be sure to have water line bypass ground area where a septic field installation might be made. The water line may come into the house foundation area either through a foundation wall or below the footing and up through a vertical run of pipe. Consult your water supply source as to both the need for a specific type of shut-off valve at point of entry and the provision at this point of a means of draining the entire system to prevent freezeup in a nonoccupancy period. A stop-and-waste valve can be used to provide both functions—shut-off and line-drain. Such a valve includes a drainage opening as part of the valve construction. Some plumbing codes will specify the exact type of valve needed at the point of entry, whether globe, gate, or compression type.

The normal practice, although there is no specific reason why in the absence of a code requirement, is to position the domestic water heater close o the water supply entrance. Or vice versa, to bring the water supply line to enter the home as near as possible to the water heater which must, usually, be close to the home heating plant to make convenient use of the flue connection. But, aside from conventional practice, it does make good sense from the standpoint of the home occupant to have house entrance valve, line drainage valve, domestic water heater and water softening equipment, if any, grouped near each other and in a readily accessible location. If a curb meter is not used, this location is also the proper place for your meter where it can be easily read. Such a water-use center will also make easier the addition of any piping needed for future home expansion.

Your water supply distribution system to service various water-using fixtures will be in the form of two parallel piping runs, one for hot water, the other for cold. The same principle of main lines plus branches to individual fixtures is used in a manner roughly comparable to the house main and waste branches of the DWV system. For your supply mains, use the same size pipe as the supply main of the house entrance, 3/4 inch. Individual single-line runs to sill-cocks (outside hose-bibb faucets) should also be 3/4 inch as should the piping related to the water heater. Hot/cold supply mains should be run approximately 10-to-

12 inches apart, located so that lateral or branch runs are reasonably short and so branch connections are relatively accessible and not too close to wood framing members. These supply mains generally run perpendicular to the floor-ceiling joist direction; they may be suspended below floor joists in a one-story home, run through second-floor or ceiling joists in a one-and-a-half or two-story home. In some areas, plumbers prefer to keep supply mains in the basement or crawl space area for one-and-a-half and two-story construction taking 2nd story branches off the main just as they do for first-floor fixtures. Your plumbing subcontractor will quickly suggest what he believes the proper way to run mains for the home design you've selected.

At fixture locations, the branch supply lines terminate in fixture shut-off valves which are usually of the tee-type having through-passage connections for short lengths of flexible tubing runs to fixture faucets or mixing valves. Water supply branch runs are generally of 1/2 inch pipe while tubing connections are 3/8 inch. The lateral or branch terminations to all fixtures and shut-off valves (except the cold water line that goes to water closets) need a short extension of pipe running vertically above the fixture shut-off valves (see illustration). This upward extension is usually about 12-to-16 inches high, is kept within the wall stud space and is called the air chamber or expansion chamber. The purpose is to provide an air cushion within the piping to avoid "water hammer," the pipe noise that sometimes comes with rapid water shut-off.

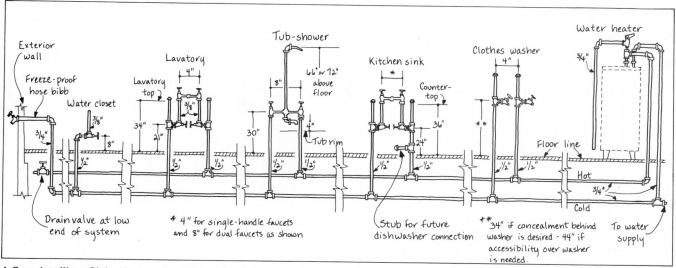

A Complete Water Piping System should be as simple as this sketch indicates. Unfortunately, in any given actual installation, the piping must turn corners and cross rooms. Still, this diagram shows the different parts, fixtures and accessories required for a complete water pipe installation. It also indicates the common dimensions above floor line for the fixture stops or shut-off valves.

This type of installation, sometimes referred to as a dual-pipe system, is the most common for single-family homes. Some luxury homes are equipped with a return hot-water line to the heater. The circulation through this line means that when any hot-water faucet is turned on, the water is hot almost immediately.

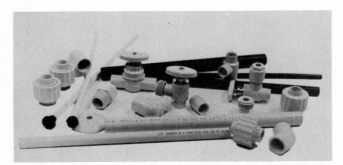

Plastic Water Pipe and Fittings, now being distributed through many home retail centers and lumber-supply stores, offer a ready selection of supplies plus instructions for their use. Shown is the PB (polybutylene) tubing and CPVC (chlorinated polyvinyl chloride) fittings made by Genova Products. The tubing is relatively flexible for easier installation. Both tubing and fittings meet the requirements of the National Sanitation Foundation for potable water conveyance.

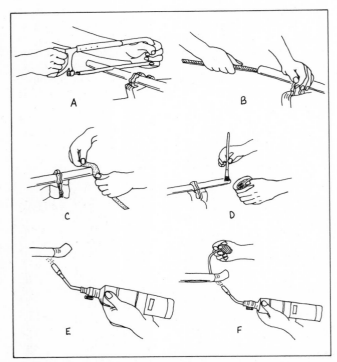

Soldered Cooper Tubing Joint is basically a six-step procedure as indicated in these sketches adapted from the illustrations contained in instruction sheets prepared by Nibco, in conjunction with its line of copper fittings. A hacksaw is used to cut the tubing to length (A) and the burr on the inner edge of the tubing is smoothed down (B) with a rounded file. The outer end of the tube where the fitting is to be placed is polished with a strip of fine sandpaper (C) and followed with a brushed-on coat of paste flux (D). The fitting is slipped onto the tubing end and heated with a portable torch (E). When hot, solder is applied to top of tubing near fitting (F) and torch kept on the joint until the solder flows completely around.

In planning the water piping supply mains and branches, remember that at every fixture, the cold water line must come up to the fixture on the right side as you stand in front of the fixture facing the faucets. Your planning of branch terminations at fixture locations should be done observing certain common dimensional practices with respect to rough-in dimensions (see illustration). Yet at the same time, realize that these are standard dimensions for more or less standard fixtures or products. The growing selection in types of plumbing fixtures as outlined in Chapter 41 make it mandatory that you make your selection at least of the *type* of fixture to be used in advance of the time that plumbing rough-in work is to be done. Then, in making this definite fixture determination, check the manufacturer's or supplier's catalog to verify that the fixture you've selected will be accommodated by the rough-in dimension that you've tentatively planned on using. This is particularly applicable in regard to some of the newer types of tub-and-recess units and stall shower units.

Pipe Materials and Workability

In the past, bell-and-spigot style pipes in both clay and cast iron were just about the only kinds of pipe used in house sewer and drain lines. Cast iron was the material for soil lines and soil stacks-and-vents while galvanized iron was used for branch waste lines and vent runs. Galvanized was also the standard for water supply lines. That situation has changed radically.

Copper was the first nonferrous material to gain headway in residential plumbing stallations. In many areas now, copper is the principal material used for both DWV and water-supply piping. Within the past few years, rigid plastic

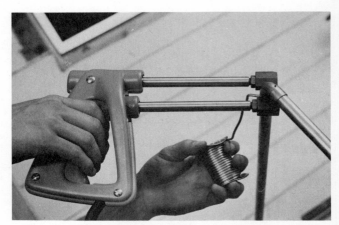

An Electric Soldering Tool designed for use on copper water pipe installations has been introduced by Nibcoware. The tool provides flame-free soldering and thus avoids the scorching of nearby framing members. Heat is concentrated in two carbon electrodes controlled through a pistol-grip release. The replaceable tips are good for use on about a thousand joints. Check your supplier for rental availability.

pipe in several types has been given approval by many building codes and has been receiving widespread acceptance by those in the plumbing trades.

Different tools are required and somewhat different cutting-fitting procedures are involved with the newer piping materials. From the standpoint of ease of working or handling, as well as the need for special tools, cast iron and galvanized steel are the more difficult and time-consuming. Plastic pipe is by a considerable degree the lightest in weight and handling ease but is also the easiest to join and the fastest to install. The quality of plastic piping has been proven in literally thousands of mobile homes. Supplies and fittings for plastic pipe are commonly available in all parts of the country. Where plastic is permitted by building codes, it is highly recommended for owner-builders.

Local building code approval of plastic water supply piping is not as widespread as that for drainage-waste-vent use. Be guided here by local practices. The savings and ease of working with plastic pipe are not sufficient reward for the frustrations and arguments that could ensue if the local officials don't think very well of plastics.

Cast iron pipe is heavy, very slow to cut, and requires a poured joint of melted lead. With proper equipment the melting and pouring of such joints in soil stacks is fairly easy but properly filling a horizontal joint takes some skill. Have your plumbing subcontractor make the joints in the parts of your system requiring cast iron.

Heating and Brazing Outfit is made by Mapp Products in two models or kits. At left, gas cylinder with adjustable fuel regulator, hose length, torch and medium-duty high-velocity brazing tip (other tips available for special work). At right, premium quality brazing kit and carrying case.

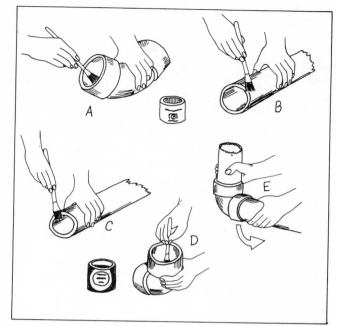

Joining DWV Plastic Pipe can be accomplished in just a few steps with a brush. First, the bed of the plastic pipe socket is brushed with a cleaning agent (A); same is done for the outer rim of the pipe to be inserted (B). Next, a special welding solvent is brushed on the pipe rim (C) and inner side of the socket (D). The joint is then completed by simply inserting the pipe in the fitting socket (E) with a tightening, twisting motion.

Sockets are provided on all fittings, which come in a full range of types including a splicing collar. Plastic pipe comes in plain 10 foot lengths, and is cut to proper length for use with an ordinary carpenter's handsaw.

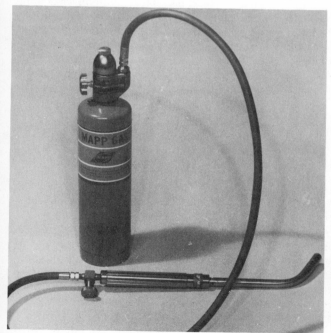

Galvanized iron pipe for water lines and black pipe for gas lines involve threaded connections. You can probably rent or borrow a manual threader. Fittings come pre-threaded female; your part is measuring pipe, cutting to length, and threading the male pipe end. The connection is lubricated with joint compound, tightened by pipe wrench. A bit time-consuming but not difficult.

In some building supply retail stores, you'll see supplies of prethreaded pipes. Even though they seem to come in a wide range of lengths, avoid them. They're designed more for repair and replacement, not for new construction. In addition, they usually sell at a substantial mark up above the price of full-length unthreaded pipe.

Copper pipe is more often than not called tubing. It comes in three types. The heavy-duty Type K and a lighter Type L are for water supply lines, both come in either rigid or flexible-bendable tempers. Type DWV, as you might guess, is intended for drainage-waste-vent use. Cutting of copper is done with a wheel cutter or fine-toothed hacksaw. Inside of the cut pipe must be deburred using a rounded file on the larger sizes, a burring hand tool on smaller ones. A series of copper or bronze fittings is available for use with each type of connection, and may be either soldered or flared. Clean metal is essential for soldered connections. The fitting and pipe ends are softly fine-sanded and a flux applied. Fitting and pipe end are jointed, heated with a plumber's tank-supplied torch or a portable propane torch. With well-distributed heating, the solder flows into the joint to surround the pipe.

Installing Plastic Piping in stud framing. Pipe is sized so largest diameter normally used (3 inches) fits within dimensions of 2×4 studs and no special framing is required.

Flared copper joints are often used where a torch cannot be safely handled or where the joints may be subject to later disconnecting. A special flaring tool is used to increase the tubing's diameter at the very end. This creates a flared flange grasped by a threaded flange nut previously slipped over the tube end. The flange nut threads into the fitting or into the female part of a splicing connector.

Plastic pipe is simplest to cut and join. A wheel tube cutter or hacksaw does the cutting. A cleaner is brushed on both pipe and fitting to remove surface gloss. A welding solvent brush-applied, or using container dauber, is given both pipe end and fitting; the two are brought together, given a slight twist and held in contact for about a 15-second hardening process. Where plastic piping meets other types of pipe material, special transitional fittings should be used.

Plastic pipe for DWV use comes in two principal types that are now generally accepted: ABS and PVC are the abbreviated names for Acrylonitrile-Butadiene-Styrene and Polyvinyl Chloride piping materials. With respect to water supply piping, the commonly available products are a combination of Polybutylene (PB) tubing with fittings molded of Chlorinated Polyvinyl Chloride (CPVC). The PB tubing is suited for water systems not exceeding 100 psi pressures and 180° F temperatures.

The supply picture on plumbing pipe and fittings is undergoing change. Plumbing suppliers, traditionally supplying only to tradesmen, may be a good source, but you must know what to order . . . there's little to guide you except your plumbing subcontractor. On the other hand, an increasing number of building supply establishments are offering complete assortments of plumbing parts and supplies. The manufacturers of these parts are packaging them, and furnishing display racks plus information on what situations they are used for. A few manufacturers are furnishing all parts needed for certain types of common installations in kit form—a bathroom rough-in kit or a lavatory trim and tubing-stop kit. While you may pay a slightly higher price for kit and packaged materials, you benefit by having specialized instructions and by having there in one package all the parts you're likely to need.

Miscellaneous Provisions

With respect to gas line plumbing, first discuss the use of gas appliances with your local gas utility company. Not the customer representative but the new-building or builder's-planning representative.

Your first consideration is for availability. Don't plan to use gas if the availability is contingent upon completion of any new supply mains or sources. Proceed with gas appliance or heating plans only if the representative can assure you, preferably with a commitment in writing, that when your new home is completed it will be connected and provided with gas service.

Approximately the same procedure should be followed

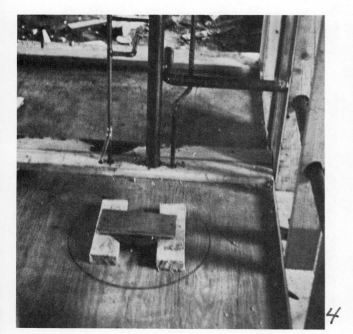

DWV Piping Run Details are illustrated in this group: (1) upper vent pipe is offset in the attic space and a wood brace nailed to rafters serves to hold the 3-inch vent section penetrating the roof; (2) an offset in the waste line through the second floor joist space allows the piping run to miss an obstruction in the stud space immediately below; (3) waste-vent piping at the clothes washer location where a between-studs recessed metal box enclosure contains the water shut-off valves; (4) plastic pipe stack of 3 inches diameter is well within 2×6 framing behind the water closet; note board cover protection for the closet flange on the floor.

in rural areas with suppliers of liquified petroleum (LP) gases such as propane or butane.

The next point of our planning discussion relates to the meter and its location. Increasingly, outside meters are being used so meter-readers won't need to enter the home. While this is desirable, you should check with the company for a desirable meter location consistent with your house plans. It should be accessible but unobtrusive.

The piping from the street gas main to the meter and a short extension into the home is done by the gas company. The piping from this point in basement or utility room is your responsibility. A single 3/4 inch black pipe is run parallel or perpendicular to framing members and brought to a stub end (capped) just inside the wall surface point at the appliance location.

Piping For Your Fireplace may be desirable. It's mostly a matter of extending your gas appliance piping (water heater and/or furnace) below the floors or through the walls to the fireplace location so that either a gas lighter or set of gas logs can be installed. Here are a few details: (1) coil of copper tubing is end of underground run from furnace, and connection is being made to black steel pipe which must be used above ground in building; (2) using small tubing cutter to cut the tubing off to proper length; (3) attaching flaring tool to flare the end of the tubing; (4) tightening up the transition fitting with a wrench. The black pipe end is just long enough to project through fire brick into fireplace opening.

24 Electric Service and Wiring

Your next guidance expert, and partial subcontractor, is the electrician. As with plumbing work, separate permits may be needed for electrical work in your locality and permits might be issued only to licensed electricians. But whether this is the case or not, hiring an electrical subcontractor to handle the initial service entrance work and to guide the balance of the wiring will pay off—both in saved time, and prevention of wiring mistakes or improper material purchases that would not be OK'd by your local inspector.

Finding such a qualified electrician to act as your subcontractor is not difficult. It involves pretty much the same legwork as in finding a plumber. You can (1) contact electrical subcontracting firms who specialize in new residential construction in your area; (2) ask the local building official or inspector; or (3) inquire of counter men at local electrical supply firms who supply primarily electrical contractors rather than consumers.

Electrical contractors vary in size of their operations from a one-man, do-everything repair specialist to a well-staffed residential and commercial contracting organization. As with the plumbing subcontractor you may find that the technican best suited to help you is a smaller almost one-man electrician working entirely in new home construction, or a moonlighting electrician regularly employed by an electrical contracting firm doing principally residential wiring work. Whichever, he should be familiar with local electrical practices and with your local building officials.

The National Electrical Code (NEC) is the single most widely observed code for electrical installations of all kinds. It calls for neat, workmanlike execution of the mechanical part of the work. In addition, the code recommends that those local authorities or officials having jurisdiction make a determination as to who's qualified to do the work on the basis of three points:

(1) competent knowledge and experience of installation methods;
(2) established practices of qualified journeymen in a particular area;
(3) programs available in trade schools having training courses for apprentices and journeymen.

Just what little details might not be considered "neat and workmanlike"? Here are a few examples of what could be termed a careless installation:

□ nonmetallic cables installed with twists or kinks;
□ concealed runs not grouped and irregular or diagonal exposed runs of cables;
□ noticeable droop or slack between supports on suspended runs;
□ conduit bends with flattened areas;
□ wiring difficult to sort or not organized in enclosures;
□ any improvisation of supports, fittings, hangers, straps.

So, as the owner-builder you should apply the same criteria here as in the plumbing work, and use as intended the parts and pieces involved. Errors or poor workmanship can result in hazardous conditions that can threaten serious injury to your family. It might be noted, however, that in new construction normal practice is for an entire installation to be completed before the current is switched on. This makes it even more difficult to locate and correct an error.

Division of Work

Electrical service to a home from a utility pole or underground cable system comes via a group of three relatively heavy-duty conductors. At the house, there is a service entrance head that may be wall-mounted or eave-mounted or may project above the roof level on a pole mounting. It may also come underground to a service entrance enclosure and meter base (see illustration).

Normally, the local electric utility's crew will make the service drop connections at the utility pole or underground transformer plus the wiring runs to the service entrance head and meter base. From this point on, the wiring is done by the electrician.

In considering the logical division of labor between you and your electrical subcontractor for the various parts of the electrical system and subsystems, your subcontractor should probably install and connect the following . . . mostly front-end items:

- □ service head mounting pole or bracket, or enclosure and meter base;
- □ conduit or direct through-wall cable to the main disconnect switch-and-fuse box;
- □ conduit or cable through interior from the main switch to the distribution panel;

Electrical Service Entrance may be overhead or underground. Shown here is a typical entrance enclosure with meter base for an underground service drop. At right, meter and enclosure cover in place once home has been completed.

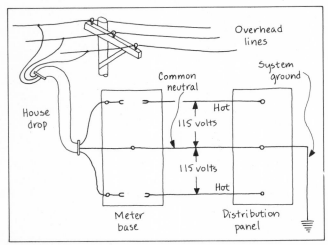

Three-Wire Electrical Service with overhead service drop and feeder to main distribution panel. This service provides 115-volt electricity for normal usage plus 230-volt service for special heavy-duty appliances such as electric water heaters, ranges and clothes dryers.

- □ conduit or cable from the distribution panel serving as feeder to any branch distribution center;
- □ provision for and connection to system ground.

The foregoing work would involve organizing the distribution centers with circuit breakers in accordance with the planned circuitry developed in the electrical diagram, and making wiring connections at the panels once the circuits have been installed.

This division of work would assure that the service entrance met with utility company requirements, and would enable skilled, knowledgeable hands to handle the heavy conductor portion of the installation in a code-approved manner. The circuitry work with the later installation of outlet receptacles, switches, and fixtures—easier but more time-consuming, routine and repetitive work—would be done by you. Then, with circuitry work completed, the eletrician could check the work out thoroughly and complete the final circuit connections at the distribution panel(s).

Service entrance and distribution panel equipment may vary from one locality to another. A particular electrical utility company can decide it wants things this way or that way . . . and wants this or that equipment used. Thus, the locally qualified electrician knows installation details that an outsider would find difficult to come by.

Most of homes of 2,500 square feet or less can be served by a single distribution panel or branch circuit center. The panel, physically, is in the form of a metal enclosure box that recesses into a stud space; the panel face leaves exposed the front faces of individual circuit breakers and the switches that control them. The panel may or may not have a hinged cover plate or door. Within the enclosure, the primary elements are bar conductors that permit connection in parallel of a number of breaker-type circuit protection devices. The number accommodated depends on the size of the enclosure selected, and the circuitry needs of the specific home.

In a few areas and with small minimum-cost homes, there's an inclination to continue the practices of the past and use fuses as circuit-protection devices instead of circuit breakers. While fuses will still perform their intended function, the extra expense of the circuit-breaker panel is more than warranted by its convenience.

Arrangements for accommodating breakers may include a primary section for double-pole breakers used with 3-wire 230-volt circuits and a secondary section for single-pole breakers controlling regular 115-volt circuits. Another type of breaker arrangement uses all single-pole breaker components but provides for side-by-side mounting and bridging of operation switches for 230-volt circuits.

Whatever the breaker arrangement, the owner-builder should be guided by local practices in the choice of panel equipment. The circuit-breaker concept is that an overload or overflow of current will cause the breaker to interrupt the circuit continuity, stopping the flow of current completely. By pushing a reset button or switch (which has an

Electrical Demand Factors and Load Calculation

Ckt. No.	Location	Lighting Outlets	Conven. Outlets	Estimated Watts	Amperes	Conductor No. & Size	Watts Load
1-G	Dining, Laundry, Living	4	3	1250	15		
2-G	Entry, Kitchen, Bath No. 2	5	1	1250	15	3-#14	
3-G	Hall, Den, Bedroom No. 1	3	4	1100	15		
4-G	Bedroom No. 2, Bath No. 1	3	4	900	15	2-#14, 1-#12*	
	NOTE: General lighting circuits total 4500 watts or 3.00 watts/sq. ft.						
5-A	Kitchen, Dining		4	1000	20	2-#12	
6-A	Kitchen, Laundry		4	1000	20	2-#12**	
7-A	Dining, Laundry		3	750	20	2-#12	
8-A	Garage-Workshop		3	1250	20	2-#12	
				8500			
			First	3000	@ 100%		3000
			Balance:	5500	@ 35% (approx)		2000
9-I	Range: 12kw model, max demand 8kw		1			2-#8, 1-#10	8000
10-I	Water Heater		1	4000	20	2-#10	
11-I	Bathroom Heater		1	1500	20	2-#12	
12-I	Furnace (1/4 & 1/200 HP motors)		1	600	20	2-#12	
13-I	Automatic Washer (1/6 HP motor)		1	450	20	2-#12	
14-I	Dishwasher		1	1000	20	2-#12	
				7550	@ 75% (approx)		5700
							18,700

Calculated load for service size: Watts (18,700) divided by Volts (230) = Amperes (81.3) = 100-ampere service
Watts (18,700) divided by Volts (230) = Amperes (81.3) = 100-ampere service

---

* This #12 conductor is neutral common to circuit No. 11-I
** One of these #12 conductors is neutral common to circuit No. 13-I

on-off indication), the current flow is restored. If the circuit is definitely shorted, the breaker will interrupt again. If the breaker goes into action due to a temporary overload, normal function will continue but the user is warned of the overload by the break. Thus, circuit breakers help pinpoint electrical problems.

As mentioned above, the size of the home and the number of circuits (and circuit breakers needed) will determine the size of the distribution-panel enclosure. Obviously, homes having a greater number of 230-volt appliances and 115-volt equipment requiring individual circuits will need more distribution panel space. Your electrician will be able to assist in your choice of a adequate size enclosure, capable of handling present and future needs. This can be done more easily if you have prepared a detailed load chart that indicates all immediate facilities plus possible likely future additions.

In homes that run larger than 2,500 square feet of living area, it may be desirable or necessary to supplement the main distribution panel with one or more branch centers containing over-current protection devices. This is most applicable in homes where there is a grouping of heavy-load outlets, as for a kitchen-laundry-sewing-workshop area remote from the furnace-utility and water-heater area of

Home Circuit Listing and Load Estimate for a 1,750 square foot one-story home to assist in making your own load calculation. Circuit numbers are grouped into general purpose, appliance and individual circuits. Estimating practice may vary somewhat in different areas; inquire about local practices from electric utility company.

---

which the main distribution center is normally located. Your electrician will guide you on this. A branch distribution center is simply an extension of the main panel, but does require a properly sized feeder cable for connection with the main distribution center.

Symbols and Wiring Diagram

Your home's floor-plan drawing shows several different kinds of electrical outlets. It accurately locates these outlets, tells what purpose they serve, and indicates which are switch-controlled and where the switch outlets are to be located. For example, a ceiling light symbol (circle plus four short lines at compass points) is usually connected by a dashed line going to a nearby wall symbol (circle with two short parallel lines perpendicular to wall plus an "sw" adjacent). The latter is the symbol for a single switch and the dashed line shows what outlet that switch controls.

Allowable Wiring in Electrical Boxes

Box Size (inches)	Maximum Number Of Conductors			
	No. 14	*No. 12*	*No. 10*	*No. 8*
1-¼ X 3-¼ octagonal	5	5	4	0
1-½ X 4 octagonal	8	7	6	5
1-½ X 4 square	11	9	7	5
1-½ X 4-11/16 square	16	12	10	8
2-1/8 X 4-11/16 square	20	16	12	10
1-3/4 X 2-3/4 X 2	5	4	4	4
1-3/4 X 2-3/4 X 2-½	6	6	5	4
1-3/4 X 2-3/4 X 3	7	7	6	4

Note: shallow boxes, less than 1-½ in. deep should not be used in new construction.

Box Capacities for Wiring depend upon conductor sizes. Chart indicates the maximum number of conductors allowed by box size.

Study the floor-plan drawings in your set of plans and you will soon learn the meanings of the various symbols. No problem there. But what the floor plans do not show is how these various outlets are connected together in circuits. So you need an additional drawing or sets of drawings to indicate circuits according to wiring runs from the main distribution panel.

A wiring circuit is a dual set of wires, one "hot" or positive conductor and the other a neutral conductor. If the circuit is to provide current to a relatively heavy-duty, 115-volt appliance or piece of equipment, that load is apt to be all that set of wires should bear. This, then, is an

Accessory Items With Wiring Devices in the form of a checklist and in purchase orders. Many of these items included will not be needed until the electrical fixture and device connection work is done. This checklist was prepared by Safeguard Electrical Products, producers of housewire.

WIRING MATERIALS CHECKLIST FOR TYPICAL HOME

DESCRIPTION Typical Use Room Area/Sq. Ft.	*Bath or Utility* 50-60	*Bedroom or TV* 125-150	*Bedroom, etc.* 200-240	*Family/Rec.* 340-380
No. 12/2 Conductor (with Ground) Safeguard Type NM Plastic Jacket	50 Feet	100 Feet	125 Feet	150 Feet
2-hole Wall Straps	use at 2-to-3 ft. intervals where cable needs support			
Steel or Plastic Boxes—With NM Cable Clamps and Ground Attachment				
Octagon or Round for Lighting Fixtures	1	2	2	2
Outlet Boxes for Duplex Receptacles	1	4	6	6
Switch Boxes—1 Gang or 2 Gang to match switches	1 or 2	1 or 2	1 or 2	1 or 2
3-½" Nails (if not provided with boxes)	4	10	14	14

Finish Wiring Devices

15A-120V Single Pole Switch	1	1	1	1
(If switching in two locations is desired use 3-Pole	OR			
switches and 3 conductor grounded Safeguard Type NM	2	2	2	2
OUTLETS—Duplex Parallel Slot 15A-125V	1	4	6	6
Switch Wall Plates, Single Pole	1 or 2	1 or 2	1 or 2	1 or 2
Duplex Wall Outlet Plates	1	4	6	6
Solderless Wire Connectors (for No. 12 Wire)	Minimum 6	6	8	12
1/2" Type NM Cable Connectors	2	4	6	8

*SPECIAL APPLIANCE WIRING CIRCUITS**

Electric Dryer or Electric Hot Water Heater

  25' or 50' No. 10/3 Conductor (With Ground Wire Type NM or
    UF Plastic Jacket Cable)
  One—30 AMP Dryer Outlet
  One 3/4" Cable Connector
  Six—2-Hole Cable Straps (One for 4-5')
  One—30 AMP 220 Volt Circuit Breaker*

Electric Range or Electric Furnace

  25' or 50' 8/3 Conductor (With Ground Wire
    Type NM or UF Plastic Jacket Cable)
  One—50 AMP Range Outlet
  One—3/4" Cable Connector
  Six—2-Hole Cable Straps
  One—50 AMP 220 Volt Circuit Breaker*

*Maximum Conductor Capacity: 10/3—30 amps 8/3—40 amps 6/3—60 amps
SOURCE: Safeguard Electrical Products Corporation, from Safeguard House Wire in Pick-Me-Up Carton

individual circuit. Other circuits can connect multiple outlets, the number dependent upon the load that you can expect from each.

The multiple outlet circuits are of two types: appliance branch circuits intended for connecting one or more small portable appliances, such as those typically used in a kitchen; and general-purpose branch circuits intended primarily for lighting and convenience outlet connections. It should be noted that the NEC requires a kitchen to have a least two appliance circuits. These must be rated at 20 amperes each and this means use of No. 12 size wire. The requirement for two such circuits does not mean they must serve the kitchen only. Each circuit be a kitchen outlet supplemented by other outlets in the nearby rooms to which appliances might be connected; for example, a laundry or bathroom. But no lighting outlets should be on these circuits. At least one 20-amp circuit is also an NEC requirement for the laundry area. As indicated, this circuit can also serve the kitchen or another nearby area. Outlets on these circuits may also service pantries, dining rooms, breakfast areas, workshops, or hobby-craft rooms.

With the help of your electrician, a load-calculation chart for the home should be prepared. HUD's Manual of Acceptable Practices cites several load-computation examples, derived from the NEC, for single-family dwellings. The computations simply list the expected appliance loads plus a formula figure of 3 watts/square foot for general purpose circuits in a 1,500 square foot home.

Your load-calculation chart should be organized to demonstrate each circuit's load so that you not only come up with the computation, as NEC does, but also have a circuit-by-circuit listing indicating just what outlets are connected to what circuits (see illustration).

With the load-calculation chart organized by circuits, it's easy to go one step further and prepare either a single complete wiring diagram showing all the circuits together in one drawing or sketch, or to prepare one diagram showing all individual 115-volt and 230-volt circuits plus a series of sketches for the appliance and general-purpose circuits.

To help indicate areas of construction (floor, ceiling, exterior walls or partitions) in which circuit wirings are located, the circuit sketches can be drawn on an isometric basis as suggested for the plumbing diagrams in the previous chapter (see illustration). Be sure that your diagram, sketches, and load chart indicate circuits in which a common neutral is shared by two or more conductors. This practice offers wire savings for the neutral conductors, and is made easy by the use of 3-wire cables. The NEC indicates

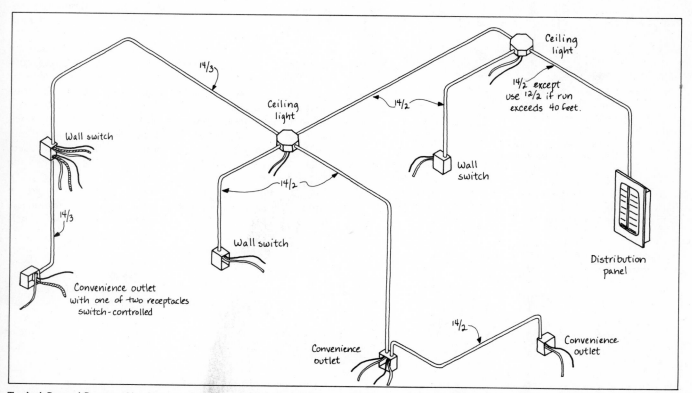

Typical General Purpose Circuit in a residential wiring system begins at the distribution panel and works its way out through wall and ceiling construction framing to various outlets. Wall switches, of course, are usually in the same room with the outlet they control but convenience outlets such as the two in the bottom right of the sketch can be in other rooms. Wiring runs can be of nonmetallic sheathed cable or individual conductors pulled through conduit.

that a multi-wire branch circuit may have two or more ungrounded conductors having an electrical potential difference between them plus "an identified grounded conductor connected to the neutral conductor of the system and having equal potential to the ungrounded conductors". Basically, in single-family homes, the multi-wire usage is

generally limited to 3-wire cables or 3 wires in a conduit run sharing a common neutral. A 3-wire single-cable or conduit run takes the place of a two 2-wire run by sharing a common neutral wire. This type of wiring saves wire and installation time for runs going to same or nearby areas, if outlets are to be on different circuits. These 3-wire runs can also be used to advantage if one outlet of a duplex convenience outlet will be switched-controlled and the other is always hot. It should be clear by now that circuit runs should be laid out according to what outlets may conveniently be connected through what walls, partitions and floor or ceiling areas, rather than on a room-by-room basis.

Tools and Wiring Supplies

For electrical rough-in work, you'll be needing several common wood-cutting and fastening tools—a power drill, hammer, keyhole saw, wood chisel. Then, you'll want a couple sizes of screw-drivers, a hacksaw, and a lever-jaw or offest wrench. In fact, several types of gripping wrenches or pliers are desirable for specific connection details. If you're installing conduit, a conduit-bender is required. With respect to the portable drill, it should really be a 3/8 or 1/2 inch capacity drill rather than the common, light-duty 1/4 inch size. Why? You want a drill that can quickly cut 1 inch diameter holes through framing lumber. A right-angle extension drive for the drill will prove useful for making straight-through holes and in tight quarters.

For roughing-in work, the principal supplies needed are metal boxes, cable connectors and cable . . . or boxes, conduit connectors and conduit. Add a supply of cable or conduit straps when nailing to framing. Plus some cross-joist metal straps for ceiling boxes. Your electrician will guide you as to convenience and to switch outlet boxes with side-plates or other integral devices which allow direct nailing to sides of studs. If nonmetallic sheathing is used, select boxes that have built-in cable clamps to save the time of attaching cable connectors.

Commonly available everywhere, steel boxes are in widest use. But molded plastic boxes have seen limited use in a few areas. However, avoid experimentation. If plastic

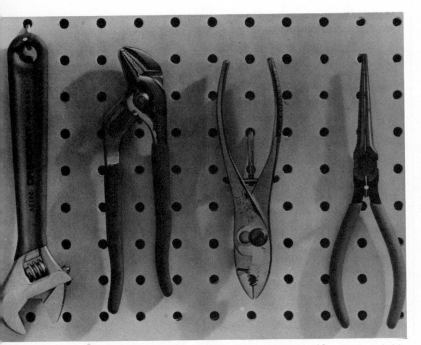

Good Gripping Tools are essential for electrical wiring work and this assortment by the Crescent Company indicates the types commonly used (l to r): adjustable wrench, offset pliers, standard pliers and needle-nose pliers. The wrenches, called "crescent wrenches," have a hex-shaped jaw and tension spring for a solid grip and come in choice of five sizes. Tongue-and-groove pliers have an adjustable opening, aligned teeth and come in 7-to-14 inch sizes. Slip-joint pliers are available in six types with wire-cutting capability and are a general purpose tool. Long needle-nose pliers provide gripping ability in tight or narrow places where fingers won't go. Also handy for forming eyes on wire ends.

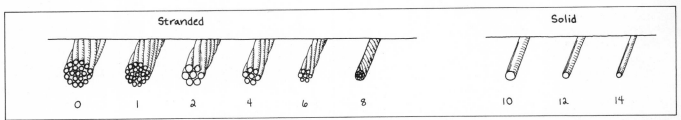

AWG Electrical Wire Sizes used in residential service drops and home wiring systems are shown above, the "AWG" referring to the American Wire Guage standard involved. In use, wires are sized to meet electrical demands of the circuit and service entrance wires are sized to meet the total anticipated load of the home. In practice,

No. 14 conductors are used in lighting or general purpose circuits, No. 12 conductors in appliance circuits, and the sizes of conductors in individual circuits are tailored to fit the individual appliance being served.

boxes and accessories are not used much in your area, forget them. Use steel.

A few additional tools and suitable connect-up supplies will be needed later for receptacle, switch, and fixture installation. These will be described in Chapter 42.

The bulk of your cable will be 2-wire, using No. 14 size wire for general-purpose circuits. A limited quantity of 3-wire No. 14 will be needed and also a limited amount of 2-wire No. 12 size conductor cable for appliance and individual circuits. Certain electrical heavy-duty appliances such as water heaters or air conditioners will probably need No. 10 size conductors, while the range and clothes dryer outlets will a cable composed of two No. 8 conductors with a No. 10 neutral. Practices vary slightly in conductor/cable specifics and this point should be checked with your electrician as you go over your load calculation chart with him.

Electrical conductors for residential work are of copper in either stranded or solid form with an insulation covering. The exceptions are the large bus bar conductors in breaker enclosures and bare conductors included in cables for grounding. Conductors in the smaller American Wire Gauge (AWG) sizes are generally single strands of solid wire, while larger sizes are stranded (see illustration). As you'd expect, the larger sizes have greater load-carrying capacity.

There is a possibility you may encounter aluminum building wire in dealing with your supply sources. It was used to some extent during the period 1965-71 when copper was in short supply. At present, the acceptability of aluminum conductor wire is being questioned by the U.S. Consumer Product Safety Commission. Avoid using it.

Load-carrying ability in electrical circuits is calculated in amperes. In preparing your load calculation chart and using it to arrive at an overall ampere rating, remember the basic electrical equation, amperes times volts equals watts.

Choice Of Wiring Methods

Both cable and conduit have been mentioned. You will choose between them. Some building codes still exclude nonmetallic sheathed cable although it is really the standard type, used in a great majority of new homes across the country.

Nonmetallic sheathed cable (Type NM) has multiple conductors, each insulated, covered with a paper wrap and an outer plastic sheathing (see illustration). Similar in appearance at first glance is Type UF cable which has a sheath of molded thermoplastic material of high resistance, making this type of cable suitable for underground use.

The metal conduit normally used in residential wiring is thin-wall tubing. The electrical rough-in work involves placing the tubing and fastening it to boxes with connectors, but the conductor wires are not installed until after installation of wallboard.

Nonmetallic sheathed cable is simpler and faster to install than conduit and it now meets the wiring standards of the National Electrical Code and the One-and-Two-Family

Dwelling Code. Do not confuse this type of cable with the flexible metallic sheathed cable more often called "armored cable." While commonly seen in retail stores, it is used principally in remodeling, rewiring, and wiring extension work rather than in new construction.

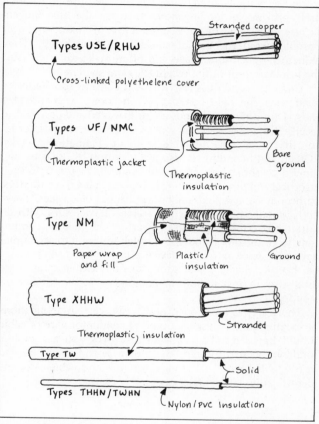

Cable and Conductor Insulations are designated according to the specific materials involved, shown here are those encountered most frequently in residential wiring work. In terminology, a "cable" may be either a single conductor in stranded form or a combination of conductors each insulated from the other. Characteristics or purposes of the various types (top to bottom): USE. RHW, an underground service entrance cable for direct burial, may also serve as an aerial cable for service drops; UF/NMC is a nonmetallic sheathed cable designed for wet indoor locations and underground direct-burial feeder service to lamp posts, patio lights or landscape lighting; NM cable is nonmetallic sheathed cable, the most economical, and is most widely used for residential wiring. It comes in sizes 14, 12, 10, 8, 6, and 4 in two-conductor cable with or without ground and in three-conductor cable, with or without ground; XHHW is a heat-resistant conductor suited for applications up to 167°F in wet locations and 194°F in dry locations; TW insulated conductors have excellent insulating properties, high resistance and silicone surface treatments for easy snaking through conduits; THHN and THWN types have thinner insulating covers without loss of insulating or operating qualities.

All wiring runs from the distribution panel to and sometimes through outlet boxes. The wiring runs are attached to the boxes in the knock-out holes provided and are either clamped in place or provided with screw-type box connectors. Only the knock-out holes that will be used for connections are knocked out. The bare grounding wires of each cable must be attached to the box's grounding screw or to the box edge using an appropriate grounding clip. No grounding wire is used with conduit because the tubing itself provides grounding continuity for the box and enclosure units. One tip on your selection of boxes: wherever possible avoid the use of so-called shallow boxes. They reduce the enclosure space and often make more difficult the installation of outlet receptacles and switches.

Thin-wall conduit is less stiff and considerably easier to bend than the rigid conduit, which comes with threaded ends. Thin-wall tubing ends are unthreaded and designed to receive either crimp-on or screw-clamp connectors in order to fit to boxes. Flexible conduit (sometimes called "Greenfield" conduit) is also available but its use is usually limited to short runs from wall or ceiling outlets to such electrical units as recessed light fixtures, fans or ventilators, bathroom heaters and similar appliances or devices. These units usually have a rough-in frame or enclosure with an outlet box either attached or nearby. The flexible conduit runs from the box through the rough-in frame to accommodate later hookup of the device after wall or ceiling board has been applied. Similar short runs of flexible conduit are used also to install built-in equipment in the kitchen or laundry.

There are, as mentioned previously, certain applications or locations where a special type of conductor wire or cable should be used. The following list gives you a complete rundown on the different types of wire and cable involved in residential work. All conductor wire and cable carry the identification letters described.

In Common Use

Type NM. Nonmetallic sheathed cable and multiple plastic-insulated conductors as previously described. This cable is suited to new construction wiring or rewiring of old installations, exposed or concealed. It may be installed in masonry voids that are reasonably dry. It is available usually in sizes 14 to 10 (solid) and 8 to 4 (stranded). Not suitable for burying in the ground, for service entrance use, or for damp locations; often called "Romex".

Type NMC and **Type UF.** Similar in makeup but having greater resistance. Former is for use where there is danger of corrosion; latter is for underground feeder use. These cables may be used indoors or out, in dry or wet or corrosive locations, but they should not be buried in concrete or aggregate.

Type SE-U. This is service entrance cable suitable for overhead service drops. It may also, codes permitting, be used for interior runs from the meter or entrance box to main or branch distribution panels. Type SE-U may also serve individual circuit runs to heavy-duty appliances such as ranges, ovens, dryers and water heaters.

Single Conductor Electrical Wires for Residential Building Applications

Types RH, RU, RW and RHW. All are rubber-insulated conductors which are now considered outdated by the following plastic-insulated types.

Types TW, THW and THWN or THHN. With the thermoplastic insulation in which the "W" inclusion signifies suitability for damp or wet locations and the letter "H" denotes suitability for high-heat locations. An "N" suffix denotes a special nylon-coated insulation 30 percent less thick than standard and designed for rewiring of existing conduits;

Type USE-RHW and Type XHHW. These wires are encased in cross-linked polyethylene insulation resistant to both oil and water. The former is designed for underground service entrance use and for interior runs from meter or entrance box to main or branch distribution centers. Should not be buried in concrete or aggregate but may be used for aerial service entrance.

With respect to the specific conductors included in a cable, the identification numbering shows both the number of conductors (2 or 3) and their wire size. For example, a 14/2 designation means two conductors each of size No. 14 wire. The plastic insulation in 2-wire cable is color-coded, black for connection to the hot-side terminals of fixtures or receptacles (brass), white for connection to the neutral-side terminals (silver). In 3-wire cable, the extra conductor is a hot line and its plastic insulation is red. In some cables containing an insulated ground conductor the insulation covering is green; this connects to box screws and bonding terminals of switches and outlet receptacles which have been daubed with green paint.

Installing Rough-In Boxes

Whether your wiring is to be cable or conduit, the initial step in installation is the same—nailing up of outlet boxes. Proceed with both your floor-plan drawing and load-calculation chart in hand. When locating a box, think also of the wiring runs coming to that box and adjust the box location somewhat to make your cable or conduit runs straighter or easier.

Start with boxes for the individual circuits first, both 230-volt and 115-volt. Follow with boxes for small appliances. If your chart has made use of numbered circuits, you can mark the framing member nearby with this circuit identification. Ceiling boxes nailed up with cross-joist straps are easier to run cable or conduit to than boxes nailed to sides of joists. In nailing up boxes, be sure to allow the front box edges to project beyond the face of the framing member by the wallboard thickness (1/2 inch usually). Boxes with integral side brackets automatically make this projection.

As you proceed give due consideration to the wiring to or through each outlet box. You may find the outlet is in a rather difficult position. It might seem easier to handle the several wiring runs in a different location. In such instances, consider the possibility of using a junction box in the attic, crawl space or basement—some accessible location. Bring your wiring runs to the junction box, then run a single cable or conduit to the particular outlet. Later, when wiring connections and fixtures are installed, the junction box receives a blank cover plate.

The floor-plan drawings which are part of your house plans, if obtained from one of the nationally known plan services, undoubtedly shows proper convenience outlet frequency as required by the NEC. For your information, the following four rules give code provisions for outlets in all principal rooms but not including bathrooms, utility rooms or basements:

☐ on walls 2 feet or more in length space outlets so that no point along the floor line of the wall is more than 6 feet, horizontally, from an outlet;

☐ built-in partition units such as bar counters or room dividers are counted as "walls";

☐ bathrooms should have at least one convenience outlet adjacent to the lavatory;

☐ outlets intended for individual circuits should not be counted when planning spacing; in case of movable appliances such as clothes washers, the individual circuit outlet should be within 6 feet of the appliance location.

Installing Cable Connections

The easiest tool for cutting wire and cable is the slightly diagonal pincers known as side-cutters. Equip yourself with both medium and medium-large sizes. You'll also want a good steel tape-rule and professional-quality wire strippers.

Your electrician, while assisting you with the electrical-circuit diagrams and load-calculation chart, will have indicated verbally the rough or approximate routes that box-to-box cable lengths might take. Now, as you're about to start installing cable along these routes, you will find it easier to proceed systematically circuit by circuit, beginning each at the circuit end most distant from the distribution panel and working back toward it.

Cable comes in packaged reels that usually have some opening that tears or cuts out to permit unreeling so that the balance of the cable remains within the package. You must decide on a path through the framing for each length box to box. Cable running parallel to framing members can be strapped to the sides of the framing members. If cable

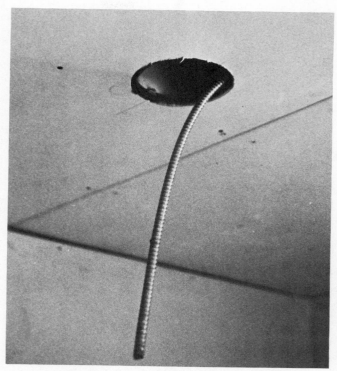

Rough-in Enclosure for recessed lighting fixture in ceiling with flexible conduit lead (sometimes called "greenfield") left hanging from ceiling junction box; wiring will be run from the box through this cable at the time fixture is being connected.

runs perpendicular to framing members, run it through a series of drilled holes. Your electric drill should use a 3/4 inch drill bit for passage of single cable lengths and a 1 inch bit for occasional situations where it may be desirable to fit two cable runs through the same hole.

To start a circuit, place the reel package close to the next-to-last outlet box on the circuit. Eye the path you intend to follow to the last box. Proceed to drill passage holes as required, keeping holes near the center of 2X4 studs and about 2 inches hole edge to joist edge . . . from the top edges of ceiling joists and the bottom edges of floor joists. Where adjacent holes occur, allow 3/4 inches of lumber between hole edges.

Now, thread the cable length from the reel along the route chosen proceeding towards the last box. When you reach it, take a knife and remove the cable sheathing and paper wrap, being careful not to let the knife penetrate into conductor insulation. Choose appropriate knock-out hole and hammer the blank inward, prying it off with a screwdriver to break it. Loosen inside cable clamp and lead conductor wire ends through the clamp until the sheath is just past the clamp, then tighten it to the cable. Loosen the box ground screw, cut off the cable's ground wire to suitable length, and fit it around the ground screw and tighten. Don't strip the insulation coverings from the conductors but simply fold them back so they're within the box space.

Now work backward along the cable length, pulling the cable straight without tension and without twists. No further supports are needed through the framing holes. When strung along joist or stud sides, cable support is provided by cable straps at intervals. Horizontal runs of cable strung along joists will need straps every 3-½-to-4-½ feet to maintain a straight run without sags. Vertically along stud sides you will need a strap near the stud top if the cable comes from above, or near the stud bottom if it comes from below. In addition, a strap may also be required near the outlet box since the NEC calls for a support strap within 12 inches of every cabinet, box or fitting.

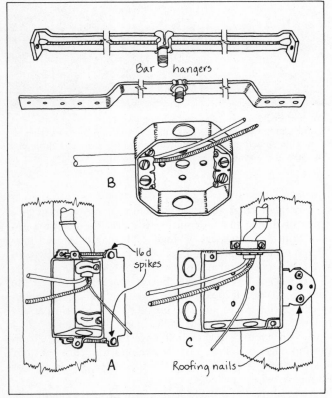

Most Common Types of Outlet Boxes used in a residential installations: (A) used predominately for switch outlets, sizes 1-3/4 by 2-3/4 inches on the face and usually 2½ or 3 inches deep with either side flaps or spike holes for nailing to studs; (B) a typical 4×4 inch octagonal box, 1½ inches deep with a large center hole for direct mounting to bar hangers that nail to lower edges or to sides of ceiling joists; (C) a 4×4 inch square box, 1½ inches deep with nailing side flap and used for convenience outlets. Boxes come with installation devices that either bring the front box edge flush with framing members or project inward 3/8 or 1/2 inch to penetrate wallboard.

Check with your electrician regarding use of staples. Certain types of staples are approved for use with nonmetallic sheathed cable; if available and allowed by your local code, the staples are easier to hammer into place than support straps.

When you reach the last cable length going to the distribution panel, bring it to the distribution enclosure's stud space or adjacent stud space; cut it off leaving about two feet of extra length and just let it hang loose without strap or staple fastening. Your electrician will want to organize and group these cable lengths for proper entry to the enclosure.

You'll encounter certain areas where everything becomes a bit crowded. There may be duct runs, waste-drain and water supply pipes that take up stud-space, leaving tight quarters for needed cable runs. In such locations, you can install the cable into shallow notches in the stud faces. The NEC indicates, however, that with such notching, a stud-width steel plate at least 1/16 inch thick should be used to cover the cable notch protecting the cable from later wallboard nail penetration.

As you proceed with cable lengths for a circuit, you will come to a point where an adjacent circuit run will be following the same path. Try to foresee where any such doubling or tripling of cable runs might occur and in drilling holes or providing strap supports for the first run, make sufficient space allowance for subsequent cable runs.

Also as you proceed, check each box location with your floor-plan drawing to make certain you placed the box properly. Especially with respect to height. The practice in many drawings is to indicate the outlet height only if it differs from standard . . . and standard height is either 12 or 16 inches for convenience outlets and 48 inches above floor line for switch outlets. Heights are to box centers.

If code requires your electrical installation to be thin-wall conduit, your initial installation need is for a suitable tubing bender. One tool used widely for this purpose is a handled device that slips over the tubing end. The user pulls the handle while holding the conduit in place with floor blocks or a vise. It takes practice to apply a positive and quick spurt of muscle, following through with steady pressure until just the right point, in order to obtain a smooth uniform bend without flattening or deforming the tube.

A fishing tape and reel are required later to pull conductor wires through conduit. On many electrical jobs, the wire pulling is not done until after wallboard or paneling is completely installed. For the owner-builder, wire pulling is suggested before application of wall finishes. Reason: it is considerably easier for the amateur electrician to pull wires when he's able to see the conduit runs through which they're being pulled. All wires in a given run of conduit should be pulled at once; the fishing tape is not so easy to operate if a conduit run with bends has wires already in it.

Before pulling any wires, go over the entire circuitry with drawing and chart in hand to make certain the tubing runs have been accurately made. Verify and check each run for the conductor wires it will contain. It's much easier to correct errors at this point than after wires have been strung.

In electrical terminology, there is a distinct difference between "grounded" and "grounding." The current-carrying conductor that has a white or neutral grey color (or in sizes above No. 6 has white marks at terminals) is a neutral conductor. It runs through the circuitry back through the distribution panel and perhaps to the service entrance, to be attached to a single system ground. This may be provided by a clamp on the cold-water main-supply line coming up from underground. In other cases, it may be connected to an outdoor ground pipe driven adjacent to the meter location. Such an electrical system is a "grounded" system. In addition, it is now required practice to provide what amounts to emergency "grounding" of all electrical system enclosures, boxes, switches, receptacles, lighting-fixture metal parts. This is done by grounding wires screwed or clipped to outlet boxes. Remember colors. White or grey for neutral conductors with a system ground connection at only one point. Green for enclosure, fixture and box grounding wires.

The exception to this rule for conductor insulation colors occurs with cable runs to switch legs. A switch is an interrupting device in a hot line to a fixture or device. Later, in Chapter 42, the appropriate coloring of the white or grey conductor in a switch leg will be described during discussion of connecting-up procedure.

Certain runs can be of 3-wire cable (or conduit containing two hot conductors and one neutral to serve two circuits). As the NEC explains, such 3-wire circuits can supply a load that would need four conductors if 2-wire circuits were used. And the percentage of voltage drop is only half as great in 3-wire circuitry as in 2-wire. However, in using 3-wire conductors or cable for two circuits, each "side" should be suitably balanced by an approximately equal number of outlets or probable load. Voltage drop or loss is greater for longer conductor runs. Minimize lowered voltage wherever possible, by keeping runs as short as possible.

Note the difference, too, between this type of 3-wire circuitry which has 115 volts per side with no outlets providing service to 230-volt devices or equipment, and the 3-wire circuits using heavier conductor sizes to provide 230-volt service on individual circuits.

Once you've wired a circuit, later wiring will come easier and go faster. After your longer-lighting and general-purpose circuits have been completed, follow with the small appliance circuits. It's only a little harder to work with the No. 12 size conductors or cables than those used earlier. They're stiffer and bend to slightly longer radii.

Finally, you reach the individual circuits and must use of heavier-duty cable or conductors, in the No. 10 to No. 6 sizes. These conductors are stiff. Hard to cut and twist for terminal connections. Ask your electrician about these runs and make sure he checks them on his next visit.

Ground Fault Interrupters

A 1975 series of revisions in the National Electrical Code resulted in some new requirements for residential electrical systems and their use of grounding-type outlet receptacles.

While the grounding system as evidenced by the use of 3-hole receptacles for 3-prong plugs gave protection to circuits and appliances in case of serious short or overload, it was possible for electric current to leak to the grounding channel in small amounts insufficient to trip protective breakers, but more than adequate to cause serious shocks to people. The grounding system, in other words, doesn't protect people against shocks from touching parts of outlet boxes, tools or equipment with grounding leakage.

The device developed to meet this hazard is called a "ground fault interrupter." It constantly monitors the grounding circuit and when it detects any small flow of current in the range between 5 and 15 milli-amperes, it interrupts the circuit, shutting it off. Thus, a person who touches such a faulty grounding part or cover may induce a more direct flow of such small current to ground through his body. He'll receive an initial shock but the interrupter operates within 1/40 of a second and so the victim can then free himself and thereby avoid serious shock injury.

GFI protection is now required by NEC on all 15-amp and 20-amp receptacle outlets installed in bathrooms, or outdoors or within 15 feet of swimming pools. Also for any outlets used to connect submersible pumps or fountains. GFI-protective devices come in two forms—a circuit breaker that installs in a distribution panel and protects an entire circuit, and a standard GFI outlet receptacle that gives protection only to the devices plugged into that particular outlet. The owner-builder should note that such GFI protection is also NEC-required for outlets for temporary wiring at construction sites. Both types of GFI protective devices contain a reset button to bring the device back into readiness again after the fault has been corrected, and a test button to determine whether the device is operable and in working order. The test button should be pushed regularly to verify that the GFI protection is in effect.

Signal Circuits

Commonly called bell or intercom circuits, these signal circuits according to the NEC supply energy "to an appliance that gives a recognizable signal." Such a signal might be the doorbell, buzzer, chime, code-calling system, signal light, intercom-music system, speaker wiring, or various alarm or detection device connections.

For doorbell, door-chime and radio-intercom-music systems, light-duty insulated wire conductors can be strong and stapled into place without need for any sheathing, conduit or other special protection. For door-chime purposes, the common conductor remains the same as it has been for years, AWG No. 18 size wire. But whereas it used to come

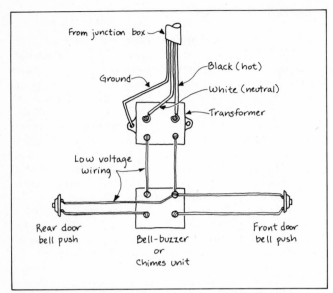

Doorbell Diagram indicates typical transformer connections to house electrical system for low-voltage equipment. Low voltage wiring is usually No. 18 conductor size commonly called bell wire; it can be stapled to framing and run to the push botton locations without need for any terminal boxes or other protective measures. Best practice is to run bell wiring along mid-faces of studs and joists.

with a waxed spiral wrapping today's bell wire is usually plastic-wrapped.

For intercom-music equipment designed to incorporate

branch stations in various rooms and at entry doors, check the manufacturer's specifications and instructions. The wiring runs between stations and to the main control unit will usually involve multi-wire cable with a specific number of color-coded conductors of a specific size.

Another type of low-voltage wiring installed in many new homes is that used for telephone service at several locations withing the home. Prior to installing, check with your local telephone company to find out what their practice is with new homes. In some cases wiring is strung and stapled into place much like other signal circuits. In other cases, the phone company may want to have short runs of conduit from a telephone outlet location to an accessible space such as an attic or crawl space.

Except for telephone wiring, the signal circuits at some point or other will require connection to line voltage of 115 volts. In the case of intercom-music equipment this is usually done at the main control panel which comes with a rough-in enclosure or mounting bracket to which an outlet box is attached. This is then wired in with the house circuitry just like a general-purpose outlet. The same may apply for fire- and burglar-alarm devices.

The signal system for door-chimes or bells-buzzers usually operates on 24 volts. A transformer is needed to provide this low voltage. Door-chime suppliers can furnish small transformers for this purpose. They may mount by screws adjacent to an outlet box or junction box, or may be equipped with an integral connector that fits a box knock-out hole. Bell wire runs then are made from the transformer's output terminals to the front and rear entry doors, with the leads being brought down to small drilled holes adjacent to the door jambs on the knob side.

25 PLan for Electric and Gas Appliances

This point in construction marks the proper time to shop for home appliances, because certain appliances require specific openings in the construction and in the location of electrical outlets or gas pipes at specific locations.

Home-appliance connections to a home's electrical system vary. The differences are indicated in definitions given in the National Electrical Code:

(1) fixed appliance—fastened or secured at a specific location;

(2) stationary appliance—not easily moved;

(3) portable appliance—easily moved from one place to another in normal use.

Applying these definitions to major home appliances, it's understandable that electric ranges and laundry units are "stationary" while counter cooking units and wall ovens are "fixed." In wiring terms this means that built-in cooking appliances are generally connected up permanently by junction box and flexible cable to a home's wiring system. In contrast, stationary and portable appliances have no permanent electrical connection but employ a plug-in connection to a wall outlet.

Criteria used by some lending institutions in determining whether home appliances can be covered as part of a new home's long-term mortgage sometimes distinguish between permanency or portability of the appliances. The decision by a specific lender to allow such inclusion may hinge on the permanent connection idea . . . thus, built-in cooking units and all gas pipe-connected units might be included while plug-in units might not. Check this specific point before doing any shopping for your new homes' appliances.

Appliance Selection

The appliances of your choice may require for their use a modification or special provision in the wiring that will serve them. It is best to decide, therefore, on the types of appliances you will be using before continuing. This chapter will assist in your home appliance selection by pinpointing some of the appliance trends that have been occurring, and by illustrating some of the newer types of appliances.

For a long time, home appliances were all stationary but portable. Many families took appliances with them when they moved. Some still do. But after World War II came a big boom in single-family home construction and the era of

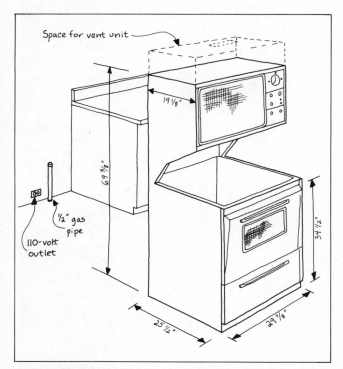

Space for vent unit

19 1/8"

69 3/8"

1/2" gas pipe

110-volt outlet

34 1/2"

25 1/2"

29 7/8"

Appliance Dimensional Data and connection details vary for different brands and models of major appliances. Modern Maid gas range with eye-level oven shown comes in a variety of styles. Unit slides into opening between cabinets with just half inch clearance for built-in look.

built-in appliances . . . cooking tops, ovens, dishwashers, refrigerators. The "built-in look" gained popularity, first in luxury homes and, by the early 1960's, in all but the lowest-priced economy homes. (built-in appliances do cost more).

But the 1970's have seen a gradual swing away from built-ins in favor of "slide-in" appliances—free-standing stationary appliances that have been carefully designed with straight sides and square corners to fit a counter opening of a certain dimension. The result is a "built-in look" but without the extra expense of actually recessing the unit in a counter or wall. Slide-in or slip-in appliances allow the owner to have his cake and eat it, too, in that he gets the popular built-in appearance but he can still take his appliance with him when he moves, if he so desires.

Another trend important to owner-builders has occurred for laundry appliances. In new homes the old-time laundry picture of a couple of laundry trays in the basement and an outdoor drying line is obsolete. Although wringer clothes washers are still being sold, very few find their way into new homes. Automatic clothes washers are either included or space provided for them in virtually every new home. Further, the idea of a laundry pair . . . washer plus dryer . . . has taken hold and even economy homes today

usually provide sufficient space for both washer and dryer. And where space is not sufficient, manufacturers have devised ways that the dryer can be stacked over the washer . . . two appliances in the floor space of one.

In addition laundries have ascended from the basement to the first floor and, in increasing numbers of homes, to the second floor. More home plans are providing space for laundry appliances closer to the point of clothes changes, the bedrooms and bath, rather than in the kitchen or utility room.

Gas Or Electricity

Due to the energy situation today, the choice of fuel or power for home appliances has become somewhat more clouded. The starting point in your selective process on appliances will begin, in most cases, with the gas company. In most areas, gas has been the more economical both with respect to heating plants (furnaces, boilers and air conditioners) and cooking and laundry appliances. Whether this will continue is anybody's guess. But the fact appears at present that natural gas resources may become limited in their capacity for new home connections. Gas-main exten-

Slide-In Ranges are popular due to fewer installation details in comparison with built-in cooking units. Shown here, at left, Hotpoint's 30-inch self-clean oven model available with or without oven door window. At right, Frigidaire's ceramic-top 30-inch double-oven model with black-glass door on bottom oven, also a free-standing range for slide-in installation.

sion in some areas already has been curtailed. The only reliable guidance for an owner-builder is through direct application for service with the local gas utility company.

Both gas and electric utility firms are making every effort to encourage energy conservation. Not only among their present customers in existing homes but also among new home builders and occupants. The accompanying recommendations for, and increased HUD-MPS requirements on, the amount of insulation for new homes (see details in next chapter) have helped electric utilities get more home heating and water-heating installations because added thermal resistance of the home has resulted in more competitive operational costs.

Utility choice and energy conservation factors appear to be without solution in the near future. The only recommendation possible is that you investigate the situation thoroughly, in advance, in the area where you're planning to build. And try to obtain an advance commitment from the appropriate utility, stating that you will be able to connect at or before the time of occupancy. The same counsel might be given to those whose new homes are located beyond gas mains and who are planning to use liquified petroleum or bottled gas. Make sure of your supply first.

Appliance Selection Factors

As implied earlier in this chapter, one of the first decisions facing the owner-builder is whether to go to built-in

Smooth-Top Ranges are also becoming the choice of many cooks because of their neat appearance and easier cleaning. The ceramic-top unit at left is made by Corning; models have conventional heat controls for use with any utensil, or thermostatic controls for greater cooking efficiency but require pans with flat bottoms. In the center, a 35-inch wide glass-ceramic cooktop by Hotpoint with two large 2200-watt heating areas and two small areas each half that wattage. In the photo right, a smooth cooktop model by O'Keefe & Merritt with the four cooking areas contained within a polished metal frame.

kitchen appliances or free-standing ones. If it is to be built-ins, then the specific appliances must be selected in order to learn the proper accurate rough-in dimensions and the location of the junction box with its flexible lead. The same advance accuracy on accommodation space and box location (or gas line location) may also be necessary with certain slide-in appliances.

Free-standing range-and-oven appliances generally run less in cost than separate wall ovens and cooking tops. Within the past year or two, there's been a newcomer in cooking appliances called the "set-in" or "drop-in." This is a compact economy-model with oven below the surface cooking units, designed to fit a counter and face-front opening in the base cabinets (see illustration). The set-in units require precise openings and a specific junction box location.

In shopping for home appliances, be aware that the ordinary retail appliance stores and discount retail busi-

nesses are not likely to show built-ins or set-ins. Their orientation is toward the appliance replacement field rather than new construction. As an owner-builder, you should shop for appliances at your local utility company and also at the nearest appliance manufacturer or distributor outlet serving home builders. Another good reason for so doing . . . possible discounts. Try to make contact with and work through the builder's representative in your area for the appliance manufacturer or his distributor. Obviously, if the proper contact is made with such a representative, it could well be a factor in the choice of an entire complement of appliances. But be warned, also, that purchases through builder-representative channels may require full payment within 30 days of delivery.

When considering appliance brands, do so in three separate categories: food storage and preparation appliances; food clean-up and disposal appliances, and laundry appliances. The reason for separation into such groups is that there are some excellent appliance products made by manufacturers who limit their production to just one or two types of appliances. They may offer units in one group or another rather than all three.

Laundry Appliance Twins, or go-together clothes washers and dryers, have found rapid acceptance in past few years. At left, Maytag-made units in a compact under-stairs installation with a folding door to screen off view of the appliances when not in use. In the center photo, spacing-saving Frigidaire units are only 24 inches wide by 65-3/4 inches high and the vertical combination fits a variety of closet or cabinet conditions. At right, separate Hotpoint units mounted with aid of a special stack-rack.

Supplementary Considerations

The foregoing discussion of home appliances deals primarily with major appliances. There are also secondary appliances, mostly electrical in operation, receiving increased attention by home builders due to high customer acceptance. Or because they are required in order to meet building codes or standards.

For example, the HUD-MPS's require that kitchens and bathrooms have ventilation of one type or another . . . if natural ventilation via window openings, the free-vent area must be at least 5 percent of the floor area of the room. And the alternative to natural venting is mechanical ventilation by an exhaust fan or range hood. The MPS's specify that kitchen exhaust fans must be capable of furnishing air flow at the rate of at least 15 air changes per hour and bathroom exhaust fans, 8 changes per hour. Kitchen range hoods need to be at least as long as the range and have a capacity of 40 cubic feet per minute (cfm) per lineal foot of hood length, or 50 cfm for peninsular hoods.

Vent fans and range hoods are secondary appliances of the permanent or fixed type. For electrical connection these units will require a nearby junction box as specified in the manufacturer's literature. Very often, depending on the type of unit, the manufacturer will provide roughing-in frames or enclosures (sometimes with junction boxes attached). So it is imperative to proper installation to select such units early and purchase them in time so that rough-in assemblies can be installed while electrical wiring is being done.

Exhaust air ducts are another consideration for vent fans and also clothes dryers. Such ducts are usually run to points outside the home structure (see alternative illustration in Chapter 22). Under certain conditions, however, bathroom fans may be vented into properly ventilated attic spaces. All clothes dryers need duct connection to vent the exhaust air. For clothes dryers located on exterior wall, venting is merely a matter of drilling a 4 inch round duct hole at the proper position for direct fitting of a short flexible duct to the appliance. An outside deflector fitting allows the air to exhaust but keeps weather out. If you want to locate it on an inside partition, check the situation out with your electrician and appliance supplier so that proper dryer venting can be worked out.

In many ways the following assortment of secondary appliances, now available for built-in installation in new homes, are comparable to exhaust fans and range hoods (but are not required by codes or standards):

Kitchen	*Laundry*
food mixer-blender	ironer for cabinet installation
microwave oven	recessed fold-down ironing board
trash compactor	sewing machine in cabinet installation
can opener	(see illustration in Chapter 33)
food waste disposer	*Bathroom*
barbecue grille	wall or ceiling heater
rotisserie	heat-lamp or sun-lamp fixture
toaster	tub water-circulation pump

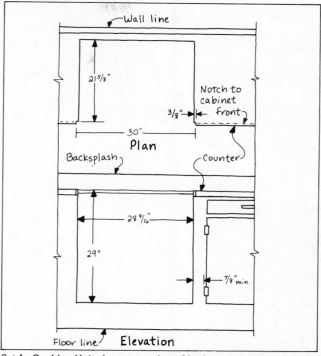

Set-In Cooking Units involve cutting of both counter and cabinet facing openings such as those shown in this sketch. Cut-out work is generally simpler than for separate countertop ranges and built-in wall ovens. The set-in units are range-oven combinations that remove easily from the cabinets for servicing.

The warranty-and-service provisions now being offered by manufacturers and dealer-distributors for a wide range of both portable and built-in appliances are, at this writing, undergoing change. New provisions benefitting purchasers will be forthcoming soon, as a result of passage in early 1975 of the Magnuson-Moss Warranty Act for consumer products.

The law doesn't say warranties must be given to the purchaser. But it says when they are, they must be given in clear language and with clear channels through which the purchaser may go in obtaining service or complaint adjustments. Thus warranty-and-service for home appliances is becoming an important guideline in making the original purchase. The new law is aimed at providing more uniform and open warranty-service procedures, without disturbing already well-established warranty and customer-relations programs. One channel that deals with appliance-customer problems is an industry-wide program called MACAP, the Major Appliance Consumer Action Panel (see Reference List for address).

Optional Appliance Choices commonly seen in moderate-to-high priced homes. Upper left, Hobart's KitchenAid built-in under-counter dishwasher; next, a trash compactor, one of two models available from Whirlpool. The microwave ovens by Litton Industries are available as part of complete range-oven units or separately as countertop or wall built-in models. Final photo is of Hobart's instant hot water dispenser, handy for convenience foods.

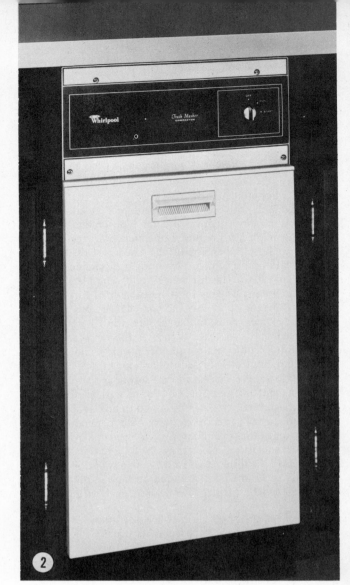

26 Insulation and Energy Saving

Nearly everyone has become an energy saver. Builders throughout the country are packing more thermal insulation into ceiling, wall and floor spaces that ever was thought possible or justifiable.

In late 1974 the U.S. Department of HUD altered its Minimum Property Standards (MPS), reducing the allowable maximum heat transmission rates through various parts of a residential structure. And the changes also tightened up certain related requirements aimed at reducing heat losses or, for air conditioning purposes, heat gains.

An accompanying chorus from insulation manufacturers swelled in volume and advertising scope during the early days of the energy crisis. The song sung was that great savings in operational costs could result from using maximum thicknesses of their thermal product.

And the advertisers were right, because for the owners of existing homes, greater insulation value would mean a lower rate of escalation in utility heating bills. In new construction, with the already higher standards in thermal resistance, there are no direct savings. Only the knowledge that operating costs of heating and cooling will tend to be somewhat lower than what they might otherwise be. And the knowledge that greater insulation is apt to produce a more salable home. The day may not be very far off when the documentation of a home's past performance in energy usage may become a part of every home sale.

With the trend towards constantly higher fuel and utility service costs, the new emphasis on energy savings may mean just this: the slight extra time and relatively small extra expense in making a new home really tight against heat loss and heat gain will do much in assuring interior comfort with the greatest efficiency. It is possible, too, that present talk of an income tax concession for maximum home insulation may materialize to give additional future benefits.

Areas of High Heat Gain or Loss

Reducing heat loss or heat gain involves more than just installing as much thermal insulation as possible in walls and ceilings. There are other places where the losses and gains need minimizing.

□ Windows-Doors—a significant area of loss-gain due to single glass panels and infiltration. You can minimize by attention to flashing strips and, when insulating, filling in small spaces; after siding, do a tight caulking job; select good-quality windows with insulating glass or built-in storm sash and use thermal-type entrance doors.

□ Foundations—provide insulation on the inside of foundation walls including behind band- or box-joists. Use crawl space vents that can be closed in winter; apply efficient foam-board insulation on outside of exposed portion of basement walls, or better, apply furring strips on the interior side with the foam-board between the strips and cover with wallboard or paneling.

□ Shade—where possible and practicable, provide shade for sunny east-south-west walls and windows. Use roof overhangs, shade trees, sun-screens or interior drapes; try to be flexible since shade makes for easier cooling in summer yet sunshine coming in through windows in the winter helps to somewhat reduce winter heating load as well as affording a pleasant interior atmosphere.

□ Equipment—look for ways to determine efficiency of heating and cooling equipment such as data on comparative performance. Choose equipment with useful features such as a summer fan switch for days when mild cooling through just air circulation will work well; plan to maintain heating plant with periodic filter changes, proper lubrication, balanced register adjustments.

□ Ducts—provide adequate sealed thermal insulation around all ducts running through nonheated or noncooled spaces, a practice that also helps reduce air-movement noise.

Insulating Walls and Ceilings

For most wood-framed homes, then, the amount of insulation to use when being built is . . . as much as possible. The maximum for 2X4 stud walls is insulation 3-½ inches thick but you can gain additional value by choosing an insulating sheathing. In ceilings, joists may be 2X6's or 2X8's, and in either case, use insulation 6 inches thick.

The terminology you'll encounter on insulating materials relate to "R-value." This is given as a number such as R-11 or R-19. The number represents the resistance to heat flow and the larger the number, the greater the resistance. The two sample figures given here are the values for the most common types of batt and blanket insulation of mineral wool or glass fibers. The 3-½ inch thick material is rated as R-11 while the 6 inch thick is R-19.

The difference between batt and blanket insulation is simply the form in which it comes. Batts are in relatively short lengths while blankets come in rolls for cutting to the desired length. Both types are available to fit framing member spacings of 16 and 24 inches.

The HUD-MPS requirements on insulation vary according to a home's location in the country. In specifying the minimum allowable heat transmission, the values for winter heating purposes are based on degree-days of the location. For summer cooling, heat transmission maximum values go by the number of cooling hours over 80° F. Actually, the MPS criteria if considered from both heating and cooling aspects, nearly balance. That is, homes in northern climates insulated to meet heating needs will be more than adequately prepared for cooling purposes, while homes in southern climes with insulation to meet cooling needs will need no additional work for heating purposes.

It should be noted here that in connection with the MPS minimums on insulation there are also MPS provisions on transmission values for doors-windows, for floors over unheated basements, garages or crawl spaces, for basement or crawl-space foundation walls and for concrete slab-on-ground floors.

With respect to insulating of crawl spaces, there are two ways to do it. With closable crawl-space vents, insulation material should be placed at the band- or box-joists beginning at the underside of the sheathing and extending down over the face of the foundation wall to the ground. If crawl-space ventilators cannot be closed or if the home is in the northern tier of states, it is probably advisable to insulate the floor joist spaces. Ask your local insulation supplier about practices in the area regarding floor insulation.

In selecting your insulating material, you'll want to give attention to providing a vapor barrier. Such a barrier is needed on the *warm* or interior side of the insulation with respect to heating operations. The interior of a home is the source of much moisture in the air, resulting from showers, laundry, dishwashing, cooking, and other normal household functions. Such air-laden moisture can penetrate construction materials and, at lower temperatures, may result in condensation that impairs the effectiveness of insulating materials and is conducive to wood deteriorization. The flow of air-laden moisture into construction materials can be easily stopped with a continuous wall-and-ceiling barrier. Such barriers in the form of film, foil, or special treatment

Extra Insulating Value for exterior stud walls using high-efficiency insulating sheathing, back of which is seen at right before placement of fiberglass insulation between studs. The white sheathing material is called Styrofoam, by Dow Chemical Company.

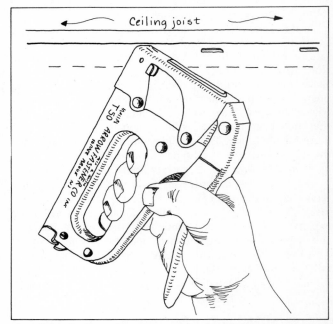

Manual Stapler, made by Arrow, is a key tool for installing of batt or blanket insulations. The stapler's emitting edge is used to push insulation flange in place for quick stapling while the installer's other hand helps hold up the material.

are provided in many batt and blanket insulations. If a nonbarrier insulation is used, a polyethylene plastic film should be applied over the interior faces of the stud and joist spaces. The film is easily stapled into place.

Installation Procedures

Blanket-type insulation material is probably one of the easiest of all building materials to install in new homes. The only tools needed are: razor-blade type cutting knife; pair long-blade scissors; stud-height measuring stick, and folding ruler or tape-rule; pair of step-ladders and scaffold plank;

manual staple-gun and supply of staples; helper's T-shaped hold-up device.

Start with ceilings. Ceiling blankets are best cut to length right in the room where they will be applied. Use your sawhorse-plank working table. Measure joist space from exterior wall to partition. Apply ceiling blankets from below stapling blanket flanges to bottom edges of joists. Try to keep barrier side taut and even across the joist space. Have your helper hold up loose end as you work to it. With scissors, snip flanges at point where blanket goes over partition. Work from wall to partition or partition to partition so blanket joints occur over a wall or partition. At exterior walls, attach blanket ends in such a way that the

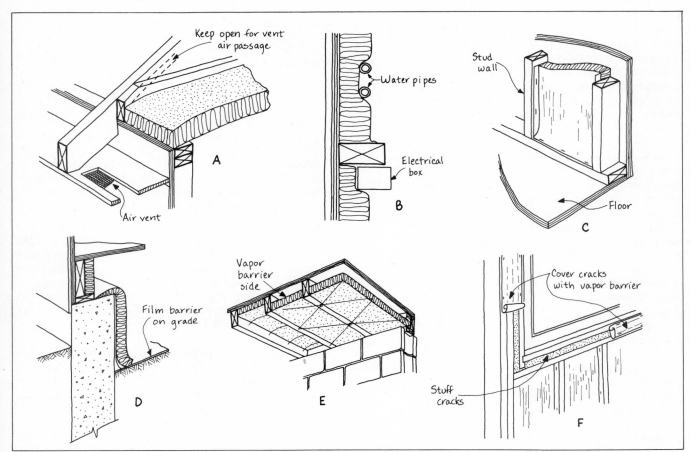

Insulation Application Tips illustrated in these sketches have been culled from the many illustrations in an *"Insulation Manual"* prepared by the NAHB Research Foundation, an affiliate of the National Association of Home Builders. In sketch (A), ceiling insulation should be brought across top wall plate of exterior walls, being careful to allow about an inch of space under roof sheathing for free air movement from the soffit vents. In (B), insulation should be carried around the backs of pipes, ducts and electrical boxes. If batts or blankets are not full thickness as in (C), the flanges should be stapled to stud faces with back of insulation touching the sheathing or siding; with full-thick material, flanges are stapled to stud edges. In either case, a stapled, snug fit should be made at top and bottom. Sketch (D) shows insulation placement for interior side of crawl spaces; where crawl spaces are vented, it may be more desirable to insulate the floor by placing blankets between floor joists and held in position by either of two types of wire supports (another alternative: chicken wire applied to joist bottoms). Final sketch indicates how narrow openings at window and door framing should be stuffed with strips of insulating material and vapor barrier covers provided. Insulating batts and blankets should have integral vapor barrier, kept on the room side when installed.

blanket's top edge is slightly depressed; this provides air ventilation space over the blanket between eave-soffit area and the attic.

Do the entire ceiling before beginning on the stud-space insulation. Be sure to fill in all open spaces in the framing such as around masonry chimneys. Cut insulation strips to fit the 2 inch opening between the faces of the chimney and the nearest framing members forming the chimney opening.

Insulation of the exterior wall stud spaces is less awkward than the ceiling work. Use your precut stud-height measuring stick and cut a number of blanket lengths at a time. Begin at a building corner and work down the exterior wall proceeding around the building. Start stapling at the top. Be sure to press insulating fibers back from the barrier cover at both top and bottom so that the cover material can be stapled to the top- and sole-plates. Stretch barrier cover taut over stud-spaces and be sure that flanges at least meet or, preferably, overlap at the studs.

Blanket flanges should be kept smooth and staples should be spaced no more than about 5 inches apart. When you come to piping or wiring runs in the exterior walls, keep the insulation behind such runs between the cables or pipes and the exterior sheathing. Same for any heating-cooling duct runs.

Be alert for any small openings or crevices, cutting strips of the fibrous material to stuff into the opening. And as you go, watch for small tears in the barrier cover material and repair them immediately (so you won't forget where they are) with electrical-type adhesive tape.

Keep children away from insulation work. The fibers don't get along very well with human skin. You and your helper should probably be equipped with gloves. Also, if you're working in tight or closed spaces with little air circulation, you may want to use a breathing mask over nose and mouth.

Insulating For Noise Reduction

All of the foregoing relates to insulation for thermal purposes. Batt and blanket insulation materials can also be helpful for reducing noise transmission.

Noise reduction in floors and walls is a design factor in planning attached single-family or multi-family residential construction. But even in single-family detached homes, there may be a few room situations where sound transmission from one room to another may be annoying. An obvious example might be if you've a kid, or an adult, who's a high fidelity or rock nut.

Here a few other reasons why the owner-builder may wish to take some extra steps for the reduction of noise transmissions.

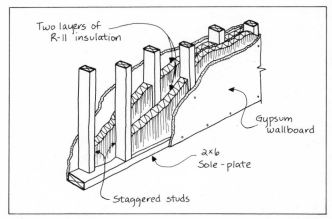

Insulating for Noise Control. Shown here is an effective method for reducing noise transmission between rooms—a double-studded wall framing with staggered studs and insulating blankets placed within studs. Other aids: avoid through-wall piping or electrical connections, minimize the room's door cracks, and double the gypsum-board wall layer.

□ minimizing possible noise from bathroom use where bath or powder rooms may be adjacent to living-dining areas;
□ keeping one or more bedrooms especially quiet for sleeping purposes;
□ muffling the high decibel sounds that emanate from groups or parties in recreation rooms.

Noise is transmitted from room to room in two ways: vibration of structural members between the rooms, and through cracks or other openings. So to minimize such noise you need to adequately separate vibrating structural members and to seal door cracks or any other openings . . . and avoid any piping or cable-box parts having a common touch or opening on each side of the wall. Back-to-back plumbing fixtures and electrical outlet boxes are common offenders.

One common way to provide optimum noise reduction between rooms is to double up on partition members. Stagger the studs in the two partition units so they are nailed to different top- and sole-plates. The installation of insulating blankets between the staggered members will furnish even greater noise reduction (see illustration).

Reducing the amount of outdoor noise transmitted though exterior walls into the home poses a somewhat different problem. Your full-thick thermal insulation will, of course, help greatly. But you may wish to take further outdoor steps if you have a nearby noise source that can be offensive. Earth berms are particularly helpful and other landscaping procedures can also be effective, such as planting groups of shade trees or providing fences.

27 Gypsumboard Drywall Interior

Gypsumboard is one of several names used to describe an interior wall-ceiling finish material that comes in sheets 4X8 to 4X14 feet in size. It is available in 1/4, 3/8, 1/2 and 5/8 inch thicknesses and consists of a rigid solid gypsum core paper-covered on both sides and long edges.

It's often called plasterboard or simply drywall. The latter term comes from an earlier common reference to cement-plastered interiors as wet-wall construction. Strictly speaking, other forms of sheet materials are also included under the term "drywall" . . . fiberboards, plywood, hardboard and various types of composition board. But mostly, in residential building circles, drywall means gypsumboard.

One difference between gypsumboard and other dry sheet materials is its greater fire resistance. There are different types of gypsumboard for serving different purposes. Most common in both single- and multi-family new home construction are:

□ standard tapered-edge (long edges only) wallboard;
□ insulated backing board with bright aluminum foil bonded to the back face as a vapor barrier and reflective insulation;
□ predecorated wallboard with patterned or textured vinyl or paper sheet bonded to front face and no further finish needed; rounded or beveled edges on long dimension;
□ core-board, usually with square edges, factory-laminated to serve as unsupported partitions or demountable walls;
□ fire-rated wallboard using a core material having greater fire resistance;
□ water-resistant type wallboard suited to bath-kitchen use or as a base for application of ceramic or other tile.

Gypsumboard is practically a commodity like cement, brick or lumber. You really couldn't tell the difference among gypsum wallboard products if they weren't labelled. Prices of the wallboard will be competitive and pretty much the same within any area.

However, in making a chioce as to the type of wallboard to use and the size sheets, there will be some differences in what your local supply sources will carry in stock. Nearly every source will carry the wallboard type most commonly used, standard tapered-edge sheets in 1/2 inch thickness and in 4X8 to 4X12 sizes. You might wish to depart from the standard 1/2 inch sheets for the walls of the utility room, heating closet or the common wall between the house and an attached garage. In these locations, building codes frequently specify that wall construction should merit a fire-resistance rating. Type X fire-rated gypsumboard in 5/8 inch thickness applied to both sides of a 2X4 stud wall merits a one-hour fire-resistance rating. Doubled layers of 5/8 inch Type X merit a two-hour rating. Wood floor/ceiling construction with single or doubled Type X ceiling finish receives the same ratings. Inquire of your local building official to learn what specific locations may require use of fire-rated wall-ceiling materials and whether your planned use of gypsumboard will meet the requirements. It's possible that the local code might specify gypsumboard plus some type of noncombustible asbestos-fiber board as a surface covering.

Planning The Work

The first factor to consider before applying any wallboard to walls or ceilings is construction inspection. Completion of all interior framing, wiring, plumbing and ductwork that's going to be concealed within the walls or elsewhere must be viewed by the building inspector. The inspector or inspectors, if separate for electrical and plumbing, want to see how these various installations have been made. There may be tests that have to be run. Be sure that you give proper notification on each inspectable aspect to the appropriate agency or department.

Now, for layout of the gypsumboard work, some guides to drywall installers advise planning your sheet positions in such a way that the length of the long tapered-edge joints is minimized. But, for an owner-builder, the opposite is believed best. Tapered-edge joints are designed for taping-cementing and usually result in uniformly even and flush-wtih-surface joint finishes. For the inexperienced, it's the butted-end joints that cause difficulties in finishing. So, as a rule-of-thumb in planning, prepare a layout sketch sheet for

Application of Gypsum Wallboard

Thickness of Gypsum Wallboard (Inch)	Plane of Framing Surface	Long Dimension of Gypsum Wallboard Sheets in Relation to Direction of Framing Members	Maximum Spacing of Framing Members (center-to-center) (In Inches)	MAXIMUM SPACING OF FASTENERS (center-to-center) (In Inches)		Nails[1] — To Wood
				Nails[1][2]	Screws[3]	
	Horizontal	Either Direction	16		12	No. 13 gauge, 1-3/8″ long, 19/64″ head No. .098 gauge, 1-1/4″ long. Annular ringed 5d, cooler nail
1/2	Horizontal	Perpendicular	24	7	12	
	Vertical		24	8	12	
	Horizontal	Either Direction	16	7	12	No. 13 gauge, 1-5/8″ long, 19/64″ head No. .098 gauge, 1-3/8″ long. Annular ringed 6d, cooler nail
5/8	Horizontal	Perpendicular	24	7	12	
	Vertical	Either Direction	24		12	

Fastening Required with Adhesive Application

1/2 or 5/8	Horizontal	Either Direction	16	16	16	As required for 1/2″ and 5/8″ gypsum wallboard, see above
		Perpendicular	24	12	16	
	Vertical	Either Direction	24	24	24	
2-3/8 (3/4 total)	Horizontal	Perpendicular	24	16	16	Base ply nailed as required for 1/2″ gypsum wallboard and face ply placed with adhesive
	Vertical	Either Direction	24	24	24	

1. Where the metal framing has a clinching design formed to receive the nails by two edges of metal, the nails shall be not less than 5/8 inch longer than the wallboard thickness, and shall have ringed shanks. Where the metal framing has a nailing groove formed to receive the nails, the nails shall have barbed shanks or be 5d, No. 13-1/2 gauge, 1-5/8 inches long, 15/64-inch head for 1/2-inch gypsum wallboard; 6d, No. 13 gauge, 1-7/8 inches long, 15/64-inch head for 5/8-inch gypsum wallboard.

2. Two nails spaced not less than 2 inches apart, nor more than 2-1/2 inches apart and pairs of nails spaced not more than 12 inches center-to-center may be used.

3. Screws shall be No. 6 with tapered head and long enough to penetrate into wood framing not less than 5/8 inch and metal framing not less than 1/4 inch.

Application Specifics for Gypsum Wallboard in this chart were taken from the One and Two Family Dwelling Code. The chart indicates two ways of sheet placement, two framing member spacings, and the nail sizes and spacings for various wallboard thicknesses when used with the different placements and spacings.

ceilings, minimizing butt-end joints. Further, where they must occur, try to position sheets so that the butted joints are in nonvisible or non-light-reflecting locations.

As a rule, you probably won't really need layout sketches for your walls. The usual 8 foot to 8 foot 3 inch interior wall height tends to simplify placing of sheets on walls. The common practice is for 4 foot wide sheets to be applied horizontally across the studs. You will still want to give attention to butt-end joints, however, keeping them few and in relatively unobtrusive locations.

For a ceiling layout use tracing paper over your floor plan to sketch out the room areas and then, working with graph paper having parallel lines emphasized at 4 foot intervals, adjust the sheet positions and sizes to best accommodate the room area. Remember that the long sheet dimension should run across the ceiling joists. Remember, too, that the longer 12 or 14 foot sheet lengths can help to eliminate butt-end joints but are a little difficult to handle on ceiling applications, especially in tight quarters. And although the long sheets will take some bending, breakage is possible, particularly when the handling is awkward.

End joints should be staggered in much the same man-

Approximate Quantities of Drywall Supplies

Amount of gypsumboard in sq. ft.	Drywall nails needed * in lbs.	Powder type cement in lbs.	OR	Ready-to-use cement in gals.	Perforated joint-tape in ft.
100	.6	6		1	37
200	1.1	12		2	74
300	1.6	18		2	111
400	2.1	24		3	148
500	2.7	30		3	185
600	3.2	36		4	222
700	3.7	42		5	259
800	4.2	48		5	296
900	4.8	54		6	333
1000	5.3	60		6	370

* with 7 in. spacing on ceiling and 8 in. spacing on walls
SOURCE: *Handyman's Guide,* "How to Install and Finish Sheetrock Gypsum Panels," United States Gypsum

Estimating Gypsum Wallboard Needs will be easier using this chart adapted from "How to Install and Finish Sheetrock Gypsum Panels" issued by the United States Gypsum Company.

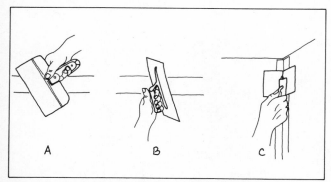

Drywall Taping-Cementing of joints and corners is simplified and more likely to produce good results when proper hand tools are used. Here are three key tools which the Marshall Trowel Co. believes will aid any drywall applicator: a wide blade-knife of 5 to 5 inches for applying cement and imbedding the joint reinforcing tape (A); a slightly concave steel trowel (B) for spreading a broad strip of cement over the tape; and an inside-corner trowel (C) which can be used for tape smoothing and cement application in wall and wall-ceiling corners.

ner, done with plywood floor and roof decking. Don't plan to put a 4 foot wide sheet in a space that is 3 foot 11-7/8 inches or even 4 foot 0 inches. It won't fit and you'll break the sheet edges. You need a 1/4 inch clearance, either in width or length, to fit in a sheet.

You may hear or read about the better quality that is possible with double-layered or laminated gypsumboard. Or with glue-nailing application of gypsumboard. Granted that

in either case a more rigid and solid-seeming wall will result. But the extra value gained is not likely to warrant the extra time and expense. Unless, possibly, the more rigid wall is being used as part of noise-transmission reduction efforts. Another slant that may reach you concerns the added insulation value you can gain with foil-backed gypsumboard. Understand that bright aluminum foil as a reflective insulation only has thermal value if an air-space of about 1 inch depth is adjacent to the foil. If your walls and ceilings have thermal insulating batts or blanks with full thickness and flanges applied over framing member edges, there won't be any air-space behind the gypsumboard and the foil backing will not have any insulative value.

A final consideration in planning gypsumboard installation is deciding where you wish to omit it in favor of other types of wall or ceiling finishes. You may wish to choose other finishes or other materials for accent walls, for different wall-ceiling treatments in different rooms, more washable surfaces in kitchens or bathrooms, more economical materials in closets or storage areas. Check the variety and direct-to-framing application methods for such finishes in Chapters 28-through-31. Of course, gypsumboard can provide an excellent base for the application of certain other finishes using adhesives.

Tools And Equipment

Two different sets of tools will be required for the two-phase job of applying the wallboard sheets and finishing the joints and corners with tape and cement.

Simple carpenter's tools handle the first phase—hammer, proper size-type wallboard nails (see chart) and a good utility thin-blade knife. Plus your sawhorse-and-planks working table. You will also need your measuring rules, a steel square and a 4 or 5 foot long steel straight-edge. A keyhole saw and power jigsaw will be useful for cutting openings for electric boxes.

For application of ceiling sheets, you'll want one or two T-braces, whose length is not quite floor-to-ceiling height so that the T-brace can hold up one end of a sheet after you and your helper get it up into position.

You will also find good use for a rasp or surface filing tool and a sandpaper block. Purpose: to smooth-cut edges, taking off the ragged paper edges. In addition, you can rasp down at a slight angle the face corners of butt-ends so that a slightly better butt-end joint is possible.

Don't plan to do the second phase, taping-and-cementing, until all of your gypsumboard has been applied and is in place. And have a thorough cleanup after the completion of that work. Gypsumboard cutting leaves a fine white powder and an accompanying dust when disturbed. Do yourself and your nostrils a favor by thoroughly sweeping up when the wallboard nailing has been completed.

Your supplier of gypsum wallboard will also have available rolls of perforated joint tape and containers of joint cement in dry form; just mix with water. He'll guide you as to approximate quantities needed, and to appropriate containers for mixing and handling.

A proper set of blades or trowels is needed to obtain a professional-quality finish on the taped-cemented joints. Three types are suggested: a 4-to-6 inch wide joint-cement knife, an inside-corner trowel, and a long steel trowel having a slightly concave curvature designed especially for joint finishing (see illustration).

There may or may not be a need for certain types of metal trim pieces. This will depend upon the details of how the gypsumboard comes up to meet windows and doors and whether or not the home has any room-to-room openings, generally referred to as "cased openings." Such openings require the use of metal corner bead trim at both edges and extending fully around the opening. The corner bead gives a straight, not-subject-to-damage edge which can be cemented for a smooth corner. The same corner bead is used wherever a room's walls might turn an outside corner. Inside corners of a room are taped-cemented like a joint except the tape is creased to fit the corner.

Metal trims of various styles are also used to provide a ends to the wallboard at the doors and windows that may not receive casing trim. And the trim also is suited for use where gypsumboard ends and some other wall or ceiling finish begins. If metal trim is to be applied, add a pair of tin-snips, or sheet-metal shears and a hacksaw, to your tool list.

Application Methods

Whoever delivers your gypsum wallboard will probably place a pile for the entire home in the middle of the largest room, just where the load hazard to the floor framing is apt to be the greatest . . . unless you give specific instructions as to where you want it. But don't expect your supplier to place proper amounts on a room-by-room basis. Try to have a third of the total order delivered into the living or family room, and the remaining two-thirds split between the two largest bedrooms.

The sheets present a handling problem, particularly if larger sheets are ordered. They come packed two to a package, face-to-face to each other with paper wrapping on the edges. Carrying two sheets at a time around the house means two men with extra muscle. Carrying one sheet at a time around the house can mean a few damaged sheet faces. The supplier's men can give you some help by depositing the order in key spots, near where it will be used.

Normally, drywall applicators do all of the ceilings before beginning on the walls. It.allows them to get the scaffolds out of the way for the wall work. Otherwise, it doesn't make much difference whether ceilings or walls come first. Wall nail-up is easier insofar as handling the sheets but wall sheets need more measuring-cutting to fit openings and outlet boxes. There is one decided advantage for the ceilings-first procedure. This allows the top wallboard sheets, with a long tapered edge, to fit up to the

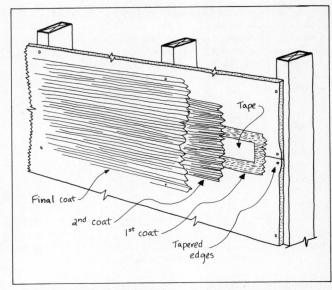

Unobtrusive Wallboard Joints are obtained only by following a step-by-step procedure with at least overnight drying time between steps. The first cement coat is for embedding the perforated tape. The second coat provides a broad cover for the tape. The third coat, broader still, tapers out the cement to an extremely thin feather edge.

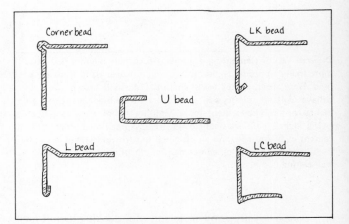

Metal Trim Shapes for gypsum wallboard installations. The trim pieces, generally supplied in 10 foot lengths, are of galvanized or zinc-coated steel to give hard damage-resistance to wallboard corners and edges. Corner beads protect outside corners. The beads having flared angles (L, LK and LC) are used for edge protection, the flaring providing space for joint cement finishing. Designations here are used by the Gypsum Association, and some suppliers may use other names for the beads.

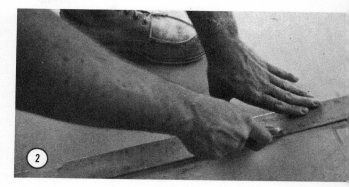

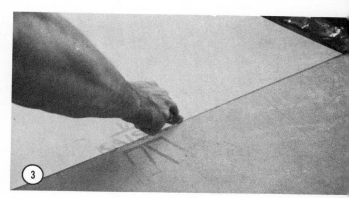

Drywall Installation Details in this series of photos are excerpted from booklet issued by Kaiser Gypsum Company. In photo (1) a storage pile of 4×14 foot gypsum wallboard sheets which come to the job packaged in pairs to help protect the room sides of the sheets. Gypsum wallboard can be cut quite easily using a utility knife (2) with a steel straight-edge to score the covering paper. In (3) the cut-off portion is broken partly off and the knife is used again to score through the bottom paper cover. In (4), sheets are first applied to ceilings with a minimum of two men to position and nail large sheets. Next as in (5), the top wall sheets are held up so top edge meets ⟶

ceiling sheet. And may enable a slightly straighter and truer ceiling-corner joint than is possible when the ceiling sheets butt to the wall sheets.

When applying sheets, be sure that you do not fit them in tightly to the framing or to each other. Changes in moisture content can cause minor expansion, just enough to bulge the wallboard in certain places. Allow a uniform 1/8 inch space between sheet edges and between an edge and a part of the framing.

With a normal ceiling height running slightly over 8 feet, the application of two parallel 4 foot wide sheets horizontally will leave a space of from 1 to 3-½ or 4 inches at the bottom. Fill this space with strips of gypsumboard cut from waste and nailed to the sole-plate as well as studs. This area will later be covered by base trim.

Be sure the ivory-colored paper face is toward the room since this is the finished surface. The grey paper covering is for the backs of the sheets. When cutting openings or cutting to length, always keep the ivory face up not only to avoid marring or scratching but also to avoid paper tears. When scoring with a knife and breaking, or when sawing, the underside of the sheet always has a little more ragged

edge from which the paper sometimes tears off. This is OK for the back side but it defaces the front, making extra touch-up cement work, besides looking like hell.

With respect to nailing and nail spacing, you may encounter conflict. A building code may say one thing, a manufacturer's instructional material another, and your local supplier or trades-people yet another. If a question arises, check the local building inspector to find out what drywall applicators in the area use.

The nailing chart reproduced in this chapter shows the nail and nail-spacing provisions of the One-and-Two-Family Dwelling Code. Authoritative recommendations from wallboard manufacturers suggest the following nail schedule for 1/2 inch thick gypsumboard:

- □ use 1-1/4 inch long, 12½-gauge annular-ring nails with a 1/4 inch head diameter, or;
- □ a 5d cement-coated, 13-gauge nail with 15/64 inch head;
- □ space nails 7 inches apart on ceilings and 8 inches on walls keeping edge nails between 3/8 and 1/2 inch from the wallboard edges.

Nails should be driven so that the final stroke sets the

the ceiling board. A drywall hatchet shown here has a larger-than-normal round head suited for properly indenting nail heads. In (6), a cut-out for an electrical wall outlet can be done with a keyhole or jig saw and in (7), broad knife being used to embed tape in first coat of joint cement. One excellent consideration shown in photo (6) is the care used in locating switch boxes at the exact point where the horizontal gypsumboard sheets meet, thereby simplifying the switch cut-outs and allowing smooth cement finish as a base for switch wall plates. Horizontal sheet application on walls is preferred to vertical placement.

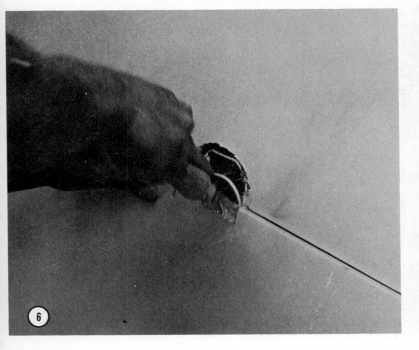

Drywall Details worth noting include the use of metal corner beading (left) at all wall openings which are not to be framed for door hanging. These are called "cased openings" in some areas even though the metal beading takes the place of casing trim. Accuracy in marking-cutting for electrical outlet boxes allows a neat installation fully covered-concealed by the wall plate.

head in a slight dimple, but avoids breaking the paper from driving it in too far or too strong a hammer stroke. Also avoid driving nails at an angle. When nailing, use the free hand to press the wallboard tightly against the framing as the nail is driven home.

On this latter point, getting wallboard tight to the framing, some drywall specialists employ a so-called "double-nailing" method. This procedure uses two nails at each nail location. The two are separated by about 2-to-2-½ inches. With double nailing, single nails are still used along the sheet edges as with single nailing. But the spacing increases to 12 inches and the recommended procedure is to nail a first series of single nails from the center of the sheet outward at 12-inch intervals, completing all single nails, before coming back and going the same route with the added nails.

Some applications of gypsumboard are made using specially designed wallboard screws that need only 12 and 16 inch spacings for ceilings and walls, respectively. The screw application gives a tight fit with framing but the owner-builder will usually find nailing easier.

A smooth, ridgeless, and uniform taping-cementing job is easy to achieve with patience and perseverance. It is a three-step process of applying first a tape bedding coat, then a wider tape-covering coat, and finally a broad, still-wider trowel-finished coat. Wait between applications for the previous coat to dry.

At the time of the tape-bedding coat, the nail-heads are each "spotted" with a small smooth dab of cement. At the time of the tape-covering coat, a second and somewhat broader dab is applied over the nail spots. Following the second or tape-covering coat, take a close look in good light to note minor imperfections, ridges, low spots, etc. Smooth down such places lightly using medium-coarse sandpaper with a sandpapering block.

The broad joint following the third troweled-on coat should be uniform in width. It can be spread just a bit wider on butt-end joints than on tapered-edge joints. And with fine sandpaper, you can smooth down the final joint with a vibrating sander. That is, if irregularities are still noticeable. Go once more with another finish coat. When sanding, use only light pressure near noncement paper areas which are easy to scuff. When sanding, use a nose-mouth filter mask.

Working in an area of gypsum dust may be more hazardous to the worker's health than it was once thought. While manufacturers don't list the ingredients of the gypsum core as with foods and drugs, there is good reason to believe the core content includes some asbestos fibers. At least one manufacturer's gypsumboard literature so indicates and has the warning that breathing asbestos dust may cause serious bodily harm. That company recommends use of wet-sanding or sponging of finished joints rather than dry sanding. And it suggests that in working in a dusty atmosphere, the worker use eye-protective goggles as well as a respirator similar to that approved by the Bureau of Mines.

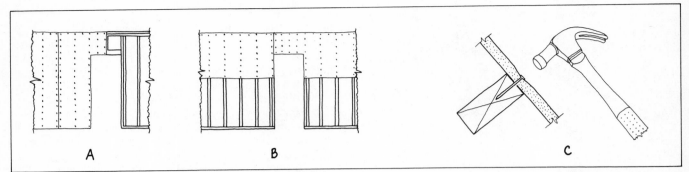

Gypsumboard Application in vertical sheets (A) is appropriate for the base layer in a double-layer lamination but for normal single-layer work, the horizontal application on walls (B) is preferred; it provides a stronger wall and reduces the number of joints that need tape-cement. Vertical sheet application may be suitable for vinyl-covered wallboards. In nailing gypsumboard, normal spacing of nails is 8 inches on walls and 7 inches on ceilings. Nail the sheets first at intermediate points and work out towards the edges. Attempt to center every nail in the framing member since nails that come close to the member's edge are apt to split the wood and have little holding power. Dimple the nails as in (C) without damaging or breaking the paper cover. Keep nails at least 3/8 inch from the sheet's edges or ends.

28 Prefinished Panels and Ceilings

For more than two decades, there's been steady growth in the use of various sheet, tile and plank materials that come with factory prefinishes and in a constantly widening selection of patterns. The growth in both simulated and real woodgrain patterns has been particularly phenomenal. Every day there are more and more woodgrain "specie" names to fool Mother Nature.

Originally, wood paneling in homes was comprised only of solid wood boards, usually 3/4 inch, or 25/32 inch thick, applied individually. This type of board paneling is now difficult to find, its place having been taken over for most new home construction by plywoods, hardboards and, more recently, particleboards. In addition to some use as a sheet backing material for woodgrain panelings, particleboards are being offered with a variety of surface treatments in smooth, textured, splintery, sand-scuptured and other prefinishes.

Hardboard panelings, too, have spread beyond the woodgrain types and are now available in an ever-broadening array of simulated carved-wood, molded, wood end-block, brick, marble, shingle, stucco, travertine, terra cotta and stone prefinished surfaces.

Paneling finishes not only extend over a wide range, so do prices. There's apparently no correlation between price and type of material; all materials have inexpensive thin sheet panelings as low as $5 per 4X8 foot sheet and more expensive, thicker 1/4 and 5/16 inch panelings that may cost $30 or more a sheet.

Materials, Trim and Tools

By far the most commonly available as well as the widest ranging in cost are the woodgrain panelings in plywood and hardboard. Owner-builders who must watch every nickel of housing materials expenditure, will do well to shop a number of different types of retailing establishments that now sell paneling. It isn't so much that one kind of retailer will have lower prices across the board but that at regular times through the year some excellent buys become available in the form of close-outs or stock reductions on overstocked items or less popular colors and patterns.

One warning . . . watch out for cheaper panelings which may take the form of thin 1/8 and 3/16 inch sheets, and some imported materials. The thin panelings may have reasonably good surfaces and appearance but in new construction they aren't appropriate for direct application over framing without some sort of backer board.

There's another factor to watch out for in panelings of any price. That's a color tone variation panel to panel that isn't too noticeable when you look at just a few panels but really can be exasperating when you are standing up the panels around a room and are trying to obtain fairly close color-tone match, panel to panel.

Yet another factor worth at least a fleeting thought is noise transmission through paneled walls. Thin panel sheets applied directly to both sides of a stud wall make a fairly good transmitters of sounds from one room into the other. If such noise transmission will be objectionable, better consider applying gypsumboard backer sheets or going to a staggered-stud and insulated partition (see previous chapter). Similarly, use fire-resistant gypsumboard if so desired.

For installation, the usual carpenter's tools are all that's needed—hammer, handsaw, electric saw, steel square, your three rules, a level and plumb-line. Also proper nails, a nail set, and colored putty-stick that matches or blends with the paneling color. For application of prefinished moldings, a good miter box. A drill and keyhole saw will be handy for cutting panel openings for outlet and receptacle boxes.

Since paneling is usually applied in a limited number of rooms, and to walls only, a stepladder can take the place of scaffolding. In ordering the material, allow 5-to-10 percent extra beyond the estimate in order to allow for damaged or poor color-match sheets. The excess can be used for cabinet backing or other applications.

Have your paneling delivered so that the sheets will be stored for at least several days before being used. This will allow the paneling to become acclimated to the home's heat or moisture conditions. However, time the delivery at least a week after the final coats of gypsumboard cement or

Panelings in Light or Dark Tones should be selected with an eye for the degree of daylighting in any given room. Shown here are some prefinished Weldwood panels made by U.S. Plywood Corp. In (1), narrow 2-inch planks separated by 1/8-inch grooves in light hickory design; (2) random 4-6-8-inch planks in pastel-toned "Candyland" style panels; (3) strong grain emphasis in this "Teak 4" style with 4-inch planks; and (4) the "Shadow Oak" style is a random plank pattern whose prefinish involves a light-and-shadow technique.

plastering veneer have been finished, to allow curing time. Provide a flat storage space for the paneling delivery. Pile the panels face-to-face and back-to-back with 2X4 or board spreaders about every 8 to 10 panels, thus avoiding panel curl.

Choose nails to suit the paneling, either finish nails that can be set in the paneling and color-puttied to blend with the panel prefinish or colored wallboard nails that match the paneling grooves and which will be left exposed. Nails about 1 inch in length are suited for nailing direct to studs

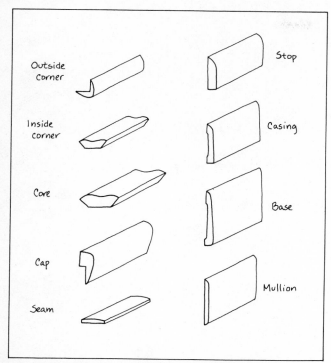

Outside Corner

Inside corner

Core

Cap

Seam

Stop

Casing

Base

Mullion

Prefinished Moldings are companion products with prefinished woodgrain panelings. Shown here are the common types used to cover seams and joints at ceilings, floors, corners, as well as to protect panels from kicks and bumps. Designed in a range of grains and colors to harmonize (if not exactly match) the panelings, they usually have a surface that resists dirt and allows wipe off with a damp cloth.

while 1-5/8 inch long nails should be used for application over furring or backer-board materials.

Have Adequate Blocking

In paneling walls, 4X8 sheets are normally used and it's easy to see that when applied vertically the panel joints should fall on studs. So you have the top and bottom edges nailed to plates, the side edges to 4 foot studs, and some nails to intermediate studs.

Well, it doesn't always work out that way. In the first place most new homes have floor-to-ceiling heights that run a few inches over 8 feet, and if the wall paneling is started at the ceiling, there will be a gap at the floor. This gap can be covered by baseboard but it leaves the sheets shy of the sole-plate for nailing. So some 2X4 blocks atop the sole-plate are needed.

Then, the 4 foot stud placement doesn't work out exactly and, for intermediate nailing, the panels can't be shifted in order to have grooves fall over studs. So where do you nail? The answer: into the blocking. For any kind of vertically grooved materials where you have to nail through the grooves, you'll find it best to start right off by cutting blocks to fit between the studs. Run two horizontal rows of blocking so that the vertical height is divided into three approximately equal spaces. If quite thin sheets are used, make it four equal spaces with three rows of blocking. If paneling occurs on exterior walls, nail in the blocking so the 3-½ inch side of the 2X4 faces the room and is flush with the stud edges; this allows the insulating material to remain behind the blocking.

An alternative to cut-in blocking is the application of 1X2 or 1X3 furring strips over the face edges of the studs. Position the furring rows the same as the cut-in blocking would have been, two or three rows depending on paneling thickness. With furring strips, you'll also have to nail strips to the wall top-plate and at the bottom near the sole-plate.

Application of paneling can also be accomplished using an adhesive method over plywood or gypsumboard backing, or by glue-nailing direct to the framing members. The glue or adhesive methods should be considered only for situations where normal blocking or furring cannot be provided. The methods do involve extra work and the glue or adhesive use can get messy and be a problem with any prefinished material.

If panelings are to be installed on a basement wall, the furring-strip method of wall preparation is nearly always used and the space between furring strips is used for applying an insulation board material (see Chapter 48).

Paneling Application

Start your installation work in a less-important room, and in a least-noticed corner. As you will have already discovered, the first time you begin doing a new job there are little slips and minor mars to contend which are quickly overcome as you adjust to doing the work. So, with paneling, you'll make your saw over-cuts and slight corner chips on the first panel or two you nail up.

With the paneling in the room ready to be applied, stand the sheets up along the walls on which it will be placed. Inspect how the color tone runs panel to panel. Also the grain variations. Move panels to other positions to match up or blend with adjacent panels. Number the panel backs in order and restack. Now, you're ready to begin.

(1) When starting at one corner of the room, don't assume the adjacent wall is plumb to the one you're starting on; check plumbness with your 4 foot level before putting initial sheet up; then when sheet is in position, tack at the top and once again check the plumbness, which is important in the first sheet since following sheets will be guided by it.

(2) Since ceiling corners may not be exactly true either, place the first panel leaving a gap of about 1/8 inch to ceiling finish and same for following panels; this will take care of any minor ceiling irregularities.

(3) To aid getting sheets to right height and alignment,

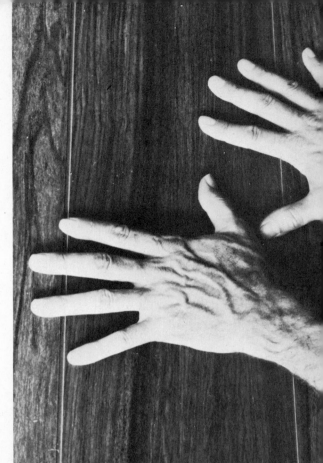

Solid-Lumber Paneling, an alternative to sheet materials, is not as widely used as it once was. Shown here are narrow tongue-and-groove panels by Simpson (left) and wide rough-sawn boards known in some areas as barn boards. Solid D&M (dressed and matched boards) have one advantage for owner-builders over sheet materials and that is the ease with which such boards can be used to assemble cabinet doors and drawer fronts.

use small blocks at the bottom for the sheet to rest on while being positioned.

(4) When you come to electrical switch and outlet boxes, measure their wall location from the ceiling (allowing for the gap) and from the adjacent nailed-up panel; mark the location on the new sheet for cutting prior to nailing the panel up.

(5) No matter what type of nails you use, avoid driving the nail so deep that the hammer head dents the groove edges; later, use the nail set to finish driving the nails—colored nails flush with the groove surface,

finish nails slightly below the groove surface for subsequent puttying.

(6) In nailing, apply first nails at the top of the sheet thereby allowing slight readjustment as the sheet hangs in order to obtain good joint fit.

(7) In making door-window opening cuts, give due thought to at exactly what point you wish the panel edges to come with the proper trimming; use care in marking and remember it's easier to cut panels for a joint occurring over the door or window than to cut out the entire opening accurately from one sheet.

(8) Electric circular saws are fastest for cutting but not necessarily the most accurate in sawing exactly up to a mark; electric jigsaws may be used but are a little more difficult in following a mark closely. In either case, if a power saw is used the sheets should be cut face down and this means having a smooth, non-marring surface to cut on. The face-down position accommodates the power saw blade cutting direction from bottom upward.

(9) Prefinished paneling takes careful handling to avoid chipped edges and corners; watch every step you take

Tips for Glue-Up Application of hardboard panelings: (1) studs or furring strips (in basement application) are first given bead of adhesive and panel is pressed into position carefully so a minimum of shifting is needed after glue contact; (2) apply uniform steady hand pressure to seat in the adhesive; (3) tack-nail with finishing nails at top of sheet leaving heads exposed for later easy removal; (4) use a padded block following a 15-to-20 minute interval to reapply pressure in a final adhesive-setting procedure. Paneling shown is the Masonite Corporation.

191

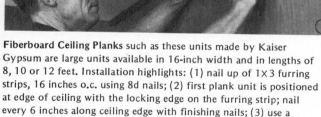

Fiberboard Ceiling Planks such as these units made by Kaiser Gypsum are large units available in 16-inch width and in lengths of 8, 10 or 12 feet. Installation highlights: (1) nail up of 1×3 furring strips, 16 inches o.c. using 8d nails; (2) first plank unit is positioned at edge of ceiling with the locking edge on the furring strip; nail every 6 inches along ceiling edge with finishing nails; (3) use a manual tacker or stapler to staple successive planks along tongue edge after first locking with previous plank; (4) applying trim molding and (5) the finished plank look. A similar alternative plank product is seen in (6), planks grooved to give a tile look on the ceiling.

Apply Panels With Care for Details and caution to avoid damaging the panel prefinish. This plywood paneling installation uses Georgia Pacific panels: (1) circular electric saw for cutting but note that the panel is face down on the saw horses because the blade tips cut upwards; (2) a compass is used to trace the irregularities of adjacent brickwork thereby scribing an irregular mark on the panel which, when cut, will allow the panel to follow the contours of the bricks; (3) 5/8 or 3/4 inch drill corners of a small cutout area to start, followed by a keyhole saw (4) or power jig saw to cut to the exact lines of the cutout.

while carrying sheets, keeping your eyes on the panel corners; watch how you set the panel down and what you lean it against.

(10) Don't apply moldings until all panels have been nailed and nails set; prefinished moldings are recommended with prefinished panelings.

(11) Take your time to get accurate measurements and molding cuts; use moldings around all door and window openings, at ceiling and floor levels to conceal panel edges; also use them at inside or outside room corners and where paneling joins with other materials.

(12) Where moldings change directions at 90°, use a miter-box to get accurate 45° cuts.

Prefinished Ceiling Materials

The ceiling tiles on display in lumber-supply retailers are of wood-fiber materials and are designed for relatively easy application. But they have very little value for sound-deadening or noise-reduction within a room.

Acoustically rated ceiling tiles are available in both tile and drop-in panel form for suspended ceilings. These tiles or panels have perforations of various sizes and pattern arrangements. When offered as an acoustical material, noise-reduction ratings will be given. The cost of these materials may run substantially more, perhaps even double that of ordinary fiber ceiling tiles.

In most instances the ceiling tile installation is best handled by the use of furring strips. The alternative would be for a plywood or gypsumboard sheet backing and the application of the tiles by adhesive. Furring strips are nailed at 12 inch centers for the typical 12X12 inch ceiling tiles. The strips run perpendicular to the joists. They accommodate the fiber tiles which have tongue-and-groove edges. Acoustical tiles are of different composition and may come only with square or beveled edges, and perhaps require a backing material for adhesive placement.

Suspended ceiling installations with drop-in panels have had little use in single-family homes. Where they have been used extensively, however, is in conjunction with luminuous lighting fixtures or light panels. Further details on this installation are provided in Chapter 35.

The manufacturers of ceiling finishes are providing some innovations in application methods. Because, under certain truss conditions, it is difficult to obtain a true and level base with furring strips, one manufacturer of ceiling finishes now offers a metal-channel method of attachment. The lightweight steel furring channels receive metal cross-tees which, in turn, accommodate the tile units. The channels are self-leveling, rigid, and eliminate the need for shims or wedges to level the furring.

Ceiling Tile Materials Required
(per hundred sq. ft.)

	TILE SIZE	
	12 X 12 in.	12 X 24 in.
1X 3 furring strips	140 lin. ft.	140 lin. ft.
8d furring nails	1.7 lbs	1.7 lbs
ceiling tile	2-½ cartons	2-½ cartons
1/2 or 9/16 in. staples or 1-1/8 in. blued lath nails	450	350
cove molding	room perimeter plus 20%	room perimeter plus 20%

A Guide To Ordering Tiles in square foot and two square feet sizes shows the other materials needed for the installation. Quantities given are for an area of 100 square feet. The number of tiles needed? If you estimated a hundred of the smaller tile units, you're right!

Suspended Ceilings are particularly appropriate in combination with ceiling lighting (see Chapter 35). Shown is suspended ceiling using Armstrong products: left, a close-up of metal channels and cross tees that support the ceiling tiles. The grooved-edge 1X4 foot tile material is placed followed by the supporting cross tee fitted into the tile slot and resting on the channels. The 4 foot long units lay up fast as you work your way across the room. When a tile needs cutting to finish a row, use the leftover piece to start the next row.

Two Types of Thin Brick Finishes suitable for interior accent: at left, individual "Hearth Brick" wall covering units applied with adhesive are 3/16-inch thick, of mineral composition and have the texture and fire-resistance of real bricks. These thin units are made by the GAF Corp. and are applied without mortar fill for the joints. At right, fiberglass-reinforced molded bricks in panel form made by Masonite's Roxite division. The panels have invisible seams, are available in choice of colors and may be used inside or out.

With wood furring strips, fastening of tiles with staples is faster and easier than nailing. And hammer dents are avoided. A typical gun stapler is used with 9/16 inch staples for the usual 1/2 inch thick ceiling tiles (staples are driven through the flanges which are less than half as thick as the tiles).

Before beginning any ceiling work, you'll want to draw up at least a rough layout sketch, a ceiling plan with exact room dimension outline and center-lines drawn in two directions perpendicular to each other. This permits a layout that will result in north-south border tiles being equal and east-west border tiles similarly equal. If the room has wall offsets or is otherwise irregular, a more accurate sketch may be needed to adjust the initial tile placements to come up with the desired borders. It's desirable, where possible, to have border units at least a half-tile in size.

Your nailing up of the furring will be aimed at accommodating the tile layout you've planned. In rectangular rooms, it will work out thus:

☐ if the end-wall of the room to which the furring strips butt is an odd number of feet (such as 13 feet 8 inches), then the first furring strip will be along the room center-line from end-wall to end-wall (and the border tile parallel to the furring will be about 10 inches on each side for a 13 foot 8 inch wide room);

☐ if the end-wall is an even number of feet (12 feet 6 inches, for example), then the first two furring strips should be located 6 inches on each side of the center-line (and the border units for this example would be 9 inches wide).

Border tiles are easily cut using a utility razor-blade type knife and your steel square as a cutting guide. Don't worry about lack of stapling space along cut edges next to the wall. A cove or other molding should be applied to conceal the crack along the wall. The molding is nailed through the wall finish and into the framing plate and thus provides adequate support for the tile's cut edges.

Other Materials You Can Choose

Each year new kinds of wall or ceiling finish materials come on the market. Some don't last either because of lack of acceptance or because the producing companies fail or decide to withdraw the material from the market. But gradually many such innovations do continue to be sold and eventually become readily available on a countrywide basis.

One type increasingly more popular through the years is a wood-fiber board having a lightly textured linen finish that receives paint or wallpaper quite well. It comes in 8 foot widths and various lengths and can thus be used for full wall-length installation without joints . . . but watch it, you may have difficulty getting it into the rooms where it will be used. Other fiberboard materials are available, some with prefinishes, and with various types of sheet joint treatments suggested in the manufacturer's literature.

One form of fiberboard material seemingly more and more popular has a cork or burlap surface. Another form gaining acceptance is gypsumboard in predecorated form; its room face is covered with a vinyl surfacing. While these specialized sheet materials are not as widely distributed and stocked as woodgrain panelings, inquiries can be made through your lumber and building supply retailer, who may have a partial stock and can readily order other similar materials.

Use of cork as a wall-surfacing material is expanding, with a growing assortment of styles, colors and textures available. It is being used for special wall applications in study rooms, children's rooms, dens and other locations. It is popular partly because of its thumb-tackability but the material also has sound-deadening properties as well as a highly attractive appearance. Cork panels that do not come mounted on a backing can be applied with adhesive to a plywood, gypsumboard or fiberboard backing material.

Another type of wall product still new in its distribution is called "tackboard." Its derivation is from a commercial product sold to schools along with chalkboard and used to tack up samples of student work and reference materials. Vinyl- and burlap-covered tackboard sheets are well-suited for children's rooms. Their surfaces and backing allow penetration by thumb or map tacks and, upon later removal, the surface holes tend to close and be unnoticeable. When inspecting or selecting the various types of newer wall-ceiling finish materials, be sure to ask for installation information in advance. The methods vary according to specific materials or manufacturers.

Thin Brick Installation using bricks, adhesive and sealer made by the Z-Brick Company. Steps are: (1) spread 1/6 inch coat of mortarlike adhesive; (2) press brick into place wiggling, slightly to seat; (3) smooth adhesive between bricks with narrow brush; (4) apply one or two coats of sealer to make surface washable.

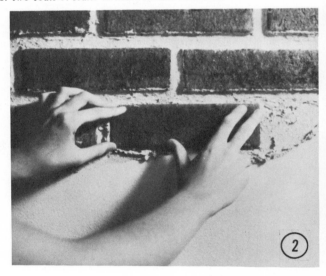

29 Kitchen and Bathroom Finishes

Many traditions carry over from yesteryear. One principally related to bathrooms is the once common installation of "all-tile" bathrooms. It was thought in the late 1930's and 1940's that fastidious cleanliness of almost operating-room purity was needed in all parts of bathrooms. And to some degree this carried over to kitchens, particularly in the homes of the more well-to-do. Believe it or not, it was once carried to the extreme of not only tiling the full walls and floors of some bathrooms, but ceilings as well!

Since the 1950's many changes have come about in bathrooms in new homes although the plumbing fixtures have remained reasonably comparable, at least in appearance. Free-standing lavatory basins have disappeared and the only pedestal models seen today are in antique shops. Wall-hung lavatories may be heading in the same direction because of the continued popularity of vanity lavatory cabinets and of the rapid growth in synthetic integral basin counters. Synthetics in the form of acrylics and polyesters have also come to other fixtures, as will be seen in the Chapter 41 discussion of plumbing fixtures.

For walls and ceilings and floors of bathrooms the trend has been towards more decor, less sanitation. This is partly the result of better plumbing fixtures but it also has to do with comfort, visual appeal, and the relationships between bathrooms and glamor or personal vanity, and between kitchens and informal family rooms.

At any rate, kitchens and bathrooms in today's new homes are given much decorating attention and as a result have become rooms where function and utility are no longer the dominant factors as far as materials are concerned.

An owner-builder who may feel at a loss when it comes to kitchen-bath decorating and color schemes need only visit the nearest kitchen display at the local lumber-supply or home-center retailer. In many such display centers, he will find not only ample assemblies but also expert kitchen design people who are prepared to help him with coordination of kitchen-bath materials, fabrics and floor coverings. You may also consult the bibliography provided here for decorating-idea books.

And there is need for coordination. Bathroom items are now offered in a wide range of colors and patterns that include floor tiles, wall tiles, wallpapers, cabinet counter-basin, cabinet doors, shower-curtain fabrics, window-curtain fabrics, plumbing fixtures-in-color, toilet seat designs, throw rugs or full carpeting, bath accessory styles. So, any expert color/pattern design aid you can get, take. Or, take it if it makes sense to you. Otherwise, shop for design assistance elsewhere. You won't have to hunt very far.

In planning the use of certain materials in kitchens and baths it should be stated that today's assortments of such materials include some very very expensive items, and you will be wise to always inquire about per-unit or per-square-foot cost of such and such. In addition, ask about availability. Some sample displays indicating wide choice are backed by narrow stocking practices and there may be delivery delays for items not stocked.

Keeping in mind trends in this field and also taking cognizance of practices followed by thousands of home builders in recent years, the following wall-finish factors in kitchens and bathrooms might be given due thought by the owner-builder interested in stretching his dollars.

☐ Wall areas where water repeatedly collects in heavy amounts with potential damaging effect on wall construction are caused principally by just two plumbing fixtures—bathtubs and stall shower units. Other plumbing fixtures have undergone many design-installation improvements through the years and rarely initiate water problems.

☐ Still, moisture-laden air in kitchens and bathrooms comes from showering and cooking and, although quickly dissipated by forced-air heating systems, there is a possibility of some air-laden moisture condensing on walls and ceilings.

☐ In kitchens, a special problem around the cooking area involves airborne grease vapors and spatterings, so that wall areas near to ranges and ovens are apt to be grease collectors despite the best efforts of range hoods.

☐ The foregoing would indicate the advisability of having wipable wall finishes, but not necessarily surfaces that

Coated Fabric Wall Coverings are both washable and strippable. They come in some surprising designs, as shown here: at left the unusual Davilla pattern on a reflective hammer-textured metallic finish and at right, the Chantilly design, a wet-look floral. Both patterns are from the Sanitas collection which includes hundreds of stylings.

are completely impervious to penetration by moisture. In short, complete floor-to-ceiling tiled walls around the room indicate affluence rather than necessity.

Thus, gradually but increasingly, imperviousness and sanitation are no longer the prime requisites for kitchen and bathroom wall finishes; decor is being given vastly increased attention.

Choice of Materials

The first choice among home buyers and home builders for bathroom walls and floors continues to be ceramic tiles. These glazed clay-base units have great surface resistance as well as withstanding stains and discoloring. They are available in many rich and bold colors, plus the traditional pastels. And newer offerings include various patterns and textures. These, along with details of new and easier installation methods, are discussed more fully in the following chapter.

Probably the second most popular type of wall finish in bathrooms, and second to paint in kitchens, is wallpaper.

Texture on Bathroom Walls complements decor. Shown on the left, bath walls covered with Marlite's Barnside, a plastic finish hardboard simulating barn siding. At the right, Roxite brick-like plastic panels contrasts with the plush carpeting in a shower bathroom.

This of course needs backing, and by far the common practice for wall construction in these rooms is to apply gypsumboard sheets to the framing just as in other rooms. Then specialized bath-kitchen finishes (including ceramic tile) are applied over the wallboard.

Fabric and vinyl wallpapers having excellent surface washability-durability characteristics are well suited to kitchen-bath use. And there are no longer limitations in color or pattern with these easy-wipe, easy-clean wall coverings. A large number of companies are now offering them in ever-expanding assortments. Check Chapter 44 for details on wallpapers and similar coverings.

Patterned-colored vinyls now come factory-applied as a prefinish on gypsumboard sheets. It's called "predecorated wallboard" and similar prefinishes are available from a few companies for plywood, fiberboard and particleboard. As yet, these prefinished boards do not have wide distribution but samples or literature on them may be available in lumber-supply retailers.

One long-used material for economical bath-kitchen use which has recently seen improvement in design and style-selectivity is prefinished hardboard. Not the same kinds of prefinished hardboards having woodgrain surfaces, as described in the previous chapter. But hardboards having an extremely durable glazelike prefinish that makes the surface closer to tile than to wood paneling.

These glazelike hardboards were first offered (and still are) in 4X8 sheets with the surface grooved in 4X4 inch "tile" squares. This product was commonly called "tile-board." Then came the marbilized patterns with the same glazelike prefinish and no grooves. Both products were offered in lighter pastel colors only. More recently, new styles in darker shades have been added by some companies. And 5X5 and 5X6 foot sizes are now available, permitting installation without seams in bathtub recesses.

The prefinished glazelike hardboards install with adhesive over a suitable backing material such as gypsumboard. Their joints, corners and edges are trimmed in color-matching metal moldings in various shapes to fit junctures (see illustration). A few lines of prefinished hardboards have unusual pattern themes such as ferns, lace, multiple-lines, metallics, antiqued and textured woodgrains.

One newer kind of specialized wall product is the rigid molded-plastic tub recess panels. These are components installed with adhesive over a solid backing but designed to fit a standard 2-½X5 foot tub recess without seams and with just a sealant bead needed at the tub line.

All of these specialized wall finishes are accompanied by

199

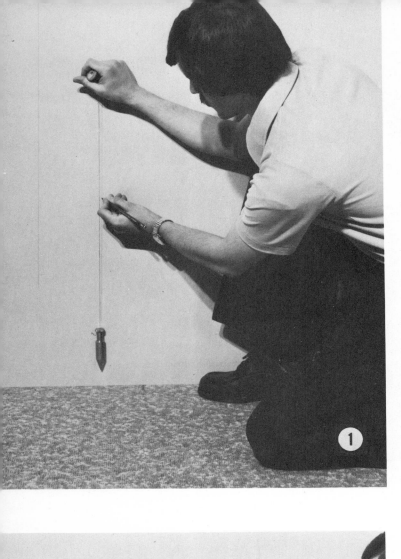

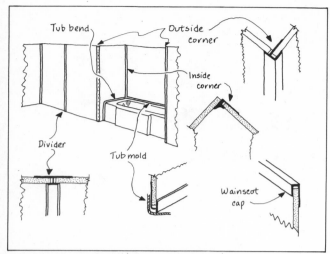

Hard-Surface Hardboard Panels are a relatively inexpensive method of providing an easily washable surface over all or part of the bath-kitchen walls. Once called "Tileboard" because it came with tile squares grooved in the panel surface, the sheets found today in retail home supply stores are more apt to have marblized patterns in choice of colors. They are also available in solid colors. And installation is by adhesive plus color-harmonizing metal molding trim.

manufacturer's instruction sheets. Methods of application may vary according to the material. With some panels, caulking of seams, joints, corners and along molding edges

may be recommended for high moisture areas. If such is the case with the material you choose, follow the instructions because the product, while it may have an extremely resistant surface, might also have vulnerable edges.

To sum up with just a few suggestions on keeping material costs in rein, the following options are offered because they appear to represent the rather happy combination of installation ease and limitations on the use of more expensive materials.

- Use a complete premolded, reinforced plastic tub-and-recess unit and/or premolded reinforced plastic stall-shower components.
- Use limited ceramic tile for floor surfacing and for low wainscot wall applications using adhesive for bonding (details in next chapter).
- Use a patterned material on walls above wainscots applying predecorated wallboard or applying wall-coverings to gypsumboard backing.
- Complete the room with high lighting-value luminous suspended ceiling having some drop-in prefinished and washable panels (details in Chapter 35).

With appropriate color and material choice coordination, you'll come up with a well-decorated, attractive bathroom or kitchen suited to the functions required while still easy to keep spic and span. Floors for these rooms have only been touched upon. Your selection might well involve (and probably will) those considerations on resilient and soft floor coverings found in Chapters 37 and 45.

Wainscot Paneling, another way of finishing walls in bathrooms and kitchen dining areas. Smoothly finished hardboard panels in wainscot size have now been packaged by Maonsite's Marlite division in kit form for easier installation. The main steps are: (1) getting off to a vertical start through the use of a plumb reference line; (2) the Marlite panels are placed and held in position on the wall by the use of special edge clips; (3) a cap-mold follows panel placement to provide trim along the top edge; and (4) the completed installation gives a highly attractive yet easy-clean appearance. Applicable in dens, dining, and other rooms as well as the kitchen and bath.

30 Ceramic Tile Application

There's little doubt that ceramic tile walls and floors, with a long history of good performance, have found long-lasting acceptance in new homes and provide a key sales feature for existing older homes.

But in addition to tradition the product also has a strong status-quo-preserving team in tile contractors, union craftsmen, and association of tile manufacturers. Most architects, many home builders, and a large number of building supply establishments will tell you, if asked, that ceramic tile work can be done only by a highly skilled and experienced craftsman. And that the only way tile work can properly be done on residential sites is by laying floor tiles over a 2-inch thick concrete subfloor base, and wall tiles to a 3/4-inch thick metal-lath-reinforced scratch, mortar and bond coat base.

Don't believe them. They're wrong.

There's been but limited acknowledgement among building professionals that a good-quality, first-class installation of either floor or wall tiles can be accomplished using the adhesive method direct to backing board, without any concrete or mortar base. And the adhesive method is one entirely suitable for use by amateur tile workers, as it is also for professionals. There are literally thousands of tile shops, do-it-yourself stores, lumber-supply retailers, home centers and catalog merchandisers who have been selling ceramic tiles to home owners for years. A very high proportion of these installations have been made using the adhesive method over old walls or floors. So, there's no need to be concerned about doing your own tile work.

In fact, once you've shopped several retailers and seen the variety in tile styles and patterns, you may desire to use tiles in places other than the bath or powder rooms. It makes good sense in a number of areas. For entrance foyer floors, for fireplace facings, for back-counter decor in kitchens, for planters and counter surfacing of room dividers, and numerous other possible applications.

Choosing Tile

The owner-builder shopping for ceramic materials will soon note three general types of ceramic units:

- individual 4×4 or 4-¼×4-¼ inch square tiles usually in the 1/4 to 5/16 inch thicknesses plus matching half-tiles and trim units;
- mosaic tiles mounted on loosely woven cloth or fabric backing in small sheets of about 2×2 feet, the tiles being about 1 inch in size and uniformly spaced for grouting;
- irregularly shaped tiles having about the same surface area per tile as the 4 inch square units but mounted on cloth-backed sheets that fit and mesh together the design pattern for grouting.

Tiles also are available in some rectangular sizes but their use is more in commercial and institutional buildings so they are not usually stocked by retailers for home use.

Because the smaller mosaic tiles are primarily used on floors, they're sometimes called floor tiles. Actually, the mosaics can be applied on walls and the other, larger tiles can be used on floors.

Trim tiles, which may or may not be available in matching colors and patterns, usually come in the following styles and for the following purposes:

- caps—for top edges of wainscot walls or tub-recess walls;
- cove base—for easy-clean curve joint at floor level;
- corners—rounded inside coves and outside corners.

On the subject of corner units, these have declined in use in home construction, with many inside corners simply being grouted joints. Some tile manufacturers offer tile units that at first glance appear to be field tile, but which actually have one or two round edges to become self-trimming tiles for top or side edges of tile areas and for outside corner use.

As suggested in the previous chapter on kitchen-bath

Custom Tiled Shower has an overhead recessed light, adjustable shower head and single-dial water control. Standard tile units plus accessory trim shapes are used with a standard cement-mortar bed installation.

wall finishes, the trend has been in recent years to emphasize decorative possibilities in these rooms. In selecting ceramic tiles bear in mind the need for color coordination with other room materials, but also consider that ceramic tiles are not likely to be changed for a long time. They should, therefore, receive careful selection.

You may find that the tile products of a few manufacturers have special preparation to make them simpler to use or apply. For example, one company puts little integral lugs along two edges of each tile. The purpose is to give accurate parallel alignment of adjacent tiles and to separate the tiles uniformly so that later grouting will result in uniform joints. The lugs make the setting of tile quicker and assure a better joint job.

Another product with built-in assistance for the tile worker is called the "Redi-Set" system because it involves applying sheets or panels of tiles that are already pre-grouted. You grout only the joints between the panels and you apply the silicone rubber grout using a caulking gun.

Wall Backing For Tile

While other wallboard materials may be suitable as a base for adhesive-applied ceramic wall tiles, the suggested material is gypsumboard. Ask your supplier if he can furnish 1/2 inch thick water-resistant-type gypsumboard for use in your tub recess or shower stall wet areas. Regular gypsumboard may be used on other bathroom walls and also in kitchens.

Just in case the supplier won't order a small quantity of this water-resistant wallboard, use regular gypsumboard sheets but give them a coat of penetrating sealer or shellac. Apply the sealer after sheets have been cut to size but before nailing up. Allow a day for the sealer to dry. Apply it to both faces and all edges.

Before applying the gypsumboard, check the framing with a long straightedge and your 4 foot level. The Tile Council of American specifications indicate that the backing surface shouldn't have an out-of-plane variation more than 1/8 inch in 8 feet. It also states that corners and door jambs where tile is to be fitted should likewise come within the above tolerance. This is not an unusual limitation and comes well within the normal range of expectation in residential wood framing.

In respect to tub recesses and shower stalls, the tub or shower base fixtures must be set, their drains connected, before the wallboard is applied. Bring the gypsumboard down to about 1/4 inch from the top of the tub lip or shower-base flange in such a way that the inside of the lip or flange is flush with the wallboard (see illustration). This permits a down-lapping by the ceramic tiles. You may have to provide furring or blocking at this point in order to bring the wallboard to this position.

For recesses and stalls, cut the gypsumboard sheets so the edges adjacent to the tub consist of full 1/2 inch thick material and not the slightly thinner tapered edges. Joints and nail-heads should not be treated with tape and cement. Cut edges around pipes or bath accessory openings should be caulked flush with a waterproof, nonhardening compound.

Use The Right Tools

Don't try to do the job with make-shift tools just because the tile area is limited. The money you save in not buying a few specialized tile-working tools will be lost in damaged materials and a poor-looking job. You should have tile nippers and cutting accessories for your electric drill, a rented lever-type tile cutter if you have a substantial area to do, cheesecloth for wiping joints, and solvent for grout clean-up. Plus a properly-notched adhesive-spreading trowel.

Your regular tool complement will yield certain items for tile installation use—4 foot level, chalk-line, light hammer and tapping blocks, caulking gun and your three rules. Adhesive and edge caulking materials will be purchased at

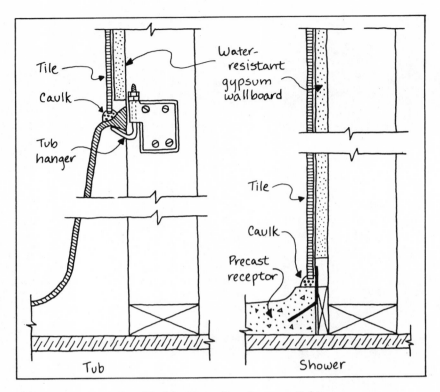

Tile-Fixture Juncture Detail indicates how tile units are applied to gypsumboard base in an adhesive installation and carried down almost to the tub or shower rim. The remaining space is then caulked with white compound designed for tub-joint application.

same time as tiles. Adhesive comes in premixed pails ready for use while the grout normally is in powder form for mixing with water. The latter, however, may not be the case with some newer grouting materials.

If you're planning to install ceramic tiles over a considerable area, you may wish to inquire further about the possibility of obtaining premixed grouting in cartridge form for use in a caulking gun, and whether an air-operated grouting gun might be available in your area for rental.

For floor applications, one extra tool needed is a floor roller similar to that used for resilient floor-covering sheet materials . . . a three-segmented carpet-covered roller that weighs about 150-175 pounds and may probably be rented from a floor-covering dealer.

In ordering tiles, figure your wall or floor area to be covered and allow 5 percent extra for cutting waste. And use some caution in purchasing or ordering adhesives and grouting material. Give preference to a tile brand in which

Pregrouted Sheet Tile Installation begins with spreading adhesive on dry wallboard and placing first tile sheet; then in (3), a pipe hole is being cut with tile nippers; in (4) last sheet is applied on back wall and now comes upper sheets; the special inside-corner strips are pressed (5) into recess corners, then grouting between sheets and at tub edges is applied with caulking gun that dispenses same silicone rubber material with which the sheets are factory-grouted. Final photo indicates touch-up using spray solution and cheesecloth pad for wiping grouted joints.

Ceramic Tiles in Prerouted Sheets is newest product of the American Olean Tile Co. Shown here is the two-carton set of 8 tile sheets, with two tub legs, corner strips and a few extra tiles. This kit assembles into a complete tub-recess wall finish for a standard five foot bathtub.

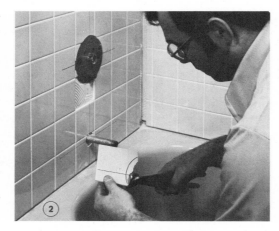

the tile manufacturer also offers his own brand of adhesive, caulking and grouting materials. You're assured in such cases that the materials are appropriate for the tiles. Where a tile manufacturer offers no such application materials, check his literature to find out what brands or chemical materials he suggests.

There are basically two sorts of adhesives designed for tile applications. Both are organic, one intended for use only in areas characterized by limited or intermittent moisture conditions, and the other for areas likely to have prolonged periods during which water resistance must be maintained.

For specific guidance on these adhesives, check the adhesive label to verify that the material meets the following application standards: *Organic Adhesives For Ceramic Tile*—ANSI A136.1, Type I for prolonged water-resistance, Type II for intermittently moist or dry. This is a nationally recognized standard by the American National Standards Institute. Which leads to mention of another standard you may have occasion to refer to, *Water-Resistant Gypsumboard*—ANSI A108.4.

Tile Application Know-How

Give attention to your layout planning. Measure dimensions where tiles are to be placed, divide by tile unit dimensions to arrive at marginal distances; plan to start tiles in a way that will avoid narrow tile cuts at the margins. Plan for the use of full tile units at certain prominent, easily viewed places such as outside wall corners or at tub flange on tub-recess walls.

As part of the tile layout work, mark straight clear reference lines. On walls, make sure of the level or the plumb of starting reference lines. On floors, verify the parallel-to-wall and perpendicular reference lines. These beginning points must be accurate or later tile rows will tend to magnify the errors cumulatively, until the discrepancy becomes quite noticeable along the cut marginal tile units.

When cutting tiles to fit around pipes, inserts or bath accessories, allow about 1/8 inch caulking space. Accurate-to-mark cuts are made bit-by-bit, a little at a time, using your tile nippers. Make accurate, full-round holes by using your electric drill and an appropriate circular drilling bit or saw. Also suited for larger holes, a handsaw that's called a "rod saw," which uses carbide-coated hacksaw blades.

Tile straight-line cutting can be done with a small tile scoring tool and a manual break. For cuts close to tile edges, score and use the tile nippers to break off at the score line. For much cutting, rent or buy a lever-cutter that operates on tile in much the same way as a paper cutter.

The tiles must be set firmly into the adhesive. Press initially with fingers but follow with light tapping on a wood block or piece of plywood that extends over several tile units. Tap block to bring tile units into a single plane of alignment.

Grout only after all tiles are set and have been thoroughly cleaned. Surface dirt can find its way into grout material and stain or discolor it. Follow grout-mixing instructions and use grout application and wiping procedure suggested. The aim is to wipe evenly and neatly so that a uniform-width joint results. If your tiles have been accurately positioned and aligned in the same plane, then the grouting procedure should be easy to accomplish.

When grouting, it pays to do at least a partial cleanup of excess grout as you go, using a manufacturer-recommended grout solvent. At final cleanup it's easier to remove a thin excess mark than a full-strength thick mark that was left to dry on the tile.

In wiping the grouted joints, attain good smooth surfaces by using the same consistent wiping strokes, using the cheesecloth pads and shifting the cloth constantly as the pad fills with excess grout. Have your work adequately lighted, and provide ventilation when using solvents. For final wiping strokes to achieve added smoothness, apply a bit of solvent to a fresh pad or to your fingertip. Curing time for the grout varies with grout material and atmospheric conditions. Allow ample time before beginning final cleanup.

The last step in completing the installation is applying caulking material between the tilework and the tub, lavatory, or other adjacent fixtures including those pipes, faucets or control units that penetrate the tiles. Here, too, uniformly caulked joints are desirable and can be obtained by wiping with a solvent-daubed pad, but be sure to use the proper solvent for the caulking material.

Tips For Floor Tiles

The single-layer plywood subfloor deck widely used in conventional wood-frame residential construction is not sufficient as a base for ceramic floor tile installations. An added layer of exterior-type plywood or of suitable underlayment material is suggested (details in Chapter 32).

However, if your new home followed the recommendation in Chapter 9 for use of the APA glued-plywood floor system, it made be satisfactory for direct application of tiles without added underlayment. The glued-plywood system should employ an appropriate grade of plywood having laminations with exterior-type glue and, preferably, 5/8 inch thickness over 16 inch joist spacings.

In layout planning for mosaic tiles, try to adjust the tile sheets and central starting lines so that sheet joints don't fall any closer than 3 inches to a wall and also so they do not coincide with joints in the underlayment or floor deck. In adjusting the lines, test the right-angle juncture by layout of several tile sheets along central lines in both directions before any adhesive is applied.

The laying procedure for mosaics will involve placement of all full tile sheets before cutting any sheet margins. The suggested method is to apply adhesive only for an area of full tile sheets, a quarter of the room at a time. Be sure to use a corrugated paperboard resting base for the adhesive container in order to avoid spills on the tiles already in place.

Tile sheets should be butted so that the joints at sheet edges match up in thickness with the joints within the field of the sheet. Lower sheet into adhesive by placing one edge carefully and letting the balance roll out. Try to avoid sliding the sheets; press them down firmly to adhesive contact. The installer can walk on the tiles but had better place a protective paperboard mat in order to avoid catching shoe soles or heels on tile edges.

After cutting and placing the marginal sheets, mark and cut for fitting around plumbing fixtures or floor registers. The installation is then completed by rolling tiles with the flooring roller, and then allowing the adhesive to set for needed curing time before going to the tile cleanup, grouting, and caulking work in the usual manner.

The procedure is essentially the same for larger patterned tile that comes mounted on backing sheets. Or for individual tile units. Somewhat more care must be used in stepping or walking on the larger tile units since the entire weight may fall on a single tile. Play safe by using paperboard, or better still, hardboard mats about 3X3 feet in size that can easily be moved around.

Where coved base tile units are to be applied on the wall, the floor tiling installation should be done first and a suitable margin width provided to accommodate the coved tiles.

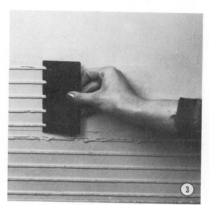

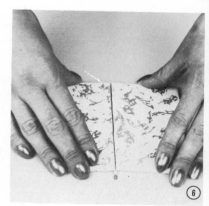
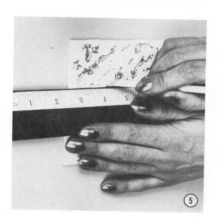

Fashion-Styled Tiles from England in convenient do-it-yourself packaging, now sold in this country by the H&R Johnson Company through home center and lumber-supply stores. Somewhat simplified, the Johnson-recommended steps are: (1) start with a plumb line and next a straight-edge (2) in the form of a horizontal story-pole so that tile joints are level and plumb; make appropriate guide marks on the surface. Next in (3), use a notched adhesive spreader for applying the adhesive. In (4), tiles are placed by tilting slightly in order to have tight-touching butts. For cutting tile as in (5), score with a special scoring tool then place the tile (6) on a counter edge and gently break off at the score mark. After tile placement, apply grouting mix (7) with a sponge pad working the grout into the tile grooves. Then (8), following initial drying of grout, wipe the excess off from tile faces using cheesecloth.

31 | Closet and Storage Facilities

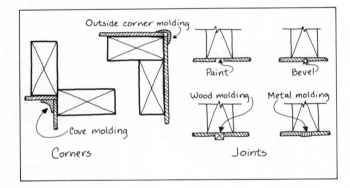

Corners

Joints

Hardboard Wall Treatment Details suitable for closet and storage room use. At left, covering corner edges with cove and corner moldings. And in the four right-hand sketches, alternative methods for handling of joints in the hardboard material.

Home builders have, in the past, applied gypsumboard drywall in all closets and behind all other types of wall coverings. But some site builders and many producers of factory-built housing have found that closet walls and, to a lesser extent closet ceilings, are a logical place to apply other drywall sheet materials that offer cash economies.

As a result it is not unusual to find some newer homes in which closets are lined with different wall-ceiling materials, often with exposed nail-heads, slender batten strips over joints, plus plywood or particleboard shelving with the edges left raw. Much of the raw appearance disappears with the overall application of high-hiding-power acrylic and latex paints. In short, some economizing in the wall-ceiling finishes of storage closets is not out of place in an average single-family home, and for the owner-builder this savings may permit more money to be spent on closet fixtures and convenience facilities.

Different Kinds of Boards

One of the new board products most rapidly increasing in use is particleboard, which has pretty much the same broad range of nonstructural sheet applications boasted by plywoods and hardboards. One type of particleboard well suited to closet-storage use is called "flakeboard" in many areas, because its surface clearly defines the individual wood chips, giving a flakelike appearance.

Since their introduction to the commodity sheet board market several years ago, particleboard prices have run somewhat less than the lowest cost plywoods. And the particleboards for closet, shelving and other storage facility uses have a slight advantage over plywoods in their uniformity of appearance, splinterless surface, minimized grain raise, and the elimination of larger voids in their edges. Particleboards have been especially accepted by new home builders for shelving and by cabinet makers for kitchen and bathroom cabinet applications.

A second, highly underrated sheet or board product available in lower price ranges is named fiberboard, although more often than not it is referred to by the trade names of the two largest-volume manufacturers, Homasote and Upson boards. These fiberboards are advantageous in that they are available in 8 foot widths allowing full-size cuts in closet-storage areas and the minimizing of seams or board joints. Large-size pieces, however, must be cut slightly shy (1/8 to 1/4 inch) in order to allow tilting into place. This might prove a problem in tight quarters.

Fiberboards and hardboards are also offered with factory prefinishes that could be a small time saver by cutting out some of the painting. Using inexpensive prefinished trims in corners and around the closet-interior edges of door frames will provide further economies in closet installations.

When choosing materials and finishes remember that most closets have very poor daylighting, even with doors open. As a rule, light and bright finishes are preferred to medium or darker ones. With walk-in wardrobe closets, normal practice is to install a ceiling light fixture, pull-chain or door-switch operated. This closet lighting provision might also be made with other closets to good advantage.

Perforated hardboard, having a series of small holes equally spaced in each direction, is very useful in some closet or storage areas because of the wide range of hooks, racks, hangers and other inexpensive accessories available for insertion through the holes. This type of hardboard often goes by one manufacturer's trade name "Pegboard." It is usually stocked by retailers in 1/8 and 1/4 inch thicknesses.

Considerations When Installing

Before starting to apply closet-storage wallboards, make another check of your framing to ensure that block backing is available at the points needed for the particular wall material being used. It may be desirable to provide an extra stud, or perhaps between-stud blocks, when using closet shelve ledgers or mounting hardware.

Apply board products using nails designed for wallboard, in the 1-to-1-1/4 inch range. Nailing is usually done on these materials with 6-to-8 inch nail spacings to intermediate studs or supports and with 4-to-6 inch spacings along sheet edges or joints. A wide range of color in wallboard nails is readily available for use with prefinished boards; you can come very close to matching colors so that the exposed nail heads become inconspicuous.

In cutting wallboard holes in sheet or board products that have prefinishes, you have to be more careful than when cutting similar openings in gypsumboard. First, the prefinished materials need cutting and handling on a smooth surface so that no surface marring occurs, a distinct hazard with some of the prefinished fiberboards. Secondly, the openings need to be cut more accurately to that cover plates extend over the cut opening. You can't go back to an oversize opening and patch it up with joint cement, as you do with drywall.

In addition to wall finishes in bedroom wardrobe closets, clothes-hanging and shelf provisions must be made. Usually, a single 12 inch wide shelf is placed along the back wall of the closet at a reachable height (see illustration). Just in front of and below the front shelf edge, a closet pole furnishes the means for using coat and clothes hangers.

Shelf supporting hardware is readily available at lumber-supply retailers and home centers for shelves alone, for shelves plus the closet pole, and for the complete shelf-and-pole installation. The latter, in metal assemblies, come with necessary mounting accessories and are factory prefinished so that no painting is necessary. Wherever possible, mounting nails or screws should penetrate into studs or backing. In some cases where there is no backing at the correct location, blind-fastening devices such as toggle-bolts or Molly anchors will be needed.

Substantial weight can accrue to a shelf or pole filled with stored items. Shelf supports at the two ends of a closet shelf are sufficient in small 2-to-4 foot wide closets. But in walk-ins or wider closets using longer shelves, the supports should be no more than about 3 feet apart. Round wood closet poles about 1-¼ inch in diameter provide sufficient

strength for up to 4 feet, but beyond that dimension there should be added central support. Closet poles 1-3/8 inch in diameter will hold full clothes loads up to about 5 feet before central support is needed. You can follow the same approximate guidelines for metal clothes rods unless other allowable spans are given on the package. Metal rods with chrome or stainless finishes have a slight advantage over wood poles in that clothes hangers slide more easily on the bright finishes.

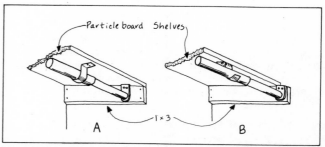

Metal Closet Shelves available in a series of adjustable-width sizes to fit nearly all closet conditions make shelf installations easy. These sketches show details of shelf units made by Kinkead Industries but other units are of comparable design and installed similarly. The adjustment distance is about 12 inches. Metal wall brackets provide support for both shelf and hanging rod. Sketch in lower left shows typical shelf heights in closets, the lowest height being intended for use by children. Where wall brackets cannot be screwed to studs, use of any of the wallboard fasteners (lower right) is recommended.

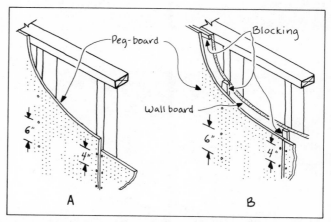

Perforated Hardboard Panels give functional aspect to wall finish in storage areas because the holes accommodate a wide range of hooks and racks. The panels and accessories are produced by several companies but the best known is called Pegboard, a product of the Masonite Co. Shown at left with suggested nail spacing is the material applied direct to studs. At right in (B), blocking is placed over the studs where the wall has wallboard. The blocking permits engaging of the accessory items in the holes.

Aside from prefinished metal shelves, there are several alternatives. Most lumber-supply companies carry stocks of prefinished shelves of various sizes both in colors and wood-grains. On the inexpensive side is unfinished particleboard. And 1X12 inch boards are still available, although in shelf applications such boards have a tendency to cup or warp.

If you choose unfinished wood or wood-fiber materials, the installation should be made, of course, in advance of the painting-decorating work. If, however, the choice is for metal hardware and prefinished shelving, the installation can wait until the painting and decorating have been completed.

Vinyl-Coated Steel Rod System for storage rooms and wardrobe closets can really organize the keeping personal and household effects. First photo shows attachment points in a typical walk-in closet with hardboard wall surfaces. In the second view, the shelf-racks are shown with clothes in place and in third view, off-the-floor shoe rack.

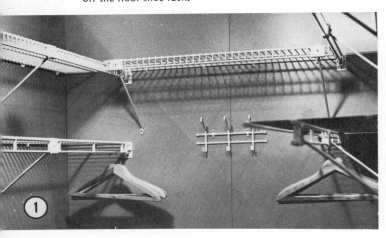

Specialized Storage Areas

Some of the special-purpose closets included in most new homes are a foyer or entry closet, linen closet, kitchen pantry, utility-cleaning closet. The latter is sometimes referred to as a broom closet and it serves to store vacuum cleaners, dust mops and other house-cleaning equipment. Cabinets adjacent to the laundry equipment usually provide space for storage of detergents and other clothes-cleaning supplies.

Foyer closets are commonly equipped with the same type of shelf and pole as wardrobe closets.

In the past linen closets had a combination of shelves above, drawers below . . . the latter usually being three closet-wide drawers resting on the floor and installed in built-in form with a trimmed face-front and wall-to-wall top, serving as a shelf or counter. In most new homes today, drawers have given way to more economical shelves. The normal installation consists of five or six shelves. Shelves usually have about 16-to-18 inches vertical spacing for the lower shelves and 12-to-14 inches for the two or three upper shelves. All are full closet depth, ordinarily between 2-and-2-½ feet.

Whether drawers serve a useful and convenient function in linen closets is no doubt arguable. For those owner-builders who may be interested in having such shelves, it might be noted that some millwork suppy sources can furnish two-, three- and four-drawer stacks having face-fronts and tops and specifically designed for closet installation. Another and perhaps slightly lower-cost alternative might be small wood chests of drawers available in unfinished furniture departments or stores. There may be a problem in getting the right size to fit the closet.

Pantry closets are fully multiple-shelves with variation in shelf spacings. Some pantries with hinged access doors also are equipped with door shelves. Or you may consider a full floor-ceiling height series of revolving shelves. Hardware including top and bottom pivot brackets and shelf flanges are readily available. You supply the center pole which is of 3/4 inch steel pipe.

Utility or cleaning-equipment closets usually include one or two back-wall shelves and some coat or other hooks at the sides. In these closets a perforated hardboard is especially appropriate. The various accessories that fit into the perforations make an easy job of organizing the closet's contents.

In basementless homes, furnaces and water heaters may be in first-floor closets. The materials used on floor-walls-ceiling of such heating closets are subject to safety requirements contained in building codes. The owner-builder should check his local code on this point early in the framing stages, so that proper accommodations can be made for installing correct materials.

Among the points to consider regarding heating closets are: specified room clearance needed on all sides of heating appliances; method and arrangement of connecting appliance smoke pipes to chimneys or vents; surface material on floor-walls-ceiling that may require special material or covering to meet fire-resistance rating specified; and provision for closet ventilation or fresh air for combustion purposes. It might be noted that the needs of some building codes can be met by the use of 5/8 inch thick fire-resistant gypsumboard on walls and the installation of asbestos millboard or metal coverings on floor and ceiling surfaces.

Closets alone are inadequate for storing the ever-growing array of household, yard-care and recreational items deemed necessary for today's families. New homes are

Typical Wardrobe Closet using Stanley-made metal adjustable shelf and hanging-rod units, all wall mounted.

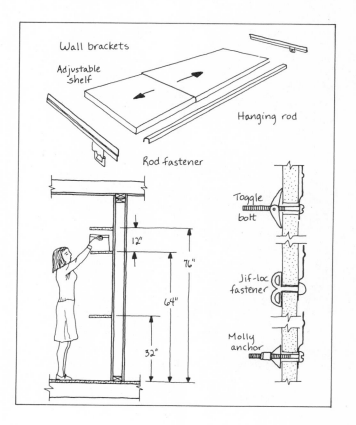

Metal Rod, Wood Shelf and Blocks is probably the easiest and least expensive method for installing closet shelves. The round metal rods, such as those made by Stanley which are sketched here, telescope one part into the other to give a degree of adjustability. An accessory midpoint hanger fastens to the shelf bottom in either of two ways: (A) for wide shelves and (B) for normal foot-wide shelves where you want the hanging rod slightly in front of the shelf edge.

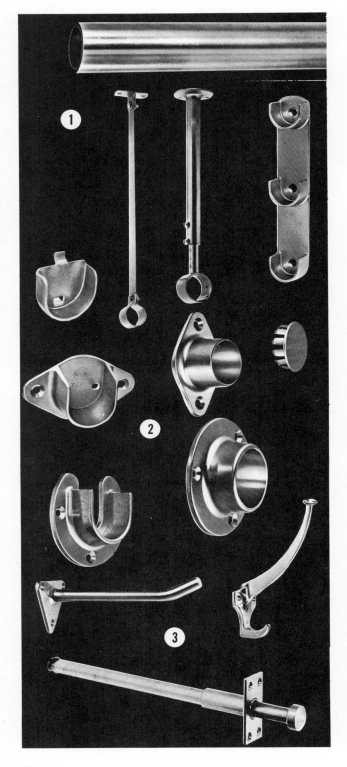

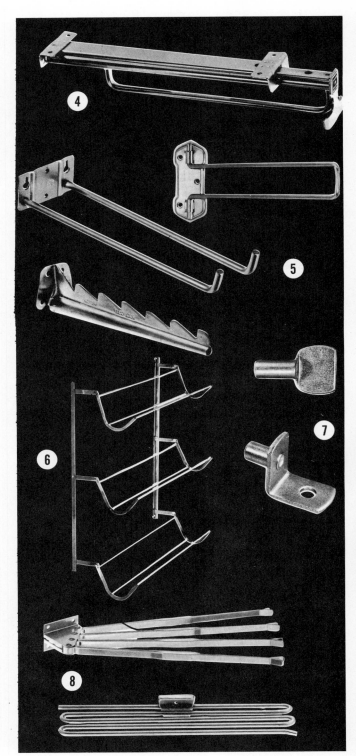

often purchased or built not only because new rooms are needed for new children but due to more and better storage space requirements to hold the accumulating sports equipment, hobby materials-activities, maintenance tools, party utensils and other vital accessories.

Basements are one solution; in basementless homes, an accessible unfinished crawl space may be improved to provide storage. In other homes, an attic access opening or pull-down attic stairway may be very helpful in storing possessions less frequently used.

Since housing designs will vary greatly, as will the types of spaces available for storage, an owner-builder will perhaps have to use his imagination in fixing up or adapting places for storage. Here are a few guidelines for your imagination-at-work:

□ prime requirement for any storage space is a flat floor surface so that stored items can be easily shifted or moved aside to get at others;

□ access door should be relatively wide to permit large items or boxes to be carried in;

□ in basements, it's very easy to contain the storage clutter by installing a simple stud wall and door to separate the storage room from the rest of the basement;

□ don't forget a special storage place for outdoor items, either in or adjacent to your garage or carport, but be sure the storage space is weathertight and lockable.

Closet and Storage Room Hardware in a sturdy quality line, the collection shown from the Knape & Vogt Company. The identifying numbers indicate: (1) chromed or stainless steel tubular hanging bars and center or stack hanger supports; (2) various styles of satin or polished chrome mounting flanges; (3) long, standard and retractable hooks; (4) clothing carrier that slides out from its under-shelf mounting; (5) swinging garment bracket and a double-pronged hook; with a notched bracket below for clothes hangers; (6) wall-mounted shoe-rack with hole-type shelf brackets at the right; (8) skirt and slacks holders.

32 Flooring and Underlayments

At the stage of construction represented by this chapter, the owner-builder should have already arrived at a planning decision as to his preferred floor finishes. Now, with the home fully enclosed and interior wall finishes completed, final plans should be firmed up for the exact types of floors in various locations.

Now, while the structural floor deck or subfloor can still be modified if necessary for any special flooring materials, the supplementary provisions should be made. Normally, the only extra work necessary for most of today's popular floor coverings and finishes is simply a smoothing-out surface preparation most easily accomplished by the use of sheet or board materials designed with just that purpose in mind . . . underlayments.

Until you begin to look for floor coverings or finish materials, you wouldn't believe the wide assortment that's available. Popularity of the various kinds of coverings-finishes varies considerably by geographic area. Presently acceptable to new home buyers are . . . hardwood strip or parquet floors, resilient vinyl-asbestos or all-vinyl tiles, wall-to-wall carpeting, vinyl sheet flooring and several types of hard surfaces including ceramic tiles, brick, slate and stone floors for certain special areas.

Practice in the past for floor installations was governed by the widespread use of plastered interior walls. All wood cabinet and hardwood flooring work could be done only after a lengthy period of drying-curing time for the plaster. In contrast, with gypsum wallboard, only two-to-three days drying are needed and work is not held up. But there is now another consideration that did not apply in the homes built in the era of plaster. That is the wide use of prefinished flooring materials. It is desirable today to hold off with final floor coverings until all other work is completed in order to avoid damaging or staining the floor coverings or finishes.

So, at this point, you ask yourself: "Am I a traditionalist who wants unfinished hardwood flooring installed throughout my home, or am I a contemporary who wants prefinished flooring materials, which I can install later?" If the former applies, then the structural floor needs no prepara-tion and you can turn to Chapter 38 for further details on the choice and installation of hardwood floors.

If, however, your answer indicates resilient or soft floor coverings, then now is the time to prepare their base using appropriate underlayments.

What Floor Finishes Where?

Public preferences in floor coverings and finishes have, like most other things, undergone changes in recent years. While some regions . . . notably those in mild climate areas . . . still hold regional preferences, there are many points of agreement around the country. Many home-builders are aware of the following factors and feel them to be the principal directions in which floor coverings and finishes are moving.

Homes for Mid- to Upper-Income Families

Use of hardwood flooring continues to be popular in many rooms and there's been a steady growth in preference of darker-tone and special types (such as pegged planks) of prefinished hardwood floors in some rooms, notably the family room or den.

Continued preference is being exhibited for hard-surface floors of tile or masonry materials for entrance foyers, fireplace hearths and porches or patios; ceramic tile continues as a high-preference type for baths and powder rooms; quarry tile seems to be gaining in acceptance for foyers, entrances and porches.

Wall-to-wall carpeting of living rooms and bedrooms shows a rapid climb in popularity over the past two decades; more recently, there's been a gradual increase of interest in the use of stain-resistant carpetings for family or dining rooms and kitchens.

A slow but gradual increase in the use of high-fashion deluxe patterned vinyl sheet materials in rooms other than kitchens has been noted.

Homes for Low- to Middle-Income Families

There's been an almost universal preference and practice of using low-maintenance resilient floor coverings in both sheet and tile form for kitchens, dining areas, hallways and, in economy homes, in bathrooms and entryways.

A rapid growth has occurred in the preference and use of wall-to-wall carpetings applied to single-floor construction supplemented by proper underlayments.

Hard-surface materials have seen only limited use, primarily in main bathrooms and small entry areas.

Underlayment Materials, Methods

For a long time, 1X6's or 1X8's laid diagonally across floor joists provided a subfloor, the lower part of what was routinely called double-floor construction. The hardwood flooring was the upper part, except in kitchens and bathrooms where other floor treatments were involved. Resilient coverings in the form of linoleum, and later asphalt tiles, were used in kitchens. But the subfloor boards were not suited for direct applications of these materials and there was also needed a little height gain to bring floor levels up to the surface of the normal hardwood surface thicknesses. Result was the application of underlayment material. Initially, plywood with one clean-smooth face and

hardboards were utilized until the increased amount of usage brought about the introduction of specially designed underlayments. Within recent years, additional materials have become available for underlayment applications.

While plywood sheathing materials have largely replaced boards as a subfloor material in most areas, the unevenness, roughness and other irregularities of plywood sheathing grades has continued the need for underlayments that provide a suitable base for resilient or soft floor coverings. The value or need for underlayments has been recognized in some building codes and in the HUD-MPS requirements.

Choice of an underlayment material is to be made from the following four . . . sanded-plywood, hardboard, particleboard and fiberboard. The use of particleboard has grown quickly because of its low cost and lack of sheet curvature. Underlayments vary in thickness. Plywood and fiberboard materials are generally 3/8 inch, hardboard underlayment is 1/4 inch, and particleboards are either 1/4 or 3/8 inch. One newer type of fiberboard material designed especially for carpeting underlayment is 1/2 inch thick and has some insulative value.

Before applying underlayments, the subfloor or structural floor should be swept very clean. Underlayments should not be applied over on-grade or below-grade concrete floors. They can be applied with nails or staples. Spacing of the fasteners will depend on board thickness and the recommendations of the manufacturer or trade associa-

Useful Underlayment Tips shown in this group include the following suggestions from underlayment board manufacturers: at left, Kaiser's carpet board underlayment has a 1X2 wood strip serving as a measuring device in layout and cutting work; in the center, an installer of Armstrong hardboard underlayment material is using matched cover to provide the thin gap desirable between underlayment sheets; at right, the hardboard sheets are being nailed so that nails penetrate into floor joists.

Underlayment Guidelines for Particleboard in this series of pictures furnished by the National Particleboard Association. In (1), the particleboard sheets delivered to the job site should be stacked flat on 2×4's off the floor and be given a few days before use to adjust to the home's climate. Preparatory to placing particleboard, scrape the subfloor or deck (2) free of all wallboard joint cement, drippings or other floor surface accumulations and (3) use a patch cement to fill in gouges, holes or surface deformities. In figuring how the sheets should be laid out (4), avoid placement so the underlayment joints occur over or even close to the plywood joints below. The adhesive method (5) of application gives a superior job and here an ordinary paint roller is being used to apply the casein-type adhesive. Follow recommended practice in nailing (6) trying to hit the floor joists and keeping nails at least 3/4 inch away from the edges.

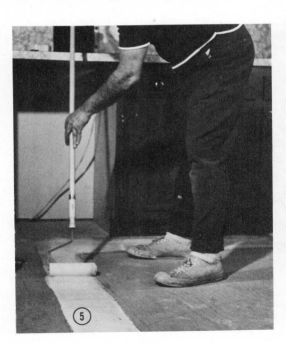

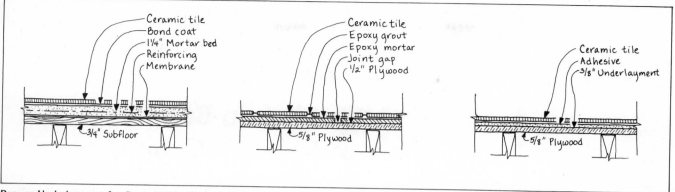

Base or Underlayment for Ceramic Tile Floors is shown in three different techniques, the sketches adapted from drawings included in the "Handbook for Ceramic Tile Installation" issued by the Tile Council of America. At the left, the use of a 1-1/4 inch thick cement mortar bed with 2×2-inch, 16×16-gauge welded wire mesh reinforcing. The membrane suggested is 15 pound building felt or 4-mil polyethylene film.

In the center sketch, the plywood subfloor should be overlaid with exterior-type plywood leaving a quarter inch gap between sheets to give a suitable base for an epoxy mortar and grout installation designed for commercial and high-quality residential installations.

At the right, the simpler floor preparation for tile installation using organic adhesives is quite suitable for ordinary residential use. Underlayment sheets should be carefully nailed so adjacent sheets are flush or within 1/16-inch of each other. Underlayment should be exterior grade plywood or other underlayment material suited to below-tile application.

tion of the material involved. The National Particleboard Association suggests that where plywood subfloors are to be covered with particleboard underlayment, the plywood should be 5/8 inch thick and the underlayment board 3/8 inch. Thinner 5/16 or 1/4 inch particleboard underlayments are permissible with thicker subfloor boards or plywood.

In light residential, non-fire-resistive construction, this minimum recommendation of 1 inch total floor-plus-underlayment thickness may be excessive. Check local practices on underlayment thicknesses before settling on adherance to the above guideline.

At this point, the reader is referred back to Chapter 9 on floor framing and the recommended application there for the American Plywood Association's glued tongue-groove floor system. If a suitable thickness and grade of plywood subfloor material was selected at that time, the system provides a finished deck surface that requires no underlayment application for receiving resilient or soft floor coverings.

Floor Prep For Hard Surfaces

Hard surfaces normally do require some sort of special subfloor preparation. The very first consideration which may or may not apply in your case is structural strength, and ability to carry the hard-surface load. The thinner hard-surface materials such as ceramic and quarry tiles are relatively light in weight when laid by the adhesive method to a plywood structural floor or over an underlayment material. But tile applications, and those of other masonry materials which might be laid in mortar atop a concrete base slab, will probably require added strengthening of the floor framing. This point was discussed briefly in Chapter 9.

It might be applicable for fireplace hearths as well as for bathroom, kitchen, and entrance-foyer floors.

Again, in connection with the concrete bases for such hard-surface floor materials, local practice becomes involved. Check your working drawings with the local building authority or inspector for floor modification to accommodate hard-surface materials. In most cases, the subfloor area will have to be lowered by blocking and probably doubling of floor joists at the perimeter of the area. The lowering will allow pouring of a 2 inch thick mesh-reinforced slab that provides the floor base. In no case should any masonry materials or tiles be applied directly to ordinary subfloor construction without due consideration for the floor loads involved.

Whether ceramic tiles in the regular square or rectangular form or in smaller mosaic styles are to be used, accepted practice in most areas has been to provide a concrete base. But as the description in Chapter 30 pointed out, this is not necessary with the adhesive method of application.

Now, with ceramic tiles, there's a third alternative possible. The recommended specifications of the Tile Council of American include provision for laying floor tiles in a cement mortar bed 1-1/4 inch thick and reinforced by 2×2 inch, 16×16 gauge welded wire mesh or by conventional metal lath (see illustration). This alternative method involves a lighter load and floor modification may be minimized. In placing this or the conventional concrete base, first apply a layer of waterproof paper or plastic film over the subfloor area.

Incidentally, just to keep the terminology straight, the use of the word "concrete" above means mixing of portland cement with both fine and coarse aggregates. Mixing "cement mortar" involves just the portland cement and fine aggregate (sand, no gravel).

33 Kitchen-Bath-Laundry Cabinets

Cabinets are a mixed bag. Some name-brand cabinets are sold on a national basis. Yet each region has a certain number of kitchen cabinet manufacturers who distribute their products only in certain market areas. While a few cabinet producers focus almost exclusively on top-quality products intended primarily for luxury homes, most cabinet manufacturers offer several lines with sliding price ranges.

Retailers . . . lumber-supply dealers, kitchen dealers and catalog or discount houses . . . usually carry only one manufacturer's line and this makes comparison shopping a bit more difficult. While a regional or local manufacturer may produce units of comparable quality to national brands, the selections in styles, types, sizes and accessories are likely to be more limited. It's suggested that owner-builders will do well by at least obtaining from some national manufacturers (see appendix) their product literature and names of nearest dealers in order to compare with products distributed locally or regionally.

The broad range of cabinet styles and factory prefinishes is almost too great to attempt categorizing. You'll find wide variations in traditional, contemporary and foreign styles with cabinet hardware in as many or more choices.

Most cabinets sold are preassembled and prefinished. Woodgrains predominate, in a full range of light to dark tones. Some are real wood, some are grain patterns on substrates. The latter is a cabinet-and-furniture industry term meaning base material such as particleboard, hardboard or plywood. And some cabinets are a product involving combination materials with perhaps particleboard sides and bottom, hardboard backs and molded plastic doors.

A Component System

The magazine photos you see of finished kitchens, bathrooms and other areas of a home with cabinets give the impression of really fine cabinet craftsmanship. Not just

Fine-Finish Kitchen Cabinets in a series of six highly appealing styles made by Riviera Products, three of which are illustrated above: at left, the Contemporary design plain flush faces and concealer door-drawer pulls; in the center, the Sangria design in rich dark tones and color-coordinated hardware; at right, the light-toned woodgrain of the Homestead style equipped with early American hardware.

fine furniturelike finishes, but careful customization to fit the particular dimensions of an individual home's kitchen space. No suggestion of cabinet mass production.

The part above about craftlike character is really true. The part about custom pains to produce individualized cabinetry is misleading. That fine array of cabinet work you see in the finished installation actually involves a series of standard components that fit together. The component units are offered in a complete assortment of sizes so their assembly in any given home can fit almost any kitchen

situation. And by the judicious use of filler accessories, the installation achieves that custom appearance.

So the owner-builder doesn't by any means have to be an on-site furniture craftsman. In fact, even among pro-

Match Up Kitchen-Bath Cabinets are available from some cabinet manufacturing firms. Shown here is the Aquarius line produced by Triangle Pacific: at left, kitchen units with concealed door-drawer pulls; at right, bathroom vanity and wall cabinets match those in the kitchen.

Budget-to-Deluxe Cabinet Types produced by two different cabinet divisions of the Tappan Company. At left, the Kemper division's Eton contemporary style cabinet available in full range of sizes for

budget-minded builders comes in both dark and light finishes with antiqued brass hardware. At right, the Quaker Maid division's Campaign style cabinets with brass corners and recessed pulls.

wall cabinets

single double

9W	27W
12W	30W
15W	33W
18W	36W
21W	42W
24W	48W

End view — 12" / 30"

angle wall cabinet

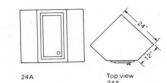

24A

Top view
24A

24" / 12"

wall corner cabinets

Single door	Double door
24WC	39WC
36WC	42WC
	48WC

range cabinets

End view — 12" / 21"

24R (Single door)
27R
30R
33R
36R
42R
48R

base cabinets

single double drawer sink bases

   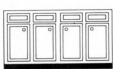

12B	30B	15D	9T	54SB 12"—30"—12"
15B	36B	18D	Tray	60SB 15"—30"—15"
18B	42B	24D	Left	66SB 15"—36"—15"
21B	48B		only	72SB 18"—36"—18"
24B				84SB 24"—36"—24"

Full shelf in sink bases except under sink—no back.

range bases and sink cabinets

 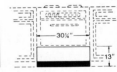

30RBS	300RB
36RBS	Stack-on
42RBS	Range base
	28¼" high

30¼" / 13"

RPF
Fronts for under-counter oven and range units.

base cabinets

lazy susans

36LS
Lazy Susans are shipped without finished ends.

36" / 24"

whatnots

Base Whatnots
BWN

84" cabinets
oven cabinets

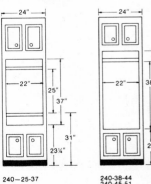 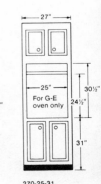

240—25-37

240-38-44
240-45-51

270-25-31
270-44-50

24" / 22" / 25" / 37" / 31" / 23¼"

24" / 22" / 38" / 44" / 20¼"

27" / 25" For G-E oven only / 30½" / 24½" / 31"

Cabinet Sizes—Types To Choose From plus the sink fronts, peninsula units, filler components and full-height cabinets needed to round out any custom kitchen installation. These units comprise the line manufactured by the Kitchen Kompact Company which is marketed in most parts of the country as "Plaza One" or "Glen-

wood" cabinets. Wall cabinets are reversible for right or left installation; base cabinets come hinged left but can be simply reversed by moving hinge screws to predrilled locations. Tall oven and broom cabinets can vary from 81 to 84 inches high simply by trimming down the 4 inch top rail to the desired height.

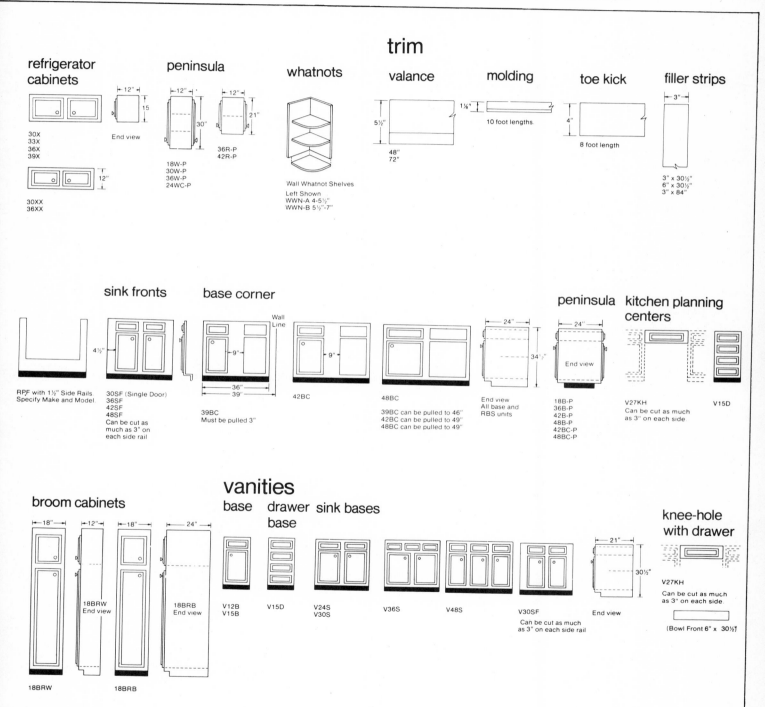

Kitchen Details: Popularity Factors

Most Acceptable Cabinet Styles		Most Popular Appliance Colors	
Modern	45.1%	Yellow/Harvest Gold	55.5%
Early American	24.7	Green/Avocado	14.8
Spanish	17.4	White	13.0
English	4.4	Brown/Coppertone	6.3
Rural American	2.3	Red/Orange/Poppy	1.0

Most Common Shape Of Kitchen		Type Of Floor-covering Preferred	
U-shape	38.7%	Sheet vinyl	47.9%
L-shape	36.7	Vinyl asbestos	27.9
Corridor (2 wall)	16.8	Carpeting	21.6
Island type	3.8	Solid vinyl tile	10.4
Pullman (1 wall)	2.4	Ceramic/Quarry tile	5.5

*Type of Eating Facilities
Provided Within The Kitchen*

Small but adequate area of some type for sit-down eating	30.2%
A complete area for dining with the use of table and chairs	26.0
Sit-down dining in a combined kitchen and family room area	17.2
No eating; food preparation only in kitchen	15.4
Use of a counter-top area with stools	9.4

NOTE: with homes selling under $35,000, 57% indicated desire for separate dining room in addition to above; in homes above $35,000, about 90% did.

Kitchen Amenities, Features And Added Appliances Desired

All homes . . . range hood with exhaust fan, window over sink, over-cabinet soffits finished, utility closet and separate pantry storage

Under $35,000 . . . free-standing range, utility closet

Over $35,000 . . . dishwasher, garbage disposer, built-in cooking units

Other Frequent Mentions . . . luminous ceilings, planned storage wall, cabinet for small appliances, planning desk

Miscellaneous Preferences For Cabinets & Counters

Cabinets of all-wood (75%) preferred over wood with plastic facing (23%)

Counter-tops of plastic-laminate (85%) preferred over ceramic tile (11%)

Kitchen sinks about even between stainless steel and enamel or porcelain but most (76%) prefer double-compartments and single-handle faucets (67%)

fessional builders on-site cabinet-building work is a thing of the long-ago past. The installation of preassembled, prefinished cabinet components is both a relatively fast and simple task.

The cabinet component method, which has already won almost universal acceptance for kitchen cabinets and for vanity-lavatory cabinets in baths and powder rooms, has also gained much ground in recent years for providing much needed storage and shelf space adjacent to the laundry equipment.

Before you get too involved in planning your own kitchen or laundry, it would be worthwhile to learn just what expert planning assistance is available to you. You can obtain excellent planning information in booklet form from some appliance manufacturers. For further details in a reference text, there's the *Kitchen Planning Guide for Builders & Architects*, available from Structures Publishing Company.

A third avenue of assistance, a person-to-person one, may be available to prospective customers of certain suppliers of cabinets or appliances such as utility companies, kitchen or lumber-supply dealers. Some such retail firms employ a kitchen design expert often one who has earned the title of "certified kitchen designer" from the American Institute of Kitchen Dealers.

While there are some noticeable differences in workmanship from one cabinet producer to another, as a rule the quality differences in comparably priced cabinets are quite small. A few manufacturers offer great selection in types, sizes and styles. There are differences in the guidance or instructional information offered. But the organization that will provide the owner-builder with attentive planning assistance will also aid him with any installation problems that may occur.

And the chances are pretty good that at least one unanticipated problem will occur. Cabinets require coordination in the piping and wiring runs that are made to both appliance and plumbing fixture locations. Cabinet components may and frequently do need adjustments in position or cutting of side or back parts to fit the dimensions or fittings of built-in appliances. So, prepare yourself for some unplanned discrepancies or details that need adjustments while the installation work is going on.

The basic kitchen planning concepts revolve around a very simple arrangement of three common-to-all-kitchens center areas: the food preservation-storage area (refrigerator), the food preparation and cooking utensil area (range-oven), and the food mixing and cleanup area (sink-dishwasher).

The floor-plan sheet of your set of working drawings will

Preferences of Home Buyers with respect to kitchen details is given in this condensed chart. The information resulted from a survey conducted among home builders by the Bureau of Building Marketing Research in which the builders were asked to give the product types and features that were included in their best-selling homes.

normally indicate the placement of these center areas. It's also the practice to show in the drawings the elevations or front views of all kitchen-bathroom-laundry walls where cabinetry occurs. Although it would seem that these drawings have already done your kitchen planning for you, actually the drawings show only typical cabinetry in a general way. You must take these drawings with you to obtain more detailed cabinet-component planning aid either from the kitchen deisgner or your source of supply. Because specific dimensions, specific components, specific styles and finishes must be planned and ordered. You will also have certain options and there are also likely to be some prohibitions or certain cabinet types that are inappropriate or won't fit.

For these planning-ordering procedures you will have some choice of either drawer or door types for floor-mounted units. You will choose, too, among alternative cabinet details in other respects. Depending upon the particular brand or line of cabinets, you may have some choice in the type of sink front or sink cabinet. Or some option you may not wish to have included immediately, but for which provision must be made now.

You will also have to make a final decision by this time on your choice of cooking and refrigerator appliances. With refrigerators, it's a matter of the height and width dimensions so that base cabinets can be brought to the point for adequate refrigerator space and so your over-refrigerator wall cabinets are of proper height (see illustration for standard dimensions).

On cooking appliances, you'll have to settle your choice on slide-in, set-in or built-in units as described in Chapter 25. A different cabinet procedure and different types of

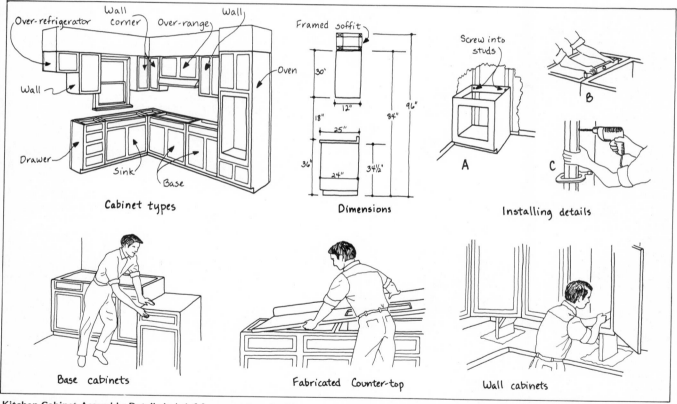

Cabinet types

Dimensions

Installing details

Base cabinets

Fabricated Counter-top

Wall cabinets

Kitchen Cabinet Assembly Details in brief form are given in this series of sketches. Upper left, a typical L-shaped assembly of cabinets identifies the different types. Normal vertical heights are given in the center sketch. Installation is begun with base cabinet units, key steps being: (A) wood screws, not nails, are used to anchor cabinets to the wall; (B) check each cabinet for level using shims where needed to adjust for floor or wall irregularities; (3) predrill holes for wood screws fastening frames of two adjacent cabinets using C-clamps to hold frames firmly until screws are driven top and bottom. (Three lower sketches) Check each cabinet's model number and size to verify its position in the assembly. When all base units have been fastened and leveled, place the fabricated counter-top units attaching with screws driven through cabinet frames into underside of countertop. Omit installing sink or cooking units until cabinet assembly is completed. Last come the wall cabinets and you can use the counter surface (protected with paper) to brace up the wall units to desired height while fastening screws. Use care in handling cabinets to avoid mars and scratches to the prefinish. Use clean hands in handling and use cabinet carton paperboard to protect counters and cabinet faces against damage while you're working.

Sketches in this group were adapted from illustrations contained in instruction guide booklets prepared by two leading cabinet manufacturing firms: Kitchen Kompact and Riviera Products.

cabinet components must be ordered to fit each of these three types of appliances.

Installation Is Easy (Sort of)

It will take time. But a lot of it will be measuring, marking, adjusting, and thinking time. You will want to proceed carefully, at least to start. One reason is to avoid small errors because wood screws are being used for component connections. Wood screws provide firm and secure fastening, but they should be used with predrilled holes. Once you've predrilled a hole at a certain position, it's difficult to make a minor adjustment of the cabinet by moving it slightly and drilling another hole.

Another reason for proceeding slowly is the cabinet prefinish. Any time you're installing prefinished units you have the problem of avoiding tool contact on prefinished surfaces and need caution in handling to avoid bumping and scratching. And damaging of corners or edges.

There is no particular wall preparation to be made. Your soffit-type framing and wallboard covering work will have been done unless your kitchen is to have a suspended ceiling. The principal preparation need is simply a quick check of wall surface trueness with your 4 foot level. You will be able through the use of thin wedges or shims to adjust cabinet components properly to minor irregularities in the wall surface. But if any part of the wall where cabinets are to be positioned is seriously out of plumb or substantially uneven, you may have to provide some ad-

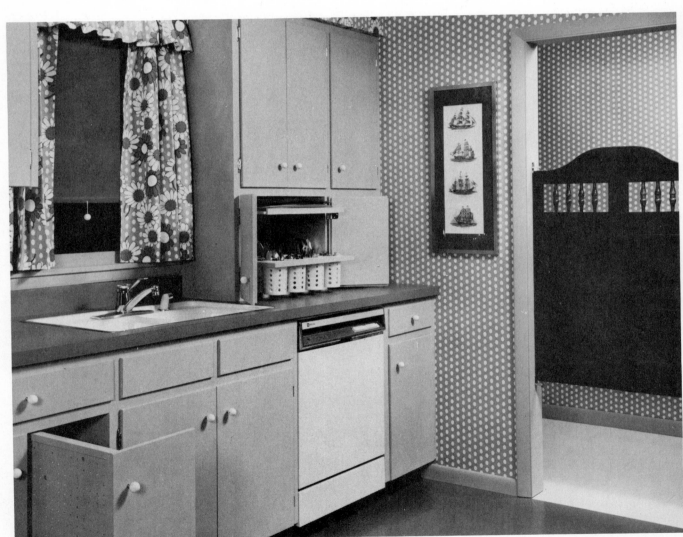

Cabinet Storage Ideas are disseminated in the literature of appliance firms as well as cabinet companies. Here, the Maytag built-in dishwasher has some nearby cabinet conveniences. In the area between wall and base cabinets, a minicabinet has been added with slide-out shelves for placemats and silverware, the latter contained in restaurant-type cannisters for easy transfer from the dishwasher.

Vanity Lavatories, a full range of economy-to-deluxe models now standard for new home bathrooms. Shown here, left, is an economy unit by Eljer featuring an acrylic-finish molded plastic top with integral basin. At right, Formco's "Lexington" model vanity with early American styling which comes in three woodgrain finishes and with matching wall cabinets if desired. Choice of 2- and 3-door sizes in this deluxe line which features self-closing hinges, white ceramic door pulls and a washable vinyl interior finish.

vance blocking. With normal new construction of framing and drywall finish, fortunately, the need is probably unlikely.

As you may have gathered a key factor in cabinet installation is the units' levelness and plumbness. There's sound reason here. Unless they are level, plumb, square, and firmly fastened, problems are apt to occur with the sliding of drawers and the latching or fit of doors.

Kitchen cabinets are designed for screw fastening to walls, whether they be wall or base cabinets. And for screw fastening of one adjacent component to the others. Long wood screws are used sufficient to penetrate the wall finish and to go securely into studs or other framing members. Depending upon the particular type of cabinet construction, the points of location for screws may vary one manufacturer to another. Some furnish cabinets with predrilled holes but the locations may not work out for your framing. A cabinet manufacturer may also recommend installation of cabinets to horizontal furring strips placed over the wall finish and nailed to studs. In normal practice, it is advisable to drive screws just partially to walls, but tightly to each other as the components are assembled. Then the combined units can be shimmed as needed and the wall fastening screws tightened. Your cabinet supplier will, of course, have suggestions appropriate for a given line of cabinets and his installation tips should be given careful consideration.

One particular aspect of the kitchen cabinet work on which you should consult your cabinet supplier relates to the installation of a range hood . . . assuming that such a ventilator is going to be installed. Hoods vary in the position of their duct connection, which goes up through the over-range cabinet interior space to connect with the duct

outlet you've previously roughed in. Your cabinet supplier will usually be willing to cut in proper duct-size holes if you provide him with an accurate location and duct-size sketch. He'll be willing, that is, if the cabinets come out of his stock, but he may not offer this service if the cabinets are shipped to the job from a producer's plant or from a warehouse. Don't worry about it. Cutting of duct holes in top, bottom and shelf is no big deal.

The cabinet installation sequence may be either of two types. You can start at a corner and proceed along one wall to the other end, or start at an appliance or fixture cabinet and proceed outward from it. The former method may be better suited for wall cabinets while the latter might facilitate installation of base cabinets. The latter method is simpler where cabinets need cutting-fitting to plumbing or electrical rough-in locations; it is easier to get the proper fit and placement before adjacent cabinets are in position.

Just a word about accessories. Most cabinets makers offer certain types of cabinet accessories. Very often the accessories make the cabinet space more useful or allow easier access to certain items. Check also what your lumber-supply or home-center retailer has in cabinet hardware and accessories. You may wish to equip yours with cup racks, retractable towel bars, pad-sponge holders, spice racks, towel bars, cutlery trays and similar specialties.

Bath and Utility Cabinets

Very few new homes, except possibly those in the save-every-nickel-possible class, use wall-hung lavatory fixtures in either the main bathroom or secondary ones such as the powder room or master-suite bath. What was once the routine cast-iron or pottery wall-hung unit has largely given way to the newer basin-equipped vanity lavatory cabinet.

Vanity cabinets are built of the same sort of materials and in the same preassembled manner as kitchen cabinets. And most kitchen cabinet manufacturers also make vanity units for bathrooms.

There are some recent changes, however, in the counter and basin portion of vanities. Earlier, the common practice was to furnish plastic-laminate counter surfaces like in kitchens, and lavatory basins were set into these counters using metal application rims. Then, some plumbing fixture producers began offering rimless basins for counter installation. And more recently, the vogue has switched to a complete integral counter-basin-backsplash unit of molded acrylic plastic. Competition has flourished in these vanity

lavatories with one-piece marblized tops. Some low-priced vanity units cost little more than what a quality wall-hung lavatory used to run.

The added advantage of the under-lavatory cabinet space should not be underestimated. It has eliminated the unsightly plumbing connections and helped develop bathroom interior decoration.

A second type of bathroom cabinet has also been changed to fit in better with the idea of bathroom decor. That is the old traditional medicine cabinet. Once limited in finish to white enamel and a mirror door, bath wall cabinets are offered in a wide range of styles and types. Some are designed for recessing into stud spaces or prepared wall openings, some for surface mounting. There are bath cabinets with mirrors, without mirrors, and in pairs with mirrors between them. There are also narrow cabinets for

China or Marblized Tops are offered in some lines such as the vanities made by Universal-Rundle Corporation. At left is a vitreous china top and at right, the acrylic-faced top which is sometimes referred to as "cultured marble" because of the colored veinings.

The company has developed an easy-mounting system for its acrylic fiberglass lavatories, which have a warm-touch surface, come in six colors, and clean easily.

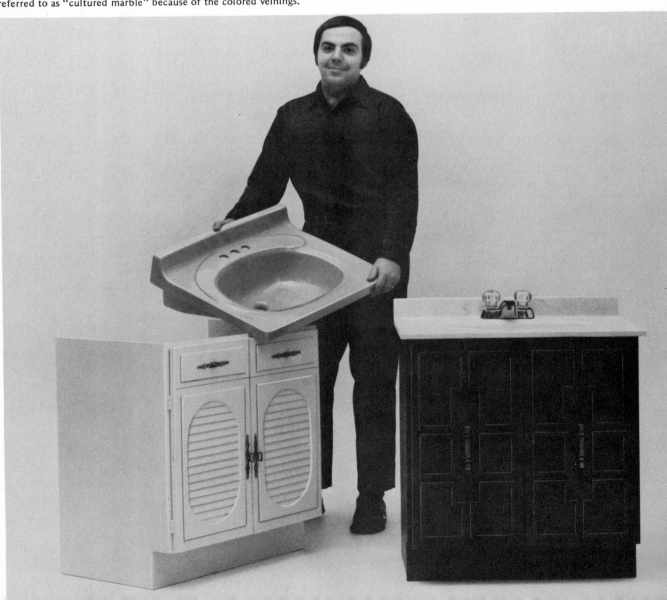

fitting into wall areas at the sides of vanity lavatories and also for fitting into corners of such recesses. There are various door styles including plain blank doors that can be wallpapered over and doors that match those of the vanity units.

The top-of-the-line mirrored wall cabinets are sometimes referred to as "ensembles" and generally consist of dual "his" and "her" units. The doors of such pairs may be mirrored and positioned (hinges towards each other) so that they can be used as wing mirrors with a central, fixed mirror between them.

Middle-line cabinets are offered in two common styles: a rectangular door-mirrors with diffusion-type light fixture above the mirror and sliding door-mirror operation or hinged mirror-door cabinets equipped with light fixtures at each side. More economical cabinets consist of single mir-ror-doors on recessed cabinets without lights.

Obviously, if your choice in bath wall cabinets is for a recessed type, that decision should have been made earlier so that proper framing for the recess and (if lights are involved) electrical outlet would have been provided prior to installation of the bathroom wall finish. Cross-stud blocks should be cut and nailed in between studs at the appropriate heights and a stud cripple also placed to accom-modate cabinet width. These blocks have their edges flush with stud surfaces and the wallboard is brought to the four edges of the openings. Cabinets designed for recessing have a flange that projects beyond the opening so that no further trimming is needed.

Shelving Plus Doors?

Recently, a few companies have begun selling just cabinet doors. These are of molded plastic in very real simulations of wood-molded or paneled doors. Sales, for the most part, have been to mobile-home and modular home manufacturers whose mill shops produce inexpensive cabinetry that is faced with these luxurious-looking door and drawer fronts. One other somewhat similar line of laminated-plastic door-and-drawer fronts can be found on the remodeling market for replacing the fronts of old cabinets.

The availability, even though at present on a limited basis, of such prefinished door-and-drawer fronts suggests that an owner-builder can save some cabinet money by building, in effect, some simple shelving and framing then mounting the prefinished facings.

Wall shelf assemblies with such doors are not too difficult to design and screw together for wall mounting and door hinging. Base cabinets are somewhat more complex and need adequate regular spacing of vertical shelf sepa-rator-members to do the twofold job of providing needed support for the counter-top components, and providing a base for side-mounting of drawer slides.

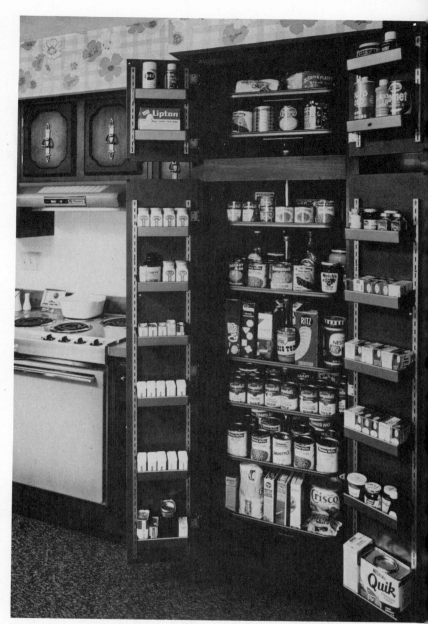

A Tall Cabinet Pantry results from installing revolving tray units in both upper and lower portions of this ceiling-high kitchen cabinet. Trays, mounting column and door racks are made by Amerock Corporation, hardware manufacturers.

34 Counter Surfacing Components

For years, kitchen counter surfacings came and went, each with perhaps some slight improvement over foregoing materials. Then came plastic laminates.

The high-pressure, dense, smoothly surfaced and highly resistant 1/16 inch laminates took over the counter surfacing market after World War II and has dominated it ever since with the possible exception of the west coast's new luxury housing in which counters of ceramic tiles provide the principal alternative.

But there's one particular approach to the counters in your new home that can be recommended. That is to use laminate-surfaced counter components precision-fabricated to fit the specific installation you're planning.

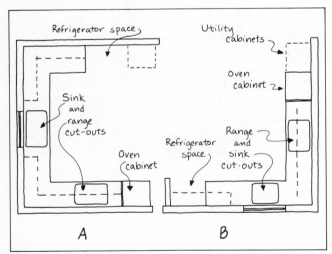

U-Shaped and L-Shaped Kitchens are probably the most workable and efficient types for many homes. In sketch (A), the U-kitchen saves steps yet leaves one side open for an adjacent dining-in-the-kitchen area. The L-kitchen in sketch (B) is also convenient for kitchen duties and is often seen in luxury-home installation supplemented by a peninsula snack counter, island sink or range. A third type (not shown) goes by the name of "corridor kitchen" but is not recommended for most families because its narrowness means traffic conflict and inconvenience for informal eating.

In your material shopping, you'll encounter in lumber and home supply stores certain thin laminates or plastic materials for on-site surfacing of rough counters. Don't buy them. Don't plan on surfacing your own kitchen counter. Or bathroom vanity. You have so many things on which to spend your time and this is one where you'd best avail yourself of the skills and special machinery that countertop shop fabricators have.

There are literally thousands of cabinet and countertop shops around the country specializing in mounting surfacing materials on counter base materials in a way that cannot be matched by hand-crafting. And the prices are competitively low so that shop-fabricated counter components represent an excellent dollar value. The separation of this chapter from that on kitchen-bath cabinets is intended to emphasize to owner-builders the desirability of using a custom-tailored, shop-fabricated, high-pressure-laminate countertop installation.

If by some chance your kitchen cabinet supplier has difficulty in supplying you with names or locations of two or three different counter-top fabricators in the area, you might address an inquiry to the National Association of Plastic Fabricators (see appendix).

Your Preliminary Preparation

While you may have inspected various countertop surfacing samples during your cabinet shopping, and even if the cabinet supplier is going to handle the countertop order, a very accurate measurement and drawing must be made to communicate exact actual dimensions to the fabricator. He cannot work just from the working drawing floorplan alone. But he can work from your drawing showing the exact kitchen cabinet components to be assembled.

You will probably be asked to measure and verify the exact inside-surface to inside-surface measurements in your kitchen, laundry or wherever the counter units will be placed. It is worth taking your time and making certain of the dimensions given the fabricator in order to avoid a later

Front Counter Edges having a plain square-edge design are seen in the Kemper-made cabinets, wall, and island types shown at the left. In the other photo, the Formco cabinet has a counter-top installed which is commonly called a "post-formed counter." This refers to a

rounded cove where the counter surface meets the backsplash surface and it may also mean the inclusion of a no-drip front edge sometimes called a "roll edge."

frustrating misfit that only shows up once you've begun the installation process.

Probably a 6 foot folding rule and a steel square are the best tools for determining exact inside dimensions and the squareness of the wall inside-corners that the counter-top must abut. Then, armed with the dimensions and the cabinet component drawing, see if the shop fabricator needs any further details. One such detail might be whether 1X3 or 1X4 wood furring strips are needed across the cabinets' top edges in order to adjust the counter's front edge to the proper height.

Countertops are designed to provide suitable covers for a wide range of base cabinet styles, so be sure that your cabinet component drawing indicates proper cabinet depth and dimensions. The following might be considered standard dimensions, but there are likely to be some departures from these figures in certain areas of the country. Postformed backsplash (integral counter surfacing coved upward) is usually of a 4 inch height. Normal countertop depth from front edge to wall surface is 24-½ or 25 inches. This dimension coordinates well with the depth of many kitchen base cabinet units built to a 24 inch depth from front frame face to rear face. Lipped or lapping doors and drawers may add 3/8 to 5/8 inch, leaving a typical countertop edge overhang of about a half inch.

In verifying your countertop dimensions, check the specification sheet for the appliances you've selected and make certain of either the clearance needed with cabinet sides and counter or the roughing-in dimensions of openings

needed in the countertop. Normal clearance for the slide-in types of free-standing appliances is about 1/2 inch on each side.

Types Of Countertops

The most widely used high-pressure plastic laminate for counter surfacing work is a polyester such as that sold under the trade name Formica. Some fabricating shops employ melamine surfacings.

In bonding the surfacing material to the base material, which is either particleboard or plywood in 3/4 inch thickness, the shop fabricator may offer finished components in either of two types:

- □ self-edged—a flat counter base with square edges, the front edge having an added wood strip bonded to the bottom of the base material to give greater thickness to the front facing edge; the surfacing is also applied to face and edges of a 4 inch high backsplash section (or higher if desired) which bolts or screws to the rear edge of the countertop;

- □ postformed—done with a special fabricating machine that, after proper grooving, bends the backsplash up under heat and pressure to form the counter cove and also bends the front facing surface down into a rounded roll-edge so that the surfacing is continuous and leakproof; usually included in the front roll is a hidden T-mold insert giving the front edge a slightly raised, no-drip characteristic.

Needless to say, the coved back and the no-drip front are desirable features and the slight extra cost of the post-formed countertop is worthwhile.

As mentioned above, your counter opening dimensions must be given accurately. These include not only the larger openings for sink or built-in cooking units but also any smaller openings planned for such items as a built-in chopping block or cutting surface, built-in blender-mixer, built-in can-opener or toaster. Obviously, these items must be preselected, and you'll have to obtain the manufacturer's specification sheets for the models chosen.

Supplementary suggestions at this point regarding arrangements for built-in items: first, make sure your model selection is made from up-to-date literature or specifications; second, it pays to order the appliance or built-in unit as soon as possible even though it may not be installed until a later date. The reasoning? Manufacturers do change models without prior notice. Some models are more popular and stocks run low. Order and ask for immediate delivery so that you know you'll have the unit when the time comes to install. Or, if stock runs out, you will at least be forewarned in time about new or replacement models to be able to make your opening provisions fit the new units. Then, follow through and have some lockable place where the items can safely be stored.

Installing The Countertops

The order in which you position adjacent counter components may be important, depending on the layout. Inquire of the fabricator whether he prepared the components for placement in a certain order.

Normally, countertop sections are designed to butt to each other. They are fastened down with undercounter clamps that can be drawn tight. At counter corners, the joints in the counter sections or components may be mitered, or the juncture may be between the front edge of one counter component and the side of another. With postformed coved and roll-edged counters, the mitered corners are nearly always used.

With respect to fastening countertops to the base cabinets, wood screws are used driven from below, in the cabinet space, upward into the counter base material. This will ordinarily require drilling of screw holes before starting the screws and some sort of weighting on the counter will be needed to place holes accurately. Do all butting or joining of the countertop sections and draw clamps tightly before proceeding with screw fastening. Also make sure component sections align with the wall surface and are in close contact with it. Before drawing fastening screws tight, check counter levelness with your 4 foot level and place shims, if needed, to bring the surface to level.

Some suppliers or fabricators provide paper or film protection for counter surfaces. Install such countertops with the protective covering in place. If none is provided, obtain suitable adhesive-backed covering material and apply to the surface in order to minimize possible surface damage during the balance of construction work.

Other Counter Materials

At one time, and perhaps still, there were certain kitchen supply sources or fabricators able to furnish continuous stainless steel countertops. They can and do perform excellently for this purpose, but because they cost considerably more than the pressure laminate materials their use has been limited primarily to luxury homes.

Linoleum has been long outdated even as a floor covering. It never did prove very durable for counter use. Of the older materials, ceramic tiles alone still finds support. Its application on countertops resembles the adhesive method of application described in Chapter 30. However, ceramic tile counter surfacing requires special edge-trim shapes which may not be readily available in all parts of the country.

Maple cutting block sections and other ceramic or plastic cutting surface materials may be obtained as cabinet accessory items from cabinet suppliers. Some are equipped with metal rims for recessed installation in countertops.

35 Kitchen-Bath Luminous Ceilings

Why luminous ceilings? In short, they make sense in kitchen-bath-laundry areas.

These areas can make good use of the same sort of high-level fluorescent lighting, available at relatively low cost, that is so universally popular in office and commercial buildings.

In new homes, the added cost for a suspended ceiling system plus the needed number of fluorescent fixtures amounts to more than just the cost of a couple of conventional kitchen-bath light fixtures, but the benefits in terms of better lighting for important home working areas are worth the extra expense.

The precision metal grid suspension systems now being widely distributed for home applications are the result of years of development work in the commercial lighting field. Suspension wires are attached to the structural ceiling and hang down to hold firm a series of metal channels and cross-tees that form a grid for the lay-in of ceiling materials and translucent lighting panels.

It's possible, of course, to provide a complete expanse of translucent panels entirely across the ceiling. But this requires multiple lighting fixtures and produces a higher level of illumination overall than may be desired or desirable. Usually made of plastic, the translucent panels come in a choice of patterns and light transmission capabilities. With the systems developed by some manufacturers, the lamp-holding fixtures attached directly to the metal grid members, while with other systems the fixtures are mounted to ceiling framing in the conventional way. Electrical outlet boxes are attached and wallboard applied as usual. Painting of the ceiling finish a flat white increases its reflectivity and raises the illumination level. Unpainted wallboard often turns yellow.

Fluorescent lamps bring two advantages—bright nonglare light level with relatively low wattage, and long lamp life that reduces attention or lamp replacement.

In a kitchen, the translucent panels can be arranged to bring more light to the individual working centers ... food preparation and cleanup, food cooking, and food storage. In kitchens, where cooking is accompanied by vapors that leave a grease residue, the lay-in or drop-in ceiling materials as well as the translucent panels can be removed and cleaned with ease, and without neck strain.

In terms of light value, incandescent bulbs require 500 percent higher wattage in order to provide equivalent foot-candles delivered by fluorescent lamps. And one manufacturer of luminous ceilings reports that lamp life with fluorescents might run to about 9,000 hours, while incandescent bulbs have an expected use of little more than 500 hours.

Planning Your Installation

In kitchens, the luminous or suspended ceiling grid will normally extend from soffit face to soffit face at a point just above the cabinet-top level.

The formula or rule-of-thumb for spread of lamps is that horizontal lamp spread should be double the vertical distance from luminous panel to the lamp. Example: with 1 foot vertical distance ceiling panel to tube, the lamp bases should be mounted 2 feet o.c.. This is for a continuous series of luminous panels in which the lamp bases would be end-to-end for the room length.

A continuous luminous ceiling is a highly attractive room feature but most owner-builders, operating on a strict budget, will probably opt for a ceiling installation that consists of at most half luminous, half drop-in ceiling finish panels.

Most metal grid suspension members are fabricated to be installed on 2 foot spacings. Luminous and drop-in ceiling finish panels are available in 2X2 feet and 2X4 feet sizes. Grid-attaching lamp fixtures in single- or double-lamp types usually come to fit the 2X4 feet grid unit and receive 48 inch fluorescent lamps. Where islands of luminous panels are provided at various kitchen centers, there should be a minimum of two lamps and the luminous area should be at least one fourth the area over which light is expected to be spread.

In planning for kitchens that are open on one side to

Full or Partial Luminous Ceiling can be provided with the same suspended grid installation. Shown at left is a combined partial installation using Kaiser-made grid components and drop-in fiberboard ceiling panels supplemented by translucent acrylic panels

for diffusing the fluorescent lamps installed above them. At right, a complete luminous ceiling with grid system laid out on the diagonal using square-cut acrylic sheets and Westinghouse deluxe warm-white fluorescent lamps mounted on the upper ceiling.

dining or family rooms, it is probably desirable to have the ceiling outlets wired to two wall switches and to split the connections of the lamp bases. This will furnish two levels of lighting for the kitchen . . . a high and bright level for working purposes . . . and a medium brightness for normal come-and-go activities for dining.

You'll want to prepare a ceiling plan sketch so that you'll know where to position main channels and cross-tees. The purpose here is essentially the same as described for ceiling tile layout sketches in Chapter 29, to obtain adequate and uniform border widths. To make the sketch, use graph paper and draw a scale plan of the ceiling looking either down or up. First, make an accurate outline of the entire ceiling area, with your lines representing the faces of walls or soffits. Next, figure the best position for the main metal runners. Normally, these will run parallel to each other 2 feet apart and also parallel to the length of the room or perpendicular to the direction of ceiling joists.

Whether or not added main runners are needed depends on the ceiling area dimensions; for a space whose overall width is 6 feet or less, no further main runners are needed. Wider spaces will require added runners at 2 foot intervals. With this spacing, then, fix the main runner positions so that overage is divided evenly for border units at each side.

Similarly, plan the positioning of cross-tees which may

be placed at either 2 foot or 4 foot spacings with most systems. Again, figure the positions to give equal border segments.

With the grid layout sketched in, now figure your lamp base placement or mounting. Normally, the 48 inch lamp bases will be used but this really isn't necessary. Lamp bases may be screw-mounted directly to ceiling surfaces with screws penetrating into ceiling joists. With some manufacturers, lamp bases or fixtures can be purchased along with the other ceiling parts; with others the fixtures have to be purchased separately from an electrical supply house. Flourescent lamps come in 2, 3 and 8 foot sizes as well as 4 foot, and fixtures for these lamp sizes are readily available.

Supplies and Tools Needed

Use your detailed ceiling grid sketch to make a list of the various ceiling parts and materials you'll need. The metal parts will consist of the following, calculated to fit your lineal foot requirement:

☐ main runners—these usually come in 23 foot lengths and have integral or separate devices for splicing end-to-end;
☐ cross-tees—in 2 foot and/or 4 foot sizes as needed to fit the layout sketch and the ceiling panels to be used;

□ wall angles—these right-angle L-shaped metal members come prepunched for nailing to wall surfaces along perimeter, providing a ledge on which panels rest;

The other materials needed will include appropriate quantitites calculated from your layout sketch of these items:

□ lamp-bases—2-lamp fixtures in most cases will suit, but 1-lamp and 4-lamp fixtures are also obtainable;
□ hanger wire—for main runner suspension; also buy splicing connectors if these are not integral with runners;
□ translucent/opaque panels—select type and pattern in the sizes needed to fit sketch layout.

In estimating lineal feet of main runners needed, be sure to allow some excess. This is to permit adjustment of runner placement to accommodate the cross-tees at desired location.

Selection

Depending upon the particular manufacturer's system ordered, you may have considerable choice in styles or types of panels. To give you an idea of the range of choices possible, the following materials list is offered by one manufacturer who has pioneered in developing luminous ceiling products.

Translucent

□ frost-white, 50,000 hours translucency without color change
□ multi-color decorative laminates: spatter, leaves, butterflies
□ half-inch eggcrate plastic louvers for through venting
□ semi-translucent half-inch thick styrene foam

Grid Suspension Installation for owner-builders is made fairly simple for owner-builders. In this series, the grid parts, solid panels and light fixture modules are those made by the Armstrong Cork Company. The principal steps are: (1) nail wall angles so they are level and at the desired ceiling height; (2) attach hanger drop wires to suspension hooks and screw into joist bottoms at 4-foot intervals; (3) attach drop wires to the main runners making sure the runners are at the same level as the wall angles; (4) next, snap the cross tees into place to accommodate holes in the main runners; (5) lay in the 2×4 foot prefinished ceiling panels; and (6) a 4-lamp (2-lamp fixtures also available) fluorescent module fits the runner and cross-tee grid.

Opaque

- smooth-finish half-inch molded styrene foam
- choice of three styles of 3/4 inch thick acoustical mineral fiber-and-glass board with or without washable film surface

A few suspension-system manufacturers are offering a considerably wider assortment of ceiling finish materials both in the prefinished fiberboard types described in Chapter 28 and also in the acoustical materials having specific noise-reduction and sometimes fire-resistive ratings.

Your regular carpenter tools will be used and no specialized equipment required. This means hammer, chalk-line, 4 foot level, blade-type knife, pliers, screwdriver. A hacksaw is apt to give better cuts and square edges than ... eet-metal shears. Use the hacksaw carefully to avoid scratches on the metal parts' exposed surfaces. Use a hand file to remove cutting burrs on the edges. Two ladders with a scaffold plank between them is advised to allow movement while you're in the process of fastening hangers and runners.

The removable-blade utility knife is for cutting of panel materials. Many will fit in the grid without cutting but border panels will have to be cut to fit. Use a metal straightedge to guide the knife. The plastic translucent panels can be cut by the score-and-break method. If you haven't done this before and have only a relatively small quantity of plastic panels to cut, stick to the handsaw method. Incidentally, glass is not desirable for use in the metal grid spaces because of the breakage hazard.

Installation Guide

Measure uniformly around the room's ceiling the distance down vertically to the level at which the suspended ceiling surface should come. Make marks about every 4 foot and adjust marks to level.

Next, the wall-angle members. Cut to size with hacksaw and drill side holes for nails or screws at stud locations. Nail spacing at every other stud is fine. Now, mark the wall angles for the main runners, sometimes called the T channels. Check your layout sketch for wall distance to first cross-tee and cut main runners accordingly.

Use No. 14 galvanized steel wire for hanging runners using ceiling hooks and running to holes punched in runners. Wall-angles will support runner ends. Hangers should be spaced every 3-to-4 feet with ceiling hooks penetrating into ceiling joists. Use care to position main runners so that the attachment holes for cross-tees are in correct perpendicular alignment.

With main runners in place, proper positioning of ceiling-mounted lamp-bases can now be made. Attach the lamp-base fixtures screwing to ceiling joists or drilling ceiling finish and using toggle-bolts, Molly, or Jif-loc fasteners.

Comfort dictates use of low-noise lamp-bases or fixtures. These fixtures have the ETL-type balasts and are A-rated for noise. Avoid the C-rated slimline tubes and bases. The

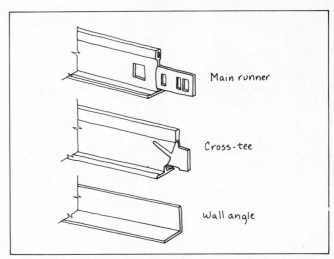

Suspension Grid Components for either a prefinished ceiling panel or luminous lighting installation consist of these metal components. The slotting and connection details may vary from one manufacturer to another so ask for instruction booklets.

ETL ballasts should also be of the rapid-start type, for prompt light-up when switched on.

The next step is locking in cross-tee members. The cross-tees are made with an interlock design that engages holes punched in the main runners. Follow the manufacturer's instructions for inserting the tees and making the interlock. Cross-tees for the side margins or border areas will have to be cut to fit between runners and wall angles.

It's suggested that both translucent and opaque ceiling panels remain in their packages and stored until all electric fixture wiring work has been completed (see Chapter 42). Check the packages to make certain you have the proper quantity of each, in undamaged condition. The object here is to minimize handling prefinished ceiling panels. These are easy to lay-in and cut-fit to margin size in the final cleanup stages of construction.

When the panels are ready to be placed, check the manufacturer instructions regarding panel edge-holding. In small rooms, opening-closing the door may cause the ceiling panels near the door to lift slightly or move. Some manufacturers provide fold-down tabs or furnish attachment clips that will keep the panels in position.

Degree of lighting intensity is at least partly a matter of personal preference, but since fluorescent lamps are an unknown quantity to most people the following may serve as a guide to brightness:

- for high intensity illumination in working areas such as in kitchens or laundries, use 40 watts (4 foot lamp) for every 8 square feet of area to be lighted;
- for medium intensity lighting as for bathrooms and hobby areas, use 40 watts for each 12 square feet of area to be lighted;
- for low intensity levels as in hallways or entry foyers, use 40 watts for each 20 square feet of area.

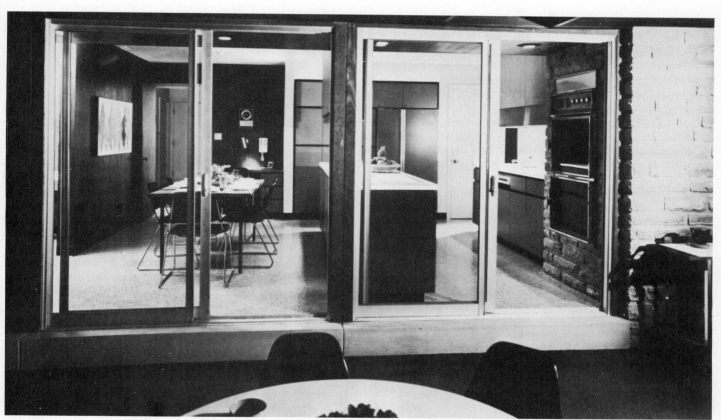

Supplementary Lighting Tips culled from information furnished by the lamp division of Westinghouse: at left, counter lights for counter areas supplement the general ceiling illumination at sink, range locations; at right, down lights in the ceiling and small spots at the art wall and the desk. Westinghouse lighting engineers say a luminous ceiling simulates daylight and creates a feeling of spaciousness because the light is uniform throughout the room. And the farther the tubes are from the diffusing material, the better the light distribution. Cool white lamps enhance blues and greens and are not advisable for use in kitchens and bathrooms, where they tend to give undesirable effects. Instead, use warm white lamps that enhance yellows, oranges and reds.

36 Interior and Closet Doors

First, let's talk room passageway doors. When you open and close such a door to go in or out of a room, it seems like there's nothing much to it. But to properly hang a door for smooth operation in varying climatic condidtions is not as simple as it may appear.

Not every carpenter can do a good job of door-hanging. He must have certain skills in handling sharp cutting tools and precision in every step of the site-hanging procedure. The relative scarcity of these skills is attested to by the rapid acceptance among home builders of all kinds of factory-assembled, machined, and prehung door units— units in which processing of hinge and lock mounts on both doors and frames are done almost entirely by automatic machinery.

To hang a door a trim carpenter must be able, with the aid of nothing more than a circular table-saw, a miter-box and a couple sawhorses at the building site, to carry out the following assortment of procedures:

- □ notch and chisel out frame jamb members to receive the flush-mounting butt hinges;
- □ cut jamb members at their bottoms to proper height above rough or finish floor;
- □ assemble frame, place in opening, wedge or shim to plumb and level, nail into place;
- □ cut door to height, plane to fit frame including slight bevel-planing on lock edge, ease the sharp corners;
- □ measure and notch-chisel the hinge recesses on door edge to match those on the frame with proper clearances at top and lock edges (see illustration);
- □ mount hinges, hang and test door to verify clearances, removing and replacing if door cannot be properly adjusted due to twist or warp;
- □ cut and miter door stops, nail into position on frame;
- □ bore door in two directions, chisel out opening for lockset and face-plate recess;
- □ install lockset mechanism in door, mark frame for strike-plate, chisel strike-plate recess and install strike-plate, install lockset trim;
- □ cut, miter and nail up casing trim on both sides of the door;

- □ test door operation for case of swing and correct with adjustments for any binding or improper latching.

The foregoing procedure, described in just a few lines, can take a very good trim carpenter between 3 and 4 hours per door. An unskilled person might take another hour or two, but wouldn't be able to come up with as neat and clean an installation every time as the skilled tradesman. Remember, these are passageways in which even small discrepancies become noticeable.

In contrast, a relatively unskilled carpenter can take a prehung interior door, remove any wrapping or temporary fasteners, unhinge the door, slip the split-jambs apart, put them in the opening, tack, plumb-level, nail, rehinge the door, apply door stop if separate and mount lockset ... all in a matter of about 20-to-25 minutes.

So, the factory precision-assembled prehung door component is a boon to professional and amateur builders alike. It's a real time saver.

Where and Why Prehungs Are Used

Prehung door units come in a full range of conventional passage-door sizes. Most are made with a door height of 6 feet 8 inches, a standard residential height. Most common door widths for bedrooms, bathrooms and other rooms are 2 feet 4 inches, 2 and 6, and 2 and 8. Other widths from 1 to 3 feet may be available depending on the individual supplier's stock.

As a rule, prehung doors cost substantially more than the door, frame and trim materials might run for on-site hanging. But consider the built-in labor you're saving. Some owner-builders may find their suppliers have a compromise between site-hanging and prehung. This may be in the form of "precut" or "prefitted" door packages, which run slightly less than prehung units. But they provide all necessary parts, pieces and trim, precut to size and miter for relatively rapid job assembly.

Prehung interior door units may also be used for closets. Either in the form of single doors for walk-in or linen closets or for wider openings in bedroom wardrobe closets where double-door units can be obtained in knocked-down form. These latter units are not as widely distributed; check your supplier on this particular item.

Most wide-opening wardrobe closet installations in new homes currently make use of the bi-fold type of operation with four door panels per opening. Sliding doors in pairs are also popular for wardrobe installation for a similar reason . . . they make clothing accessible and visible from the full width of the opening.

Aside from speed and ease of installation, prehung doors have other benefits for the owner-builder. Uniform quality standards are observed by door manufacturers adhering to the production requirements of Commercial Standard PS 32-70 for "Hinged Interior Wood Door Units." The Standard specifies the member dimensions, thicknesses, jamb-head joinery, hinging details, machining, clearances, bracing of units for shipment and other details.

Practices vary, however. Normally, split-jamb construction is used so the installer can use the same door with varying wall-finish thicknesses from perhaps 1/4 or 3/8 inch up to perhaps 7/8 inch. One-piece jambs for use with just a single thickness of wall finish are also produced and available at slightly lower cost.

Another method of preparing prehungs is to route the components and bore for locksets in such a way that the door can be reversed from top to bottom in the frame, thereby allowing the same unit to serve for an installation that will be either right- or left-handed.

While on the subject of handedness . . . and this is applicable no matter what kind of door unit or mounting is used . . . you're apt to run into confusion about what right-handed or left-handed door installation means. The consensus is:

Standing on the hinged side of the door so that you are facing the door which opens by coming towards you, it's a right-hand door when the knob and latch are on your right and a left-hand when they're on your left. Some manufacturers use the terms left-hinged and right-hinged . . . applicable when facing it from the hinged side.

Prehungs are usually available with a prime coat of paint, but increasingly home builders are using prefinished units with factory prefinishes applied to door, jambs, stop and casing trim. In some cases, the prefinished is a woodgrain pattern of vinyl cladding. Precut door packages may also be available with prefinished members or in primed form.

There's been some refinement in protecting prehung door units from weather and damage. Most door unit manufacturers now ship prehungs individually in polyethylene-wrapped film. Bracing, strapping and protective cartoning supplement the wrap and help protect the units in transit and handling. The wrapping also helps to stabilize the

Prehung Door Units are delivered to the job in assembled form including trim and may have a prime coat or be already prefinished. Many door unit fabricators provide a waterproof wrapping. Shown here, a prehung door made by U.S. Plywood Corp. being installed in the framed opening. Wedge, plumb, nail, apply opposite side's trim and the job's done.

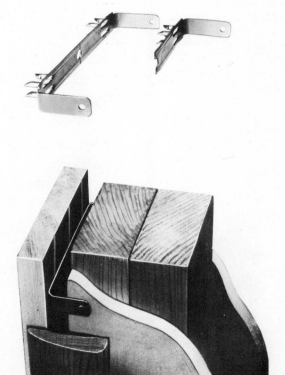

Site-Hanging Door Aid for mounting door frame in rough opening— these special jamb-width clips made by the Panel Clip Company.

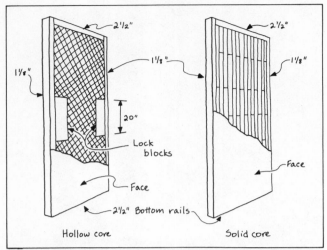

Residential Door Types of wood construction employ either of the two types of core construction shown here. Hollow-core doors in 1-3/8 inch thickness are the norm for most single-family homes for interior passage-door use. Solid-core, 1-3/4 inch thick doors are used principally as entrance doors. However in many areas, the practice has been to use either the thicker or heavier doors for interior passage use in luxury homes because of their better feel and reduced likelihood of warp or twist. In the hollow core construction, the core material may vary considerably from light wood egg-crate stock to equi-length sections of paperboard tubing. Core construction will include a pair of solid lock blocks for normal lockset locations for either right or left swing. Cores in solid doors may vary, too. Alternatives for the wood stave pieces shown might be a single sheet of particleboard or plastic foam board.

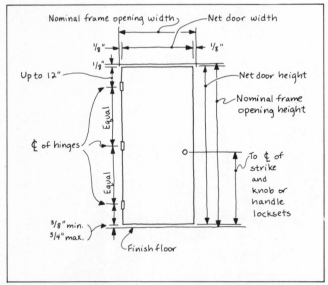

Typical Door Dimensions and hardware mounting locations are indicated in this sketch adapted from HUD's Manual of Acceptable Practices. The height of the center-line of the lockset is normally 40 inches above door bottom, which distance is the mid-point for 6 foot 8 inch high doors. Height for deadlock bolts (now shown) is 60 inches.

moisture content changes and thereby keeps the door units less subject to damage in shrinking-swelling movements.

Installing Prehungs

With solid jamb units and with some split-jamb types, the manufacturer's policy is to furnish the trim casing mounted to the jamb on one side of the door (usually the hinged side) and precut but loose for the other side. Normally, the casing trim in such cases involves premitered splined-and-glued corners for strength and resistance to shrinkage in the mitered joint. With other manufacturers, the split-jamb construction allows the casing trim to be premounted on both door sides, the jamb sections being separated for installation purposes.

Where solid type jambs are used, the plumbing-shimming method can be simplified through use of special metal clips that attach to the back of the door-frame, four or five clips to each side of the jamb. Clip ends are then bent on both door sides for nailing through the wallboard and into studs (see illustration).

As a rule, for a complete installation, you will have to select and order interior door locksets separately from the prehung units or precut packages. The doors will be pre-bored and the lock-side jambs prerouted, but the lockset hardware is not furnished.

Door Construction and Selection

Practically all interior doors in single-family homes are hollow-core units. The hollow core contains some type of corrugated, cell or strip construction so that the two face skins remain parallel. Faces are glued to the core material. Interior doors are 1-3/8 inch thick although luxury homes occasionally use 1-3/4 inch thick doors, the normal thickness for exterior units.

Solid wood strips are used in interior door construction at the door edges including top and bottom rails. Two solid wood lock-installation blocks occur at lock height along each side of the door (see illustration).

Solid wood strips throughout the area under the door skins make the door a "solid-core" door, normally used only in entrance door units.

When shopping for interior doors and when deciding on the type of doors needed for closets and wardrobes, keep in mind that you can go either of two routes in your selection for any given nonpassageway opening. The alternatives are:

☐ door-and-hardware separate—where sliding or bi-fold closet door operation is desired, hardware kits are bought to be mounted with doors purchased elsewhere or separately;
☐ door-hardware combined in a packaged set—applicable usually to bi-fold door units which use metal or plastic doors rather than wood.

If you wish to use hinged wood doors for closets, you may be able to obtain the sizes needed in prehung door units. Some prehung suppliers offer hinged units with only one side trimmed for this purpose. If the prehungs aren't available for that size opening, then hinged wood doors will have to be hung at the job.

The recommendation here is to consider bi-fold operation for all of your bedroom wardrobe closets. The bi-fold operation is usually smooth and opens up the full breadth of the closet. But expect to encounter cheaper products offered; don't buy blind. Consider a packaged set or hardware only when the supplier is able to show you an operating display so you can feel the door, test how it glides, what opening is left when it's closed, and what sounds it might make while being opened and closed.

Sliding doors of the paired by-pass type, two-panel, or four-panel installations, are also appropriate for wardrobe use with the possible advantage that doors of this type can be obtained with completely mirrored surfaces. Or mirrors can be mounted on panel faces. Full mirrored sliding doors, however, pose an extra expense. Be a bit skeptical on this. Mirrors are heavy and may affect door operation.

Jambs on Prehung Doors may vary slightly depending upon the individual fabricator or manufacturer. The three most common jamb types: (A), the solid jamb in which the door unit is made for specific thickness of wall finish; the split-jamb in (B) adjusts to a limited extent to different wallboard thicknesses and has a separate door stop to cover the jamb opening; the door stop in (C) is integral with the split-jamb.

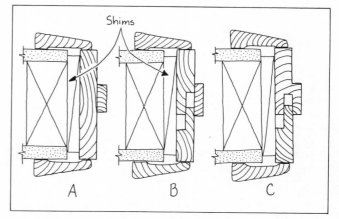

Bi-Fold Doors for Wardrobe Closets have enjoyed rapid growth in residential use because they open fully to give ready access to all of the closet's contents. Shown here are two different types of bi-fold units of steel construction made by Leigh Products. On the left, the door panels have an embossed 3-dimensional texture (inset shows close-up) as a result of leather-like graining in the metal itself. Other styles include full or partial louvered, mirrored and traditional-panel. On the right, a smooth panel white finish on one series of bi-folds which permits wallpaper covering to match walls.

There are sliding-door hardware sets available for pocket-type installations in which the door disappears within the wall. Such installations are sometimes used where home planners feel a hinged-mounted door's swing will interfere with the door's use. The pocket-type installation requires special provision in the wall framing. The rough openings needs to be about double that of normal door width, and the opening height must be adjusted to accommodate the header or mounting used by the door hardware. The first-time owner-builder should probably avoid pocket-door installations and opt for some other type even though it may not be as convenient.

Door Handling, Fitting, Hanging

Store your door units or doors lying flat on a level surface and, if they are not wrapped, cover the pile to keep the doors clean. When installing, handle the doors carefully (watch the door corners). Carry them. Don't drag prehung units on the floor.

Hold off installing any doors until at least a week after completion of drywall taping-cement work . . . longer if veneer or full plaster is used. After door delivery, allow 5 to 7 days time for the doors to become acclimated to your home's humidity conditions before removing the protective covering and hanging.

Check the delivered doors to make certain of your size selection because you're limited in the amount that you can trim from any door edge. With prehungs, no trimming of doors is possible; either it fits the rough opening or it doesn't and has to be sent back for replacement by the correct size. While some prehung door manufacturers may

---

Bi-Fold Door Ruggedness demonstrated. A characteristic of louvered, molded, structural foam doors made by Como Plastics. The lightweight doors, which look and feel like wood, won't warp, shrink, rust or dent according to the maker and can be painted or antiqued with a woodgrain finish. At the right, one of a line of five bi-fold door units in factory-finished metal made by U.S. Plywood Corp. Models fit any size opening from 18 inches to full room width and come 8 feet high as well as the standard 6 to 8.

fit doors with about 1/8 inch clearance, the National Wood-work Manufacturers Association recommends 3/16 inch as the fitting clearance for site-hung doors in order to allow for swelling in damp weather.

Mounting

Use three hinges, not two, per door. Top, middle and bottom. This is now standard for residential doors. The hinges should be recessed so their surfaces are flush with the jamb and door edge. Keep hinges in vertical plumb alignment. With unfinished natural doors, it's advisable to immediately apply a prime or sealer coat including the top, bottom and jamb edges.

Hinged Pairs. Within one opening, you can mount a pair of hinged doors, right-and-left hand, so they latch at their meeting point. Ordinarily, doors used in this way are the regular 1-3/8 inch thick hollow-core doors and they are mounted very much the same in a door frame as any conventionally hinged passageway door.

The main difference comes at their meeting point in the center. Some type of friction latch and latch-strike are needed; hardware is available for this purpose. If the double-door installation is one in which the right-hand door is the side usually used, it may be desirable to omit the left-hand knob and provide lever latches recessed in the door edge top and bottom to hold the left-hand door firmly in position.

Hinged door pairs are offered in prehung units by some manufacturers and can be ordered through retail outlets.

Sliding Pairs. Overhead track for roller-wheel door hangers plus floor-mounted door guides are the usual items combined for bypassing sliding door pairs. Hardware for such installations comes in packaged sets according to the number of doors (two, three or four) and width of opening. Doors are purchased separately and are usually of the passageway hollow-core type.

One of the key points of installation is the ability to make small adjustments in door height and plumbness after the door units are hung. These adjustments are usually possible through the hardware design. One such design uses of diagonally slotted screw holes for attaching roller hangers to the door backs. A useful feature in some hardware sets is a dial mechanism used in conjunction with one door-hanger; the dial has an offset center so that twisting the dial adjusts the door height up or down to a proper fit with the jamb.

One detail to note in a sliding door installation is the front facing at the top. If the door frame is trimmed in the conventional way, with casing mold, it leaves exposed the sliding track face and the slight space above the door top. This can be corrected in either of two ways: order a hardware set with an integral front fascia that projects downward and conceals the hangers and door tops; or

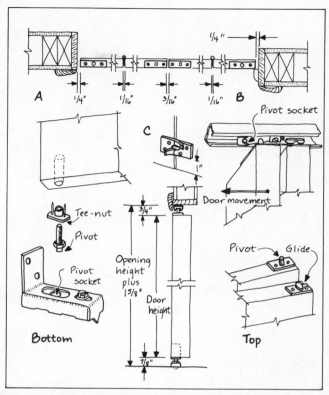

Bi-Fold Door Mounting Details are given in these sketches adapted from the instruction sheet issued by the hardware manufacturer, the National Manufacturing Company. Sketch (A) shows door mount so faces are nearly flush with the wall surface; sketch (B) indicates an alternative recessed mount with the use of door stop trim. In either case, door clearance dimensions are the same. Sketch (C) indicates door-closure alignment aid screwed to bottom of meeting panels on the inside. Side sketches indicate pivot mount details for bottom door edges (left) and top edges (right).

provide narrow blocking along the frame's front edge so that casing trim can extend downward about 1-to-1-1/4 inch, sufficient for concealment.

One word of caution. Some sliding door track-and-hangers sets are of reversible design, the same track and hangers being usable for paired doors either 1-3/8 inch thick or 3/4 inch thick. If your paired doors are anywhere close to the normal 6 foot 8 inch standard door height, panels 3/4 inch thick are likely to prove unsatisfactory because of eventual warp or twist, or lack of rigidity.

Folding Doors. These also operate on overhead track but a pair of door hangers support a pair of hinged panels, rather than a single door as in the sliding operation. The hangers pivot, permitting the hinged edges of the door panels to move out toward the operator. Certain types of bi-fold hardware use a bottom track also but preferred installations have bottom pivot sockets at the opening jambs only. This

permits floor coverings, including carpet, to fully extend into the closet.

Bi-fold hardware is readily available in packaged sets to fit various width openings. The door panels to be used with such hardware may be of conventional interior hollow-core construction, louvered door panels, or some type of custom-built frames with special sheet coverings. The hardware will generally be adjustable for panel thicknesses ranging between 1 and 1-3/4 inch.

Complete hardware-and-door packages are also available, as previously mentioned, in prefinished steel door units or with doors made of a high-impact molded plastic material such as polystyrene. Plastic doors may have steel-reinforced edges.

Folding doors can be set so their outer surfaces are flush with adjacent wall surfaces or they can be set near the center of the door frame with door stops applied (see illustration).

With either sliding or folding doors, the owner-builder should give a close look at any provision included in the packaged set of materials for door cushions. These are small rubber or plastic bumpers that absorb the noise of door closings. Use care, too, in figuring height of door-floor clearance to allow proper functioning after floor coverings have been installed.

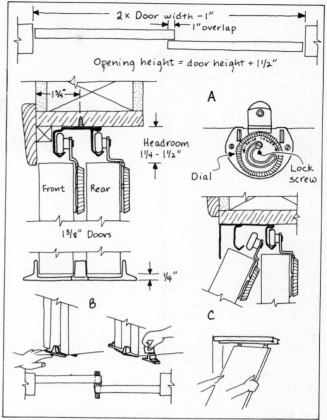

Sliding Door Hardware for use in bypass types of door installation illustrated here in sketches derived from the "How To Install" folder issued by Stanley Hardware. Other makes of hardware are comparable in most details. The top drawing indicates door overlap and at left a cross-section through the head and track portion of the door. Detail (A) indicates a dial hanger adjustment feature for proper leveling and door fit after the doors are hung. The sketches at (B) show how bottom door guides are handled and sketch (C) indicates an alternative fascia-type track plus the tilting needed to insert the hangers in the track.

Custom Bi-Fold Door can be installed by use of standard bi-fold hardware fitted to a job-made door with hardboard facing. Shown here, such a door installation using Masonite's "Provence" paneling. Each 4X8 foot sheet has three long, narrow panel sections with fine dimensional detailing. The panel-covered bi-fold doors match the same panels used on the walls of this dining room providing concealed storage space for china and table linen.

37 Resilient Floor Coverings

Made in two basic types, square tiles and rolls of sheet materials for seamless or one-seam installations, resilient floor coverings have become very popular in new homes.

There are two main reasons for their increased use: steady reduction in necessary care and upkeep; and regular introduction of new styles and an increased range of colors and patterns. As with some wall-finish materials, fitting in floor coverings with room decor is now considered important for resilient floor materials.

The new easy-care characteristics are evident in the preponderance of vinyl materials and the near-disappearance of linoleum and asphalt tiles from flooring retailers' stocks. And the latest move, adopted competitively by major floor covering manufacturers, has been the introduction and emphasis on glossy, high-polish vinyls known as "no-wax" types, with a cushioning underlayer that provides comfortable footing.

Decor, fashion and motif have become highlighted as new style-color-pattern introductions are made industrywide on a regular semi-annual basis in the market showings for professionals. This style evolution includes a broadening of floor tile simulations . . . that is, an adaptation of the appearance of a wider range of hard-surface materials in embossed, two-dimensional vinyl surfaces. The simulations include brick, stone, hardwood-parquet, mosaic and other ceramic tiles. This expansion has brought, within the past three years, a very wide-ranging assortment of simulations depicting the delicate-pattern high-glaze ceramics with an historic foreign past. Particularly popular in new homes today are the tiles and sheet goods whose patterns simulate the floor tiles in the older buildings of the glamor countries—Spain, Morocco, Brazil and Mexico. Surface embossing of these vinyl coverings does more than just add depth to the surface; it contributes a mystique factor.

To comprehend the flavor of these coverings, the owner-builder's family should browse a few floor-covering shops. Just an inkling of both the trends and the variety can be garnered from some of the pattern names used by floor covering manufacturers use.

Tarsia	Casa Mila
Bisque	Capricorn
San Rogue	Tranquility
Ceramique	Dutch Royale
Alvarado	Castilian
Topiary	Delpaso
Rio Verde	Faience
Hibiscus	Cortina
Durango	Quadrille
Cameroon	Sandridge
Iberia	Plaza Roma
Regency Square	Ambrosia

And while the above names apply to the multicolored glazed-tilelike patterns, the following list indicates the range of other simulated hard-surface floorings:

Swirl Mosaic	Antique Brick
Travertine	Edgewood
Ticonderoga Slate	Pebbled Onyx
Vermont Flagstone	Maison Parquet
Trojan Marble	Mexican Agate
Hampshire Brick	Native Stone
Quarry Tile	Kiln Brick

Get ready for yet another facet of floor coverings that's on the way . . . the no-wax cushioned vinyl line by Armstrong called "Solarian". Its patterns and colors are supplemented by new lines of color-matched-blended cotton fabrics and vinyl wall coverings.

Floor Planning Tips

Most brands of flooring materials offer easy maintenance, attractive styles, ready availability, and long wear.

But you want to go a step further in your planning and take a closer look at the samples and the individual brand claims. Note the differences in product types. Cushioned vinyl designed for a softer-underfoot characteristic comes with various cushioning materials. Distinguish, here, between the cushioned product and one with thicker backings. Some foam-backed vinyls can given an unsatisfactory "mushy" feeling when walked over.

Two other properties you might ask about that are the quieting effect on heel-tap sounds and surface traction or slip resistance.

In connection with easy upkeep, don't expect to find maintenance miracles. Even the best of resilients need regular attention by: frequent dusting or vacuuming; damp-mopping with appropriate light detergents followed by film-removing rinse; and avoiding tracked-in grit or sand particles and indentations or scratches from furniture. With respect to the last point, plan to use entrance mats to control the grits and glides, and casters or leg cups to hold off the dents.

The type of subfloor on which resilients are to be applied is essentially any wood-plywood-underlayment surface characterized by uniform smoothness and no irregularities that would show ridges or hollows. For new construction, the underlayment procedures described in Chapter 32 are recommended. Where resilient floor coverings are being considered for application to basement, lower-level or porch concrete floors, use caution. Some manufacturers recommend that their products *not* be applied to concrete slabs-on-ground or below grade. Others may have a special preparation procedure to be used with their products with these subfloor.

Installing Large Sheets

Vinyl sheet materials come in 6, 9 and 12 foot wide rolls although any given manufacturer's line may not be available in all three widths. The wider rolls will allow installation of a continuous one-piece floor surface in many rooms. No crevices or seams at all. But if you find a pattern or style you like in narrower widths, there is a suitable procedure (see illustration) for tight seams using sealing cements. Installation of a one-seam floor is less awkward than the handling of a single sheet.

In ordering your materials, make sure your measurements or calculations on room size are correct and that you allow sufficient margins. Include all room offsets or doorways so that the dimensions are figured to the outermost points. If the resilient material is for floor surface only, allow about 3 inches extra in length and width. If the sheet material is to be coved up at the wall base or cabinet bases, allow about 8 inches extra for a 4-to-4-½ inch cove. Coving of the sheet material takes time and care. And very exact cutting at corners. For the first-time owner-builder, it's a complicating method being used where a simpler-faster method can be employed with almost as desirable a result. The alternative method is to lay flooring sheets to wall or cabinet edges, and apply a color-blending vinyl cove base in separate strips.

Use a removable-blade utility knife for cutting; avoid those that are just light metal holders for regular double-edge razor blades. Buy instead a knife with half handles that unscrew to allow blade changes and whose blades are about 1/32 inch thick instead of razor-blade thin. Also avoid knives that have a sharp curve and are usually called linoleum knives.

Where there are cabinet corners or room corners for which the sheet material must be accurately cut and fitted, the best procedure is to first cut a paper or cardboard pattern that you can apply on a "try-and-see" basis. After you have cut a good pattern, then use it to mark and cut the floor covering material.

Some sheet materials resist folding or bending damage. Others don't. Be careful in folding or bending as you reach the stage where you're trying to get close fits at corners (see illustration).

Cutting work for an irregularly shaped one-piece floor surface may be easier and less subject to error if a plan sketch is prepared showing room outlines and crossed perpendicular center lines. The latter are then transferred to the floor surface by chalk-line. These central reference lines then permit you to accurately measure and mark from the reference line to any room or cabinet point, noting down each measurement on the sketch. It will save you going back to recheck a measurement.

In transferring your sketch measurements to the floor covering material, use a china crayon for marking on the covering surface; it will easily wipe off. In starting the markings, make allowance for the pattern lines. Pattern lines should be accurately parallel with or perpendicular to wall and cabinet edges.

When marking and cutting (leaving in the excess allowance) has been completed, roll up the covering material so the roll's length is parallel to the room's long dimension. Carry the roll in and unroll but don't force it into any corners or to meet any edges. Just allow the material to curl up along the edges. Adjust so the pattern is running true and so excesses are about equal at various points. You're now ready for adhesive application.

Pull back the covering over about half the room and apply adhesive in this uncovered area. Roll back the covering material onto the wet adhesive. Now, fold back the other half, apply adhesive and re-cover. Now proceed to the outer edges making final trim cuts and fitting cuts for corners or floor inserts (see illustration).

Installing Floor Tiles

Tiles are simpler to place than sheet materials. In many of the new tile designs and patterns, the square tile effect is lost because the tile edge butting is so close and the pattern matching so accurate that the butt lines all disappear.

Tiles have a way of separating from adhesives if it is at

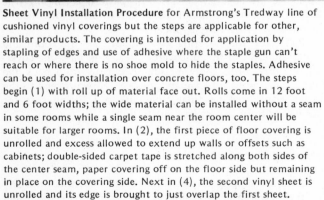

Sheet Vinyl Installation Procedure for Armstrong's Tredway line of cushioned vinyl coverings but the steps are applicable for other, similar products. The covering is intended for application by stapling of edges and use of adhesive where the staple gun can't reach or where there is no shoe mold to hide the staples. Adhesive can be used for installation over concrete floors, too. The steps begin (1) with roll up of material face out. Rolls come in 12 foot and 6 foot widths; the wide material can be installed without a seam in some rooms while a single seam near the room center will be suitable for larger rooms. In (2), the first piece of floor covering is unrolled and excess allowed to extend up walls or offsets such as cabinets; double-sided carpet tape is stretched along both sides of the center seam, paper covering off on the floor side but remaining in place on the covering side. Next in (4), the second vinyl sheet is unrolled and its edge is brought to just overlap the first sheet.

Photo (6) is a close-up of the overlap indicating that the sheets have been adjusted for pattern match. A utility knife is used to cut out a U-shaped section from the excess extending up the wall or cabinet at both seam ends so that the seam area will lie flat on the underlayment. And then in (7), the knife with the help of a steel straightedge is used to cut through both vinyl sheets to produce a perfectly butted seam. Photo (8) indicates lifting of sheet edges to pull out top paper covering from the carpet tape and pull away the trimmed off portion of the under vinyl sheet. In (9), seam sealing cement or adhesive is being applied.

The installation is completed by trimming at borders and fitting around cabinet corners. Shown here in (10) is an upward knife cut of the floor covering at an inside corner in order to permit covering to be fitted tightly down. In photo (11), an outside cabinet corner is to be trimmed and the corner cut is started at the floor line. A steel straightedge (12) is used for cutting along wall or cabinet and the floor covering sheet is turned back (13) to allow application of adhesive or cement. Finally a manual staple gun is used with 3/8 to 9/16 inch long staples spaced at about 3-inch intervals. Edge and staples are then covered with a base show molding strip.

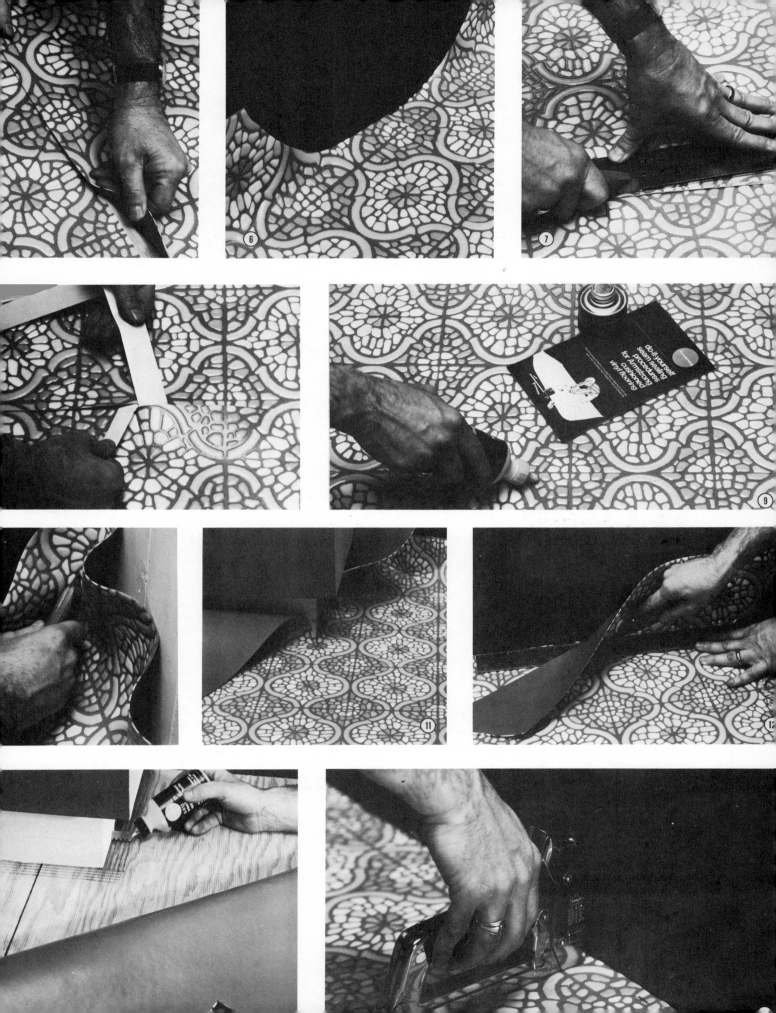

Floor Tile Square Foot Coverage

For 9" × 9" Size			For 12" × 12" Size	
1/8", 9" × 9"				Sq. Ft. of 12" × 12"
No. of Cartons	Pieces	Sq. Ft.	No. of Cartons	1/16", 3/32" & 1/8"
1	80	45	1	45
2	160	90	2	90
3	240	135	3	135
4	320	180	4	180
5	400	225	5	225
6	480	270	6	270
7	560	315	7	315
8	640	360	8	360
9	720	405	9	405
10	800	450	10	450
11	880	495	11	495
12	960	540	12	540
13	1040	585	13	585
14	1120	630	14	630
15	1200	675	15	675
16	1280	720	16	720
17	1360	765	17	765
18	1440	810	18	810
19	1520	855	19	855
20	1600	900	20	900

SOURCE: Azrock Floor Products Division, "Manual of Installation"

Ordering Floor Tiles is usually done by the carton and this chart will help you convert your floor square footage into cartons needed to cover.

all damp; origin either from below or from above. To avoid dampness, the manufacturer's recommendations usually call for installation only over wood subfloors or underlayments and, in the case of crawl-space foundations, there should be a minimum of 18 inches vertical distance from the bottom of the floor joists down to the earth surface of the crawl space. If your distance is less, you may wish to dig out excess dirt or do two damp-prevention jobs: cover the crawl-space earth with a polyethylene film; and apply an asphalt felt layer to the subfloor using 15 pound building felt applied with adhesive.

Resilient flooring tiles, whether made of vinyl-asbestos or of all-vinyl, are laid following the same room-by-room procedures. A start is made with chalk-lines at or near the central part of the room, two lines perpendicular. Same starting method as you might have used for ceiling tiles or luminous ceilings.

Adhesive application is best done a quarter of the room at a time. When the adhesive gets to the proper stage of feeling "tacky" but without adhering to the testing finger-tips, it's ready for tile laying. In applying adhesive with a notched trowel, be sure that the spreading is relatively uniform with sufficient adhesive in the ridges to obtain a sure grip on the tiles but not so much that it will squeeze out through the tile joints. Begin adjacent to the center lines and proceed tile by tile to the room edges. After all full tiles are laid, go on to next room quarter.

After all full tiles are laid, border tiles are marked and positioned. Be sure to check the borders by accurate measurement and cutting. Don't get too tight a fit with the wall or cabinet edge; cut to fall about 1/16 to 1/8 inch shy. This slight gap will be covered by the cove base.

Tile installation work should generally not be done at temperatures lower than about 65° F. It's a good idea to store the tile cartons in the same area they are to be used, several days in advance of installation. If your new home hasn't yet completed the heating installation and outdoor temperatures are running lower than the above level, postpone the tile installation until you are able to run the heating plant and warm up the interior.

Cove Base and Trim

With most tile and sheet installations, the only trim is around the edges. Metal moldings or wood thresholds are used at floor edges that occur in doorways, or where the covering meets other types of floor surfaces.

Along walls and along the toe-space of kitchen or vanity cabinets, the conventional trim material is vinyl cove base. This is in the form of a .08 gauge thickness of solid vinyl strips having a preformed cove along one edge and a slightly rounded finish on the other. The strips come in 4 foot lengths. Heights for residential use are 2-½ and 4 inches, but

Steps in Laying Floor Tiles are just about the same whether all-vinyl or vinyl-asbestos tiles are being used. Cutting of all-vinyl tiles is easy with a scissors while the vinyl asbestos type tiles may better be cut with scoring tools or a tile cutter. Layout of starting center lines is important to get good tile alignment and photo (1) indicates careful measurement to obtain proper perpendicular center lines. In (2), tile units are temporarily laid out to check border widths and thus verify suitable position for center lines. Once the lines are established and marked on the underlayment, adhesive is spread (3) with a brush or notched adhesive trowel keeping within one quarter of the room. A short wait may be needed (4) until the surface of the adhesive feels tacky to the touch rather than wet.

Tile units are started at the juncture of the center lines and work of laying unit by unit proceeds toward the outer edges (5). When all field tile have been laid carefully butting each new tile to the adjoining tiles, it's time to work on the border tiles. First, in (6), the full tile piece to be cut for border installation is held on top of last full tile for marking. A line drawn across edge marks allows accurate cutting (7) and then in (8), the cut border piece is slipped into place first butting it to the last previous tile. For many resilient floor covering installations, vinyl cove base is an appropriate trim that lends a hand in floor maintenance by keeping floor corners clean. In (9), cove base is being applied and in (10), the final step: rolling the tiles in both directions using a heavy steel floor roller.

6 inch material is also available. You can choose from a wide range of solid colors in order to obtain a suitable match with your floor pattern. Some suppliers may also carry the vinyl cove base in woodgrain patterns.

The cove material is installed with floor covering adhesive. You apply it to the back of the cove base strips, and for this you need your sawhorse-and-plank working table. After adhesive is back-applied, the cove base strip is lifted into position, given a downward pressure with the fingers to make tight contact of the cove edge with the floor covering surface. A small wallpaper roller can be used over the base strip to ensure tight, uniform contact.

At inside room or cabinet corners, the cove base strip is marked and an inverted "V" is cut in the coved portion only (45° legs on the "V"). The strip is then bent and pressed into the corner, the "V" coming together to look like a mitered cut. Outside corners are best handled with premolded corner units available as an accessory with the base.

At the juncture point of cove base and door casing trim, you'll want your base to butt to the casing's outer edge. Apply the base to come to the edge of the opening and later, when the casing is being applied, mark the base and cut it off vertically to fit the casing edge.

Your tile installation may be enhanced by the inclusion of another form of resilient flooring trim material called "feature strips." They may be available only in a company's vinyl-asbestos line of tiles. The feature strips come in the same thickness as the field tiles and in 1/4, 1/2, 1 and 2 inch widths. The strips are 2 feet in length and are ordinarily available only in a range of solid colors. They're laid simultaneously with the field tiles and thus the owner-builder desiring to use feature strip trim must have his strip pattern coordinated with the field tile in sketch form before beginning the work. This is another way to blend floor coverings into your room's decor.

38 Hardwood and Other Floors

The days are long gone when a new home had hardwood floors throughout the house except in bathrooms. Today many professional home builders limit the use of hardwood to bedrooms. This seems to be not just a matter of cost . . . because hardwood flooring is really not that expensive . . . but a result of changing times and preferences as well.

Times do change. New-home customers today often prefer their to have floors to be part of the room decor. They apparently like to choose patterns and colors; for example, plain level-loop carpetings are outnumbered by blends, textures, and sculptured styles.

But there have been changes in hardwoods, too. It wasn't very long ago that your principal choice in hardwood flooring was a strip width between 2-¼ and 3-¼ inches wide. And between oak and maple, either one finished in a single light tone. Today, you can select from a variety of prefinished hardwood floorings—strips, planks and parquets. And the color range of these prefinishes extends to medium and even some darker tones.

Unfinished strip flooring is not particularly difficult to lay. It requires careful nailing to avoid both bent nails and split material. Also, some selectivity of strips must be exercised to prevent extreme variations, one strip to another, in graining and color tone.

But the process is time consuming. Floor-nailing tools are of considerable help, but the flooring material is still subject to damage from damp weather and, once installed, needs to be sanded and finished promptly to avoid scars or stains that may be difficult to remove. In a completed home, hardwood floor finishes tend to show dust easily. And the omission of rugs in traffic areas will tend to broadcast heel-tapping steps through the house.

For the first-time owner-builder, time and trouble can be saved by avoiding the use of unfinished strip floorings. If you want hardwood floors in some rooms, investigate what can be obtained in prefinished floorings. Many of these, especially the plank and parquet styles, are very appropriate in family rooms and dens.

Handling and Installation

Try to have your flooring delivered in dry weather. Then, take some time to store it right. Place it in a well-ventilated location but don't store in open sunlight or in a dry-heated room. Place the pile on a piece of building paper or film and keep the bundles relatively open so air can circulate around them. You wish to avoid much moisture fluctuation for the flooring because it comes with about a 7-or-8 percent moisture content. If it acquires much more before being installed, it will later be subject to shrinkage when the home is heated. And if somehow it becomes dryer, there may be a danger of buckling once installed.

Like resilient tile floor coverings, hardwood strips or other types should not be laid directly to concrete slabs on or below grade; the same 18 inch minimum vertical distance from grade to bottom of floor joists applies with hardwood. Strip flooring can be laid on a concrete subfloor using wood blocks laid over a continuous coat of mastic. If, however, you have in mind the possibility of applying hardwood flooring in a basement recreation room or on the concrete floor of the lower level in a split or bi-level home, forget it. It's not worth taking the chance. These below-grade installation involve, nine times of ten, above-average dampness.

Avoid laying your hardwood flooring any time there is standing water in the basement area of the home or in an unexcavated area. Any concrete, brick or other masonry work involving cement or mortar should have had ample time to thoroughly dry before commencing flooring work.

With a nailed application, use 15 pound building felt over the subfloor. But for floors over crawl spaces, use a moisture barrier such as polyethylene film or roll roofing paper, instead of the asphalt-impregnated felt.

The secret to nonsqeaking hardwood floors is in the nailing. Firm, secure strips do not squeak. Floors that are not sufficiently nailed are the ones most likely to turn up loose strips, to buckle, and to squeak. If the subfloor is of inch boards, the preferred board installation is laid diago-

Nailing Schedule for Strip Hardwood Floorings

Flooring		Nailing	Spacing
Type	Size		
Tongue & Groove, blind-nailed	25/32 by 3-¼ in.	7d or 8d screw-type or cut nail *	10 to 12 in. apart **
	25/32 by 2-¼ in.	ditto	ditto
	25/32 by 2-0 in.	ditto	ditto
	25/32 by 1-½ in.	ditto	ditto
Tongue & Groove, blind-nailed over sub-floor	1/2 by 2-0 in.	5d screw-type, cut or wire casing nail *	10 in. apart
	1/2 by 1-½ in.	ditto	ditto
	3/8 by 2-0 in.	4d wire casing nail	8 in. apart
	3/8 by 1-½ in.	ditto	ditto
Square-Edged, nailed thru top face	5/16 by 2-0 in.	1-inch, 15-gauge barbed flooring brad, preferably cement-coated	2 nails each 7 in.
	5/16 by 1-½ in.	ditto	ditto
	5/16 by 1-1/3 in.	ditto	1 nail each 5 in. on alternate sides

* Machine driven barbed fasteners of size manufacturer recommends are acceptable
** If subfloor is 1/2 in. plywood, fastenings to be driven into each joist, with an additional fastening in between
SOURCE: National Oak Floor Certified Oak Floors Association, Specification Manual

What Nails for Strip Flooring of various thicknesses and installation methods are proper is shown in this schedule. The recommended data shown comes from the National Oak Flooring Manufacturers Association.

nally with 1/4 inch spacing between boards. With a plywood subfloor, the preferred application is minimum thickness of 1/2 inch, using plywood with exterior-type glue. With a plywood subfloor, hardwood strips should be nailed through the plywood into joists with an additional nail between joists.

To avoid excess drying out of flooring at certain areas where the floor is directly over a basement furnace or uninsulated duct runs, provide a minimum of 1/2 inch thick insulation board or, if the thickness of this material is objectionable, use a double layer of 30 pound asphalt or asbestos felt paper. Or provide regular duct insulation.

Hardwood flooring laid too tightly against walls or framing can buckle. Allow at least 1/4 inch expansion space where the flooring comes up to all vertical surfaces.

Wide plank flooring is highly attractive. But its physical characteristics are even more demanding than strip flooring and even more subject to changing moisture or dampness conditions. Planks are installed with a combination of blind nailing (same as for strip flooring) and face fastening. The latter consists of set face nails with holes filled with plastic wood or wood cement and, at plank ends, wood screws which are hole-recessed and the holes filled with wood plugs. Plank floors are not for someone in a hurry to move into a new home.

Prefinished Floorings

Prefinished planks are a different story. And so are the other prefinished strip and parquet flooring products.

The most apparent difference between site-finished hardwood floors and prefinished flooring products is the darker wood tones available with the prefinished products. Often, the prefinish has a deep rich tone quite in tune with the rich wood finishes now so widely available and popular in wood panelings. This, among other factors, has made prefinished hardwood floors widely accepted by home builders for use in paneled family rooms, library-dens, and TV rooms. One type of prefinished flooring that has found unusually broad acceptance is the simulated plank style introduced by the E.L. Bruce Company as "Ranch Plank" flooring. It is prefinished 2-¼ and 3-¼ inch strip flooring that is end-matched but has factory-installed walnut pegs at the strip ends to simulate the real pegging of plank floors. A similar style is available without the pegs.

Prefinished block floorings come in a variety of styles and also in a range of 3/4, 1/2 and 5/16 inch thicknesses. The thinner types are usually intended for adhesive application. These are offered in true parquet patterns, in blocks made up of strip pieces, and in herringbone-style installations using rectangular blocks. And one company offers a prefinished plank flooring in random lengths and plank widths of 3, 5 and 7 inches, with factory-installed pegging, intended for adhesive application. Sizes of the wood blocks vary from 9X9 inches up to 12X12 inches, depending upon the style. In some company lines, the style or pattern may be offered with a preapplied adhesive; all you do is peel off a protective paper for immediate application to a prepared subfloor.

The various prefinished floorings are offered usually in the medium brown colors but are also available, in a few lines, in either darker or lighter colors. One newer prefinished plank in medium and dark brown shades comes with a distressed surface finish complemented by wrought-iron nail-heads.

Other Floors

Aside from hardwood floors, resilient, and soft-floor coverings, the principal other material installed in new homes is ceramic tile. Details on ceramic tile are included in Chapter 30.

In moderate-cost and luxury-class homes, entrance foyers, fireplace hearths, and other special floor areas may be floored with slate, brick, marble or other types of hard-surface materials. Normally, these require setting beds similar to the concrete or reinforced mortar beds prepared for ceramic tiles. For the owner-builder of a low- or mid-priced home, the utilization of such masonry types of floors is not recommended.

It isn't a matter of the skill needed to install. Rather, the owner-builder should ask himself the question: "Will the extra effort and extra cost of such floors be worthwhile to me either in utilization advantages or in the overall increase in the home's value?"

In most cases, the answer to such a question is "no." And for those who might like the appearance of brick, tile, slate, mosaic or parquet without the extra effort and attention entailed, they may find satisfactory substitutes in the simulated patterns available in sheet-vinyl floor coverings.

Strip Flooring Installation highlights given in this series of photos: (1) after building felt has been stapled down, first hardwood strip is face-nailed at the starting wall with the tongue towards the room; (2) as work proceeds, blind nailing is done easier and more uniformly using a fiberhead hammer to drive cartridge-clip nails with this angular nailer; (3) final strips in the room are also face-nailed and a pry-bar used to draw the strips up to those previously laid.

39 Applying Interior Trim

Literally, wood moldings have been around for centuries. So long, in fact, they were once spelled mouldings. The crafting of wood strips into intricate shapes with handmade wood-block knives was an art brought into this country during the revolutionary period, and perfected in the colonial homes built by carpenters who were their own designers.

In colonial days—and still found today in fine authentic-reproduction details in new luxury homes—moldings were used to convert plain wall surfaces into paneled rooms. Long before today's woodgrain paneling was born, moldings applied to wall surfaces were the means for identifying a room as one which received extra attention, effort, and the best craftsmanship.

For a long time before labor/material costs entered the picture, moldings served in several ways—to conceal cracks, to protect against wall damage, and as a purely decorative device. Sometimes the particular application served more than one purpose.

Today, moldings still work in much the same way but a growing awareness of economy has tended to diminish the purely decorative aspects and emphasize the functional purposes. Additionally, the need to protect wall surfaces has diminished through the use of better materials and the more durable prefinishes. Still, some of the old protective methods still find present-day applications unchanged . . . such as the baseboard-and-shoe protection at floor level and the chair-rail protection in dining rooms.

The Shapes You Work With

Trim work consists almost 100 percent of cutting, fitting, and nailing moldings into place. Once these wood strips were 100 percent clear wood (pine, oak, or mahogany), nailed into place with casing or finish nails, nail heads set for puttying, priming and enamel coats. Now, trim work may vary considerably from that once-universal practice. Moldings have taken simpler shapes. Many come with factory prefinishes. Metal and plastic moldings are in wide use but serve as supplements to unfinished wood rather than replacements.

Your first reaction to all the different sizes and shapes of unfinished and prefinished moldings on display in a lumber-supply retailer's racks would well be to wonder where all these various things go. A division of the various molding shapes into *functional* and *decorative* types will help organize the array of sizes and shapes.

A functional molding is simply one that serves the purpose of covering and trimming what would otherwise be an unsightly crack. A decorative molding is one applied for its visual effect or for effecting a certain design pattern.

There should be a relationship between the molding shapes you select and the places where they will be used. The molding shape names indicate this, to a degree. There should also be a relationship between the style of molding selected and the style or design theme of the home. You would choose traditional shapes of casing trim, for example, for trimming openings of paneled doors, while smoothly curved moldings would be more appropriate for flush doors.

Don't mix molding shapes. Match up the kind of trim material you select with the basic style of your home. If your home has flush doors, use the smooth-surface or ranch-type moldings for window casings and baseboards. You may at times run into difficulties. Such as having muntined* windows shown in the drawings but no paneled doors. Try to be alert to such discrepancies and be consistent in your use of styles.

What Cracks To Cover?

The principal places you will use trim . . . where cracks in the construction need to be concealed . . . are the door-window casings and the floor-wall joints where baseboard-and-shoe moldings are required. Most other trim items are associated with specific added installations. If the installa-

*window panes separated by strips

tion is made, you'll need the trim, otherwise not. Into such a category fall the following items:

Paneling and tile—cap, edge and corner trim;
Fireplace—wall face and mantel trim;
Stairs—handrail and base trim.

One other situation requiring concealment moldings is the point at which differing surface materials meet or join. This commonly occurs on floors where carpeting meets wood or resilient or tile. Sometimes the floor joint of differing materials can be covered with a conventional wood threshold strip. At other floor junctures, metal trim pieces may be more appropriate. Obtain these various trims from flooring suppliers.

A variety of built-in equipment or various kinds of built-in wood facilities such as shelves, drawers and other types of cabinetry will require some form of trim to cover their joining surfaces. With some such products the facing may have an integral trimmed design or a separate edge trim may be furnished with the product. In the case of wood built-ins, the owner-builder will have to select the type of molding he believes best suited to the application.

Trim is needed for an open passageway. Such as an opening from living room to dining room or to a hallway where there is no passage door. These are commonly referred to as simply "cased openings" and that term indicates how they're trimmed. A flat square-edged piece of board, milled and sanded smooth, and free of knots is called a "casing." For a normal stud wall with half inch wall finish material on each side, a casing member 3/4 or 25/32 inch thick by 4-1/2 inch wide would be fitted into the doorway opening at head and both jambs. Nailed into position level and plumbed in much the same manner as a door frame, the casing then has its edges trimmed (and the crack with the wall-finish concealed) by casing moldings.

A simpler and less expensive way to finish off such openings is simply to carry the drywall gypsumboard material right around the opening. This is done by applying strips of gypsumboard in place of the casing members at head and jambs. Then, to give the corners a straight edge for the edge-cementing, a metal corner bead is applied as described in Chapter 27.

Door and Window Trim

If you've followed the suggestion earlier to use prehung or prefit doors, your door trimming work is already completed because the trim was part of the package. And the package instructions would have included guidance on installing the trim items.

For those owner-builders who may have purchased door frames and doors separately and have hung the doors at the job site, casing trim for door edges can now be applied along with trim of the same style for windows.

The usual procedure in applying door casing is approximately as follows:

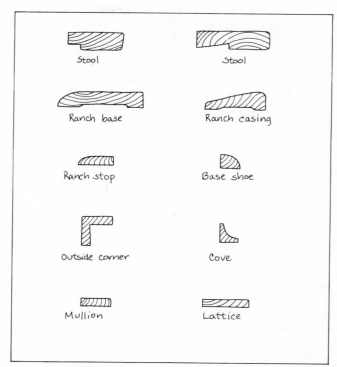

Common Molding Trim Shapes in smooth-surfaced contemporary styles. Most lumber-millwork suppliers will also carry a similar group of moldings of traditional designs better buited for Colonial and Early American home styles, particularly where interior-exterior doors are paneled.

(1) Start with one side's jamb strip, mitering the top to 45° and then measuring accurate length to the finished floor surface. Allow 1/4 inch set-back of the edge of the molding from the corner edge of the casing or door-frame.

(2) After cutting to exact length, nail into place using casing or finish nails and nailing through trim and wallboard into studs.

(3) Next, measure and cut head member with 45° miter cuts on each end and measure-cut jamb member on other side.

(4) Position the two members just cut and note the fit of the miters; if need be, remove to sand or slightly under-cut the miter in order to obtain a straight-tight fit line on the face of the molding.

(5) Nail second jamb member up observing same set-back from jamb or casing corner edge.

(6) Place head member in position and nail lightly at center with proper set-back. Then, first at one corner followed by the other, use one hand to pull down the member to a tight miter fit with the jamb member and, while holding firm, nail near the corner.

(7) Proceed around the opening with added nails so that nail spacing is about every 12-to-15 inches.

One additional suggestion that old-time trim carpenters would really frown on (but then, this is not the day of the old-time carpenter): to make sure your mitered corners remain tight after painting and do not separate and need later putty-filling and repainting, have a little plastic can of Elmer's white casein glue (or some comparable brand) handy. Just before placing the head member, apply a fair amount of the glue to the miter cuts of the head member. Then, nail it up tight, as before, and wipe off the excess glue with a rag. Follow with two finish nails. If you haven't already nailed miters together, predrill the holes. At one corner, one nail comes down vertically starting in the top edge of the head member and penetrating into the jamb member through the miter joint. A second nail starts in the edge of the jamb member, is slightly offset to miss the first nail, and is driven through the miter joint horizontally to penetrate the head member. Do the same at the other head corner. This will prevent miter-joint separations. Set all nail heads and fill with wood-filler.

Windows

Windows at one time were built or assembled right in the openings. Perimeter frames, sash balancing weights, sash

insertion, window hardware, then the glazer with its glass. And just before the painter was ready, a trim carpenter came in to trim a window out with first some boxing or blocking, then a sill and under-sill apron, wide casing trim to cover weight spaces, and finally the application of the head, often with a decorative cornice.

Most of the foregoing work is no longer done simply because it or some other process is being incorporated into fully assembled window units during the factory panel production or into a prepared opening at the job-site. The preassembled window in most cases has its exterior trim already in place and on the interior its casing members are part of the window construction. They are designed so that their edges come flush with the interior wall finish once the window unit has been properly installed. All that's needed is a few strips of casing trim . . . narrow trim similar to that on the door openings is quite suitable . . . to conceal the crack with the wallboard joint. In some types of windows, a finish sill-member and apron may be used (see illustration).

While window details vary somewhat from one window manufacturer to another, in most cases the owner-builder will have a choice as to how the window is trimmed . . . full picture-frame trim entirely around the opening or casing applied to jambs and head while the sill is trimmed with a stool and apron. In either case, applying casing trim moldings is very similar to applying the same moldings to trim door openings. In deciding on trim for window sills, the best procedure is to ask your panel or window supplier for literature that gives specification details and drawings of typical window installation. Follow the window manufacturer's sill recommendations. Final note: stool-type sill was once considered a "must." It no longer is.

Baseboard, Shoe, and Other Trims

In the past, 8-to-20 inch flat baseboards were used and decorated with supplementary cap molds. Today, baseboard moldings commonly range from 4-1/4 down to 2-1/2 inches. Sometimes they come with a supplementary shoe mold, sometimes not.

Normal baseboard molding has a square-edged bottom which fits near the floor surface. A small rounded 1/2X3/4 inch molding is nailed to the baseboard and is slender enough for pretty close adjustment to floor irregularities. With wall-to-wall carpeting, the shoe molding is sometimes used to conceal the carpet edge which is brought up to the face of the baseboard.

Don't feel that you're omitting something that should be there if you apply a casing type molding at the baseboard without a shoe-mold. Today's method of floor construc-

---

An Accurate Precision-Cutting Miter Box is an essential tool for interior trim installations. Here, a couple under-braces and two flat 2X6's added to the sawhorse top provide a convenient base on which the miter box is mounted.

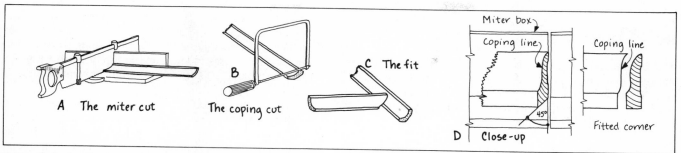

Making A Coping Cut is claimed by many skilled trim carpenters to give a better right angle molding joint than two 45° miter cuts. In a coping cut, one molding member (the right-hand one in the fitted corner sketch) is cut to length with just a square end cut. The second molding strip is first cut on a 45° degree miter as in (A). Then using the front edge of the miter cut as a guideline, the coping saw (B) is used to follow this edge at right angles to the molding face to permit an accurate fit to the first molding strip.

tion, using plywood sheathing plus underlayment material for resilient and soft floor coverings, has minimized floor irregularities so that one reason for the shoe-molding is pretty much eliminated. It will still, however, make corner-cleaning or vacuuming easier.

Application of the baseboard trim should follow, not precede, the dooring casing work since the base moldings butt up to the thick edges of the door casing trim. The same applies if windows extend to the floor or near the floor. It's better to trim out the sill before the baseboard material is applied.

At room corners, trim carpenters nearly always employ 45° mitering of baseboards at outside corners but prefer a coped joint for inside corners. Coping a joint is easier than trying to get a tight fit by mitering on the inside corner work. It also seems to produce a joint having less chance of opening up due to shrinkage. The method for coping is to cut one member with a square cut and then cut the other member square to the first but along the line of the face edge of a 45° cut (see illustration).

Selection

Most new homes, except perhaps those in the higher price ranges, will get along very nicely without purely decorative moldings. But just so you won't feel short-changed in this department, here's a quick rundown of the remaining types of wood moldings still generally available today through lumber-supply retail outlets.

Crown and bed moldings. Generally have a curved face shape and edges that have been machined to about 60/120° angles. The intent here is to make application possible at wall-ceiling corners that cross this juncture on an angle. Their function was originally to conceal plaster grounds. With the increasing use of gypsum wallboard and taped-cement wall-ceiling corners, the use of crown or bed moldings has diminished.

Cove Moldings. Somewhat similar to crown-bed moldings

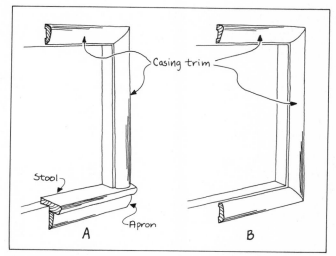

Two Types of Window Trim Methods are shown in these sketches. In sketch (A), the conventional sill stool and apron method appropriate with traditional trim styles. Sketch (B) shows the simpler picture-framing method with casing trim used on all four window edges.

in that they're sometimes used at wall-ceiling corners; they're smaller and cost less. The 3/4 X 3/4 inch cove mold remains a general-purpose cabinet installation trim, but larger cove molds see little use in new homes.

Quarter/Half Rounds. Now general-purpose moldings, probably used more with cabinet and shelf installations than for any other purpose.

Chair Rails. Still are very popular in certain rooms such as dining rooms, dens, libraries and family rooms, with or without wainscot paneling. Also suited to foyers and hall-ways or other locations where relatively straight-back chairs may stand and rub against wall surfaces.

Base Caps. Seldom used any longer with baseboards.

Door Stops. Still found when door jambs with integral stops are not used.

Mullion Moldings. Remain in common use to cover joints between individual window units that are installed side-by-side. However, the growing practice has been for window manufacturers to include mullion strips factory-applied in preassembled window combinations.

Picture Moldings. Like crown-bed moldings, these hark back to plastering days when hanging a picture on a nail in the plastered wall often meant a cracked wall. The solution was a picture molding nailed through the plaster into studs near the ceiling and small copper or brass hooks were used over the moldings to hang the pictures.

Corner Moldings. In right-angle shapes for protecting outside corners against damage. These see some use today in conjunction with plywood and other paneling materials.

Brick and Shingle Molds. Exterior moldings designed to trim bricks and shingles where they meet wall construction.

Drip Cap Molds. Also intended for exterior use at the heads of windows and doors, applied over the exterior sheathing but under head flashing and siding to help shed water. In many cases today, the drip cap or a substitute for it are incorporated as part of the assembled window unit.

Mill Stock. In full-rounds and squares they have certain specialized uses, more often than not in conjunction with special cabinet and built-in woodwork installations. In this general class too are the various parts and shapes that comprise stair assemblies or supplements.

Relatively new in the field of trim and moldings are cap molds designed for plywood or hardboard edges. Available, too, for pure decoration are a wide range of carved wood moldings. And then there are full assortments of different types of metal or plastic-covered prefinished trim members for use with thin paneling materials.

40 Furnace, Controls, Registers

Though much work yet remains to be done on your new home's interior, you will no doubt be giving thought to completion timing and occupancy. You'll want to be readying certain things before cooler weather sets in. And one of the "musts" before you can begin thinking of occupancy is the home's heating system. And what provisions are to be made, if any, for summer cooling or air conditioning.

Your heating rough-in work as outlined in Chapter 22 consisted entirely of duct installation where runs occurred within walls, floor joist spaces, or over ceilings. It was suggested that in connection with this work you work out duct sizes with your heating subcontractor so that the same ductwork would be of adequate size for distribution of cool air either from a winter-summer conditioner in a combined unit or on a heating-now, cooling-later basis.

At the risk of being repetitious, it again should be stated that with proper ductwork installed for your heating system, it is a relatively easy matter to select a furnace that permits addition of a cooling coil in the furnace supply plenum, and the installation of a related condenser unit at an outdoor location.

Now, going on to the heating installation and what's necessary to bring it to the operable stage, what are the prerequisites? The first requirement, the electrical service entrance and distribution wiring should already have been completed, inspected and either hot or ready for immediate utility-line connection.

As the second prerequisite, your basement's concrete floor must be poured and finished. Then you can properly and permanently set the furnace in position, bring ductwork to it, wire the controls and connect it to the power outlet. Refer to Chapters 42 and 46 for further details.

In Chapter 22 the subject of cooling was just touched on briefly. There we indicated that duct rough-in work should really include the provision for slightly larger duct sizes so that cooled air could be distributed in the same ducts as the heated air. The presumption is that you will have conferred with your heating subcontractor on this point and will have decided on duct runs suitable for either system even if an additional duct run or two might be needed later to accommodate proper return air flow. This is a fairly simple procedure often used in 2-story homes where it may be desirable to use high-level return register locations for cooling and low-level locations for heating.

Also in Chapter 22, mention was made concerning the various sources where heating-cooling equipment can be purchased. The presumption at this stage is that you've given consideration to the purchase and, in conjunction with your heating subcontractor's counsel, have decided on the general type of equipment to be used.

Now, with the time ready for taking delivery on the furnace and/or air conditioning unit, you've got to get down to brass tacks, firm up the order, spell out which accessories you want, and know exactly what duct and plenum conditions have to be met.

However, you may at this stage want to obtain some further guidance in the choice of equipment brand and the supply source. Understand this . . . heating subcontractors are usually dealers for only one or possibly two brands of heating-cooling equipment. Your agreement with him may or may not have specified a brand of heating equipment that he supplied. In such cases, you may have to take what he can offer; to keep your options open on the kind of equipment selected, make your subcontract agreement indicate that this choice is subject to your approval. And the objective of your choice should be not only to obtain a good performing unit but, if you're choosing a forced-air furnace, you want it to be easily adaptable for cooling purposes.

Your furnace consists essentially of four major elements: fuel-injection or power-connection section; fire-box or heat-exchanger section; blower compartment, and control devices. It's possible to arrange these components vertically within an outer metal casing, and you'll have a furnace called the "high-boy" model. Take the same components and place them into a more compact enclosure with the blower compartment along the side of the heat-exchanger and you have a "low-boy" model furnace used mostly in basement installations. Arrange the components for horizontal flow of air and you have a furnace designed to be

Standard Installation Clearances for Heat-producing Appliances[1]

These clearances apply unless otherwise shown on listed appliances. Appliances shall not be installed in alcoves or closets unless so listed. For installation on combustible floors see footnote 2.

RESIDENTIAL TYPE APPLIANCES For Installation In Rooms Which Are Large[3]		Above Top of Casing or Appliance (Inches)	From Top and Sides of Warm-Air Bonnet or Plenum (Inches)	Appliance From Front[4] (Inches)	From Back (Inches)	From Sides (Inches)	CHIMNEY CONNECTOR (Inches)	VENT CONNECTOR[5] (Inches)
BOILERS AND WATER HEATERS[6]	**FUEL**							
Steam Boilers—15 p.s.i. Water Boilers—2500°F. Water Heaters—200°F. All Water Walled or Jacketed	Automatic Oil or Combination Gas and Oil	6	—	24	6	6	18	—
	Automatic Gas	6	—	18	6	6	—	9
	Solid	6	—	48	6	6	18	—
FURNACES—CENTRAL								
Gravity, Upflow, Downflow. Horizontal and duct Warm Air—250°F. maximum Limit Control	Automatic Oil or Combination Gas and Oil	6[7]	6[9]	24	6	6	18	—
	Automatic Gas	6[7]	6[7]	18	6	6	—	9
	Solid	18[8]	18[8]	48	18	18	18	—
	Electric	6[7]	6[7]	18	6	6	—	—
RANGES—COOKING STOVES		[9]				Front Side / Other Side		
Vented or Unvented	Oil	30	—	—	9	24 / 18	18	—
	Gas	30	—	—	6	6 / 6	—	6
	Solid—Clay lined Firepot	30	—	—	24	24 / 18	18	—
	Solid unlined Firepot	30	—	—	36	36 / 18	18	—
	Electric	30	—	—	6	6	—	—
CLOTHES DRYERS Listed Types	Gas	6	—	24	6	6	—	1
Listed Types	Electric	6	—	24	0	0 one side	—	—

1. Standard clearances may be reduced in existing construction only by affording protection to combustible material as shown below.
2. An appliance may be mounted on a combustible floor if listed for such installation or if the floor is protected in an approved manner.
3. Rooms which are large in comparison to the size of the appliance are those having a volume equal to at least 12 times the total volume of a furnace and at least 16 times the total volume of a boiler. If the actual ceiling height of a room is greater than 8 feet, the volume of a room shall be figured on the basis of a ceiling height of 8 feet.
4. The minimum dimension shall be that necessary for servicing the appliance including access for cleaning and normal care, tube removal, etc.
5. The minimum dimension shall be 18 inches for gas appliances not equipped with draft hoods, except clothes dryers. The dimension may be 6 inches for listed gas appliances equipped with draft hoods and for boilers and furnaces equipped with listed conversion burners and with draft hoods. A vent connector of listed Type B or L venting material may be used with listed gas appliances with draft hoods and may be installed at clearances marked on the material.
6. For a listed oil, combination gas-oil, gas or electric furnace this dimension may be 2 inches if the furnace limit control cannot be set higher than 250°F., or this dimension may be one inch if the limit control cannot be set higher than 200°F.
7. The dimension may be 6 inches for an automatically stoker-fired forced warm-air furnace equipped with 250°F. limit control and with barometric draft control operated by draft intensity and permanently set to limit draft to a maximum intensity of .13-inch water gage.
8. To combustible material or metal cabinets. If the underside of such combustible material or metal cabinet is protected with asbestos millboard at least 1/4 inch thick covered with sheet metal of not less than No. 28 gage, the distance may be not less than 24 inches.

Clearances Required for Heating Plants and vent-chimney connections are provided in this chart adapted from a one in the One-and-Two Family Dwelling Code.

Maximum Reduced Clearances (Inches), with Specified Forms of Protection[1]

TYPE OF PROTECTION — Applied to the Combustible Material Unless Otherwise Specified and Covering All Surfaces Within the Distance Specified as the Required Clearance With No Protection (Thicknesses Are Minimum)	_ Where the Required Clearance with no Protection is:											
	38 Inches			18 Inches			12 Inches		9 Inches	6 Inches		
	Above	Sides and Rear	Chimney or Vent Connector	Above	Sides and Rear	Chimney or Vent Connector	Above	Sides and Rear	Chimney or Vent Connector	Above	Sides and Rear	Chimney or Vent Connector
(a) 1/4" asbestos millboard spaced out 1"[2]	30	18	30	15	9	12	9	8	5	3	2	3
(b) No. 28 Manufacturers' Standard gage steel sheet on 1/4" asbestos millboard	24	18	24	12	9	12	9	8	4	3	2	2
(c) No. 28 Manufacturers' Standard gage steel sheet spaced out 1"[2]	18	12	18	9	6	9	6	4	4	2	2	2
(d) No. 28 Manufacturers' Standard gage steel sheet on 1/8" asbestos millboard spaced out 1"[2]	18	12	18	9	6	9	6	4	4	2	2	2
(e) 1-1/2" asbestos cement covering on heating appliance	18	12	36	9	6	18	6	4	9	2	1	6
(f) 1/4" asbestos millboard on 1" mineral fiber bats reinforced with wire mesh or equivalent	18	12	18	6	6	6	4	4	4	2	2	2
(g) No. 22 Manufacturers' Standard gage steel sheet on 1" mineral fiber bats reinforced with wire or equivalent	18	12	12	4	3	3	2	2	2	2	2	2
(h) 1/4" asbestos cement board or 1/4" asbestos millboard	36	36	36	18	18	18	12	12	9	4	4	4
(i) 1/4" cellular asbestos	36	36	36	18	18	18	12	12	9	3	3	3

. Except for the protection described in (e), all clearances should be measured from the outer surface of the appliance to the combustible material disregarding any intervening protection applied to the combustible material.
. Spacers should be of noncombustible material.
SOURCE: One-and-Two-Family Dwelling Code, 1975 edition, pp. 88-90

hung from floor joists in crawl spaces or to rest on ceiling joists in attic spaces. Most new homes employ low-boy or high-boy models in basements, and high-boy models in utility rooms or closets on the first floor of basementless homes. Sometimes a basementless home employs a vertical furnace in which the supply air flows downward for distribution through an under-floor duct system; these are called counter-flow models. Their use has been predominantly for one-story homes built on concrete floor slabs-on-the-ground.

Safety Factors, Features

Your heating-cooling plant and the home's electrical system are the two most hazardous-to-your-health installations in a home. The dangers are fire and explosion. As a consequence, building codes have detailed provisions covering the safety aspects of heating-cooling and electrical systems.

In this respect, the owner-builder can get a rough idea of how detailed these provisions may be from a brief rundown of the provisions contained in the One-and-Two-Family Dwelling Code for the installation of a conventional direct-fired, blower-forced warm-air furnace.

(1) Do not locate it downstream (in airflow direction) from a refrigerant evaporator or cooling coil unless the heating unit is UL-listed for such use.
(2) The location of such an evaporator in the air discharge duct of a furnace requires that furnace to be approved for operation at a certain static pressure.
(3) Fuel-burning furnaces must have adequate combustion air supply and "adequate" depends on room size and heating capacity of the furnace in BTU/hour.
(4) Combustion air must have airtight separation from the furnace's fan or blower plenum.
(5) A working space of at least 30 inches deep must be provided in front of a furnace and it must be at least 2 feet wide for access to the temperature-limit control and the vent collar on the furnace.
(6) In addition to working space, installation clearance dimensions must be observed for front, sides, back and distance-to-chimney; these can be reduced if certain protective measures are taken (see chart).

Features and Accessories

Though your choice in furnace brands and features may be limited because the purchase has been handled through your heating subcontractor, your knowledge of available features can be of assistance to him in determining the proper model or brand. And if you're handling the furnace purchase through some other source, you'll also need to know just what features can be obtained.

The main working element in a furnace is its heat exchanger. This is the heart of the system and the element is subject to extreme temperatures. Modern heat exchangers are designed to resist corrosion, blistering, cracking. Steel is the most common heat exchanger material and it is treated or coated to be not only tough and temperature-resistant but also long-lasting and durable. Inspect in advance, if possible, the manufacturer's warranty on the heat exchanger. Also, of course, the assembly as a whole.

With gas or oil fuels, a second important element in the functioning of a furnace is the burner assembly. Burner opening ports or flame facilities vary in design but the intent is the same, to maintain uniformity in flame, ignite quietly, and burn without developing hot spots or uneven flow. One recent improvement with some furnaces is the use of electric-spark ignition thereby eliminating the need for an ever-burning pilot, and thus conserving fuel.

Furnace safety features usually include an automatic shut-off device in case fuel service is interrupted. Limit switches are standard, shutting off burners if the unit overheats.

Electric blower-and-motor assemblies are comparable one furnace make to another. But in light of recently rising electric rates, a few manufacturers have started to make use of the more efficient-electrically permanent split-capacitor type of motor in place of the traditional shaded-pole type.

Another alternative that may be offered with certain furnace brands is an extra-cost feature in the form of a two-stage high/low gas burner. It has a low-level of flame (and gas usage) during periods of mild weather and the high-level flame comes on only during severe weather periods.

Nearly all furnace manufacturers will offer certain types of furnace accessories. These may be company-brand accessories or outside brands. Your heating subcontractor may have certain accessory brands he recommends for use with any type of furance. The two principal ones are humidifiers and air cleaners. Neither are essential for a heating system but they do add a measure of interior comfort.

Humidifiers. These introduce moisture vapor into the circulating warm air, and help prevent a heated home from becoming excessively dry—a direct cause of dry skin, scratchy throats and, for some people, impaired breathing. The use of humidifiers may also provide a better interior atmosphere for furniture and plants and help reduce static electricity.

Humidifiers come in several types, some more effective than others. They're offered in a range of sizes to fit home size or furnace capacity. A pipe connection to the cold water supply is needed. A humidistat control device permits

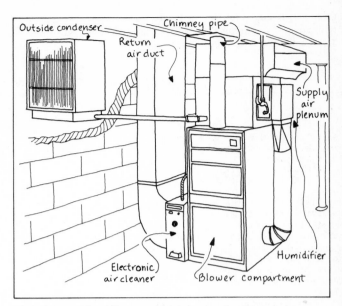

Typical Assembly of Components that comprise an up-to-date yearround air conditioning and heating installation. This arrangement with a humidifier and electronic air cleaner is a deluxe installation with an upflow air direction in the heating unit for basement installation.

automatic operation, turning the device on when more moisture-in-the-air becomes needed. Inquire, if purchasing, about problems with water residues and rust that may apply depending on the characteristics of your water supply.

Air Cleaners. Available in two principal types, electric and nonelectric. What, you say, is the need for air cleaner accessories when every furnace has its own air filter near the blower? The answer is that ordinary air filters remove particles of dust and dirt. But these particles, the air cleaner people say, comprise only the larger particles that amount to about 15 percent of all particles in the air. They say its the smaller particles that cause many problems, including those involving air-carried allergens and bacteria. It costs you nothing to obtain air cleaner literature and to weigh for yourself the possible benefits versus the extra cost.

In electric air cleaners, the removal of particles is handled by oppositely charged plates. Nonelectric air cleaners function by using one or more filtering principles—straining, diffusion, impingement, interception and entrapment of a wide range of particle sizes.

Air cleaners are said to reduce household cleaning chores. Both humidifiers and air cleaner devices attach either to the furnace itself or to an adjacent duct plenum chamber. The humidifier goes onto the supply side with its moisture-adding device inserted within the airstream that goes out to room registers. Air cleaners are installed in a return-air plenum or at the return-air flange connection to the furnace.

Domestic water heaters to provide a home's hot water supply are *not* furnace accessories though they are often installed immediately adjacent to the furnace, and share the chimney vent connection. Water heaters are part of the home's water piping system and within the work jurisdiction of the plumbing trades (see Chapter 41).

Central Cooling and Alternatives

Central cooling equipment gives more uniform comfort throughout a home than does the use of one or more room air conditioners. Central cooling also adds to a system's cost. A rule-of-thumb is that a complete winter-summer conditioner will cost nearly double what a warm-air furnace will cost. This is really a very rough guide due to the fact that in northern climates a small-capacity cooling unit is combined with a high-capacity heating unit while in southern climates, that combination is reversed.

The already-mentioned alternative is installation of a heating unit now that is designed for easy addition of cooling equipment components in the future. If the cooling function is merely deemed desirable at some uncertain or remote future date, then perhaps the most reasonable answer is to size the ducts for cooling and be sure that the furnace chosen allows adequate plenum space for the cooling modification.

Another option that might be appropriate for new homes in the more northern areas of the country, or homes having excellent natural shading from direct sunlight, is the forced-air attic cooling method. Appropriate for locations with relatively few above-80° days, such a system involves the installation of attic or roof-structure fans which exhaust room or attic air. The provision of eave-soffit, gable, or roof vent openings is primarily to eliminate attic moisture that can damage insulation. With powered or forced ventilation through such openings attic-heat buildup is avoided. And an attic ventilating system can be designed to also draw in air from various rooms and exhaust it. Such an exhaust arrangement sets up a circulation pattern that will bring cooler night air into the home.

Another cooling alternative involves use of the furnace's blower. Many furnaces come equipped with a "summer switch" that can be used to manually turn on the blower only. No heating flame, just the blower. This circulates room air. And the cool air introduced into certain rooms by window air conditioners or room units installed in walls can be circulated around the home by the heating system's blower and distribution ducts.

Air Flow and Heat Controls

The present practice in forced warm-air heating is to carry ducts to heating registers located at or near the home's outdoor perimeter as explained in Chapter 22. This procedure helps distribute the warm air over the coldest

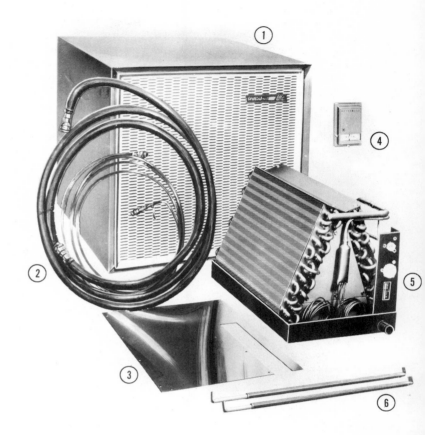

Add-On Cooling Components for a central warm air furnace, now in kit form from McGraw-Edison Company. The various items identified are all included and a complete step-by-step set of instructions is provided.

room surface, the exterior wall. And the register is often placed under a window to counter the added heat loss of the wall.

Obviously, there are some rooms such as the kitchen or perhaps a bathroom where cabinets or plumbing fixtures may interfere with the placement of heating registers at or near the exterior walls. But in living rooms, bedrooms, family rooms, entrance foyers and dens or studies, the perimeter register can be accommodated.

Air flow through registers can be adjusted in two ways— a volume of air can be blown into the room by means of an adjustable damper on the register; and the direction and spread of the air-flow pattern can be adjusted by the louver blades that form the register's cover-grille area. For normal under-window registers, the blades are usually adjusted to fan the air out in an upward direction to cover as much wall surface as possible, in addition to the window surface.

Similarly in foyers, kitchens or bathrooms where a register is apt to be away from an exterior wall or window, the register blades can be set to direct the air toward the exterior wall, toward the opening side of an exterior door or in whatever direction may seem best suited to that specific register.

For temperature control, the heating system is equipped with a remote thermostat. This is simply an on-off switch which is air-activated according to the air temperature. It goes on at a certain temperature when the room air needs heat, goes off when that heat need has been satisfied. The thermostat can be set manually to obtain the desired comfort level.

Your thermostat location should be in a central part of the home in a living or family room or central hallway. It should be located at about chest or shoulder height and at some point where it won't be subjected to air drafts when

doors or windows are opened. It's no problem choosing a thermostat location. Ask your heating subcontractor and he'll indicate one or two optimum locations. But this should be done at time of ductwork installation so that you can include low-voltage wiring from furnace location to thermostat location when your wiring work is being done (see Chapter 24).

Furnace Installation

The placement of most basement and closet furnaces is simply a matter of suitable dolly transport carrier from delivery truck into the home. Or a little muscle, or both. In concrete-floored basements, warm-air furnaces rest on the concrete directly leveled-and-plumbed by shims. In closet installations over wood floors, the furnace rests on a protective mat of sheet metal or asbestos millboard unless the heating unit has been approved for direct placement on combustible materials.

After positioning and leveling, the furnace supply-and-return plenum chambers are mounted. These will have been shop-fabricated either by your heating subcontractor or a sheet-metal shop. The furnace will have metal-flanged collar projections for these connections. The plenums are simply enlarged sheet metal enclosures or ducts to which one or more standard-sized ducts can be connected. And the plenum must be sized properly to fit the furnace flanged opening.

Branch ductwork or individual duct runs to the register locations were completed as part of the rough-in work described in Chapter 22, but near the central support beam of the home the branch duct ends have been left open. The duct connections to these open ends will be made to fit openings properly provided in the main supply duct, which has also been shop-fabricated in one or more sections.

From the heating plan you worked out with the heating subcontractor to guide rough-in work, he will have taken off the correct supply duct dimensions and branch opening locations. The main supply duct then will be fabricated in either of two ways. For smaller compact homes, the main supply will probably be a uniformly rectangular size throughout its length. There will be branch outlet openings with connecting flanges at each opening. In larger homes or where the house design is not just a simple rectangle, the main supply duct is apt to be fabricated in a volume-reduction manner. This means it starts off at the furnace plenum connection with a relatively wide-or-deep duct which, after one or more branch take-offs, is reduced in width or depth. Further reductions in size may occur as the supply main reaches more distant branches. The branch connections are often curved off the main supply by means of 45° elbow connections that provide smoother air flow into branches.

With fabrication work done in a well-equipped shop by an experienced duct fabricator, you should have little difficulty in mounting the plenums, hanging the main supply

Cooling Coil for furnaces in low-ceiling basements is this "FlatTop" design by York indicated on the left. Right photo indicates traditional A-shaped coil.

with sheet metal straps from the joist bottoms and connecting up the branches. All fitting of plenum or duct over flanges is followed with sheet metal screw fasteners. It is the practice of may heating subcontractors to insure against duct air leakage by wrapping each joint with a heat-resistant adhesive tape. In the case of some air-conditioning installation, all supply and branch ducts not only have wrapped joints but are provided with complete wrap-around duct insulation. The purpose is not only to avoid duct heat loss or heat gain but also to reduce the system's air-passage noise level.

The final step in conjunction with your duct distribution system is to attach room registers. These are fastened with sheet metal screws to the duct ends but this is frequently not done until all floor coverings including carpeting have been installed and the system is ready for final balancing and adjustment.

In most installations one step remains: connecting up the return air duct. This will normally be a straight rectangular duct run that connects up from two to four return branches. These branches normally occur near the central part of the home and may involve just a very short run from the main return to a floor grille, or vertical branches in partitions to wall grilles in first and second floor rooms or halls. The return air duct installation is essentially a duplicate of the supply runs but in a shorter, more direct route. The main return comes to a plenum which fits the return-air opening flanges at the blower compartment of the unit.

Furnace Hookup and Adjustments

Though it's quite possible you have the skill for making electrical and fuel-line connections to your furnace, this work should be handled by your heating subcontractor. The reasoning? The connections are few but important. The expert installer will take the time to inspect each connection carefully, making the connections in just the right manner. It will take him a relatively short time to do so. Your rough-in wiring work should have brought an electrical outlet on an individual circuit for furnace use, and it should be adjacent to the furnace location. Your plumbing rough-in work should have included installation of a black-pipe gas line from the meter location to the furnace location; or, for an oil or LP-gas installation, provision of proper-sized copper tubing from the tank location to the furnace.

Your heating subcontractor can easily make the connections, and will have the required fittings for changing from rough-in provision to the furnace itself. At the same time, he will want to make certain adjustments or settings to the furnace's fan or blower switch and the limit switch. He'll

connect up the wiring leads from the thermostat location and also connect up the thermostat. While he may start up the unit to test the various functions, he will also probably want to hold off final adjustments until such time as all registers have been installed and the home is ready for occupancy. At this later time, he will also make the final smoke-pipe connections including that for the water heater.

First-time startup of a heating system involves accurate knowledge of the equipment involved and the various control adjustments that need to be checked and revised. Your heating subcontractor probably enjoys this adjustment work more than any other part of a heating installation, will therefore be conscientious in getting the equipment to operate as it should. He will be equipped with certain instruments that will help him check adjustments and settings. And a part of his work at this time will involve system balancing, a procedure that makes adjustments to register dampers so that the various sections of your home receive a suitable flow of supply air, and a sufficient steadiness of return air flow is established.

A part of your agreement with your heating subcontractor should involve provision for his return to check the system's operation after it has been functioning for a four-to-eight week period. And you would be well advised to make arrangements, if possible, for him to make annual check-up visits before the start of each heating season.

Solar Energy As A Heat Source

At this writing, there have been roughly three years of widespread research and publicity about entirely new methods for harnessing the sun's energy and converting it to residential heating needs. Despite the publicity and despite the fact that since early 1974 there's been a Solar Energy Industries Association, there is presently no system developed that is very much beyond a prototype or experimental stage.

There have been a number of homes, new and old, that have been provided with some sort of solar energy conversion equipment. Yet, these installations have functioned only in furnishing *supplemental* energy since the solar energy system is almost always accompanied by a backup, conventional system needed for periods of high heat load or continuously cloud days. The installations have further been characterized by relatively high initial costs.

Nevertheless, the caliber of companies and research technicians who are working diligently on solar energy applications suggests that there may be some excellent possibilities in the not-too-distant future, and that costs may be reduced sufficiently to enable some sort of solar energy system practical for everyday single-family housing.

41 Plumbing Fixtures and Trim

Any home owner who has ever received a bill from the tradesman who just replaced his kitchen sink faucet has taken the first step to becoming a plumber.

Plumbing is said to be one of the building trades requiring top skills. Hogwash. The ability to use a pipe wrench, gas torch, and some common sense in installing plumbing fixtures, waste fittings and supply-valve connections, is more a matter of doing-to-learn rather than learning-to-do.

Like other trades, the mystique is coming out of plumbing work and this is being accomplished mostly by the adoption of up-to-date merchandising methods on the part of plumbing supplies manufacturers. Once plumbing fixtures and their connecting parts had limited availability. Plumbing wholesalers would sell only to plumbing contractors and not to anyone walking in off the street. Now, the distribution picture has changed entirely. You can pick up a sink or lavatory or tub or shower and all you need in order to connect it is right there at your nearest lumber-supply retailer, hardware or home center outlet. What's more, you can pick it up package by package, with just the right amount of connecting parts in a single package to make a single fixture installation!

Buying plumbing supplies in kit form from a retail outlet will probably mean paying a slightly higher price than would purchasing through a plumbing wholesaler supply house (if they'll take your account). Your plumbing subcontractor may also act as a dealer for certain plumbing fixtures or supply. Talk with him about your purchasing alternatives. But first let him know you have other places you can buy from. One nice feature about kit purchases . . . the package gives you the installation instructions in detail including diagrams of how the parts fit together.

At this stage of construction, your waste-drain and water supply piping is just about complete, at least that part of it concealed within the framing. And now, you're ready to proceed with fixture installation, except that your bathtub and metal or plastic stall shower unit may already be in place because they needed to be fitted to partition framing.

How should you proceed? Probably by a room-by-room procedure in which the fixture mountings and pipe connections are all done within a given area before you proceed to the next area. The actual fixtures, the optional ones an owner-builder may choose, and the number of them will vary considerably according to the home's design. But for descriptive purposes the features listed here are those considered typical and which usually occur at least once in every home.

☐ Bathroom—three-fixture grouping consisting of toilet or water closet, tub-with-shower and lavatory. This also basically, applies to a powder room in which the tub is omitted and also to a shower-bathroom in which a shower receptor or stall unit replaces the tub;

☐ Kitchen—the sink is the principal installation here, but brief consideration is given to the two most common built-in sink accessories . . . dishwasher and garbage disposer;

☐ Laundry—may be part of the kitchen or bathroom area but the plumbing provision is off by itself and consists of connections for an automatic clothes washer and often a dryer;

☐ Water Heater—in basement, utility room or closet, and usually close to the incoming water supply line.

Now, even before the fixture mounting and piping connections, there's the fixture-and-trim selection. Perhaps you have already settled on the size and general type of fixture that you want for each location. But this choice has to be firmed up now to a specific size, model number and color. Plus the specific valve or operating trim.

The Installation Parts

Each fixture mounting relates to some structural part. Bathtubs are hung on supports or fastened directly to wall framing. Stall shower receptors rest on subfloors while metal/plastic shower cabinets are contained by framing but are secured to the receptor. Lavatories may be wall-hung units but more commonly are supported by vanity cabinets.

Sinks are generally cabinet-mounted. Clothes washers are stationary appliances that connect to plumbing lines through hoses.

With certain fixtures, there are three groups or sets of parts, each with a plumbing term to describe them:

- tubulars—the pipe sections, P-traps and connection units that run from a fixture's drain outlet-and-overflow to connect to the wall drain-waste stub, traditionally of chrome-plated brass but also now in plastic;
- supplies—the small and flexible water pipes and stop-valves that connect between the fixture valve(s) and the wall water-supply stubs;
- trim—the above-fixture operating handle(s) for a mixing valve or for individual hot/cold faucet valves; the units include mounting nuts and cover trim for attaching the trim to the fixture.

There are variations in the above parts to fit them to different types of fixtures. Lavatory and sink parts are

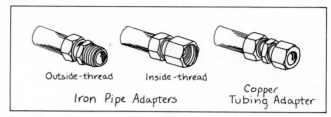

Transition Fittings allow the installer to change from one type of piping material or connection method to another. Shown are common fittings for transitions in water supply piping; a wide range of similar fittings will handle other piping and pipe-change situations.

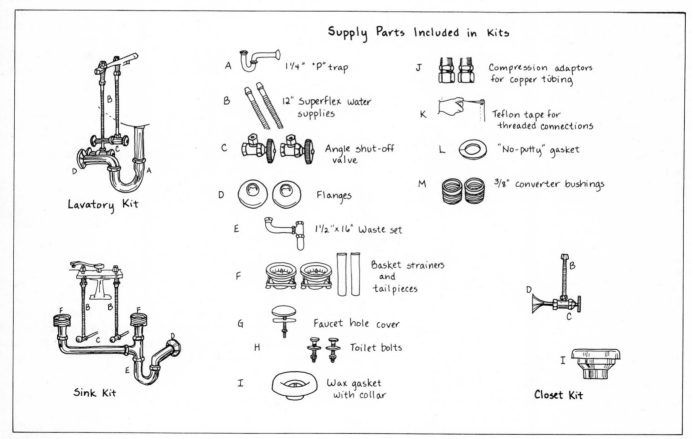

Trap and Water Supply Accessories, sometimes called fixture supplies and trim, can now be purchased in "all-together" packages that provide the do-it-yourself installer with the proper selection of parts or fittings for a single installation. Shown here are the elements that comprise lavatory, sink and water closet kits made and packaged by the King division of Jameco Industries. The letters in each kit sketch refer to the Supply Parts listing. Many manufacturers of plumbing supplies now package products in this convenient manner and include detailed instruction sheets.

roughly the same except that for kitchen sinks the popular style has a double-bowl or double-compartment sink which employs a dual-drain tail-piece (tubular). Water supply lines to kitchen sink and lavatory fixtures having separate faucets have traditionally been spaced 8 inches apart for the sinks and 4 inches apart for the lavatories. While this spacing is still usually observed in rough-in piping or wall stubs, the spacing no longer holds for fixtures that will be trimmed with single-handle mixing valves. So slight variations occur with each fixture and reference must be made to both the fixture provision for type of trim desired and to the needs of that particular type of trim. Flexible supplies can now also be obtained in plastic, as well as chromed brass or copper; fixture valve parts and fittings are of bronze with a chrome finish on exposed parts although molded, clear plastic handles have become widely popular.

As a rule, the best route in selecting fixtures and trim fittings is to compare brands and see what line of fixtures most appeals to you. If possible, stick to just one or two brands rather than choosing a different brand for each fixture. Ask your plumbing subcontractor for suggestions. In choosing colored fixtures, remember that there is good color match between fixtures of the same brand but noticeable variation in the same color when fixtures of different manufacturers are compared. After you've settled on the fixtures, proceed in choosing trim fittings. Then your needs for the tubulars and supplies will be apparent.

One factor to keep in mind here—and this information is something you can probably get from your plumbing subcontractor—your choice in these parts and components should be something your local building inspector or official has seen before and is familiar with. In many areas, the newer plastic products are being accepted rapidly and are desirable for the owner-builder, but they may not yet have found acceptance with the local authorities. Remember that your objective is to install products that will let your plumbing installation pass inspection without hassle or delay.

The use of certain materials or products should be on a match-up basis. For example, this means that your normal plumbing installation might have: brass tubulars/supplies with a cast iron/steel pipe DWV system; brass tubulars/supplies with a copper DWV system; PVC tubulars and CPVC/PB supplies with a PVC or ABS plastic DWV system.

Bath Area—Tub and Shower

Many bathtub installations include the piping and water-mixing arrangement for supplying a shower head as well as the tub-filling spout.

Bathtubs were once almost 100 percent of enameled cast iron although, for a time, many low-cost homes used enameled steel. Both are still used but within recent years there's been a rapid increase in use of reinforced molded plastic tubs.

With the plastic tubs has come a new concept . . .

complete tub-and-recess components either in a single one-piece assembly or in 3- or 4-member components that assemble quickly at the job. One-piece plastic stall shower units are also coming into vogue.

The porcelain-enameled cast iron tubs (as well as the newer molded plastic units) come in a range of sizes that varies from one manufacturer to another. The usual widths are 2-½ to 4 feet. Lengths, 4 to 6 feet. Typical tub depth is 12-to-15 inches above floor level. A variety of special sizes or types, such as sunken models, have been introduced in recent years but are principally sold in the luxury home market. Porcelain-on-steel tubs come in limited sizes, usually 4-½ or 5 feet long, 2-½ feet wide, and 15 inches deep.

Reinforced fiberglass plastic tubs first came into common use around 1970. These one-piece tub-and-recess units solve the problem of getting a watertight joint between wall surface and tub edge. The recess walls may or may not extend to full ceiling height depending on what individual manufacturer offers. In some cases, the unit may include a ceiling as well and this also applies to the tub-and-recess types that come in component sections for job assembly.

Cleaning and maintenance of the molded plastic units require nonabrasive materials. The manufacturers usually recommend just the ordinary liquid household detergents. Users of the fiberglass tubs report that the surfaces are warmer to the touch, don't soil as quickly as conventional porcelain, and are quite easy to clean. The plastic units usually include molded-in soap holders and sometimes seats as well.

Most bathrooms in smaller stock-plan homes are likely to include provision for a 5 foot long recessed bathtub and, in second or master bathrooms, stall showers that are 3 feet square. Before shopping for fixtures know what sizes are called for and whether or not a wall-change or modification will accommodate a different size.

Fiberglass tubs are considerably easier to handle. A complete tub-and-recess unit in one piece weighs under 200 pounds while the conventional cast iron tub by itself runs more than 300 pounds. Perhaps more significant to an individual owner-builder is the saving in wall-finish work that the one-piece or 4-component tub-and-recess assembly provides. This alone might be worth the extra cost that plastic units run over conventional fixtures. A further advantage to the molded-plastic type fixture is ease of repair at the site in case of damage. Plastic repairs kits help fix up any damaged spots, which could prove a real delay and cost-adjustment factor for porcelain-finish fixtures.

Bath Area—Lavatory and Closet

In most new homes, vanity lavatory units are used in main bathrooms and powder rooms. Wall-hung lavatories have diminished in use and, in many cases, have given way to synthetic molded plastic material used with the vanity cabinets rather than the traditional china or porcelain-enameled cast iron fixtures.

 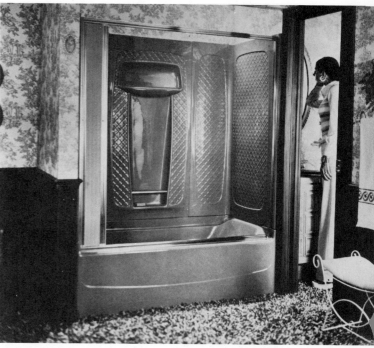

Reinforced Fiberglass Bathtubs have become popular among professional builders. At left is a complete one-piece molded tub-and-recess unit by Universal-Rundle. At the right, Borg-Warner's four-piece set consisting of molded plastic tub and three recess panels which come in a single carton for assembly at the site.

Fiberglass plastic fixtures are warm to the touch, clean easily using liquid detergent and are much lighter in weight than conventional cast iron tubs. Most molded tub units include integral soap dishes or shelves and grab-bar handles. Some models offer a ceiling or top component for building-in, as in the left photo.

The molded plastic counter-and-basin units come in two types: acrylic-faced and cast methacrylate, both of which were initially introduced with veining that simulated a polished marble surface. As a result, these units have come to be known as "synthetic marble" countertop lavatories.

Vanity lavatory cabinets install just like kitchen cabinets. Slide into position, level, and screw to framing members. Plumbing connections are made after the cabinet is in place and the counter-lavatory attached to the base cabinet.

Toilets

At first glance in plumbing fixture displays, you might say . . . "Well, the old W.C. hasn't changed very much from the old days." In appearance, you would, in most cases, be correct. In materials, internal parts and other respects, you'd be wrong. Just in the past few years there have been a considerable number of changes. Mostly for the better.

Vitreous china is still the standard material for closet bowls but some manufacturers are now offering an injection-molded ABS-plastic toilet tank whose special liner has an insulative quality that reduces or eliminates condensation on the outside of the tank.

There are significant differences in the method of trap-ping and flush-functioning of water closets. And as might be expected, the better it functions, the more it costs. A wash-down closet is the least expensive but the noisiest. A reverse-trap closet has quieter siphon action, is less likely to clog than the washdown type, but is still not much more in cost. Best of the three common types is the siphon-jet closet with a larger trapway and more of the bowl surface water-covered for less chance of fouling, less clogging, and quieter operation (see illustration).

All three main types of closets conform to a standard 12 inch rough-in dimension . . . 12 inches from the face of the wall to the center of the closet connection flange. One factor you may wish to consider in your selection is the advantage of the elongated bowl. This style brings the front rim of the bowl 2 inches further into the room although the rough-in dimension remains the same. The elongated bowl is more comfortable to the sitter, more attractive and, because of its greater interior water surface, more sanitary and easier to keep clean.

Two additional types of water closets, not widely available in retail outlets, are the so-called low-profile one-piece units and the wall-hung residential closets. Both are relatively expensive, see more use in luxury homes, and are to be avoided by the economy-minded owner-builder. In the same class is the bidet, a feminine hygiene floor-mount

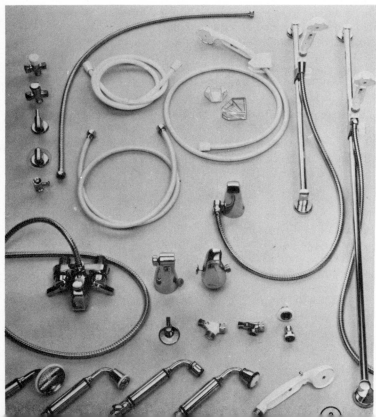

fixture widely used in Europe and South America. If interested, owner-builders can obtain data from any of the major plumbing fixture manufacturers (or find more information in *Book of Successful Bathrooms*).

One quite recent innovation in toilets is a water-conserving type which uses substantially less water for flushing purposes. Usually, 30-to-45 percent of all water used in a home goes for flushing toilets. A toilet saving 30 percent of the flushing water could be a worthwhile fixture, especially in high-water-cost areas. These fixtures use a special flushing action with a smaller tank.

Kitchen Sink Area

If you're like most new home owners, you will choose a stainless steel sink. Once made of enameled cast iron like bathtubs, kitchen sinks are now predominantly of stainless steel. With stainless, you get a greater choice in style and function. One sink manufacturer offers a dozen different styles of two-compartment models, three different three-compartment sinks, and a couple that include surface space for a built-in mixer-blender.

Choose your sink and valve fitting trim together. This will involve a decision between separate control faucets for hot/cold water or a single-handle mixing valve control. In either case, the trim fitting is a one-piece assembly, but the drilling on the sink fixture must accommodate the type of trim fitting chosen.

If you opt for a garbage-grinding disposer unit for installation with the sink, you will have to choose a sink whose drain connection will permit attachment of the grinder unit.

Dishwashers involve different requirements. Your rough-in piping need not include a special drain or supply connection since these can be run from the sink as long as the dishwasher is to be located in the normal next-to-sink location. Dishwashers employ a small waste hose whose

flow is under pumping pressure; the connection is generally made to the tubular P-trap for the sink using a tubular that has a tap-in fitting for that purpose. Select the tubular now whether you plan to install a dishwasher immediately or some time in the near future.

Incidentally, if a dishwasher will be included in the future, make certain that your cabinet space on one side or the other of the sink (preferably the right) is of sufficient width to accommodate a built-in dishwasher. This will normally mean a clear interior space 24 inches wide, or wider.

Types of Toilets in cross-section to show how their design and operation vary. The toilet's flushing efficiency is dependent on both the flushing mechanism and the bowl design. The three principal types are: WASHDOWN ... least costly toilet but also the noisiest; it has smaller exposed water surface and thus a larger area of the bowl subject to staining or contamination; in some areas, local authorities will not approve this type; REVERSE TRAP ... this type has a rear rounded trapway for more efficient flushing action and more exposed water surface for less bowl staining; SIPHON JET ... still more water surface and less interior exposed china surface; the trapway, engineered to be larger than that of reverse-trap toilets and more rounded, results in better flowing action.

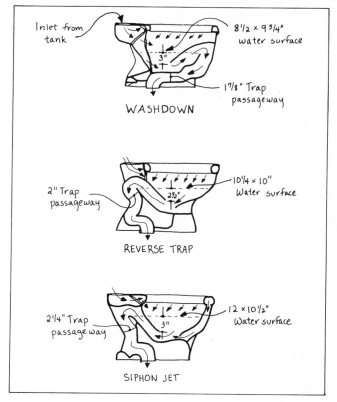

Up-To-Date Shower Equipment includes the following items: (1) plastic-molded cabinet shower unit made by Gerber Plumbing Fixtures with a lock-together panel system that needs no supplemental fastening; the shower's rounded corners make cleaning easier and its stone receptor is dip-resistant and leakproof; (2) a single-handle shower control by Delta Faucet Company is called "Scald-Guard" because it has a valve admitting cold water first; (3) assorted types of hand-held flexible pipe shower units; these Ondine-made shower-heads and their various mounting accessories allow custom arrangement in tub or shower stall; (4) pulsating water flow is the latest innovation in shower heads; this head by Moen is said to give a massagelike feeling but it has a shift lever that converts operation to normal flow.

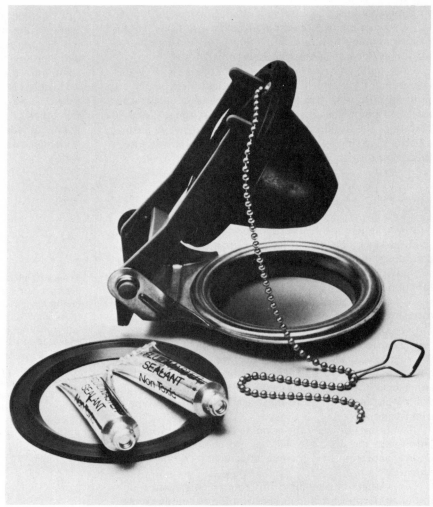

Anti-Siphon Ballcock and Outflow Valve overcomes the cause of leaky or dripping toilet valves. The ballcock (left) is made by Fluidmaster and is adjustable for tank water height. It has double "O-rings" to insure a tight water seal and its valve is made of stainless steel and Celcon plastic to provide corrosion-free service. No rod or floatball required. The outflow valve is of the flapper type made of vinyl and hinged so it can't become misaligned; the valve seat cements to the tank opening.

Dishwasher and mixer-blender installations in the sink area also require a 115-volt electrical connection, so wiring to an outlet box should have been provided if these built-in units were indicated on your kitchen plans. If the units are not to be installed immediately, simply tape the wiring leads, fold within the outlet box and provide a blank cover plate for the box.

If you chose your sink model early and gave the dimensions to the countertop fabricator, your sink mounting hole cut-out is already provided. If this wasn't done and you have a hole-less counter already installed, you can still make the cut-out using a power jig-saw to make a continuous cut by means of rounded small-radius corners.

When purchasing or selecting the sink, make sure you find out how that model attaches to the counter. In some cases the sink will be a rimless model that needs a separate mounting rim and clamping devices. In newer model sinks, built-in rims simplify the installation work and the sink has integral attachment points for clamping to the counter (see illustration).

Adding to a sink's initial cost but having added value in one way or another are some sink accessories which may or may not be available from your sink source. These include:

soap or lotion liquid dispenser
water purifier
instant hot water dispenser (with choice of temperature)
undercounter water chiller
hardwood cutting board over a sink compartment
remote drain control for sink-top mounting.

Laundry and Utility Area

Every new home used to be built with a laundry tub, or "tray" as it was frequently called. Way back it was a two-compartment tray. Then, when wringer-washers became popular, it was usually a single-compartment unit. These are still available and sometimes in some areas still provided in new homes. But in most new homes, the laundry tray or deep sink has disappeared since today's automatic clothes washers make it unnecessary. For those homemakers still interested in doing hand washables, trays or deep sinks are available; another possible alternative is a kitchen sink having two compartments, one of which is about 10 inches deep.

Within the past few years a more startling change in laundry facilities has occurred in many new home designs and stock plans. That is the placement of laundry appliances and a small cabinet area on the first floor rather down in the basement. And in some new home designs the laundry area and appliances are located near the bedroom-bath

part of the home rather than the kitchen-utility area. Obviously, with automatic washer-dryers, laundering has become a chore which doesn't need constant working at but is more often done by the homemaker on an intermittent-visit basis to the appliances while in the process of accomplishing other household duties.

The plumbing connections for an automatic washer differ from those for standard plumbing fixtures. Water supply lines, hot and cold, are brought to the washer location. Supply stubs are bracketed to an inch-board or 2X4 nailed between stud spaces at a height of about 40 to 42 inches above the floor, sufficient to be above the normal height of the appliance. To these stubs are connected individual manual valves with threaded spouts for standard 3/4 inch hose connections. The appliance comes with such hose and fittings. The drain-waste connection for a washer is an upright open-ended 2 inch waste pipe which comes up to about the same height as the supply lines; from the washer, a drain hose slips into the open end of the pipe.

New Water Closet Features include water savings design and tank-condensation prevention. At left is the "Conserver" model two-piece closet by Briggs which operates on 30 percent less water than a conventional closet without affecting the efficiency of the flushing action. Center photo shows the lightweight "ThermoTank" design by Universal-Rundle which is made of molded ABS-plastic and weighs only 8 pounds; it has an inner liner to prevent moisture collection on the outside. At right, a low-silhouette closet by Borg-Warner, equipped with a molded ABS tank on a siphon-jet china closet. In use, it flushes with only 3½ gallons rather than 5 gallons required by conventional closets.

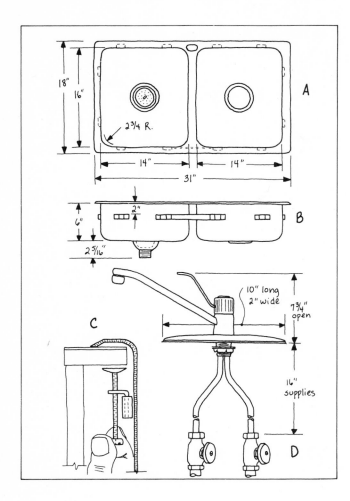

Kitchen Sinks for countertop drop-in and their fittings vary considerably in their installation dimensions according to sink model and fitting chosen. Shown are the dimensions for a typical 2-compartment stainless steel sink such as the narrow-ledge Model 3118 by Zeigler-Harris in sketch (A) which is designed for a single-handle faucet. Ledge sinks with wider back-rims for supply and hose-spray fittings are offered by sink manufacturers as well as the narrow-ledge types. Sink sketch (B) shows in elevation a sink having twin bowls of same 6-inch depth but some sink producers offer deeper bowls on one or both sides. Sketch (C) indicates typical rim-mount to countertop with a series of bolts that slip through brackets which come attached to the sink exterior. In sketch (D), a one-handle faucet for wide-ledge mounting; this "Chateau" model by Moen features extra long supplies for direct connection to stops.

The domestic water heater, source of a home's hot water supply, is usually located near the furnace or heating-cooling unit. This permits running of the vent from a gas water heater to the smoke pipe between the furnace and the chimney. Involved in this run, too, is a draft diverter to protect the pilots of these gas appliances from chimney down-drafts and flame-out.

No venting is needed with an electric water heater and, thus no need for it to be adjacent to the furnace. But otherwise the plumbing or running of supply pipes and installation of overload protection is essentially the same for either type of fuel.

Choose your water heater carefully and consult with your plumbing subcontractor on the purchase. The first matter is proper sizing for your present and future family needs. Utility companies and water heat manufacturers usually have some sort of easy reference chart in which you can check your family size and find an appropriate size heater-and-tank.

One confusing factor on water heater selection: tank sizes for electric water heaters seem to run larger than for gas. This is due to a difference in the rate of heating water for gas and electricity. Gas heats water faster. A tank of a given size thus takes less time to come back to a usable level after hot water usage. This ability to heat up a fresh supply is known as the appliance's "recovery rate." Due to this

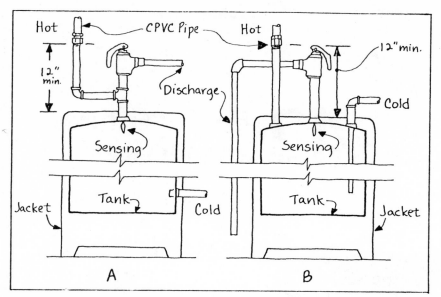

Water Heater Connections may vary somewhat according to local codes or practices. Shown here are alternative piping arrangements at the top of the heater, both installations in visible positions for easy inspection, check and maintenance. CPVC plastic water pipe can be used on hot water lines as well as cold and for water as high as 180°F but the plumbing code may require connections to be made at a certain distance from the heater, typically 12 inches as shown here. Transition fittings are used where the metal pipe changes to plastic.

slower recovery for electric water heaters, it has become the practice to provide larger tanks for the electric type water heaters.

In most areas of the country, preference has been for gas water heaters because of lower costs, lower initial appliance cost and lower monthly usage cost. How long this favorable-to-gas economic situation will prevail in any given area is anybody's guess.

Accident-Prone Areas

The bathroom and the utility room or area are the two prime hazard areas in your home.

The bathtub and shower fixtures, particularly, are dangerous for both children and adults. The U.S. Consumer Product Safety Commission not long ago sponsored a research study that revealed slips and falls were the most common cause of tub-and-shower-related injuries, but that burns from scalding water could be even more serious. A copy of the report is available from CPSC (see appendix).

And in connection with gas water heaters, CPSC has issued a special "Fact Sheet" (No. 65) describing some of the safety factors relating to these appliances. The sheet points out that voluntary industry standards observed by most water heater manufacturers now include provisions for certain safety features (see illustration). The "Fact Sheet" gives tips for the home occupant on proper use and maintenance including suitable settings for water temperature control.

42 Electric Fixtures and Devices

Supplemental Lighting a functional nature above; thin-tube fluorescent fixtures attached to under side of kitchen wall cabinets provide good working light over counter surfaces; other desirable rooms: entrance foyers, bathrooms, utility-laundry rooms, dens or hobby rooms.

A lamp, in electric lighting circles, is not something that sits on a table and sheds light but rather the light bulb or fluorescent tube itself. Tradition has it that the incandescent bulb is most suitable for home use while the fluorescents see use only in stores, offices and schools.

Actually, there have been residential fluorescent fixtures available, the most commonly seen a circular tube used to a considerable extent in kitchens. However, most lighting fixtures are designed for incandescent bulb lighting.

As mentioned in Chapter 35, fluorescents are a logical choice where relatively high levels of light are desirable. The availability of fluorescent tubes in a "warm white" types has long since met earlier objections of color distortion on food and skin.

Your choice of electric fixtures is in part a matching of the type of fixture to its location and use, and partly a matter of selecting a style that suits your room decor. The latter is particularly true of fixtures for dining areas, family rooms, and hallways. Lighting in living rooms and bedrooms tends to be provided by portable lamps on the floor or table.

There are roughly three large categories of electric lighting fixtures designed for permanent attachment to electrical outlet boxes and operated by manual or automatic switches. These include fixtures in which style or decorative value outweighs the functional aspect of lighting efficiency; fixtures which emphasize fulfilling a certain function but have decorative considerations; fixtures whose purpose is almost entirely utilitarian in nature.

In the first category would be those lighting fixtures commonly used in front entry foyers, porches, staircase halls, living-dining rooms and perhaps one or more outdoor lights. In the second category, you would include typical hall, bedroom, bath and study-den fixtures. And in the third class would be lighting fixtures in the kitchen, laundry, utility room, basement and garage.

Bedrooms have become something of a special situation with the common solution a plug-in table lamp for use on vanity tables, desks or drawer chests. Many new home builders provide no wall or ceiling light fixture in these rooms but often have at least one convenience outlet wired to a wall switch at the bedroom door. In some cases, wardrobe or walk-in bedroom closets are equipped with ceiling lights either pull-chain, door-switch, or wall-switch operated.

Nearly all conventional lighting fixtures, except recessed types, are mounted via screw attachment to outlet boxes. With ceiling outlet boxes, frequent practice employs a box hanger strap that nails to the framing and incorporates a threaded stud that serves as a base for fixture support.

Recessed fixtures, designed so that only a thin fixture cover and glass insert are visible from within the room, are furnished with metal rough-in enclosures that contain the lamp holders. These enclosures, often furnished with

Suggested Home Lighting Levels

| Room Size | A. Surface and Pendent Fixtures* | | B. Recessed Fixtures* | C. Wall Lighting** |
	Minimum Size of Shield	Minimum Bulb(s) or Watts per sq. ft.	Minimum Wattage or Watts per sq. ft.	Length of light source; or Wattage and spacing of fixtures
VERY SMALL (Up to 125 sq. ft.)	12" to 15"	One 100-watt or Three 40-watt	150-watt fixture for each 75 sq. ft. floor area or fraction thereof	6' or 75-watt fixtures on 3' centers
AVERAGE (125 to 225 sq. ft.)	15" to 17"	One 150-watt or Four 40-watt	150-watt fixture for each 75 sq. ft. floor area or fraction thereof	8' to 12' or 75-watt fixtures on 3' centers
LARGE (Over 225 sq. ft.)	17" to 22"	100 watts for each 100 sq. ft. *footnote	150-watt fixture for each 75 sq. ft. floor area or fraction thereof	16' to 20' or 75-watt fixtures on 3' centers

*More than one fixture is usually needed on ceilings and/or walls for minimum general lighting. Dining area fixture should provide predominant downlight on table.

**Fixture recommendation applies to lighting one long wall. For most effective design, consult electric utility, lighting fixture distributor, or manufacturers' booklets.

mounting straps, must be nailed to the framing work during the electrical rough-in work (see Chapter 24). Openings are cut in the wall-ceiling board to fit closely around the metal box; later the cover trim conceals this rough edge.

All electric lighting fixtures are designed to employ only a certain maximum wattage in lamps used with the fixture. The limitations in size/wattage of lamps are usually indicated on the label or the fixture and should be observed when lamping the fixture.

Your choice of fixtures is best made at an electrical supply store which has a lighting fixture display. Some electrical supply firms with such displays are mostly frequented by the home-buying customers of builders or electrical contractors. The fixtures are marked with retail prices. Contractors and builders, when ordering fixtures chosen by their customers, get discounts from the marked prices. When you shop for fixtures in these stores, remember that you are a builder and entitled to the normal builder discount; if they say you don't have an account with them, say you're thinking about opening up one or that this job will be on a cash basis.

Switches and Receptacles

You know what a switch is. A receptacle, electrically speaking, is something you plug into . . . that part of the outlet box assembly to which wiring is connected and which will receive an electrical plug. Switches and receptacles are pretty much alike in the way they mount to

Guidelines for Lighting Intensities are given in this chart prepared by the American Home Lighting Institute. The chart was issued prior to the focussing of attention on energy conservation and the wattage intensities given may accept a bit of trimming in the interests of lower utility bills.

the boxes. They come equipped with screw tabs and often with screws also, the tabs being properly spaced to fit predrilled and prethreaded holes in the outlet boxes.

To complete the electrical system installation which you began by installing boxes and wiring runs, you now must obtain the lighting fixtures, switches, receptacles and perhaps a number of special devices and connect them properly to the wiring and to the boxes for support. The final step will then be the installation of fixture trim, switch, and receptacle cover plates.

The procedural order is not especially important, but to accustom the owner-builder's hands to the stripping of wire leads, following the electrical circuit sketches and screwing the various devices into place, it's suggested that you begin in the bedroom areas where the lighter No. 14 gauge wire is used and the switch circuits are simple. Proceed room by room, circuit by circuit. That is, start in a remote bedroom at the end of one circuit and proceed to work, outlet by outlet, back on that circuit toward the distribution center. Then, start with another bedroom circuit. When all branch, general-purpose or lighting circuits have been completed, proceed with the small appliance circuits to kitchen-dining-laundry areas. Then, to the individual circuits that receive receptacles such as the clothes wash outlet and the 230-volt range and drywer outlets. Then, conclude with the devices that connect to your low-voltage signal circuits.

One word of counsel with respect to certain lighting fixtures hung on walls or ceilings. If they are reasonably large or movable, it may be advisable to omit connection of the fixture until such time as painting, wallpapering and other decorating work has been completed. If you think a fixture will get in your way, wait until decorating is finished; if you're in a hurry to have electrical service in operation before decorating, tape the wiring leads to such omitted fixtures but join up the other parts of the circuit.

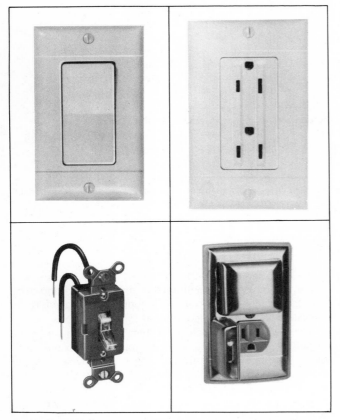

Switch and Outlet Devices for control of or access to the home's electrical system come in a variety of types and styles. Shown here are devices produced by the Sierra Electric Company. Upper left is the fashionable wall switch which operates on the rocker-arm principle; at right is a matching convenience outlet receptacle and wall plate. (Note: both plates are same size but photo size was different.)

Bottom left photo shows a Sierra toggle switch with pigtail connections. Called "double-insulated" because it is totally enclosed by nonmetallic insulating materials and all live conducting parts are hidden to give a "deadback" electrical construction.

Lower right photo indicates a convenience outlet with protective cover plates for outdoor use. The Sierra-made outlet cover is in corrosion-resistant stainless steel with a PVC gasket to prevent moisture intrusion when outlet is not in use.

In choosing switch and receptacle devices, you want to make sure they are properly rated and meet approval of Underwriters Laboratories. This latter is indicated by a UL label or by a notation of "UL-listed." The devices should carry the same rating as that for the circuit on which they're used, normally, 15-amperes for general purpose lighting circuits and 20-amperes for small appliance circuits.

Back a few years, you could choose from brown or ivory cover plates for switches and receptacles; there was only one style. Today, you have a choice of devices as well as a wide choice in color or finish of the cover plates. Do not mix types of devices, and mix the colors or finishes of the cover plates not at all or very judiciously. One limited selection method might be to use ivory in all painted-wall-papered rooms except bath-kitchen-laundry-utility rooms where chromed cover plates would be used. Rooms having woodgrain paneling would be provided with dark-brown cover plates. This is an individual matter but once you've noted the wide choice available, you'll see the need for exercising some restraint.

Among the various specialized types of switch units readily available, and which you may consider to be desirable at specific points, are:

(1) standard-toggle, nonmercury, quiet operation;
(2) rocker-arm for arms-full, elbow-touch operation;
(3) lighted toggle that stays on when lights are off;
(4) full-range dimming for incandescent lamps;
(5) delay-action light that stays on until you get in the house or up the stairs;
(6) key-operated lights giving manual control for normally automatic devices.

In all probability, you will be well advised to purchase convenience outlet receptacles of the 3-hole grounding types which will accommodate either 3-prong or 2-prong plugs. The National Electrical Code requires all receptacles on 15- and 20-ampere circuits to be the grounding type. This is a fairly recent broadening of earlier provision for grounding-type receptacles only in wet or hazardous locations. But the requirement is part of a continuing move to have all small appliances equipped with the grounding-type plugs.

Connecting Up The Devices

Screw terminals on electrical devices have long been used, but solderless connectors have become common only in the last decade. In new housing, the combination of these connecting methods with other rough-in time savers such as built-in cable clamps and ground screws have helped speed the work of making wiring connections and, as a rule, have resulted in better-than-solder electrical contacts. Incidentally, these mechanical methods for firmly securing connected wire have also made the work easier for owner-builders.

Switches and receptacles are available with screw terminals on the back of the device or on both sides. Or, they can be obtained with holes on the back into which pre-stripped wires are pushed to engage friction contact points. The length of the proper stripping is marked on the receptacle. In some newer devices, an insulated body is equipped with prestripped pigtail wires for connection.

In most cases you are better off using the side-terminal or pigtailed devices. The side-terminal type has two screws per terminal, a convenience where an "in" wire and an "out" wire must connect to the same terminal. While these various devices all meet the National Electric Code requirements, there may be local code regulations that tend to favor one type over another. Check this with your electrical subcontractor to determine the switch-receptacle units commonly used in your area.

There are several types of solderless connectors but the principal one referred to here, and in common use with No. 14 and No. 12 wire sizes, have a plastic body and a spiral tension-wire insert. The wire leads to be connected are first twisted together tightly, ends trimmed and inserted into the connector end, which is then twisted on firmly (see illustration). They're sometimes called "wire nuts." These connectors will be used for nearly all lighting fixture connections plus connection of through-circuit connections at outlet and junction boxes.

With respect to connections of heavier than No. 12 conductor size, other types of solderless connectors include the split-bolt or cable-clamp. Ask your electrician just where there may be a need for these. In most homes, the runs of heavy wire are straight-through runs on individual

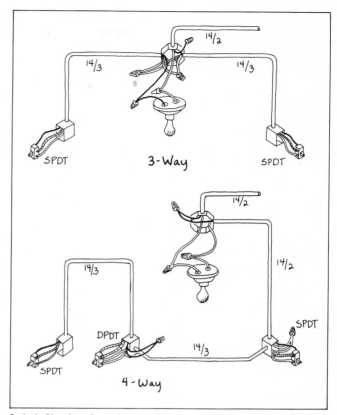

Switch Circuits where the same lighting outlet is to be controlled from more than one location such as at the top and bottom of stairs. In the sketch, the striped conductor represents the hot red-insulated conductor in a cable, black is for the black-insulated and the white for white or grey insulation of the neutral conductor. In these cases, as required by the National Electrical Code, the neutral is serving as the return conductor from switch to outlet and should have its white or grey insulation painted blue at the switch and outlets.

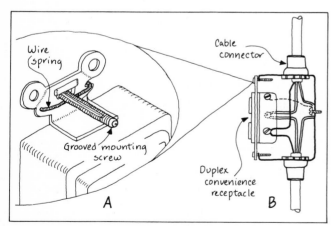

Receptacle Grounding Detail indicates two methods of providing adequate electrical bonding of the switch or outlet receptacle to the electrical box to maintain grounding continuity. In sketch (A), a built-in wire spring is provided in some devices so proper box contact is made when the device is screwed to the box. In sketch (B), an alternative method. The dashed line which represents a bonding jumper wire from the bonding screw terminal to the box ground screw. The National Electrical Code requires bonding of all electrical system enclosures such as raceways, cable armor, cable sheath, frames, fittings and other noncurrent-carrying metal parts.

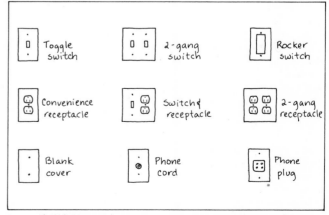

Types of Wall Plates for Devices come in a wide range of styles, finishes and colors. Shown: standard-sized plates and common two-gang or combination devices.

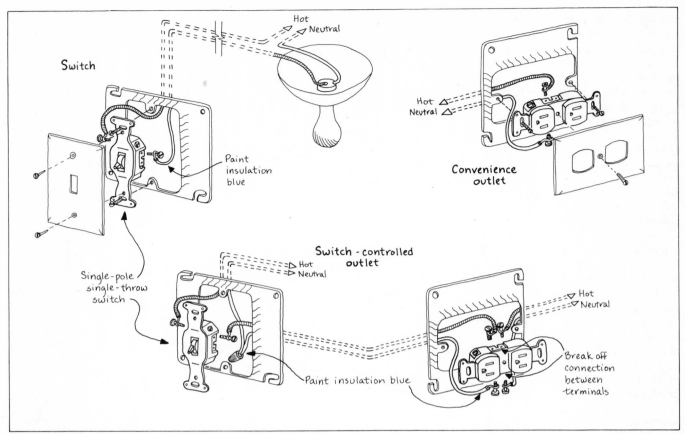

Typical Outlet Device Connections between wiring conductors and switch or receptacle devices. Upper two sketches show a single lighting switch as the left and a regular duplex convenience outlet at the right. The devices have screw terminals on the sides for easy through-wire connections. Lower sketch shows how a connecting link between terminal screws can be broken so that one receptacle can be hot, the other switch-controlled. This method is useful in rooms where table or floor lamps are to be turned on-off with a wall switch. Note: grounding connections and receptacle bonding jumper have been omitted from these sketches.

circuits or feeder lines and the boxes or enclosures where they connect have screw-terminal connection provisions.

You will no doubt encounter one or two situations in your home's circuitry where there are three or four wire leads that need connecting together, and the wire nuts won't handle this bulk properly. In such cases, where soldering of conductor leads is indicated, use a relatively heavy-duty soldering iron or gun, not the light-duty iron often associated with electronic or radio kits. And use resin-core solder, which is not the same kind of bar solder used for sheet metal work. Resin-core solder contains its own flux. Here are the principal points to be observed in making such wire connections:

(1) The wire leads out of a box or enclosure should be a minimum of 10 inches long; strip about 1-to-1-¼ inches of the insulation off each lead.

(2) With your wire stripper or a knife, scrape the exposed copper wire lengthwise a half dozen times going around the wire surface in order to remove any film or oxidation.

(3) Twist the wires together equally, not one around the other or two around one; begin twist by hand and conclude tightening with pliers; using side-cutters, trim the ends of so twisted wires are about 5/8 or 3/4 inch long.

(4) Allow solder iron to preheat for at least two or three minutes then apply the iron to the twisted wires and keep the contact heating for 30-60 seconds before applying solder (more time for thicker twists).

(5) Apply solder to the twist, not the iron; keep iron in contact with twist while you turn the twist and let the solder flow into the interstices; the solder should not bulk up but should appear to thin out and spread.

(6) After twist has cooled to allow handling, apply plastic electrical tape in spiral winding; start by folding over end of twist and spiral toward the insulation; all parts of the twist should have about three layers of tape

covering at any point and the tape should extend at least an inch over the insulation.

One point of emphasis on applying the wire nuts to connect conductors: be sure you're using the proper size nut for the wires involved. Also, make the wire twist compact, tight, and not too long. The twist should be about 3/8 inch long for No. 14 and about 1/2 inch long for No. 12. This lets the nut twist tight on the wire and the lower part of the nut project down over the insulation. Twist the nut as tight as you can by your fingers but don't apply any further tool force. Use care to avoid even slightly loose nuts. And tuck all leads back into the outlet box or enclosure. Connected leads should lie along sides of boxes, having been folded to fit. Don't just cram them haphazardly back into the box.

As a standard rule, black wires connect to black, red to red and white or grey to white or grey. Bare wires in cables or green pigtails connect to green terminals on boxes or devices to give grounding continuity. If no green grounding terminal is on the box, use a slip-on clip (see illustration).

There's a major exception to the above color-code matching. It occurs at all switches. As you know from the rough-in work described in Chapter 24, the two conductors connecting the switch device are both hot lines, the switch being an interruption in the hot line run to a certain outlet. The practice is to run (for example) the cable to the controlled outlet, with another cable run to the switch. Then the black hot lines are spliced at the outlet box. The return leg from the switch to the outlet device is white or grey but the conductor ends are given a touch of blue paint at both the switch and the outlet (see illustration).

A few tips about tools and techniques. Ask to see your electrician's hand tools, mostly to check their quality. You'll want two or three sizes of screw drivers, a pair of lineman's pliers for twisting the conductors and clipping their ends. A pair of good-quality diagonal wire clippers (sometimes called side-cutters) for general wire cutting work. And a good-quality wire-strippers with notches identified for wire size.

Special emphasis here about grounding continuity. This is an important aspect of box and enclosure connections and switch-receptacle devices in the National Electrical Code. The Code refers to the procedure as "bonding" and this defines a procedure at each outlet box or enclosure to make certain that the bare wire grounding lead from each cable is connected to the box's green-painted screw terminal or to a terminal on a box-clip. And each switch-receptacle device has either a green-painted terminal or green wire lead also needing connection to the box terminal. A bonding jumper is used from a screw-terminal device to the box terminal (see illustration). In some areas, the type of non-metallic sheathed cable supplied may have a green colored conductor (or green with yellow stripes) instead of the bare wire. These *grounding* connections, it should be understood, need interconnection through the home to give continuity back to the service entrance where

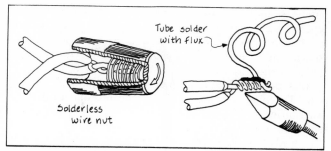

Conductor Splicing is the term used to describe connecting up of two or more conductor wires. The solderless wire nut method is faster and easier and in new construction it eliminates the sometimes troublesome solder-iron heating. However, it is probably not possible to eliminate soldering 100 percent.

Wire nut usage involves proper length stripping of conductor insulation, scraping wire for clean contact, twisting of ends together prior to placement of the nut which is then twisted on tightly. Wire nuts must be chosen to fit conductor sizes; the nuts contain a spiral wire insert within the plastic enclosure.

In soldering, the preheated or electric iron is held to heat the wire first and then the solder is touched to the wire, not the iron. Easiest solder is the tube type with resin-type flux.

the grounding conductor is connected to the system ground. And it should be clear that these interconnections are in the nature of an emergency path and are completely separate from the wiring system's neutral (white or grey) conductor. The grounding connections in a box or enclosure should be arranged in such manner that the removal of a fixture or receptacle will not disturb the continuity of the grounding wires.

In connecting up lighting fixtures, there's a right way normally evident in the color of the insulated pigtail leads coming from the fixture. But in certain cases there may be no leads or identification of screw terminals. The normal next place to check is the screw-shell of the fixture into which the lamp bulb screws. The lead from this outer shell should be connected to the neutral conductor, the white or grey colored insulation.

Special Outlets and Devices

After all 115-volt, 15-amp and 20-amp lighting and convenience outlet circuits have been accounted for as well as the 115-volt individual circuits, there remain certain outlets which require either special devices or special handling. These are: appliances or equipment using 230-volts; outlets for transformer connections, and outlets to be protected by ground fault interrupters.

Range-Dryer Outlets

Receptacles for wall connection of electric range and electric clothes dryers have come to be called range-dryer outlets simply because these are the two most common types of stationary appliances requiring plug-in connection for 230-volts. Some room air conditioners also require this voltage and a range-dryer receptacle is suited for use with that appliance, too.

This outlet receptacle takes a special kind of 3-prong plug. The plugs are the same but the receptacles may be rated differently. The range installation will normally use a receptacle rated at 50-amperes while the clothes dryer usually needs one at 30-amperes. The individual circuit conductors to these outlets, of course, will have been wired with proper conductor size to handle these ratings. The wire sizes involved in 230-volt circuitry is normally of stranded rather than solid conductor wire. The receptacles have terminal clamps designed to accommodate stranded conductors. But in some areas, it may still be the local practice for the stripped strands to be soldered together before placing in the receptacle clamps. Check this with your electrician.

Transformer Outlets

The most common electrical signal system operating on low voltage and requiring connection to house voltage through a transformer is the bell-push wiring for door chimes or buzzers.

The usual practice provides two push-button locations, the front and rear doors. To indicate which door needs answering, a bell-buzzer combination can be used or a door-chime unit which has different ringing characteristics or tones for each door.

The outlet for the transformer need not be specially provided. The transformer can be mounted on the outside of any outlet box or junction box. However, the box should be an accessible one in case the transformer has to be replaced. In a basement home, the transformer may be connected on an exposed box; in a basementless home it can be wired to a ceiling-joist-mounted box.

Range and Dryer Receptacle is wired with heavy-duty cable and needs secure mounting. Use of a 2X4 backing block between studs is suggested. Receptacle has screw terminals. The stranded conductors should be twisted and bound with solder before shaping the wire end to fit the terminal.

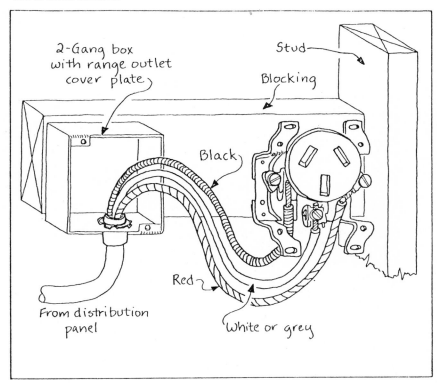

Ground Fault Interrupter is combined with a duplex convenience outlet in this Leviton-made device which should be used for outdoor outlets and in other hazardous locations where the entire circuit is not protected by a GFI-type breaker at the circuit distribution panel. The interrupter is sensitive to leaking current protecting against the possibility of serious shocks. It includes a test button to verify proper operating condition.

Transformers are available that mount directly into a box knock-out hole with two pigtail leads coming through the hole. Then, low-voltage leads to the door location attach to screw terminals on the transformer body outside of the electrical box.

Ground Fault Interrupters

As explained in Chapter 25, GFI devices are required by the National Electrical Code in certain house locations. The outlets to be protected are those in bathrooms, outdoors, and serving submersible pumps, fountains or swimming pools. One type of device that can be used is a GFI circuit breaker which, when mounted in a distribution panel with other breakers, protects an entire circuit. Another device is a GFI receptacle that installs in an outlet box and protects only that outlet.

GFI receptacles and breakers come in 15-amp and 20-amp ratings. The receptacle needs a 2-½ inch minimum depth box and is equipped with its own cover plate (see illustration).

Smoke Detector

The 1975 edition of the One-and-Two-Family Dwelling Code contains a newly added provision for making mandatory the installation of at least one smoke detector. It must be UL-listed for adequate sensing of both visible and invisible particles of combustion and for sounding an alarm when such particles are detected.

While some smoke detector models run on small batteries, the probable interpretation in building codes for these devices will be that the detector must be connected to the home's electrical system in new construction.

Smoke detectors are designed to be sensitive to the particles that spread through the air when a fire is in its incipient stage . . . early detection. From a practical viewpoint, the most dangerous situation occurs when the occupants are asleep. Thus, the normal placement of a single detector might be in a hallway near the sleeping areas of the home. Normally, the outlet for connecting a smoke detector would be a ceiling outlet (see illustration).

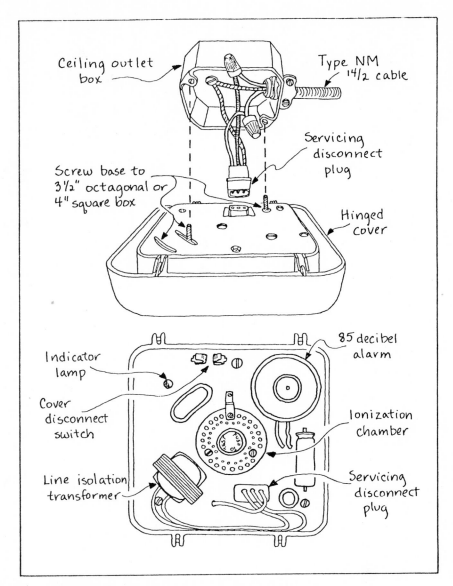

Smoke Detector unit, now required by some building codes, is an alarm device sensitive to particles of smoke that usually precede fires. Detector shown is a 6×6-inch square unit called the "Home Sentry" and made by General Electric. This type mounts to an ordinary ceiling box; the recommended location is in the hallway leading to sleeping rooms.

Other Devices

There are innumerable other electrical devices that can be hooked up to your home's wiring system. Many that you see in retail stores or supply firms are designed for replacement purposes in older homes.

The attempt here has been made simply to cover the basic and most common items and those optional extra electrical items that appear to be quite popular or are becoming code-required. There are radio-intercom units, built-in hi-fi or music systems. There are also a number of small kitchen appliances available in built-in models such as mixer-blenders and toasters.

Your option on these additional electrical accessories should be exercised early so that suitable provision can be made in the concealed wiring system. Once that provision for outlet connection has been made, you can always install the appliance or accessory itself at a later stage.

Connecting Up Appliances

As explained earlier, the practice with major home appliances is to provide a wall plug-in receptacle if the appliance is easily removable. This is a characteristic of conventional ranges and refrigerators which simply rest in place on the floor. And for clothes washers and electric clothese dryers. And room air conditioners that fit in windows.

But other types of appliances are rather difficult to move because they are pipe-connected or have permanent mountings to other construction parts. Examples might be water heaters, gas clothes dryers and ranges, wall-insert conditioners and cabinet-built-in ovens and cook-tops.

These built-in appliances are connected up by flexible cable or conduit leads from the appliance to nearby junction boxes positioned for that purpose. Terminal connections are made at the junction box and the appliance. Then the appliance is slipped in and fastened to its mounting. A similar procedure is followed with recessed lighting fixtures and other built-in electrical accessories.

With gas-operated clothes dryers and range-oven units, the rough-in plumbing work will have included the bringing of a gas pipe to the appliance position, as noted on the appliance's specification sheet. But these two appliances also require a regular convenience electric outlet at the location also. An electric dryer employs the same electrical receptacle for 230-volts as used for the range. With either type of dryer, an added necessity is a 4 inch diameter vent to the outdoors, usually of flexible metal tubing and available in kit form with clamp-rings to fit the dryer collar and an outside downward-flow deflector-cover for the vent opening on the outside.

Gas water heaters require the gas supply pipe connection plus a vent connection that usually is made to the larger-size combustion smoke pipe running from the furnace to the chimney as described in Chapter 40. Electric water heaters require 230-volt connections but unlike ranges or dryers, the outlet connection to the heater is by flexible cable or conduit rather than by a receptacle and plug. Check with your electrician for advice concerning electric water heater connections.

Room air conditioners designed for window installation generally come equipped with cords and plugs for plug-in to wall receptacles. Smaller capacity conditioners operate on 115-volts and need only a nearby convenience outlet, preferably on a 20-amp circuit. Larger capacity models operate on 230-volts and require an individual 3-wire circuit and range-dryer receptacle. Some conditioner manufacturers offer built-in wall models equipped with metal rough-in sleeves that are normally fitted into framing openings during early stages of construction. The units may be equipped with cords and plugs but can also be connected by short flexible cable or conduit runs to a concealed junction box.

Signal Circuit Outlets

In moderate-cost to upper-bracket homes, it's become common practice to prewire a home for telephone service and for TV antenna connections. Neither of these wiring systems have any direct connection with a home's electrical wiring. However, the owner-builder who desires to make such provisions can do so quite easily. And it does make the use of telephones and TV sets in the homes more convenient, particularly when there are to be multiple phones or sets or where it may be desired to move the set from one location to another.

The easiest way to do this is to install regular metal or

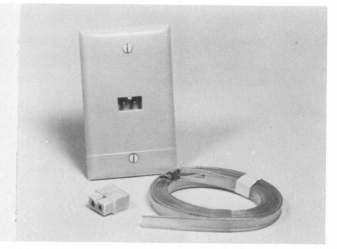

Signal Circuit Devices include these units that allow convenient hook-up of telephone and TV/FM receivers. At left, receptacles or jacks, wall plates and cord plugs in choice of colors for 4-prong plug-in portable telephones. At the right, receptacle-plate, 300-ohm twin-line cable and plug for TV/FM antenna cable. If several locations are to be prewired for plug-in antenna use, the proper signal-splitting devices should be used with the cable runs. Devices shown are made by Sierra Electric and other manufacturers.

plastic outlet boxes as you would for convenience outlets. While it's possible to install the phone cable or antenna wire itself, it is easier and more flexible to fit specific needs if you simply provide the channels in wall-framing spaces through which the wire or cable can be pulled.

What you do is this. Install the rough-in boxes where you wish the TV antenna and telephone outlets to be. Then use lengths of thin-wall conduit fitted with conduit connectors to the outlet boxes and the other ends extended down into the basement or up into the attic space. With antenna outlet locations, it is better to use 1/2 or 3/4 inch polyethylene tubing also using conduit connectors at box fittings. Extend the tubing runs to the attic space. In each case then, the phone or antenna installer can run wiring or cable through basement or attic spaces to the conduit or tubing ends, then through these to the outlets. Receptacles and plugs for making connections of phones and TV sets to the outlets are readily available from your electrical supply source.

Electrical Safety

An operating electrical system is a potential hazard to the home's occupants. An improperly installed or improp-erly connected system is particularly dangerous. In install-ing the wiring and various devices or appliances in new construction, there is limited hazard because the bulk of the work is done before the service entrance connections are completed and the main switch turned so the current becomes available to the system.

Nevertheless, you should consult with your partial elec-trical subcontractor about the safety aspects of the installa-tion. And about any testing of the circuitry that should be made once the installation is completed. If you followed earlier suggestions in Chapter 24, he will be making the connections himself at the main distribution panel includ-ing the breaker installation and circuit identification. You should plan to be present with him at this time to verify just what connections you've made with each circuit, and to aid him in running circuit tests.

Electrical safety after occupancy also presents a poten-tial hazard for occupants, particularly for families with small children and pets. The U.S. Consumer Product Safety Commission (CPSC) has issued a series of bulletins and reports concerning various aspects of home safety. Three that cover certain aspects of electrical installations in the "Fact Sheet" series are: No. 16 on extension cords and wall outlets; No. 57 on smoke detectors; and No. 62 on elec-trical appliances, circuits, devices, and other system details.

43 Hardware, Interior Accessories

The new code requirement for use of at least one smoke detector in every new home as mentioned in the previous chapter is just one indication of a general trend in the past few years to make homes safer. Safer against fire, against accidents, and against intrusion.

This latter safety factor, apparently stems from increased owner-occupant anxiety due to growing crime rates, and has resulted in an assortment of new hardware and accessory products being introduced in the past few year. These products are designed to make it more difficult for would-be intruders to enter a home. Or to sound an alarm that will alert owners to any intrusion attempts.

Most of the newer safety-security devices come with detailed installation instructions. Some of the products are intended for use in new homes, some for use as replacements or supplementary measures in existing homes. Illustrations in this chapter indicate some of each type. In choosing hardware intended for new construction but having due thought and added attention to the desired level of home security, you may well save yourself the trouble of adding further protective devices later. This is particularly true of entrance door locksets.

Guarding Against Intrusion

At one time most home entrance doors had deadbolts to assure double-locking protection. Then came a period when simplified installation of locksets just by drilling and faceplate mortising brought about the widespread and nearly universal use in single-family homes of the tubular or key-in-knob lockset.

Now a growing number of new home entrances are provided double-protection once again with supplementary hardened steel-insert deadbolts controlled by steel-reinforced cylinder-lock mechanisms. These are in addition to the regular lockset and virtually assure the home owner that his entry doors cannot be tampered with or have its locks pried off. Yet this same entrance door hardware is also designed to allow quick panic exit from inside with just a twist of the door knob or lock thumb-turn in a single-handed operation.

But just high-quality and secure door locks may not be sufficient. If you have to open an entrance door in order to answer a ringing door bell, you may still desire the protection of a door-chain guard that allows only partial door-opening to see who's there and what's wanted. This function can sometimes be better handled by other accessories . . . a small door-insert viewer that gives you a wide-angle peep at the visitor or an entrance door with glass lights using clear or one-way mirror glass. Or door-answering can be accomplished electronically and remotely with a built-in intercommunication unit.

If you really wish to be determined about this, there are more sophisticated measures you can take. There are some intrusion-guard home systems available that sound an alarm when an intruder tries to gain entry at any window in addition to the entrance doors. Sensing devices at these locations send signals to a central control panel. The main interior alarm horn or bell may have a supplementary outside unit for also alerting your neighbors (in case of your absence). And some of these systems include provision for smoke-sensing devices so that an alert can also be sounded in case of fire. Such wired signal systems aren't cheap. One manufacturer's kit contains the control panel with the means for testing, 12 door-window magnetic sensors, 6 fire-detector sensors and a remote external alarm. The whole kit has a price tag close to $500. A single fire or smoke detector as described in the previous chapter costs about $40, should meet the requirements of NFPA Standard No. 74 (sponsored by the National Fire Protection Association) and should be connected to the home's electrical system.

Be cautious in buying fire-and-intrusion protection equipment. These units have developed very rapidly since about 1972. As a result, there are some inexperienced companies involved in selling these units along with some quick-buck or fly-by-nite characteristics. Look for evidence of both product and manufacturer reliability. (For detailed information consult *Total Home Protection*, a Successful Book.)

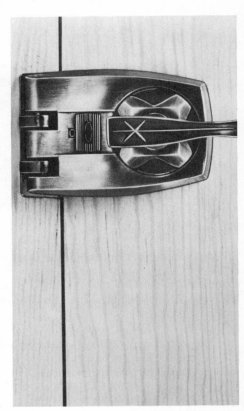

Entrance Door Locksets stress home security and the newer models such as these units include high-quality pin-tumbler cylinder locks and deadbolts. Other features that are sometimes included are heavy-duty steel cylinder housings and better mounting methods that resist forceable cylinde removal.

At left is Schlage Lock's "Meteor-G" lockset with the double protection of a half-inch-throw deadlocking latch and a separate

one-inch-throw deadbolt with armor plate under the outside rose trim. The two photos at the right show the inside and outside of the "SuperGuard II" entrance door set made by the Ideal Security Hardware Corporation. The handle design keeps the key cylinder from being wrenched off and the unit is mounted with through-bolts having concealed screw heads.

Interior Door Locksets

If you followed the recommendation to use prehung interior doors, those units in all probability were delivered with all hardware except the locksets. However, the doors and jambs would be predrilled to accommodate tubular locksets.

The selection of locksets, their style and finish, may involve more time than it takes to install them. With predrilled holes and premortised recesses for face- and strike-plates, installation shouldn't take more than about 10 minutes per door.

Although this door-knob hardware device is called a "lockset," that term often applies accurately only to bathroom door units which do have a locking mechanism. The frequent practice is to use units on bedroom and other interior doors which do not lock but have a latching function. They are sometimes called "passage locksets."

The true interior door lockset may be used anywhere where privacy is desirable, but the usual locations are bath-rooms, powder rooms and storage rooms or attic doors. The units designed for bathroom use normally have a one-sided locking handle, either a button in the knob center or a small lever. This is placed on the bathroom side of the door. Read your lockset installation instruction sheet (one comes with every set) and you'll discover that part of the package is a small opening on the hall side of the door, provided so that in case of emergency (especially involving children), the locked bathroom door can be opened by a narrow lever inserted through the small opening.

Where closets have hinged doors, you can obtain, if you wish, dummy knobs for use with friction latches, the knobs matching interior locksets in style and finish.

Locksets are available in a broad assortment of styles and metal finishes. Some manufacturers also offer cabinet and bathroom accessory hardware in designs that match the style and finish of lockset hardware (see illustration). Locksets also come in units with lever-type door handles rather than knobs.

If your doors are not predrilled for locksets or prerouted

for plates, inquire of your lockset supplier about the availability, on a rental basis, of a suitable installation kit or jig. A number of leading manufacturers of door hardware make such kits. They're usually intended for builder use and contain a precision guide for drilling holes, proper size boring bits, latch and strike mortising markers.

Bathroom Accessories

Certain minimal bathroom and powder room accessories are built-in or preinstalled in every new home. The standard items are towel bars, soap or soap-toothbrush holders, toilet-tissue holders, garment hooks and sometimes bathtub or shower grab bars.

The latter item requires special attention. Bathtubs are hazardous and the scene of numerous home accidents. Some accidents have been contributed by insecure or haphazard mounting of grab-bar accessories, which are sometimes made part of a soap-dish recess. Unless these have firm backing and sufficiently solid screw mountings, the grab-bar may provide a false sense of security to the tub-user. They must resist the considerable pressure-leverage of a person's full weight, or nearly so.

Grab-bars are excellent assist devices that will prevent accidents if properly placed and firmly fastened. This means, at minimum, long wood screws for mounting with the screws going into solid backing blocks rather than being fastened simply to wallboard (see illustration). However, check your bathtub selection if you're planning to use one of the newer reinforced plastic-molded tub or shower units. You'll likely find that grab-bars are molded right into the one-piece assemblies.

The other accessories are also screw-mounted and can be fastened to wallboard by means of toggle bolts, Molly anchors or Jif-loc devices. With towel bars, the screw-mounting is often by means of a concealed bracket over which the towel-bar base fits with a set-screw tightener. Towel bars come in a choice of several lengths; select to fit your needs.

If your bath or powder room has a vanity lavatory, the probability is that it came equipped with cabinet hardware and nothing further is required. Face-height medicine cabinets are often considered bathroom accessories because they are sold through the same outlets and made by accessory manufacturers. Considerations regarding these bath cabinets are given in Chapter 33.

One electrical accessory commonly used in bathrooms is a ventilating exhaust fan. HUD-MPS's require all habitable rooms including kitchens and baths to have a natural window ventilation area that is at least 5 percent of the room's floor area. If such window opening area is not provided (such as in the case of an inside, no-window bath or powder room), then a mechanical exhaust fan must be provided and it must be sized to furnish 15 air changes per hour in kitchens and 8 air changes per hour in bathrooms. There is an alternative to the exhaust fan for kitchens; range and oven hoods with exhaust-duct connections may be used in lieu of the fan. Bath-kitchen exhaust fans come in wall and ceiling models and require duct connections to the outside (see Chapter 22). A combination fixture often used in bathrooms is a light-and-fan unit controlled from the same wall switch.

Window and Cabinet Hardware

Windows previously involved piecemeal assembly at the site beginning with the installation of the frame. Later came the insertion of sash units and weights or balances. Still later, after painting and glazing, came the installation of operating and locking hardware. No longer.

Today, nearly all new homes use preassembled and precompleted window units comprised of frames, sash, glass, hardware and screens. They even include bright labels on glass panes so construction men can see that the glass is already in place. As a result, the majority of new homes need no window hardware.

What may be needed for windows, however, is storm

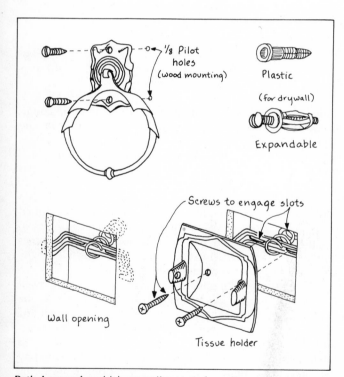

Bath Accessories which are wall-mounted usually require secure fastening preferably where screws can penetrate into studs. But towel rings or bars and tissue holders cannot always be so located or provided-in-advance with backing blocks. Shown here are mounting methods suggested by the Amerock Corporation. In upper right, small drywall anchoring devices. For tissue and soap holders, a spring-loaded metal screw base can be slipped into the opening, the spring keeping tension on while screws are engaged.

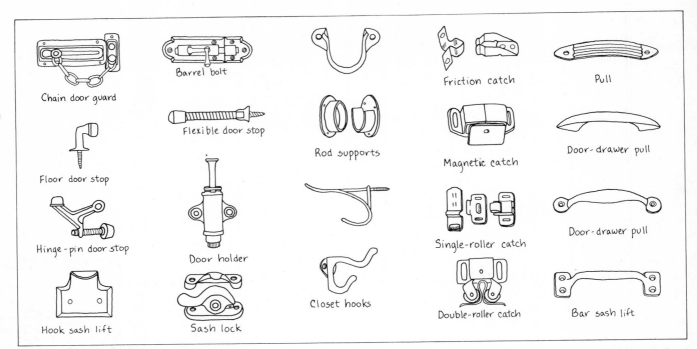

Utility Hardware for a variety of home uses. Many cabinets or other products now include appropriate hardware. In other cases, utility hardware items such as these may be needed. Lowest cost units are usually those having a zinc-coated finish while more expensive are the one with chrome or brass finish.

sash and, if not related to the window units, mounting hardware for the storm sash. Hardware for shop-fabricated storm sash is readily available and includes sash hangers, corner braces, sash adjuster bars and turn-button holders.

Another supplementary type of window hardware that is needed soon after occupancy, if not before, is associated with curtains and drapes. In recent years, there have been a number of new kinds of window treatments popularized; cafe curtains, for example. So, there are a number of different kinds of curtain-drape mounting methods and appropriate hardware for them. Your best bet in shopping for such window hardware is to look in retail shops selling drapery and upholstery fabrics.

Cabinets are somewhat similar to windows in their need for hardware. Most of the cabinets in a typical new home are kitchen bath units that come completely assembled, usually prefinished and more-often-than-not fully equipped with hinges, door-drawer pulls and latches.

In those instances where an owner-builder decides to build his own cabinets or mount prefinished cabinet doors on site-built shelves, the choice of appropriate cabinet hardware will be one of style selection more than anything else. Cabinet hinges and pulls are sold in a wide range of styles-shapes-finishes, all aimed at complementing the design or decor of the cabinets themselves.

The most common cabinet door hinges are the semi-con-cealed type in sizes to accommodate varying door lip conditions. The amount of offset (outward projection from the edge of the door opening) is usually 3/8 inch. The hinges screw into the face-frame of the cabinet and into the back side of the door. Some cabinet hardware lines offer hinges with a self-closing feature.

Door pulls are mounted by a pair of machine screws which come with the pulls. They're driven through drilled holes in the door or drawer and go into threaded holes in the pull. Most pulls are designed to mount with two holes drilled 3 inches apart. In some lines, matching-style single-unit pulls or pendants are available for drawer use.

When cabinets are site-built, cabinet drawers are available in both metal and molded plastic. In either case, the drawer unit needs a facing or drawer front to match the cabinet doors. If you decide on prefinished cabinet doors, the same source will have matching drawer-fronts. In kitchen and bathroom applications, drawers see everyday use and need smooth effortless operation. Ball-bearing roller-equipped side-mounted drawer slides are suggested.

For your kitchen cabinets particularly, investigate available hardware accessories. Available either from the cabinet manufacturer or separately from regular hardware sources, these hardware items often give an extra measure of convenience. The items include cup-hanging racks, towel holders, counter-insert chop-blocks, spring-balanced pull-up mixer shelves, revolving trays for corner cabinets, and many other devices. In every case, you'll find installation instructions with the accessories.

Electrical Accessories

While certain built-in electrical home accessories were described in Chapter 42, there are a few additional considerations that might be touched on briefly here.

The rules in the National Electrical Code applying to loads on branch circuits designed to serve portable appliances and lighting are: the wattage rating of any one portable or easily-movable appliance for plug-in should not exceed 80 percent of the branch circuit rating; the wattage rating of a fixed appliance continuously attached to a branch circuit should not exceed 50 percent of the branch circuit rating.

Now, these rules mean that any individual portable appliance should not exceed 2,440 watts (80 percent of the total 1,800 watts allowable on a 20-ampere, 115-volt circuit). And any fixed appliance should be limited to a maximum of 900 watts if connected to a 15-ampere circuit or 1,200 watts if to a 20-ampere circuit.

Within this 900/1,200-watt maximum are a variety of small electrical appliances that are optional accessories. They include:

☐ exhaust fans and range-oven hoods;
☐ electric heaters and heat lamps;
☐ food mixers and blenders or combination units;
☐ garbage-grinding sink disposers.

Used more in luxury-class homes are several additional electrical accessories that may be of interest to the owner-builder.

☐ built-in vacuum cleaning systems;
☐ intrusion-and-fire alarm systems;
☐ radio-music and music-intercom systems;
☐ garage-door operators, manual-switch or automatic.

These more complex and expensive accessories are varied in their installation requirements. Most require some minimal prior electrical provision, often just a nearby electrical outlet. Similar items with greater wattage ratings than mentioned above will require prior installation of an individual circuit.

This type of equipment comes with detailed instructional information. Depending upon the nature of the accessory, there may be roughing-in accessories with the package. The only counsel is to decide on which of these various or other electrical accessories you wish to include at an early stage of construction so that you don't have to go back and cut into already completed work.

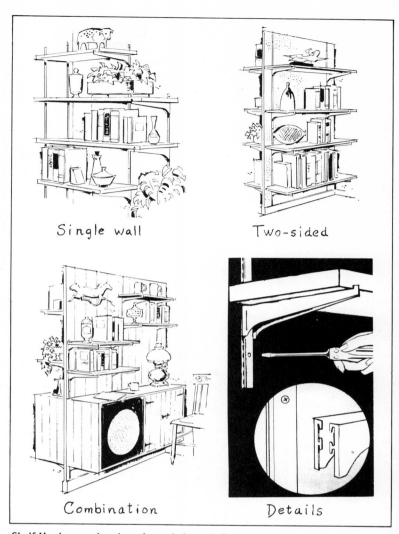

Shelf Hardware using slotted metal channels for wall-mounting and slot-fitting metal support brackets has become quite popular for home use. Shown here, an improved shelf line by Stanley Hardware, unusual in that it can be used for double-sided application on a room divider as well as for the normal single-wall application. In lower right a close-up sketch of mounting details.

44 Painting, Stain and Wallpaper

Do-it-yourselfers have long found painting and papering a "fun" chore where the biggest difficulty encountered was often simply a matter of reaching decisions on what paint, what color, what pattern, what paper to use.

The continuing trend of home owners doing their own decorating work has been aided by better paint technology and better painting tools and equipment. Similar developments but more recent ones have occurred in wallpapering. In both cases, owner-decorators are finding more paint/wallpaper stores catering to their needs with greater selection range and more instructional information.

There's yet another factor that's been creeping into the newer types of paint/wallpaper stores. It's the influence focussing on decorating design. The boutique approach. More information is being provided the customer on design elements, color choice factors, reflectance values, decorating coordination and other characteristics. And if you indicate a desire, you'll find through such stores, for a fee, a professional decorator's individualized counsel without the need for hiring him/her for a complete interior design job.

Before you begin to think this is a snap, there are a few things of which to be wary. With painting, particularly, some elementary precautions should be observed. Paints and stains are being made in a much broader range of formulations than ever before. There are considerations such as flammability, vapor inhalation, skin effects and other possible hazards to the person using the various painting products and solvents. The best general advice is to READ THE LABEL. Paint and stain containers have labels that describe in some detail the surface preparation, use, and cleanup. But the labels also contain (sometimes in fine print) facts about the formulation, its possible hazards, and suitable remedies for misuse.

In general, household paints, finishes and related products are harmless if: ventilation of the working area is adequate; direct inhalation of fumes or vapors is avoided; contact with the skin is minimized; and, children are kept remote. All materials should be checked for their specific flammability. Also, because of possible subsequent fire hazard conditions, prompt cleanup, rag disposal, and care in paint storage away from heat sources, is advised.

If you're an owner-builder completing his new home, you already have the stepladders and planks needed as painting scaffolds. Also required for floor protection are drop-cloths. Your painting tools will consist of an assortment of high-priced brushes ranging from a 1-½ inch wide trim brushes to 3-½ or 4 inch brushes for surface work. Your large-area wall-ceiling surfaces are best done with paint rollers after edge-painting by brush.

Sundries needed include paint pails, roller trays, mixing sticks, paint-drop removal rags. Then, there will be occasional need for sandpaper, wire brush, scraper-knife, putty, wood-filler, spachtling compound, steel wool, brush-cleaners and solvents.

Paint spraying? Possibly. The spray method of application has been used extensively by some professionals, especially in nonresidential fields. These pro's have sophisticated equipment including air compressors and an assortment of nozzle accessories that lend specialized spraying capabilities to the equipment. Home-type paint sprayers were introduced a number of years ago but appear to have had limited distribution until just recently. There have been a number of innovations in spray methods and the equipment designed for home use. One of the more promising innovations is the introduction of professional-quality sprayers that operate electrically and need no air compressor (see illustration).

Two primary characteristics apply to paint spraying. First, the procedure is fast. Once you've grasped the little knack of smooth uniform movements of the spray head, the time needed to coat a given surface is substantially less than the application time with either brush or roller. Second, the paint spray is more difficult to control with respect to areas that you don't want to paint. This means more masking preparation and better floor-cabinet-door protection. (For more specific details on surface preparation and paint applications, consult *Book of Successful Painting*.)

Painting Interior Walls-Ceilings

When today's newer painting materials are used, painted surfaces are durable and retain their good appearance for a considerable period. Application doesn't pose a particular problem. A very high percentage of all paint jobs give the owner-painter complete satisfaction.

Failure is most apt to occur in connection with proper surface preparation, and this seldom applies to the painting of new construction work. Paint should not be applied to a surface for which it was not intended. Or a surface in improper condition. The frequent presence of moisture due to condensation or leakage spells potential paint problems. Dry conditions mean painted surfaces are not likely to develop problems.

The kind of paint chosen for a specific purpose depends considerably on the nature of the surface. In a typical new home built along the lines described in this text, the probability is that the bulk of your interior painting will be in connection with wallboard ceiling-wall finishes in all rooms and halls; interior wood trims and unfinished millwork items; and woodgrain finishes for cabinets, trim, panelings. But if you've also followed this text's suggestions for use of prefinished materials, your work with trim and woodgrain material will be minimal.

Oil-based, solvent-thinned paints were the only type used in new homes for decades and decades. And while there may be many knowledgeable painting experts who still give oil-based paints top rating, it is probable that for typical single-family home use with the owner-occupant doing the work, latex paints are preferable.

There's no question that latex paints have become highly accepted among do-it-yourselfer painters. Why? Well, they're very easy to apply without streaking or thin spots. Time after time, they give a professional-looking job. In addition, they're quick drying. Paint brushes and rollers clean up with just soap and water. Also (and don't underrate this point), an owner-painter can stop, admire, answer the phone, get a snack and a beer and come back to paint without any overlap problems.

The early variety of latex paints were called "rubber-based" but this term has been outdated by the coming of synthetic-based materials . . . vinyl, polyvinyl-acetate (PVA) and acrylic types. These are not all alike or even alike in one category, brand to brand. Follow, therefore, the procedural advice given on the paint container by the manufacturer. And this should be especially carefully observed with the priming or initial paint coat. Very often the latex paint needs no special primer, just use the regular paint as a self-priming coat. Latex paints are less affected by moisture and dampness than oil-based paints but still some caution is recommended. They may be used on a damp surface or applied in very humid weather, but the drying times will be longer.

One precaution applies to new gypsum wallboard interior applications: these fresh surfaces have a considerable amount of surface dust, and latex paints do not adhere well to dirty or chalky surfaces. Before starting on fresh wallboard with your prime coat, use a vacuum or hand-dust with a damp rag the complete room surfaces . . . and before you do that, sweep up the floor.

No doubt you've heard/seen in latex advertising about something to the effect that "one coat is sufficient to cover." There may be some truth to that claim when the paint is applied over old or previously painted walls. It is not applicable to new, unpainted surfaces. If a fresh surface and the prime coat team up pretty well without excessive or spotty absorption, your second coat of paint can be the finish coat.

Similarly, the number of coats will depend at least partially upon your application technique. If you "brush out well" or really spread your roller load, then the coating is apt to be thinner and more likely to need a subsequent coat. The technique that seems to work best with many paints is to prime-coat thoroughly but not to excess. Then, use a "flow on" application for the second coat keeping the application on the thick side but not so thick that there are runs, drips, or other accumulations.

In most instances, flat paint is selected for wall and ceiling surfaces and semi-gloss (sometimes called "satin") for related trim work. High gloss tends to be used on cabinets or utility areas where washability may be desirable. Where wall paint is of a self-prime type, it can also be used as a prime coat for the trim work. Semi-gloss trim enamel, also latex-based, is available in the same color ranges as the wall-ceiling flat paint.

One word about another type of synthetic-based paint, the alkyds. Alkyd paints-enamels are often suggested for wall-ceiling and trim applications because they wash better and are more resistant to damage than latex paints. Like latex types, they're also nearly odorless. But they do require solvents for cleanup rather than soap-and-water. Another point about washability. Latexes and oil-based paints are also "washable" in the sense that they will resist damage and are cleanable when the whole room is to be washed clean at certain maintenance periods. Paints such as alkyds, that offer a greater degree of washability, are a good choice at certain locations such as doorways, where there is frequent staining or finger-marks that must be repeatedly wiped, washed and perhaps solvent-cleaned.

In closets and storage areas, the most frequently used wall finish is gypsum wallboard, an extension of the same wallboard used in other room areas. Such closet-storage areas are painted in the same manner or usually with the same paint as the room with which they're affiliated.

However, in some cases, closet and storage area walls have different wall finish materials—hardboard, plywood, particleboard. Unfinished or perhaps prefinished. All three types of wall surfaces have characteristics that differ from wood trim or paint-grade lumber. They tend to vary in absorbency and appear sometimes to lack uniformity in their absorbency. The prime coat should be an appropriate primer-sealer. Often a penetrating type of sealer is appropriate as the initial coat in order to produce a uniform base for paint. If semi-gloss or high-gloss enamels are used in closet-storage areas, use an enamel under-coater as the prime coat. The use of light colors in closets and storage rooms is desirable in order to obtain better visibility, with or without closet lights.

Wood and Special Finishes

The two main areas where natural wood finishes might be selected by the owner-builder are floor finish for hardwood flooring, and unfinished wood cabinets and trim. Each requires a different kind of product although at one time both used to be given the same good old stain and yellowing varnish routine.

You may still elect to use stain and varnish. But a more modern, nonyellowing treatment is advised. Alkyd varnishes may be slightly paler than the older resinous varnishes although the latter do have somewhat better resistance. Epoxy varnishes are characterized by good color and

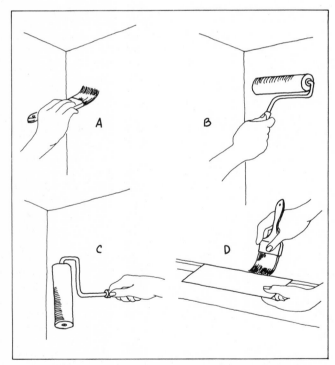

Painting Procedures are highlighted in these sketches: begin at ceiling level brushing on paint just below ceiling line and also at corner edges (A). Then, use a roller for application (B), rolling upward towards the brush-finished area. In new sections, apply paint and again keep working towards the previously finished area. As you cover the surface, make final roller strokes at right angles to the earlier ones (C). When wall surface has been covered, go back to the brush for bottom finishing (D) using a cardboard or metal protector for woodwork.

alkali resistance. Urethanes have better abrasion resistance but require careful surface preparation. Shellac is sometimes used on floors but has low resistance to water, alcohol and abrasion.

Among floor finishes in the satin or semi-gloss class, there are varnishes having a flattening effect added to avoid the bright sheen associated with regular varnishes. Penetrating sealers come into this category; they are essentially varnishes which have been thinned and are intended for wipe-off application. That is, they're brushed on or applicator-applied and the surplus immediately wiped away with rags. After two or possibly three applications, they can be buffed to a very attractive soft sheen and have good color fastness, easy reapplication to worn spots, and fair abrasion resistance.

Wood trim and cabinets which will take natural wood finishes tend to be rare in new home construction. Trim and cabinets are often prefinished. In other cases, the unfinished clear moldings and trim have subdued grain patterns that don't lend themselves to natural finishes. However, where such treatment is desired a wide choice of stains and wood finishes are available, including many that provide light-toned or blonde effects. And the old stain-plus-varnish treatment has given way in wood finishes to more specialized products. Stains with alkyd bases now outnumber oil-based stains. And the color tints have provided a considerably broader selection of wood tones than used to be the case when stains were simply allied to species of woods—walnut, mahogany, birch and maple. In addition to just pigmented stain finishes, there are a variety of antiquing stains that simulate old finishes.

Standard procedure with pigmented stains is a two-coat application. With some open-grained woods, an additional finish coat may be desirable. With some products, the recommended final coat will be a clear sealer.

With most new homes, there will be a variety of additional surfaces that need a special type of paint . . . metal or iron work, masonry, plastic surfaces. Check first the accompanying chart for appropriate type of paint and then check the label for instructions with these special surfaces.

Paint Application Tips

(1) The general practice is to start painting on ceilings, then walls, then doors-windows and trim. On walls and doors-windows, work from the top down. Most pro painters work toward the wet edge or previously painted area but the reverse technique may be better with quick-drying paints.

(2) Use a brush whose width is appropriate for the surface widths encountered. The advantage of a good-quality paint brush is its ability to resist repeated cleanings and maintain flexible bristles.

(3) In manipulating your brush, brush first in one direction, say up and down; then, follow with a horizontal brushing for better coverage and uniformity. Avoid

excessive brush pressure, which tends to separate and deform the bristles.

(4) Be alert to the need for surface preparation and for what the paint label suggests; if there's any grease on a surface, consider it a prime enemy and attack it with a detergent or solvent remover.

(5) Metal and masonry surfaces are most apt to need specific preparation work before painting. Look for corrosion on metals, oil on aluminum and crystalline deposits of a powdery consistency on masonry.

(6) Drywall taping-cementing should dry about two days before being painted. If you plastered with a veneer plaster, allow about 10 days curing time and if your home had a standard 3/4 inch thick plaster job, allow 30 days drying time before decorating.

(7) Don't fuss with painting on a real hot-and-humid or damp-rainy day. There's plenty of other work to be done. This is especially true with latex paints, which really should be used on dry days when temperatures are between 55 and 90 degrees all day.

(8) Don't apply additional coats until the previous one is dry; a slightly tacky touch isn't dry. Ventilate well to speed the drying and check the normal drying time given on the paint can.

(9) Paints labelled "house paint" or "interior paint" indicate simply a general-use paint suited to several types of surfaces and intended as a final coat as well. But enamels of varying types and trim paints intended for woodwork need more attention with their under-coat in order to avoid the roughness associated with grain-raise of the wood.

The paint colors chosen should coordinate well with the general decorating scheme planned. For those who wish to approach the painting work in more detail regarding color selection and coordinating methods employed by professional interior designers, reference is made to the *Book of Successful Painting* (see appendix), where the subject is covered much more fully.

The Wallpaper Situation

It has a long history; not to be traced here. But wallpaper was once the mark of the home-of-the-elite. There was a period during the 1940's when it declined in use, and it was slow to revive in the late 40's and early 50's because new-home emphasis was on large volumes of small compact houses.

Wallpaper today is a more acceptable and desirable interior treatment than it's ever been. And from the standpoint of design and decor, much more imaginative.

In fact, wall "coverings" is today a more appropriate term to use because there's been, in effect, a revolution in range of designs, in colors and types of patterns, in surface treatments and in the introduction of other-than-paper materials, notably the fabric backings and the extruded

Wallpaper Estimating Guide

Room Dimensions	Height of Ceiling				No. Rolls for Ceiling
	7 Ft.	8 Ft.	9 Ft.	10 Ft.	
6 X 10	8	9	10	11	2
6 X 12	8	10	11	12	3
8 X 10	9	10	11	12	3
8 X 12	9	11	12	13	3
9 X 10	9	11	12	13	3
9 X 12	10	12	13	16	4
9 X 14	11	12	14	16	4
9 X 16	12	13	15	17	5
10 X 10	9	11	12	13	4
10 X 12	10	12	13	15	4
10 X 14 (12 X 12)	11	13	15	16	5
11 X 11	10	12	13	15	4
11 X 12	11	12	14	16	4
11 X 16	13	14	16	18	6
14 X 14	13	15	17	19	7
16 X 18	16	18	20	23	9
16 X 20	17	19	22	24	10

Wallpaper Estimating Chart for typical two-foot wide ready-trimmed paper. Columns under various ceiling heights indicate the number of single rolls required. Deduct a single roll for every two average windows or doors. Paper packed in double rolls helps minimize waste in pattern match-up; ask your supplier about this.

vinyl surfaces. Not to mention new wall covering application aids in the form of pretrimming and prepasting.

Wallpaper seems to give more of a custom look. And a warmer, "lived-in" appearance. The wide choices of pattern and color tend to reflect the individuality of the household members. Wallpapers have become a business involving great creativity.

Yet, there are guidelines to be followed in color and pattern combination and in coordination with solid-color paints. And make no mistake about that; most professional interior decorators do employ a combination of pattern and solid color which gives a more effective background than either one alone.

There are changes occurring in the way wallpapers are sold and marketed. More and more wallpapers lines are being produced as consumer-aimed, do-it-yourself products. In some stores, wall coverings are part of the interior decor package of carpeting and drapery fabrics. In some locales, the new pretrimmed/prepasted coverings are sold in a box. Ready at home, the owner-decorator takes the roll out of the box, fills the box with water, cuts the roll to slight over-length then runs it through the box (which has been placed on the floor below the section where the strip will be applied) and lifts it up into place on the wall, sliding it to adjust to the previous strip. Not much to it except care in handling, alignment, and trimming of top and bottom edges.

Two words coming into prominent usage in connection with wall coverings are "scrubability" and "stripability". These terms convey the added durability provided by the surfaces and backings; surfaces that resist much harsher treatment than just mere washing, and backings that permit easy removal and replacement, or removal to take-with-you when you move!

Papering Tools

A table roughly 3×6 feet, standing about 48 inches high if possible, and having a clean smooth surface, is the prime piece of equipment needed to apply wall coverings. You will, if you have much papering to do, be able to make use of added table space but your first table is for unrolling, marking and cutting, plus spreading of paste if the covering is not prepasted.

Cutting is best done with a blade-type utility knife and a metal straight-edge is necessary. Your wallpaper supplier may have professional-type tables and straightedges available on a rental basis.

A wide 8 or 10 inch paste brush (not paint brush) is used to apply wall size, adhesive or vinyl paste. Paste is available in either dry-powder form for water mixing or in premixed pails. A short bristle brush 12 inches long is used in long brush sweeps to smooth out papers and tuck into corners. A window squeegee of soft rubber can also be useful for this purpose with the heavier or thicker wall coverings. You'll need some pails or buckets, one for mixing up the paste and the other to hold clean warm water for cleanup.

Wallpapering tools are sometimes offered by retailers in kit form at reasonable cost. These are usually of minimum quality but they may be satisfactory if you have just limited papering work to do. With the prepasted and pre-trimmed papers, check the manufacturer's instructions with respect to the use of regular wallpaper seam rollers. Some manufacturers do not recommend this tool to be used on coated, covered or fabric-backed coverings.

Papering Tips

(1) Before starting your work, write down for your permanent household file, the run numbers and style numbers of the wallpapers you're using; these are apt to appear on the roll backs or wrappings and there may be a future occasion when added material is needed and you want these specific numbers to make phone-ordering easy.

(2) Paper design employs three types of pattern match: straight across horizontally strip to strip; drop match in which there is a diagonal descent in the pattern strip to adjacent strip; and random match where there is no match-up needed. If you've chosen a paper with a relatively large pattern, you may save on waste by cutting one strip from a roll, taking a new roll to cut the second match-up strip and then going back to the initial roll for the third strip.

(3) No particular surface preparation is needed with gypsum wallboard that's been taped-cemented except dust removal. However, if there appears to be a likelihood of replacing the paper in the foreseeable future, it is probably advisable to apply a wall size that will seal the spackled areas and facilitate paper removal. Such a size can be easily brushed on using clear shellac.

(4) Try using an ordinary wire cooking whisk for mixing adhesives or paste and reducing the lumps.

(5) In cutting strips to approximate wall height, always allow about a 2 inch excess at both the ceiling and the base so trimming cuts can be scribed properly to the minor irregularities of the surfaces that the paper meets. In cutting several strips at a time, make sure of proper match-up of pattern and number the order of application on the back of each strip.

(6) Apply paste evenly starting with the bottom 2/3's of the strip, which you then fold; start hanging the strips in an inside room corner allowing the paper to turn the corner by about a half inch . . . make sure the initial strip is plumb by measuring along the wall 23-½ inches and dropping a plumb line at the mark using your 6 foot level or a plumb bob . . . each wall should have a plumb line for its first strip;

(7) In placing adjacent strips to butt the previous one, be gentle. Wise old decorators say that many types of papers have a memory; if you press or push or pull them too hard, they stretch for now but will eventually come back to their original dimension. So, if your first attempt at a good butt line doesn't quite make it, don't stretch or tug at the strip but instead, lift it from wall contact and reposition.

(8) If you're finishing a wall with a strip wider than necessary, don't carry it around the room corner. Pre-cut it lengthwise to give a half-inch corner turn and make the first strip on the next wall overlap the corner turn after being plumbed.

(9) There's no reason why wall coverings can't be used on ceilings. Application is the same but a bit more uncomfortable, taking some hold-up assistance; papered ceilings should be done before walls but the application follows the same excess-and-trim method.

(10) Work with clean hands; use a damp cloth around your hand to help to gently slide or adjust the strips to correct position; wipe off spills or accidents of adhesive to the paper face immediately, using another damp cloth.

45 Wall-to-Wall Carpeting

When you shop for carpeting, shop for a possible installer at the same time. Selling home carpeting is an extremely competitive business. Many carpeting retailers will quote you prices on an installed basis as well as for carpeting alone. The installation work, in all likelihood, is handled by a small independent carpet layer who regularly does work for that seller.

The competitive situation is often so close in many locations that you can obtain an installing price that is a very nominal add-on figure to the yardage price. And this is apt to be even more the case as the carpetings you're looking at go up in price.

Your best prices, though not necessarily the best buys, will come from the larger chain-type discount retailers and home centers. If an installed cost is not quoted by the retailer, ask about recommending an independent carpet layer.

The point to this is twofold. You can very often find an excellent carpeting buy that includes the installation work at just a slight added increment; and installation of jute-backed carpeting over padding to tackless strips requires stretching tools and some cutting-seaming skills; with this type of carpeting the typical owner-builder may be saving a little installation money to make some mistakes with spoilable materials in areas where it shows.

Now, in the same breath, it should be mentioned that the newer foam-backed carpetings are frequently being laid using carpet tapes or adhesives. And this type of installation is well within the capabilities of the owner-builder. The decision about which type to use might revolve about the nature or use of the carpeting. If yours is a household in which there are several children prone to roughhousing games and various indoor athletic activities, your carpeting might best be installed by the tack-down or newer tackless border strip methods. If the carpeting is apt to receive less strenuous use, the foam-backed materials with tape or adhesive could be entirely appropriate.

Choice Of Carpet Type

As you visit various carpeting retailers, you'll soon discover that most will fit into either of two categories.

☐ The older rug-and-carpet type—in a store often part of or associated with a furniture retailer. Emphasis is on traditional practices; the products tend to be high-quality and also high-priced; the store's personnel have great sales knowledge of carpeting fibers but little to contribute with respect to self-installation methods. In fact, they'll probably recommend against doing it yourself and the bulk of their products will be jute-backed traditional carpeting styles.

☐ The newer carpeting merchandiser—a retailer more apt to show you roll stock than sample books; a place where you'll hear more talk about the synthetic fibers such as nylon, acrylic and olefin; where sales persons will have suggestions for reaching a carpet layer or for self-installation methods. Much of this retailer's stock will be in rubber-vinyl-urethane backed carpetings that do not need separate paddings.

The above categorization doesn't mean to imply that the newer products and synthetic fibers are to be preferred to older fibers and materials such as rayon and wool. There have been many improvements in treating materials, tufting-weaving methods, and carpet backings that have resulted in better products than ever before. But wool does have a powerful competitor in some synthetic fibers that have outstanding durability, stain resistance, and washability.

Most carpetings sold today are made on tufting machines. Like a sewing machine, they insert the stitches or loops of pile fiber into a backing material. There's considerable variety in the way these loops can be arranged (see illustration). The varying of the heights of cut or looped pile fibers (or a combination) can produce textured and sculptured surfaces.

Weaving is the older but still widely used method of producing carpet and consists of intermingling fill yarns with warp yarns. The names traditionally associated with carpets like Wilton and Axminster refer to methods of combining yarns. Among newer methods of manufacturing are needle-punched construction and fusion-bonded carpets. The former results in a flat felt-like surface often imprinted with patterns; the latter is used principally for commercial carpeting because it results in a dense, strong heavy-duty material.

Carpeting quality is usually a matter of how well a carpet performs and the principal factors in producing good performance are the pile height, its density, and the toughness of the fibers. Carpeting experts say its a combination of these factors that should govern your choice. Like, the tougher the fiber, the less density needed.

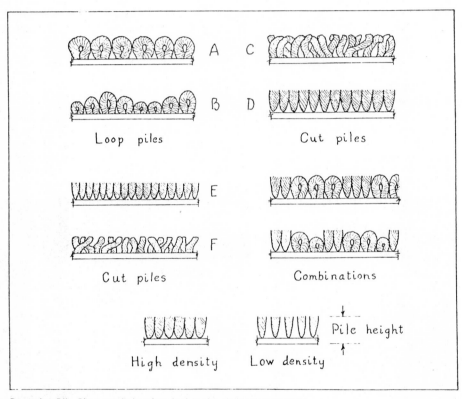

Carpeting Pile Characteristics sketched in the above illustrations identify the principal methods of tufting carpets. Shown are: level-loop (A) and multi-level loop (B). With the latter, the carpeting may have a sculptured pattern or effect. The main forms of cut piles are shag (C) and dense saxony (D) each having relatively long tufting. Shorter tufted cut piles may be more properly called plush (E) and frieze (F). Some carpetings employ various combinations of loop and cut piles. These sketches adapted from "A Consumer Guide to Carpeting," a useful booklet available from Allied Chemical Home Furnishings. In tufted carpetings which account today for more than 90 percent of the yardage being sold, the yarns are threaded through a multitude of needles extending across the tufting machine. These needles are forced through the backing material forming loops or tufts that may be sheared as in cut piles. Older and now lesser-used carpet making methods include woven Axminsters, Wiltons and velvets as well as knitted carpeting.

They say the first decision should be one of style . . . whether a plush, a shag or some other type of carpet is desired for the specific applications you have in mind. Then, with this decision made, begin comparing fibers in the style groups you've selected. The general rule is to seek deeper piles and denser ones but remember that shag-like carpetings are intentionally made with low densities to achieve their effects.

When choosing style or type, consider the wear that a carpet will get. You'll probably choose the most beautiful carpet for your living room but if this room sees heavy family traffic instead of being just a visitor's parlor, then you'll perhaps favor an anti-soiling plush and avoid light-toned solid colors. In a family room, a dense anti-soil carpeting may be appropriate with perhaps a spatter or tweed pattern to help conceal minor soils. An extra-dense even-surface carpeting of this type can be extended into the kitchen. Carpeting in the kitchen is one of today's newer trends. Bedroom carpets see the lightest duty. A good place to economize.

In shopping, you'll find ample literature to describe the properties of various carpeting fibers. Just to familiarize you with the names and terms, here's a brief rundown.

☐ Nylon—Strong, man-made fiber in a relatively economically produced carpeting; long life, very popular, it has excellent crush-and-abrasion resistance.
☐ Acrylic—While often mistaken for wool because of its feel, it is light, bulky and offers fair crush-and-abrasion resistance.
☐ Wool—Oldest type of carpeting, it's a natural fiber, dyes well and features very good resiliency. Warm, cozy and comfortable but highest in price of all fibers.
☐ Olefin/Polypropylene—The newer indoor-outdoor types

Foam-Backed Carpetings, like foam-backed or cushioned resilient floor coverings, are easy to install. Basic suggestions shown here come from Armstrong, a leading producer of floor coverings. At room border, mark along edges on both the flooring underlayment and the wall base (1) with a piece of chalk leaving marks that will transfer to the carpet's foam backing when it is pressed into the corner. The carpeting is then folded back and cut (2) along the transferred marks. Most foam-backs have factory precut edges that assure straight seams and the use of double-faced carpeting tape (3) for adhering to underlayment is required only at seams and door openings. Armstrong also suggests using a bead of special adhesive (4) in what the company calls an "Econo-Fast Installation System." The adhesive is designed to release the carpeting for removal without scraping.

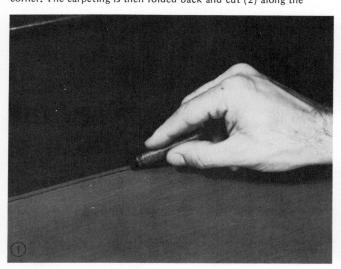

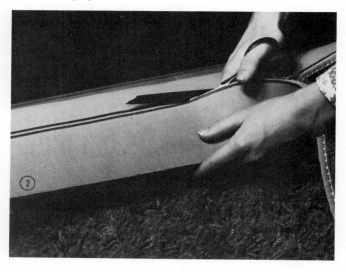

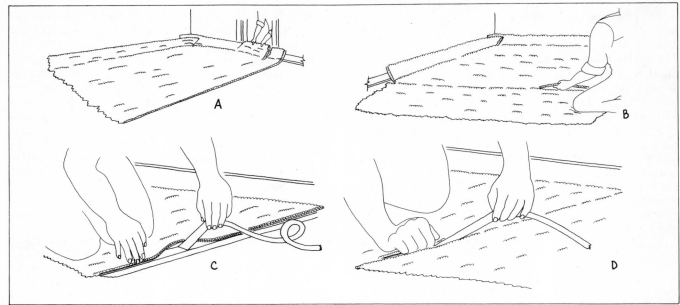

Main Carpet Installation Steps where the one-seam method of laying foam-backed carpeting is used is shown in this group. The steps as suggested in the Armstrong do-it-yourself installation brochure are: unroll a greater-than-room-length strip of carpeting to cover about half the room (A). The excess length is left but short cuts are made in the material at room corners and doorways. Then the second strip of carpeting for the other half of the room is stretched into place

(B) and its edge brought to alignment abutting the edge of the first strip. Double-faced carpet tape is placed in two rows on each side of the seam leaving the top paper protective strip in place. After the tape has been pressed to the floor uniformly, the top paper protection is removed first on one side (C) and the carpeting pressed down, then on the other side (D) and the press-down on the other side completes the seam.

of carpeting with high resistance to stains, soils, fading and abrasion; popular for kitchens; economical but limited in its range of use.

☐ Polyester—Has good abrasion resistance and is less static-prone than other synthetics. It offers an unusual sheen in appearance but, like the acrylics, seems to be seeing less use today than in the past.

Assurances Of Quality

Some manufacturers are offering a warranty of guarantee with their carpet products. This may concern its wear and a provision might include something to the effect that if any given area is abrasively worn more than a certain percentage within a given period of time, it will be replaced. One manufacturer of fiber materials provides a guarantee with respect to control of static electricity.

However, the probable most significant factor affecting your choice . . . especially for certain rooms . . . might be whether the carpeting conforms to the requirements of the U.S. Flammable Fabrics Act. Inquire of your carpeting supplier whether the material you're selecting meets the Act's acceptance criteria, which are incorporated in the Standard for Surface Flammability of Carpets and Rugs (DOC-FF 1-70).

It's possible also that your lending institution may want some assurance of quality of a wall-to-wall carpeting installation; acceptance in this respect might be to choose carpeting that meets HUD-MPS's and in this case, carpeting is covered along with carpet cushions in two FHA "Use of Materials Bulletins" (UM-44c and UM-47).

Carpet Installation Factors

Tackless strips appear to be the most common installation method used. Strips have rows of projecting pins on their up-side, which are angled towards the wall when the strips are nailed or glued to the floor along the room perimeter. The pins firmly grip the stretched carpeting and the excess is trimmed off flush with the wall. Edges can be concealed by a 3/4-round molding nailed to the baseboard just above the carpeting.

Tacking was once the most common method . . . turning the carpet edges under at the room perimeter and tacking the turned-down edge adjacent to the shoe molding or to the baseboard before applying the shoe. Stretching is also done with the tacking method but holding the stretch is a line of stay tacks about 2 feet in from the walls, followed by trimming and edge tacking.

Padding is placed under carpeting to lengthen the

carpet's life as well as to soften the impact of walking and thus provide foot comfort. Padding of hair, felt, rubber-coated jute and cellular rubber have been used, but much of the cushion material used today uses synthetic foam molded into a waffle-like form.

The surface to which carpeting is applied should be smooth, relatively uniform, and ridgeless. The normal underlayment materials described in Chapter 32 are suitable. Where separate cushion or padding is to be used, it should be stapled to the underlayment and the joints seamed with tape. Avoid coinciding seams with carpeting. Certain types of padding materials should be laid with a light stretch using a regular carpeting knee-kicker.

With most cushion- or foam-backed carpeting materials, an adhesive application is used rather than the tackless strip technique. Adhesive materials designed for carpeting applications should be used. They come in two types, in cans or containers similar to that employed for resilient floor coverings, or double-covered adhesive tape. Called carpet tape, this method is an easy one appropriate to most rooms. Where unusually rough use may be involved, the cushion-backed carpetings should probably be applied with the overall adhesive application. Check with your carpeting supplier on this.

Plan your carpet layout to use a minimum number of sections and a minimum of seams. If practicable, keep the seams in out-of-traffic locations. Always lay your carpeting in the same direction; that is, don't butt the end of a fresh roll to the side of a previous roll.

On jute-backed carpeting and separate cushion installations, use knee-kick stretchers unless the manufacturer indicates by label that such should not be used. Stretching in large areas may be best done by a powered device perhaps available on a rental basis. Stretching in both length and width directions should produce a uniform appearance without any diagonal bias.

Normal jute-backed carpeting over padding ordinarily involves sewing of seams. Use a No. 18 waxed linen thread. This is bottom sewing of the backing mterial; your supplier also should have raw-edge sealing latex for application to raw edges before sewing.

Much easier seaming is possible with the cushion-backed carpetings using the double-faced tapes or continuous beads of carpeting adhesive. Such seams can be "set" by the use of sandbags or similar weighting-down overnight.

Take your time in installing, as you should in selection. Carpetings will provide you with many years of service, given a decent installation and adequate maintenance. The many new developments in fibers, construction and treatments have, as mentioned earlier, brought a much wider range of properties. But in some cases, the properties may not be good ones. For example, what's the allergy situation in your family? You may wish to have a certain child's room or perhaps the entire home carpeted in nonallergenic-fiber carpeting. What about your habits with moths? Some carpet fibers make great moth food. Then, there is the shock hazard, with some carpetings being notable for their static electricity, if untreated. There are also some questions to be asked about shedding or pill-rolling or small blow-away tufts . . . these are all no-no's. And there's furniture denting. This reflects the carpet's lack of resilience or bounce-back . . . ask about it. You'll also want to know about color-fastness and ability to take repeated carpet shampoos or cleaning without fading or other adverse effects.

46 Walks, Drive and Landscaping

Access convenience is important. Your home will see a lot of coming and going. You can make it simpler and avoid built-in irritations by planning ahead. Of course, you want it to look good; but convenience in day-to-day movements gets top billing.

The first consideration goes to autos. Despite gas prices, unemployment, and everything else you have to worry about, auto travel will still be heavily involved in your to-and-fro movements.

You may have followed the counsel given in Chapter 5 for preparing your driveway for use during the construction period. This should be done by establishing at that time the driveway layout. But often this doesn't get done because there are a multitude of other things to get going when a home starts construction. Often, just barely sufficient rock base and gravel are provided at the street or road entrance and for a short distance into the lot. So, the subject will be dealt with here in more detail.

You should determine at once the need or desire for an auto turn-around. This does take extra surfacing but offers real convenience. You don't realize how often you come and go by car until you have to back out every time. But turn-arounds can also have added value in other ways. Properly laid out, they can serve as parking areas for visitors. They come in very handy for car washings and maintenance. With multiple-car families, the turn-arounds ease the inevitable shuttling or shuffling of cars to get the right one out. The suggestion here is that you trim your costs somewhere else, but don't omit from your driveway a place to change driving directions.

Consider a semi-circular drive with two street or road entrances-exits only if your lot has ample width. This in-one-way and out-the-other pattern works better for front-entering garages than with side-entrance ones. The latter appear to be best served by a wide drive that goes beyond the garage entrance to furnish turn-around space to the rear.

Don't try to economize on driveway width. A 10 foot wide drive is sufficient for just driving, but when visitors park on the drive, they'll have to get out on the grass or planting area. Where any curvature is involved, a couple extra feet in width is desirable to avoid cars going off the drive. A long drive doesn't have to be fully paved, or all paved in the same type of surfacing. Concrete pavement is the most desirable because of the smoothness of the surfacing and the low maintenance. But these desirable qualities are best appreciated and most needed in the drive and turn-around areas closer to the home.

Driveway paving, as suggested earlier, should really be a two-stage process. First the digging out of the earth to permit placement of a base layer of 6-to-10 inches of crushed stone. Second, the pouring of concrete or laying of a blacktop surface layer *after* the base stage has had 8-to-12 months to compact and settle. This waiting period, while cars and trucks are compacting your gravel base, will produce a more stable concrete or blacktop surface that will show considerably less minor cracking and almost no pavement break-off areas where base settling is the cause. If your home-site is of hard, dense soil and the driveway digging goes to undisturbed earth, the waiting period can be trimmed down to perhaps 3 to 4 months.

In providing a driveway base, note the difference between crushed stone and gravel. Most gravels ordered from a building supply dealer are washed gravels graded for size. The individual pieces are rounded. When packed, they continue to slip or mesh rather easily. For your driveway base, order crushed stone which has irregular rock shapes that bind together solidly. The bottom portion of your base layer can be old crushed concrete but add some medium-size stones to it. Later, just before the drive is to be surfaced, add some fine stone and crown the base with a raised center . . . 2-to-2-½ inches for a 10 foot wide drive and about 4 inches for an 18 foot drive.

Flat Slabs and Entrance Stoops

Your order of procedure for the remaining concrete work may vary with the individual home and the condition of the ground or concrete base. As a general rule or prac-

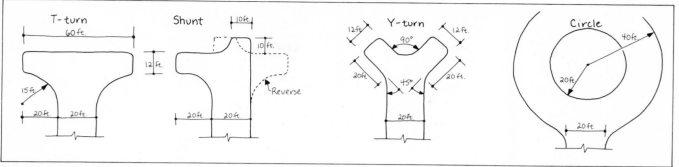

Driveway Patterns with turnaround space or extensions for turning purposes are shown here, adapted from the designs illustrated in HUD's Manual of Acceptable Practices. All right angle turning corners need a minimum radius of 15 feet. Curvature in the main length of the driveway is inconvenient for cars that back out, so maintain alignment. Driveway width minimum is 8 feet.

tice, the order of priority is . . . basement and garage floors . . . entrance stoops and steps . . . walks and drive-way . . . patio.

When a concrete subcontractor is doing the work for a home builder, all of the above may be completed within a single 2-or-3-day period. With an owner-builder, who will be involved with preparatory work with each part, it makes more sense to do the work a step at a time. The principal consideration is to prepare sufficient work to accommodate about 11 or 12 cubic yards of concrete, the normal amount of a single ready-mix truckload.

Pouring-finishing of concrete flat slabs is quite a bit different from the earlier concrete work done for footings and possibly foundation walls. Flat slab work does require proper finishing, the proper type of finish at the necessary finishing locations. There's nothing difficult about finishing work, with just one exception; it does take some skill and practice to use a steel finishing trowel at just the right stage of dryness to produce a uniform and smooth-hard-dense surface without leaving any trowel ridge marks.

Now, before you have doubts about your concrete finishing ability, it should be said that the only place you really need such a good, hard, dense smooth surface is your basement floor. Outdoor slabs are better finished by a troweling plus a light brushing. In most areas, you will encounter no problem in obtaining the name and phone number of a moonlighting cement finisher or subcontractor who will appear on your job while you're pouring the concrete and will handle the finishing work for you. Observe the expert in action on your basement floor; then, you should be able to handle the balance of finishing work where the troweling-edging-jointing work is given the final brushing that eradicates minor irregularities in troweling and gives a slight coarseness to the surface. Just sufficient to keep the outdoor slabs from becoming slippery when wet.

Concrete walks are normally placed directly on graded earth but if you have some sand, gravel or crushed stone handy from other work, apply a thin layer to the graded area. Use 2X4's for forming the walways, setting on edge and nailing to regularly spaced stakes. Set the forms to give walks a slight slope away from the building for surface drainage. A slope of about 1/4 inch per foot.

Place your walks for convenient usage. With home mail deliveries curtailed or made to street mail boxes, the old need for a walkway from home to street may be eliminated. Let your driveway handle walkers up to the point where they can conveniently proceed to the front entrance. Make your entrance walk from drive to stoop about 4 feet wide, sufficient to accommodate couples walking. The traditional 36 inch wide walk is fine for rear doors but for front entry use it confines visitors to single-file.

For the two working entrances, front and rear, there is no hard surface quite as durable or satisfactory as concrete. The only possible exception for some homes might be a raised outdoor wood deck (see Chapter 49).

Many people find great attraction in walks and entrance steps-stoops of brick, flagstone, masonry or patio blocks. Don't do it. Or if you do, be prepared to do considerable maintenance work every 2 or 3 years and to have some harsh irritable language gush forth about the surface irregularities during periods between maintenance periods. The irregularities are apt to be more pronounced in northern areas of the country.

Basement Floor Installation

Basement and garage floors are much alike. Both inside the house. Both extend wall to wall and need only intermediate strike-off forming. Both rest on the ground and need to have a suitable base course preparation. They're also alike in that because they're part of the house, you're particularly anxious to get them installed as quickly as possible whereas the balance of the outdoor concrete can afford to suffer a few delays.

(1) The grade in the basement (or garage) should be leveled

smooth and low spots filled with crushed stone or gravel; fill any mushy holes with stone or gravel; bring the grade up to allow a 4 inch slab thickness.

(2) If your earth base is almost constantly wet, dig it out sufficiently for a base course of 4 to 6 inches of gravel or stone and then cover it with a layer of polyethylene film before pouring. If it appears to be excessively wet, check whether you installed the outside-foundation drain tile (Chapter 8) and what the outlet situation is for this tile; you may have to pump out the basement area before preparing the base and once again before pouring. If excessively wet and no outside drain tile were placed, you had best consider placement of interior perimeter tile running to a basement sump pump.

(3) Depending on size or shape, your slab is best poured in sections; if the basement is quite small, a single row of 2X4's on edge down the approximate center will let you pour one section (half the basement) first, get it struck off and floated; then the other half can be poured, struck off, floated, the 2X4 removed and void filled with concrete. In larger basements, three or even four sections are suggested; the 2X4 strike-offs must be set, of course to proper grade;

(4) At the perimeter, 1/2 or 3/4 inch thick felt-type asphalt-impregnated concrete joint strips 4 inches wide are set along the basement wall and held in place by temporary stakes or shovel-fulls of gravel; these rest on footing top, help accommodate slab expansion (they're sometimes called expansion joint strips) and at the same time they act as the strike-off edge along with your section 2X4's.

(5) If adjustable basement columns were used, you will probably want to place a sheet-metal piece around the base of the columns in order to keep the adjustability; trim the metal so it rests on the footing and comes up to about a half inch above floor line.

(6) With respect to plumbing items at floor level, you'll want to check and correct the placements of sump-pump pit cover, floor drain outlet, waste and sewer clean-outs. Place floor drain about an inch below your concrete surface grade and slope the surrounding slab down to this drain. If height of other items is off, dig out or block up to the correct level; clean-outs should project above floor line sufficiently to permit plug removal.

(7) Be certain that your base course is pretty well compacted before concrete is placed, and wet it down before pouring; the slab normally doesn't need reinforcing unless there are a number of soft areas. Use 6X6 inch wire mesh over the entire floor area; cut mesh from rolls in 8, 10 or 12 foot lengths; spread concrete about 2 inches deep, place mesh, then follow with balance of the concrete.

Owner-builders may run into some hassle when ordering ready-mix. The ready-mix supplier wants to be sure your job will be ready to take the concrete without delay and that you will have adequate manpower to handle the concrete almost as fast as the truck operator can dish it up. In many cases, there is a demurrage or service charge in connection with any delayed trucks.

In ordering the concrete, be certain the supplier knows what the application consists of. There are different concrete proportionings for different applications. In the case of residential floors and flat slab work, the aggregate size

---

Concrete Steps and Drives are easiest to maintain and keep looking neat through the years. At left, integral steps of concrete flanked by planter boxes. At right, a straight concrete drive with parallel walk.

should be in the 3/4 to 1 inch size plus sand, and the wetness or slump be in the range of 2-to-4 inches. Basement floor concrete, installed after framing construction work, is generally placed through basement window or door openings; be prepared inside the basement with a high-sided contractors' wheelbarrow for distributing the mix.

Practices and terminology vary somewhat with respect to ordering concrete and specifying its quality. In some locations, the practice is to order concrete of a 5-bag mix or

a 7-bag mix, etc. In other places, the concrete is commonly described by the compressive strength it is intended to develop after curing . . . for example, a concrete which develops 3,500 pound compressive strenth per square inch at 28 days following pour is suitable for floors, walks, entrances and driveways.

In this connection, the Portland Cement Association suggests the use of cement weight per cubic yard and recommends the minimum cement content for basement floors of 540 pounds of cement for 3/4 inch aggregate size and 520 pounds for 1 inch aggregate size. Your supplier can be counted on to tell you what he usually supplies for the type of installation you're making.

While the concrete floor or slab can be walked upon the next day after pouring, it shouldn't really be used until it is sufficiently cured. This normally will mean keeping traffic off and keeping the surface damp for a period of 3 to 5 days, the longer period being necessary if the weather is hot and dry.

Forming for Concrete Steps is done with 2X6's and braced by 2X4 diagonals to ground stakes. Two cheek forms at sides are partially held in place by a series of riser forms. Note the beveling on the bottoms of riser forms to facilitate tread troweling and riser form removal.

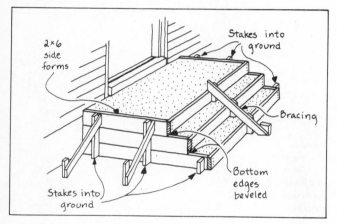

Concrete Porch Steps

At house entrances (except for sliding patio doors which generally have direct access to a patio as described in Chapter 49), the concrete or masonry work can be divided up if the owner desires. For example, the basic steps and porch can be installed at once, adding decorative supplements such as planter boxes or other details later. However, if porches are more than just a couple steps off the ground,

Concrete Step Finishing begins with float and steel trowel on the platform and step treads. Top riser form is then removed carefully to avoid corner breakaway of concrete. Riser face is floated (left photo) and followed by troweling plus the use of an inside-corner trowel (right photo). Outside corners of the steps may be finished either with an outside-corner trowel or with an edger plus steel trowel.

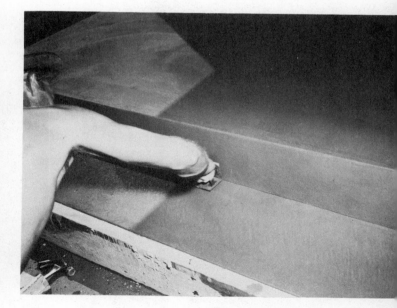

it's advisable that the steps and porch slab be immediately provided with handrails. Ornamental iron and aluminum railing materials, parts, and attachment devices are readily available in lumber-supply and home center retailers. The logical way to approach this job is to plan, in sketch-to-scale form, your porch and steps. Obtain railing literature showing parts and pieces so that you can make up your order to fit the need. If the railing parts include insert pieces for the concrete, these will provide a firmer fastening then fittings which require later drilling of holes to accommodate the fastening devices. Most ornamental iron/aluminum suppliers furnish straight and angle railing sections (4 to 10 feet in length is typical), newel posts that attach to the concrete and support the railings, and a choice of scrolls or ornaments to fit the railing sections and posts. The same suppliers will also usually carry matching ornamental columns for supporting porch roofs.

At the time outdoor concrete work is being done, the patio or outdoor deck area should be given some attention. If it is to be of concrete, it can have a base preparation and pour identical to that used for your driveway. Or there are a variety of designs and surface finish methods that a

Shape and Branch Characteristics to seek in selecting landscaping shrubs. Other considerations: growth habits and degree of attention or maintenance required. HUD's Manual of Acceptable Practices suggests that initial sizes of new trees and shrubs should be sufficient for their intended function and gives these specifics: 1½ to 2 inches caliper minimum for shade trees, a minimum of 4 to 5 feet height for evergreens, a minimum of 3 years growth for fast-growing shrubs and 5 years growth for slower ones. Often a few mature plants in a group will result in better appearance than a profusion of spread-out small ones.

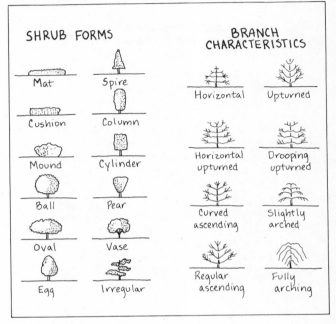

Outdoor Wood in permanent installations is highly attractive but when used in contact with or near the ground, the wood should have a preservative treatment. Shown here are two different kinds of wood units used outdoors and both have had a factory-applied special "Wolmanizing" pressure treatment by the supplier, the Koppers Co. In the preservative treatment, salts are forced into the wood under extreme pressure in a process that leaves the wood clean to the touch and with a natural weathered appearance. At left, treated dimension lumber for use in a wood entry deck; at the right, treated round wood posts set side-by-side in concrete footings to provide earth-retaining borders.

concrete patio slab can be given (see appendix). If the decision is to delay the concrete patio work, leveling-grading and base course work could be done now to allow compaction time.

Serious consideration at this time might be given to the alternative of a raised, off-the-ground, outdoor wood deck to serve as patio and outdoor living room. Such decks are especially appropriate for use outside of sliding patio doors of family rooms, dining rooms or kitchens. Wood decks are constructed on concrete footings and piers (see Chapter 49). If such a deck is planned, now is the time to grade the ground, dig footing holes, provide forming for low piers and pour them, while other concrete work is being done.

Grading, Grass and Plantings

Shortly after your home's foundations were completed, the backfilling work was done by tractor or bulldozer and at the same time, most of the dirt excavated was leveled off the give a definite slope away from the house. Perhaps the excavator put aside, in a separate pile, black topsoil. If so, don't touch that just yet.

With your rough grade just about where you wish it to be from the backfill-machine-grading work, you can proceed to rake and pulverize the top two inches or so within an area around the home. This should be done only after the digging necessary for entrance steps, porches, walks and the house end of your drive. The object is to do the preliminary cleanup and ground preparation so that after pouring of concrete steps-walks-drive, the only work needed is spreading of topsoil and seed. It doesn't pay to have general dirt moving, raking, debris gathering, and hauling-away work done over fresh concrete.

The next step in your logical procedure will be the provision of protective devices for existing trees and shrubs. This is needed only where it turns out there is more than about 4-5 inches of fresh graded dirt placed over the existing or former ground level around trees and larger shrubs. To assure that adequate moisture reaches the roots of such trees and shrubs, a low protective wall should circle the plant at a distance of about two tree trunk diameters. For smaller trees or shrubs, just a ring of galvanized sheet metal for temporary hold-back of grading dirt is all you need, or try a permanent and attractive tree well wall of bricks, masonry blocks, railroad ties, or other materials.

In checking existing shrubs, you may wish to note any that have excessive branch length so that the branches fan out widely and droop to reach near to the ground. Such shrubs need cutting back and this can be done as you place a dirt retain ring around their bases. A close cropping of these branches brings a rebirth of the shrub and a revived, healthy appearance to the plant.

If you have a relatively large number of existing trees within fairly close proximity of your home, it is probably desirable to consult a tree specialist about removal of dead branches and a general pruning. This not only im-

proves their appearance but can help to stimulate further and better growth.

If you plan to plant any new trees or shrubs, have them delivered now. Ask for planting instructions at time of purchase. Make any preparatory provisions for border edgings or plant wells so that there's no later digging or fussing around a new plant after its been set into position.

On new homes where financing is insured by FHA/VA and where HUD-MPS's apply, the provisions for landscaping provide:

> Plant materials shall be provided to enhance the appearance of buildings and grounds, provide necessary screening, help separate incompatible use areas, arrest erosion and reduce noise. Quantities of trees and shrubs shall be sufficient to fulfill the needs of the property, as interpreted by HUD, based on professional site design analysis and the customary planting treatments in the general locale.

Too often the above general requirements lead to what became known to home builders as the "FHA tree" plus a couple of scrawny, mandatory small evergreens at the house entrance.

The wise owner-builder will include in his planning budget and house-cost estimate a reasonable sum for new planting materials, especially shrubs and bushes. And at the same time, he'll recognize the advantage in the gradually improved home appearance attainable with a small but regular year-in, year-out program of adding new plantings.

Outdoor Paving

While there's no substitute for outdoor concrete as far as cleanliness, durability, and low maintenance, an excellent alternative for driveway paving is plant-mixed blacktop or asphalt topping laid to a thickness of about 2 inches over a well-graded, crowned, and compacted base course.

If you've previously installed a crushed rock or stone base with some finer mesh material on top and given it a chance to settle or be compacted, it can now receive the blacktop. This material should be purchased on the basis that the installing crew provide the fine crushed-stone top layer, compact it with a road roller, and then lay the blacktop mix. This job requires specialized equipment and should not be attempted by the owner-builder with hand tools. Many hard-material dealers carry bags of premixed blacktop material, but these are useful mostly for patching purposes.

Pay attention to the stone base to be sure it is raked into proper shape. If driven upon during construction, the auto wheel tracks will depress the stone. If these depressed areas aren't raked out and a suitable shape of round crown provided in the base course, the blacktopping will turn out crownless and include the wheel depressions. Such depressions hold water after a rain and tend to be the places where cracking first occurs and becomes most serious.

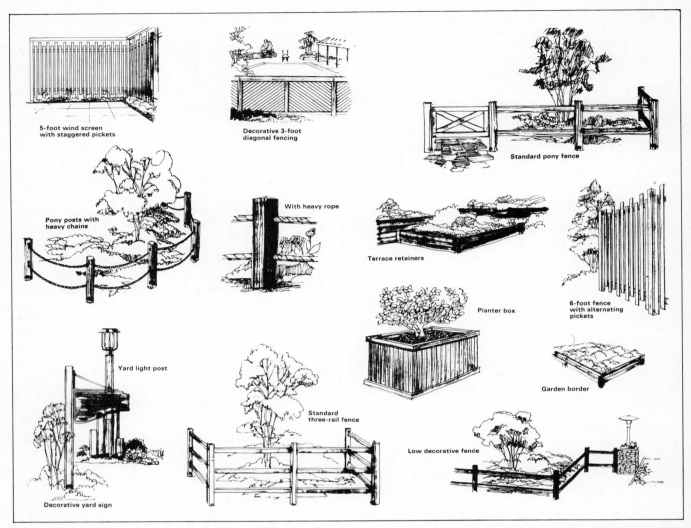

Split Red Cedar with a special rustic look which weathers to an appealing neutral grey is a versatile outdoor wood. These sketches suggesting appropriate applications for this low-maintenance species were taken from a "Creative Ideas" brochure issued by and available from the Potlatch Corp.

Concrete Driveway Tips

(1) The subgrade or base for your driveway pavement is important. When your home site is relatively high and well-drained, the hard undisturbed earth makes a good base. But where topsoil has been removed and/or grading work has brought loose material, the driveway base should be excavated and filled with stone or other suitable granular material.

(2) The advantage derived from placing a base course and driving on it for 4 to 8 months before paving is that it allows time for ground settling and for potential trouble spots to appear in the base that can be remedied before paving.

(3) Run the crushed stone or fill material about a foot wider on each side of the driveway than the pavement width; this prevents under-cutting of the slab and subsequent possible breakage by surface drainage off the slab.

(4) Alternatives to crushed stone as a base might be such locally available materials as slag, mine tailings, some kinds of coarse sand and mixed sand-gravel. Broken-up concrete sledged down to manageable sizes is a good base material but needs the addition of some fine stone on the top.

(5) A 4 inch thick slab is sufficient for single-width drives of about 10 feet; make the slab slightly thicker (5 inches) for drives of 16-to-18 feet wide. Use 2X4's to form slab edges except where a curve in the concrete is needed such as at turns or entrance aprons where 1X4's can be bent to the desired radius. Use 2X6's or 1X6's for the 5 inch thickness, keeping the bottom edges slightly below grade.

(6) Wet down the subgrade in advance or the dry ground will be absorbing moisture from the concrete and the concrete then sets up too fast for the finishing work; sprinkle it thoroughly with a hose but not so much that muddy spots or standing water remain.

(7) For ease in shoveling the concrete that needs lifting or placement, use a pointed shovel; switch to a square-ended shovel for spreading, leveling and spading. The latter involves placing the shovel's concave upper side to the form and holding the handle vertically with shovel corners against the form, pumping the shovel up and down in short strokes along the form. This produces smooth concrete next to the shovel's back side and when the shovel is removed, the smooth concrete goes against the forms so that when forms are removed no concrete voids occur.

(8) Use a straight 2X6 for "striking off" the spread concrete; this is done by placing the 2X6 across the forms on edge and see-sawing it back and forth to level the concrete down to form heights and to move the excess forward; strike a second time with a slight tilt of the 2X6 to raise fine stone to the surface.

(9) After striking, if you've planned for a crown in the pavement, shovel some added concrete to the center area using a fanning-out motion with the shovel; have a bullfloat ready to smooth the center area down working the float with a motion towards the slab center; also have ready an inch-board that will reach from form-to-form across the slab whose bottom has been cut by saw to the slightly-rounded crown shape; use this to test frequently that enough extra concrete has been spread in the center area to form the crown.

(10) The foregoing work should be done as rapidly as possible with a minimum of float work to get the concrete surface brought to the proper crowned shape. Now, as a preliminary aid to the concrete finisher, trim the slab edges along the forms with a 1/2 inch radius edging tool . . . just one pass along the edge to cut the bond between the slab edge and the form edge before the concrete stiffens.

(11) Final finishing of the surface, jointing and brushing must await proper set of the concrete once all the surface water has left and there's been a noticeable stiffening sufficient to sustain the weight of the finished on his finishing boards.

Driveway slabs need curing similar to basement floors and concrete walks and steps. Use burlap cloths kept wet or cover with polyethylene film. Just so the surface remains moist.

After 3 to 5 days of curing time, protective covers can be taken off, forms removed, grading dirt brought to the slab edges.

Now, finally, your yard is ready for final application of the topsoil that's been saved, or the bringing in of fresh black dirt for seeding. Or, in some areas having sod farms, you may decide to buy sod in place of seed and come up with an instant lawn.

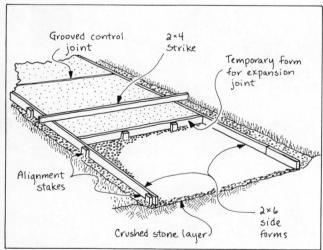

Forming-Pouring Concrete Drives is a procedure similar to that involved in concrete walks or patio slabs. Earth is graded, side or edge forms are staked out and aligned, then concrete is poured and struck off level. For driveways, a 4-to-6 inch layer of crushed stone base is highly desirable. The 2X6 side forms should be aligned straight using a mason's line and a transit-level for elevation. Provision for the water surface drainage should be either by a cross-slope of about 1/8-inch per foot of driveway width or by a crown in the center having a comparable slope to each edge.

Procedures in Pouring-Finishing Slabs are given in this series of a dozen photos. In the first group, the procedure begins after forming and grade preparation. First the fill-in gravel base is tamped to compact it (1) followed by wetting down the grade (2). Wet concrete from the ready-mix truck chute is then dumped within the forms and spread using a square shovel (3). Leveling is followed by see-sawing a strike-off board to bring the surface smoothly even with the top edges of the form boards. Then, the finisher uses a large bullfloat (4) to fill small voids and raise the concrete fines to the surface.

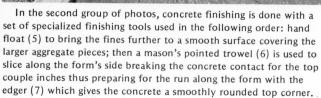

In the second group of photos, concrete finishing is done with a set of specialized finishing tools used in the following order: hand float (5) to bring the fines further to a smooth surface covering the larger aggregate pieces; then a mason's pointed trowel (6) is used to slice along the form's side breaking the concrete contact for the top couple inches thus preparing for the run along the form with the edger (7) which gives the concrete a smoothly rounded top corner.

At regular intervals along the walk or slab, usually from 3½ to about 6 feet, a joint is cut using a board for a straight-edge guide (8). The jointer tool is designed to place a slightly rounded V-groove in the concrete which is about 3/4 inch deep. This is sometimes referred to as a control joint because its function is to control any cracking that may occur. A crack in the joint is more desirable (if cracking must occur) in the joint where it can be suitably filled with a joint sealer.

Final finishing work is indicated in the final group of photos. After edging and jointing comes the working of the slab's surface which is by now drying out and becoming free of surface water. A float (9) first roughs up the setting surface slightly giving it a properly moist and textured top 1/8-inch which is then brought to a final smooth and slick surface by a steel finishing trowel (10). The finisher works the surface using the trowel at a slight tilt and with even pressure in a sweeping motion. Back and forth across in a semi-circle smoothing out previous trowel marks. Final troweling is best accomplished when the top surface looks nearly dry. Outdoor walks and drives left trowel smooth are apt to be slippery underfoot in wet or snowy weather. Broom trowel work (11) for a slightly coarse texture. Last step (12) uses strips of burlap kept wetted down to cure the slab for a period of 2 or 3 days.

47 Your Mortgage Loan

Approaching construction completion time, you're ready to have your final inspection by building authorities and to obtain your permanent amortized mortgage loan. In connection with the legalities of the mortgage and the documentation that accompanies it, you'll encounter a number of new and perhaps confusing terms.

In the initial chapter on home financing it was pointed out that the arrangements made at that time were not for an immediate mortgage but rather a conditional one. That is, what you would have received from the lending institution was some form of *firm commitment* for the institution to provide you with such a mortgage loan at some time in the future when the home construction work had been satisfactorily completed.

In the meantime, this firm commitment had immediate value because it led to the availability of money for construction purposes either in the form of an interim loan by the same lender or for a construction loan by some other lending institution. Now, with the home completed, inspected, and certified for occupancy, the entire property (home and land) can serve as the collateral for a long-term mortgage loan, the proceeds of which will serve to pay off and close out the interim or construction loan.

An amortized mortgage . . . the way nearly all residential mortgages are written . . . calls for repayment of the loan and interest in monthly installments at the interest rate and over the period of time specified in the mortgage contract. During the initial early period of the loan when the debt and interest charges are the largest, more of your monthly installments are for interest. As the loan matures, the percentage going for interest is diminished and the percentage applying to repayment of the principal amount increases. The amount of principal that has been repaid at any given time is sometimes referred to as the amount of owner's "equity" in a home. But it is obvious that an owner-builder also has the value of the labor he contributes as equity in the home.

In some states, the security instrument is a trust deed instead of a mortgage. The borrower deeds the property to a trustee under terms similar to those of a mortgage and when the loan has been fully repaid, the trustee returns the deed to the owner.

Final Inspection

Your home usually will not be acceptable to the mortgage-loan officer until it has received its final inspection although, there are some lenders that do not stand upon this formality.

And practices vary on final inspections. You should ask the building inspector (if you're in a fairly large municipality, go to the building department head), at the time of your last plumbing-heating inspection, exactly what further work must be completed for the final inspection.

In many communities, you will need a certificate of occupancy before you will be able to move in. Usually such a certificate is not issued until after the final inspection. The owner-builder is usually eager to move in as quickly as possible even though all interior work may not be entirely done. Very often, what is impossible to achieve through normal channels can sometimes be worked around on an informal basis, when discussed and arranged well in advance. If you've been unusually diligent in adhering to building department rules on permits, notices, and other approval procedures, the building official will probably try to be helpful to you when it comes to the time you'd like to move in.

Before collecting your papers for the visit to the mortgage lending firm, you'd be wise to make a recheck of the engineer's lot survey and plot-plan drawing. Go measure once again the dimensions shown on the plot-plan drawing to make certain that the reality which has been constructed is in the exact position the drawing indicated it should be. Also verify some of the other details that may be shown on the plot-plan drawing. Are the sewer-water lines correctly shown? What about the gas and electric service lines . . . are they correctly indicated? It is especially desirable to fix accurately the location of underground lines so that in case of any future digging, you know just what might be encount-

A. U.S. DEPARTMENT OF HOUSING AND URBAN DEVELOPMENT	B. TYPE OF LOAN	
	1. ☐ FHA 2. ☐ FMHA 3. ☐ CONV. UNINS. 4. ☐ VA 5. ☐ CONV. INS.	
DISCLOSURE/SETTLEMENT STATEMENT	6. FILE NUMBER 7. LOAN NUMBER	
If the Truth-in-Lending Act applies to this transaction, a Truth-in-Lending statement is attached as page 3 of this form.	8. MORTG. INS. CASE NO.	

C. NOTE: This form is furnished to you prior to settlement to give you information about your settlement costs, and again after settlement to show the actual costs you have paid. The present copy of the form is:

☐ ADVANCE DISCLOSURE OF COSTS. Some items are estimated, and are marked "(e)." Some amounts may change if the settlement is held on a date other than the date estimated below. The preparer of this form is not responsible for errors or changes in amounts furnished by others.

☐ STATEMENT OF ACTUAL COSTS. Amounts paid to and by the settlement agent are shown. Items marked "(p.o.c.)" were paid outside the closing; they are shown here for informational purposes and are not included in totals.

D. NAME OF BORROWER	E. SELLER	F. LENDER

G. PROPERTY LOCATION	H. SETTLEMENT AGENT	I. DATES	
		LOAN COMMITMENT	ADVANCE DISCLOSURE
	PLACE OF SETTLEMENT	SETTLEMENT	DATE OF PRORATIONS IF DIFFERENT FROM SETTLEMENT

J. SUMMARY OF BORROWER'S TRANSACTION		K. SUMMARY OF SELLER'S TRANSACTION	
100. **GROSS AMOUNT DUE FROM BORROWER:**		400. **GROSS AMOUNT DUE TO SELLER:**	
101. Contract sales price		401. Contract sales price	
102. Personal property		402. Personal property	
103. Settlement charges to borrower *(from line 1400, Section L)*		403.	
104.		404.	
105.		Adjustments for items paid by seller in advance:	
Adjustments for items paid by seller in advance:		405. City/town taxes to	
		406. County taxes to	
106. City/town taxes to		407. Assessments to	
107. County taxes to		408. to	
108. Assessments to		409. to	
109. to		410. to	
110. to		411. to	
111. to			
112. to		420. **GROSS AMOUNT DUE TO SELLER**	
120. **GROSS AMOUNT DUE FROM BORROWER:**		*NOTE: The following 500 and 600 series section are not required to be completed when this form is used for advance disclosure of settlement costs prior to settlement.*	
200. **AMOUNTS PAID BY OR IN BEHALF OF BORROWER:**		500. **REDUCTIONS IN AMOUNT DUE TO SELLER:**	
201. Deposit or earnest money		501. Payoff of first mortgage loan	
202. Principal amount of new loan(s)		502. Payoff of second mortgage loan	
203. Existing loan(s) taken subject to		503. Settlement charges to seller *(from line 1400, Section L)*	
204.		504. Existing loan(s) taken subject to	
205.		505.	
Credits to borrower for items unpaid by seller:		506.	
		507.	
206. City/town taxes to		508.	
207. County taxes to		509.	
208. Assessments to		Credits to borrower for items unpaid by seller:	
209. to		510. City/town taxes to	
210. to		511. County taxes to	
211. to		512. Assessments to	
212. to		513. to	
220. **TOTAL AMOUNTS PAID BY OR IN BEHALF OF BORROWER**		514. to	
		515. to	
300. **CASH AT SETTLEMENT REQUIRED FROM OR PAYABLE TO BORROWER:**		520. **TOTAL REDUCTIONS IN AMOUNT DUE TO SELLER**	
301. Gross amount due from borrower *(from line 120)*		600. **CASH TO SELLER FROM SETTLEMENT:**	
302. Less amounts paid by or in behalf of borrower *(from line 220)*		601. Gross amount due to seller *(from line 420)*	
303. CASH ☐ REQUIRED FROM OR ☐ PAYABLE TO BORROWER:		602. Less total reductions in amount due to seller *(from line 520)*	
		603. **CASH TO SELLER FROM SETTLEMENT**	

HUD-1A (6-75) AS & AS (1323)

Disclosure Settlement Statement required by HUD for property sale closings was aimed at enlightening property buyers about the many various details involved in the transaction and their probable costs. When the Real Estate Settlement Procedures Act (RESPA) first went into effect in mid-1974, the government received a multitude of hardship complaints about the way the Act operated from lenders, realtors and home-builders who had to use the RESPA forms and comply with the Act's provisions. These criticisms centered on the increased paperwork the Act required, the delays and a resulting increase in a borrower's costs rather than the expected lowering.

At present writing, bills are before the Congress which will

L. SETTLEMENT CHARGES	PAID FROM BORROWER'S FUNDS	PAID FROM SELLER'S FUNDS
700. SALES/BROKER'S COMMISSION based on price $ @ %		
701. Total commission paid by seller Division of commission as follows:		
702. $ to		
703. $ to		
704.		
800. ITEMS PAYABLE IN CONNECTION WITH LOAN.		
801. Loan Origination fee %		
802. Loan Discount %		
803. Appraisal Fee to		
804. Credit Report to		
805. Lender's inspection fee		
806. Mortgage Insurance application fee to		
807. Assumption/refinancing fee		
808.		
809.		
810.		
811.		
900. ITEMS REQUIRED BY LENDER TO BE PAID IN ADVANCE.		
901. Interest from to @ $ /day		
902. Mortgage insurance premium for mo. to		
903. Hazard insurance premium for yrs. to		
904. yrs. to		
905.		
1000. RESERVES DEPOSITED WITH LENDER FOR:		
1001. Hazard insurance mo. @ $ /mo.		
1002. Mortgage insurance mo. @ $ /mo.		
1003. City property taxes mo. @ $ /mo.		
1004. County property taxes mo. @ $ /mo.		
1005. Annual assessments mo. @ $ /mo.		
1006. mo. @ $ /mo.		
1007. mo. @ $ /mo.		
1008. mo. @ $ /mo.		
1100. TITLE CHARGES:		
1101. Settlement or closing fee to		
1102. Abstract or title search to		
1103. Title examination to		
1104. Title insurance binder to		
1105. Document preparation to		
1106. Notary fees to		
1107. Attorney's Fees to		
(includes above items No.:)		
1108. Title insurance to		
(includes above items No.:)		
1109. Lender's coverage $		
1110. Owner's coverage $		
1111.		
1112.		
1113.		
1200. GOVERNMENT RECORDING AND TRANSFER CHARGES		
1201. Recording fees: Deed $; Mortgage $ Releases $		
1202. City/county tax/stamps: Deed $; Mortgage $		
1203. State tax/stamps: Deed $; Mortgage $		
1204.		
1300. ADDITIONAL SETTLEMENT CHARGES		
1301. Survey to		
1302. Pest inspection to		
1303.		
1304.		
1305.		
1400. TOTAL SETTLEMENT CHARGES (entered on lines 103 and 503, Sections J and K)		

The Undersigned Acknowledges Receipt of This Disclosure Settlement Statement and Agrees to the Correctness Thereof.

_____   _____
Buyer or Agent   Seller or Agent

NOTE: *Under certain circumstances the borrower and seller may be permitted to waive the 12-day period which must normally occur between advance disclosure and settlement. In the event such a waiver is made, copies of the statements of waiver, executed as provided in the regulations of the Department of Housing and Urban Development, shall be attached to and made a part of this form when the form is used as a settlement statement.*

HUD-1B (5-75)   AS & AS (1323)

modify the original Act's provisions perhaps by channeling many of these items towards the lender with the end effect of reducing the borrower's direct payment costs but probably resulting in higher but tax-deductible charges by the lender. The original Disclosure Statement form reproduced above, though perhaps not applicable because of modifications, will still serve to indicate to owner-builders and property buyers the many fees and charges that can be involved in a real estate transaction.

ered below the surface on your lot or close to its boundaries.

Include on the plot drawing any supplementary installations that may have been made subsequent to the time the plans were prepared, such as patio or deck, swimming pool, garden walks, landscape features. Whatever you actually did to provide value in the home may be something more than what the original drawings indicated and which was the basis of your preconstruction appraisal. If substantial value beyond the original plans has been added, be certain that such additions-modifications are brought to the lender's attention for possible change of the appraised value of the home.

You will also, prior to the visit to the mortgage-loan office, collect the records indicating you have paid your construction service and labor-material bills. Depending upon a state's lien laws, this must often be done in an organized manner, using suitable lien forms. The statute is often referred to as a "mechanics' lien law" and on construction work it provides a supplier or subcontractor with a legal right in the ownership because he has contributed to the building's value by way of the labor and/or materials he's furnished. He has that right until he is paid in full for his materials or services. The idea is simply to prevent transfer of ownership of a building until the materials/services have been paid for.

While it's sometimes a local practice in a given area to withhold final payment to suppliers or subcontractors until incompleted work has been finished as promised, or damaged material replaced or adjusted, the owner-builder should know in advance his state's lien law and what effect it may have on the completion of his home for mortgage approval purposes. In most lien-law states, the instrument which gives the owner clearance after his supplier-and-subcontractor bills have been paid is a Waiver Of Lien. This is a signed statement by the supplier or subcontractor stating he is now and for all time in the future waiving his right of lien in the specific building or construction job indicated.

The Settlement Procedure

The Real Estate Settlement Act of 1974, new as it is at this writing, has already undergone some modification by the federal administering agency, the U.S. Department of HUD, in the way the Act is being carried out. There have been some revisions proposed by a Congressional subcommittee and the Act has received widespread criticism. Undoubtedly there will be further changes in a short period of time.

RESPA, as the Act is called, was designed as a consumer protection measure which would help to spell out in advance all of the various fee and charge amounts made when a real estate transaction occurs. It's clear that the Act applies to a sale where house-and-land are involved. But apparently the rules and regulations do not appear to cover construction loans unless they include provisions for a take-out mortgage.

Your construction loan lender or the mortgage lending institution with whom you're dealing will be able to give you up-to-date facts about RESPA disclosures and how the Act applies to your particular case, if it does.

Earlier, in Chapter 7, mention was made of insurance protection for the owner-builder against job hazards and accidents or other liabilities. Now, as the opening of your home and its permanent mortgage approaches, your lender will need to know the nature of your continuing insurance program. This is provided in the form of a comprehensive policy known as a "home-owner's insurance policy." This is not to be confused with mortgage insurance and title insurance, both of which may be part of the mortgage closing phase.

Discuss home-owner's insurance with your lender to see just what provisions he feels should be included and the total amount of the policy. He might suggest the use of a newer type policy in which the amount increases through the years in a regular pattern intended to conform with the normal growth in home valuation and with inflationary costs. Shop around at insurance companies; compare features and rates.

Coverages vary with a home-owner's policy. Some offer certain standard or mandatory provisions plus a series of optional coverages. Among the more common provisions are the protection against loss due to fire, windstorm or hail, aircraft accidents, glass breakage, snow-ice damage, civil disturbances, theft and falling objects. There may be clauses relating to accidents involving the home's mechanical systems . . . plumbing, heating, electrical. And to body injuries of other people on the premises. Still another form of insurance required by some lending insitutions is life insurance on the principal breadwinner so that mortgage payments are protected in the event of a family crisis.

In regard to total amount of insurance, your guideline should be your home's present appraised value plus some sort of consideration for constantly inflating building costs. Try to estimate the replacement cost of the home if all work were done by a contractor.

The federal government has two types of insurance programs of interest to some home owners in locations where there's possible danger from flooding and from burglary or robbery. Your local mortgage lender can find out for you whether the Department of HUD's flood insurance program is applicable to your home if it is located in a flood-plain area. The burglary-robbery insurance might apply to homes within certain high-crime areas of cities. Details on either program are available from regional HUD offices.

48 Basement and Garage Facilities

The probability is that the working drawings for your home, if it has a basement, show nothing in the way of partitions, electrical or plumbing provisions beyond a basement light outlet or two and perhaps a floor drain or waste cleanout. This is more or less normal practice.

It you are going to have any facilities beyond a mere minimum in the basement, it's up to you to modify the drawings to accommodate what you wish to install, and this could range from the addition of a 20-ampere appliance circuit to your workshop location, to piping and electrical needs for a sump-pump. And, in case your plans have no provision for washer-dryer installation on the first or second floors, the laundry facilities should be provided in one form or another in the basement. More about that a bit later.

For any basement, the three most usual rooms or areas include a recreation or play room, a home workshop-repair room and a storage room. The fourth would be the laundry if not already located upstairs.

To make proper provisions, both in the beginning and now that the home's nearing completion, it helps to focus your planning attention, at least to the extent of determining where the various use areas will be located and then following through with certain minimal partition and equipment installations.

The following general suggestions are given just in case you've not had previous living experience with basements. These are not hard-and-fast rules but simply a few things that other people have discovered (mostly the hard way) about the basement use.

□ Plan your recreation-play room as to be as convenient as possible to the basement stairs, since it will be the most frequented basement room. The most desirable arrangement encloses and dresses up the stairway, which enters directly into the rec/play room with the rest of the basement out of sight.

□ Try to have larger-than-basement windows in the

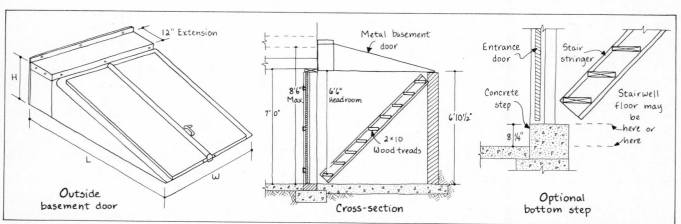

Outdoor Basement Stairs provide convenient passage from the basement directly outdoors. Retaining walls and slab should be poured (or walls laid of block) at the same time that the home's foundation walls are built (see Chapter 8). Shown here are the typical details for using metal basement door units made by the

Bilco Company. The same firm also makes the metal stair stringers for these installations, the owner-builder providing the 2×10 wood treads. Door sizes come in a suitable range to accommodate most basement wall conditions and/or ceiling heights.

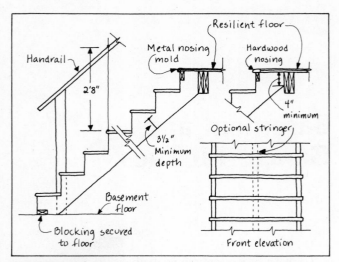

Simple Open-Stringer Stairs are generally used in more economical new homes from the main floor to the basement. Shown here are typical details for such stairs as suggested in HUD's Manual of Acceptable Practices. Dimension lumber is used for stringers, rails and blocking. Treads may also be the same or they may be of 5/4-inch thick round-nosed tread stock.

recreation and workshop rooms so that each room will have some degree of daylight; this can be done, if the outside grade level is high, by the use of deep window-wells. Daylighting is not needed in either the storage area or the laundry, but the latter does need good artificial lighting.

☐ Check the building code requirements relating to any partitions around the furnace and water heater area; you may need to meet clearance and surfacing requirements.

☐ Avoid placing partitions, present or future, too close to plumbing-heating-electrical elements such as sump pumps, water meter or shut-off valves, waste-sewer clean-outs. Give an inch or two extra clearance to mini-mize access problems for operational parts of mechanical systems.

☐ A direct basement-to-outdoors door is highly desirable. It's no problem on sloping lots where good use can be made of sliding patio-doors on the lower side. On flat or other home sites, a basement areaway can be provided at the time foundation walls are being built, and complete prefabricated metal stair units and weather-tight top enclosures can be assembled within and atop such area-ways.

☐ Where possible, plan your workshop area close to outdoor access and also close to any unexcavated area whose crawl space can serve as a lumber-materials storage space.

If you've built most of your home yourself, there's one thing you're bound to have . . . a quite extensive collection

of tools and equipment plus surplus lumber, plywood, paneling and other items you've saved for possible future use. Now, while the basement is relatively free of the clutter that's bound to come with moving in, take a half or full day to provide the minimum aids for organizing of basement space. These minimums might be the follow-ing . . . one to three ordinary 2X4 partition wall sections that will divide off the rest of the basement from your workshop and storage area . . . and the provision of or-ganized laundry space.

On the workshop-storage partitions, include door open-ings and door frames for these two separate rooms or areas. Apply inexpensive fiberboard or hardboard sheets to the *interior* or room sides of the partitions, your dress-up work on the rec/play room side of the partitions can come later, once you've moved in.

Extend electrical wiring runs through floor joists and stud spaces to provide at least one connected-up duplex convenience outlet and one ceiling light outlet in each room. Install bracket-type shelving supports on the parti-tions inside the rooms; wide deep shelves in the storage room and an assortment of several narrower-width shelves in the workshop area. Make this much of an organized start now and you'll be in good shape at move-in time.

Laundry Provisions

As mentioned earlier in Chapter 25, an increasing proportion of new homes are including automatic clothes washing-drying equipment and associated cabinetry in first-floor closets, hallways or utility rooms. And sometimes in second-floor locations convenient to upstairs bedrooms.

Conveniences

If you've relegated Mom to the basement for the handling of some of her hairier chores, then the least you can do is fix up a proper place for your "laundress":

Clothes Chute. In the working-drawing stage when modi-fications are easily made, include a clothes chute in the form of a direct-drop, galvanized metal duct within the framing. About 6X10 or 8X12 inch duct will handle clothes, bedding materials and other items; the framing can be blocked out in a hallway or bedroom closet; metal chute doors are available to trim the opening. Provide a basket holder or wire cage at the chute bottom.

Laundry Tray. Tight budgets that won't permit inclusion of automatic clothes washers-dryers should provide a laun-dry tray; make it a double-compartment tray and allow room adjacent to one side for a second-hand clothes washer if nothing else; manual washing and wringer washers require sorting counter space so provide 3-to-4 lineal feet of counter-plus cabinet storage space.

Drying Area In and Out. Indoors, convenience calls for two or three clothes-line reels which retract the lines when not in use; install in a warm part of the basement adjacent to main supply duct for the heating system; outdoors, install in a sunny area a large circular multiple-line unit in a concrete-filled posthole. These are great for small washes and longer lines can be strung from the house for large washes.

Electrical and Equipment

After completing your basement partition work extending your wiring to outlets in the workshop and storage areas, you should consider what additional electrical runs might be desirable so that they will be done and completed for your final building inspection. This could avoid your taking out additional electrical or plumbing permits later for the additional modification or extension work.

That portion of your basement wiring serving the workshop and laundry area should be on 20-ampere circuits. If a clothes washer will be used at the laundry area, its outlet must be on an individual circuit. For all electrical wiring in the basement, including those outlets originally planned for the furnace and water heater, it is best to keep the outlets at or above a point about 48 inches above the floor. Almost no basement is 100 percent safe against flooding or back-water at some time or other. If you have wiring close to the floor, basement flooding might cause serious electrical damage. There's another factor here, too. Some basements, though not subject to flooding, are subject to dampness, particularly in summer humidity. To safeguard people in the basement against shocks provide basement electrical circuits with ground fault interrupter protection as described in Chapter 42. Such protection is mandatory for outlets serving sump pumps.

The latter, incidentally, are now commonly in the form of submersible units that rest down in the sump itself which is provided with a flat cover plate. Only the wiring cord and the water ejection pipe are seen, although in some installations the pipe may run outdoors below floor level.

Sumps in the basement may have pits of poured concrete or of masonry blocks. They should allow easy admission of water through some openings. The top is a removable cover either a flat concrete slab or a circular concrete catch-basin ring with metal cover. Provision must be made for connecting up ejection pipe which runs outdoors to a suitable drainage area and for a short pipe sleeve section through which the electrical cord and plug can run from pump to nearby outlet.

Wall Shelf Standards and Brackets for organized storage space in basements, garages and other areas. This system is made by Spacemaster Home Products. At left is a ceiling joist suspended installation in a basement. In the center, color-coordinated units for use in children's rooms. At right, a wall cross-bar and snap-on hook system suited to tool storage.

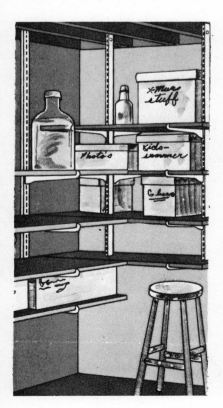

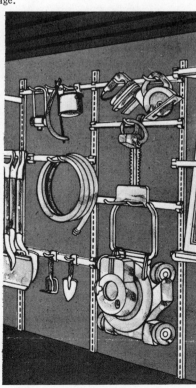

Garage Requirements

With an attached garage and often with a carport, the local building code will require that there be some form of fire resistance provided in the wall construction between garage and living space. If this requirement has not been previously mentioned or checked, it probably can still be done by the application of proper board materials. This is one of those often overlooked details that can cause delay in obtaining approval following final inspection.

The usual requirement on fire resistance between living space and garage is for a wall that has either a 1-hour or 1-½-hour resistance rating. This requirement will apply usually only if the wall is common to both spaces and without any breezeway, porch, entrance or other similar space between.

Such a fire-resistance rating can be achieved fairly easily by the use of fire-resistant type of gypsumboard in the 5/8 inch thickness or a layer of asbestos-cement or asbestos-millboard. There are usually local practices in the building of these fire-walls between garage and home so inquire what the normal practice is. The local code may also require a fire-rated entrance door if there's a passage-door in the wall.

Your garage needn't be completely finished with wallboard and other finish materials on the inside in order to pass final inspection, except for the fire-rated wall. Nor need it be finished to pass approval or final inspection of the lending institution for mortgage purposes.

Allow at least a full day for the installation of a single garage door and perhaps 1-½ days for a double garage door or two singles. But you must have the openings prepared, all framed to the proper dimensions so that the only non-hardware work is the final nailing up of door stops. Hardware consists of hinges, brackets, track, overhead support braces and balancing springs.

There are hardware-and-door kits and hardware-only kits where you furnish the door panels. Avoid the latter. The complete package provides hardware that matches the door-panel weights and other features are usually incorporated in the panels which you probably would not include in self-made panels such as factory weatherstripping, locks, light panels and prime coat. Step-by-step instructions come with the packaged door units.

As far as the type of door, you decide. There are wood

panel doors, metal doors and plastic doors. There appears to be little difference in operation. The doors made of reinforced fiberglass plastic sheets are translucent and give good daylight within the garage.

Switch-operated or remote electronically controlled garage door operators are real convenience accessories. Once considered a pure luxury, the garage-door operators now are more looked upon as a security feature since the driver doesn't have to leave the car until it is inside the garage and the garage door is closed.

There is another aspect worth considering also, back strain. Lifting some garage doors manually takes real effort despite the manufacturer's claims of balance and light weight. Steepness of driveway slope and hopping out of the car in bad weather are other arguments favoring a garage-door operator.

Costs for a door operator can range between $100 and $200 depending on features included, and on the model size or horsepower needed for the particular weight of door. Manual switch-operated units will run less than the remote radio-controlled-from-the-car models. Most doors have a safety device that reverses or holds the door if it encounters any obstruction in its travel. And most have a off-switch in case of malfunction that allows manual lifting of the garage-door. The devices come in component form and are relatively easy to install by following the specific instructions given with the package.

You will need, of course, an electrical outlet near the central part of the garage ceiling, preferably a 20-ampere outlet on an appliance circuit. The components include a traveler track suspended from the ceiling, the door-connecting linkage, motor assembly, signal receive and inside switch, and a remote-signal sender for car mounting.

Garage Storage

Like basements, garages suffer from storage clutter. Especially in homes without basements.

Your best bets to avoid garage clutter are wall aids that facilitate storage by making the various items readily accessible. The two principal wall aids are shelves and hooks-racks. Both are easy to install in any of several ways, and are made even easier through the use of well-designed shelf and rack hardware.

Storage shelves 16-to-24 inches deep front to back offer very good storage. You can use large corrugated-board cartons to organize smaller items by contents. Shelves of this depth are best built with 2X4 vertical frames in which cross-members both brace the uprights and serve as shelf supports. The vertical frames can be nailed to wall studs. Particleboard shelves provide strong support for stored items and also offer easy paintability. Vertical frames for 3/4 inch particleboard shelves should be spaced about 36 inches maximum but this can be upped to 4-½ or 5 feet if added framing supports the front and rear edges of the shelving boards.

Insulation and Paneling in the basement can bring added comfort and livability when rooms are being completed on the lower level. Shown here, foam-type insulation board produced by Zonolite/Grace Construction Products is placed between 2X3 furring strips nailed to basement block walls using masonry nails. After furring-insulation work is completed, the walls are finished using hardboard or woodgrain plywood panels nailing through the vertical grooves into the furring strips. For exterior walls it is advisable to add a cement parge coat and dampproofing membrane to the outside of the foundation wall if the wall is of masonry blocks.

49 Patios and Outdoor Decks

Poured Concrete Patio divided by finish joints into approximately 4-foot squares laid out on a diagonal to the home. Wood bench has steel pole supports embedded in the concrete. Concrete patios such as this are excellent for the use of outdoor furniture and barbeque equipment with their smooth footing. They wash down easily with a garden hose and need very little year-in, year-out maintenance.

You can gain great visual and emotional satisfaction from an attractive patio or elevated wood deck just outside your home. Even if your family is, like most, a busy and active group with very limited time to sit down outside and unwind, still just having the place to do so is important. Add the fact that patios and decks are superb when acting as host-hostess and you've several good reasons for inclusion in your new home.

As you know from the home-garden magazines, outdoor living facilities can be extremely luxurious. But for a family operating on a tight budget, the costs for simpler patio/deck building materials are quite reasonable. The enjoyment possible from this outdoor improvement will be realized long after the added cost has been forgotten.

Nevertheless, don't skimp. An 8X10 foot concrete slab on the ground down two steps from your sliding-glass door is not a patio. It's too small for its intended use and too plain to be attractive. Your minimum basic construction should be at least 400 square feet in area, 20X20 feet if built square. But don't do that. For some reason, odd-shaped, irregular patios seem to work better and look better.

Another factor . . . whatever your outdoor construction material or combination of materials, provide some *height* variances. For instance, keep the floor surface at least 4-to-6 inches above the surrounding ground to facilitate cleaning. And provide raised-above-floor planter areas, step cheek-walls or other permanent construction details that will incorporate top surfaces wide enough for sitting (about 12 inches minimum).

One further detail with any patio or patio-to-be: minimum electric facilities in the form of at least one switch-controlled-from-inside lighting fixture and one outdoor-type convenience outlet.

Basic Materials

Here's a flat-out statement that some will argue with. For your outdoor floor construction, there are only two types of materials that you should consider using: poured concrete with a self-surface or as a base for any floor-walk areas resting on the ground; or naturally rot-resistant or chemically treated wood for suspended floor construction that rests on concrete footings.

These are the only two types of floor construction that provide a smooth surface suitable for furniture utilization and shifting, and present few if any problems in short and long-term maintenance.

Smooth troweled concrete and milled-surface wood may not have for you the visual appeal of flagstones, brick, pebbled-concrete or colored patio blocks or coarse rough-sawn lumber. But in the long haul of usage, their better surfaces for sitting and furniture plus simplified cleaning and repair will rate higher in most people's estimation than mere visual appeal.

An attractive concrete patio of irregular shape and perhaps nonrectangular jointing or wood inserts is as simple to form and pour as your regular outdoor walks and drive. Include with your patio slab, two or three small planter or step areas and maybe a built-in bench. Use the same care in preparing subgrade and drainage slope as you did in your driveway; and the same attention to forming and form-bracing that you did with your entrance steps and platform.

With respect to planter boxes, step cheeks and benches, it sometimes simplifies the work to combine masonry blocks laid in mortar and filled with concrete for vertical elements. Outdoor masonry work, remember, does require capping of the top surface crowned for drainage and provided with a drip edge. The object is to avoid water collecting on top of the masonry where it can filter down into the interior crevices.

Wire or metal lath-reinforced concrete can really be a sculpturing material for a creative worker. Among the numerous possibilities for outdoor applications and landscaping devices are:

▢ slotted fence posts to hold timber rails;

▢ plantbed rims and raised planter boxes;
▢ platforms and shelves for potted or portable plants;
▢ integral-with-floor legs for wood-plank or slab seats;
▢ garden or fountain pools.

Some of the above can be formed and cast in place, in other cases, a forming mold can be prepared to cast and recast multiple units.

Wood Outdoor Decks

There's been a long-standing practice among owners and builders of vacation-leisure homes that is gradually being adopted for outside areas of prime residences, particularly those in wooded or rocky areas. It involves elevating a home's ground floor level somewhat so that entrances to the home...main, rear and/or patio...are served by wood-plank decks and steps. The deck level is at least 1-½-to-2 feet above the ground or more. And the entire ground or yard area is left in its natural state with minimal grading and lawn, if any.

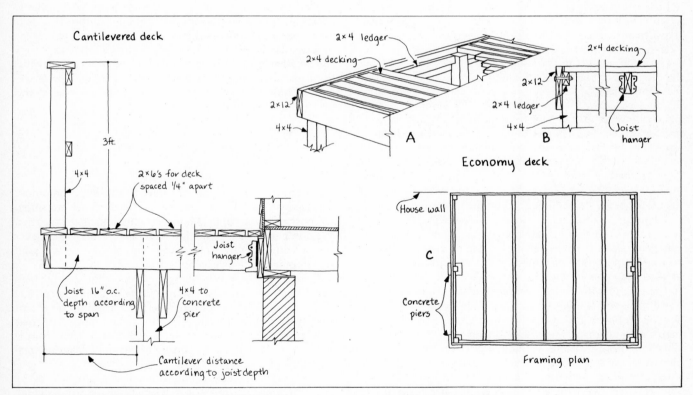

Deck Construction Details showing a few possibilities for the owner-builder. Deck support comes from the 4X4 posts resting on concrete piers. The boxed-in framing shown in sketch (A) makes for a neat installation and permits later adding of rails or seats attached to the outer face of the 2X12 band joists. A time-saver in assembly work is the use of metal joist hanger clips (B). Sketch (C) indicates the plan of deck framing to show how inner portion may be supported by the house wall.

A cantilevered deck is particularly advantageous where the ground slopes sharply away from the home as indicated in the lefthand sketch. The length of projection beyond beam supports depends on the length of span from the house to the beam and the size joists used. Your lumber supplier will be able to assist in determining a suitable span and cantilever deck projection.

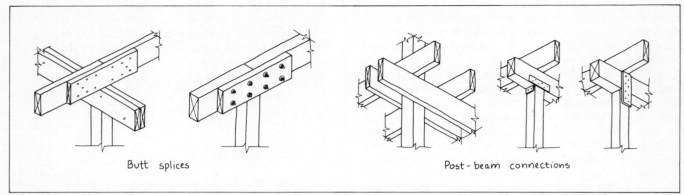

Butt splices   Post-beam connections

Deck Support Splicers-Connections for outdoor raised-deck construction may be any of several types. Shown here are typical common methods of nailed or bolted splices and at the right, paired beams on both sides of support posts, metal beam-post connector plates and plywood splice plates. Beam and joist spacing will depend upon lumber grade used; your lumber supplier can help regarding the spacing dimensions required.

This natural landscape treatment is sometimes supplemented by such features as rock gardens, ground-cover patches, timber or rail-tie terracing and perhaps oriental-style gravel and bark beds along with appropriate shrubs. Low maintenance is one of the objectives of this landscaping, which works very well with elevated decks.

A main factor in building outdoor decks is suitable lumber. Only a few species are naturally resistant to various deteriorization factors. Redwood and cedar are the commonly available rot-resistant types. However in recent years, a few companies have begun distributing preservative-treated lumber through retail outlets for outdoor residential use. One leading company calls their preservative-treated material "outdoor wood" and offers a range of pole and post products in addition to the treated lumber. High-pressure preservative treatments are an outgrowth of the old creosote days of railroad ties and bridge timbers.

Mention of creosote brings up the assortment of wood sealers and other preservative coatings available in nearly any paint store. Used properly, they can do an adequate job in some applications of lumber outdoors. But the pressure-treated materials provide deeper chemical penetration and are apt to provide longer trouble-free service, particular if the lumber will have ground contact.

You will probably also want to check into the range of hardware and fastening devices now on the market in rust-resistant metals. These include not only galvanized or aluminum nails and zinc-coated bolts and screws, but also a variety of wood fasteners or connectors in zinc-coated or stainless steel. And there's also operating hardware in the form of hinges, door or gate latches, and similar items for outdoor use in resistant metals.

For your outdoor deck work, the probability is that nominal 2 inch lumber will be used extensively. But don't overlook the fact that the outdoor species or treated woods are also available in board form, nominal 1 inch thicknesses for shelving, siding, railing applications, and to meet other needs.

One consideration factor in planning outdoor facilities is a storage place convenient for patio-deck furniture and other put-away-for-the-winter items. One good idea is to simply include an outdoor closet or storage enclosure, roof and weather protected. It can be located to serve as a wind or visual screen for the patio or deck. A three-sided, shed-roof enclosure that attaches to the house or side of the garage is easy to build.

Outdoor Wood Construction Tips

In outdoor woods you may have a selection of smoothly surfaced or rough-sawn textured surface; either are suited to most outdoor applications with this principal exception ... don't use rough-sawn for handrails or seating surfaces unless you take care to remove potential splinters and sand down some of the coarseness.

In dimension woods, there's considerable strength and your deck designs can often be made more attractive through judicious use of cantilevering. Basically, this means that floor planks and steps needn't be supported at their very ends. However, any extensive degree of cantilevering needs to be calculated to be sure of adequate load-supporting capability.

With certain species, inquire about sap presence or be alert for sapwood areas or cracks; this is worth watching with firs, pines and eastern softwoods. avoid the use of sap-spotted or sap-stained materials where they will come into possible contact with skin or clothing.

For least deflection or springiness of floor planks, use 2X3's or 2X4's on edge, spacing them 1/8 or 1/4 inch apart by means of small fiberboard or hardboard spacers. Toe-nail

the pieces into beams below that are spaced about 4 feet apart; more economical and yet quite firm underfoot are 2X4's or 2X6's laid flat with under-supports spaced no more than about 3 feet o.c.

For strength and holding power in fastenings use zinc-coated or hot-dip galvanized nails and bolts (terminology varies in different locations). Aluminum fastenings do not perform as well in strength situations although they are entirely satisfactory in many applications such as nailing of pickets to a fence. If the mounting situation prevents nail penetration more than about an inch, use galvanized threaded or ringed nails.

Treatment of wood with water repellent liquids by brush or dip application will prevent absorption of surface moisture and help the wood resist staining; it may be entirely appropriate for uses where the wood members have good air circulation. And don't forget that you can employ wood stains to obtain the desired color in outdoor woods.

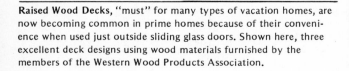

Raised Wood Decks, "must" for many types of vacation homes, are now becoming common in prime homes because of their convenience when used just outside sliding glass doors. Shown here, three excellent deck designs using wood materials furnished by the members of the Western Wood Products Association.

APPENDIX A. SELECTED REFERENCES

In Part I below are listed various texts which have been published in new or revised editions since 1970. The author has selected these references as probably the most helpful to prospective owner-builders and recommends them for supplemental reading; many of them may be available in local libraries.

In Part II, a listing by title is provided covering booklets, brochures, manuals and guides to the use of various building materials and products. These have been chosen by the author for their helpfulness to owners desiring to do their own installation work.

PART I

Anderson, L.O. *Wood-Frame House Construction*, L.A. Craftsman Book Co., 1973.

———— *How To Build A Wood-Frame House*, N.Y. Dover Publications, 1973.

Banov, Abel, and Lytle, Marie-Jeanne. *Book of Successful Painting*, Farmington, MI, Structures Pub. Co., 1975.

Browne, Dan. *The Housebuilding Book*, N.Y. McGraw-Hill Book Co., 1974.

Charney, Len. *Build A Yurt—The Low-Cost Mongolian Round House*, N.Y., Macmillan Co., 1974.

Dalzell, J. Ralph (rev'd: F.S. Merritt). *Simplified Concrete Masonry Planning & Building*, N.Y., McGraw-Hill Book Co., 1972.

Dezettel, Louis M. *Mason's & Builder's Library* (2 vols), Indianapolis, Theo. Audel & Co., 1972–74.

Dietz, Albert G. *Dwelling House Construction*, Cambridge, MA, MIT Press, 1974.

Durbahn, Walter E. *Fundamentals of Carpentry*, Chicago, American Technical Society.

Galvin, Patrick J. *Kitchen Planning Guide For Builders & Architects*, Farmington, MI, Structures Pub. Co., 1972.

Harrison, Henry S. *Houses—Illustrated Guide To Construction Design & Systems*, Chicago, National Institute Of Real Estate Brokers, 1973.

Jones, Rudard A. *Basic Construction & Materials Takeoff*, Urbana, IL, Small Homes Council, 1970.

Lytle, R.J. and Marie-Jeanne. *Book of Successful Fireplaces*, Farmington, Mich., Structures Pub. Co., 1971.

Maguire, Byron W. *Carpentry For Residential Construction*, Reston, VA, Reston Pub. Co., 1975.

Manas, Vincent T. *National Plumbing Code Handbook*, N.Y., McGraw-Hill Book Co.

Mix, Floyd M. *House Wiring Simplified*, South Holland, IL, Goodheart-Willcox Co., 1973.

Neal, Charles D. *Do-It-Yourself House-Building Step-By-Step*, N.Y., Macmillan Co., 1973.

Ray, J.E. *The Art of Bricklaying*, Peoria, IL, Charles A. Bennett Publrs, 1971.

Reiner, Laurence E. *Methods & Materials of Construction*, Englewood Cliffs, NJ, Prentice-Hall Inc., 1970.

Ring, Alfred A. *Real Estate Principles & Practices*, Englewood Cliffs, NJ, Prentice-Hall Inc., 1972.

Smith, Ronald C. *Principles & Practices of Light Construction* Englewood Cliffs, NJ, Prentice-Hall Inc., 1970.

Ulrey, Harry F. *Carpenter's & Builder's Library* (4 vols), Indianapolis, Theo. Audel & Co., 1970.

Wass, Alonzo. *Methods & Materials of Residential Construction*, Reston, VA, Reston Pub. Co., 1973.

Watt, John H. *Handbook of the National Electrical Code*, N.Y. McGraw-Hill Book Co.

Wilson, J.D. *Practical House Carpentry*, N.Y., McGraw-Hill Book Co., 1973.

PART II

Chapter 1. Home Mortgages
Financing the Home (A1.3—25¢), Small Homes Council, Univ. of Ill.
Home Mortgage Insurance (HUD 43-F-3), U.S. Dept. of Housing & Urban Development
Quick Facts About MGIC Residential Mortgage Loan Insurance, Mortgage Guaranty Insurance Corp.

Chapter 2. Homesite Purchases
Buying Lots From Developers (164C—45¢), Consumer Info. Service
Fundamentals of Land Design (B3.0—25¢), Small Homes Council, Univ. of Ill.
Know the Soil You Build On (USDA Agric Info. Bulletin No. 320—15¢) Superintendent of Documents

Chapter 4. Planning Construction
Business Dealings With the Architect & the Contractor (A2.0—25¢) Small Homes Council, Univ. of Ill.
Everything You Wanted to Know About Plywood (25¢) American Plywood Association
House Construction—How to Reduce Costs (174C—25¢), Consumer Info Service

How to Work With Tools & Wood ($1.25), Stanley Tools Div.

Selecting Lumber (D7.0—25¢), Small Homes Council, Univ. of Ill.

Southern Pine Use Guide, Southern Forest Products Association

Tools and Their Uses (192C—$1.95), Consumer Info. Service

Manual of Acceptable Practices, U.S. Dept. of HUD Regional and Field Offices

Wood-Frame House Construction (181C—$2.60), Consumer Info. Service

Chapter 5. Lot Details
Solve Excess Water Problems, Advanced Drainage Systems Inc.

Chapter 6. Building Approvals
One and Two Family Dwelling Code ($8), Building Officials & Code Administrators International Inc.

Soils and Septic Tanks (USDA Agric Info. Bulletin No. 349—15¢) Superintendent of Documents

Chapter 7. Site Preparation
Prevention & Treatment of Construction Damage to Shade Trees (TN #1—25¢), Small Homes Council, Univ. of Ill.

Chapter 8. Building Foundations
Making Basements Dry (177C—25¢), Consumer Info. Service

Recommended Practices for Building Watertight Basements with Concrete (15¢), Portland Cement Association

Recommended Practices for Laying Concrete Block (90¢), Portland Cement Association

Troweling Tips and Techniques (50¢), Marshalltown Trowel Co.

Chapter 9. Ground Floor
APA Glued Floor System (U405-874—25¢), American Plywood Association

How To Framing Sheets 1-Thru-14 on Use of Plywood (25¢), American Plywood Association

Chapter 10. Wall Framing
Manual for House Framing (WCD-1—$1), National Forest Products Assn.

Wood Framing (F3.0—25¢), Small Homes Council, Univ. of Ill.

Chapter 13. Chimneys, Fireplaces
ABC's of Installing a Safe Chimney for Fireplaces and *Installing Instructions,* William Wallace Div.

Chimneys and Fireplaces (F7.0—25¢), Small Homes Council, Univ. of Ill.

Fireplaces and Chimneys (169C), Consumer Info. Service

Heatilator Installation Instructions—Heat Circulating Fireplace and *Fireplace Simplified Systems,* Heatilator Fireplace Div.

Chapter 15. Roof Flashing-Accessories
Built-Up Roofing Details (TN #2—25¢), Small Homes Council, Univ. of Ill.

Construction for Attic Ventilation (TN #9—50¢), Small Homes Council, Univ. of Ill.

Chapter 16. Asphalt Shingles
Good Application Makes a Good Roof Better, Asphalt Roofing Manufacturers Association

Roofing Materials (F12.3—25¢), Small Homes Council, Univ. of Ill.

Chapter 17. Wood Shingles-Shakes
Roof and Wall Shingling Made Easy, Red Cedar Shingle & Handsplit Shake Bureau

Chapter 18. Doors and Windows
Easy Window Installation, Andersen Corp.

How to Create Your Own Beautiful Window Fashions ($1), Graber Co.

Insulating Windows & Screens (F11.2—25¢), Small Homes Council, Univ. of Ill.

Selecting Windows (F11.1—25¢), Small Homes Council, Univ. of Ill.

Chapter 19. Exterior Sidings
Redwood Siding Application (3A4-1), California Redwood Association

Rigid Vinyl Siding Application, Society of the Plastics Industry

Siding & Paneling—Specifications, Installation Recommendations, Western Red Cedar Lumber Association

Wood Sidings (182C), Consumer Info. Service

Chapter 20. Exterior Coatings
How to Paint Your Wood Home, National Paint & Coatings Association

Selection & Application of Caulks, Sealants & Putties, National Paint & Coatings Association

Chapter 21. Framing Details
Stair Manual—Guide to Planning Residential Stairways (CSM-1081) Morgan Building Products Div.

Chapter 22. Heating Installations
Cooling Systems for the Home (G6.1—25¢), Small Homes Council, Univ of Ill.

Heating the Home (G3.1—25¢), Small Homes Council, Univ. of Ill.

Home Heating (172C), Consumer Info. Service

Home Heating-Cooling with Electricity (TN #10—25¢), Small Homes Council, Univ. of Ill.

Chapter 23. Plumbing Installations
How to Do-It-Yourself in Plumbing, Waxman Industries Inc.

How to Install U/R Fiberglass Plumbing Fixtures, Universal-Rundle Corp

LP-Gas Handbook of Technical Data, Fisher Controls Co.

Plumbing (G5.0—25¢), Small Homes Council, Univ. of Ill.

Recommendations & Installation Procedures (253102—$1.50), Genova Plumbing Products

Chapter 24. Electrical Wiring
Electrical Wiring (G4.2—25¢), Small Homes Council, Univ. of Ill.

How to Do-It-Yourself in Electrical, Waxman Industries Inc.

Interior Wiring (278C—$1.45), Consumer Info. Service

Wiring & Cable Guide, Safeguard Electrical Products Corp

Chapter 25. Appliance Planning
Built-In Dishwasher Installation Guide, Maytag Co.

Dishwashers (2201-00035—45¢), Superintendent of Documents

Washers & Dryers (2200-0079—45¢), Superintendent of Documents

Chapter 26. Insulation & Energy
Energy Savings Calculator (0-598-981), Federal Energy Administration

How to Insulate for Maximum Economic Returns, Certain-teed Products Corp

How to Save Money by Insulating Your Home (FEA-346-D), Federal Energy Administration

Insulation Manual: Homes, Apartments ($4), NAHB Research Foundation

Insulation of Wood-Frame Structures (WCD-7—$1), National Forest Products Association

Making the Most of Your Energy Dollars (NBS-C13.53.8—70¢), Superintendent of Documents

Noise Control in Residential Construction, Owens-Corning Fiberglas Corp.

Chapter 27. Gypsumboard Drywall
Using Gypsumboard for Walls & Ceilings (6A-201-71), Gypsum Association

Chapter 28. Wall-Ceiling Finishes
Application Specification for Fiberboard Ceiling Tile, Acoustical & Board Products Association

Ceilings—A Practical Way to Beautify Your Home (KGC-455), Kaiser Gypsum Co.

How to Install the Easy Ceilings, Boise Cascade Wood Products Div.

How to Install Wall Paneling, Georgia-Pacific Corp.

Today's Hardboard & How to Handle It, Acoustical & Board Products Assn.

Your Guide on How to Panel a Room, Masonite Corp.

Chapter 30. Ceramic Tiles

Installation Instructions for Easy-Set Ceramic Tile, American Olean Tile Co.

Chapter 31. Closets, Storage

How To Install Metal Shelves, Stanley Hardware Div.

Indoor Storage (C5.12—25¢), Small Homes Council, Univ. of Ill.

Chapter 32. Flooring, Underlayments

How to Install Particleboard Underlayments, National Particleboard Assoc.

Chapter 33. Cabinets, Counters

Cabinet & Countertop Installation/Care Instructions, Riviera Products Div.

Cabinet Ideas, International Paper Long-Bell Div.

How to Install Kitchen Cabinets, IXL-Westinghouse Div.

Kitchen Planning Standards (C5.32—25¢), Small Homes Council, Univ. of Ill.

Laundry Areas (C5.4—25¢), Small Homes Council, Univ. of Ill.

Organize Your Storage Areas for Convenience & Efficiency (CM-636), Amerock Corp.

Chapter 36. Interior Doors

How to Install Sliding Doors and *How to Install Folding Doors*, Stanley Hardware Div.

Chapter 37. Resilient Flooring

A Consumer Guide to Resilient Flooring, Congoleum Industries

Azrock Manual of Installation, Azrock Floor Products Div.

Do-It-Yourself Guide to Installing Cushioned Vinyl Flooring, Armstrong Cork Co.

How to Install 12-foot Wide Do-It-Yourself Floors, Armstrong Cork Co.

Chapter 38. Hardwood Flooring

Guide to Oak Floors, National Oak Flooring Manufacturers Association

Hardwood Flooring Handbook (303), National Oak Flooring Manufacturers Association

Chapter 39. Interior Trim

How To with Prefinished Wood Mouldings, Western Wood Moulding & Millwork Producers

Chapter 40. Heating-Cooling Equipment

Fuels & Burners (G3.5—25¢), Small Homes Council, Univ. of Ill.

Room Air Conditioners (Consumer Info Series No. 6—45¢), Superintendent of Documents

Chapter 41. Plumbing Fixtures

Everything You Need to Know About Bathrooms But Didn't Know Enough to Ask Eljer Plumbingware Div.

Chapter 42. Electrical Fixtures-Devices

Planning Your Home Lighting (USDA Home-Garden Bulletin No. 138—20¢) Superintendent of Documents

Chapter 44. Paint & Wallpaper

Heritage Decorating Project Kit (75¢), Sherwin Williams Co.

Paint & Painting (188C), Consumer Info. Service

Chapter 45. Carpeting

A Consumer Guide to Carpet, Allied Chemical Home Furnishings-Fibers Div.

Carpet Facts Book, Hercules Inc. Home Furnishings Div.

Carpet and Rugs (149C—55¢), Consumer Info. Service

How to Install Do-It-Yourself Carpet, Armstrong Cork Co.

Chapter 46. Outdoor Improvements

Better Lawns (204C—40¢), Consumer Info. Service

Cement Mason's Guide to Building Concrete Walks, Drives, Patios, Steps ($2.50), Portland Cement Association

Creative Ideas with Split Cedar, Potlatch Corp.

How to Build a Driveway of Ready-Mix Concrete (15¢), Portland Cement Association

Redwood Garden Structures You Can Build, California Redwood Association

Chapter 47. Mortgage Loan Closing

Settlement Costs—A HUD Guide (45¢), Superintendent of Documents

Chapter 48. Basement & Garage

Garages and Carports (C5.9—25¢), Small Homes Council, Univ. of Ill.

Chapter 49. Patios and Decks

Concrete Improvements Around the Home ($2.25), Portland Cement Assn.

Construction Guide for Exposed Wood Decks (166C—$1.25), Consumer Info Service

Decks, Patios, Fences, Southern Forest Products Association

Fences, Decking, Storage, Western Wood Products Association

Outdoor Wood, Koppers Co. Inc.

Redwood Deck Construction (3C2-5), California Redwood Association

The Outdoor Room, Western Wood Products Association

APPENDIX B.

The following companies, agencies and organizations have contributed in one way or another to the information presented in this book and thanks for their contributing efforts is hereby acknowledged.

Acoustical & Board Products Assn., 205 W. Touhy Ave, Park Ridge IL 60068

Advanced Drainage Systems Inc, 1880 MacKenzie Dr, Columbus OH 43220

Allied Chemical Home Furnishings-Fibers Div, 1 Times Square, New York NY 10036

American Biltrite Inc, Amtico Flooring Div, Trenton NJ 08607

American Land Title Assn., 1828 L Street NW, Washington DC 20036

American Olean Tile Co., 1000 Cannon Ave, Lansdale PA 19446

American Plywood Assn., 1119 "A" Street, Tacoma WA 98401

American Standard Plumbing-Heating, P O Box 2003, New Brunswick NJ 08903

Amerock Corp, 4000 Auburn St, Rockford IL 61101

Andersen Corp, no-street-needed, Bayport MN 55003

Armstrong Cork Co, Liberty & Charlotte Sts, Lancaster PA 17604

Asphalt Roofing Manufacturers Assn, 757 Third Ave, New York, NY 10017

Automated Building Components, 7525 NW 37th Ave, Miami FL 33159

Azrock Floor Products Div, P O Box 531, San Antonio TX 78292

Bilco Co, 37 Water St, New Haven CT 06505

Bird & Son Inc, no-street-needed, East Walpole, MA 02032

Boise Cascade Wood Products Div, P O Box 4463, Portland OR 97208

Borg-Warner Corp, Plumbing Products Div, 201 E Fifth St, Mansfield OH 44901

Bradley Corp, P O Box 348, Menomonee Falls WI 53051

Briggs Div. Celotex, 5200 W Kennedy Blvd, Tampa FL 33622

Bruce, E.L. Co., P O Box 16902, Memphis TN 38116

Building Officials & Code Administrators International Inc, 1313 E 60th St, Chicago, IL 60637

California Redwood Association, 617 Montgomery St, San Francisco CA 94111

Carrier Air Conditioning, Carrier Pkwy, Syracuse NY 13201

Certain-teed Products Corp, P O Box 860, Valley Forge PA 19842

Chamberlain Mfg Corp, 845 Larch Ave, Elmhurst IL 60126

Clopay Corp, Clopay Square, Cincinnati OH 45214

Closet Maid Corp, P O Box 304, Ocala FL 32670

Coastal Abrasive & Tool Co, P O Box 337, Turnbull CT 06611

Como Plastics Inc, subsid PPG Industries, Columbus IN 47210

Congoleum Industries, 195 Belgrove Drive, Kearny NJ 07032

Consumer Information Service, Public Document Distribution Center, Pueblo CO 81009

Corning Glass Works, Appliance Dept., no-street-needed, Corning NY 14830

Crown Aluminum Div, P O Box 61, Roxboro NC 27573

Delta Faucet Co, P O Box 31, Greensburg IN 47240

Elkay Mfg Co, 2700 South 17th Ave, Broadview IL 60153

Eljer Plumbingware Div, 3 Gateway Center, Pittsburgh PA 15222

Exxon Chemical Co, Nevamar Laminates Div, Odenton MD 21113

Farmers Home Administration, USDA Publication Services, Washington DC 20250

Federal Energy Administration, 12th & Penn Ave, NW, Washington DC 20461

Fisher Controls Co, McKinney Div, Box 900, McKinney TX 75069

Flintkote Co, 480 Central Ave, East Rutherford NJ 07073

Fluidmaster Inc, 1800 Via Burton, Anaheim CA 92805

Formco Inc, 7745 School Rd, Cincinnati OH 45242

Formica Corp, 120 East 4th St, Cincinnati OH 45202

Frigidaire Div GM, no-street-needed, Dayton OH 45401

GAF Corp, 140 West 51st St, New York NY 10020

Garlinghouse Co, P O Box 299, Topeka KS 66601

General Bathroom Products Corp, 2201 Touhy Ave, Elk Grove Village IL 60009

General Electric Co, Suite 309, 2100 Gardiner Lane, Louisville KY 40205

Genova Plumbing Products, 300 Rising St, Davison MI 48423

Georgia-Pacific Corp, 900 SW 5th Ave, Portland OR 97204

Gerber Plumbing Fixtures Corp, 4656 W Touhy Ave, Chicago IL 60646 .

Goodrich, B.F. General Products Co, 500 S Main St, Akron OH 44318

Grace, W.R. Construction Products, 62 Whittemore Ave, Cambridge MA 02140

Graber Co, Graber Rd, Middleton WI 53562

Gypsum Association, 1603 Orrington Ave, Evanston IL 60201

Heatilator Fireplace Div, P O Box 409, Mt Pleasant IA 52641

Hercules Inc, Home Furnishings Div, no-street-needed, Wilmington DE 19889

Homasote Co, Box 240, West Trenton NJ 08628

Home Building Plan Service, 2235 NE Sandy Blvd, Portland OR 97232

Home Planners Inc, 16310 Grand River, Detroit MI 48227

Hotpoint Div, Suite 309, 2100 Gardiner Lane, Louisville KY 40205

Ideal Security Hardware Corp, 219 East 9th St, St Paul MN 55101

International Paper Long-Bell Div, P O Box 8411, Portland OR 97207

IXL-Westinghouse Div, Route No. 1, Elizabeth City NC 27909

Johns-Manville Sales Co, Greenwood Plaza, Denver CO 80217

Johnson, H & R Inc, State Highway 35, Keyport NJ 07735

Kaiser Gypsum Co, 300 Lakeside Drive, Oakland CA 94604

Kemper Div Tappan, 701 S "N" St, Richmond IN 47374

King Div Jameco, 248 Wyandanch Ave, Wyandanch NY 11798

Kinkead Industries, 5860 N Pulaski Rd, Chicago IL 60646

Kitchen Aid Div Hobart, no-street-needed, Troy OH 45373

Kitchen Kompact Inc, KK Plaza, Jeffersonville IN 47130

Knape & Vogt Inc, 2700 Oak Industrial Dr NE, Grand Rapids MI 49505

Kohler Co, no-street-needed, Kohler WI 53044

Koppers Co Inc, Koppers Building, Pittsburgh PA 15219

Leigh Products Inc, no-street-needed, Coopersville MI 49404

Leviton Mfg Co, 59-25 Little Neck Pkwy, Little Neck NY 11362

Litton Industries, 400 Shelard Plaza South, Minneapolis MN 55426

Magnolia Products Div Beneke, P O Box 1387, Columbus MS 39701

Mannington Mills Inc, no-street-needed, Salem NJ 08079

Mapp Products, P O Box 105, Springfield NJ 07081

Marlite Div Masonite, no-street-needed, Dover OH 44622

Marshalltown Trowel Co, P O Box 738, Marshalltown IA 50158

Masonite Corp, 29 N Wacker Drive, Chicago IL 60605

Master Plan Service, 89 East Jericho Turnpike, Mineola NY 11501

McGraw-Edison Air Comfort Div, 704 N Clark St, Albion MI 49224

Modern Maid Div McGraw-Edison, Box 1111, Chattanooga TN 37401

Moen Div Stanadyne, 377 Woodland Ave, Elyria OH 44035

Morgan Building Products Div, CEE, no-street-needed, Oshkosh WI 54901

Mortgage Guaranty Insurance Corp, 600 Marine Plaza, Milwaukee WI 53201

NAHB Research Foundation, P O Box 1627, Rockville MD 20850

National Association of Plastic Fabricators, 4720 Montgomery Lane, Washington DC 20014

National Disposer Co Div Hobart, no-street-needed, Troy OH 45373

National Fire Protection Association Assn, 470 Atlantic Ave, Boston MA 02210

National Manufacturing Co, P O Box 577, Sterling IL 61081

National Forest Products Assn., 1619 Massachusetts Ave NW, Washington DC 20036

National Oak Flooring Mfgrs. Assn, 804 Sterick Bldg, Memphis TN 38103

National Paint & Coatings Assn, 1500 Rhode Island Ave NW, Washington DC 20005

National Particleboard Assn, 2306 Perkins Place, Silver Spring MD 29010

National Plan Service, 435 West Fullerton Ave., Elmhurst, IL 60126

Nautilus Industries, 926 W State St, Hartford WI 53027

Nibco Inc, 500 Simpson Ave, Elkhart IN 46514

Norwood Mills, 2101 Kennedy Rd, Janesville WI 53545

NuTone Div Scovill, Madison & Red Bank Rds, Cincinnati OH 45227

Owens-Corning Fiberglas Corp, Fiberglas Tower, Toledo OH 43659

Panel Clip Co, 24269 Indoplex Circle, Box 423, Farmington MI 48024

Pease Co, 900 Forest Ave, Hamilton OH 45023

Pease Ever-Strait Door Div, 7100 Dixie Hwy, Fairfield OH 45014

Portland Cement Association, Old Orchard Rd, Skokie IL 60076

Potlatch Corp, P O Box 5414, Spokane WA 99205

Red Cedar Shingle & Handsplit Shake Bureau, 5510 White Bldg, Seattle WA 98101

Riviera Products Div Evans, 1960 Seneca Rd, St Paul MN 55122

Rockwell Admiral Group, 1701 E Woodfield Rd, Schaumburg IL 60172

Rockwell Bldg Components Div, P O Box 798, Morgantown WV 26505

Rolscreen Co, 100 Main St, Pella IA 50219

Safeguard Electrical Products Corp, 360 Hurst St, Linden NJ 07036

Schlage Lock Co, P O Box 3324, San Francisco CA 94119

Sherwin Williams Co, 101 Prospect Ave NW, Cleveland OH 44115

Sierra Electric Co, P O Box 85, Gardena CA 90247

Simpson Timber Co, 900 Fourth Ave, Seattle WA 98164

Small Homes Council, U of Illinois, One East St. Mary's Rd, Champaign IL 61820

Society of the Plastics Industry, 250 Park Ave, New York NY 10017

Society of Real Estate Appraisers, 7 S Dearborn St, Chicago IL 60603

Soil Conservation Service, USDA Public Services, Washington DC 20250

Southern Forest Products Assn, P O Box 52468, New Orleans LA 70150

Spacemaster Home Products Div, 2501 N Elston Ave, Chicago IL 60647

Stanley Door Systems, 2400 E Lincoln Rd, Birmingham MI 48012

Stanley Hardware Div, 195 Lake St, New Critain CT 06050

Stanley Tools Div, 195 Lake St, New Britain CT 06050

Structures Publishing Company, Box 423, Farmington MI 48024

Superintendent of Documents, U.S. Government Printing Office, Washington DC 20402

Tel-O-Post Co, P O Box 217, Linesville PA 16424

Temco Inc, P O Box 1184, Nashville TN 37202

Tile Council of America, 360 Lexington Ave, New York NY 10017

Triangle Pacific Cabinet Corp, 4255 LBJ Freeway, Dallas TX 75234

Universal-Rundle Corp, Box 960, New Castle PA 16103

Upson Co, no-street-needed, Lockport NY 14094

U.S. Department of Housing & Urban Development (HUD), 451 7th St SW, Washington DC 20410

U.S. Gypsum Co, 101 S Wacker Dr, Chicago, IL 60606

U.S. League of Savings Associations, 111 E Wacker Dr, Chicago IL 60601

U.S. Plywood Div Champion, 777 Third Ave, New York NY 10017

Waxman Industries Inc, 24455 Aurora Rd, Bedford Heights OH 44146

Western Red Cedar Lumber Assn, Yeon Bldg, Portland OR 97204

Western Wood Mouldings & Millwork Producers, P O Box 25278, Portland OR 97225

Western Wood Products Assn, Yeon Bldg, Portland OR 97204

Westinghouse Electric Corp, Gateway Center, Pittsburgh PA 15222

Westinghouse Lamp Div, 200 Park Ave, New York NY 10017

Whirlpool Corp, Admin Ctr, no-street-needed, Benton Harbor MI 49022

Wickes Lumber Div, 555 N Washington Ave, Saginaw MI 48607

William Wallace Div, Box 137, Belmont CA 94002

York Div Borg-Warner, P O Box 1592, York PA 17405

Z-Brick Co Div VMC, 2834 NW Market St, Seattle WA 98107

Glossary—Index